IRELAND

Richard Nowitz, APA Publications

Ondine - film locations : ~~Beara Isl~~
Bere Island, Beara, Co. Cork
Castletownbere, Dursey Island, and
Puleen Harbour

Executive Editorial Director   David Brabis
Chief Editor   Cynthia Clayton Ochterbeck

THE GREEN GUIDE IRELAND

Editor	Gwen Cannon
Principal Writer	Roxanne Besse
Production Coordinator	Allison M. Simpson, Anna Wilson
Cartography	Alain Baldet, Michelle Cana, Peter Wrenn
Photo Editor	Cecile Koroleff, Lydia Strong
Proofreader	Gaven Watkins
Layout & Design	Tim Schultz, Frank Ladd
Cover Design	Ute Weber, Laurent Muller

Contact Us:

The Green Guide
Michelin Maps and Guides
One Parkway South
Greenville, SC 29615
USA
☎ 1-800-423-0485
www.michelintravel.com
michelin.guides@us.michelin.com

The Green Guide
Michelin Maps and Guides
Hannay House
39 Clarendon Road
Watford, Herts WD17 1JA
UK
☎ (01923) 205 240
www.ViaMichelin.com
travelpubsales@uk.michelin.com

Special Sales:

For information regarding bulk sales,
customized editions and premium sales,
please contact our Customer Service
Departments:
USA   1-800-423-0485
UK   (01923) 205 240
Canada 1-800-361-8236

Note to the reader
While every effort is made to ensure that all information printed in this guide is
correct and up-to-date, Michelin Maps and Guides (Michelin Tyre PLC; Michelin
North America, Inc.) accepts no liability for any direct, indirect or consequential
losses howsoever caused so far as such can be excluded by law.

One Team …
A Commitment to Quality

There's just one reason our team is dedicated to producing quality travel publications—you, our reader. We want you to get the maximum benefit from your trip—and from your money. In today's multiple-choice world of travel, the options are many, perhaps overwhelming.

In our guidebooks, we try to minimize the guesswork involved with travel. We scout out the attractions, prioritize them with star ratings, and describe what you'll discover when you visit them.

To help you orient yourself, we provide colorful and detailed, but easy-to-follow maps. Floor plans of some of the cathedrals and museums help you plan your tour.

Throughout the guides, we offer practical information, touring tips and suggestions for finding the best views, good places for a break and the most interesting shops.

Lodging and dining are always a big part of travel, so we compile a selection of hotels and restaurants that we think convey the feel of the destination, and organize them by geographic area and price. We also highlight shopping, recreational and entertainment venues, especially the popular spots.

If you're short on time, driving tours are included so you can hit the highlights and quickly absorb the best of the region.

For those who love to experience a destination on foot, we add walking tours, often with a map. And we list other companies who offer boat, bus or guided walking tours of the area, some with culinary, historical or other themes.

In short, we test and retest, check and recheck to make sure that our guidebooks are truly just that: a personalized guide to help you make the most of your visit. After all, we want you to enjoy traveling as much as we do.

The Michelin Green Guide Team

PLANNING YOUR TRIP

INTRODUCTION TO IRELAND

SYMBOLS

🙂 **Tips to help improve your experience**

🙂 **Details to consider**

👓 **Entry Fees**

👣 **Walking tours**

⊶ **Closed to the public**

🕐 **Hours of operation**

🕐 **Periods of closure**

CONTENTS

DISCOVERING IRELAND

HOW TO USE THIS GUIDE

Orientation

To help you grasp the "lay of the land" quickly and easily, so you'll feel confident and comfortable finding your way around the region, we offer the following tools in this guide:

- Detailed table of contents for an overview of what you'll find in the guide, and how it is organized.
- Map of Principal Sights at the front to the guide, showing the starred places of interest at a glance.
- Detailed maps for major cities and villages, including driving tour maps and larger-scale maps for walking tours.
- Map of Regional Driving Tours, each one numbered and color coded.
- Principal Sights ordered alphabetically for easy reference.

Practicalities

At the front of the guide, you'll see a section called "Planning Your Trip" that contains information about planning your trip, the best time to go, different ways of getting to the region and getting around, basic facts and tips for making the most of your visit. You'll find driving and themed tours, and suggestions for outdoor fun. There's also a calendar of popular annual events in Ireland. Information on shopping, sightseeing, kids' activities and sports and recreational opportunities is also included.

LODGINGS

We've made a selection of hotels and arranged them within the cities, categorized by price to fit all budgets (see the Legend at the back of the guide for an explanation of the price categories). For the most part, we selected accommodations based on their unique regional quality, their Irish feel, as it were. So, unless the individual hotel embodies local ambience, it's rare that we include chain properties, which typically have their own imprint. If you want a more comprehensive selection of accommodations, see the red-cover *Michelin Guide Great Britain and Ireland*.

RESTAURANTS

We thought you'd like to know the popular eating spots in Ireland. So we selected restaurants that capture the local experience—those that have regional flavor and local atmosphere. We're not rating the quality of the food per se. As we did with the hotels, we selected restaurants for many towns and villages, categorized by price to appeal to all wallets. If you want a more comprehensive selection of dining recommendations in the region, see the red-cover *Michelin Guide Great Britain and Ireland*.

Attractions

Principal Sights are arranged alphabetically. Within each Principal Sight, attractions for each town, village, or geographical area are divided into local Sights or Walking Tours, nearby Excursions to sights outside the town, or detailed Driving Tours—suggested itineraries for seeing several attractions around a major town. Contact information, admission charges and hours of operation are given for the majority of attractions. Unless otherwise noted, admission prices shown are for a single adult only. Discounts for seniors, students, teachers, etc. may be available; be sure to ask. If no admission charge is shown, entrance to the attraction is free.

If you're pressed for time, we recommend you visit the three- and two-star sights first: the stars are your guide.

STAR RATINGS

Michelin has used stars as a rating tool for more than 100 years:

   ★★★ Highly recommended
   ★★ Recommended
   ★   Interesting

SYMBOLS IN THE TEXT

Besides the stars, other symbols in the text indicate tourist information 🅸; wheelchair access &; on-site eating facilities 🍴; camping facilities △; on-site parking 🅿; sights of interest to children Kids; and beaches ⚓.

See the box appearing on the Contents page for other symbols used in the text.

See the Maps explanation below for symbols appearing on the maps.

Throughout the guide you will find peach-coloured text boxes or sidebars containing anecdotal or background information. Green-coloured boxes contain information to help you save time or money.

Maps

All maps in this guide are oriented north, unless otherwise indicated by a directional arrow. See the map Legend at the back of the guide for an explanation of other map symbols. A complete list of the maps found in the guide appears at the back of this book.

Addresses, phone numbers, opening hours and prices published in this guide are accurate at press time. We welcome corrections and suggestions that may assist us in preparing the next edition. Please send your comments to:

Michelin Maps and Guides
Hannay House
39 Clarendon Road
Watford, Herts WD17 1JA
UK
travelpubsales@uk.michelin.com
www.michelin.co.uk

Michelin Maps and Guides
Editorial Department
P.O. Box 19001
Greenville, SC 29602-9001
USA
michelin.guides@us.michelin.com
www.michelintravel.com

Principal Sights

WHEN AND WHERE TO GO

Driving Tours

  See the Driving Tours map p 11.
The touring programmes outlined below and shown on the map have been devised to help you plan visits to the main cities Dublin and Belfast, Cork and Sligo, and important attractions nearby. A grand tour including all the major sights is also provided (tour 8) although you may find you want to linger longer in some places to enjoy the scenery, the warmth of the people and their take on life!
Itineraries all start and end at a convenient port of entry by air or sea. Overnight stays shown in bold.

① DUBLIN AND ITS SURROUNDINGS – ONE WEEK

Dublin demands at least two days for its many attractions and vibrant atmosphere, after which, it is good to foray into the countryside to see some of the country's major sights – the stunning prehistoric monuments of the Boyne Valley, great houses and gardens, Early Christian Glendalough in its remote valley, busy country towns and charming seaside harbours. From **Dublin**, head north to picturesque Howth, the aristocratic desmesne of Malahide and bustling **Drogheda,** the nearby prehistoric grave sites of Newgrange and Knowth, and the tranquil setting for the decisive Battle of the Boyne.
West of the capital, follow the road to the vast Anglo-Norman castle at Trim, the splendid Palladian mansion of Castletown, and Curragh: the heartland of Irish horse-breeding and racing near **Kildare**. Then proceed to the Great House at Russborough, and climbs up into the Wicklow Mountains, to the highly evocative monastic remains at Glendalough. After a night in the seaside town of **Wicklow**, return to **Dublin** via the magnificent gardens of Powerscourt and the capital's attractive southern suburbs.

② ASPECTS OF ULSTER– ONE WEEK

Northern Ireland comprises only six of Ulster's nine counties: to get a view of the whole province, consider a longer itinerary (*see Tour 7*). This route takes in the major towns, wonderful natural landscapes and array of man-made attractions including a number of world-class museums.
Head east out of **Belfast**, pausing at the fascinating Ulster Folk and Transport Museum, to the coastal resort of **Bangor**. On the way to St Patrick's town of Downpatrick, visit the great houses and gardens of Mountstewart and Castle Ward before driving on to **Newcastle**. Continue through the spectular Mourne Mountains before arriving at Ireland's holy city of **Armagh**. The less grand but equally interesting country houses of Ardress and The Argory are worth a detour on the way to Lough Neagh, Ireland's largest lake. From here, consider calling in at the Peatlands Park to learn about local wildlife and turf-cutting, before going to Ardboe to see the High Cross, and the archetypal plantation towns of Cookstown and Draperstown, visiting the Ulster-American Folk Park on the way to the last walled city to be laid out in Europe, **Londonderry**. Follow the coastal road east through Portrush and Portstewart

Carnlough in the Antrim Glens

H. Champollion/MICHELIN

to the spectacular Giant's Causeway and the pretty seaside resort of **Ballycastle**. Return to **Belfast** via the imposing landscapes of the Antrim Glens and the corniche of the Antrim Coast Road.

③ SIGHTS OF THE SOUTHEAST – ONE WEEK

Follow in the footsteps of the Anglo-Normans as they spread across Ireland, building great castles, churches and abbeys, and relish one of the great sights of ancient Ireland: the holy hill of Cashel. The Republic's second city, Cork, has its own distinctive character, while the southeastern coast is renown for its beauty.

From the ferry port of Rosslare, and the Viking city of **Wexford**, make your way to Johnstown Castle and the Irish Agricultural Museum, drive through the National Heritage Park to the old towns of Enniscorthy and New Ross, past the lovely abbey ruins at Jerpoint to medieval **Kilkenny** (2 nights), one of Ireland's most compelling towns.

The Rock of **Cashel** is simply magical: enjoy! From here, head south through Caher with its castle and Fermoy with its splendid river crossing to the Republic's second city, **Cork** (2 nights) From Cork take the road east along the coast to Cobh overlooking the broad waters of Cork Harbour, and on via delightful old Youghal to the southeast's other Viking city of **Waterford**, renown for its opera festival and lively cultural life.

A ferry crosses Waterford Harbour to the abbeys, gardens, castles and beaches of the Hook Peninsula. The return is then direct to Rosslare.

④ THE SOUTHWEST – COUNTIES CORK, KERRY AND LIMERICK – TEN DAYS

The Southwest corner, with its rocky peninsulas stretching far into the Atlantic, the country's highest mountains and lush inland landscapes, is perhaps the most alluring region for visitors to Ireland.

From Shannon Airport, follow the road to 15C Bunratty Castle and its Folk Park to the Republic's third largest city, historic **Limerick**. Explore the country towns of Kilmallock and Mallow on the way to bustling **Cork** (2 nights). The coastal road west of Cork takes you through attractive fishing villages and little maritime towns like **Kinsale**. More coastal delights include Skibbereen, Skull and **Bantry** on its great sea-inlet, Bantry Bay - famous for its fish. The splendidly scenic coastal road, the Ring of Beara, runs round the Beara Peninsula, to pretty **Kenmare**. The panoramic Ring of Kerry offers wonderful views of the glorious Iveragh Peninsula to the distant drowned mountain top of Great Skellig Island, once an austere monastic retreat, before reaching the world-famous lake and mountain setting of **Killarney** (2 nights). From here, continue to the Gaelic harbour town of Dingle and the tip of the Dingle Peninsula with its beehive huts and panoramic views of the wave-battered Blasket Islands, before turning inland via Tralee, Ardfert Cathedral and Glin Castle. Return to **Limerick** and Shannon.

⑤ GLORIES OF GALWAY, CONNEMARA AND SLIGO – ONE WEEK

Connemara sometimes appears to consist more of sky, sea, bog and lake than firm ground, despite its mountains, including the splendidly rounded Twelve Bens - very different from the

Horse and cart in the Burren

J. Malburet/MICHELIN

bleak arid limestone landscapes of the Burren and lively city of Galway.

From Knock airport, head north to the cheerful regional capital of **Sligo** with its many associations with W B Yeats. From here, head west to north Mayo through vast stretches of bog, to Stone Age vestiges at Ceide Fields and high cliffs of **Achill Island**.

An essential detour is made for Castlebar and its state-of-the-art National Museum of Country Life at Turlough, on the way westwards to the elegant town of **Westport** to visit Westport House, one of the finest Great Houses in the West. From the road southwest, you will see St Patrick's holy mountain, Croagh Patrick. Continue south through the Sheffry Hills, round the end of the fjord-like Killary Harbour and past the opulent 19C country house of Kylemore Abbey to charming little **Clifden**.

Archetypal Connemara landscapes can be enjoyed on the way to Inverin with its air service to Inishmore, the largest of the **Aran Islands**, where Gaelic is spoken very fast and life is steeped in traditional ways.

Back on the mainland, it is tempting to linger at the vibrant city of **Galway**. The south of Co Galway includes the strange moonscapes of **The Burren** and the lofty Cliffs of Moher, some of the tallest in Europe.

The tour returns to Knock via Ennis, the miniature capital of Co Clare, the Heritage Town of Athenry and the little cathedral city of Tuam.

6 THE HEART OF IRELAND, THE UNKNOWN MIDLANDS – ONE WEEK

As well as outstanding monuments like the great monastic complex of Clonmacnoise and the enigmatic earthworks around Tulsk, this itinerary introduces the inquisitive visitor to a few hidden treasures: castles and country houses, bustling small towns off the tourist trail, unexpected uplands, the banks of the Shannon, and one of the country's most extensive and well-preserved boglands.

Head northwest out of **Dublin** to Trim withs its great Anglo-Norman castle, to the prehistoric burial mounds of Loughcrew and the ancient seat of the Pakenham family at Tullynally, before arriving at the midland market town of **Mullingar** for the night.

Co Longford has some intriguing features, notably the delightful estate village of Ardagh. Co Roscommon boasts Strokestown House which has its own estate village and an authoritative Famine Museum, and the small town of **Boyle**, graced by handsome abbey ruins. From here, head south to Tulsk, where the Cruachan Aí visitor centre provides an insight into the mysteries of the Celtic past, then continue to Ballinasloe and **Athlone** at the southern end of Lough Ree on the River Shannon.

The monastic precinct of Clonmacnoise is one of the great ecclesiastical sights of Ireland, as is the extraordinary little Romanesque cathedral of Clonfert. This itinerary now leaves the Shannon for the little Georgian town of **Birr**, the anteroom to the great house and grounds of the Birr Castle Desmesne. To the East of Birr rise the green summits of the relatively little visited Slieve Bloom Mountains, while to the northeast, close to little Tullamore, lies the vast, strange, and potentially perilous expanse of Clara Bog. From here, it is a straight run back to **Dublin**.

7 ULSTER ODYSSEY – TWO WEEKS

A near-comprehensive tour of the old province of Ulster, including the six counties of Northern Ireland and three over the border in the Republic, takes in the quiet countryside of Cavan and Monaghan, and the wild scenery of Donegal's coast and mountains.

From **Belfast** take the road to the old coastal resort of **Bangor**. Visit the great houses and desmesnes at Mountstewart and Castle Ward before taking the ferry across the mouth of Strangford Lough to St Patrick's city of Downpatrick, and heading for the seaside town of **Newcastle**.

Snake your way through the lovely Mourne Mountains to **Armagh**, another holy city, the seat of both Archbishops of Ireland. The following day, head south-west into the Republic through Monaghan and Cavan, before turning northwest to the Fermanagh Lakeland and its little capital, **Enniskillen**.

After Belleek with its famous pottery, you cross into Co Donegal. West of Donegal town rise the dramatic cliffs of Slieve League where the village of Glencolumbkille is perched, still breathing the spirit of its founder St Columba. From here, the route heads inland to the tweed town of Ardara and north via Glenveagh National Park to the quiet little resort of **Dunfanaghy** in the lee of Horn Head.

Take the N56 back past the ancient fortress of Grianan of Aileach to the renowned walled city of **Londonderry** in Northern Ireland. Divert to the **Sperrin Mountains** for the Ulster-American Folk Park. East of the mountains there is the typical plantation settlement of Cookstown, a famous High Cross at Ardboe on the shores of Lough Neagh, the country's greatest lake, and the 17C planter's house of Springhill. Drive north to Draperstown, another plantation settlement and continue to the favourite seaside resorts of **Portrush** and Portstewart. The Giant's Causeway and the Causeway Coast demand a day of anyone's time, and a choice of accommodation is available at **Ballycastle**.

The return to **Belfast** is along the Antrim Coast Road through the superlative landscapes of the Glens of Antrim, with a final stop at the great Anglo-Norman castle at Carrickfergus.

⑧ IRISH HIGHLIGHTS, A GRAND TOUR – TWO WEEKS

The very best that Ireland has to offer to the first-time visitor.

From **Dublin**, drive out to one of the country's finest mansions, Russborough, and on through the Wicklow Mountains to the monastic ruins of Glendalough in their deep wooded valley, before arriving at the historic

city of **Kilkenny** (2 nights). Spend a day absorbing the atmosphere of Ireland's Acropolis, the Rock of **Cashel** before heading for the Republic's second city, **Cork**, and then west on to **Killarney** (2 nights) in its incomparable setting of lakes and mountains. The classic drive around the Iveragh Peninsula, the Ring of Kerry, is an experience not to be missed, nor is the Dingle Peninsula, with its ancient stone huts and enclosures, and views of the rocky Blasket Islands.

Old **Limerick** is an up-and-coming place, while Co Clare offers its little capital, Ennis, the mighty Cliffs of Moher and the weird limestone landscapes of the Burren.

North of The Burren is one of the country's most attractive towns, **Galway**. From here, make your way to **Clifden** through what many regard as the most Irish of landscapes: the bogs, shining lakes, and rounded mountains of Connemara. Pass close to St Patrick's mountain, Croagh Patrick, to **Westport**. After Castlebar and the excellent Museum of Country Life at Turlough, follow signs to the busiest town in the northwest, **Sligo**.

Northern Ireland is entered at **Enniskillen**, in the heart of the glorious Fermanagh Lakeland. An essential stop on the way to the walled city of **Londonderry** is the Ulster-American Folk Park. Do not miss what is perhaps the country's greatest natural attraction, the Giant's Causeway, before driving on to the province's capital, **Belfast**. Return to **Dublin** along the **Boyne Valley** with its battle site and magnificent prehistoric monuments.

Slea Head on the Dingle Peninsula

Bord Fáilte, Dublin

Themed Tours

HISTORIC ROUTES

Sarsfield's Ride

This historical route (70mi/113km signed) makes a wide loop around Limerick along byroads through small villages and unspoilt countryside, following the route taken by General Patrick Sarsfield when he set out to intercept an English siege train. In August 1690 King William III of England was encamped at Caherconlish 8 miles east of Limerick waiting for the arrival of heavy siege guns from Dublin, while his army besieged Limerick. Acting on information from a deserter, Sarsfield slipped out of King John's Castle in Limerick with 600 cavalry and headed northeast along the right bank of the Shannon via Bridgetown, fording the river upstream of Killaloe Bridge, which was held by the Williamites. At about this point he was joined by local guides who showed him a route by Kiloscully and Ballyhourigan Wood, pausing to rest before climbing over the Silvermine and the Slievefelim Mountains via Toor and Rear Cross. From Doon they continued south along the county boundary to Monard, and turned west. In Cullen they discovered the password for the Williamite camp was Sarsfield: so after midnight, they travelled the last 2 miles to Ballyneety and destroyed the siege train.

Siege of Kinsale

The sites of the various camps and engagements of the opposing forces are marked by a dozen signs erected by the roadsides around Kinsale.

SCENIC ROUTES

Several **Scenic Routes**, designated by the local Tourist Boards, are marked by signs *(Slí)* – **Inis Eoghain Scenic Drive** in Donegal, **Arigna Scenic Drive** around Lough Key near Boyle, **Slea Head Drive** on the Dingle Peninsula, the **Ring of Kerry** round the Iveragh Peninsual west of Killarney, the **Ring**

of Beara round the Beara Peninsula west of Glengarriff.

LITERARY ROUTES

Those interested in literary affairs may like to explore the places where **Oliver Goldsmith** spent his childhood (*see Athlone*), or visit the towns where **Anthony Trollope** lived during his residence in Ireland or follow the trail of sights associated with **Patrick Kavanagh**.

Ideas for your Visit

Always allow plenty of time when touring Ireland: part of the enjoyment is stopping for an idle chat, a pint of Guinness or to take in spectacular views.

SUGGESTED ITINERARIES

2-day Breaks

Dublin City

Begin with a visit to **Trinity College** and that masterpiece of Irish art, the **Book of Kells** before going up **Grafton Street** and its side streets enjoying the buskers and Dublin's elegant shopping area. Wander around the gardens of **St Stephen's Green** before returning to the streets off the north side to find a place for lunch. In the afternoon visit the **National Museum** or the **National Gallery**, walk through **Merrion Square** and admire the Georgian houses, notably **Number Twenty Nine**. Spend the evening exploring **Temple Bar**. On the second day explore the old town and the art in the **Chester Beatty Library**. Alternatively, book a guided tour of **Dublin Castle** or look into **Christ Church Cathedral** or **St Patrick's Cathedral**. After lunch take the bus to **Kilmainham Gaol** for a lesson in recent Irish history and pop in to admire displays in the **Irish Museum of Modern Art** installed in the **Royal Kilmainham Hospital**.

Kilkenny

Visit **Kilkenny Castle**, its park and the **Kilkenny Design Centre**. After lunch drive out for a deep plunge into **Dunmore Cave**. Head south down the Nore Valley to the magnificent ruins of **Jerpoint Abbey**, calling in on **Inistioge**, and on over Brandon Hill to **Graiguenamanagh** on the River Barrow.

Sligo

Visit the **Niland Gallery**, one of the best displays of paintings by Jack B Yeats, and stroll through the Abbey ruins. After lunch, take a boat trip on **Lough Gill** visiting the lake isle of **Innisfree** and **Parke's Castle**.
Drive through **Yeats' Country** to the tomb of William Butler Yeats at **Drumcliff** in the shadow of Benbulben and **Lissadell,** home of Countess Markievicz, before turning inland to **Glencar Waterfall**.

3-day Breaks

Cork City

Highlights include the **English Market**, **Grand Parade** and **St Patrick's Street**. Admire the exuberant architecture of William Burges at **St Fin Barre's Cathedral**. After lunch cross the river to try your hand at ringing **Shandon Bells** and see how criminals were treated in **Cork City Gaol**.
On the second day take a trip to **Blarney Castle** to kiss the **Blarney stone** and make a round trip to **Mallow** and **Fermoy** on the beautiful **Blackwater River**.
On the third day drive out to **Fota House** and the **Wildlife Park**, make a lunchtime visit to **Cobh** and end the day sampling whiskey at the **Old Midleton Distillery**.

Westport and District

Stroll round the charming little town, and the **Quayside**, a good spot for lunch, then visit **Westport House**. Drive west to explore the **Murrisk Peninsula** which presents some of the most beautiful landscapes in the west of Ireland – **Croagh Patrick** and **Killary Harbour**.

Take the road north to the **Marian Shrine at Knock** and the **Museum of Country Life** at Turlough near Castlebar.

Enniskillen

Stroll through the town and visit **Enniskillen Castle** and its museums. In the afternoon tour the stately rooms of **Castle Coole**.
Drive southwest to **Florence Court**, another less austere country house with flamboyant plasterwork, and the **Marble Arch Caves**, part of which is visited by boat.
Make a tour round the shores of **Lower Lough Erne** taking in **Devenish Island**, **Castle Archdale** and **White Island**, the **Janus Figure**, **Belleek Pottery**, the **Cliffs of Magho viewpoint** and **Tully Castle**.

Londonderry

Walk round the walls and visit the **Tower Museum**, the **Cathedral** and **Long Tower Church**.
Make a tour in the **Sperrins Mountains** – **Roe Valley Country Park**, **Glenshane Pass**, **Dungiven Priory**, **Wellbrook Beetling Mill**, **Beaghmore Stone Circles**, **Ulster Plantation Centre** in Draperstown, **Springhill**, **Ulster History Park**, **Sperrin Heritage Centre**, **Ulster American Folk Park**, **Gray's Printery** in Strabane.
Make tour north round the **Inishowen** (**Inis Eoghain**) **Peninsula** – visiting the many prehistoric and early Christian relics – **Grianán of Aileach**,

Touring in the traditional way by horse-drawn caravan

Bord Fáilte, Dublin

NITB, Belfast

Cruising at Erincurragh in the Fermanagh Lakeland

Carrowmore High Crosses, Clonca Church and Cross – visit **Malin Head**, famous from the shipping forecasts, and **Fort Ree Military Museum**.

4-day Breaks

Dublin and District

For two days explore Dublin City as described above.

Drive south into the **Wicklow Mountains** – to **Russborough** or **Powerscourt** – and further south to the monastic ruins at **Glendalough**.

Take the motorway north via Slane to the **Newgrange** in the **Boyne Valley** and return via **Trim** and **Tara** or **Malahide** and **Newbridge House**.

Killarney and District

Wander around the town centre and explore the **National Park** on foot – **Knockreer Demesne** and **Ross Castle** – or by car – **Muckross House**, **Muckross Friary** and the **Muckross Peninsula**, and **Torc Waterfall** and **Ladies View**.

Take a guided tour through the **Gap of Dunloe** if it is a fine day, or drive round the **Ring of Kerry**, enjoying the fine views of the landscape.

Go north to the **Dingle Peninsula**, part of the Gaeltacht, which has many relics dating from a former way of life.

Limerick and District

Visit the treasures in the **Hunt Museum** and walk up to the **Castle** and **St Mary's Cathedral**.

Drive northwest into Co Clare to visit **Bunratty Folk Museum and Castle**, **Quin Friary**, **Knappogue Castle** and **Cragganunowen Centre**.

Make a round trip south of Limerick visiting the prehistoric remains at **Lough Gur Interpretive Centre**, the walled town of **Kilmallock** and the childhood haunts of de Valera in **Bruree**, before returning down the Maigue Valley via **Croom**, **Monasteranenagh Abbey** and charming **Adare** with its thatched cottages.

Drive north via Ennis and Ennistimon to the barren landscape of the **Burren** – the **Cliffs of Moher**, **Lisdoonvarna**, **Corkscrew Hill** and **Aillwee Cave**.

Belfast and District

Visit the city centre and the **waterfront**. Try to take into **St Malachy's Church** and the **Oval Church** before lunching in the **Crown Liquor Saloon**. In the afternoon visit the **Ulster Museum** and take a stroll in the **Botanic Gardens** with its two glass houses.

Drive out east to visit the **Ulster Folk and Transport Museum** at Cultra; after lunch explore the architectural and horticultural splendours of **Mount Stewart** on the east shore of **Strangford Lough**.

Head south up the **Lagan Valley** to learn about a traditional Irish industry in the **Lisburn Museum**. Visit charming **Hillsborough** and the plants and shrubs at **Rowallane**.

Drive north via Ballymena and Ballymoney to marvel at the volcanic columns of the **Giant's Causeway**. In the afternoon drive south along the **coast and glens of Antrim**.

5-day Break

Galway and District

Stroll round the medieval city centre and in the afternoon take the road to **Aughnanure Castle** and the charming fishing village of **Oughterard** on **Lough Corrib**.

Take the road up the east shore of **Lough Corrib** via **Annaghdown** and **Ross Errily Abbey** to **Cong**.

Take the road west through **Connemara** to **Clifden,** returning by the coast road.

In Kiltartan country south of Galway visit **Athenry**, a heritage town, **Thoor Ballylee**, once the home of William Butler Yeats, and **Coole Park**, where Lady Augusta Gregory resided.

Book a day-trip to **Aranmore**, the largest of the **Aran Islands**, where tourism has softened the once harsh island way of life.

Longer Breaks

For periods of a week or more see Driving Tours.

Activity Holidays

The Irish Tourist Board provides information on all kinds of holidays and summer schools. 👍 See also *What to Do and See.*

Horse-Drawn Caravan

The caravan provides accommodation as well as a leisurely way of exploring the Irish country roads:

Slattery's Horse-drawn Caravans, 1 Russell Street, Tralee, Co Kerry. ☎ 066 21722; Fax 066 25981

Mayo Horsedrawn Caravan Holidays Ltd, Belcarra, Castlebar. ☎ 094 903 2054; Fax 094 903 2351

Boating and Cruising

Ireland is blessed with many lakes and waterways, and is surrounded by sea. The waterways suited for cruising include the River Shannon, Shannon–Erne Waterway and Lough Erne; canal barges are recomended on the River Barrow, the Grand Canal and the River Shannon. Details of local operators are given in the relevant chapters.

It is recommended that boat operators be members of the Irish Boat Rental Association (IBRA).

www.waterwaysireland.org
www.sailing.ie
www.waterbasedireland.ie

Walking, Cycling and Horse Riding

Holidays – chauffeur driven even – can be organised around a variety of activities that includes tracing ancestors, gardens and golf.

Tailormade-Ireland. ☎ 059 916 1473 ; www.tailormade-Ireland.com

Irish Language and Culture

Several course are on offer in the Irish speaking districts (Gaeltacht) either specialising on language or combining language with culture, including workshops in tin-whistle playing, set-dancing, sean-nós singing and hill-walking, lectures on Irish folklore, poetry reading and concerts of traditional music; cultural activity courses on archaeology, marine painting, celtic pottery, Bodhrán playing etc.

Oideas Gael, Gleann Cholm Cille, Co Donegal. ☎ 074 973 0248; Fax 074 973 0348; www.oideas-gael.com

Food

Various country hotels have set up cookery schools. One in particular offers A Taste of Irish Cooking.

Berry Lodge, Annagh, Miltown Malbray, Co Clare. ☎ 065 708 7022; www.berrylodge.com

For other options, check:
www.discoverireland.com

OTHER WAYS OF EXPLORING

In addition to the ideas listed below, you may like to check out rail and bus trips from the major towns organised by Irish Rail Service (Iarnród Éireann), Northern Ireland Railways, Bus Eireann and Ulster Bus (👍 *see Getting There*).

By Tourist Train

There are a few tourist railways in Ireland that occasionally operate

Making Irish soda bread

Bord Fáilte, Dublin

steam trains on the national network. Advance booking is essential.

Railway Preservation Society of Ireland (RPSA), PO Box 1/1, Larne, Co Antrim BT40 1UU. ☏ Belfast 028 260803 or Dublin: 01 280 9147; www.rpsi-online.org

Irish Steam Preservation Society Ltd, Steam Museum, Stradbally, Co Laois. www.irishsteam.ie

By Cycle

Ireland is an ideal place to cycle because much of the country is gently undulating. Bicycles can be taken on planes, trains and buses so travelling around is straight-forward. There are also various tour operators offering well-organised group itineraries and independent holidays - *see What to do and See: Cycling.*

Irish Tourism.com Ltd, River House, Killarney Road, Newcastle West, Limerick. ☏069 77686; www.irishtourism.com

Northern Ireland Tourist Board, www.discovernorthernireland.com/cycling_holidays.aspx

The Táin Trail

The trail (365mi/585km) retraces as closely as possible the route through the Midlands from Rathcroghan to the Cooley Peninsula and back taken by Maeve's armies in pursuit of the Brown Bull of Cooley, a tale told in the *Cattle Raid of Cooley (Táin bó Buailgne)*, one of the great Irish legends.

The circular route can be joined at any point as it passes through historic places of interest – on the northern leg, starting from Rathcroghan, the trail goes through Strokestown, Longford, Fore, Kells, Louth, Dundalk and Omeath to Carlingford; on the southern leg, starting in Carlingford, it runs through Monasterboice, Slane, Kells, bypasses Mullingar, and continues through Kilbeggan, Clara, Athlone and Roscommon to Rathcroghan.

On Foot

Ireland has over 30 waymarked routes *(yellow arrow and walking figure)* following disused roads, lanes and forest trails across the country.

As the weather can change quickly it is important to let someone know where you are going and when you are expected to return, to be properly equipped with suitable clothing, compass, maps and guidebook. In addition to the trails described below, you will find others listed in the appropriate chapter– Beara Way *(see Kenmare)*, Burren Way *(see The Burren)*, Mourne Trail *(see Mourne Mountains)*, Wicklow Way *(see Wicklow Mountains)*.

The Bangor Trail

This is an old drovers' trail (approx 20mi/32km) in the west of Ireland from Newport on the shores of Clew Bay northwards through the Nephin Beg Mountains to Bangor Erris. This area of northwest Connacht consists of hills encircled by an vast area of trackless bog, without trees or houses, nothing between the heather and the sky but the occasional shepherd or farmer.

The Cavan Way

In north-west Co Cavan between Blacklion and Dowra (6mi/26km) over the hills to Shannon Pot, the source of the River Shannon, and then mainly by road to Dowra where it links up with the Leitrim Way *(see below)*.

The Dingle Way

This walk (104mi/168km) starts and finishes in Tralee and takes in the beautiful scenery of the Dingle Peninsula, although the stretch between Tralee and Camp is unexceptional.

The East Munster Way

This walk (44mi/70km) starts from Carrick-on-Suir, passes through Clonmel and finishes in Clogheen in Co Waterford; it includes forest tracks, open moorland and a river towpath.

The Kerry Way *(Slí íbh Ráthach)*

This is the longest walk (133mi/214km) which can be walked clockwise or anti-clockwise, starting and finishing in Killarney. It winds through the Macgillycuddy Reeks before reaching the coast at Glenbeigh and running south and east through Caherciveen, Waterville, Derrynane, Sneem and Kenmare.

The Leitrim Way *(Slí Liatroma)* Consists of old and new tracks (30mi/48km) from Drumshanbo, along the east shore of Lough Allen at the foot of Slieve Anierin, through Dowra the first town on the River Shannon, up the Owennayle Valley, over a moorland plateau, past Doo Lough (panoramic views), through lowland and forest, over the Tullykeherny Plateau and down a country road into Manorhamilton.

When To Go

CLIMATE

Extreme temperatures are rare in Ireland but there is the possibility of rain throughout the year. The southeast enjoys the most sun and the east coast is drier than the west.

WEATHER FORECAST

Information about the weather is available in the Republic of Ireland on ☎ 01 842 5555, in the national press, or at www.ireland.com/weather/

For forecasts affecting Northern Ireland, the Met Office operates Weathercall, ☎ 09014 722 077 (premium rate call); www.meto.gov.uk

Sign of fair weather

THE BEST TIME

The sunniest months are May / June, the warmest are July / August, so the best time to visit Ireland is the summer, the season of festivals.

WHAT TO PACK

As little as possible! Cleaning and laundry services are widely available. Most personal items can be replaced at reasonable cost. Try to pack everything in one suitcase and a tote bag. Porter help may be in short supply, and new purchases will add to the original weight of your bags. Take an extra tote bag for packing new purchases, shopping at the open-air markets, carrying a picnic, etc. Be sure luggage is clearly labelled and old travel tags have been removed. Do not pack medication in checked luggage, but keep it with you. Rain gear and an umbrella are a must!

KNOW BEFORE YOU GO

Useful Web Sites

The Internet is a useful source of information to enable you to make the most of your visit.

www.irlgov.ie
Republic of Ireland government

www.tourismireland.com
All-Ireland tourism body promoting Ireland overseas

www.ireland.com
Irish Times, daily newspaper

www.rte.ie
Irish radio and TV

www.beo.ie
Irish language magazine

www.12travel.com
Information on regions, towns, accommodation, tours, helpful tips, interactive maps etc

www.emigrant.ie
Irish Emigrant Publications, Cathedral Building, Middle Street, Galway. ☎ 091 569 158; Fax 091 569 178; info@emigrant.ie

www.discovernorthernireland. com
Northern Ireland Tourist Board, 59 North Street, Belfast BT1 1NB. ☎ 028 9023; Fax 028 9024 0960 and at 16 Nassau Street, Dublin 2, ☎ 01 679 1977; Fax 01 679 1863

Tourist Offices

TOURIST ORGANISATIONS

For information, brochures, maps and assistance in planning a trip to Ireland contact the following tourist information offices:

Irish Tourist Board (Bord Fáilte) offices situated outside Ireland

Australia
Level 5, 36 Carrington Street, Sydney, NSW 2000. ☎ 029 299 6177; Fax 029 2996323; www.tourismireland.com.au

Canada
2 Bloor Street West, Suite 3403, Toronto ON M4W. ☎ 1 416 925 6368; Fax 1 416 925 6033; www.tourismireland.com

Japan
International Place, 26-3, Sanei-cho, Shinjuku-ku, Tokyo 160-0008. ☎ 03 5367 6525; www.tourismireland.com

New Zealand
Level 6, 18 Shortland Street, PO Box 279, Auckland 1001. ☎ 0649 977 2255; Fax 0649 977 2256; www.tourismireland.com

Nordic Region/Denmark
Nyhavn 16, 3rd Floor, DK 1051 København K. ☎ 33 15 80 45; www.tourismireland.com

South Africa
c/o Development Promotions, Everite House, Level 7, 20 De Korte Street, Braamfontein 2001 Gauteng. ☎ (27) 11 339 4865; Fax (27) 11 339 2474; www.tourismireland.com

Liffey River, Dublin

United Kingdom
103 Wigmore Street, London W1U 1QS.
☎ 020 7518 0800; Fax 020 7493 9065.
James Millar House, 7th Floor,
98 West George Street, Glasgow
G2 1PJ, ☎ 0141 572 4030;
Fax 0141 572 4033;
www.tourismireland.com

United States
345 Park Avenue, 17th Floor,
New York, NY 10154. ☎ 212 418 0800;
☎ 212 371 9052;
www.tourismireland.com

**Northern Ireland Tourist Board
(NITB) offices situated outside
Ireland**

North America
551 5th Avenue, Suite 701,
New York, NY 10176. ☎ 212 922-0101;
Fax 212 922-0099.

United Kingdom
All Ireland Information Desk,
Britain Visitor Centre,
1 Regent Street, London SW1Y 4XT (personal callers and written enquiries only).
☎ 020 8846 9000 (British Tourist
Authority); www.visitbritain.com

If phoning from abroad, the county
code for the Republic of Ireland is 353,
and for Northern Ireland 44.

**Irish Tourist Board (Bord Fáilte)
offices situated in Ireland**

Irish Tourist Board (Bord Fáilte)
www.ireland.travel.ie
Baggot Street Bridge, Dublin 2.
☎ 01 602 4000 (callers within Republic of Ireland only); Fax 01 602 4100
53 Castle Street, Belfast BT1 1GH.
☎ 01232 327 888; Fax 01232 240 201
8 Bishop Street, Derry BT48 6PW.
☎ 01504 369 501; Fax 01504 369 501

**Northern Ireland Tourist Board
(NITB) offices situated in Ireland**

Northern Ireland Tourist Board
www.discovernorthernireland.com
St Anne Court, 59 North Street, Belfast
BT1 1NB. ☎ 028 9023 1221;

Fax 028 9024 0960
16 Nassau Street, Dublin 2.
☎ 01 679 1977; Fax 01 679 1863.

LOCAL TOURISM ORGANISATIONS

Regional Tourism Organizations offices situated in Ireland

Dublin Tourism
Dublin Tourism Centre, Suffolk Street,
Dublin 2. ☎ 01 605 7700;
www.visitdublin.com

South West Tourism
Grand Parade, Cork. ☎ 021 425 5100;
Fax 021 425 5199; www.corkkerry.ie

Ireland West Tourism
Aras Failte, Forster Street, Galway.
☎ 091 537 700; Fax 091 537 733;
www.irelandwest.ie

**East Coast and Midlands East
Tourism**
Dublin Road, Mullingar, Co West-
meath. ☎ 044 934 8761;
Fax 044 934 0413;
www.eastcoastmidlands.ie

South East Tourism
41 The Quay, Waterford.
☎ 051 875 823; Fax 051 876 720;
www.southeastireland.com

North West Tourism
Aras Reddan, Temple Street, Sligo.
☎ 071 916 1201; Fax 071 916 0360;
www.irelandnorthwest.ie

Shannon Development
Shannon Town Centre, Co Clare.
☎ 061 361 555; Fax 061 363 180;
www.shannonregiontourism.ie

Regional Tourism Organizations offices situated in Northern Ireland

Derry Visitor and Convention Bureau
44 Foyle Street, Londonderry
BT48 6TE. ☎ 028 7137 7577; Fax 028
7137 7992; www.derryvisitor.com

The Kingdoms of Down
40 West Street, Newtownards, Co
Down BT23 4EN. ☎ 028 9182 2881;
Fax 028 9182 2202;
www.armaghanddown.com

Fermanagh Lakeland Tourism
Wellington Road, Enniskillen BT74 7EF.
☎ 028 6632 3110; Fax 028 6632 5511;
www.fermanaghlakelands.com

Causeway Coast and Glens
11 Lodge Road, Coleraine BT52 1LU.
☎ 028 7032 7720; Fax 028 7032 7719;
www.causewaycoastandglens.com

LOCAL TOURISM ORGANIZATIONS

The addresses and telephone numbers of the Tourist Information Centres to be found in most large towns and many tourist resorts in Ireland are identified by the 🚹 symbol in the chapters in the *Discovering Ireland* sections; some are open only during the summer months. The centres can supply town plans, timetables and information on sightseeing, local entertainment and sports facilities. Many have bureau de change facilities and a hotel reservation service.

International Visitors

IRISH EMBASSIES

www.foreignaffairs.gov.ie

Australia
20 Arkana Street, Yarralumla, Canberra, ACT 2600.
☎ 06273 3022; Fax 06273 3741;
irishemb@cyberone.com.au
(Consulate General) – Level 30,
400 George Street, Sydney, NSW 2000.
☎ (612) 9231 6999;
Fax (612) 9231 6254

Canada
Suite 1105, 130 Albert Street, Ottawa,
Ontario KIP 5G4. ☎ 613 233 6281;
Fax 613 233 5835

Denmark
Østbanegade 21, DK-2100 Copenhagen. ☎ 035 423 233; Fax 035 431 858

Finland
Erottajankatu 7A, 00130 Helsinki.
Postal Address: PL 33, 00131 Helsinki.
☎ (09) 646 006; Fax (09) 646 022

Japan
Ireland House 5F, 2-10-7 Kojimachi,
Chiyoda-Ku, Tokyo 102-0083.
☎ (03) 3263 0695; Fax (03) 3265 2275

New Zealand
Level 7, Citibank Building, 23 Customs
Street EASt, Auckland. Postal address
PO Box 279, Auckland 1001.
☎ 09 977 2252; Fax 09 977 2256

Norway
Haakon VIIs gate 1, 0244 Oslo.
☎ (47) 2201 7200; Fax (47) 2201 7201

South Africa
1st Floor, Southern Life Plaza, 1059
Schoeman Street, Arcadia 0083,
Pretoria 0001.
Postal address PO Box 4174 Pretoria
0001. ☎ (27) 12 342 5062; Fax (27) 12
342 4752

Sweden
Ostermalmsgatan 97, PO Box 10326,
100 55, Stockholm.
☎ 08 66 18 005; Fax 08 66 01 353

United Kingdom
17 Grosvenor Place, London
SW1X 7HR. ☎ 020 7235 2171;
Fax 020 7245 6961. Passport Office,
106 Brompton Road, London SW3 1JJ.

United States
2234 Massachusetts Avenue NW,
Washington DC 20008-2849.
☎ 202 462 3939; Fax 202 232 5993;
www.irelandemb.org

FOREIGN EMBASSIES AND CONSULATES IN IRELAND

Australia
Fitzwilton House (7th floor), Wilton
Terrace, Dublin 2. ☎ 01 664 5300;
www.australianembassy.ie

Canada
Canada House, 65 St Stephen's Green, Dublin 2. ☎ 01 478 1988; Fax 01 478 1285; cndembsy@iol.ie

Denmark
121-122 St Stephen's Green, Dublin 2. ☎ 01 475 6404; Fax 01 478 4536; amb@um.dk

Finland
Russell House, Stokes Place, St Stephen's Green, Dublin 2. ☎ 01 478 1344; Fax 01 478 3727; sanomat.dub@formin.fi

Japan
Nutley Building, Merrion Centre, Nutley Lane, Dublin 4. ☎ 01 202 8300; Fax 01 283 8726

New Zealand
37 Leeson Park, Dublin 6 ☎ 01 660 4233; Fax 01 660 4228; nzconsul@indigo.ie

South Africa
Alexandra House, Earlsfort Centre, Earlsfort Terrace, Dublin 2. ☎ 01 661 5553; Fax 01 661 5590; information@saedublin.com

Sweden
13-17 Dawson Street, Dublin 2. ☎ 01 474 4400; Fax 01 474 4450; ambassaden.dublin@foreignministry.se

United Kingdom
29 Merrion Road, Ballsbridge, Dublin 4. ☎ 01 205 3700; Fax 01 205 3885; management.dubli@fco.gov.uk; www.britishembassy.ie

USA
42 Elgin Road, Ballsbridge, Dublin 4. ☎ 01 668 8777; Fax 01 668 9946; www.dublin.usembassy.gov

DOCUMENTS

Visitors entering Ireland must be in possession of a **valid national passport** (except British nationals). In case of loss or theft report to the appropriate embassy and the local police.

Visitors who require an **entry visa** for the Republic of Ireland or Northern Ireland should apply at least three weeks in advance to the Irish Embassy or the United Kingdom Embassy. Useful information for US nationals on visa requirements, customs regulations, medical care etc for international travel is contained in the booklets *Your Trip Abroad* and *Safe Trip Abroad*, from www.travel.state.gov Visitors from outside the EU wishing to drive in the UK or Ireland should apply for an **International Driving permit** (♿ *see Getting There: by Car*).

Visitors from outside the EU should have comprehensice travel insurance in case of accident or ill-health. Visitors from EU countries should carry a **European Health Insurance Card (EHIC)**, and have adequate travel insurance for the duration of their stay. In case of the loss or theft of any document, report it to the local police.

CUSTOMS REGULATIONS

Tax-free allowances for various commodities are governed by EU legislation. Details of these allowances are available at most ports of entry to the Republic of Ireland / United Kingdom, and from customs authorities. It is against the law to bring into the Republic of Ireland firearms, explosives, illicit drugs, meat and meat products, plant and plant products (including seeds). It is against the law to bring into the United Kingdom drugs, firearms and ammunition, obscene material featuring children, counterfeit merchandise, unlicensed livestock (birds or animals), anything related to endangered species (furs, ivory, horn, leather) and certain plants (potatoes, bulbs, seeds, trees).
Customs and Excise, Passenger Terminal, Dublin Airport, Co Dublin. ☎ 01 844 5538; Fax 01 844 5420
Customs and Excise, Custom House, Belfast BT1 3ET. ☎ 028 9056 2600 or 028 9023 4466; Fax 028 9056 2972
HM Customs and Excise ☎ 0845 010 9000 (National Advice Helpline);

☎ 020 7620 1313 (HQ); 020 7928 3344 (switchboard)

For US nationals returning to the US after travelling abroad there is useful information in the leaflet *Know Before You Go* available as a downloadable pdf from www.cbp.gov/xp/cgov/travel/vacation/kbyg/

DOMESTIC ANIMALS

No animals, pets or other, may be brought into the Republic of Ireland, except from the United Kingdom. Domestic animals (dogs, cats) with vaccination documents are allowed into the United Kingdom (Great Britain and Northern Ireland).

Department of Agriculture, Food and Rural Development, Agriculture House, Kildare Street, Dublin 2. ☎ 01 607 2000

HEALTH

In Ireland hospital treatment is available in emergencies but is not free of charge except to nationals of the country. Emergency help can be obtained from the Casualty Department of a hospital, from a pharmacy/chemist. For emergencies dial 999. Nationals of non-EU countries should take out comprehensive insurance. National of EU countries should apply to their own National Social Security Offices for **Form E111** (not obligatory for UK nationals; proof of identity only necessary) which entitles them to medical treatment under an EU Reciprocal Medical Treatment arrangement, provided treatment is sought from a doctor in Ireland whose name is on the Health Board Panel of Doctors (list available from the local health board). Information is available from the Aviation Health Institute on precautions to take before and during air travel; on DVT and air travel, on transmission of disease inflight, on radiation and inflight medical incidents; on deaths and incidents of air-related problems **Aviation Health Institute** – www.aviation-health.org

Accessibility

Some of the sights described in this guide are accessible to disabled people – ♿ indicates at least partial access for wheelchairs.

The **Michelin Guide Great Britain and Ireland** indicates hotels with facilities suitable for disabled people. Information on tourism, accommodation, transport and activity centres is available from several organisations:

♦ **Everybody's Hotel Directory** – www.everybody.co.uk – On-line directory which gives useful information about accommodation for all room types (including wheelchair access) in Ireland.

♦ **Irish Wheelchair Association**, Blackheath Drive, Clontarf, Dublin 3. ☎ 01 818 6400; Fax 01 833 3873; info@iwa.ie; www.iwa.ie

♦ **Comhairle**, 44 North Great George's Street, Dublin 1. ☎ 01 874 7503; Fax 01 764 7490

♦ **Disability Action**, Portside Business Park, 189 Airport Road West, Belfast BT3 9AD. ☎ 028 9029 7880, ☎ 028 9066 1252, 028 9029 7882 (textphone); Fax 028 9029 7881; hq@disabilityaction.org; www.disabilityaction.org

♦ **Radar**, 12 City Forum, 250 City Road, London EC1V 8AF. ☎ 020 7250 3222; Fax 020 7250 0212; minicom 020 73500 4119; radar@radar.org.uk

♦ **Holiday Care**, Imperial Buildings (2nd Floor), Victoria Road, Horley RH6 7PZ. ☎ 01293 774 535; Fax 01293 784 647; holiday.care@virgin.net; www.holidaycare.org.uk

♦ **Tripscope**,The Vassall Centre, Gill Avenue, Bristol BS16 2QQ. ☎ 08457 585 641, ☎ 44 117 939 7782 (from outside the UK); Fax 0117 939 7736, Fax 44 117 939 7736 (from outside the UK); enquiries@tripscope.org.uk; www.tripscope.org.uk

GETTING THERE

By Air

Many international airlines operate flights to the international airports in Ireland – Dublin, Shannon, Knock and Belfast. All airports are linked by bus to the neighbouring towns.

Information, brochures and timetables are available from the airlines and from travel agents. Fly-Drive schemes are operated by most airlines.

Aer Lingus
www.aerlingus.com

British Airways
www.britishairways.com

British European
www.flybe.com

British Midland
www.flybmi.com

Easyjet
www.easyjet.com

Manx Airlines
www.manx-airlines.com

Ryanair
www.ryanair.com

By Sea

Details of passenger ferry and car ferry services to Ireland from the United Kingdom and France can be obtained from travel agencies or from the main carriers. Information about ferries to the offshore islands is given in the *Discovering Ireland* section of the guide.

Brittany Ferries
www.brittany-ferries.com.
General enquiries ☎ 021 4277 801 (Ireland); 0873 665 333 (UK).

Irish Ferries
www.irishferries.com.

General enquiries ☎ 0818 300 400 (Ireland); 00353 818 300 400 (Northern Ireland); 08705 17 17 17 (UK)

Stena Line
www.stenaline.com
☎ 0870 570 7070

P&O Irish Sea
www.poirishsea.com.
Larne ☎ 0870 24 24 777;
Dublin ☎ 01 800 409 049

Swansea Cork Ferries
www.swansea-cork.com
Reservations: ☎ 021 483 6000 (Ireland); 01792 456 116 (UK)

By Rail

Irish Rail Service, (Northern Ireland Railways and the various British railway companies operate train services between the major cities in Ireland and the United Kingdom.

Iarnród Éireann / Irish Rail
Online timetables and ticket reservation; ☎ 1850 366 222; www.irishrail.ie.
Talking timetable 1890 77 88 99
Iarnròd Eireann Travel Centre,
35 Lower Abbey Street, Dublin 1.
☎ 01 703 4070
Tours (1-4 days) by train and coach.
Advance booking essential;
www.railtours.ie

Ferry crossing the Irish Sea

R Holzbachova, Ph Benet/MICHELIN

Dublin Tourism Centre, Suffolk Street, Dublin 2 or opposite Connolly Station; ☏01 856 0045

CIE – national coach / rail / Dublin Bus operator. International and national routes, timetables, fares on www.cie.ie

🚃 **Northern Ireland Rail**
Online timetables and journey planner; www.translink.co.uk
Central Station, Belfast BT1 3PB.
☏ 028 9066 6630(enquiries)
international services and short breaks
NIR ☏028 9024 2420

By Coach / Bus

Regular coach services operate between the major Irish towns and the major cities in Great Britain and the Continent via the car ferry ports at Rosslare, Dublin Ferryport and Larne.

Bus Éireann
www.buseireann.ie; www.infopoint. ie/buse/
Store Street, Dublin 1. ☏ 01 836 6111, 01 830 2222; Fax 01 873 4534

Dublin Bus (Bus Atha Cliath)
www.dublinbus.ie
☏ 01 873 4222

Ulsterbus
www.translink.co.uk
Europa Bus Centre, Glengall Street, Belfast BT12
5AH. b 028 9066 6630 (enquiries)

By Car 🚗

👆 For additional information about driving in Ireland see *Getting Around*.

Nationals of EU countries wishing to drive in Ireland require a **valid national driving** licence; nationals of non-EU countries require an **International Driving Permit (IDP)**. This is obtainable in the US for US$10 from the National Auto Club, 1151 E Hillsdale Boulevard, Foster City CA 94404; www.thenac.com or from a local branch of the American Automobile Association. ☏ 1 800 622 2136. Nationals of other non-European countries should check before leaving their home country.

It is necessary to have your vehicle's **registration papers** (log-book) and an approved **nationality plate**. Vehicle **insurance cover** is compulsory. Although no longer a legal requirement, the International Insurance Certificate (Green Card) is the most effective proof of insurance cover and is internationally recognised by the police and other authorities. In the case of loss or theft of any document, report it to the local police.

CAR HIRE / RENTAL

There are car rental agencies at airports, railway stations and in all large towns throughout Ireland. European cars usually have manual transmission; automatic cars need to be specified at the time of booking.

Before crossing the border between the Republic and Northern Ireland it is important to check that the insurance cover extends to the other country. It is cheaper to return a hire car to its pick-up point than to leave it elsewhere.

MAPS AND PLANS

For Route Planning use Michelin Map 712 Ireland and the Michelin Atlas Great Britain and Ireland; both show the major roads (N or A) and many of the minor roads (R/L or B).

GETTING AROUND

📍 *See also Driving Tours Map on p 11.*

Driving in Ireland

The road network consists of few motorways, some high standard major roads, some older ones with an inside lane for farm vehicles, and some which are narrower. In the peatlands where the road surface may be undulating it is necessary to moderate your speed.

On the Sky Road, Connemara

HIGHWAY CODE

- The **minimum driving age** is 16 years in the Republic of Ireland and 17 in Northern Ireland.
- Traffic drives on the **left**.
- Traffic on main roads and on roundabouts has priority.
- The driver and front-seat passenger must wear **seat belts**. Rear-seat belts must be worn where they are fitted; children under 12 must travel in the rear seats.
- Full or dipped **headlights** should be switched on in poor visibility and at night; use **sidelights** only when the vehicle is stationary in an area without street lighting.
- It is obligatory to carry a red warning triangle or to have hazard warning lights to use in the case of a **breakdown** or **accident**.

Speed limits Republic of Ireland:
30mph/48kph: in built-up areas
60mph/96kph: on country roads
70mph/112kph: on motorways
Northern Ireland:
30mph/48kph: in built-up areas
60mph/96kph: on country roads
70mph/112kph: on dual carriageways and motorways

PARKING

There are multi-storey car parks in towns, disc systems, parking meters and paying parking zones; in the last two cases, small change is necessary and in the last case tickets must be obtained from the ticket machines and displayed inside the windscreen. In Northern Ireland city centre parking may be restricted and the usual regulations are as follows:

- Double red line = no stopping at any time (freeway)
- Double yellow line = no parking at any time
- Single yellow line = no parking for set periods as indicated on panel
- Dotted yellow line = parking limited to certain times only

PENALTIES

In the Republic
Parking offences may attract an on-the-spot fine. Drivers suspected of **speeding** are liable to an on-the-spot fine. Drivers suspected of **driving while under the influence of alcohol** are liable to be checked with a breathalyser and to prosecution.

In Northern Ireland
Failure to display a parking paid ticket may result in a fine. Illegal parking is

liable to Penalty Charge Notice and, in some cases, to the vehicle being clamped or towed away.

Drivers suspected of **driving while under the influence of alcohol** are liable to be checked with a breathalyser and to prosecution.

Drivers suspected of **speeding** are liable to prosecution; there are warning signs (camera) beside the road and speed cameras (yellow) which are activated by speeding vehicles.

ROAD SIGNS

The colour code for different types of road signs is as follows:

- blue for motorways
- green for major roads
- black on white for local destinations
- brown for tourist signs

NATIONAL (REGIONAL) IDENTIFICATION LETTERS

In the Republic of Ireland the vehicle registration number consists of two figures representing the year of registration, a letter indicating the county of registration and the individual registration number (1 or more figures). The international symbol is IRL.

Since 2001 in Great Britain and Northern Ireland the number plates on new vehicles must conform to a standard typeface and size and a British Standard (with GB and EU symbols as permitted options). The individual

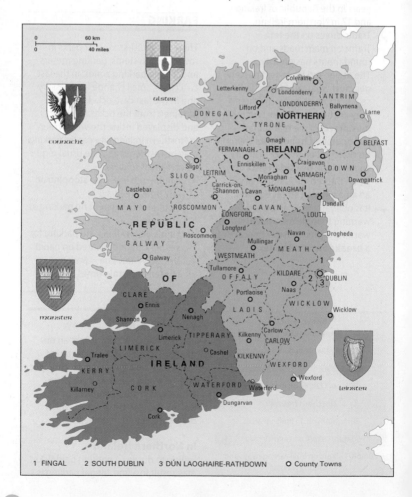

1 FINGAL   2 SOUTH DUBLIN   3 DÚN LAOGHAIRE-RATHDOWN   O County Towns

registration number consists of a two-letter area code, a two-number age code and a three letters selected at random.

ROAD TOLLS

Tolls are levied on the East Link Bridge (Dublin) which spans the Liffey estuary, the West-Link Bridge (Dublin) which runs north–south on the western edge of the city, on the M1 Drogheda By-pass and the M4 Kinnegad-Enfield-Kilcock road.

PETROL/GAS

Most service stations have dual-pumps; **unleaded pumps** are identified by a green stripe or green pump handles.
Petrol prices in the Republic (2006):
- Unleaded: 117.7c
- Diesel: 111.9c

Petrol prices in Northern Ireland vary, being cheaper near the border but the following are a guide:
- Unleaded: 95.9p
- Diesel: 98.1p

MOTORING ORGANISATIONS

In Ireland and the UK accident insurance and breakdown service schemes are organised by certain motoring organisations for their members. Members of the American Automobile Club should obtain the brochure *Offices to serve you abroad*.

Automobile Association (AA)
www.aaireland.ie
56 Drury Street, Dublin 2.
☎ 01 617 9999; Fax 01 617 9900

Automobile Association (AA)
www.theaa.co.uk
☎ 09003 401 100 (AA Roadwatch),
☎ 00 44 161 495 8945 (international enquiries)

Royal Automobile Club (RAC)
www.rac.co.uk ; www.rac.ie
RAC UK (Head Office), RAC Motoring Services, 8 Surrey Street, Norwich NR1 3NG. ☎ 020 8917 2500
Postal address: RAC Motoring, Great Park Road, Bradley Stoke, Bristol BS32 4QN. ☎ 08705 722 722 (Customer Services)

Europ-Assistance
www.europ-assistance.com
IDA Business Park, Athlumney, Navan, Co Meath. ☎ 0870 737 5720 (Customer Services); customerservices@europ-assistance.co.uk
HQ, Sussex House, Perrymount Road, Haywards Heath, West Sussex, RH16 1DN.

WHERE TO STAY AND EAT

Where to Stay

(🪙 *See the Places to stay map pp 36-37*)

A variety of different types of accommodation are available in Ireland. Hotels and restaurants are described in the Address Books within the *Discovering Ireland* sections. 🪙 *See the cover flap for coin ranges.*
In town centres **parking** can be a problem but many hotels have a car park on site or a short walk away.
In a small town the only hotel often doubles as the **local disco** and it may be very noisy until the early hours on a Saturday night, especially if there is a wedding party in the house.
At **breakfast** most types of establishments offer a light Continental-style breakfast of coffee and bread and jam as well as the traditional cooked breakfast. In larger establishments there may be a choice for the first course of cereal, porridge, stewed or fresh fruit, yoghurt and fruit juice, followed by a main dish usually of eggs or fish, followed by toast and marmalade, accompanied by tea or coffee.

Places to stay

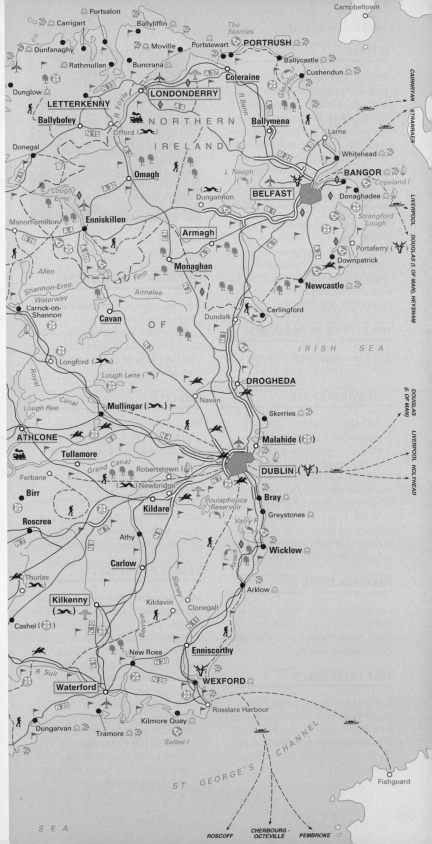

HOTELS

Traditionally hotels tend to be medium to large establishments, where the bedrooms have en suite facilities and a full-range of services. The terms hotel and guesthouse are used fairly loosely, usually at the whim of the proprietors, and apply to a broad range of accommodation.

GUESTHOUSES

The term guesthouse describes a smaller operation than a hotel, with fewer facilities, that generally appeals more to visitors on holiday than to those on business. The properties vary from modern purpose-built premises to Georgian and Victorian houses.

INNS / PUBS WITH ROOMS

In the smaller towns and villages the local inn often has rooms to let.

BED & BREAKFAST

The distinction between Bed-and-Breakfast places and guesthouses is often blurred but the traditional Bed-and-Breakfast is a family-run affair, offering one or two bedrooms at a moderate price. This simple form of accommodation is found all over Ireland in properties ranging from a simple bungalow to a great house. Staying in an Irish home provides an opportunity to share in Irish family life.

FARM HOLIDAYS

Being a predominantly agricultural country, Ireland has a great range of farms, many of which welcome visitors in the summer season.

SELF CATERING

In many parts of the country, particularly the tourist districts, there are purpose-built holiday villages consisting of a cluster of well-appointed cottages. 🕯 *See Low-Budget Accommodations below.*

A welcome sign in Kenmare

UNIVERSITY RESIDENCES

Accommodation in **universities** (single rooms and self-catering apartments) is available during school vacations, particularly in Dublin, Cork, and Galway. 🕯 *See Low-Budget Accommodations below.*

HOSTELS

There are 50 **youth hostels** in the Republic and six in Northern Ireland. 🕯 *See Low-Budget Accommodations below.*

CAMP SITES

Ireland has many officially graded caravan and camping parks with modern facilities and a variety of sports facilities.

USEFUL ADDRESSES

www.goireland.com – the **Accommodation Booking Service** developed for the Irish Tourist Board (Bord Fáilte) and the Northern Irish Tourist Board (NITB), and their networks of regional tourist boards. Information on flights, ferries, special interest holidays. ☎ 00800 369 87412 in Ireland; 0800 783 8359 from the UK; 1 888 827 3028 from US.

Other affiliated organisations include:
- ◆ **Irish Hotels Federation**, 13 Northbrook Road, Dublin 6. ☎ 01 497 64 59; Fax 01 497 4613; www.irelandhotels.com

◆ **Manor House and Irish Country Hotels**, 1 Sandyford Office Park, Foxrock, Dublin 18. ☎ 0818 281 281 from within the Republic of Ireland; 1877 905 6789 toll-free USA; +353 295 8900 from elsewhere; www.manorhousehotels. com

◆ **The Hidden Ireland** – Accommodation in historic Irish houses – P O Box 31, Westport, Co Mayo. ☎ 01 662 7166 or 098 66650; Fax 01 662 7144, 098 66651; www. hidden-ireland.com

◆ **Ireland's Blue Book** – Irish country houses and restaurants affiliated to the Historic Hotels of Europe /America – 8 Mount St Crescent, Dublin2. ☎ 01 676 9914; Fax 01 631 4990; www.irelands-blue-book.ie

◆ **Irish Farm Holidays** – 2 Michael Street, Limerick. ☎ 061 400 700; Fax 061 400 771; www.irishfarm-holidays.com

◆ **Town and Country Homes Association** – publishes *Bed and Breakfast Ireland* (€10) – Belleek Road, Ballyshannon, Co Donegal. ☎ 071 98 22222; Fax 071 98 22207; www.townandcoutry.ie

◆ **Elegant Ireland** – Exclusive rented castles, country houses or cottages in Ireland – 15 Harcourt Street, Dublin 2. ☎ 01 475 1632; 01 475 1665; Fax 01 475 1012; www. elegant.ie

◆ **Premier Collection of Ireland** – Guesthouse accommodation promoted by Irish Cottages and Holiday Homes Association. ☎ 01 205 2826; Fax 01 293 3027; www.premierguesthouses.com

◆ **Irish Cottages and Holiday Homes Association** – Self-Catering Accommodation Guide *(€6.50; £5)* listing over 5 000 holiday cottages and houses to rent – Bracken Court, Bracken Road, Dublin 18. ☎ 01 205 2777; Fax 01 293 3025; www.irishcottageholidays.com

◆ **Dining in Ireland** – online directory of restaurants produced by the Restaurants Association of Ireland. www.rai.ie

Simple **Low-Budget Accommodation** is available in hostels (single, twin and 4/6-bedded rooms) at the following addresses:

◆ **Independent Holiday Hostels Ireland**, 57 Lower Gardiner Street, Dublin 1 ☎ 01 836 4700; Fax 0 836 4710; www.hostels-ireland.com

◆ **Kinlay House** – budget accommodation in the centre of town. ☎01 679 6644 Dublin; 021 450 8966 Cork; 09 156 5244 Galway. www.kinlayhouse.ie

◆ **Barnacles Hostels** – 19 Temple Lane, Temple Bar, Dublin2; ☎01 671 6277 and 10 Quay Street, Galway; ☎091 568 644. www. barnacles.ie

◆ **Northern Ireland Hostelling International**, ☎ 028 9032 4733, www.hini.org.uk

◆ **An Oige** (Youth Hostel Association) ☎ 01 830 4555; www. irelandyha.org

◆ **Usit** –Student travel specialists and information centre. Hostel / hotel booking service ☎ 01 602 1904. www.usit.ie

◆ **Marketing University Summer Accommodation** (**MUSA**), Accommodation Office, University of Limerick ☎ 061 202 360; Fax 061 202 188

◆ **Accommodation Office**, Trinity College, Dublin 2, ☎ 01 608 1177; Fax 01 671 1267; www.tcd. ie/accommodationandcatering

◆ **Irish Caravan & Camping Council**, P O Box 4443, Dublin 2. Fax 098 28237 (brochures); www. camping-ireland.ie

Where to Eat

Ireland offers a huge range of places to eat from top-class restaurants offering high quality produce and the latest in the culinary art through wine bars, bistros, brasseries, to fast food outlets such as pizzerias, cafés and fish and chip shops. Many historical sights, like National Trust properties (Northern Ireland only), also provide lunch and tea.

EATING OUT

Restaurants are usually open at lunchtime from noon to 2.15pm depending on their location, and in the evening from 6.30pm to 10pm. Many close one day a week and they may close early (between 7pm and 8pm on Sundays and Mondays in Northern Ireland). It is always advisable to book in the evening, particularly at the weekend. A usual evening meal in a restaurant consists of three courses but in many places it is acceptable to eat only a starter and a main dish or a main dish and a dessert. Portions are usually generous. A meal is usually accompanied by an alcoholic or non-alcoholic drink and followed by tea or coffee. Filter coffee is rare in the less expensive restaurants. Most restaurants serve bottled water - still or sparkling - but tap water will be provided on request.

SPECIALITIES

Being an agricultural country, Ireland produces very good home-reared meat, particularly beef and lamb, and excellent dairy products – local cheeses, butter and cream. Near the coast there should be a good choice of fish; salmon is usually available everywhere. In the less-expensive restaurants the menu may not offer much in the way of fresh fruit and vegetables but the potatoes are usually very good. Look out for soda bread, for potato cakes (even at breakfast), for oysters and Guinness, for black pudding – a speciality in Co Cork and for carrageen – a form of seaweed which is used in savoury and sweet dishes.

TIPPING

Tipping is optional but it is very common to leave 10% when the service is particularly pleasing. Usually Value-Added Tax (VAT) and service (12.5%) are included in the bill. Some restaurants will leave the total open on a credit card slip so that customers can add a tip to the bill.

AND ALSO ...

If you are unable to find suitable accommodation or a pleasing restaurant among the establishments listed in the Address Books listed in the *Discovering Ireland* sections, consult the **Michelin Guide Great Britain and Ireland** which provides comprehensive coverage of hotels, guesthouses and restaurants.

WHAT TO DO AND SEE

Ireland is naturally well-endowed with a variety of different physical environments for outdoor **sports and leisure activities**. The long and indented coastline provides facilities for bathing, scuba-diving, wind-surfing, sailing, sea-angling and deep-sea fishing. The many inland lakes and waterways are good for cruising, canoeing and water-skiing and attactive to anglers. For golfers there are both inland and links courses. The magnificent mountain ranges which fringe the Atlantic coast from north to south provide exhilarating locations for walking, rambling, orienteering and mountaineering. Hunting and horse racing are concentrated in the flatter, agricultural counties of the south and midlands; pony trekking is country-wide.
Information on all the activities listed below is available from the Irish Tourist Board (Bord Fáilte) and the Northern Irish Tourist Board (NITB).

Outdoor Fun

ADVENTURE SPORTS

Climbing and Mountaineering

Information on mountaineering, rock climbing and orienteering is available from the following organisations:

- **Mountaineering Council of Ireland**. www.climbing.ie
- **National Mountain and White-water Centre**, Tiglin, Devil's Glen, Ashford, Co Wicklow – Courses in caving, canoeing, hang gliding, hiking, mountaineering, orienteering, rock climbing, snorkelling and surfing. www.tiglin.com
- **Tollymore Mountain Centre**, Bryansford, Newcastle, N Ireland. www.tollymoremc.com

AIRBORNE SPORTS

Gliding

Irish Hang-Gliding and Paragliding Association. www.ihpa.ie or www.uhpc.f9.co.uk (for Northern Ireland)

Parachuting

Irish Parachute Club www.skydive.ie

EQUESTRIAN SPORTS

Association of Irish Riding Establishments (AIRE)

www.aire.ie

- **Equestrian Holidays Ireland** www.ehi.ie
- **Hunting Association of Ireland** Hunting with hounds. www.hai.ie

HERITAGE

Historic Properties

- **Dúchas** – The Irish Heritage Service is the State body responsible for the protection and conservation of the natural and built heritage. It offers a **Heritage Card**, providing unlimited admission to all sites managed by The Office of Public Works, available at most properties or from Dublin Tourism. **Dúchas Education and Visitor Services**, 51 St Stephen's Green,

Paragliding at Portrush

NITB, Belfast

Dublin 2. ☎ 01 661 3111. www.heritageireland.ie

- **Heritage Towns** – Some 25 towns have been designated Heritage Towns because of their architecture and history or particular character, which is illustrated in the local heritage centre. www.heritagetowns.com
- **Historic Monuments** In Northern Ireland are the responsibility of the Department of the Environment.
  Environment and Heritage Service : Built Heritage: www.ehsni.gov.uk/built
- **National Trust** – The Trust owns over 200 historic house and gardens and 49 industrial monuments and mills in the United Kingdom. Members may use their membership cards to visit NT properties in Northern Ireland. Annual membership offering free admission to all NT sites is available at most sites. **Head Office in Northern Ireland**, Rowallane House, Saintfield, Ballynahinch, Co Down BT24 7LH. ☎ (44) 28 9751 0721; www.nationaltrust.org.uk

Museums and Art Galleries

- **National Museums & Galleries of Northern Ireland (MAGNI)**. ☎ 028 9038 3000; www.magni.org.uk
- **Northern Ireland Museums Council**: ☎ 028 9055 0215; www.nimc.co.uk

Nature Reserves and National Parks

Ireland has four **national parks** – Glenveagh, Connemara, Wicklow Mountains and Killarney – in the Republic, many **forest parks** and **country parks** managed for public use and recreation, and numerous **nature reserves** (wildfowl sanctuaries, peat bogs and sand dunes) on both sides of the border :

- **National Parks and Wildlife Service** ☎ 01890 202 021 from Ireland; +353 1 888 2000; www. npws.ie or www.environ.ie
- **Birdwatch Ireland (BWI)**, Co Wicklow. ☎ 01 281 9878; www. birdwatchireland.ie
- **Irish Peatland Conservation Council**, Co Kildare. ☎ 045 860 133; www.ipcc.ie
- **Royal Society for Protection of Birds (RSPB)**, Belvoir Park Forest, Belfast BT8 4QT. ☎ 028 9049 1547; www.rspb.org.uk/nireland/

LAND SPORTS

Cycling

Cycling is becoming increasingly popular in Ireland, as a result, it is easy to hire a bicycle almost anywhere in Ireland.

- **Walking Cycling Ireland**. www. irelandwalkingcycling.com **Tour operators:**
- **Irish Cycling Safaris**, Belfield Bike Shop, Belfield House, University College Dublin, Dublin 4. ☎ 01 260 0749 ; Fax 01 716 1168 ; www. cyclingsafaris.com
- **Irish Cycle Hire**, Unit 6 Ardee Enterprise Centre, Co Louth. ☎041 685 3772; www.irishcyclehire.com
- **Cyclewest Ireland**, 12 Dun Na Mara, Renmore, Co Galway. ☎091 761 707; www.cyclewest.com
- **Killary Tours**, Leenane, Connemara, Co Galway. ☎ 095 42276. www.killary.com
- **Ireland Rent-a-Bike**, Emerald Alpine, 1 Patrick Street, Limerick. ☎ 061 416 983. www.irelandrentabike.com

Golf

A complete resource available online - including details of some 417 courses and specialist Tour Operators: www. golf.ireland.ie

- **Golfing Union of Ireland (GUI)**, Carton Demesne, Maynooth, Co Kildare. ☎ 01 601 6842; Fax 01 601 6858; www.gui.ie
- **Irish Ladies Golf Union (ILGU)**, 1 Clonskeagh Square, Dublin 14. ☎ 01 269 6244

Rambling

The Irish Tourist Board publishes brochures on the **national way-marked ways** in the Republic of Ireland. Detailed information sheets for individual long-distance walks are also available. Waymarked ways are reserved for walking as they are unsuitable for horses or mountain bikes. ☺ If you have a dog with you, it should not be brought on ways which cross farmland; any dog seen chasing domestic animals is likely to be shot.

- **Walking Cycling Ireland**: www.irelandwalkingcycling.com lists various tour operators across.
- **Walking in Northern Ireland**. www.geographia.com/northern-ireland
- **East–West Mapping**, Ballyredmond, Clonegal, Enniscorthy, Co Wexford. ☎053 937 7835; Fax 053 937 7835; http:// homepage.eircom.net/~eastwest/

Shooting

In the Republic of Ireland permits are available from the Department of the Environment and Local Government. In Northern Ireland permits are available on application to the Forestry Service – www.forestservice.ni.gov.uk

- **National Parks and Wildlife Service**, 7 Ely Place, Dublin 2. Tel 01 888 2000; www.npws.ie/PermitsLicences/
- **District Forest Office**, The Grange, Castlewellan Forest Park, Castlewellan BT31 9BU. ☎ 028 4377 2257
- **District Forest Office**, Inishkeen House, Killyhevlin, Enniskillen BT74 4EJ. ☎ 028 6634 3123

RACING

Horse Racing

There are racecourses dotted across much of Ireland. Those in the Dublin area include The Curragh, Punchestown, Leopardstown and Fairyhouse. The most popular festivals are **Fairyhouse** *(Easter)*, **Killarney** *(May)*, **Curragh** *(June)*, **Killarney** *(July)*, **Galway**, **Tramore** and **Tralee** *(August)*, **Galway** and **Listowel** *(September)* and **Leopardstown** and **Limerick** *(December)*.

Irish Horseracing Authority, Thoroughbred County House, Kill, Co Kildare. ☎ 045 842 800; Fax 045 842 801; www.hri.ie

Greyhound Racing

There are 18 race tracks for this popular evening entertainment: Ballyskeagh, Cork, Dublin, Dundalk, Dungannon, Enniscorthy, Galway, Kilkenny, Lifford, Limerick, Londonderry, Longford, Mullingar, Newbridge, Thurles, Tralee, Waterford and Youghal.

Bord na gCon, Irish Greyhound Board, Limerick. www.igb.ie

WATER SPORTS

Ireland Waterways was set up under the British Irish Agreement (1999) to co-ordinate the management and promotion of inland navigable waterways. www.waterwaysireland.org

Canoeing and Kayaking

The many lakes and rivers provide good sport, as does the sea!

- ◆ **Irish Canoe Union** www.irishcanoeunion.com
- ◆ **Irish Sea Kayaking Association (ISKA)**. www.irishseakayakingassociation.org
- ◆ **National Mountain and Whitewater Centre**. www.tiglin.com

Fishing

The Irish Tourist Board lists details on Game Angling, Sea Angling and Coarse Angling, River Trout Angling, Pike Angling, River Moy Angling, Lough Derg Fishing Guide.

The Fisheries Board provides details of coarse fishing, sea fishing, pike fishing, flyfishing, salmon and trout fishing in Ireland.

Fishing permits are available in Northern Ireland from tackle shops and fishery authorities

- ◆ **Central Fisheries Board**, Swords Business Campus, Swords, Co Dublin. ☎ 01 884 2600; www.cfb.ie
- ◆ **Shannon Fishery Board**. www.shannon-fishery-board.ie
- ◆ **Angling News**. www.anglingnews.net
- ◆ **Fisheries Conservancy Board for Northern Ireland**, 1 Mahon Road, Portadown, Co Armagh, BT62 3EE. ☎ 028 3833 4666; www.fcbni.com

Sailing / Cruising

There are sailing marinas all round the coast of Ireland and on the inland lakes. All yacht clubs are linked to the Irish Sailing Association which lists racing, training and cruising activities on its Web site:

- ◆ **Irish Sailing Association** www.sailing.ie
- ◆ **Water activities in Ireland** www.waterbasedireland.ie
- ◆ **Saii Ireland Charters**, Trident Hotel Marina, Kinsale, Co Cork; ☎ 021 477 2927; Fax 021 477 4170; www.sailireland.com
- ◆ **Waveline Cruisers Ltd**, Quigley's Marina, Killinure Point, Glassan, Athlone, Co Westmeath. ☎ 090 648 5711; Fax 090 648 5716; www.waveline.ie
- ◆ **Celtic Canal Cruisers Ltd**, Tullamore, Co Offaly. ☎ 0506 21861; Fax 0506 51266; www.celticcanalcruisers.com

R Holzbachova, Ph Benet/MICHELIN

Fishing at Maam Cross in Connemara

- **Sail Northern Ireland**, Carrickfergus Marina, The Marina 3 Quayside, Carrickfergus, Co Antrim BT38 8BE. ☎02893 366666; Fax 02893 350505

Sub Aqua Diving

Ireland has a beautiful underwater coastline, particularly on the west coast where the Gulf Stream brings an abundant marine life into the clear Atlantic waters.

- **Irish Underwater Council**, 78A Patrick Street, Dún Laoghaire, Co Dublin. ☎ 01 284 4601; Fax 01 284 4602; www.irishunderwater-council.com
- **Activity Ireland Dive Centre**, Caherdaniel, Co Kerry. ☎ 066 947 5277; www.activity-ireland.com/padi/

Swimming (and Bathing)

There are swimming pools in the Leisure Centres of most of the larger towns and seawater baths in many seaside resorts.

Water Skiing

Irish Water Ski Federation (IWSF), Cork PB & WSC, Agherinagh, Dripsey, Co Cork. www.iwsf.ie

Surfing

The best conditions are to be found on the northwest and the mid-west coasts; good conditions prevail on the north, southwest and south coast; the east coast is practicable only during a storm or strong southerly winds. Surfboards are available for hire.

- **Irish Surf Association**, Easkey Surf Centre, Easkey, Co Sligo. ☎ 096 49428. www.isasurf.ie
- **Irish Sailing Association** – *See Sailing above.*

Windsurfing

Some of the most popular places for windsurfing or sailboarding or board-sailing are in northwest Ireland on the coast of Co Mayo at **Easky**, where the Tiki Cold Water Classic was held in 1997, and on the coast of Co Donegal at **Bundoran**, where the European championships draw great crowds.

Sailing at Carrickfergus

- **Irish Wind Surfing Association** www.sailing.ie/windsurf/
- **Oysterhaven Centre** (sailing/windsurfing course) Kinsale, Co Cork. ☎ 021 4770 738. www.oysterhaven.com

Spas

The only active spa resort in Ireland is **Lisdoonvarna** in The Burren, which has been popular since the 19C. The water, containing magnesia, iodine and iron, is reputed to promote healing.

THALASSOTHERAPY

The abundant supplies of seaweed on the Irish coast are used not only as food but also in hot seaweed baths at Enniscrone west of Sligo and for therapeutic purposes at the outdoor baths in Ballybunnion north of Tralee and at Waterworld in Bundoran in Co Donegal, where you can enjoy various health treatments using heated sea water, local seaweed and sea water drench showers.

RETREATS

Ireland's beautiful natural landscapes provide perfect settings for retreats, yoga centres and health farms.

- www.retreats.org.uk
- www.sustainable.ie

Activities for Children Kids

Sights of particular interest to children are indicated in this guide with a Kids symbol. Some attractions may offer discount fees for children.

Ireland is a great place for children. There are swimming pools and leisure centres in the major towns, bathing beaches on the coast and adventure centres in the Wicklow Mountains and at Westport House.

A number of the old railways are being brought back into services. The longest is the **Tralee-Blennerville Railway**, and there are shorter rides on the **Fintown Railway** in Co Donegal, the **Foyle Valley Railway Centre** in Londonderry, in Downpatrick and on two former peat bog trains – the **Clonmacnoise and West Offaly Railway** near Birr and the narrow gauge railway at **Peatlands Park** between Dungannon and Lough Neagh. There are model railways at the **West Cork Model Railway Village** near Clonakilty and the **Fry Model Railway** at Malahide.

A great selection of vintage vehicles is on view at the Museum of Transport in Clonmel, the National Transport Museum in Howth Castle north of Dublin, the Museum of Iriish Transport in Killarney and the **Ulster Folk and Transport Museum** near Bangor. Other delights for the mechanically minded are the **Great Telescope at Birr Castle**, which has been restored to working order, and the **Tayto Potato Crisp Factory** near Armagh. Most children enjoy watching the demonstrations of old crafts at the open-air museums – **Muckross Farms** near Killarney, **Ulster Folk and Transport Museum** near Bangor and the **Ulster-American Folk Park** north of Omagh in the Sperrin Mountains. They are also likely to enjoy seeing how their ancestors lived in earlier centuries at the **Craggaunowen Centre** near Ennis where the *Brendan* is on view, at the **Lough Gur Interpretive Centre** south of Limerick, at the **Irish National Heritage Park** near Wexford and the **Ulster History Park** north of Omagh in the Sperrin Mountains.

Dublin Zoo, **Fota Wildlife Park** and **Belfast Zoo** present a variety of animals to view. Connemara ponies roam wild in the **Connemara National Park** and there are herds of deer in several parks – **Glenveagh National Park** in Co Donegal, **Doneraile Wildlife Park** near Mallow and **Parkanaur Forest Park** near Dungannon. There are many riding schools offering the chance of a **pony ride** or you can take a trip in one of the **jaunting cars** in Killarney.

The action of water on the landmass has produced several caves which can be safely explored – **Aillwee Cave** in the Burren, **Mitchelstown Cave** near Caher, **Dunmore Cave** near Kilkenny, **Crag Cave** near Tralee and **Marble Arch Caves** near Enniskillen.

Calendar of Events

FEBRUARY

All Ireland Irish Dancing Championships – Open to competitors from Ireland and abroad. **Different town every year**

MARCH

17 March: St Patrick's Day Parade – 4-day spectacle of fireworks, carnival, marching bands and theatre. **Dublin and all major towns**
Feis Ceoil – Classical music festival for aspiring instrumentalists and singers. **Dublin**

St Patrick's Festival, a week-long celebration of Ireland's national day

Bord Fáilte, Dublin

APRIL

All Ireland and International Dancing Championships – Competition involving over 4000 dancers from everywhere in the world (6 days at Easter). **Different town every year**

Pan Celtic International Festival – Inter-Celtic poetry, dancing, musical and arts extravaganza. **Letterkenny, Donegal**

MAY

Bantry Mussel Fair – Seafood festival promoting the mussel industry; free street entertainment. **Bantry**

Fleadh Nua – Folk festival of musicians, singers, dancers, wrenboys, biddy boys, strawboys, all woven together in a rich cultural pattern. **Ennis**

Castle Ward Opera – Performed at an elegant Georgian country house. **Castle Ward**

Irish Open Golf Championship. Different venue each year

MAY / JUNE

Raft Race Weekend – Bands, street theatre, parachute displays and the Raft Race, raising funds for the RNLI. **Portrush**

Writers' Week – Ireland's oldest literary festival with workshops, exhibitions and a book fair. **Listowel**

National Country Fair – Ireland's premier country sports event and country fair for all the family. **Emo Court Co Kilkenny**

JUNE

Fleadh Amhrán agus Rince – Traditional festival of song, music and dance. **Ballycastle**

16 June: Bloomsday – Annual celebration of James Joyce's great novel *Ulysses* – readings, re-enactments, music, theatre, street theatre. **Dublin**

Galway Hookers' Regatta (*Crinniú na mBád*) – Traditional boat gathering and regatta on Strangford Lough. **Portaferry**

Irish Country Lifestyle Festival – Game fair, carriage-driving, clay pigeon shooting, dog shows; Irish Medieval Festival. **Shanes Castle, Co Antrim**

JUNE–JULY

County Wexford Strawberry Festival – Eating strawberries and cream, arts and crafts exhibition, Irish dancing and mumming, horse and greyhound racing, band recitals. **Enniscorthy**

JULY

Willie Clancy Summer School – Major festival of traditional Irish music (particularly *uilleann* pipes) and dance. **Milltown Malbay**

James Joyce Summer School – Lectures, seminars and social events in Newman House, St Stephen's Green, where Joyce himself studied (*2 weeks*). **Dublin**

Twelfth of July Parades – Bands, banners and brethren of the Orange Order celebrating the anniversary of the Battle of the Boyne. **Belfast**

International Rose Week – International rose Trials. **Belfast, Dixon Park**

Galway Arts Festival – Theatre, dance, music and street entertainment, Ireland's premier multidisciplinary arts festival (*10 days*). **Galway**

MICHELIN

Lambeg Drums, an impressive sight in the marching season in Northern Ireland

JULY–AUGUST

Loughcrew Garden Opera – In-the-round production in Loughcrew Gardens. **Loughcrew**

Yeats International Summer School – Lectures and seminars. **Sligo**

All-Ireland Intermediate Road Bowls Finals – Ancient game, played only in Co Armagh and Co Cork, in which competitors used to throw cannonballs. **Armagh**

AUGUST

O'Carolan Harp and Traditional Music Festival – Performance of his works, international harp competition, Irish music, ceilis, concerts, song and set dancing, many open-air events (ᵭ *see Boyle*). August Bank Holiday. **Keadew**

Steam Engine Rally – Stradbally Steam Museum (ᵭ *see Abbeyleix*) annual steam and vintage show. August Bank Holiday. **Stradbally**

Kerrygold Horse Show – International team jumping competitions held at the Royal Dublin Society ground in Ballsbridge; equestrian and social event of the year. **Dublin**

William Carleton Summer School – Irish literature workshops. *(4 days)* **Clogher Valley**

Kilkenny Arts Festival – 10 days of music, visual art, theatre, literature, children's arts and outdoor events. **Kilkenny**

10-12 August: Puck Fair – One of the oldest street festivals in Ireland, centred on a billy goat enthroned in a chair, with a traditional horse fair, busking, open air concerts, parades and fireworks. **Killorglin**

Gathering of the Boats *(Crinniú na mBád)* – Galway hookers' regatta. **Kinvara**

Clifden Connemara Pony Show – Grand showing of the Connemara poy, Ireland's only native pony. **Clifden**

Fleadh Cheoil na hEireann – Traditional Irish music – playing, talking, singing, dancing or listening *(7 days)*. **Different venue each year**

Ould Lammas Fair, a traditional horse fair held in Ballycastle in the Antrim Glens

NITB, Belfast

Rose of Tralee Festival – Bands, parades, dancing horse racing and other activities, celebrating the art of being Irish *(see Tralee)*. **Tralee**

Ould Lammas Fair – Oldest traditional Irish fair with horse trading, street entertainment, competitions and market stalls. **Ballycastle**

AUGUST / SEPTEMBER

Lisdoonvarna Matchmaking Festival – Ireland's biggest singles event with music and dance and horse racing *(late August to early October; ᵭ see The Burren)*. **Lisdoonvarna**

Appalachian & Bluegrass Music Festival – Ulster American Folk Park

National Heritage Week / European heritage Open Days – Walks, lectures, exhibitions, music recitals, pageants and demonstrations involving many community and national organistions. **Nationwide**

All Ireland Hurling Finals – Annual national hurling championships at Croke Park. **Dublin**

Clarinbridge Oyster Festival – Food and stout, music, dance. **Clarinbridge** Map 712 – F8

Laytown Strand Races – Unique horse race held annually in East Meath at low tide. **Laytown**

All Ireland Football Finals – Annual national Gaelic Football championship finals at Croke Park. **Dublin**

International Oyster Festival – World Oyster-opening Championships, held in the pubs, oyster tasting, music, song and dance. **Galway**

Aspects Irish Literature Festival – Celebrates the best of local, national and international literature. **Bangor / Belfast**

SEPTEMBER / OCTOBER

Waterford International Festival of Light Opera – Competitive musical festival for amateur musical societies held at the Theatre Royal. **Waterford**

Listowel Race Week – Steeplechases, Last week of September

Dublin Theatre Festival – Best of world theatre and new productions from all the major Irish companies. **Dublin**

OCTOBER

Cork International Film Festival – Ireland's oldest film event established to present the best of international cinema and to serve as a platform for new Irish cinema. **Cork City and region**

O'Carolan Harp and Cultural Festival – Harp and instrumental workshops and competitions, traditional Irish music concerts, step and set dancing, traditional festival Mass in Irish, seminars and lectures. **Nobber**

Kinsale International Gourmet Festival – The best of fine food and wines in a convivial party atmosphere with music, dance and wine tasting. **Kinsale**

Great October Fair – One of the three great country fairs of Ireland for buying and selling horses. **Ballinasloe** Map 712 – H 8

Cork Jazz Festival – Great jazz and an imperative rendez-vous for the greatest names in this genre. **Cork**

Baboro - International Arts Festival for Children– Workshops, storytelling, theatre. *(6 days)*. **Galway**

OCTOBER / NOVEMBER

Wexford Festival Opera – Production of rare operas and other cultural activities *(10 days)*. **Wexford**

Belfast Festival at Queen's – Largest arts festival in Ireland: music from classical to folk and jazz, drama, ballet and cinema. **Belfast**

Shopping

Ireland produces a number of articles which have an international reputation, such as **Waterford Crystal**, **Aran sweaters** or **Donegal tweed**. The **Kilkenny Design Centre**, set up in the early 1960s, infused new life into domestic and industrial design in Ireland and markets a good range of craftwork (*see Kilkenny and Dublin)*. Throughout the country there are many less well-known enterprises and individual craftsmen and women producing hand-made articles. Manufacturers of textiles, glass and porcelain usually offer a tour of the factory and have showrooms and shops on the premises; their goods are often available in department stores, specialist shops in the major towns and tourist shops in the popular country districts. The *Linen Homelands Tour* visits the **Irish Linen Centre** as well as various linen manufacturers in and around Lisburn.

Some craft workers are grouped in certain regions, such as weavers in Donegal. Others congregate in the special **craft villages**, set up by the Government in Dingle, Donegal town, Blennerville near Tralee or Roundstone in Connemara.

Some folk museums and folk villages organise demonstrations of traditional crafts.

GLASS

The most famous and oldest glass factory in Ireland is in **Waterford**, but since its revival in 1951 several smaller enterprises have started to produce hand-blown lead crystal which is cut, engraved or undecorated – Cavan Crystal, Galway Crystal, Grange Crystal, Sligo Crystal, Tipperary Crystal, Tyrone Crystal. Most have factory shops where first- and second-quality pieces can be bought and many offer a guided tour of the workshops.

KNITWEAR

The thick cream-coloured (undyed) knitwear associated with the Aran Islands is the best known of Irish knitwear and is on sale throughout the country. Ireland produces a great variety of other knitted garments in a variety of textures and colours, particularly thick sweaters to keep out the wind and rain, using the traditional stitches – basket, blackberry, blanket, cable, diamond, moss, plait, trellis and zigzag.

LACE

In the 19C there were many lace-making centres in Ireland but few have survived. In most the skill was fostered by the nuns; the lacemakers of Clones and Carrickmacross have now formed themselves into cooperatives. Kenmare needlepoint lace is the most difficult to make; Clones is a crochet lace but the other centres produce "mixed lace" on a base of machine-made cotton net.

LINEN

The demand for bed linen, table linen and tea towels keeps some 20 Irish linen houses in business. The popularity of linen as an apparel fabric has revived in recent years, since blending with synthetic or other natural fibres has reduced its tendency to crease. It is now used by top fashion designers all over the world who appreciate its sheen and interesting texture, its durability and versatility – it is cool in summer and a good insulator in winter; it dyes well in bright clear colours.

Aran Sweaters to keep out the wind and rain

METALWORK

Throughout the country, and especially in the craft villages, artists are working in gold, silver, bronze, pewter and enamel to produce flatware and jewelry; the traditional Claddagh rings (👆 *see Galway*) worked in gold show a heart with two clasped hands (👆 *see Mullingar and Timolin*).

PORCELAIN AND POTTERY

The largest porcelain factory is the one at **Belleek** which produces fine translucent Parian ware and specialises in woven basket pieces and naturalistic flower decoration. Similar wares are produced by Donegal Irish Parian china. The Irish Dresden factory preserves and develops the tradition of delicate ornamental porcelain figures which originated in Germany.

Belleek Pottery – a sample of intricate craftsmanship

There are many studio potteries in Ireland producing hand-turned articles, such as those in Connemara and the Stephen Pearce Pottery in Shanagarry.

TWEED

The term was first recognised late in the 19C to describe the hand-woven woollen cloth produced in Co Donegal. Donegal tweed is still the most well-known and is now mainly produced on power looms by four firms in Ardara, Donegal Town, Downies and Kilcar. Three of these companies also employ out-workers using hand-looms; most have also diversified into the production of knitwear and ready-made garments or into weaving with other natural fibres – linen, cotton and silk. The original tweeds were made from natural undyed wool – grey, brown or cream. As coloured wool was produced only in small quantities from natural dyes derived from plants, lichens, turf, soot and minerals, it was introduced as speckles when the wool was carded.

Avoca Weavers were founded in 1723, the Kerry Woollen Mills later in the 18C. Foxford and Blarney were started in the 19C.

WOODWORK

There are a number of craftsmen producing hand-turned articles such as bowls, lamp stands and ornaments; the unique pieces are the graceful and delightful carvings produced by artists from skeletal pieces of **bogwood**. Some wood-turners produce musical instruments such as pipes and drums (*bodhráns*) (👆 *see Roundstone in Connemara*).

FOOD AND DRINK

The most convenient products to take home with you are Irish whiskey or a bottle of Baileys Irish Cream or Irish Mist; if you are not travelling far, you may also take along Irish cheeses and smoked salmon and other smoked fish or meat.

Sightseeing

As admission times and charges are liable to alteration, the information printed in this guide is for guidance only.

ABBREVIATIONS

Dúchas = Heritage of Ireland, Gaeltacht and the Islands; HM = Historic Monuments Branch of the Department of the Environment in Northern Ireland; NT = National Trust.

ADMISSION TIMES

Ticket offices usually shut 30min before closing time; only exceptions are mentioned.
Some places issue timed tickets owing to limited space and facilities.

CHARGE

The charge - given in the local currency - is for a single adult.
Reductions may be available for families, children, students, senior citizens (old-age pensioners) and the unemployed.
Large parties should apply in advance, as many places offer special rates for group bookings and some have special days for group visits.

CHURCHES

Many Church of Ireland (Anglican) and Presbyterian churches are locked when not in use for services.

Entertainment

TRADITIONAL MUSIC

The most typically Irish and popular form of evening entertainment is the music and singing performed in the bars in town and country. The instruments played are commonly the violin – called the fiddle by traditional musicians – the flute, the goatskin drum (*bodhrán*) and the free-reed instruments such as the accordion, melodeon and concertina; and also more recently the guitar and banjo. Traditional music has grown in importance in recent years and is played not only at sessions in pubs but also at gatherings known individually as a *céile* and at the weekly and monthly sessions held in the local branches of the national **cultural organization** – Comhaltas Ceoltóirí Éireann, Cultúrlann na hÉireann, 32 Belgrave Square, Monkstown, Co Dublin, ☎ 01 280 0295. www.cohaltas. com ℹ Information also available from Tourist Information Centres.

A feature of Irish traditional music is **dancing**, including individual old-style (*sean-nós*) dancing and particularly **set dancing**, which dates from the 18C and is, for the most part, an adaptation of military dances to existing tunes such as jigs, reels, hornpipes and polkas. The harp is now rarely played but there are two harp festivals in Keadew *(July–August)* and Nobber *(October)*. www.ocarolanharpfestival.ie; www.nobberfest.com

CULTURAL FESTIVALS

Ireland hosts a number of literary and musical festivals in honour of individual artists or groups of artists. Many are accompanied by bands and parades, horse races and regattas according to the region.

IRISH BANQUETS

For a truly Irish evening entertainment try a medieval banquet accompanied by music and poetry – Knappogue Castle; Bunratty Castle; Dunguaire Castle; Killarney Manor; Brú Ború in Cashel.

SMOKING

A smoking ban was introduced in 2004, prohibiting smoking in enclosed public places - including pubs and bars, restaurants and places of entertainment.

THEATRES

Ireland has a lively theatrical scene with theatres in many provincial towns as well as Dublin and Belfast.

Conviviality Irish style in a Doolin bar

In Dublin modern and classic plays are performed at the **Abbey Theatre** and the **Gate Theatre**.

The traditional seasonal festivals and rural way of life are evoked in music, song, dance and mime in the performances of the **National Folk Theatre of Ireland** in Tralee, which draw on the local Gaelic tradition.

Productions in the Irish language are put on by the Irish Theatre **(Taibhearc na Gaillimhe)** in Galway, which is a state-sponsored body.

CLASSICAL MUSIC

In Dublin the **National Concert Hall** (Earlsfort Terrace) has a regular programme of classical and modern orchestral music. Smaller venues offering more specialized music, such as jazz, blues etc, are to be found in Temple Bar (👁 *see Dublin*).

In Belfast the **Waterfront Hall** offers a varied programme of events.

Concerts of **chamber music** *(summer)* are given by Irish and international musicians in some of the great Irish houses; details available from the National Concert Hall in Dublin. Opera is performed in Dublin and Belfast and also at various **opera festivals**.

Discounts

If you are intending to apply for a reduced price pass, take some passport-size photos with you, and all relevant documentation to qualify for your entitlement as a senior citizen or student.

Many tourist sights offer discounts on admission charges for families, children, senior citizens, students, those accompanying someone in a wheelchair and the unemployed. Some hotels offer special rates for short breaks – weekends or 3-day stays, during the low tourist season and for bookings made online.

It is worth checking with the Youth Hostel Association for any special deals from partner companies on coach travel and flights.

SEASON TICKETS

The Heritage of Ireland (OPW) issues an annual **Heritage Card** (€21), which provides free admission to all OPW Heritage sites, available from most fee-paying sites or online from www. heritageireland.ie/en/HeritageCard/

DISCOUNT RAIL / BUS FARES

Special Rover, Explorer and Emerald Card tickets are available, which enable passengers to travel throughout Ireland, by rail only or by rail and bus; price according to the duration of the ticket

- ◆ 5 days (out of 15 consecutive days): €115.50 - south Ireland trains only
- ◆ 8 days (out of 15 consecutive days): €218 - bus + rail in all Ireland
- ◆ 15 days (out of 30 consecutive days): €375 bus + rail in all Ireland

DISCOUNTS FOR STUDENTS

Students with an **International Student Card** can apply for **Student Travelsave** to obtain reductions on Irish Rail and Bus Éireann.
USIT. ☎ Dublin: 01 602 1904; Belfast: 028 90 327 111. www.usit.ie

DISCOUNTS FOR U.S. NATIONALS

Eurorail Pass, **Flexipass** and **Saver Pass** are options available in the US for travel in Europe and must be purchased in the US, ☎ 212 308 3103; ☎ 1-800-4 EURAIL, 1-888-BRITRAIL and 1-888-EUROSTAR (automated lines for callers within the US only); www.raileurope.com/us

Books

Titles that are out of print may be obtained through public libraries in the United Kingdom.

ART

The Architecture of Ireland from the Earliest Times to 1880 by Maurice Craig (Batsford 1982)

An Introduction to Irish High Crosses, by Hilary Richardson and John Scarry, Mercier Press

Ireland's Traditional Houses - by Kevin Dunaher, Bord Failte

Irish Art and Architecture by Peter Harbison, Homan Potterton, Jeanne Sheehy (Thames & Hudson 1978)

The Irish Country House by Peter Somerville-Large (Sinclair-Stevenson 1995)

A Guide to Irish Country Houses by Mark Bence-Jones (1988)

The Painters of Ireland by Anne Crookshank and the Knight of Glin (1978/9)

Exploring the Book of Kells by George Otto Simms (1988)

AUTOBIOGRAPHY

Twenty Years A-Growing by Maurice O'Sullivan (1953, 1992)

Wheels within Wheels by Dervla Murphy (1981)

Woodbrook by David Thomson (1988)

Angela's Ashes by Frank McCourt (1997)

FICTION

Castle Rackrent by Maria Edgeworth (1800)

The Macdermots of Ballycloran, The Kellys and the O'Kellys, Castle Richmond and *The Landleaguers* by Anthony Trollope (1847, 1848, 1860, 1883)

Experiences of an Irish RM by E Somerville and M Ross (1899)

The Playboy of the Western World by JM Synge (1907)

A Portrait of the Artist as a Young Man by James Joyce (1916, 1960)

Ulysses by James Joyce (1922)
The Last September by Elizabeth Bowen (1929)
Troubles by JG Farrell (Fontana 1970)
Good Behaviour by Molly Keane (1981, 1988)
Hungry Hill by Daphne du Maurier (1983)

GEOGRAPHY

Geology and Scenery in Ireland by JB Whittow (Penguin Books 1974)
The Book of the Irish Countryside edited by Frank Mitchell (Blackstaff Press 1987)
Reading the Irish Landscape by Frank Mitchell and Michael Ryan (Town-House 2001)
The Shannon Floodlands – A Natural History by Stephen Heeny (Tir Eolas – Newtownlynch, Kinvara, Co Galway 1993)
Atlas of the Irish Rural Landscape edited by F H A Aalen, Kevin Whelan and Matthew Stout (Cork University Press 1997)
The Personality of Ireland- Habitat, Heritage and History by E Estyn Evans (Lilliput 1992)
Sun Dancing by Geoffrey Moorhouse, Widenfeld & Nicolson, – about the Skellig Isles

HISTORY

Brendan the Navigator by George Otto Simms (O'Brien Press)
The Celts edited by Joseph Raftery (The Mercier Press, Dublin 1988)
An Introduction to Celtic Christianity by James P Mackey (T & T Clark, Ltd, Edinburgh 1989)
Ancient Ireland by Jacqueline O'Brien and Peter Harbison
Ireland in Early Medieval Europe edited by Dorothy Whitelock, Rosamund McKitterick, David Dumville (Cambridge University Press 1982)
The Peoples of Ireland by Liam de Paor (Hutchinson 1986)
Citizen Lord by Stella Tillyard, Chatto & Windus – about Edward Fitzgerald
Huguenot Settlements in Ireland by GI Lee (Longman Green & Co 1936)
The Oxford History of Ireland by RF Foster

The Making of Modern Ireland 1603–1923 by JC Beckett (Faber & Faber 1966)
Citizen Lord by Stella Tillyard (Chatto & Windus)
The Great Hunger by Cecil Woodham-Smith (Penguin Books 1988)
The Identity of Ulster by Ian Adamson (Pretani Press 1982)
Twilight of the Ascendancy by Mark Bence-Jones (1987)
Hungry for Home – a journey from the edge of Ireland – by Cole Moreton (Penguin)
Fenian Fire – a British Government plot to assassinate Queen Victoria – by Christy Campbell (HarperCollins)
The Easter Rising by Lorcan Collins and Conor Kostick published by O'Brien Press
The Irish Empire - The Story of the Irish Abroad by Patrick Bishop, Boxtree - MacMillan

MYTHOLOGY

A Guide to Irish Mythology by Daragh Smyth (Irish Academic Press)
Fairy and Folk Tales of Ireland by WB Yeats (Colin Smythe 1973)
Irish Folk Tales edited by Henry Glassie (Penguin 1987)

RECIPES

Simply Delicious Recipes by Darina Allen (1989, 1992)
The Irish Food Guide by Sally and John McKenna (Anna Livia, Dublin)

TRAVEL

The Road to Roaringwater – Christopher Somerville - Harper Collins (1993) – a walk along the west coast from Malin Head to Cape Clear Island in Roaring Water Bay
McCarthy's Bar – a journey of discovery in Ireland – by Pete McCarthy (Sceptre Lir)
The Craic – a journey through Ireland – by Mark McCrum (Phoenix non-fiction)
Literary Tour of Ireland by Elizabeth Healy (Wolfhound Press Paperbank 2001)
Round Ireland with a Fridge by Tony Hawks (Ebury Press)

Useful Words and Phrases

Alt - cliff
Ard -high, height, hillock
Áth - ford
Bád - boat
Baile - town, townland, homestead
Beag - little
Beal - opening, entrance, river mouth
Bealtaine - 1 May, month of May
Boireann - large rock, rocky district
Bóthar - road
Buí - yellow
Bun - end, bottom
Cabhán - hollow
Caiseal - castle, circular stone fort
Caisleán - castle
Caladh - harbour, landing place
Capall - horse
Carraig - rock
Cath - battle
Cathair - circular stone fort, city
Cealtrach - old burial ground
Céide - hillock
Cill - church
Cloch - stone
Cluain - meadow

Cno - hill
Dearg - red
Díseart - desert, hermitage
Droichead - bridge
Dubh - black
Dún - fort
Eaglais - church
Eas - waterfall
Fear - man
Fir - men
Gall - foreigner
Gorm - blue
Gort - field
Inis - island
Lár - centre
Leithinis - peninsula
Mór - large
Óg - young
Oileán - island
Poll - hole, cave
Sagart - priest
Sean - old
Slí - route, way
Sliabh - mountain
Teach - house
Trá - beach, strand
Túr - tower
Uachtar - top, upper part

BASIC INFORMATION

Business Hours

Shops in the major cities are open Mondays to Saturdays, 9am–5.30pm (8pm Thursdays). Elsewhere there is all-day or early closing on Mondays or Wednesdays or Thursdays. Some shops may open later and may close for an hour at lunchtime.

Banks are open Mondays to Fridays (except public holidays), 10am–12.30pm and 1.30–3pm (3.30pm in Northern Ireland).

Exchange facilities outside these hours are available at Belfast, Dublin, Shannon, Connaught and Cork Airports, in some tourist information centres, travel agencies and hotels.

Electricity

The electric current is 230 volts AC (50 hertz); 3 pin flat or 2 pin round wall sockets are standard.

Emergencies

Telephone 999 – for all emergency services (no charge nationwide); ask for Fire, Police, Ambulance, Coastguard and Sea Rescue, Mountain Rescue or Cave Rescue.

Currency

NOTES AND COINS

In the Republic of Ireland the currency is the euro (€1 = 100 cent); in Northern Ireland it is Sterling (£1 = 100 pence = €1.27 at publication time).

There is no limit on the amount of currency visitors can import into the Republic of Ireland.

BANKS

Money can be withdrawn from banks using a credit card and a PIN. Since June 2002 there has been no commission charge for EU travellers on cash drawn from Cash Point / ATM machines in the Republic of Ireland.

TRAVELLERS' CHEQUES

Some form of identification is necessary when cashing travellers' cheques or Eurocheques in banks. Commission charges vary; hotels and shops usually charge more than banks.

CREDIT CARDS

The major credit cards – American Express, Visa/Barclaycard (Carte Bleue), Eurocard (Mastercard/Access) and Diners Club – are widely accepted in shops, hotels, restaurants and petrol stations.

- Amex IRL: 01 679 1200
- Amex UK: 01273 696933
- Mastercard: 020 7557 5000
- Barclay Card: 0870 154 0154

American Express Travel Services: www.americanexpress.com/uk/

Mail

Irish postage stamps must be used in the Republic, British stamps in Northern Ireland; they are available from Post Offices and some shops (newsagents, tobacconists etc).

OPENING HOURS

In the Republic post offices are open Mondays to Saturdays, 8am–5pm or 5.30pm; they are closed on Sundays and public holidays and for 1hr 15min at lunchtime; sub-post offices usually close at 1pm one day a week.
In Northern Ireland post offices are open Mondays to Fridays, 9am–5.30pm, and Saturdays, 9am–12.30pm; sub-post offices close at 1pm on Wednesdays.

Newspapers and Television

In the Republic of Ireland the national newspapers on sale are *The Irish Times*, *The Independent* and *The Examiner*. The last broadcasts in the Irish language appear on 4 television channels: RTE1, RTE2, TV3 and TG4.
In Northern Ireland the national newspapers are *The Times*, *The Independent*, *The Daily Telegraph* and *The Guardian*. There are 5 television channels – BBC1, BBC2, ITV, Channel 4 and Channel 5.

Public Holidays

On such days shops, museums and other monuments may be closed or may vary their times of admission. In the Republic of Ireland national museums and art galleries are usually closed on Mondays.
In addition to the usual school holidays at Christmas and in the spring and summer, there are mid-term breaks at Hallowe'en (1 November) and around St Patrick's Day (17 March).

- 1 January – New Year's Day
- 17 March – St Patrick's Day (Republic only)
- Monday nearest 17 March (Northern Ireland only)
- Good Friday (Republic only)
- Easter Monday
- Monday nearest 1 May – May Day Holiday (Northern Ireland only)
- Last Monday in May – Spring Bank Holiday (Northern Ireland only)
- First Monday in June – June Holiday (Republic only)
- 12 July – Orangeman's Day (Northern Ireland only)
- First Monday in August – August Bank Holiday (Republic only)
- Last Monday in August – August Bank Holiday (Northern Ireland only)
- Last Monday in October – October Holiday (Republic only)
- 25 December- Christmas Day
- 26 December (St Stephen's Day/ Boxing Day)

Conversion Tables

Weights and measures

1 kilogram (kg)	2.2 pounds (lb)	2.2 pounds
1 metric ton (tn)	1.1 tons	1.1 tons

to convert kilograms to pounds, multiply by 2.2

1 litre (l)	2.1 pints (pt)	1.8 pints
1 litre	0.3 gallon (gal)	0.2 gallon

to convert litres to gallons, multiply by 0.26 (US) or 0.22 (UK)

1 hectare (ha)	2.5 acres	2.5 acres
1 square kilometre (km²)	0.4 square miles (sq mi)	0.4 square miles

to convert hectares to acres, multiply by 2.4

1 centimetre (cm)	0.4 inches (in)	0.4 inches
1 metre (m)	3.3 feet (ft) - 39.4 inches - 1.1 yards (yd)	
1 kilometre (km)	0.6 miles (mi)	0.6 miles

to convert metres to feet, multiply by 3.28, kilometres to miles, multiply by 0.6

Clothing

Women	EU	US	UK		EU	US	UK	Men
	35	4	2½		40	7½	7	
	36	5	3½		41	8½	8	
	37	6	4½		42	9½	9	
Shoes	38	7	5½		43	10½	10	**Shoes**
	39	8	6½		44	11½	11	
	40	9	7½		45	12½	12	
	41	10	8½		46	13½	13	
	36	6	8		46	36	36	
	38	8	10		48	38	38	
Dresses &	40	10	12		50	40	40	**Suits**
suits	42	12	14		52	42	42	
	44	14	16		54	44	44	
	46	16	18		56	46	46	
	36	30	8		37	14½	14½	
	38	32	10		38	15	15	
Blouses &	40	34	12		39	15½	15½	**Shirts**
sweaters	42	36	14		40	15¾	15¾	
	44	38	16		41	16	16	
	46	40	18		42	16½	16½	

Sizes often vary depending on the designer. These equivalents are given for guidance only.

Speed

kph	10	30	50	70	80	90	100	110	120	130
mph	6	19	31	43	50	56	62	68	75	81

Temperature

Celsius (°C)	0°	5°	10°	15°	20°	25°	30°	40°	60°	80°	100°
Fahrenheit (°F)	32°	41°	50°	59°	68°	77°	86°	104°	140°	176°	212°

To convert Celsius into Fahrenheit, multiply °C by 9, divide by 5, and add 32.
To convert Fahrenheit into Celsius, subtract 32 from °F, multiply by 5, and divide by 9.

VAT

The Value-Added Tax (VAT) refund is available to non EU residents. Stores participating in the Tax Back Service must be members of the Retail Export Scheme. Details are available in major department stores.

Telephone

The telephone service in the Republic of Ireland is Eircom – www.eircom.ie Pre-paid callcards for internal and international calls from public phones are available from post offices and some shops (newsagents, tobacconists etc). Card phones are cheaper than pay phones.

It is usually more expensive (+ 30%) to make a long-distance telephone call from a hotel than from a pay phone. To make an **international call** dial 00 followed by the country code, followed by the area code (without the initial 0), followed by the subscriber's number. The codes for direct dialling to other countries are printed at the front of telephone directories.

When dialling from the Republic to Northern Ireland, dial 080 followed by the subscriber's number.

Dialling codes
00 61: Australia
00 1: Canada
00 353: Republic of Ireland
00 64: New Zealand
00 44: United Kingdom (including Northern Ireland)
00 1: United States of America

Time

In winter standard time throughout Ireland is Greenwich Mean Time (GMT). In summer (mid March to October) clocks are advanced by one hour for British Summer Time (BST), which is the same as Central European Time. Time may be expressed according to the 24-hour clock or the 12-hour clock.

Derryclare Lough, Connemara

H. Champollion/MICHELIN

NATURE

Visitors come to Ireland for many reasons: to enjoy the friendly and convivial people and their Celtic heritage, the folk music and the Guinness or, to visit the westernmost edge of the European continent – but the country's greatest draw is the wonderful scenery. For "the Emerald Isle" is wondrously green, variegated by its bare mountains and strange rock formations, stark cliffs and sandy strands, flower-rich boglands and well-tree'd desmesnes.

The Shape of the Land

Unlike the archetypal island which is supposed to rise from coastal lowlands to a mountain core, Ireland heartland is mostly low-lying country, enclosed by highland ramparts. Only from Dublin northwards is there an extensive opening of the land to the sea, a fifty-mile doorway of fertile land through which successive waves of invaders have entered the country. Overlooking Dublin from the south, the Wicklow Mountains rise to a peak of 3 035ft/925m at Lugnaquilla, but the country's highest point and the most dramatic mountain scenery are to be found in the far southwest, where Carantuohill (3414ft/1038m) and Macgillycuddy's Reeks preside over the glories of the Killarney lakeland and the Iveragh Peninsula. This peninsula is one of several, parts of a much wider set of parallel mountain folds running roughly east-west, which were violently folded in Hercynian times and which include the granites of Brittany and the Harz massif in Germany. In Ireland they also include a whole series of ranges dividing the midlands from the island's southern coastline. Their equivalents in the north are the northeast-southwest trending ranges folded in the Caledonian period and which cross to the Atlantic edge in Donegal and Connaught and leap the narrow strait separating Ulster from Scotland.

Bounded by these ancient mountain systems, the central regions of the country are largely underlaid by a much-eroded foundation of Carboniferous limestone. The basis of the rich bone-building pasturelands for which Ireland is famous, it is far from monotonous, producing such famous features as the great escarpment of Benbulben glowering over Sligo or the eerie moon-

Invermore River, Connemara

scapes of the Burren in Co Clare. Much of the midland landscape is profoundly marked by the impact of the Ice Ages. The retreating glaciers left unconsolidated deposits of clay, sand and gravel, great tracts of which remain badly drained today, though the worm-like, winding ridges of sandy gravel called eskers – deposited by streams running beneath the glaciers – have always provided dry areas in an otherwise almost impenetrable land. The ice sheets also moulded great swarms of **drumlins**, low egg-shaped mounds, most clearly visible when partially submerged as in Clew Bay and Strangford Lough. In the north, a broad band of drumlins extends right across the island, the waterlogged land around them forming a barrier to communication which may well have helped establish Ulster's distinctive identity in ancient times.

Saving the turf, Inishowen

PEAT BOGS

One of the most intriguing features of the Irish landscape is its peat bogs, the most extensive in Europe, occupying something like a sixth of the land surface, and playing an important role in the country's history, economy, and collective memory. Bogs are of two types although the peat in both is formed in water-logged conditions by the accumulation of dead and incompletely decomposed plant material. **Blanket bog** occurs in areas of high rainfall and humidity, mostly in the mountains of the western seaboard, and comprises dead grass and sedge. It is usually shallower (6ft/2m to 20ft/6m) than **raised bog**, which is more of a lowland phenomenon, occuring where rainfall is less, growing above the ground water level, formed by dome-shaped bog moss (sphagnum). This type of peat-bog, up to 19ft/12m deep, is scattered over much of the midland area, where it forms a distinctive, open and natural-seeming landscape in contrast to the farmland beyond. Raised bogs have developed over time without appreciable human interference, whereas the blanket bog has been fashioned by burning and the clearance of scrub and woodland for grazing. The history of the land is pre-

served by the peat layers revealing the nature of forests and of neolithic fields beneath the blanket bogs of the west. In more recent times, the Irish bogs have provided places of refuge for rebels and outlaws, while their inaccessibility and unfamiliarity have made it difficult for invaders to extend their control over the whole country.

The early disappearance of tree cover and scarcity of coal deposits meant that peat – known locally as turf - became the most important source of fuel. The turfs are traditionally cut with a slane, a narrow spade with a side blade set at a right angle, and laid out to dry. When thoroughly dry, they are stacked into clamps near the house. In a fine summer a family can harvest enough fuel for several years. The cuts sliced deep into the bog and the stacks of drying peat make distinctive patterns in the landscape that appear quite alien to visitors from abroad, while the sight, sound and smell of the turf fire glowing in the corner of living room or pub evokes strong emotions in every Irish heart.

Since the mid-20C peat has been harvested on an industrial scale to provide the country with electric power as well as yielding moss peat for horticultural purposes. The mechanical harvesters of the Bord na Móna (Peat Development Authority) are an impressive sight as they scrape huge quantities of sun-dried milled peat from a bog that has been drained for a period of five to seven years. The harvested peat is made into briquettes for domestic use or burned in one of five electricity generating stations.

CLIMATE

Confronting the Atlantic as it does, Ireland has an oceanic climate, tempered by the influence of the warm waters of the Gulf Stream flowing northwards along its western shores. Succcessive weather systems blow in from the southwest, bringing abundant precipitation and ever-changing cloudscapes. The temperature range is limited; it is rarely very hot nor very cold. In the coolest months of January and February temperatures vary between 4° and 7° Celsius, in the warmest months of July and August between 14° and 16°. Snowfalls are uncommon except on the highest mountains, where the total annual precipitation can exceed 2 400mm. The southwest is the wettest part of the country, the east the driest, but everywhere it is not so much the amount of rainfall, but its persistence. However, though there may not be many days without rain or a touch of drizzle, it should always be remembered that its occurrence is at least partly responsible for the freshness of the atmosphere and the luminous look of the landscape.

COAST

The country's rock foundation is most dramatically exposed at the interface of land and ocean, particularly in the west, where montainous peninsulas frequently end in bold headlands, while sea inlets and fjords penetrate far inland. The northern shore of Co Antrim boasts what is surely Ireland's most famous natural wonder, the countless clustered columns of the Giant's Causeway, formed 60 million years ago by violent volcanic disturbances. Few natural ramparts are as spectacular as the bands of shale and sandstone making up the 5mi/8km stretch of the Cliffs of Moher, rising 200m over the Atlantic breakers on the edge of the Burren in Co Clare. The limestones of the Burren leap

seaward to form the Aran Islands, where the abrupt cliffs of Inishmore, though less high, are equally awe-inspiring. The discontinuous archipelago along the western coast offers other equally

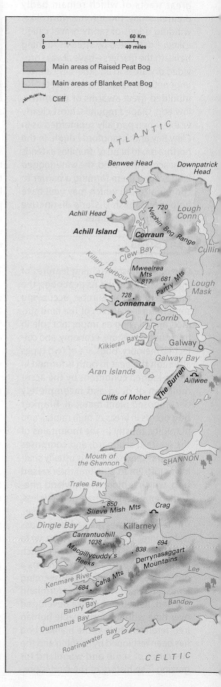

extraordinary sights, none more so than the drowned mountain-top of Skellig Michael, a rocky refuge for a hardy monastic community in the days of Early Christianity. The tallest cliffs are those of the Slieve League peninsula, where a great bastion of quartzite stands some 1 972ft/601m above the waves.

In the east of the country, coasts are characterised by splendid natural har-

New Ross, Co Wicklow

bours formed by drowned valleys, low limestone cliffs and glorious stretches of sandy beach.

FIELDS AND FARMS

Despite recent economic trends, Ireland is still very much an **agricultural country**, with more than 80% of the land used for farming. Most of this is **pasture**; Ireland has 95% of the best grassland in the European Union, but **arable farming** prospers in the drier east, notably in the Ards Peninsular in Ulster and in Co Wexford, where barley is grown on a large scale. As elsewhere in Atlantic Europe, farmland is **enclosed** rather than open, with a variety of field patterns reflecting a complex historical development. The typical field boundary is a hedgebank topped with native shrubs and trees, often allowed to grow spontaneously rather than laid to make them stockproof. And it is these leafy banks that make up for the country's lack of woodland, transforming the rolling landscape into picturesque scenery. In the rocky peninsulas of the west and elsewhere, stone is used to form boundary walls: most notably in the Aran Islands, where tiny enclosures are bounded by drystone walls deliberately built to be permeable to the strong winds. In areas of poor soil and high rainfall, "**lazy beds**" were made. These were cultivation ridges, created by laying a strip of manure and inverting sods over it from both sides. The raised

bed drained easily into the trenches on either side and its soil was warmed by the sun from the side as well as the top, highly advantageous characteristics in a cool, wet country. Lazy beds came into their own with the widespread cultivation of the potato in the pre-Famine years, and whole landscapes are marked by the wrinkled pattern of the subsequently abandoned ridges, sometimes at an elevation where cultivation of any crop would seem doomed to failure.

VEGETATION

Most of the country was originally covered in trees, particularly forests of sessile oak. Clearance for agriculture began in Neolithic times and continued until virtually no natural or even semi-natural woodlands were left. One of the last assaults on the native forest was made by the British in the 17C and 18C, on the one hand for building materials and for smelting, on the other to deny refuge to the rebellious Irish. Remnants of natural forest can be found in the southern Wicklow Mountains and around Killarney, where there are also marvellous specimens of the arbutus or strawberry tree. In the 18C considerable replanting efforts were made by many owners of desmesnes eager to landscape their estates in the English manner. Exotic trees like Scots pine, beech, sweet chestnut, monkey puzzle and cedar of Lebandon were introduced to supplement the native species. As some 6% of the land surface was held in desmesnes, the landscape impact was considerable, though it was much reduced subsequently through the break-up and parcelling-out of many estates. The fate of the Anglo-Irish so-called Big House is well known; less familiar is the felling of its heritage of trees and ornamental woodland and their conversion into ordinary farmland or monotonous plantations of conifers. Nevertheless a number of desmesnes have survived, some in the form of **Forest Parks** in public ownership, others in the hands of the National Trust in Northern Ireland.

Generations of gardeners have exploited the country's favourable, frost-free environment to create gardens famous for their broad spectrum of plants, notably in areas sheltered from the wind. Several sub-tropical paradise gardens such as Garinish Island in Glengarriff Harbour, manage to have flowers in bloom all year round. Conditions favoured by rhododendrons and fuchsias account for why these shrubs grow in woodlands and hedgerows. Ireland's botanically most fascinating landscape is perhaps the Burren, where a profusion of acid and lime-loving plants grow in harmonious co-existence.

RIVERS AND LAKES

Not surprisingly, water is ever-present in the Irish landscape. The country's rivers have a total length of 16 530mi/26 000km and lakes/loughs cover an area of 560 sq mi/1 450sq km. Ireland's low population density and the relative lack of polluting industries means that most of this water is unpolluted and well-stocked with fish and other wildlife.

The watercourses rising on the seaward side of mountains tend to be short and steep, draining straight into the sea. Those that rise inland form slow-moving lowland streams, lined by water-meadows and often widening out into lakes. The **Shannon**, the country's longest (230 mi/370 km) river behaves in this way, winding sluggishly through the midland countryside and forming the great expanses of Lough Ree and Lough Derg before discharging into its immensely long estuary below Limerick. In Ulster, **Lough Neagh** is far more impressive than the River Bann which flows through it; though shallow, it is Ireland's largest body of water, covering an area of 153 sq m/400 sq km, and teeming with eels. The country's loveliest lakeland is that which has developed along the course of the Erne, comprising countless lesser lakes as well as island-studded **Upper** and **Lower Lough Erne** themselves.

In the south, rivers rising far inland have cut their way through upland chains to reach the sea; the valleys thus formed by the Blackwater, Nore, Suir, Barrow and Slaney are often of great beauty.

Youghal Harbour, Co Cork

H Champollion/MICHELIN

HISTORY

Ireland continues to carry the scars of its troubled history more than most European countries. The Republic of Ireland enjoys booming prosperity since joining the European Union, while in Northern Ireland, efforts continue to secure peace between conflicting traditions, heart-felt ideals and deep-rooted exclusive identities which have marked the country's past.

Timeline

CELTIC IRELAND

6000-1750 BC — Stone Age; c 3000 BC hunter-gatherer people begin farming. Construction of passage graves.

1750–500 BC — Bronze Age.

500 BC–AD 450 — Iron Age; Celtic invasion from Europe; inter-tribal strife for supremacy and the title of High King (Ard Rí).

55 BC-early 5C AD — Roman occupation of Britain (not Ireland): trade links proved by coins and jewellery found.

4C–5C — Irish Celts (known as Scots) colonise the west of England and Scotland.

432–61 — **St Patrick's mission** to convert Ireland to Christianity.

6C–11C — Monastic age; Irish missionaries travel to the continent.

795 — **Viking Invasions** — Vikings from Norway and Denmark raid the monasteries near the coasts and waterways; in 841 they begin to settle.

1014 — **Battle of Clontarf – Brian Ború**, king of Munster, defeats the Danish Vikings and the king of Leinster's allied forces.

1156 — Death of Turlough O'Connor, last powerful native ruler.

1159 — Henry II (1154–89), given the title "Lord of Ireland" by Pope Adrian IV and permission to invade Ireland.

ANGLO-NORMAN IRELAND

1169 — Invited by Dermot, King of Leinster, to oust his opponents, *Strongbow* Richard de Clare lands with his Anglo-Norman army at Baginbun on the south coast. In 1171, after Dermot's death, Strongbow declares himself King of Leinster to the discomfiture of Henry II, who eventually extracts a humiliating declaration of loyalty from his over-ambitious vassal while extending English control over much of the country. England's involvement in Irish affairs was now constant, though the interests of the Anglo-Irish frequently diverged from those of the mother country and many settlers became "more Irish than the Irish".

1177 — **Anglo-Norman** invasion of Ulster by John de Courcy.

1185 — **Prince John**, "Lord of Ireland", visited the country, to which he returned in 1210.

1297 — First **Irish Parliament** convened.

1315–18 — **Bruce Invasion** – Edward Bruce, brother to King Robert of Scotland, lands at Carrickfergus with 6 000 Scottish mercenaries (gallowglasses); he is crowned king in 1316; he dies at the Battle of Faughart near Dundalk in 1318.

1348–50 — **The Black Death** kills one-third of the population.

1366 — **The Statutes of Kilkenny** promulgated to maintain the distinction between Anglo-Normans and native Irish. Prohibition of fosterage, bareback riding, hurling, the Irish language and Irish dress and patronage of Irish story tellers and poets largely fails in their purpose.

1394 & 1399 — **Richard II** landed in Ireland with an army to re-establish control.

1446 — First mention of **The Pale** to describe the area of English influence; by the 15C it was only a narrow coastal strip from Dundalk to south of Dublin.

1471 — The Earl of Kildare appointed **Lord Deputy**, marking the rise to power of the Geraldines.

1487 — The pretender Lambert Simnel crowned Edward V of England in Dublin by the Earl of Kildare.

1491 — Perkin Warbeck, pretender to the English throne, landed in Cork without the opposition of the Earl of Kildare.

1494 — Sir Edward Poynings appointed Lord Deputy: under **Poynings' Law** the Irish parliament could not meet or propose legislation without royal consent.

1534–40 — Failure of the **Kildare (Geraldine) Revolt** and the end of Kildare ascendancy.

REFORMATION AND PLANTATION

1539 — **Reformation** and **Dissolution of the Monasteries**.

1541 — Henry VIII declared **King of Ireland** by the Irish Parliament.

1556 — Colonisation of Co Laois (Queen's County) and Offaly (King's County) by English settlers.

1579 — **Desmond (Munster) Rebellion** severely crushed by Elizabeth I; confiscation and colonisation.

1585 — Ireland mapped and divided into counties; 27 sent members to Parliament.

1588 — **Spanish Armada** – After its defeat in the English Channel, the Spanish Armada, driven by the wind, sailed up the east coast of Great Britain and round the north coast of Scotland. Off the Irish coast stormy weather further depleted its ranks.

1598 — **Hugh O'Neill, Earl of Tyrone**, leads rebellion and defeats English army at the **Battle of Yellow Ford** (👆 see *Dungannon*).

1601 — **Siege of Kinsale** – 4 000 Spanish troops land in Kinsale to assist Hugh O'Neill but withdraw when besieged.

1603 — Submission of Hugh O'Neill (Earl of Tyrone) and Rory O'Donnell (Earl of Tyrconnell) at Mellifont to **Lord Mountjoy**, Queen Elizabeth's Deputy. in 1607 they sail from

Spanish Armada

Some 30 ships of the Spanish Armada were wrecked off the Irish coast between Antrim and Kerry, with an estimated loss of 8 000 sailors and gunners, 2 100 rowers, 19 000 soldiers and 2 431 pieces of ordnance.

The *Gerona*, a galleass, went down at Port na Spaniagh on the Giant's Causeway; all perished; treasures recovered by divers in 1968, are displayed in the Ulster Museum. The *Juliana, La Levia* and *La Santa Maria de Vision* all foundered at Streedagh Point, north of Sligo; over 1 300 are thought to have died. *La Duquesa St Anna and La Trinidad Valencia* was wrecked on the Inishowen Peninsula at Kinnagoe Bay. A map on the clifftop (*at the road junction*) plots the sites of the many ships that were lost during those fateful storms.

One survivor who came ashore at Streedagh, Captain Francisco de Cuellar, wrote an account of his escape from Sligo through Leitrim, Donegal and Derry to Antrim; from where he sailed to Scotland, then on to Antwerp and Spain.

Dublin Volunteers on College Green by Francis Wheatley

National Gallery of Ireland, Dublin

Rathmullan (see Donegal) into exile on the continent. This **Flight of the Earls**, marks the end of Gaelic Ireland's political power.

1607–41 — **Plantation of Ulster** under James I: Protestants from the Scottish lowlands settle in the northern part of Ireland.

1641 — **Confederate Rebellion** provoked by policies of the King's Deputy and the desire of the dispossessed to recover their land: widespread slaughter of Protestant settlers.

1642 — **Confederation of Kilkenny** is an alliance between the Irish and Old English Catholics to defend their religion, land and political rights.

1649 — **Oliver Cromwell** "pacifies" Ireland with great brutality, storming Drogheda and Wexford and sending thousands of Irish to the West Indies.

1653 — Under the **Cromwellian Settlement** most Roman Catholic landowners judged unsympathetic to the Commonwealth were dispossessed and ordered to retreat west of the Shannon.

1660 — **Restoration** of Charles II and restition of some land to Roman Catholic owners.

1678 — The **Oates Conspiracy** was a pretext for the arrest, imprisonment and even death of various Roman Catholics, among them Oliver Plunkett, Archbishop of Armagh (see Drogheda).

1685 — Revocation of the Edict of Nantes in France forces many **Huguenots** (Protestants) to flee to England and Ireland.

1688 — **Glorious Revolution:** James II is deposed; William of Orange accedes to the English throne. 13 London derry Apprentice Boys shut the city gates in the face of King James's troops; the following year the city endures a three-month siege by Jacobite army.

1690 — **Battle of the Boyne** – King William III of England and his allies representing the Protestant interest defeat King James II who flees to France.

1691 — **Siege of Limerick** – Following the battles of Athlone and Aughrim (see Athenry), the Irish army retreats to Limerick, after a siege it surrenders 'with honour' as per the military terms of the **Treaty of Limerick**; known as the **Wild Geese**, these soldiers are granted leave to sail to France; many join the French army.

ANGLO-IRISH ASCENDANCY

1695 — The provisions of the Treaty of Limerick guaranteeing Roman Catholic rights are soon ignored; **Penal Laws** *(see Religion)* impose severe restrictions on their rights to property, freedom of worship and education.

1711 — **Linen Board** established to control quality of linen for export; other "improvements" to canals, roads, urban planning contribute to growing prosperity.

1778 — **Volunteers** rally to defend Ireland against the French; support a call for an independent Irish parliament.

1782 — **Repeal of Poynings' Law** and the establishment of an independent Irish Parliament, known as Grattan's Parliament after Henry Grattan a leading campaigner for independence.

1791 — Formation in Belfast of the mostly Presbyterian **United Irishmen** to promote the idea of a republican country with no religious distinctions.

1791–93 — **Catholic Relief Acts** (👆 *see Land of saints*)

1795 — Rural violence between Protestant Peep O'Day Boys and Catholic Defenders and the foundation of the **Orange Order** (👆 *see Armagh*).

1796 — Abortive French invasion in Bantry Bay (👆 *see Bantry*).

1798 — **Rebellion of the United Irishmen** launched by Wolfe Tone; main engagements in Antrim, Wexford and Mayo; the rising was brutally suppressed; 30 000 rebels killed. Tone is captured and commits suicide in prison.

IRELAND IN THE UNITED KINGDOM

1800 — **Act of Union** and suppression of the Irish Parliament: members take up 100 seats in the House of Commons and 32 in the Upper House in London.

1803 — The abortive **Emmet Rebellion** led by Robert Emmet (1778–1803) ended with his hanging: his speech defending his actions provides inspiration to future nationalists.

1823 — **Daniel O'Connell** (1775–1847), a Roman Catholic lawyer, is elected MP for Clare after campaigning for the rights of Catholics and the repeal of the Act of Union. The **Roman Catholic Emancipation Act**, passed in 1829, enables Roman Catholics to enter Parliament.

1845 –49 — A blight destroys potato crops, leading to the **Irish**

Great Famine (1845–49)

Potato blight *(phytophthora infestans)* destroyed the potato crop on which much of the population depended. 800 000 people died of hunger, typhus and cholera. Thousands of starving people overwhelmed the workhouses and the depot towns distributing the Indian corn imported by the government; the workhouse capacity was 100 000 but five times that number qualified for relief. The Quakers did most to provide relief: soup kitchens were set up by compassionate landlords and by Protestant groups seeking converts; public works were instituted to provide employment and relief. Other landlords evicted penniless tenants (in 1847 16 landlords were murdered) or arranged for their emigration; so many died during the voyage or in quarantine that the vessels were known as coffin ships. Over one million emigrated to England, Scotland, Canada and the USA.

Marriage of Strong Bow and Eva by Daniel Mac Lise (1854)

R Holzbachova, Ph Benet/MICHELIN

Potato Famine and the deaths of an estimated 800 000 people. Even more emigrate to Great Britain and the USA.

1848 — Abortive **Young Ireland Uprising** led by William Smith O'Brien (1803–64).

1858 — Founding of the rebel **Irish Republican Brotherhood (IRB)** known as Fenians.

1867 — **Manchester Martyrs**: three Fenians are executed for the death of a policeman during an attack to release two Fenian prisoners. The conviction on doubtful evidence undermines Irish confidence in British justice.

1869 — Disestablishment of Anglican **Church of Ireland**.

1870–1933 —17 **Land Acts** transfer ownership of large estates from landlords to tenants.

1874 — **59 Home Rulers** elected to Parliament. In 1875 Protestant landowner **Charles Stewart Parnell** (1846-91) takes his seat, lobbying for home rule and landowner rights.

1879–82 — **Land League** formed by Michael Davitt to campaign for the reform of the tenancy laws and land purchase.

1886 — First **Home Rule Bill** granting Ireland autonomy to decide certain domestic matters is rejected by Parliament.

1891–1923 — **Congested Districts' Board** use funds from the disestablished Church of Ireland to build harbours, promote fishing, fish curing and modern farming methods in poor areas. In 1903 the Board

Easter Rising in 1916

While **John Redmond**, leader of the moderate Nationalists, hoped that Irish contribution to the British war effort would be rewarded by Home Rule, the more militant Military Council of the Irish Republican Brotherhood secretly organised a national uprising. Despite the capture of Sir Roger Casement and a cargo of arms from Germany, the plan went ahead. On Easter Monday columns of Volunteers marched into Dublin and seized various key sites. Outside the General Post Office, Patrick Pearse announced the establishment of a republic; the insurgents were hopelessly outnumbered and outgunned; on Saturday they surrendered. The insurrection was not especially popular but attitudes changed when the ringleaders were court martialled and executed.

is granted power to redistribute land to smallholders.

1893 — Second **Home Rule** Bill rejected by Parliament.

1905–08 — **Sinn Féin** (Ourselves) founded to promote the idea of a dual monarchy.

1912 — Third **Home Rule** Bill introduced by Asquith: fierce opposition in Ulster where 75% of the adult population represented by **Sir Edward Carson** sign a convenant to veto it. Rival militias are armed with smuggled weaponry to form the Ulster Volunteer Force *(north)* and Nationalist Irish Volunteers *(south)*.

1914 — **First World War:** postponement of Home Rule and civil strife. Irishmen volunteer for the British army.

1917 — **Sinn Féin** reorganised under Eamon de Valera to campaign for an independent Ireland.

1918 — **General Election:** Redmond's Home Rulers defeated; Sinn Féin win 73 seats.

1919 — **Declaration of Independence** in the Irish Assembly *(Dáil Éireann)*.

1919–20 — **War of Independence – Irish Republican Army (IRA)** aims to block the British administration; martial law proclaimed; the Royal Irish Constabulary reinforced by British ex-servicemen (Black and Tans) notorious for their brutal tactics.

1920 — **Government of Ireland Act** provides for partition: six Ulster counties remain part of the UK as per the will of the majority, to be ruled by a separate parliament; dominion status granted to the remaining 26 counties, which form the Free State.

PARTITION AND INDEPENDENCE

1921 — **Anglo-Irish Treaty**

1922–23 — **Civil War:** Michael Collins and the Free State Army clash with the Republicans against even the temporary partition of the country. Casualty numbers surpass those of the War of Independence. Collins is assassinated, the Republicans are defeated.

1922 — Constitution of the **Irish Free State**; the two-tier legislature comprises the Senate and *Dáil Éireann*.

1937 — Change of name to **Éire**.

1938 — Three British naval bases (Cork Harbour, Bere Island and Lough Swilly) granted under the Anglo-Irish Treaty are returned to Ireland.

1939–45 — **Second World War** (referred to as the Emergency): Éire is neutral but gives covert aid to the Allies.

1949 — Eire renamed the **Republic of Ireland**; withdrawal from the Commonwealth.

1952 — Ireland joins the United Nations.

1965 — Anglo-Irish Free Trade Area Agreement.

1973 — The Republic of Ireland and United Kingdom of Great Britain and Northern Ireland join the European Union (EU). EEC funds stimulate development in the Republic.

1998 — David Trimble and John Hume awarded the Nobel Peace Prize.

2002 — **Euro currency** goes into circulation in the Republic.

2004 — Sinn Fein fail to provide Unionists (DUM and UUP) evidence that the IRA has been decommissioned. Hope for achieving a devolved Parliament is suspended.

2005 — The Provisional IRA orders all its units to disarm and to cease all activity not related to peaceful political programs.

2006 — Official census reveals that Republic population has risen to its highest level since 1861 (4 234 925).

ART AND CULTURE

Architecture

Ecclesiastical Buildings

Romanesque (Norman)

CLONFERT CATHEDRAL, Co Galway – West door – 12C

The inner arch immediately surrounding the door is 300 years later than rest of the doorway, which consists of five rows of columns and five rows of round-headed arches framing the door, surmounted by a hood moulding containing a triangular pediment, the whole capped by a finial.

Hood moulding or tangent gable

Triangular pediment

Blind arcades with semicircular arches with a head in the top of each arch

Leaf motif on arch

Capitals

Outer pilasters decorated with **Celtic strapwork**

Scrollwork

Circular pattern

Chevrons

Diamond pattern

Finial surmounted by two flanking masks

Double rope **moulding**

Alternating masks and foliate triangles

Hemispheres in high relief

Circles and flowers

Maltese cross

Celtic **strapwork**

Gargoyles

Statue of **gate guard** resting on a corbel

Medieval

JERPOINT ABBEY, Co Kilkenny – 12C with 15C tower

Screen dividing nave into east end for choir monks and west end for lay brothers

Central tower over crossing with slight battering

Splayed window embrasures

Cloister garth

Cloister arcade

Refectory

Kitchen

Nave

Calefactory (warming room)

North aisle arcade

Chapter House

String course

Irish crenellations

Double lancet windows

Chancel

Transept

R. Corbel/MICHELIN

Gothic

ST PATRICK'S CATHEDRAL, Dublin – 13C
Construction begun in the Early English style but extensively restored in the 19C.

Tower surmounted by spire

Irish crenellations

Chancel

Flying buttress

South transept

Pinnacles

5-light lancet window

Lady Chapel / Retrochoir

Buttress

Neo-Classical

CHRIST CHURCH CATHEDRAL, Waterford – 18C

Decorated plaster vaulting

Corinthian capitals

Aisles

Aisles

Reredos with projecting pediment supported on Corinthian columns

Nave

Fluted pillars

R. Corbel/MICHELIN

Neo-Gothic

CHURCH OF THE MOST HOLY TRINITY (formerly Chapel Royal), Dublin Castle – 19C

Rib vaulting

Carved heads in the spandrels

Carved ceiling bosses

Foliate capitals

High relief figures over east window

Fan vaulting

Clustered columns

Perpendicular tracery (east window)

Carved wooden galleries

Military Structures

Norman

Motte and bailey

In the immediate post-invasion years, the Normans built timber castles, surmounting a natural or artificial earthern mound (motte). A outer stockaded enclosure (bailey) contained stables, storehouses etc. Later castles were built of stone.

Timber stockade

Tower

Motte

Drawbridge

Bailey

Ditch and rampart

R. Corbel/MICHELIN

15C-17C

DUNGUAIRE CASTLE, Co Galway – 1520 restored in the 19C

Fortified dwelling, consisting of a **tower house** surrounded by a courtyard, known as a **bawn**, enclosed by defensive wall; the main living accommodation with windows was on the upper floors.

Machicolation

Crenellations

Small and rare transomed mullion windows

Tower House

Corner tower

Bawn wall

Arched entrance

17C

CHARLES FORT, Co Cork – c 1670

Sunk battery

Traverse

Lower battery

Upper battery

Parade

Citadel

Barracks

Bastion

Bastion

Classical doorway

Causeway

Citadel

Bastion

R. Corbel/MICHELIN

Secular Buildings

16C

PORTUMNA CASTLE, Co Galway – 1518
Semi-fortified house, with symmetrical fenestration, approached through formal walled gardens.

Dutch gable

Decorative machicolation

String course

Crenellations

Corner flanking tower

Mannerist Classical doorcase flanked by gun loops

Transom window

Mullion window

17C

SPRINGHILL, Co Tyrone – c 1680 with 18C additions
Unfortified house with symmetrical facade and large and regular fenestration.

Gable end roof

Dormer window

Central doorway

Canted bay (on 18C extensions)

Central approach flanked by offices

Narrow windows flanking entrance

R. Corbel/MICHELIN

18C

GEORGIAN URBAN HOUSING

Urban terrace houses built of red brick, with 4 storeys over basement, three bays wide, with regular fenestration, composed of sash windows with wooden glazing bars. The tall windows emphasized the importance of the first floor reception rooms.

Wrought-iron
decorative balconies

Simulated stone work

Doorcase with
pillars and fanlight

Doorcases and fanlights (1740s)

Door case capped by a lantern fan light
and flanked by pillars with Ionic capitals

Door case capped by a decorated fan light
and flanked by pillars with Ionic capitals

Door case capped by a decorative fan light
and flanked by pillars with Ionic capitals
and by side lights and door scrapers

Door case capped by a decorated
fan light and flanked by pillars with
Ionic capitals

R. Corbel/MICHELIN

18C

RUSSBOROUGH, Co Wicklow – 1743-56

House in the **Palladian style** consisting of a main **residential block** linked by curved or straight colonnades to two **flanking service blocks** containing the kitchens and stables.

Parapet adorned with ornamental urns

Main house

String course

Curved colonnade of Doric columns

Main entrance surmounted by a fanlight and flanked by engaged Corinthian columns supporting a triangular pediment

Monumental gateway to stable yard

Ionic pilasters decorating the service buildings

18C plasterwork

FLORENCE COURT, Co Fermanagh – 1740s

Foliate plaster cornice in high relief

Decorative plaster panels

Dado rails

Leaf and scroll frieze in high relief

Plaster panelling in simulation of raised and fielded wooden panelling

Coffered arch soffit

Swag

Lugged doorcase

Carved stair tread ends

Ramped hand rail

Open string stair case

Fluted columnar banisters

Swan neck handrail

R. Corbel/MICHELIN

MONAGHAN MARKET HOUSE, Co Monaghan – 1791

Three-bay pedimented break front

String course on break front at level of springing of arch

Pedimented gables

Rectangular panels with swags

Quoins

Pateras (roundels) with foliated design

Blind windows

Rusticated ashlar stonework

Quoins

Rounded-headed niches

Revival styles

Medieval styles such as Gothic and Norman were revived featuring asymmetric façades and fenestration and varied rooflines.

LISMORE CASTLE, Co Waterford – 19C Neo-Gothic

Look-out turret

Hood moulding

Crenellated and corbelled parapet

Corbelling

String course

String course

Canted bay

String course

Canted bay

Window tracery

R. Corbel/MICHELIN

Although architecture in Ireland has been strongly influenced by stylistic developments originating in Britain or the continent of Europe, usually at some lapse in time, local building has many distinctive features; the medieval round towers with their conical caps have become an emblem of Irishness. Extraordinary is the array of prehistoric monuments and medieval fortified structures, while the Georgian era produced fine building in both town and countryside.

PREHISTORIC ERA

Although the first traces of human habitation in Ireland date from c 7000 BC, the first people to leave structural evidence of their presence were Neolithic farmers, who lived in Ireland from their arrival c 4000 BC to 2000 BC. Traces of their huts have been found at Lough Gur (& see Limerick).

Megalithic Tombs

The most visible and enduring monuments of these people are their elaborate **burial mounds**.

The most impressive are the **passage tombs** at Newgrange, Knowth and Dowth in the Boyne Valley, on Bricklieve Mountain, at Loughcrew, at Fourknocks and Knockmany. Each grave consisted of a passage leading to a chamber roofed with a flat stone or a corbelled structure, sometimes with smaller chambers off the other three sides and sometimes containing stone basins. It was covered by a circular mound of earth or stones retained by a ring of upright stones. Passage graves date from 3000–2500 BC.

The earliest Megalithic structures, **court tombs**, consisted of a long chamber divided into compartments and covered by a long mound of stones retained by a kerb of upright stones. Before the entrance was a semicircular open court flanked by standing stones as at Creevykeel (& see Sligo) and Ossian's Grave (& see Antrim Glens).

A third style of Megalithic tomb is known as the **portal tomb;** like Proleek (& see Dundalk), they are found mostly near the east coast of Ireland. The tomb consisted of two standing stones in front with others behind supporting a massive capstone, which was hauled into place up an earth ramp long since removed. They date from c 2000 BC.

Bronze Age Structures

Stone circles, which date from the Bronze Age (1750–500 BC), are mostly found in the southwest of the country (& see Donegal Glens, Kenmare, Downpatrick, Sperrin Mountains). The circle at Drombeg (& see Kinsale) seems to have been used to determine the shortest day of the year.

Single standing stones probably marked boundaries or grave sites. Some were made into Christian monuments with a cross or an Ogham inscription (& see Gaelige).

Glendalough

J Malburet/MICHELIN

Of similar antiquity is the cooking pit *(fulacht fiadh)* which was filled with water; hot stones were placed in the water to bring it to boiling-point.

Iron Age Dwellings

By the Iron Age, men were living in **homesteads**, approached by a causeway. A ringfort was enclosed by an earth bank *(ráth or dún)* or by a stone wall *(caiseal)* and was surrounded by a ditch. An artificial island *(crannóg)* was formed by heaping up stones in a marsh or lake. Many such dwellings were in use from the Iron Age until the 17C. There is a replica at Craggaunowen (☞ *see Ennis*. Stone forts *(cashels)* like Dún Aonghasa (☞ *see Aran Islands*) and Grianán of Aileach (☞ *see Buncrana*), although restored at various periods, illustrate the type, built on a hill with massive walls and mural chambers.

Within the homestead individual huts were built of wattle and daub or of stone with a thatched roof. In the west, beehive huts *(clocháin)* were built entirely of stone using the same technique of **corbelling** inwards to form a roof that was used in the passage graves. Similar stone huts are also found in the monastery on Great Skellig and at Clochan na Carraige on the Aran Islands. They demonstrate the use of drystone construction in a treeless land.

At the centre of the homestead there was often an underground stone passage, called a souterrain, used for storage or refuge.

IRISH MONASTIC SETTLEMENTS

Little remains of most early Christian settlements as the buildings were made of perishable material – wood or wattle and daub. The records describe beautiful wooden churches made of smooth planks constructed with great craft and skill, but none has survived.

Early monasteries consisted of an area enclosed by a circular wall or bank and divided into concentric rings, as at Nendrum (☞ *see Strangford Lough*), or into sectors assigned to different uses. The most important sector was the graveyard, since it was seen as the gateway to heaven.

Round Towers

The slender tapering round towers, just as much as symbol of Ireland as the high crosses, mark the site of early monasteries. Almost unique to Ireland, they were built between about AD 950 and 12C as bell-towers where hand bells, the only kind available, were rung from the top floor to announce the services. The towers were also used to store treasures and possibly as places of refuge; in almost every case the entrance was several feet (10ft/3m) above ground level.

Intact towers vary in height (from 50ft/17m to over 100ft/30m). All were surmounted by a conical cap, sometimes replaced by later battlements. About 65 survive in varying condition, with 12 intact. Most were constructed without foundations and all are tapered.

Tomb Shrines

Some saints' graves are marked by a stone **mortuary house** which resembles a miniature church. These structures, such as St Ciaran's at Clonmacnoise, are among the earliest identifiable stone buildings in Ireland.

Churches

Most early **stone churches** consisted of a single chamber with a west door and an east window; churches with a nave and chancel date from the 12C. None of the surviving churches is very large but there are often several churches on one site. The very large stones employed accentuate the smallness of the churches. The roofs would have been made of thatch or shingles.

The rare **stone-roofed** churches, an Irish peculiarity, employ the corbelling technique. The simplest is Gallarus Oratory; St Doulagh's near Malahide is a 13C church still roofed with stone slabs; St Columba's House, St Mochta's House, St Flannan's Oratory and Cormac's Chapel have a small room between the vaulted ceiling and the roof. The earliest examples are devoid of ornament; an exception to this rule is found on White Island in Co Fermanagh, where seven figurative slabs are attached to the walls (which may be later insertions).

MIDDLE AGES

Norman / Romanesque

The first church in the Romanesque style introduced from the Continent in the 12C, was Cormac's Chapel of 1139 at Cashel. In Ireland Romanesque churches are always small; their typical features, to which carved decoration is limited, are round-headed doorways, windows and arches. Ornament includes fantastic animals, human masks and geometric designs such as bosses, zigzags and "teeth". Cormac's Chapel has fine carvings, several series of blind arcading, painted rib vaults and the earliest extant frescoes.

Profusely ornamented west doorways are perhaps unique to Ireland, exemplified by Clonfert (after 1167), Ardfert and St Cronan's in Roscrea.

Norman Castles

The first castles built by Normans were of the **motte and bailey** type. The motte was a natural or artificial mound of earth surrounded by a ditch and usually surmounted by a wooden tower as at Clough in Co Down; the bailey was an area attached to the motte and enclosed by a paling fence. From the start of the 13C, the Normans built more solid stone donjons (keeps) which were square with corner buttresses, as at Trim, Carrickfergus and Greencastle, polygonal as at Dundrum and Athlone or round as at Nenagh. During the 13C entrance towers became more important and barbicans were added for additional defence. In the latter half of the 13C a new symmetrical design was developed consisting of an inner ward with four round corner towers and a combined gatehouse/donjon in the middle of one wall, as at Roscommon.

Gothic Churches

Gothic architecture, introduced to Ireland in the late 12C, is on a much smaller scale than elsewhere and few examples have survived. Most cathedrals show English and Welsh influences, whereas monasteries, founded by Continental

Jerpoint Abbey Cloisters

monastic orders, are built according to their usual plan of a quadrangle enclosed by cloisters bordered by the church on the north side, the sacristy and chapter-house on the east, the refectory and kitchens on the south and the store on the west, with dormitories above the east and south ranges.

Early in the 13C many cathedrals were remodelled; the two Anglican cathedrals in Dublin contain building from this period, although they have been much altered. St Patrick's Cathedral in Dublin, completed in 1254, to which a tower was added in 1372, is very English in its form and decoration.

A second period of building occurred in the 15C and coincided with the construction of many Franciscan houses in the west. Most existing churches were altered to conform to the new fashion. Broad traceried windows were inserted which let in more light and provided the stonemasons with opportunities for decoration. There is a distinctive Irish character to the capitals and high relief carving in the cloisters at Jerpoint (15C).

Tower Houses

After the Black Death (1348–50) building resumed on a more modest scale. In 1429 a £10 subsidy was offered by Edward VI for the construction of a castle or tower.

Over 70% of tower houses, which were erected by native and settler alike, are south of the Dublin–Galway axis.

The most distinctive feature is their verticality, one room on each of four to five storeys, sometimes with a hidden room between two floors.

Defences consisted of corner loop holes, battering at the base, double-stepped merlons, known as **Irish crenellations**, and external machicolations over the corners and the entrance. Most such towers, which were built between 1450 and 1650, were surrounded by a **bawn**, an area enclosed by a defensive wall. Only in the later and larger castles is decoration evident.

PLANTATION PERIOD

Plantation Castles

As the country came more firmly under English control in the late 16C, more luxurious rectangular houses were built with square corner towers, as at Kanturk (c 1603), Portumna (c 1618), Glinsk (c 1620) and Ballygally (1625). Often an existing tower house was extended by the addition of a more modern house, as at Leamaneh, Donegal and Carrick-on-Suir. These buildings show a Renaissance influence in plain and regular fenestration with large mullioned windows.

Planter's Gothic

This style was introduced in the early 17C by settlers from England and Scotland who built many parish churches throughout Ireland, a few of which survive unaltered; one of the best examples is St Columb's Cathedral in Londonderry.

Coastal Fortifications

In the Restoration period several important towns were provided with star forts; the most complete surviving fortification is Charles Fort in Kinsale (from 1671). After the French invasion of Bantry Bay in 1796 and Killala in 1798, signal towers were built on the coast. The building of Martello towers began in 1804; about 50 of these squat structures with very thick walls punctuate the coast from Drogheda to Cork and along the Shannon estuary. The so-called Joyce Tower in Sandycove, built of ashlar granite, is typical.

18C–19C CLASSICAL

Country Houses

Between the Battle of the Boyne (1690) and the Rebellion (1798) there was a period of relative peace and prosperity during which most of the important country houses were built. While Dutch gables and red brick are attributed to the influence of William of Orange, in general English and French inspiration predominated in the late 17C. In the 18C the influence was mainly Italian sources, often distilled through England and latterly Greek-inspired architects, while in the 19C the English Gothic and Tudor revivalists were influential. Most country houses were built of local stone.

The most popular style in the 18C was the **Palladian villa** which consisted of a central residence – two or three storeys high – flanked by curved or straight colonnades ending in pavilions (usually one storey lower) which housed the kitchens or stables and farm buildings.

The major architect of the first half of the 18C was **Richard Castle** (originally Cassels) (1690–1751), of Huguenot origin. Castle's many houses – Powerscourt, Westport, Russborough, Newbridge – tend to be very solid. He took over the practice of **Sir Edward Lovett Pearce**, who had the major role in designing Castletown (*see Maynooth*) and who built the Houses of Parliament (from 1729), now the Bank of Ireland in Dublin.

The influence of **Robert Adam** (1728–92) arrived in Ireland in 1770, the date of the mausoleum he designed at Templepatrick. Sir William Chambers' work in Ireland is exemplified by The Casino, Marino (1769–80), a vastly expensive neo-Classical gentleman's retreat cum folly.

James Gandon (1742–1823) was brought to Ireland in 1781 to design Emo Court. His Classical style is well illustrated by the Customs House and the Four Courts in Dublin.

The chief work of **James Wyatt** (1746–1813) was at Castle Coole but he also contributed to Slane Castle.

R Holzbachova, Ph Benet/MICHELIN

Dublin Castle in 1792 by James Malton

One of the best known Irish architects was **Francis Johnston** (1761–1829), an exponent of both the Classical and the Gothic styles, the former exemplified by Dublin's General Post Office, the latter by Dublin Castle's Chapel Royal.

Interior Decoration

Many interiors were decorated with exuberant stuccowork executed by the Swiss-Italian **Lafranchini** brothers, one of whom executed the stairwell plasterwork at Castletown. Contemporary work of similar quality was carried out by Robert West and at Powerscourt House in Dublin by Michael **Stapleton**, the principal exponent of Adam decor.

Churches

Classical details began to be used in the 17C. St Michan's in Dublin (c 1685) and Lismore (1680) by William Robinson retain some details of 17C work. The early Georgian St Anne's in Shandon in Cork has an imposing west tower with an eastern flavour. The neo-Classical rectangular building with a pillared portico, inspired by the Greek temple, was popular with all the major denominations: St Werburgh's (1754–59), St George's (1812), St Stephen's (1825) and the Pro-Cathedral (finished after 1840) in Dublin, St John the Evangelist (1781–85) at Coolbanagher by Gandon and St George's (1816) in Belfast.

REVIVAL STYLES

The Gothic Revival style first appeared in Ireland in the 1760s at Castle Ward and at Malahide Castle where two tall Gothic towers were added to the medieval core. At first Gothic features and intricate stuccowork vaulted ceilings were added to buildings that were basically Classical and symmetrical such as Castle Ward. In addition to crenellations, machicolations and pointed arches, one of the key features of the Gothic style was asymmetry. Existing medieval castles or tower houses or Classical mansions, such as Kilkenny Castle (c 1826) by William Robertson and Dromoland Castle (1826) by George and James Pain, were enlarged and reworked in Gothic or Tudor style. Johnstown Castle and Ashford Castle are later examples of such Gothicising, which was romantic in flavour but distinctly Victorian in convenience.

Some new houses were built entirely in an antiquated style; Gosford Castle is neo-Norman; Glenveagh was designed in the Irish Baronial style; for Belfast Castle, Lanyon and Lynn chose the Scottish Baronial style, which was also used for Blarney Castle House.

Gothic Revival Churches

Many early 19C Gothic churches, such as the Church of the Most Holy Trinity (formerly the Chapel Royal) in Dublin

Castle, are filled with ornament, with decorative galleries, plaster vaulting and rich oak carvings. Later the influence of Augustus Welby Pugin, who practised widely in Ireland, and JJ McCarthy promoted antiquarian correctness, as at St Fin Barre's in Cork (1862) by William Burges. McCarthy's greatest achievement was probably the completion in Decorated Gothic style of the great new cathedral at Armagh (after 1853). This was only one example, albeit an outstanding one, in the spate of building which followed the Emancipation Act when many Roman Catholic cathedrals and parish churches were constructed in eclectic Gothic variations.

19C-20C

The Gothic style was often used in the second half of the 19C for civic buildings as well as detached houses and mansions; Trinity College Museum (completed 1857) by Deane and Woodward is a classic of the Venetian Gothic revival. The Arts and Crafts movement did not find much architectural expression in Ireland; Cavan Town Hall (1908) by William Scott is a notable exception with expressive use of planes and textures. University College Dublin in Earlsfort Terrace (1912) by RM Butler and the College of Sciences in Upper Merrion Street in Dublin (1904–13) by Sir Aston Webb exemplify the Classical revival. Perhaps the most gradiose structure of this period is the hug City Hall (1906) in Belfast, a "great wedding cake of a building" (J Sheehy) with a dome and corner towers. The young Free State restored with admirable promptness the bombed General Post Office, the Four Courts and the Custom House but the record of new design is relatively poor.

Modernism

Architectural Modernism was slow to come to Ireland but an early and very striking example was the Church of Christ the King (1927) at Turner's Cross in Cork by Barry Byrne of Chicago. The changes in practice introduced by Vatican II favouring worship in the round, have inspired many exciting church designs, some of which reflect local physical features – St Conal's Church, Glenties, Co Donegal; St Michael's Church, Creeslough, Co Donegal; Dominican Church, Athy; Prince of Peace Church, Fossa, near Killarney; Holy Trinity, Bunclody. Modern civic architecture arrived in Ireland with the construction of the Ardnacrusha hydroelectric plant in 1929 and the Dublin Airport terminal building of 1940.

IRISH DISTINCTION

Towns and Cities

Early Irish villages (clachans) were formed of clusters of wattle-and-daub cottages arranged in a haphazard manner. The first towns were founded by the Vikings, invariably on estuaries; among them were Drogheda, Dublin, Waterford and Wexford. Most such places had a Tholsel (toll stall), often an arch or gateway several storeys high, where payment for rights of privilege or passage was made. Norman settlements were mostly confined to the south and east of the country. Towns were often enclosed within town walls, parts of which have survived at Athenry, Kilmallock, Youghal, Fethard and Londonderry.

The first widespread foundation of towns occurred in the late 16C and 17C during the plantations of Ulster, Munster and some parts of Leinster; they consisted of timber-framed houses, which have not survived, set out round a green or lining a street. The green was often known as "The Diamond" although rarely a true diamond shape; many such "Diamonds" survive in Ulster. In many Irish towns one of the most elegant buildings is the market and the courthouse, sometimes combined in one structure.

Town Planning

In the 18C and 19C many country landlords indulged in town planning, setting out wide streets as in Strokestown and Moy, tree-lined malls as in Westport, Birr and Castlebar, unusual formal street plans, such as the X-shape in Kenmare, rows of cottages built of local stone as at Glassan, northeast of Athlone, and Shillelagh in Co Wicklow or the picturesque thatched houses of Adare.

In the major towns elegant terraces of houses of Classically inspired design were built of local stone or red brick, some of which was imported from Somerset via Bristol. In 19C Dublin the materials used were grey brick from local clays, local limestone and grey Wicklow granite. Although most terraces were erected piecemeal and lack a unified aesthetic, the influence of the **Wide Streets Commissioners** (in Dublin from 1758) led to distinctly Irish Georgian doorways – usually flanked by columns – and ordered fenestration. The tallest windows are on the principal floor, decreasing in size towards the roofline parapet. Some later terraces by the Wide Streets Commissioners and others were more standardised – Fitzwilliam Street and Square (south side) in Dublin, and Pery Square in Limerick. Internal decoration was often of a very high standard, with Classical motifs common in chimneypieces, plasterwork and timberwork.

20C town planning in Ireland has had few notable successes. Grandiose plans for the reconstruction of Dublin following the devastation of 1916 were drawn up but never implemented. Many of the close-packed terraced streets of late 19C Belfast have been replaced by planned housing schemes of various kinds, the least succesful of which consisted of brutalist blocks of flats. The attempt to create the "New Town" of Craigavon on the British model based on the existing urban areas of Lurgan and Portadown has only been partially realised. In the South, rural prosperity and lax planning controls have led to the abandonment of the picturesque but sub-standard cabin with a scatter of comfortable but visually inappropriate houses and bungalows.

Vernacular Houses

The Irish countryside is full of buildings and other structures of traditional vernacular architecture – not only dwellinghouses and outhouses but also structures such as sweathouses and forges. The small stone sweathouses, were used to treat pleurisy and other ailments and also as a type of "sauna". A fire was lit inside and, when the interior was hot, the ashes were raked out and a layer of rushes placed on the floor to protect the feet from the heat.

The 1841 Census identified four grades of housing, of which the most modest was a windowless one-room mud cabin with a thatched roof (bothán), a type of dwelling which predominated west of a line from Londonderry to Cork. Such houses contained little or no furniture; more windows or rooms meant higher rents. The half door, which is to be found all over Ireland, allowed in light while keeping out animals.

The middle grades of house, single- and two-storey farmhouses, have survived in greater numbers, with glazed windows, hearths and a hierarchy of rooms for distinct social uses.

The Irish **long house**, in which all the rooms were interconnecting with the stairs at one end, was a style which lasted from the Middle Ages to the 18C; the one at Cratloe (see Limerick) is a rare survivor.

The box-style Georgian house with symmetrical elevation, some Classical detailing such as Venetian or Wyatt windows and a fanlit and columnated doorcase, was very popular with people of more substantial means.

Simple dwellings were often destroyed during evictions or fell into decay. Some have been discovered under layers of modernisation; others, threatened with demolition, have been reconstructed or recreated in Bunratty Folk Park, Glencolmcille Folk Village, the Ulster-American Folk Park and the Ulster Folk Park near Bangor.

Merrion Square North

B Juge/MICHELIN

Stained Glass

No medieval stained glass has survived in situ in Ireland but there was a revival of interest in this craft in the 1770s with the enamelling work of Thomas Jervais and Richard Hand, much of which was secular. The fashion for the neo-Gothic style of architecture in the 19C for both churches and houses created a great demand for stained glass; good examples from this period are St Patrick's Roman Catholic Church in Dundalk, which has glass by Early of Dublin, Hardman of Birmingham and Meyer of Munich, the east window of St Patrick's Anglican Church in Monaghan by the German FS Barff, and the altar window of the Cathedral of the Assumption in Tuam by Michael O'Connor (1801–67).

The outstanding contribution made by 20C Irish artists in this field was nurtured by the foundation of **An Túr Gloine** (the Tower of Glass) (1903–63) at the instigation of Edward Martyn and Sarah Purser.

The portrait painter Sarah Purser did designs for several windows including Cormac of Cashel in St Patrick's Cathedral, and another founder member was Michael Healy (d 1941) whose work can be seen in Loughrea Cathedral.

Wilhelmina Margaret Geddes worked for An Túr Gloine from 1912 to 1925 and works by her can be seen in the Municipal Gallery of Modern Art in Dublin – *Episodes from the Life of St Colman* (strong black line used) and in the Ulster Museum – *The Fate of the Children of Lir* (1930).

Evie Hone joined An Túr Gloine in 1934. Her work, which was often inspired by Irish medieval sculpture, includes *The Ascension* (1948) for the Roman Catholic church in Kingscourt, Co Cavan, and *The Beatitudes* (1946) for a chapel in the Jesuit Retreat House at Tullabeg near Tullamore.

Harry Clarke (1889–1931) developed a distinctive personal style as early as 1915, drawing from iconography and legends in a symbolist manner. His first public commission, 12 windows for the Honan Chapel in University College Cork, is one of his greatest works. His "Geneva Window" (1928) is in the Municipal Gallery of Modern Art in Dub-

St Wilfrid and St John Berchmans (1927) by Harry Clark

The Stained Glass Museum, Ely

lin. Just before his death he executed his most important ecclesiastical commission *The Last Judgement with the Blessed Virgin Mary and St Paul* for St Patrick's Church in Newport.

A current revival is headed by James Scanlon and Maud Cotter, both based in Cork.

Irish Art

Constantly receptive to influences from Britain and the rest of Europe and often giving them a specifically local flavour, Irish art was unsurpassed in its originality and creativity in the Early Christian era, when sculptors, jewellers, illuminators and other artists found inspiration in the country's glorious heritage of Celtic arts and crafts. A fainter echo of Celtic achievement came in the paintings and graphic arts associated with the Gaelic revival of the late 19C and early 20C, but before this, Ireland, quite as much as England, had become a stronghold of the arts and crafts of the Georgian era; the brilliant and sometimes eccentric life of the Anglo-Irish Ascendancy is reflected in the painting of the time as much as in architecture and the decorative arts.

CELTIC ART

Circles formed an integral part of Celtic art; the outline of the design was marked out on the piece to be decorated with an iron compass. Other decorative motifs were S-and C-shaped curves, spirals and swirls and zig-zags, with intricate, interlaced patterns in the interstices. Similar designs, identified by archaeologists as **La Tène**, after the continental Celtic centre found at La Tène which flourished during the last five centuries BC, are found on two granite monuments – at Turoe (🕭 *see Athenry*) and Castlestrange (🕭 *see Strokestown*) – which date from the 3C BC. They are the only two such monuments to have survived in Ireland and were probably used in religious ceremonies. They resemble the Greek *omphalos* at Delphi, a site raided by the Celts in 290 BC.

The finest Celtic pieces are designed in gold. In making a torc or neckband the goldsmith stretched the metal into long narrow strips and then twisted them around each other to make a golden rope which was then shaped to fit around the warrior's neck. The Celts made personal ornaments – brooches, horse harnesses and sword sheaths – which they often decorated with enamel favouring the colour red but also using blue, yellow and green. A regular motif in Celtic design is the triskele, a figure with three arms or legs, symbolising earth, fire and water.

Some early sculptures display a nude female figure with crossed legs, known as *Sheila-na-gig*, which owes much to pagan traditions but is usually found in or about churches. Many interpretations have been given to these often grotesque carvings which were probably linked to a fertility cult.

A Golden Age

The first important example of an illuminated manuscript is a copy of the Psalms dating from around AD600 and traditionally attributed to St Columba. Compared with later achievements, it is relatively simple, its principal feature being a large decorated initial at the beginning of paragraphs. Its ornamentation of Celtic spirals and stylised animals is further developed in the course of the 7C

Tara Brooch (8C)

National Museum of Ireland, Dublin

in the **Book of Durrow**, where a variety of coloured inks is used as well as the black of Columba's manuscript, whole "carpet pages" are given over to decoration rather than text, and the characteristic motif of interlaced bands makes its appearance. Over the next century and a half, the scribes' increasing skill resulted in ever greater intricacy and exuberance, culminating in the sublime achievement of the **Book of Kells** dating from around 800. Of equal virtuosity are a number of products of the metalworker's and jeweller's art. The almost

monumental **Ardagh Chalice** (c 700) is a masterpiece of colourful decoration; its extraordinarily elaborate base, with three friezes in gold around a central rock crystal, would have been visible only briefly when raised during Mass. In a similar way, the splendid ornamentation of the underside of the renowned **Tara Brooch** (also c 700) would have only been seen only by its owner.

Book of Kells

PAINTING

When Gaelic culture waned in the 17C the chief influences on art in Ireland were English and European. A guild of painters was founded in Dublin in 1670 but there was little development until the Dublin Society's Schools were set up in 1746 to promote design in art and manufacture. The first master, Robert West (d 1770), and his assistant, James Mannin (d 1779), had trained in France. The School's most outstanding pupil was probably **Hugh Douglas Hamilton** (1739–1808), who excelled at pastel portraits; in 1778 he visited Italy and while in Rome developed as a painter in oils.

Susanna Drury (fl 1733–70), whose paintings of the Giant's Causeway are in the Ulster Museum, was a member of the Irish school of landscape painting, which emerged in the 18C. **George Barret** (c 1732–84), who moved to England in 1763, introduced the Romantic element into his landscapes. Several Irish artists travelled to Italy. Thomas Roberts (1748–78), a pupil of the Dublin Society's Schools and a brilliant landscape artist, was familiar with Dutch and French painting and exhibited several works in the style of Claude Vernet. The dominant figure of the 18C is **James Barry** (1741–1806), who produced large-scale works in the neo-Classical tradition. He travelled widely, including in Italy, studying painting and sculpture. Joseph Peacock (c 1783–1837) from Dublin was famous for his outdoor fair scenes.

Among the visitors to 18C Dublin were Vincent Valdré (1742–1814), who painted three ceiling panels for Dublin Castle, and Angelica Kauffmann (1741–1807), who was the guest of the Viceroy, Lord Townshend for several months in 1771. In 1823 the **Royal Hibernian Academy** was incorporated by charter to encourage Irish artists by offering them an annual opportunity to show work.

After the Act of Union in 1800 many Irish artists moved to London: Martin Archer Shee (1769–1850), who became President of the Royal Academy in 1830, and Daniel Mac Lise (1806–70), a popular historical painter. Nathaniel Hone (1831–1917) spent 17 years in France painting out of doors like the painters of the Barbizon school. Roderic O'Conor (1860–1940) studied in Antwerp and in France where he met Gauguin, whose influence, together with that of Van Gogh, is obvious in his work. **Sir John Lavery** (1856–1948), who also studied in Paris, is known for his portraits, although he also painted scenes from the French countryside. Another artist who studied abroad is **Sarah Purser** (1848–1943), a prolific portrait painter and a founder of *An Túr Gloine*.

The 20C has produced several artists of note. **Jack B Yeats** (1871–1957), brother of the poet, painted his views of Irish life with bold brushstrokes in brilliant colours. **Paul Henry** (1876–1958) is known for his ability to represent the luminous quality of the light in the west of Ireland. **William Orpen** (1878–1931), who trained at the Metropolitan School of Art in Dublin and the Slade in London, became a fashionable portrait painter and an official war artist; among his Irish pupils were **Seán Keating** (1889–1977) and **Patrick Tuohy** (1894–1930). Cubism was introduced to Ireland by **Mainie Jellett** (1897–1944) and **Evie Hone** (1894–1955), who is better known for her work in stained glass.

In 1991 the National Gallery and the Hugh Lane Gallery were joined by the Irish Museum of Modern Art at Kilmainham, which is to commission works for its permanent collection.

SCULPTURE

Cross-slabs and pillar-stones

Among the earliest stone monuments are the slabs laid flat over an individual grave between the 8C and the 12C. The largest collection is at the monastic site at Clonmacnoise. Of somewhat earlier date are cross-decorate pillar-stones, some set up as grave markers. A number of them may be recycled prehistoric standing stones.

High Crosses

One of the great symbols of Ireland, the free-standing highly-decorated crosses are most numerous in the east of Ireland but they are also found in western and northern Britain. The best groups are at Monasterboice, Clonmacnoise, Kells and

Ahenny. It is thought that high crosses are the successors to small painted or bronze-covered wooden crosses used as a focus for kneeling congregations. Most stand on a pyramidal base; the head of the cross is usually ringed and surmounted by a finial often in the shape of a small shrine.

The early carving on late 8C crosses is mostly decorative consisting of spirals and interlacing. In the 9C and 10C, panels of figures appear illustrating stories at first from the New and then from the Old Testament; interestingly, such biblical figures or scenes are rare in early Christian art. Animal scenes are often executed on the base.

The 12C crosses are not a direct continuation and often lack a ring. By this date the figure of a bishop or abbot in the Continental style predominates.

Barrow - Riverine Head from the Custom House, Dublin

Middle Ages to the Renaissance

A distinctive feature of the medieval period is the box tomb found in the chancel of many churches. These often have lids bearing a carved effigy of the deceased sometimes that of his wife; while the sides are decorated with figures of the Apostles and saints. In the 15C and 16C, figures and scenes from the crucifixion were carved in high relief (*see Kildare and Kilkenny Cathedrals*). Although predominantly religious, 17C sculpture, such as the Jacobean Segrave or Cosgrave stucco tableaux in St Audeon's Church in Dublin, widened in scope to include stone and timber carved chimneypieces; there are two fine examples of the former in the castles in Donegal and Carrick-on-Suir. Renaissance-inspired 17C tombs are to be found in St Mary's Cathedral in Limerick, St Nicholas' Church in Carrickfergus and in Youghal Parish Church. Carvings from the Restoration period – fine wood relief and stone – survive, especially at the Kilmainham Hospital.

18C to the Present

The spate of building in the 18C provided much work for sculptors. The figures of **Justice** and **Mars** above the gates of Dublin Castle are the work of **Van Nost** as is a statue of George III, now in the Mansion House. **Edward**

Smyth (1749–1812), who was a pupil of the Dublin Society's Schools, created the riverine heads on the keystones of the arches and the arms of Ireland on the Custom House and also worked on the Four Courts under James Gandon and on the Bank of Ireland; he had been apprenticed to Simon Vierpyl (c 1725–1810), who worked on the Marino Casino. Vierpyl's work at the Casino includes the urns flanking the external steps; the lions adjacent are the work of the English sculptor Joseph Wilton.

The 19C saw the dominance of a taste in Greek Revival detailing; in St Patrick's Church in Monaghan there is a good collection of monuments, notably the one to Lady Rossmore (c 1807) by Thomas Kirk (1781–1845). John Hogan (1800–58) is acknowledged as a most distinguished sculptor - see his fine plaster *The Drunken Faun* in the Crawford Art Galley in Cork. Among his contemporaries, two stand out: Patrick MacDowell (1799–1870) who carved the group of Europe on the base of the Albert Memorial in London, and John Henry Foley (1818–74) who sculpted the bronze figure of Prince Albert; Foley's best work in Dublin is the O'Connell Monument and the statues of Burke, Goldsmith and Grattan on College Green. The best work of Thomas Farrell (1827–1900) is the Cullen Memorial (1881) in the Pro-Cathedral in Dublin.

The Wellington Testimonial (c 1817) in Phoenix Park in Dublin by English architect Sir Robert Smirke, has bronze reliefs on the base by the sculptors Joseph Robinson Kirk, Farrell and Hogan. The work of Oliver Sheppard (1864–1941) is strongly influenced by the Art Nouveau style. The Parnell Monument in O'Connell Street in Dublin was designed by Augustus St Gaudens in 1911. The portrait sculptor **Albert Power** (1883–1945), a resident of Dublin, was elected Associate of RHA in 1911; there are examples of his work in Cavan Cathedral, Mullingar Cathedral and in Eyre Square in Galway. The Belfast sculptor FE McWilliam (1909–92) is represented by a series of bronze figurative sculptures in the Ulster Museum.

More recent work of note includes the *Children of Lir* by Oisin Kelly (1916–81) in the Garden of Remembrance in Dublin. A pleasing aspect of contemporary urban renewal is the placing of sculpture in places where it is readily encountered by the public, who have often responded with affection and amusement.

Literature

Irish men and women of letters have made a significant contribution to English literature through poetry, novels and drama. Poetry was an art form practised by the Celtic bard and medieval monk but theatrical performances were unknown to Gaelic society. To the English language the Irish brought a talent for fantasy, wit and satire and Gaelic speech patterns. Four Irish writers have been awarded the Nobel Prize for Literature: William Butler Yeats (1923), George Bernard Shaw (1925), Samuel Beckett (1969) and Seamus Heaney (1995).

CELTIC INFLUENCE

The Celts may not have left a written literature but their oral tradition has bequeathed a rich legacy of myth and history which inspired later generations. The work of the monks in the scriptorium of a Celtic Church was to copy biblical and other religious texts and to write their own commentaries. They decorated their work, particularly the first capital letter of a chapter, with highly ornate Celtic patterns. Several of these **illuminated manuscripts**, of which the most famous is the Book of Kells, are displayed in the Old Library of Trinity College in Dublin.

One account from this early period is *Navigatio*, written in medieval Latin, an account of the voyage from Ireland to America made by St Brendan in the 6C (👆 *see Ennis*).

ANGLO-IRISH LITERATURE

The first flowering of Anglo-Irish literature came in the late 17C and 18C when George Farquhar (1678–1707) wrote his stage works, Oliver Goldsmith (1728–74) composed poetry, novels and plays and Richard Brinsley Sheridan (1751–1816) published his satirical comedies – *School for Scandal*.

The major figure of this period was **Jonathan Swift** (1667-1745) who was born in Ireland, studied at Trinity College, Dublin, and spent many years in England before being appointed Dean of St Patrick's Cathedral in Dublin where he stayed until his death. *Gulliver's Travels* is the most famous of his satirical writings on 18C Irish society. His friend and fellow student, **William Congreve** (1670–1729), meanwhile, wrote witty costume dramas, such as *The Way of the World*, which inspired Wilde and Shaw.

After spending his early childhood among his mother's relatives in Ireland, **Laurence Sterne** (1713-68), made his name in England as an innovator among novelists with *Tristram Shandy* and *A Sentimental Journey*; he is also seen as a forerunner of the stream of consciousness technique practised by James Joyce.

Many Irish writers who achieved success and fame moved to London, where they made a significant contribution to English literature and theatre. The name of the novel *Dracula* is better known than its author **Bram Stoker** (1947-1912), who worked for several years as an Irish civil servant, writing drama reviews, before moving to London as Henry Irving's manager; only his first novel, *A Snake's Pass*, is set in Ireland.

George Moore (1852–1933) described high society in Dublin *(Drama in Muslin)* and introduced the realism of Zola into the novel *(Esther Waters)*. **Oscar Wilde** (1854–1900) achieved huge success in the London theatre with his poetry, comic plays *(Lady Windermere's Fan, The Importance of Being Earnest)* and in society with his distinctive dress and style, his disgrace and prison term in Reading Gaol. **George Bernard Shaw** (1856–1950) commented on the Anglo-Irish dilemma in his journalism and his play *John Bull's Other Island* and explored the contradictions of English society *(Pygmalion)*.

IRISH THEMES

Several successful authors chose Irish themes for their work. Maria Edgeworth (1767–1849) achieved international fame and the admiration of Sir Walter Scott with her novels *Castle Rackrent* and *The Absentee*; William Carleton (1794–1869) wrote about rural life in County Tyrone. The theme of the novel *The Collegians* by Gerald Griffin (1803–40) was reworked by Dion Boucicault for the stage as *The Colleen Bawn* and by Benedict as an opera, *The Lily of Killarney*. **Anthony Trollope** (1815–82), who began his literary career while working for the Post Office in Ireland, wrote several novels on Irish themes. Canon Sheehan (1852–1913) was admired in Russia by Tolstoy and in the USA for his novels about rural life. Somerville and Ross, a literary partnership composed of **Edith Somerville** (1858–1949) and her cousin Violet Florence Martin (1862–1915), whose pen-name was **Martin Ross**, produced novels about Anglo-Irish society, *The Real Charlotte* and the highly humorous *Experiences of an Irish RM*, adapted for TV in the 1980s.

IRISH LITERARY RENAISSANCE

At this time, as part of the **Gaelic Revival** (👈 *see Gaelige*), a literary renaissance deeply rooted in folklore was taking place in Ireland. One of its early influential figures was George Russell (1867–1935), known as AE, mystic, poet and painter, economist and journalist.

The leader of this literary movement and the dominant writer of the period he old Irish myths and legends, was **William Butler Yeats** (1856–1939), who established his name as a poet and playwright and was a founder member of the Abbey Theatre. He lived for a number of years in County Sligo and came to recognise the power of the native imagination in Irish oral tradition, especially in the heroic tales and in mythological material, which greatly influenced his writing. His own understanding of the occult influenced his involvement in and interpretations of Irish lore. His *Fairy and Folk Tales of the Irish Peasantry*, first published in 1888, was followed by *Irish Fairy Tales* in 1892. Here he made the distinction among folktale, legend and myth; he was among the first writers to interpret Irish folklore. He admired Douglas Hyde because of Hyde's honest commitment to the Irish language and to native Irish lore. Yeats was part of a group of people who associated Anglo-Irish writing as part of a revival of a culture which was in danger of disappearing, to a large extent owing to social development. Another leading light in this movement was **Augusta, Lady Gregory** (1852-1932), who lived in County Galway and became friendly with Yeats. They were much influenced by one another and collected folklore together. Among her best-known works is *Visions and Beliefs in the West of Ireland* (1920), which is based

National Gallery of Ireland, Dublin

William Butler Yeats (1856-1939)

on 20 years of work int this area with Yeats. The *Kiltartan History Book* (1909) contained, for the first time, accounts and descriptions of many aspects of historical lore, unchanged from the oral narration of local people. She was one of the first to publish unedited folklore material faithfully reproducing what she had collected. In common with Yeats, she recognised the richness of folklore among the "farmers and potato-diggers and old men" in her own district, the unbroken chain of tradition and the wealth of ballads, tales and lore which played such an important part in the everyday life of the ordinary people around her in County Galway.

Some of the greatest successes written for the **Abbey Theatre** were the plays of **John Millington Synge** (1871–1909). These included *Riders to the Sea* and *Playboy of the Western World*, inspired by the Aran Islands, and *The Shadow of the Glen*, inspired by the Wicklow Mountains, where language dominates in the bleak landscape; and the pacifist plays of **Sean O'Casey** (1880–1964), *The Shadow of a Gunman, Juno and the Paycock* and *The Plough and the Stars*, written in the aftermath of the First World War.

LITERARY EXILES

The narrow-mindedness of Irish society is expressed in the drama and fiction of George Moore (1852-1933), who spent part of his early life in Paris, and even more so in the work of **James Joyce** (1882-1941), often considered to be the greatest and certainly the most innovative of 20C writers in English. The appearance of his short story collection, *Dubliners*, was long delayed because of the publisher's attempts to impose cuts. Joyce's anti-clerical and anti-nationalist views led him to leave Dublin in 1904 for exile, first in Trieste, then in Zürich and Paris. His most influential work, the vast novel *Ulysses*, recounts a day in the life of Jewish Dubliner Leopold Bloom as he moves around the city in a strange reprise of the wanderings of Homer's hero. The novel revels in the English language and pushes it to its limits, exploiting the devices of interior monologue and stream of conscious-

National Gallery of Ireland, Dublin

James Joyce (1882-1941) painted in 1934 by Jacques Blanche (1861-1942)

ness to extraordinary effect. Dwelling on the most intimate details of everyday life, it was banned not just in Ireland but in Britain and America as well. The even more monumental *Finnegan's Wake* takes these developments even further, exploiting not just the potential of English but of scores of other languages and delighting in word-play and paradox of the utmost complexity.

Much influenced by Joyce, and an associate of his during the older writer's sojurn in Paris, **Samuel Beckett** (1906-89) is remembered mainly as one of founders of the Theatre of the Absurd. Like Joyce, Beckett found life in Ireland unbearably constricting and spent most of his life in France, being decorated for his work in the Resistance in the Second World War. Unlike Joyce, Beckett honed his language to the bare minimum required to convey his grim vision of human life as an "intolerable existence not worthwhile terminating". His best-known work is the play *En Attendant Godot/Waiting for Godot*, written in French and then translated by the author himself. First produced in 1953 and provoking acclaim and bafflement in equal measure, it is the austere and apparently inconsequential tale of two tramps waiting in vain for a mysterious being who never makes an appearance.

MODERN WRITING IN IRELAND

The early 20C produced the bleak realistic poetry of **Patrick Kavanagh** from Monaghan (1904–67 *Ploughman and Other Poems*) – whose influence can be seen in the work of John Montague (b 1929 *Poisoned Lands* and *Rough Field*) and Northern poet **Seamus Heaney** (b 1939 *The Death of a Naturalist*) – and of Louis MacNeice (1907–63), who was a member of Auden's circle and an early influence on the poet / playwright Derek Mahon (b 1941 *The Hudson Letter*). Novelists included Flann O'Brien (1911–66, real name Brian O'Nolan), who wrote a famous newspaper column as Myles na Gopaleen.

The theme of the Big House survives in the work of Elizabeth Bowen (1899–1973 *The Last September*), **Molly Keane** (1897-1974) writing as MJ Farrell (1905–97 *The Last Puppetstown*), Aidan Higgins (b 1927 *Langrishe, Go Down*), Jennifer Johnston (b 1930 *The Illusionist*) and *Woodbrook* (1974) by David Thompson.

Influential writers include **John B Keane** (1928-2002), whose work is firmly set in Co Kerry – his first play *Sive* won the all-Ireland drama festival; *The Field* was made into a film in 1990 and his best novel is *The Bodhran Makers*; also **Edna O'Brien** (b 1932 *The Country Girls*), whose frank accounts of female sexuality in the 1950s were banned in Ireland on first publication and publicly burned in her home village in Co Clare, and the highly acclaimed short-story writer **John MacGahern** (1934-2006 *Amongst Women*) who grew up in Co Leitrim. *Troubles* by **JG Farrell** (1935-79) brings rare humour to the grim reality of the War of Independence. **Maeve Binchy** (b 1940) writes in lighter vane about episodes in Irish family life. **Brendan Behan** (1923-64), who was involved in IRA activity at an early age and imprisoned in both Britain and Ireland, made use of these experiences in the vivid and humorous writing of the plays *The Quare Fellow* and *The Hostage* (the latter originally written in Irish) and in his autobiography *Borstal Boy*.

Northern Irish writers Brian Moore (b 1921 *The Lonely Passion of Judith Hearne*), Patrick McCabe (b 1955 *Butcher Boy*) and Eoin MacNamee (b 1960 *Resurrection Man*) have all seen their work quickly turned into films, as have many writers from the south, including **Roddy Doyle** (b 1958 *The Commitments* and *Paddy Clarke Ha Ha Ha*, which won the Booker prize) and Colin Bateman (b 1962 *Cycle of Violence, Belfast Confidential*), or from outside Ireland such as **Frank McCourt**, who won the Pulitzer Prize in 1997 with *Angela's Ashes* about his childhood in Limerick.

Among the established pillars of Irish drama are **Brian Friel** (b 1929 *Dancing at Lughnasa*, adapted as a film in 1998), Thomas Kilroy (b 1934 *The Secret Fall of Constance Wilde*), Thomas Murphy (b 1935 *A Whistle in the Dark, Bailegangaire*) and Frank McGuinness (b 1956 *Observe the Sons of Ulster Marching towards the Somme*). Alongside them a new wave of young Irish writers is making an international impact. Encouraged by the Abbey and the Gate Theatres in Dublin, the Royal Court in London and independent theatre companies, such as Rough Magic in Dublin, the Druid Theatre Company in Galway and Red Kettle in Waterford, this new wave includes Martin McDonagh (*The Leenane Trilogy*), Conor McPherson (b 1971 *The Weir*), Marina Carr (b 1964 *The Mai*) and Enda Walsh (*Disco Pigs*).

The Gaelic Revival at the end of the 19C was responsible for the rescue of writing in Irish, which, at the start of that century had fallen to a very low point indeed. An important figure was Peter O'Leary (tAthair Peadar) (1839-1920); his folk-tale *Séadna* of 1910 eschewed archaic literary convention in favour of the vigour of the contemporary spoken language, as did the short stories of Pádraig O'Conaire (1882-1928).

Among the best-known authors is the Connemara-born Máirtín O Cadhain (1906-70), former professor of Irish at Trinity College, whose novel *Cré na Cille (The Clay of the Graveyard* - 1949*)* is the best-known prose writing in recent times. Those who lived and worked on the Great Blasket Island, off the coast of Co Kerry, have produced several works describing island life before the people left in the early 1950s. Modern Irish poetry, composed by Seán O Ríordéin, Máirtín O Direáin and Nuala ní Dhomhnaill among others, has appeared in a number of languages.

Music

Ireland is unusual in having a musical instrument – the harp – as its national emblem. Music plays a very important role in Irish life. Traditional music, song and dance are among the most vibrant aspects of Irish culture. Performances take place frequently and spontaneously in all parts of the country, and it is this very unpredictability which is responsible for much of its attraction. New songs and tunes are constantly being composed.

J Malburet/MICHELIN

The harp dominated the musical scene from the Middle Ages until it was proscribed by the English because of its nationalist allure. It was used to accompany the singing or recitation of poetry. Irish harpists, who trained for many years, were admired for their rapid fingerwork and their quick and lively technique; they enjoyed high social status. **Turlough O'Carolan** (Carolan) (1670–1738) started too late in life to reach the highest standard of skill but he was an outstanding composer, much in demand; he left over 200 tunes, which show remarkable melodic invention and are still played.

The first documented mention of mouth-blown pipes in Ireland occurs in an 11C text and the earliest depiction dates from the 15C; these pipes appear to have been primarily for entertainment purposes. The particularly Irish form of pipes, the **uilleann (elbow) pipes**, which have regulators and drones operated by the fingers, emerged in the 18C. These pipes are renowned for the unique sound produced by highly skilled musicians and are closely identified with Irish traditional music, which in recent years has become an important industry.

TRADITIONAL MUSIC TODAY

During the 20C traditional Irish music, which formerly had been played as the accompaniment to dancing, came to be valued in its own right, and is no longer confined to isolated regions. Nowadays, traditional musicians come together in pubs throughout the country for sessions which may be formal, commercial and structured, while others are informal and free of charge. Apart from the pipes, the most popular instruments tend to be the fiddle, flute, tin whistle, accordeon, concertina, melodeon, banjo, guitar, bodhrán, keyboard and the spoons.

Schools and festivals are held throughout the year with people coming from far and wide to learn an instrument or study some other aspect of Irish music. Several schools celebrate the name of a local musician, the best known being the **Willie Clancy Summer School**, which runs in early July in Milltown Malbay in County Clare. Specialist classes in regional styles of instrumental playing are also held at many schools, such as the fiddle classes in Glenties, Co Donegal, each October.

TRADITIONAL TO POP

Traditional music was popularised through the recordings made by the Irish in America and the formation of *Ceoltóirí Chualann* by Seán O'Riada in the early 1960s. This group of the highest calibre of traditional musicians created a more formalised style and generated an appreciation of Irish music. Out of this group the **Chieftains** were formed and brought Irish traditional music to a worldwide audience. In the same decade in the United States the Clancy Brothers and Tommy Makem achieved the popularisation of the Irish ballad tradition. In subsequent years many traditional music groups emerged including the **Dubliners**, the **Bothy Band**, **De Dannan**, **Planxty** and **Altan**. Members of the Brennan family of the Irish-speaking region of Donegal penetrated the realm of popular music singing in both Irish and English as the group **Clannad**, while another member of the family, **Enya**, forged a highly successful international career as a solo artist.

During the 1950s and 1960s showbands entertained in ballrooms throughout Ireland. Musicians such as **Rory Gallagher** and **Van Morrison** began their careers in showbands before pursuing solo careers. Today showband members such as Joe Dolan still have a considerable Irish following among the over 50s age group. Country/Irish music has a large fan base in Ireland. One of the most popular singers is Daniel O'Donnell who has been recording since the mid-1980s.

Traditional Irish music has influenced the bands of recent decades, so much so that Irish rock has often been described as "Celtic Rock". **Thin Lizzy** and **Rory Gallagher** were among the first to gain international celebrity. **Van Morrison** and **U2** still continue to maintain their positions on the international stage, entertaining new generations with their brand of Irish music. More recent international celebrities **The Pogues, The Cranberries**, **Sinéad O'Connor** and **The Corrs** have created a worldwide interest in "Celtic" music. **Bono** of U2 and **Bob Geldof**, exponents of cult bands, have moved onto to new venture.

Boyzone, **B*witched** and more recently **Westlife** have had huge commercial success. Boyzone members are currently embarking on solo careers; Ronan Keating has the largest following to date.

Bands who came to the fore in the 1990s making the charts in both Ireland and the UK are Northern Ireland's Divine Comedy and Ash. At the forefront of the Club Scene is David Holmes, a DJ turned Pop Star, who has gained a considerable reputation for his remixing and soundtrack work.

Bands that have not yet entered the charts have loyal fans who flock to their gigs - this underground music scene was brilliantly captured in Roddy Doyle's book *The Commitments*.

DANCE

Set dancing originated in Ireland in the 18C; it consists of figure dances, developed by travelling dancing masters, who adapted the original French dance movements to suit Irish music. Set-dancing is very popular and can be seen at many public venues; classes are held on a regular basis at hundreds of venues. Although it could not really be described as "traditional", the phenomenon of Riverdance, created in 1994 and seen on five continents, has done for Irish dance what the Chieftains did for Irish music. Other Irish dance shows have followed, including *Lord of the Dance*.

SONG

Singing forms part of many of the music festivals held in Ireland, and at least one festival is devoted solely to this art and is held each June in Ennistymon, Co Clare. Traditional singing is usually called old style *(sean-nós)* singing, and is especially closely identified with singing in Irish; songs are also sung in English in this style. Traditional songs in Irish date for the most part from the last two or three hundred years, although some are older and is the style is a good deal older still. Songs in English include recently composed songs and also many songs from the medieval ballad traditions. The style is individual, unaccompanied, free and ornate, with many regional variations. The Irish-speaking area of Rath Cairn, Co Meath, hosts the Irish-language singing festival *Eigse Dharach Uí Chatháin* in October each year.

Religion

Christianity was probably introduced to Ireland from Roman Britain or Gaul in the 4C. Palladius, the first bishop, was appointed in 431 by Pope Celestine I but his mission met with little success and it is Patrick, the country's much-revered patron saint, who is held responsible for the country's definitive conversion.

The majority (75%) of the population of Ireland is Roman Catholic but most of the country's Catholic churches are of recent date; the traditional religious sites are usually occupied by Anglican churches, a reminder that for many years the Protestant Church of Ireland was the country's established church. Many Catholic churches stand in new centres of population though others were built close to a ruined monastery where the faithful heard Mass in the Penal Days and where they continue to be buried.

NATIONAL SAINTS

St Patrick

The patron saint of Ireland was born on the west coast of Roman Britain where he was captured as a young man by Irish raiders. After six years of slavery near Sliabh Mis (Slemish in Co Down), he escaped to France and then returned to his birthplace. Inspired by a vision that the people of Ireland were calling him, he went to France to study, possibly at the monasteries of Lérins, Tours and Auxerre. In 432 in middle age he returned to Ireland to convert the people to Christianity. He is thought to have founded his first church at Saul and then travelled to Slane where he challenged the power of the High King and his druids.

In 444, after a visit to Rome, he founded the cathedral church of Armagh, still the ecclesiastical capital of Ireland, as well as many other churches. When he died, probably at Saul in 461, the country was organised into dioceses based on the petty Irish kingdoms.

Patrick is the subject of numerous tales and legends, according to which he banished monsters and drove the snakes out of Ireland.

On St Patrick's day (17 March) people wear a sprig of **shamrock** *(seamróg)*, a custom which is comparatively recent, being first documented in the later part of the 17C; it is claimed that the saint used this trefoil plant to illustrate the doctrine of the Holy Trinity.

MICHELIN

St Patrick, Bangor Abbey

St Bridget

Brigit was a Celtic goddess, whose name means "the exalted person"; it is significant that the same name is given to the most popular female saint in Irish tradition and second only to St Patrick among all the saints. This Leinster saint ("Bríd"), who died c AD 524, established a convent in Kildare *(Cill Dara* in Irish meaning "the church of the oak tree") and this may have been a sacred spot in pre-Christian times. Bridget is perceived to be the protectress of animals and crops, with which she is closely associated.

The most popular legend of St Bridget is associated with Kildare, where she wished to build a convent. The local king refused to grant her more land than could be covered by her cloak, but when she spread her garment it expanded to cover a vast area.

On St Bridget's day (1 February) it is customary to honour the saint by making straw or rush crosses *(Cros Bhríde)*, which have numerous regional variations in design and form.

CELTIC CHURCH

As continental Europe was overrun by barbarians, the church in Ireland developed a distinctive form of organisation based on monasticism. In the mid 6C and 7C a great many monasteries were founded and by the 8C the administration of the church had been taken over by the abbots. Although bishops continued to perform the sacramental duties and new bishops were consecrated, they were not appointed to particular sees.

Some **monasteries** grew up round a hermit's retreat but many were founded by the head of a clan; members of the family entered the religious life and filled the various offices, as abbot, bishop, priest, teacher or ascetic. The manual work was done either by the monks or by the original tenants of the land, married men with families, whose elder sons usually received a clerical education in the monastery school. Most monasteries were self-sufficient communities providing their own food, clothing, books, tools and horses. Some monasteries seem to have been founded on sites which had pagan religious associations; others were set up by the main highways, often on the boundaries of a kingdom.

The monastic **libraries** contained copies of the Scriptures, the early Fathers, some classical authors and some history; much early Christian scholarship was preserved in Ireland after the fall of the Roman Empire. In the scriptorium the monks made copies of existing texts or wrote their own learned works, using meticulous techniques which are well described and illustrated at the Colmcille Heritage Centre (ⓒ see Donegal Glens).

Irish monks developed a strong tradition of **asceticism** with a threefold classification of martyrdom. Ascetics seeking to contemplate the presence of God would form small monastic communities in remote places, particularly on islands like the harsh and remote rock of Great Skellig.

ROMANISATION

Following four synods held in the first half of the 12C the Irish church lost its distinctive character and was gradually reorganised on the Roman pattern. Four provinces and 33 new dioceses were created, each with a bishop. Some monastic churches became cathedrals, others were used as parish churches.

Monastic orders from the continent were introduced. The Augustinians took over earlier monastic centres to be near the people. The Cistercians chose new and remote sites in accordance with their ascetic rule, which attracted many Irish monks; by 1272 there were 38 Cistercian houses in Ireland. The Franciscans settled in the towns in the 13C; in the 15C the Observants spread to the west and north.

The Irish church was further diminished by the Normans with the encour-

---

Irish Missionary Monks

The work of monks from Ireland in re-Christianising Europe after the barbarian invasions was so extensive that it has been claimed that the Irish were responsible for saving civilisation. In the late 6C, **Columbanus** founded monasteries in Luxeuil, Annegray and Fontaines in France and Bobbio in Italy ; his disciple **Gall** gave his name to Switzerland's most renowned monastery, which has preserved a fine collection of Irish manuscripts. **Columba (Colmcille** in Irish) left his native country to found the monastery on Iona ; monks from there moved on to Lindisfarne in the north of England and to the court of Charlemagne. **Fursey** founded a monastery at Lagny near Paris, while **Johannes Eriugena** achieved renown as a philosopher at Laon. Several Irish monks went to Germany and beyond, **Kilian** to Würzburg, **Virgil** in the 8C to Salzburg, **Marianus Scottus** in the 11C to Cologne, Fulda and Mainz, and a namesake, a member of an important Donegal family, to Regensburg. The most-travelled monk, however, was probably **Brendan** (ⓒ see Ennis), who may have reached America.

agement of King Henry II and Popes Adrian IV and Alexander III so as "to extend the bounds of the Roman Church". Under the Statute of Kilkenny (1366) Irishmen were forbidden to enter English-run monasteries, and English-speaking clergy were to be appointed to English-speaking parishes.

REFORMATION

In the 16C the churches in England and Ireland were declared independent of Rome; the monasteries were suppressed. Trinity College in Dublin was founded in 1591 to provide Irish priests for the established church; although Roman Catholics were admitted to degrees in 1793, membership was confined to Anglicans until 1873. The 16C reforms were only intermittently enforced in Ireland; the majority of the people remained faithful to the Roman church and many monasteries continued until suppressed by Cromwell. Early in the 17C the Plantation of Ulster with lowland Scots introduced fervent Presbyterianism.

PENAL LAWS

Under the repressive measures introduced after the Battle of the Boyne (1690), Roman Catholics were barred from the armed forces, law, commerce, from civic office or office under the crown, from land purchase; Roman Catholic estates could pass *in toto* to an eldest son if he converted to the established church but otherwise had to be divided among all the sons. No Roman Catholic could attend school, keep a school or go abroad to school. Education was conducted in **hedge schools**, which taught Latin, Greek, arithmetic, Irish, English, history and geography; the masters, who were paid in money or kind, were respected members of the Irish community; several were poets. All Roman Catholic bishops and regular clergy were banished from Ireland, and Roman Catholic worship was forbidden. Roman Catholic priests travelled the country in disguise and said mass out of doors in remote places or in ruined monastery churches; they used sacramental

Ardagh Chalice (8C)

National Museum of Ireland, Dublin

vessels which could be dismantled to avoid detection.

DISSENTERS

Roman Catholics were not alone in suffering repression. The Scottish Presbyterians who had migrated to Ulster were frequently regarded with disfavour, though the Protestant Ascendancy could not afford to alienate them completely. The Toleration Act of 1719 granted them freedom of worship, but they continued to endure various disabilities and particularly resented the obligation to pay tithes to the established Church of Ireland; in the 18C many of them emigrated to America, though the majority remained. Their dissatisfaction with the existing order found expression in widespread support for the rebellion of 1798, when a large proportion of the membership of the United Irishmen was composed of Presbyterians. The English Quakers who came to Ireland during the Civil War period also faced discrimination of various kinds, though by the beginning of the 18C this had diminished. Like their counterparts elsewhere, and despite their generally humble beginnings, many Quakers later achieved prominence in commerce and industry.

DENOMINATIONAL FREEDOM

The Catholic Relief Acts of 1791 and 1793 finally allowed freedom of worship and education. In 1795 **Maynooth Seminary** was established for training Roman Catholic clergy. In 1820 Edmund Rice (1762–1844), a former pupil of a hedge school, obtained papal recognition of the **Christian Brothers** (👉 *see Kilkenny*), an order which established many boys' schools in Ireland. In 1831 the 18C hedge schools were replaced by the National Schools. In 1869 the Church of Ireland, a member of the Anglican Communion, was disestablished. Apart from Trinity College and two short-lived 16C colleges at Maynooth and Galway, Ireland had no medieval universities. In 1845 charters were issued to incorporate three colleges in Belfast, Cork and Galway but, owing to Roman Catholic opposition, only Queen's College in Belfast thrived. The Catholic University, founded in Dublin in 1854 with Cardinal Newman as Rector, was incorporated as University College when the National University of Ireland was founded in 1908; two years later Maynooth was also recognised as a college of the National University.

Pilgrims climbing Croagh Patrick

SLIDE FILE, Dublin

PILGRIMAGES AND PATTERNS

Since the 8C, by which time Ireland was an almost entirely Christian country, the lives of the **saints** have played a major role in popular devotion and also stimulated an entire body of related legends and lore. Saints were seen to be powerful in many spheres of life on earth and in the afterlife; in many instances, they were seen as popular heroes and heroines. Some were said to have had a miraculous birth; others wielded supernatural powers and could triumph against the enemy. Saints had healing powers and even their posessions or relics could effect a cure.

Oral tradition has been profoundly influenced by biographies of saints; the lore of saints is widespread throughout Ireland. Thousands of **holy wells**, many associated with local saints, are scattered throughout the countryside; they are said to have curative powers – of a general type or more specific – and are visited frequently, particularly on saints' days.

People still observe the feast days of local saints and the **pattern** (modern Irish *pátrún*; the word is a corruption of patron) when they make a communal visit to a holy well or other religious site under the protection of the local patron saint. In many places holy wells are associated with **rag trees**, named after the hundreds of coloured pieces of cloth attached to their branches, and used to invoke divine assistance, often of a curative kind.

Many traditional religious sites are still visited by pilgrims: Glencolumbkille on St Columba's Day (9 June); Clonmacnoise on St Kieran's Day (9 September); Croagh Patrick in July, when people climb barefoot to the summit. The most rigorous pilgrimage takes place at St Patrick's Purgatory, an island in Lough Derg (southeast of Donegal) where St Patrick spent 40 days in prayer and fasting; during the season (1 June to 15 August) pilgrims spend three days barefoot, take part in an all-night vigil and exist on one meal a day of bread and hot black tea or coffee.

Myths and Lore

Some of the best sources for understanding the Celtic mind and imagination are the Irish myths and tales populated with colourful descriptions of gods and goddesses, and the fabulous exploits of mortal heroes and heroines. Although most of the earlier stories originated in Ireland, they were written down by Christian monks.

RELIGION

The Celts seem to have acknowledged many divinities – gods of war and hunting, goddesses of fertility, harvest and healing. Among those worshipped in Ireland were Brigit, Daghdha and Cernunnos – god of animals, plants and forests, whose emblem was a set of antlers. Different tribe each venerated its own tribal god or goddess who might reside in a special sacred well and hold the power to cure and protect people who regarded not only wells, but certain springs and rivers – particularly the River Boyne – and trees as sacred, indeed, they carved images of their gods on tree-trunks. Assemblies, at which games and races took place, were held at ancient royal or assembly sites, such as Tara and Tullaghoge. The Celts buried their dead, sometimes cremated, with offerings of food and ornaments; they believed that after death they went to join their ancestors, the gods of the Otherworld, who were thought to live in sacred mounds, now known to be prehistoric burial mounds such as at Newgrange, Tara and Rathcrogan.

FAIRYLORE

The belief in the **Otherworld** is still an important factor in Irish tradition. This "Otherworld" may exist in a fort or in a mountain, under a lake or beneath the sea. Hundreds of tales and legends associated with the fairies and their world survive, as the landscape and its placenames bear witness. In Irish the fairies are called *sí* or *na daoine maithe* – the good people, or *na daoine beaga* – the little people. The fairies are said variously to be fallen angels, the ancient gods – the Tuatha Dé Danann or sometimes the community of the dead. These supernatural beings are invisible to mortals, inhabiting the earth, the air and water. The earthen tumuli – known as *rath* and *lios* – are often said to be fairy forts and sometimes fairy music can be heard to emanate from them. Many legends are told describing how the fairies "borrowed" or "stole" a mortal to assist them in some task of their own, such as nursing a fairy child or playing music at a fairy wedding. On occasions, fairies have been said to remove a mortal child, leaving one of their own in its place; when the unsuspecting parents returned from their chores, they were shocked to discover the sick or dying child in the cradle referred to as a "changeling".

BANSHEE

The Banshee *(Bean Sí)* is a solitary female spirit whose eerie cry is said to portend death. Superstition associated with the banshee is still very strong and an excuse for the retelling of many legends, often depicting her combing her long hair. One story describes how a man found her comb and brought it home; the following night he heard wailing and knocking at his window: so, catching the comb in a pair of tongs he passed it out of the window; the comb was removed by the banshee and the tongs broken as a warning that had the man put out his hand, it would have met the same fate. The banshee is associated with lamenting, keening and death. The keen *(caoineadh)* was performed by women at funerals and at wakes as part of the lament for the dead. Certain, usually older, women in the community came to the house where the corpse was laid out and took it in turns to perform the keen which was usually composed *ex tempore* and sung to music with a regular refrain during the days of the wake and later at the graveyard. During the wake people also told stories, smoked clay pipes, drank whiskey and played games. The clergy disapproved of many of the wake customs and of the keen.

SLIDE FILDE, Dublin

Castlestrange Stone

S Allegret/MICHELIN

The giddy little creature depicted here is Ireland's national fairy, the leprechaun. About two feet high – when upright! – and usually of rather wizened appearance, the leprechaun is a cobbler by trade, though he is better known as the crafty guardian of a hidden crock of gold. A mischievous player of tricks on the human race, he steals into their houses at night to create havoc in kitchen and cellar.

THE MYTHOLOGICAL AND HISTORICAL CYCLES

The stories from the four great ancient Irish cycles are arguably among the finest expressions of Irish imagination and are still a source of artistic inspiration.

The **Mythological Cycle** tells of the heroes or gods who inhabited Ireland before the arrival of the Celts and contains the story of the Battle of Moytura, the Children of Lir and the Wooing of Etain.

The **Ulster Cycle** *(Rúraíocht)* recounts the deeds of the Red Branch Knights of Navan Fort; it includes the **Cattle Raid of Cooley** *(Táin Bó Cuailgne)*, an epic poem which describes how Queen Maeve of Connaught set out to capture the famous brown bull of Cooley and how Ferdia, the Connaught champion, was defeated by the Ulster champion, Cúchulain, which translates as the hound of Culann.

The **Ossianic Cycle**, also known as the **Fenian Cycle** *(Fiannaíocht)*, is set in the time of Cormac mac Airt, who is said to have reigned at Tara in the 3C, and tells about Fionn mac Cumhaill and the Fianna, whose capital was on the Hill of Allen. The Fenian tales and lore tell of the great deeds of the Fianna or Fenian warriors.

Hundreds of neolithic tombs are called Diarmuid and Gráinne's bed *(Leaba Dhiarmuid agus Ghráinne)* in the belief that these lovers from the Fenian tales slept here during their travels in Ireland.

The **Historical Cycle**, which is also known as the **Cycle of the Kings**, is probably a mixture of history and fiction. Many place-names and sites identify with characters and episodes from mythological tales.

A vast number of tales and episodes from these cycles were central to the living storytelling tradition in Ireland until very recently. In addition to their preservation in written literature, the stories were kept alive in oral form, both in Irish and in English, and formed an important part of the repertoire of the storyteller *(seanchaí)*, a person of great social importance.

Gaelige

Gaelige, Irish or Gaelic – whichever name is used – is a subtle and extremely expressive language. Although rarely used, it has had a profound influence on the way the Irish use English, which has largely replaced it. Irish is an Indo-European language, one of the Celtic group – Scots Gaelic, the extinct Manx, Welsh, Cornish and Breton – and is closest to Scots Gaelic and Manx. Its wonderfully stylish alphabet, abandoned in the 1960s, can still be seen in old road signs and other contexts where its decorative qualities are exploited.

Once the natural language of the whole island, Irish has been remorselessly displaced by English, and today is spoken as a first language by only a small minority, some 60 000 in all. Nevertheless it enjoys official status as the first official language of the Republic, remains an important badge of Irish identity and has been consistently promoted by government and cultural organsiations since independence; over 40% of adults claim to be able to speak Irish. It has a complex grammar and a pronunciation which most outsiders find difficult to grasp; consonants may remain mute or change their sound according to their position. Even monoglot English speakers have become familiar with the use of the Irish language in official expressions; the prime minister is always referred to as the Taoiseach, the Parliament as Dáil Eireann, the Tourist Board as Bord Fáilte, the national railway as Iarnród Éireann, and all buses heading for the city centre in Dublin bear the direction An Lár.

OGHAM SCRIPT

The earliest known form of writing in the Irish language is in **Ogham script**, which now survive in the form of inscriptions on memorials to the dead dating from the 4C to 7C.

The script is based on the Latin alphabet and was probably adapted by poets and wise men before the Latin alphabet became more generally familiar in Christian Ireland. It script consists of 20 characters written as groups of a maximum of five straight lines on either side of, or horizontally or diagonally through, a central line which was usually cut into the vertical edge of a standing stone - many of which are to be found in the southern districts of Ireland.

TRANSITION TO ENGLISH

The decline in the use of Irish was caused by the gradual imposition of English law and administration in the 16C and the repressive clauses of the Penal Laws (👓 *see History*) in the 17C. Many Irish people turned to English to achieve a position in society. This trend was accelerated by the teaching of English in the National Schools, which were set up in 1831. During and after the famine (1845–49) many Irish speakers died or

Ogham Script

B Drouillot/MICHELIN

Angela's Ashes – a film adaptation by Alan Parker of Frank McCourt's autobiographical memoir of his Limerick childhood

Cat's Collection

many foreign films have been shot in Ireland and the local industry has produced some memorable works.

In 1904 JT Jameson, a newsreel cameraman, founded the Irish Animated Company (IAC); together with the American cinema, which was anxious to please the many Irish immigrants in the States, it made cinema acceptable in Ireland and launched the local industry. In 1916 and 1917 two more companies were set up – Film Company of Ireland (FCOI) and General Film Supply (GFS). It was not, however, until the founding of the Free State in 1922 that Irish cinema truly flourished in Ireland. Political events supplied the first themes such as the Easter Rising of 1916 in *Irish Destiny* (1926) by Isaac Eppel; incidents in the War of Independence feature in *Guest of the Nation* (1935) by Denis Johnston and *The Dawn* (1936) by Tom Cooper.

Perhaps the internationally best known film made in Ireland in the 1930s was the documentary *Man of Aran*. The work of an American of Irish descent, Robert O'Flaherty, it presents a compelling and beautiful picture of the harsh traditional life of the people of the Aran Islands, but is more a romantic evocation of humanity's epic struggle against the elements than an accurate record of a particular place, period, or people.

One of the earliest non-Irish films to make extensive use of Ireland as a location was Laurence Olivier's *Henry V*. Shot in 1944 as a deliberate wartime morale booster, it used the Powerscourt estate in neutral Ireland as a setting for the large-scale re-creation of the battle of Agincourt. Hundreds of local farmers hired as extras proved themselves more than adequate as stalwart cavalrymen. Plenty of other films have exploited Ireland as a background to films set elsewhere, among them Mel Gibson's *Braveheart* (1996), in which the town of Trim, its great castle and its surroundings stand in for the Scotland of rebel William Wallace. Earlier, in 1956, the little port of Youghal was transformed into New Bedford, Massachusetts, becoming the harbour town from which in *Moby Dick* Captain Ahab sets out in search of the great whale. More often, however, the cinematic role of Ireland has been as itself, or at least as a version of itself. In what is probably the most celebrated of all films with an Irish setting, *The Quiet Man* (1952), the country appears as a kind of mysterious, pre-industrial rural paradise, inhabited by quaint, stereotypical Irishmen and Irishwomen. The work of the great John Ford, himself of Irish descent, it revolves around the return to his native land of a boxer, memorably played by John Wayne, and features one of the cinema's longest fight scenes, in which Wayne and his rival brawl their way through the village from farmyard to pub. Conflict of another kind was portrayed by David Lean in *Ryan's Daughter*

(1970), in which a young married Irish-woman falls for an officer of the British garrison. Its evocation of the wild land-scapes and seascapes of the west has never been excelled.

In more recent years, film-makers from home and abroad have moved beyond this backward-looking vision of the country, taking their themes from con-temporary politics and social questions as well as from history and from litera-ture. Neil Jordan's blockbusting biopic *Michael Collins* (1996), an account of the life and times of the charismatic but doomed Republican leader, was sec-ond only to *Titanic* in its success with Irish audiences, not least thanks to the performance of Liam Neeson in the title role. Neeson was only one of several Irish stars like Gabriel Byrne, Stephen Rea and Pierce Brosnan, to emerge in this period with international reputa-tions. Jordan's earlier *The Crying Game* (1992) dealt with the relationship of an IRA gunman and a black British soldier, while his *The Butcher Boy* (1997), in which a young boy from a dysfunctional family descends into madness and murder, has been seen as a metaphor for a country still coming to terms with its troubled history. Jim Sheridan's *The Field* (1991) was equally sombre in its treatment of a farmer's refusal to let his land pass into alien hands. Previously, in 1989, Sheridan had filmed the poignant story of the cerebral palsy victim Christy Brown in *My Left Foot*, in which Daniel Day-Lewis won an Oscar for his extraordinarily moving performance. Day-Lewis also appeared in *In the Name of the Father* (1993), Sheridan's account of the failure of justice following the IRA's bombing of a Guildford pub.

The Oscar-winning *Crying Game* was based on the classic short story by Frank O'Connor, and numerous other works of literature have been translated with varying degrees of success to the screen. Among them are James Joyce's *Dubliners* (1987) by John Huston and,

Michael Collins *directed by Neil Jordan starring Liam Neeson*

Cat's Collection

perhaps surprisingly, his *Ulysses* (1967) by Joseph Strick. *Angela's Ashes* (1999), was a not altogether convincing adapta-tion by Alan Parker of Frank McCourt's best-selling autobiographical memoir of his rain-soaked and wretched Limerick childhood. A similarly grim social story is retold in *The Magdalene Sisters* (2003) set in a women's asylum run by Roman Catholic nuns.

Roddy Doyle's sensitive and sometimes hilarious novels of contemporary Dub-lin's low life have inspired *The Commit-ments* (1991) by Alan Parker and *The Van* (1996) by Stephen Frears.

Mention should also be made of the work of the expatrite director **Ken Loach** – *Hidden Agenda* (1990), *Land and Freedom* (1995), *Carla's Song* (1997) and *Sweet Sixteen* (2002). In 2006 his film *The Wind that Shakes the Barley* was awarded the prestigious Palme d'Or at Cannes for his portrayal of the struggle for freedom from occupation: in this instance the Irish Republican Army fights against the yoke of British rule (Black and Tans) in the 1920s, with intense scenes of violence on both sides.

Three Irish TV series earned great popularity in the UK – *Father Ted, The Ambassador* starring Pauline Collins and partly filmed in Ely Place in Dublin, and *Ballykissangel,* filmed in Avoca in the Wicklow Mountains.

THE COUNTRY TODAY

The prosperous economy of Ireland owes much to forceful government intervention and enthusiastic membership of the European Union in the last decades of the 20C. The effects of new-found affluence, from a high level of car ownership to individual house-building, can be seen everywhere. Social change too has been profound but at the same time many of the characteristics of the Irish way of life which so endear the country to its visitors remain as pronounced as ever, and Irish identity is far from being eroded by the country's whole-hearted entry into the mainstream of contemporary international life.

Economy

THE "CELTIC TIGER"

In the 19C, Union with Britain failed for the most part to bring Ireland the benefits, as well as many of the problems, of the Industrial Revolution. The great exception was Belfast, where the existence of the linen and food processing industries stimulated the growth of general engineering. The city joined the ranks of British industrial centres, its role confirmed in the first half of the 20C, when Harland and Wolff built liners like the *Titanic* and Short built famous flying boats. Between 1939-45, the North's economy was further stimulated by the needs of war production and by the presence of British and American military bases.

By contrast, in the years following independence, the Republic concentrated on being self-sufficient rather than on modernising its economy, which remained over-reliant on farming and on the export of agricultural products to Britain. Some stimulation came from government initiatives like the Shannon hydro-electric scheme, but the high level of emigration of people of working age was a fundamental weakness of the economy. The world depression of the 1930s and a trade war with Britain further hindered progress. Ireland's neutral stance during 1939-45 may have made political sense, but brought none of the benefits of intensified production nor of the American aid which helped restore the postwar economies of other European countries. From the 1950s onwards, however, a series of measures were taken to open up the economy and stimulate growth; tax concessions and incentives encouraged export-based, modern industries and attracted foreign investment. A further boost was given when the country joined the European Economic Community in 1972. Together with investment in research and development and the existence of a highly qualified and largely un-unionised workforce, and despite intermittent setbacks, this resulted in an astonishing economic expansion; by the 1990s, the country's growth rate was twice the European Union's average, and modern industries like chemicals and pharmaceuticals, electronics and biotechnology, and information technology constituted 75% of the total industrial output. The strength of the economy of the "Celtic Tiger" meant that Ireland was able to join the single European currency project as one of the few countries complying with the criteria set by the Maastricht Treaty of 1992. The outward migration which had been such a negative feature of Irish life for centuries came to an end and net immigration began,

Central Bank, Dublin

Ph Hurlin/MICHELIN

Skibbereen, Co Cork

many of the migrants being young professionals bringing with them expertise acquired abroad.

Northern Ireland, once in advance of the South in terms of industry and employment, has suffered like the rest of the United Kingdom from the decline in traditional heavy industries. Government sponsored initiatives have not always ended in success and the halting progress of the peace process has inhibited the inflow of investment. A mitigating factor is the exceptionally high level of employment in the public sector.

Tourism has become the Republic's second largest indigenous industry. Six million overseas visitors come here every year, drawn by unspoilt landscapes, clean rivers and lakes, peace and quiet, the Celtic heritage, and the friendly welcome extended by local people. Fishing and golf remain major attractions. The once rudimentary visitor facilities are being replaced by state of the art interpretative centres while the previous somewhat carefree attitude to conservation has given way to the meticulous work of Dúchas, the government body charged with preservation of the national heritage.

Modern tourism began with the spread of the railway network in the 19C. The mountain, lake and coastal scenery of the west particularly appealed to Victorian sensibilities. Today, more than half the Republic's visitors still come from Britain, about a million from North America, and many from the over-crowded conurbations of western Europe.

People

ORIGINS

The Irish are commonly thought of as being a Celtic people but this is more of a cultural than ethnic definition. Around 8 000BC, long before the arrival of the Celts, the coastal areas and river valleys were settled by Mesolithic hunter-gatherers who had moved across the landbridge which still connected Ireland with Scotland. The dominant Celts seem to have come in several waves during the second half of the last millennium BC, pushed to the western fringe of the continent by the expansion of the Roman Empire and pressure from Germanic tribes in Central Europe. By the time of the coming of Christianity in the 5C, the population may have amounted to a quarter of a million. Viking attacks began towards the end of the 8C but, although the Norsemen's original objective was pillage, they later settled, founding coastal towns and eventually becoming absorbed into the local population. Subsequent immigration mostly originated from Britain, the Anglo-Norman invaders and their followers being succeeded in the 16C and 17C by a planned influx of settlers and colonists. By the beginning of the 18C, perhaps a quarter of the population of just over two million was of English, Welsh and Scottish origin. Other groups, though far less numerous, added their distinctive flavour; Huguenots in the late 17C, Jews mostly in the late 19C and early 20C. Before the last decades of the 20C, the backwardness of the economy meant that immigration from non-European countries remained statistically insignificant.

DISTRIBUTION AND STRUCTURE

The country has a population of about 5 945 000, of whom 1 710 000 live in Northern Ireland, 4 235 000 in the Republic. This represents a substantial increase over the low point of about 4.5 million, reached in the early 20C, the result of a falling birthrate and continuing emigration. It is largely due to net inward migration but it is still well short of the total of over 8 million in the period immediately preceding the Famine.

The overall density compared with other western European countries is low: 52 people per square kilometre, and a large proportion of the population still live in small towns or the countryside. Villages are relatively few and the isolated family farm is the most typical form of rural settlement; many places which elsewhere in Europe would be classified as villages with a total population of perhaps a few hundred have a full range of urban functions such as a market, shops, pubs, and professional offices. Recent rural building has confirmed the scattered nature of the settlement pattern, with new farmhouses and other homes standing proudly in the middle of fields and a ribbon development of bungalows along the roads. The bigger towns all have a coastal location. Greater Dublin has a disproportionate number of inhabitants, 1,122,600 in total, Greater Belfast some 277,391. No other regional centre in the Republic approaches the capital in population size; Cork has (180 000 inhabitants) and the other cities have under 100 000.

Jaunting Car

In the Republic birth rates have fallen recently but the population is relatively young one, with more than 40% under the age of 25 and 24% under the age of 15.

RELIGIOUS AFFILIATION AND MINORITIES

In recent years, the power and authority of the Roman Catholic Church may have been sapped by recurrent scandals, but the Republic of Ireland is still a demonstratively Catholic country, with 91% of the population declaring their adherence to the Roman Catholic Church. Attendance at Mass is high, though no longer universal, and much lower in inner city districts of Dublin than in rural areas. The Church's teachings on matters such as abortion continue to command widespread respect; attempts to liberalise restrictions on termination of pregnancy have been defeated when put to referendum. Protestants, who once formed a quarter of the total population, and almost 50% of the inhabitants of Dublin, have declined in number, either through emigration or intermarriage and number around 3% of the total population of the Republic, most of them members of the Church of Ireland.

The strength of religious observance is paralleled in Northern Ireland, whose majority Protestant population is split between Presbyterians, Methodists, members of the Church of Ireland and of various minor denominations. Roman Catholics form about one third of the Northern population, a proportion which is steadily increasing.

Ethnically indistinguishable from their fellow-citizens, Travellers are perhaps the most visible minority in southern

Ireland. Previously known by the now demeaning name of "tinkers", they move their lorries and caravans from one roadside site to another and earn a living mostly from scrap-metal dealing. There are small numbers of Chinese and other Asians in both North and South, and the Republic, especially its remoter western areas, has long attracted individual residents from other European countries, particularly Germany.

Hurling

Leisure

MUSIC

Music plays a large role in Irish life; not only through the sessions of traditional music played in the bars in the evenings all over the country but also the dancing for which many of the tunes were written. Side by side with this tradition are the modern bands playing every kind of popular music (👁 see also p 96).

SPORTS

Most forms of sport are played enthusiastically in Ireland, none more so however than those which are uniquely Irish, hurling *(iománaíocht)* and Gaelic football *(peil)*. These, together with **handball** *(liathróid láimhe)* and rounders, are administered by the **Gaelic Athletic Association** *(Cumann Lúthchleas Gael)*, a largely rural movement, founded in 1884 in Thurles. The national GAA stadium, Croke Park in Dublin, with space for 80 000 spectators, is named after the Association's first patron, Archbishop Croke (1824–1902). The high point of the Gaelic sporting year comes in September, when both the hurling and football national finals are held here. The history of the Association and the exploits of the hurling and football champions are excellently illustrated in the GAA Museums at Croke Park and in Thurles.

Hurling is a fast-moving and high-scoring game of great antiquity, played by two teams each of fifteen using the long curved stick of the hurley *(camán)* to hit the cork and leather ball into or over the rugby-type goal. Allowing the ball to be handled under certain circumstances increases the excitement of the game, which can seem violent and chaotic to the non-initiated. *Camogie* is a version of hurling adapted for women participants, with a shorter playing time, teams of 12, and a smaller pitch.

Gaelic football is played with a spherical ball, uses the same pitch as hurling and has similar rules; neither game is played outside Ireland to any extent, but Australian Rules football owes much to its Gaelic ancestor.

HORSE RACING

The **horse** plays a special part in Irish life and the great Horse Fairs still figure in the Irish calendar. Breeding and racing horses have deep roots in Irish culture; the earliest races were part of pre-Christian festivals. Swimming races, which ceased only recently, also had Celtic origins, in the ritual of immersion. The focal point of Ireland's breeding, racing and training is at the Curragh in Co Kildare. There are about 28 race courses in Ireland; at Laytown Strand, south of Drogheda, the times of races are dictated by the tide and horses are often exercised on the seashore. The first recorded prize is a plate donated in 1640 by the Trustees of the Duke of Leinster. In 1684 King James II presented the King's Plate at Down Royal "to encourage the sport of horse racing". The first steeplechase, a form of race over obstacles invented by Lord Doneraile, took place in 1752 from Buttevant Church to St Leger Church near Doneraile (4.5mi/7km). In the past men challenged one another to pounding matches, in which the participants, accompanied by their grooms, had to follow the leader over any selected obstacle or admit defeat.

SLIDE FILE, Dublin

BARS AND PUBS

More varied and more interesting than its derivatives which have been such a marketing success world-wide, the Irish pub or bar remains the centre of much social life, particularly in the countryside and in small towns, where some still double as general stores. Big-city pubs in both Belfast and Dublin can be places of almost Baroque splendour, redolent with literary or political associations. Drinking and conversation remain the patrons' principal preoccupations, but more and more pubs serve good food and very few remain an exclusively male preserve. Strangers seeking company are unlikely to remain lonely for long, and the pub is the best place to enjoy fun and good talk, the famous *craic*, as well as music, traditional or contemporary.

Irish Diaspora

Forty million people of Irish descent live in the USA, 5 million in Canada, 5 million in Australia and unnumbered millions in Great Britain. Estimates suggest that over 60 million people in the world are of Irish origin. The influence of Irish people worldwide is immeasurable and disproportionate to the size of their country of origin.

The imposition of the Anglican Reformation in the reign of Elizabeth I caused a number to leave Munster for Spain and Portugal. The conquest of 1603 caused more departures to Spain and Brittany. Cromwell transported whole regiments, possibly 34 000 men, to Spain and Portugal, while many civilians were shipped to the West Indies where they could be sold as slaves. The Treaty of Limerick in 1691 was followed by the flight of the so-called *Wild Geese*, military men who, together with their wives and children, emigrated to France, where they served in the French army until 1697; some of them moved on to Spain, where three Irish regiments were formed. The most famous name among the merchants who settled on the western coast of Europe is that of Richard Hennessy, from Cork, who started the Cognac company.

The first transatlantic emigrants were mostly Presbyterians, the Ulster-Scots (known in the USA as Scots-Irish or Scotch-Irish), descendants of lowland Scots who had settled in Ulster in the 17C. Whole families emigrated early in the 18C owing to religious disability and rising rents. The Roman Catholic Irish tended to emigrate as single young adults, both men and women.

The Scotch-Irish had an influence in America out of all proportion to their numbers, particularly in the War of Independence and in education. The heartland of Ulster settlement was in the Appalachian back country; the name hillbilly derives from King William III. Many of the settlers were involved in pushing the frontier westwards and building the American railways. Over a quarter of the Presidents of the USA are descended from Scotch-Irish settlers. This Irish-American connection is traced in detail at the Ulster-American Folk Park (👆 *see Sperrin Mountains)* and Andrew Jackson Centre (👆 *see Carrickfergus)* as well as several other family homesteads. Allied military leaders in the Second World War who were of Ulster stock include Alanbrooke, Alexander, Auchinleck, Dill and Montgomery.

Following the Napoleonic Wars emigration recommenced and during the next 25 years over a million Irish men and women emigrated to Great Britain and the USA.

Emigration reached its peak during the Great Famine when Ireland lost 4 million people, through death and emigration; during the worst years about 1 million fled and another 2.5 million emigrated in the following decade. The great wave of 19C emigrants was largely composed of Roman Catholics from Donegal, Connaught, Munster and Leinster, counties which until then had not seen much emigration. Many landed first in Canada but later crossed the frontier into the USA to escape from British rule. Their descendants include John Fitzgerald Kennedy, Ronald Reagan and William Jefferson Clinton.

The numbers who emigrated to Australia and New Zealand were smaller and included some who were transported to the penal colonies.

The flow of immigrants into Great Britain has waxed and waned since the Irish

R. Holzbachova, Ph. Benet/MICHELIN – National Gallery of Ireland, Dublin

Emigrant Ship by E Hayes

established colonies in Wales and Scotland in the 5C. Many, particularly those who left Ireland during the Famine in the hope of reaching America but were too weak or penniless to continue, settled in Liverpool and Glasgow. London has a flourishing Irish community, particularly north of the river. Margaret Thatcher, Prime Minister of the United Kingdom (1978–91), is descended from Catherine Sullivan, who emigrated in 1811 from Kenmare and became a washerwoman in England.

In the 18C and 19C many Irishmen, who went to work in Britain on the canals or in agriculture and the building trade, returned home for the winter. Those who went to America or Australasia seldom returned to the mother country. Despite their rural origins most Irish emigrants settled in the big cities rather than on the land of their adopted countries.

Irish emigrants in the late 20C are highly qualified young men and women seeking employment not only in English-speaking countries such as Great Britain and the USA but also throughout the countries of the European Union. In recent years emigration has declined and immigration has increased. In 1997 there was a net inflow of 15 000 people, the highest such figure since the 1970s. Many of these people are the same highly qualified former emigrants, returning to the higher standards of living and new culturally revitalised society of modern Ireland.

TRACING ANCESTORS

Many people who visit Ireland on holiday, particularly from Australia, New Zealand and the USA, are hoping to trace their grandparents or great grand parents who left Ireland and settled abroad. This task is more difficult than it could have been owing to the destruction during the Civil War of the the national archives dating from 1174. In the latter years of the 20C a great project was set in motion to collect all the information available from parish records, tombstones and other sources throughout Ireland. Access to these computer records and assistance in tracing ancestors can be obtained through the many regional Genealogical Centres which are listed in the Address Books of the appropriate chapters in the

Ulster-Scots – Scotch-Irish

Theodore Roosevelt's mother, speaking of her family who came from Co Antrim, described them as "a grim stern people, strong and simple, powerful for good and evil, swayed by gusts of stormy passion, the love of freedom rooted in their very hearts' core. . . relentless, revengeful, suspicious, knowing neither ruth nor pity; they were also upright, resolute and fearless, loyal to their friends and devoted to their country".

Discovering Ireland sections. If you have no idea where in Ireland your ancestors came from, it is best to consult one of the national organisations in Dublin (*see Planning Your Trip*).

A good way of exchanging news or meeting long-lost relatives is to attend one of the annual clan gatherings which are held on ancestral sites by some of the 243 Irish clans.

Food and Drink

There are two Irish culinary traditions: the elaborate meals served in town and country mansions, and the simple dishes of earlier centuries.

IRISH CUISINE

The Dublin Bay prawn and the Galway oyster have a more than local reputation and the Irish have a great way with the potato, that staple of the national diet, introduced at the end of the 16C. A celebration of this great variety is the **gourmet festival** held in Kinsale.

Breakfast

The traditional **Irish Fry**, known in the north as an "Ulster Fry", consists of fried egg, sausage, bacon, black pudding, potato cakes, mushrooms and tomatoes; it is usually eaten at breakfast. Breakfast may also include kippers or kedgeree.

Fish and Meat

The king of the freshwater fish is the **salmon**, wild or farmed; as a main dish it is usually poached or grilled. Irish smoked salmon is traditionally cured with oak wood. Archaeologists have found evidence by the River Bann of a salmon weir and traces of salmon-smoking dating from 2000 BC.

The other most frequently served freshwater fish is **trout**, farmed or wild. **Shellfish**, such as crab, lobster, scallops, mussels and Dublin Bay prawns (also known as langoustines or scampi) are usually available near the coast, particularly in the southwest. Galway Bay oysters are plump and succulent.

The Irish fishing grounds produce Dover sole (known locally as Black sole), lemon sole, plaice, monkfish, turbot, brill, John Dory, cod, hake, haddock, mackerel and herring.

Prime **beef** is raised on the lush pastures in the east and south of Ireland; lamb comes from the uplands. **Pork** is presented in many ways: as joints and chops; as ham or bacon; as pigs' trotters (*crúibíní*), known in English as crubeens; in white puddings; in black puddings (*drisheen*) flavoured with tansy and eaten for breakfast. The most popular game is rabbit but hare and pheasant are also served.

Traditional Dishes

There is no official recipe for **Irish stew**, which consists of neck of mutton layered in a pot with potatoes, onions and herbs. **Colcannon** is a Harvest or Hallowe'en dish of mashed potatoes, onions, parsnips and white cabbage, mixed with butter and cream. **Champ** is a simpler dish of potatoes mashed with butter

Table laid for a Farmhouse Tea

SLIDE FILE, Dublin

to which are added chopped chives or other green vegetables such as parsley, spring onions (scallions), chopped shallots, nettles, peas, cabbage or even carrots (cooked in milk which is added to the purée). Nettles are also made into soup. To make **coddle** a forehock of bacon, pork sausages, potatoes and onions are stewed in layers. Collar and cabbage is composed of a collar of bacon, which has been boiled, coated in breadcrumbs and brown sugar and baked, served with cabbage cooked in the bacon stock.

Various sorts of **seaweed**, a highly nutritious source of vitamins and minerals, were traditionally used to thicken soups and stews. **Carrageen** is still used to make a dessert with a delicate flavour. **Dulse** is made into a sweet.

Dairy Products

Irish cookery makes liberal use of butter and cream. Ice-cream is particularly popular as a dessert. In recent years many hand-made **cheeses** have appeared on the market: **Cashel Blue** (a soft, creamy, blue-veined cheese made from cow's milk in Tipperary; milder than Stilton), **Cooleeny** (a Camembert-type cheese from Thurles in Co Tipperary), **Milleens** (a distinctive spicy cheese from West Cork), **Gubbeen** (soft surface-ripening cheese from Skull in Co Cork).

Bread

A wide variety of breads and cakes is baked for breakfast and tea. The best-known is **soda bread**, made of white or brown flour and buttermilk. **Barm Brack** is a rich fruit cake made with yeast (*báirín breac* = speckled cake).

BEVERAGES

Stout made by **Guinness** or Murphys is the traditional thirst-quencher in Ireland but the drinking of ales (bitter) and lagers is not uncommon. Black Velvet is a mixture of stout and champagne.

Although there are now only three **whiskey** distilleries in Ireland – Bushmills in Co Antrim, which produces the only malt, and Midleton in Co Cork, both owned by the same company, and Cooley in Dundalk – there are many different brands of whiskey. Their distinctive flavours arise from subtle variations in the production process.

The Flag is a patriotic drink that mixes crème de menthe, tequila and Southern Comfort—the green, white and orange of the Republican tricolor.

Irish Coffee, a delicious creation, consists of a measure of whiskey, brown sugar and very hot black coffee mixed in a heated glass and topped with a layer of fresh cream.

Whiskey or Whisky

The origins of Irish whiskey (usually but not invariably spelled with an "e") are lost in the mists of time but it was being distilled and drunk throughout Ireland by the 16C and Elizabeth I seems to have had a taste for it. Illicit whiskey *(poteen)* appeared in the 17C when the government introduced a tax on distilling (1661) and set up a department of Excisemen (Gaugers) to police the distilleries. By the end of the 17C, the substance was being exported all over the British Empire. Exports to the USA dwindled with prohibition in the 1920s and the British Empire market was closed off by the War of Independence. In 1966 the few surviving distilleries joined to form as the Irish Distillers Company and founded a new distillery in Midleton; in the early 1970s they took over Bushmills but were taken over by Pernod-Ricard in 1989.

Despite the popularity of blended whisky from Scotland, Irish distillers have preferred to maintain the lightness and fuller flavour of their traditional product, achieved by **Triple Distillation.** The grain, including the husks, is milled to produce "grist" which is mixed with hot water in a large vessel (mash tun) to release the sugars; the liquid is then drawn off. This process is repeated twice. and the liquid from the first and second mashing (wort) is pumped into vessels called washbacks; yeast is added which reacts with the sugars to produce a light brown liquid. When fermentation is complete the liquid is distilled three times. The spirit is matured in old sherry or Bourbon casks and then blended (vatted) for two or three days.

Custom House, Dublin
SLIDE FILE, Dublin

ABBEYLEIX

POPULATION 1 299

At the height of the Anglo-Irish Ascendancy in the mid-18C, Viscount de Vesci followed the contemporary trend for demolishing tenant cottages, re-housing the residents in a carefully planned new settlement at the gates of his great mansion. Scarcely changed since those days, Abbeyleix (Mainistir Laoise) is one of the best examples of this type of aristocratic estate development, preserved by its designation as a Heritage Town. But its origins are much older, since it occupies the site of a late 12C Cistercian abbey built on an earlier monastery.
🛈 *Portlaoise* ☎ *057 86 64132.*

▶ **Orient Yourself:** Abbeyleix lies on N8, 61mi/98km SW of Dublin towards Cork.
🔍 **Don't Miss:** an excursion to Emo Court.
🕯 **Also See:** ATHY, CASHEL, KILDARE, KILKENNY, ROSCREA, TULLAMORE.

Visit

Abbeyleix Heritage House

♿🕐*Open Mar-Sep, Mon-Sat 9am-5pm, (May-Aug Sun, 1-6pm).* ✆ *Donation.* 🗏 🅿 ☎ *057 873 1653 - www.heritagehouse-museum.com.*

The exhibition in the old school traces the history of Abbeyleix, its industries and role in the evolution of the region. In the walled garden of a former Brigidine convent, the **Abbey Sense Garden** has been designed and planted to appeal to touch, taste, smell, sound and sight.

ADDRESS BOOK

Morrissey's Bar – Many travellers make a point of stopping off at Morrissey's Bar, a wonderful combination of grocer's shop and pub, which, like the town itself, seems little altered since it was built.

Grantstown Lake – *8mi/13km W by R 433* – Woodland walks beside a lake (fishing).

Excursions

Emo Court★★

15mi/24km NNE of Abbeyleix by N 8, M 7 and R 422. (Dúchas) Gardens: 🕐 *Open daylight hours. House: mid-Jun to mid-Sep, 10.30am-5pm; last tour at 4.30pm.* 🕐 *Closed 25-26 Dec. House* ✆ *€2.90.* 🅿 ☎ *057 8626573*

This splendid domed Classical mansion surrounded by extensive gardens, was designed by **James Gandon** in 1792 for Lord Portarlington, a banker-cum-architect called **John Dawson**. After many years of use as a Jesuit seminary, the rotunda and superb stuccowork has been restored and re-furnished with various fine pieces and a collection of Wedgwood pottery.

A magnificent avenue of Wellingtonias, the first in Ireland, links the house to the Dublin Road; azaleas, rhododendrons and Japanese maples fashion the Clucker Garden; statues of the Seasons and a ring garden adorn the lawns; a Grapery planted with trees and shrubs descends to the lakeside walk.

St John the Evangelist in Coolbanagher *(Follow the road opposite Emo Court through the village, turn left R419)* is the only church designed by James Gandon in 1785 for Lord Carlow.

SLIDE FILE, Dublin

Stradbally Steam Engine Rally

Rock of Dunamase★
15mi/24km NE of Abbeyleix by R 245, R 247 and N 80 NW.
The rock rising straight from the plain is crowned by the extensive ruins of the O'More clan fortress, destroyed by Cromwell's army in the mid 17C. Excellent **views**★ from the summit (200ft/60m high).

Stradbally
13mi/21km NE of Abbeyleix by R 245, R 247 and N 80 SE.
In the Stradbally Market Place stands an unusual pagoda-like structure with a red roof which commemorates Dr William Perceval, a local doctor who died in 1899 after 54 years of local practice.
The **Steam Museum**★ displays a collection of old steam-powered farm machinery (1936), a few of which are brought out for the annual rally at Stradbally Hall. A narrow-gauge steam railway (1mi/1.6km) runs through the woods. ♿🕐 *Museum: Restricted opening.* ⊛ €5. *Railway: Bank Holiday Sun-Mon, 2.30-5pm. Steam Rally: August Bank Holiday weekend.* ☎ *057 86 41878/086 38 90184- www.stradballysteammuseum.com; www.irishsteam.ie.*

Timahoe
9mi/15km NE of Abbeyleix by R 430 east and a minor road N.
The fine **Round Tower**★ (96ft/29m high) leaning slightly (2ft/0.6m) from the vertical, was probably built in the 12C; it has a lovely Romanesque double doorway.
Richard Nixon, President of the USA (1969–74), whose ancestors came from the village, visited Timahoe in 1970.

Heywood Gardens, Ballinakill
3.5mi/6km SE of Abbeyleix by R 432.
(Dúchas) ♿🕐○*Open during daylight hours.* 🅿 ☎ *056 7721450 - www.heritageireland.ie*
A modern college building replaces the original mansion, but the gardens (1906–10) designed by **Edwin Lutyens** (1869–1944) and **Gertrude Jekyll** (1843–1932) survive, complete with terraces, pleached lime walk and hedges of clipped yew, an Italianate sunken garden, ponds and pergolas; walks with fine prospects of distant towers.

119

ADARE ★

POPULATION 1 042

This tiny town in fertile wooded countryside at the tidal limit of the River Maigue is particularly picturesque with its utterly un-Irish rows of pretty, colour-washed cottages with overhanging thatched roofs built in the mid-19C by the local landowner, the Earl of Dunraven, who succeeded in making his corner of west Limerick resemble something from the English shires. Adare *(Átha Dara)* is a designated Heritage Town. 🅸 *Adare Heritage Centre.* 🕓 *Open Mon-Sat, 9.30am-5.30pm.* ☎ *061 396 255.*

▶ **Orient Yourself:** Adare is 10mi/17km SW of Limerick on the N 21 Tralee road.
👣 **Also See:** LIMERICK, TRALEE.

Visit

There is more to Adare than picturesque thatched cottages: the **heritage centre** provides a historical survey of Norman invaders, medieval abbeys and the influential Dunraven family. The square tower and the south wall of the present RC **Church of the Most Holy Trinity** on Main Street were part of a monastery, the only house in Ireland of the **Trinitarian Order**, constructed about 1230 by Maurice Fitzgerald, 2nd Baron of Offaly. The 50 monks were put to death in 1539 at the Dissolution of the Monasteries. The ruins were restored by the 1st Earl of Dunraven and enlarged in 1852. The **dovecot** at the rear (restored) dates from the 14C. Adare's Anglican **Parish Church** ★ is fashioned from the nave and part of the choir of an Augustinian priory founded in 1315. The cloisters were converted into a mausoleum for the

Address Book

👣 *For coin ranges, see the Legend on the cover flap.*

WHERE TO STAY

🛏 **Berkeley Lodge** – *Station Rd. 6 rm - ☎ 061 396 857 - berlodge@iol.ie - www. adare.org.* Simple, clean accommodation competitively priced and centrally located. True 'home from home' feeling. Bedrooms at the rear of the house are quieter.

🛏🛏 **Carrabawn Guesthouse** – *Killarney Rd – 0.5mi SW on N 21- 8 rm ☎ 061 396 067; www.carrabawnhouseadare. com* 🅿 A welcoming and immaculately kept guesthouse, ten minutes walk from the town centre.

🛏🛏🛏🛏 **Adare Manor** – *113 rm, 35 suites - ☎ 061 396 566; www.adare-manor.com* ✕🅿 Imposing and impressive Gothic manor sympathetically extended with 800 acres/323ha park: fishing, golf and leisure facilities. Classic menu; bedrooms in the main house have the most character.

SHOPPING

Irish Dresden – *Dromcollogher. 20mi/32km SW of Adare by R 515 via Ballingarry and Kilmeedy.* Delicate porcelain figures representing musicians and dancers, ladies in flounced skirts, angels and figures for the Christmas crib, birds and animals. The range is cast from original master moulds from Mueller Volkestedt in Germany brought to Ireland after the original factory was bombed in WWII, with the addition of new ones of Irish inspiration. *Showroom:* 🕓 *Open Mon-Fri, 9am-1pm and 2-5pm. Factory:* 🚌 *Guided tour (20min) by appointment.* ☎ *063 83236 (Irish Dresden Ltd, Dromcolliher, Co Limerick).*

TRACING ANCESTORS

The **Irish Palatine Heritage Centre,** Rathkeale provides a **genealogical service**.

Thatched Cottages, Adare

R Holzbachoua, Ph Benet/MICHELIN

family of Quin, the Earls of Dunraven. The exuberantly neo-Gothic **Adare Manor** (1832) by the River Maigue, now a hotel, was designed in part by James Pain and **Augustus Welby Pugin**.

Adare Friary★
Access via Adare Golf Course; ask at the Club House.
The evocative riverside ruins marked by **Kilmallock Gate** are those of the Franciscan friary founded by the Earl of Kildare in 1464, and extended in 15C-16C .

Desmond Castle
Guided Tours Jun to mid-Sep by appointment. ☎ *061 39 66666.*
The strategic importance of **Desmond Catle** had dwindled when much of it was demolished by Cromwell's forces. A large square tower stands in the inner ward of the early 14C stronghold surrounded by a moat. The upper storey of the building in the southwest corner of the outer ward was the **great hall**.
Nearby are the ruins of **St Nicholas Church** (11C) and the **Desmond Chapel** (14C).

Excursions

Rathkeale
7.5mi/13km W of Adare by N 21.
The Norman tower of **Castle Matrix**★ was built in 1440 by the 7th Earl of Desmond; he and his father, the 4th Earl, are the earliest-recorded Norman poets in the Irish language. The Great Hall houses a fine **library** and objets d'art. The castle also houses an **international arts centre** and the **Heraldry Society of Ireland**.
It was at Castle Matrix that the poet Edmund Spenser, and the then Captain Walter Raleigh met for the first time in 1580 and began a lifelong friendship. �& ⓒ *Open by appointment.* ☎ *069 64284.*
The **Irish Palatine Heritage Centre**★ presents photographs, documents, articles and artefacts relating to the German Protestant settlers, their innovative farming methods, their impact on Methodism and their dispersion throughout the English-speaking world. �& ⓒ *Open mid-May to Sep, Tue-Sat 2-5pm or by appointment. Genealogy service.* ⌂ 🅿 ☎ *069 63511 - www.Irishpalatines.org.*

Irish Palatines

In 1709, following two invasions, a bitter winter, and oppression by their reinstated Catholic ruler, many German Protestants left the Rhineland area known as the Palatinate (hence their name), and travelled to England where the government promised to subsidise their ongoing journey to Carolina, USA. When allocated funds were exhausted, many were stranded in London. Finally, the Dublin government offered to take 500 families: 821 families came. Landlords were offered subsidies to accept the immigrants; some went to Counties Kerry, Tipperary and Wexford but the majority settled on the estate of Lord Southwell in Rathkeale, where their names – Bovenizer, Corneille, Delmege, Miller, Rynard, Piper, Sparling, Stark, Switzer, Teskey – sounded a foreign note. These industrious people introduced new farming practices, and being pious, God-fearing people, mostly **Lutherans** or **Calvinists,**they responded with enthusiasm to the preaching of **John Wesley**, who returned to visit them on several occasions after his first visit in 1756.

Newcastle West★
16mi/26km W of Adare by N 21.
This thriving market town, known for its spring water, takes its name from the **castle** that belonged to the **Knights Templar** before passing to the **Earls of Desmond**. The banqueting hall, now known as **Desmond Hall**, with an oak minstrel's gallery (restored) and a hooded fireplace (reconstruction), stands over a 13C vaulted stone chamber, lit by ecclesiastical lancet windows. The remains of the castle include the adjoining Great Hall *(Halla Mór)*. *(Dúchas)* 🖏🕒 *Open mid-Jun to mid-Sep, 10am-6pm (5.40pm last tour).* ☎ *069 77408.*

Askeaton
13mi/20km NW of Adare by N 21 and R 518.
On a small island in the River Deel stand the ruins of **Askeaton Castle**, probably founded by William de Burgo c 1199, with tower and walls (15C) largely intact; the banqueting hall (1440-59) erected by the 7th Earl of Desmond, was one of the largest of its kind in Ireland. North of the town by the river, are the ruins of **Askeaton Franciscan Friary**, a 15C foundation; note the depiction of **St Francis** in the northeast corner of the cloisters.

Foynes
21mi/34km W of Adare by N 21, R 518 and N 69.
Before and during the Second World War the small seaport in the Shannon Estuary was the operational base for the flying boats which pioneered transatlantic air travel. The old terminal building now houses the **Flying Boat Museum** displaying models, photographs, log books and technical equipment relating to the precursor of Shannon Airport. 🖏🕒 *Open Apr to Oct, 10am-6pm (5pm last admission).* ∞ €6. 🖾 🅿 ☎ *069 65416 - www.flyingboatmuseum.com.*

Glin Castle Hotel★
29mi/47km W of Adare by N 21, R 518 and N 69. ☎ *068 34173 - www.glincastle.com.*
A branch of the famous Fitzgerald family, the Knights of Glin have lived close to the village of **Glin** for 700 years. Their original stronghold was destroyed by Queen Elizabeth's forces in 1600, so a replacement was built (1780-85) and gothicized around 1820. The **interior** is outstanding, with superb stuccowork, excellent examples of Georgian mahogany furniture, family portraits and other paintings, and a very unusual flying **staircase** with a Venetian window overlooking the formal gardens.

ARAN ISLANDS★

POPULATION 2 000

Keeping watch over the mouth of Galway Bay are the islands of Inishmore, Inishmaan and Inisheer, great slabs of limestone linked geologically to the Burren on the mainland. People have inhabited these lonely isles since ancient times, using the limestone to build great prehistoric forts like Dún Aonghasa and Dún Conor as well as the close-knit network of drystone walls bounding tiny, flower-rich fields. Tellingly evoked in the writings of J M Synge and Robert Flaherty's classic semi-documentary film *Man of Aran*, the islanders' traditional, extremely harsh way of life lasted until relatively recently. The islands remain a stronghold of the Gaelic language. *Kilronan, Inishmore.* ☎ 099 61263.

▸ **Orient Yourself:** The three Aran Islands extend in an oblique line across the mouth of **Galway Bay**. The smallest, Inisheer is the closest (5mi/8km) to the mainland; the middle island is the slightly larger Inishmaan (6sq mi/7.77km^2); the largest, Inishmore, lies about7mi/11.3km from the coast of Connemara.

😊 **Don't Miss:** an excursion to see the stone cliff-top fort Dún Aonghasa.

👣 **Also See:** THE BURREN, CONNEMARA, GALWAY.

A Bit of History

The Aran Islands rise in natural terraces from a flat sandy shore facing Galway Bay to high cliffs (300ft/91m) confronting the Atlantic. They get less rainfall than the

---

Address Book

GETTING THERE

There are flights to all three islands from Connemara Regional Airport at Inverin *(20mi/32km W of Galway by R 336)*; they can also be reached by ferry from Rossaveel *(23mi/37km west of Galway*, and from Doolin in the Burren (Inisheer only).

Aran Islands Air Service – *Operates regular flights: up to 8 per day in summer; 3 in winter (9min). €45 Return.* ☎ *091 593 034 (Aer Arann); www.aerarann-islands.ie*

Rossaveal – Aran Islands Ferry *- Operates 4 sailings per day. €25 Return. Online booking service; bus service from Galway City Centre.* ☎ *091 568903 - www.aranislandferries.com*

Rossaveal – Aran Direct *- Operates (35min) from Rossaveal up to 3 sailings per day to Inishmore; 2 to Inishman and Inishmeer. Return €25 Bus from Galway City Centre departs 1hr 15min before ferry sailing.* ☎ *091 566 535, (Aran Direct) - www.arandirect.com*

Doolin (Co Clare) – Aran Islands Ferry *- Operates (weather permitting)*

Apr to Sep: to Inishmore (45min), 3 times daily; to Inisheer (20min), up to 5 times daily. Telephone for details. Return €40. ☎ *065 707 4455, 707 4466 (Doolin Ferry Co) - www.doolinferries.com*

GETTING AROUND

The best way to explore **Inishmore** is on foot or by hired bicycle. Regular but infrequent bus service operate along the island's main road, and minibus operators meet planes and ferries, offering tours of the principal sights. As well as the Tourist Information Centre by the harbour in Kilronan, the Aran Heritage Centre and the visitor centre below Dún Aonghasa are useful sources of information. Understanding of the island's landscape is enhanced by the meticulously detailed Map of the Aran Islands created by Tim Robinson.

SHOPPING

Aran Sweater Market, *Kilronan* – Wide range of the famous Aran sweaters with their distinctive family stitches and patterns. ☎ *064 39756; www.clanarans.com*

mainland, and are never touched by frost. Despite the lack of soil, wild flowers thrive but trees are rare: the traditional crops of rye and potatoes were grown on artificial soil created laboriously over the years by layering sand and seaweed on the bare rock. Traditionally, the white-washed cottages were thatched with straw tied down against the wind. Fishing and farming were the main activities; cows would graze the summer pastures in Connemara and winter on Aran, unlike the ponies which wintered in Connemara and worked on Aran in summer

months. Illicit whiskey and peat were imported by boat from Connemara in exchange for potatoes and limestone.

The Aran Islands have been inhabited for centuries: the ruins of great stone forts date from prehistoric times, while in the early and medieval Christian period (5C–16C), the Aran monasteries prospered as centres of culture. Today, tourism is the dominant industry, ensuring the survival of traditional crafts, notably the distinctive cream-coloured **Aran knitwear** designed using patterns of stitches that evoke elements in nature and an ancient way of life that include the women spinning the wool and men doing the knitting using goose quill needles.

Visit

Inishmore (Arainn)

The largest island (9mi/14.5km x 2.5mi/4km) is served by one road running north from the airstrip along the shore of Killeany Bay *(Cuan Chill Éinne)*, to **Kilronan** *(Cill Rónáin)* and then west to the remote hamlet of Bun Gabhla overlooking **Brannock Island** *(Oileán Dá Bhranóg)* and the lighthouse. The old tracks and walls (7 000mi/11 265km) run from northeast to southwest following natural rifts and man-made ruts created by the carting of seaweed from the shore to field. At the roadside stand square pillars topped with crosses erected in memory of islanders who died abroad or at sea. The Atlantic waves constantly batter the grim, southwestern cliffs and send spectacular spurts of spray through the "puffing-holes" at the island's eastern extremity. On the northwestern shore by Port Chorrúch, lives a colony of seals.

Kilronan

The Aran Heritage Centre, **Ionad Arann**, provides an excellent introduction to the landscape and monuments, traditions and culture of the islands. Note the currach, the seemingly frail traditional craft made of hide or canvas stretched over a frame of laths and powered by bladeless oars. ⊶*Closed for refurbishment (2006).* ☎ 099 61354 - www.visitaranislands.com

Words and Images

The Gaelic-speaking islanders are talented music-makers and story-tellers, skills encouraged by the austere life on Aran as portrayed by Liam O'Flaherty (1896-1984) in *Thy Neighbour's Wife* (1924). Local stories feature in JM Synge's play *Riders to the Sea* set on Inishmaan, and in *The Playboy of the Western World*. WB Yeats urged Synge to study the islands and 'express a life that has never found expression;' the result was *The Aran Islands* (1907), made into a film in 1924). *Stones of Aran: Pilgrimage* by Tim Robinson (1935-) is more factual.

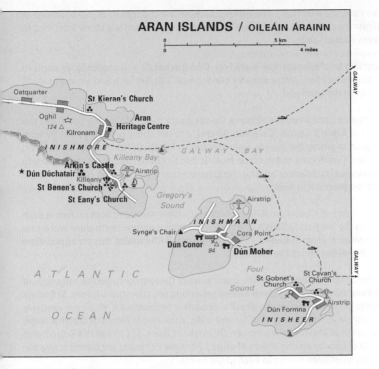

Dún Aonghasa★★★

4.5mi/7.2km W of Kilronan; 10min on foot from Kilmurvy (Cill Mhuirbhigh) Visitor Centre (Dúchas) ⓒ *Open 10am-6pm.* ⬤ *€2.10 (no charge after hours).* ☎ *099 61008.*

This great drystone fort in a spectacular setting is one of the finest prehistoric monuments in Europe, with three lines of defence. Between the outer and the middle wall, stone stakes spike the ground, set at an angle to impede attack. A square tunnel in the thickness of the wall leads into the inner compound. The inner wall, which has steps up to wall walks, describes a semicircle beginning and ending on the cliff edge. ⓒ *Take suitable clothing.*

Monuments

1mi/1.7km NW of Kilronan; bear right in Mainistir. Half way down the slope to the shore stands **St Kieran's Church (Teampall Chiaráin),** a small ruined church dedicated to **St Kieran of Clonmacnoise,** four cross-inscribed stones and St Kieran's Well.

5.5mi/8.8km NW of Kilronan. Tucked away in a hollow on the north coast overlooking a small bay is an ancient monastic site, also known as Na Seacht d'Teampall, the Seven Churches. In fact, only two ruins are churches: the larger, **St Brecan's Church (Teampall Bhreacáin),** marks the grave of St Bre-

Dún Aonghasa

125

can *(opposite west door)*. The other structures are thought to be outbuildings or pilgrim hostels. In the southeast corner of the graveyard is a stone inscribed to seven Roman saints.

2mi/3km SW of Kilronan. The Black Fort: **Dún Dúchatair**★ is a splendid example of a promontory fort, with a massive curving wall 20ft/6m high and almost as thick, guarding the headland.

1mi/1.6km S of Kilronan in Killeany. On the south shore of Killeany Bay stand the ruins of **Arkin's Castle (Caisleán Aircín)**, a tower house probably built by John Rawson to whom the islands were granted by Elizabeth I in 1588. It was fortified by Lord Clanrickard, using stone from St Enda's Church and the nearby friary to strengthen its defences against the Cromwellians who captured it in 1652, lost it and recaptured it in 1653.

1mi/1.6km S of Kilronan; in Killeany bear right; 10min there and back on foot. A path climbs the hill past St Eany's oratory (6C-7C) with a narrow north door and a slim east window. From **St Benen's Church (Teampall Bheanáin)**, there is a good **view** of Killeany Bay and of the mainland.

1.5mi/2.4km S of Kilronan. On the coast south of the airstrip, stand the early ruins of **St Eany's Church (Teaghlach Éinne)** set among countless tombstones. **St Enda** is said to be buried here on the site of a monastery he founded (c 490) from which his reputation as a teacher spread far and wide, attracting St Kieran of Clonmacnoise, St Finnian of Moville on Inishowen, St Jarlath of Tuam, St Colman of Kilmacduagh south of Galway among scores of others. As some 227 saints are buried across the island, it has been known as Aran of the Saints.

Inishmaan (Inis Meáin)

Inishmaan (3mi/5km x 1mi/2km) is the most remote of the three islands. A bleak and bare rocky plateau slopes northeast to a sandy shore, providing little shelter to the isolated houses. Inishmaan exercised a particular fascination for J M Synge, who is said to have loved one particular spot called Synge's Chair *(Cathaoir Synge)* on the western cliffs overlooking Gregory's Sound *(Sunda Ghrióra)*.

The island's main monument is the huge prehistoric fort **Dún Conor (Dún Chonchúir)** perched on high ground keeping watch over the narrow valley: its main enclosure (227ft/69m x 115ft/35m) is contained by a thick wall (17.5ft/5.65m. A second stone fort, **Dún Moher or Dún Fearbhaigh** (103ft/31m x 90ft/27m) overlooks the landing pier at Cora Point.

Inisheer (Inis Oírr)

The smallest Aran island is mainly populated along its north coast. The gentle landscape of the interior is transformed in springtime by countless daffodils. The ruins by the airstrip are those of **St Cavan's Church** *(Teampall Chaomháin)*: its east window dates from the early 10C; the chancel arch and south door are medieval. The grave of **St Cavan**, the brother of St Kevin of Glendalough, lies nearby *(NE)*. Among the central settlements stands **Dún Formna**, a stone fort (170ftx123ft/52mx37m) containing the ruins of a tower house, probably built by the O'Briens in the 14C and destroyed by the Cromwellians in 1652. Northwest of the houses are the ruins of **St Gobnet's Church** *(Kilgobnet)*: a small medieval oratory.

ATHENRY

POPULATION 1 612

Now a peaceful little market centre and a designated Heritage Town, Athenry (Baile Átha an Rí) was the scene in 1316 of one of Ireland's most savage battles of medieval times, when an Anglo-Norman force massacred a huge army of native Irish. The bloody encounter is commemmorated in the town's 14C seal, which features the severed heads of the Irish chieftains displayed on spikes above a gateway - probably the North Gate, the main feature of the defense walls built in the early 13C by the town's founder, the Anglo-Norman nobleman Meiler de Bermingham. **⏐** *Galway East Tourism, Old Church St.* 🕐 *Mon- Fri.* ☎ *091 850687 - www.athenryheritagetown.com.*

▶ **Orient Yourself:** Athenry, the town at the river ford, is in South Galway just north of the main road (N 6) between Galway and Loughrea.
🅿 **Parking:** Park by the Castle.
♿ **Also See:** BIRR, CLONMACNOISE, GALWAY, PORTUMNA, STROKESTOWN.

Visit

Athenry Heritage Centre
♿🕐 *Open 10am-6pm.* ☜ *€3.* ☎ *091 844 661.*
This museum traces the history of the town and purpose of local medieval monuments.

Athenry Castle
(Dúchas) ♿🕐 *Open Apr to Oct, 10am-6pm.* ☜ *€3.* 🅿 ☎ *091 844 797.*
Built by Meiler de Bermingham c 1239 the castle was destroyed in 1597. Among the ruins there is a central keep with a vaulted undercroft, The main entrance at first-floor level, is enclosed within massive walls and towers.

Dominican Friary
(Dúchas) Key available from Mrs Sheehan in Church Street.
Down by the river on the east side of town are the ruins of a friary founded in 1241 by Meiler de Bermingham. In 1574 the friary was confiscated and burned by the Burkes; in 1627 it reverted to the friars. After restoration, the complex was made into a university (1644), then in 1652, the friars were expelled by the Cromwellians.

127

Excursions

East of Athenry

Loughrea
11mi/18km S by R 348 and R 349.
The town on the north shore of Lough Rea facing the **Slieve Aughty Mountains** was built around a Norman stronghold c 1300 constructed by Richard de Burgo. The local **Carmelite Priory**, now in ruins, is where General St Ruth, killed at the Battle of Aughrim, is said to be buried. Part of one of the medieval **town gates** can be seen on the edge of the cathedral precinct. The neo-Gothic **St Brendan's Cathedral**★, head church of the Roman Catholic diocese of Clonfert was designed by William Byrne in 1897. Beyond a rather dull exterior is a richly decorated interior and Celtic Revival arts and crafts furnishings. The Clonfert **Diocesan Museum** displays vestments, missals and church plate. ♿ ⏰ *Open daily, 9am-9pm.* ⟲ *€2.54 (audio tour).* ☎ *091 841 212. If the museum is locked, enquire after the key at the Cathedral Presbytery.* 🅿 ☎ *091 841 212.*

St Joseph by M Healy in Loughrea Cathedral

Turoe Stone★
10mi/1.6km S of Athenry by R 348 and a minor road S from Kiltullagh to Bullaun.
The granite boulder (3ft/1m high) in the field *(right)* is presumed to be a Celtic ritual stone. Its domed cap is carved with the finest La Tène decoration in Ireland, a pattern of swelling tendrils "searching like rivulets of a great tidal stream for an outlet" (P Harbison). Other motifs include a stylised bird's head and the **triskele**.

Kilconnell Franciscan Friary
15mi/18km E of Athenry by R 348.
Extensive ruins of a monastery founded in 1353 occupy the site of an earlier complex begun in the 6C by St Conall. Note the tomb niche with the figures of six saints.

Battle of Aughrim Centre
5mi/8km S of Kilconnell by minor road. ⏰ *Open Apr-Oct, 10am-6pm (Call to confirm).* ⟲ *€2.50.* ☕ 🅿 ☎ *090 9673939.*
The Interpretative Centre incorporates various relics into a re-creation of the bloody battle of Aughrim as described by Captain Walter Dalton, one of the combatants.

Battle of Aughrim

Aughrim is the last great battle in the War of the Two Kings *(Cogadh an Dá Rí)* between King James II of England, aided by Louis XIV of France, and King William III of England and his allies. Having retreated west after the **Battle of Athlone**, the Jacobites, led by the French general St Ruth, faced the Williamites commanded by the Dutchman General Ginkel at Aughrim on 12 July 1691: 20 000 Irish, French, Germans and Walloons fought against 25 000 Irish, English, Dutch, Germans and Danish; 9 000 perished. St Ruth fell in mid-battle, in the ensuing confusion, the Williamites seized victoy fromt the Jacobites. It is said that the Williamites were buried at Clontuskert Priory; the Jacobites bodies were stripped and left to rot.

Clontuskert Augustinian Priory

10mi/16km SE of Aughrim by N 6 to Garbally and S by R 355; 5min on foot from roadside P *(left).*

The first monastery here was founded by **St Baedán** (d c 809). By the end of the 13C the **Augustinians** had established one of the richest monasteries in the diocese. Most of the present ruins are from the 15C. Note the west door with St Michael, St John, St Katherine and an abbot or bishop.

Kiltartan Country

Thoor Ballylee★

23mi/37km S of Athenry by R 348, R 349, N 6 and N 66 (sign). ♿🕐 *Open Jun-Sep, 10am-6pm.* ⬭ *€6.* P ☎ *091 631 436.*

The 16C **tower house** served as **William Butler Yeats'** summer house for 11 years, and often featured in his poetry. In the year he married Georgie Hyde-Lees, he sought a property near Coole Park, where his friend Lady Gregory resided. The local Kiltartan Society has restored the four-storey building, miller's cottage and mill wheel: the tower now houses rare editions of Yeats' works.

Kiltartan Gregory Museum

3.5mi/5km W of Thoor Ballylee by minor road and N 18 S. 🕐 *Open Jun-Sep, 10am-6pm.* ☎ *091 632346; www.gortonline.com/gregorymuseum.*

The old schoolhouse, built by the Gregory family, displays mementos of Augusta, Lady Gregory (1852-1932), co-founder with WB Yeats of the Abbey Theatre in Dublin.

Coole Park

2mi/3km S from Kiltartan by N 18.

(Dúchas) ♿🕐 *Visitor Interpretative Centre: Open Apr-Sep,10am-6pm (5pm Sep); last admission 1hr before closing.* ⬭ *€2.50.* ☕ P ☎ *091 631 804.*

In the walled garden stands a great copper beech, the **autograph tree**★, on which many of the significant figures in the Irish Literary Renaissance – William Butler Yeats, George Bernard Shaw, G Russell (AE), John Millington Synge and Sean O'Casey – cut their initials while guests at Lady Gregory's house (demolished). The **visitor centre** provides information on the national park. A forest walk *(0.5mi/0.8km)* leads to the lake, where petrified trees protrude from the water.

Kilmacduagh Churches and Round Tower★

3.5mi/50km SW of Gort by R 460.

The main landmark of the former monastic site set against the strange Burren landscape, is the well-preserved leaning **round tower**. Founded in the 7C by **St Colman**, son of Duagh, the monastery suffered many Viking attacks in the 9C-10C; after the Reformation it was acquired by Richard, 2nd Earl of Clanrickard. The 13C **Glebe House** was probably used by the abbot. The church nearby is dedicated to **St John the Baptist**. Beside the round tower stands the **cathedral** with folk art Crucifixions *(north transept).* **St Mary's Church**, across the road, was built c 1200. **O'Heyne's Church** *(NW)* contains early-13C carvings.

Dunguaire Castle★

20mi/32km NW of Kilmacduagh by minor road to Tirneevin, Killinny and Kinvarra.

🕐 *Open May to Sep, 9.30am-5pm (4.30pm last admission). Medieval banquets: daily at 5.30pm and 8.30pm.* ⬭ *Castle €4.75; banquet €50.* P ☎ *061 360 788 (Shannon Heritage Reservations) - www.shannonheritage.com.*

Facing **Kinvarra**, a charming little port, stands a four-storey **tower house** with adjoining bawn, built in 1520 by the descendants of Guaire, King of Connaught in the 7C. From the 17C to 20C, it was owned by the Martyns of Galway, and restored by Oliver St John Gogarty (1924) and Christobel Lady Ampthill (1954).

ATHLONE

POPULATION 7 691

The county town of Westmeath occupies a strategic position straddling the Shannon south of Lough Ree, in the very heart of Ireland. From an early date, the river crossing was defended by a fortress built by the Kings of Connacht. The present stronghold dates from the Anglo-Norman era. In the early days of the Free State, Athlone *(Baile Átha Luain)* was considered to be a suitable site for the capital. Though the town escaped this distinction, it is a bustling place served by good rail and road links, within easy reach of major attractions like Clonmacnoise and Lough Ree. *Athlone Castle.* *May to Sep* ☎ *090 6494630 - www.athlone.ie/tourism.*

▶ **Orient Yourself:** Athlone is located on N 6, the Dublin to Galway road, at the junction with N 55 and N 61.

☝ **Also See:** ATHENRY, BIRR, CLONMACNOISE, LONGFORD, MULLINGAR, STROKESTOWN, TULLAMORE.

A Bit of History

Siege of Athlone – Athlone was repeatedly fought over but the town's worst moment came in the course of the Williamite War, when it suffered the most devastating bombardment in Irish history. Following the Battle of the Boyne the Jacobite forces retreated to Athlone. In June 1691 the Williamite army under Ginkel made a determined assault on the bridge; Sergeant Custume, who died heroically, is commemorated in the name of the local barracks. After 10 days of sustained attack the town and castle fell; Ginkel was made Earl of Athlone; the Jacobites withdrew southwest to Aughrim.

John McCormack

The greatest lyric tenor of his day, John McCormack (1884–1945), born in Athlone, first sang in the Palestrina Choir of the Pro-Cathedral in Dublin. At 23 he made his debut at Covent Garden, and went on to perform there annually until 1914. His voice and charisma made him one of the most widely honoured and decorated singers in the world, the only Irish tenor to reach such an international standard. He was made a Count of the Papal Court for his charity work.

Visit

Market Square

Early in the 13C John de Grey, Justiciar of Ireland, built **Athlone Castle**. The curtain wall and its three fortified towers date from the late 13C. The oldest part, however, is the central polygonal **keep;** early in the 19C the upper part was altered to accommodate heavy artillery – supplemented by new defences, known as the Batteries, west of the town. A video in the exhibition centre details the Siege of Athlone and the life story of **John McCormack**. The **Castle Museum** *(in the keep)* covers local history and folk life. *Open May to Sep, 9.30am-5.30pm.* €5.50. ☎ 090 6492912.

The monumental **Church of St Peter and St Paul** was designed by **Ralph Byrne** (1937). Much of the striking stained glass comes from the **Harry Clarke** studios, while the window in the priest's sacristy is by the portrait painter **Sarah Purser**.

From the bridge, the main street curves east through town towards the site of the Dublin Gate. In a side turning *(left)* stand the remains of Court Devenish *(private)*, a Jacobean house (1620). The Bawn, a narrow street *(left)*, contains the birthplace of **John McCormack.** The **Franciscan Church** (1931) was built in the Hiberno-

Address Book

SIGHTSEEING

Athlone Cruises on Lough Ree – *90min excursion on Lough Ree / private charter.* ☎ *090 6472892*

Viking Tours – excursions in a replica Viking longship on Lough Ree. ☎ *090 6473383 - www.iol.ie/wmeathtc/viking/*

Shannon Safari – Powerboat trips on the Shannon, Lough Ree and Inner Lakes. *€20 / hr.* ☎ *090 6479558 - www.shannonsafari.ie.*

👍 *For coin ranges, see the Legend on the cover flap.*

WHERE TO STAY

🍽 **Glasson Stone Lodge** – *Glasson - 5mi NE of Athlone on N 55 - Mar to Dec - 5 rm* ☎ *090 6485004; www.glasson-stonelodge.com* 🅿 Tea and cakes on arrival; breakfast generous; bright bedrooms all with power showers.

🍽 **Riverview House B&B** – *Summerhill, Galway Rd – 2.5mi W of Athlone on N 6 -* ☎ *090 64 94532 Mar to mid-Dec - 4 rm* 🅿 Purpose-built house with a neat garden on a small tributary of the Shannon, bedrooms all ensuite. Good base for fishermen.

🍽 **Shelmalier House** – *Retreat Rd, Cartrontroy – 1.5mi E of Athlone by Dublin rd (N 6) -* 🕐 *Closed 20 Dec to 30 Jan - 7 rm* ☎ *090 6472245; www.shelmalierhouse.com* 🅿 Purpose-built accommodation with sauna/outdoor tub. Experienced owners; clean, comfortable house; bedrooms decorated to a high standard.

WHERE TO EAT

🍴🍴 **The Olive Grove** – *Athlone.* Varied menu, lunch and dinner every other day. ☎ *090 6492688.*

🍴🍴🍴 **Wineport Lodge** – *Glassan - 5mi NE of Athlone on N 55 and 1mi SW of Glassan -* ☎ *0906 439010 - lodge@wineport.ie -* 🕐 *Closed 24-26 Dec.*

EVENTS AND FESTIVALS

The **John McCormack Golden Voice of Athlone** *(late June)* is a competition for young classical singers to pay tribute to John McCormack, to bring good music to the community and to provide assistance to young singers.

Lough Ree Yaght Club Regatta - August

TRACING ANCESTORS

Dún na Sí (Fairy Fort) – Knockdomney, Co Westmeath – *Genealogy service.* ☎ *090 64 81183 - www.irish-roots.net.*

Romanesque style inspired by old Irish designs. The **Strand** along the river bank to Burgess Park provides a fine view of the weir, the eel fisheries and the old port on the west bank.

ATHY

POPULATION 5 306

Little larger than a big village, Athy (Baile Àtha) **is a bustling centre for an extensive rural area. At the beginning of the Middle Ages it was the largest town in Co Kildare, clustered round a fortified crossing of the river. Today, the Heritage Town attracts streams of visitors looking to cruise, sail and fish the River Barrow, the Barrow Line, and the Grand Canal.** 🏛 *Portlaoise.* 🕐 *Open Jun-Sep, Mon-Sat; Oct-May, Mon-Fri.* ☎ *050 22117.*

▶ **Orient Yourself:** Athy stands on N 78, and the county boundary between Kildare and Carlow.

👍 **Also See:** ABBEYLEIX, KILDARE, KILKENNY, TULLAMORE.

Visit

Town Centre

The present bridge, known as Crom-a-Boo Bridge, from the war cry of the Geraldine family, dates from 1796; White's Castle *(private)* alongside is 16C. Facing onto the main square is the **Courthouse**, the former Corn Exchange (1856), and the mid-18C **Town Hall** which houses a genealogy and heritage centre celebrating the arctic explorer SIr Ernest Shackelton, born locally, and the Gordon Bennett Car Rally. ◷ *Open Mon to Fri, 10am-5pm.* ⊛ €3. ☏ 059 8633075

The striking, fan-shaped **Dominican Church** is furnished with stained-glass windows and Stations of the Cross by the artist George Campbell (1917-79)

Driving Tour

East of Barrow Valley *20mi/32km*

▸ *From Athy take N 67 E and a minor road (right) via Burtown.*

Ballitore

The great Irish statesman and political theorist Edmund Burke (1729-97) was at school here. The **House of Mary Leadbetter** now accommodates a library and museum describing the 18C Yorkshire Quakers' sober and industrious way of life. ◷ *Open Tue-Sat, noon to 5pm; Jun to Sep, Sun, 2-6pm.* ☏ 050 723344

▸ *Take N 9 S to Timolin.*

Irish Pewter Mill, Museum and Crafts Centre, Timolin

♿◷ *Open Mon-Fri, 9.30am-4.30pm.* ◷ *Closed Good Fri to Easter Sun and 25 Dec.* 🅿 ☏ *059 8624164; www.kildare.ie/timolinpewter*

Ireland's oldest pewter mill continues to cast, spin and polish the alloy into objects of all kinds. A museum displays moulds, tools and dies used since the Middle Ages.

▸ *Continue S by N 9.*

Moone High Cross★

The scanty ruins of a 6C monastery founded by **St Columba** enclose an unusual, early 9C high cross (17.5ft/5.3m high). The slender shaft and tapering base carry a wealth of crude but very expressive carved panels of biblical scenes: one shows the Feeding of the Five Thousand with five loaves, two highly stylised eels, and a pair of smiling fish.

▸ *Continue S by N 9 to Castledermot; continue 9.5mi/16km SE by R 418.*

Castledermot High Crosses★

The site of a monastery founded by **St Dermot** is marked by two granite **high crosses** carved with biblical scenes, and a 10C **round tower** topped by medieval battlements. Ruined chancel walls recall the Franciscan friary founded by Lord Ossory in 1302.

▸ *From Castledermot take minor road E; in Graney turn left to Baltinglass.*

Baltinglass

The tiny town of Baltinglass lies at the foot of Baltinglass Hill. The main square is dominated by a memorial (1798) to Michael Dwyer, who managed to escape when his faithful comrade Sam MacAllister drew the fire of the British soldiers on himself. The first settlers were a group of monks from Mellifont; who went on from here to found Jerpoint. Beside the 19C Anglican church are the ruins of **Baltinglass Abbey**, founded by **Dermot MacMurrough**, King of Leinster, in 1148 and suppressed in 1536: six Gothic nave arches, the 19C tower and parts of the original cloisters (restored) still stand.

BANTRY★

POPULATION 2 777

The market and fishing town of Bantry (Beanntraí) stands near the head of the deep-water inlet known as Bantry Bay. Long familiar to mariners as a safe anchorage, the bay was the scene in 1796 of a dramatic episode in British and Irish history, when an attempted French invasion was frustrated by foul weather.
🛈 *Old Court House, Bantry.* 🕐 *Open Apr-Oct.* ☎ *027 50229; www.corkkerry.ie.*

▶ **Orient Yourself:** Bantry lies between Cork and Killarney (N 71) on the south shore of Bantry Bay (30mi/48km long) between Skibbereen and Glengarriff.
👆 **Also See:** KENMARE, KILLARNEY, SKIBBEREEN.

Visit

Bantry House★
♿🕐 *Open Mar-Oct, daily 9am-6pm.* 🎟 *House and garden €10; Gardens and Armada Centre €5.* ✉☎ *027 50047-www.bantryhouse.ie*

This splendidly symmetrical Georgian mansion of 1740 and its **terraced Italianate gardens** stand in superb contrast to the vast scale and wild nature of Bantry Bay. The house is full of tastefully chosen treasures: some are intimately connected with the events of 1796, for which the owner Richard White (1767-1851) was given a peerage in recognition of his role as commander of the local militia. Others are linked to Viscount Berehaven (1800-68) who travelled widely in Europe, accummulating extraordinary curiosities from Pompeii, Savonnerie carpets, Aubusson tapestries

SIGHTSEEING

Ferry from Bantry Pier to **Whiddy Island** – *Operates in summer, daily, every hour.* ☎ *086 8626734*
There are also scenic cruises of Bantry Bay.

SPORTS AND LEISURE

The inner harbour, with two slipways and safe anchorage, is an ideal location for sailing, water-skiing, wind surfing, canoeing, scuba-diving and swimming. The indoor swimming pool, children's pool and toddlers' pool and leisure centre at the **Westlodge Hotel** in Bantry are open to the public throughout the year.

EVENTS AND FESTIVALS

The **Bantry Mussel Fair** is held in May each year and the **International Chamber Music Week** in July.

Dining Room, Bantry House

Ch Legrand/MICHELIN

1796 French Armada

An expeditionary force of 15 000 French troops, commanded by General Hoche, accompanied by the Irish rebel Wolfe Tone, set sail from Brest intent on invading Ireland and expelling the British. Fog and adverse winds prevented most of the fleet from entering Bantry Bay. Then a storm blew up, impeding any attempts at landing so the ships retreated. Had the soldiers managed to come ashore, things might well have been very different, as only a scratch force of militiamen commanded by Richard White, owner of Bantry House, could be mustered.

Ten French warships were lost; the frigate *La Surveillante* was scuttled on 2 January 1797. The 17cwt/863kg French anchor, recovered by a trawler in 1964, sits by the N17 south of Bantry; a captured French longboat is now in Dún Laoghaire.

once owned by Marie-Antoinette, a Russian travelling shrine with 15C and 16C icons, and Spanish leather with which to clad the sides of the staircase. There are family portraits throughout the house, while the spectacular **dining room** is hung with those of King George III and Queen Charlotte, presented by the king at the time of White's ennoblement.
The East Stables now house an exhibition on the **1796 Bantry French Armada**.

Whiddy Island
The island has had a varied history, as its monuments tesify: Kilmore church and graveyard; Reenavanig Castle – the first residence of the White family; fortifications, including three gun batteries, erected as part of the British naval defences in 1801. An American sea plane base operated from here temporarily at the end of the First World War.

Excursions

Gougane Barra Forest Park★ *23mi/38km – half a day.*
From Ballylickey take R 584 E inland.
The approach road climbs inland between the vertical rock walls of the **Pass of Keimaneigh** (2mi/3.2km). West of the lake, the source of the **River Lee**, a **forest drive** (3mi/4.8km) makes a loop through the extensive park (walks and nature trails) which rises up the steep mountain slopes beside the tumbling mountain stream. St Finbar, the 6C founder of Cork, had a hermitage on the island in the lake. A small causeway leads to the modern island chapel built in the Irish Romanesque style.

Kilnaruane Inscribed Stone
2mi/3km S of Bantry by N 71; turn left at the Westlodge Hotel (sign).
On the hilltop stands a 9C stone pillar, possibly the shaft of a high cross. Carved panels of interlacing, a boat with four oarsmen – possibly a curragh navigating through a sea of crosses, a cross, a figure at prayer, St Paul and St Anthony in the Desert.

BIRR ★

With elegant 18C houses lining its shady streets, Birr (Biorra) is a fine example of a planned Georgian town laid out at the gates of a great house, and now a Heritage Town. The local landowners, the Parsons family, later ennobled as the Earls of Rosse, were also responsible for creating one of the richest collections of exotic trees and shrubs anywhere: one of many bequests left by a line of eminent men, innovators and inventors - another being what for many years was the world's most powerful telescope. *Brendon St.* *Open May to mid-Sep, Mon-Sat, 9.30am-1pm, 2pm-5.30pm* *057 9120110-www.shannondev.ie.*

▶ **Orient Yourself:** Birr is situated on N 52 between Tullamore and Nenagh on the country boundary SW of Tullamore in the O'Carroll country.
Don't Miss: Birr Castle and the Great Telescope.
Also See: ABBEYLEIX, ATHLONE, CLONMACNOISE, PORTUMNA, ROSCREA, TULLAMORE.

Address Book

SIGHTSEEING

Cruises downstream on the mighty Shannon – *Operate Jun-Sep, Sun at 2pm from Banagher Marina downstream to Victoria Lock, Meelick and return (1hr 30min). €10.* ☎ *057 9151112; www.silverlinecruisers.com*

For coin ranges, see the Legend on the cover flap.

WHERE TO STAY

Ring Farmhouse – *Ballinree . 2km from Birr off N62-* ☎ *057 9120976; www.irishfarmhouseholiday.com - 13 rm.* Friendly farmhouse B&B built on the site of Loretto Castle with distinctive hedges in a circle. Good location for walking in the Slieve Bloom mountains.

Maltings Guesthouse– *Castle St - 13 rm* ☎ *0509 21345 - themaltingsbirr@eircom.net -* *Closed 24-26 Dec -* Built in 1810 as a maltstore for Guinness, this establishment offers spacious accommodation; simple restaurant overlooking the river.

Ardmore House B&B – *Kinnitty.* ☎*057 9137009 - www.kinnitty.com* Ideal point for walks in the Slieve Bloom mountains and enjoy local produce sustaining farmers in the area.

WHERE TO EAT

The Thatch – *Crinkill - 1.5mi S off N 52 -* ☎ *057 9120682 - www.thethatchcrinkill.com -* *Closed Mon, Sun dinner Oct to April* . Characterful and evocative thatched pub kept by fifth generation of landlords. Open for bar lunch (busy) and restaurant dinner.

SPORTS AND LEISURE

Walking: Birr Castle Demesne, along the River Camcor, beside the Grand Canal , and in the Slieve Bloom mountains.
Boating: on the Shannon, Grand Canal.
Fishing: Shannon and Brosna rivers for salmon, pike, trout and most coarse species; River Suck and Grand Canal for pike, bream and perch.

EVENTS AND FESTIVALS

Birr Vintage Week *(late August)*: events include a Sunday parade, a Georgian Cricket Match played in period costume according to the 1744 rules; Irish Independent Carriage Driving Championships held in the Castle demesne, music, theatre, fireworks.

A Bit of History

Birr figures in the early records as the site of an important monastery, which produced the Macregol's Gospels and where the Law of Adamnan was accepted by abbots and chieftains at the Synod of Birr in 697. Owing to its central position in Ireland, Birr was referred to in the Down Survey as *Umbilicus Hiberniae*.

Until the establishment of the Free State, Birr was known as Parsonstown in King's County (the old name of Co Offaly). In 1620 the village was granted to **Sir Lawrence Parsons**. He started weekly markets, set up a glass factory and built most of the castle. In 1642 much of Birr was destroyed by fire during a siege by local clans; in 1690 it was garrisoned by the Williamites and besieged by the Duke of Berwick. During the more peaceful 18C and 19C, the town, castle and demesne were much extended. **Sir William Parsons,** a patron of Handel, enabled the composer to stage the first performance of *Messiah* in Dublin in 1742. His grandson, another Sir William, the 4th baronet, devoted much time to the late-18C Volunteers. **Sir Lawrence,** the 5th baronet, was more nationalist in political sentiment and a friend of **Wolfe Tone** but he retired from politics after the Act of Union in 1800. In the 19C the family genius was invested in **scientific discoveries** and in the 20C was directed towards the collection and propagation of the **rare botanical species** for the magnificent gardens.

Walking Tour

Birr Town★

The principal axis is **Oxentown Mall** which runs between the castle gates and the Anglican church between rows of elegant houses and mature trees. The town centre is formed by **Emmet Square**; among the best Georgian houses is Dooley's Hotel (1740). **John's Mall** is graced by a statue of the 3rd Earl of Rosse, and beside the delightful little Greek temple (1833) is the **Birr Stone**, a large limestone rock, which may once have marked the supposed meeting place of the mythical Fianna warriors near Seffin. In 1828 it was removed to a mansion in Co Clare to be used for secret celebrations of the Mass; it was returned to Birr in 1974.

Visit

Birr Castle Demesne★★

2–3hr. ♿🕐 *Open mid-Mar to Oct, 9am–6pm.* 🎧 *€9. Check Web site for telescope demonstration and summer evening concerts.* ☕🅿 ☎ *057 9120336; www.birrcastle.com*

Great Telescope, Birr

Birr Scientific and Heritage Foundation

Gardens

Each of the many walks through these pleasure grounds (100 acres/40ha) by the water or among thousands of species of trees and shrubs is a sheer delight. Highlights include the tallest box hedges or the flora from China and the Himalayas. Extensive herbaceous displays adorn the terraces below the crenellated 17C **castle** *(private)*.

Great Telescope★★

In the 1840s, the 3rd Earl of Rosse built a telescope named the **Leviathan of Parsonstown**, providing a more extensive view of space than was hitherto possible. Its mirror (72in/183cm) was cast in a furnace built at the bottom of the castle moat, and fired with turf from nearby bogs. Astronomers came from far and wide to use the telescope, considered to be the most powerful for 60 years, until 1908.

Galleries of Discovery

Part of the stable yard is given over to an account of the brilliant family achievements – the building of the first-known example of a wrought-iron suspension bridge by the 2nd Earl; the construction of the great telescope and the discovery of distant galaxies by the 3rd Earl; the invention of the steam turbine engine by Charles Parsons in the 1890s; the pioneering work in photography by Mary Countess of Rosse in the 1850s; the world-wide plant-collecting expeditions conducted by the 5th and 6th Earls.

Driving Tours

Slieve Bloom Mountains★ *Round tour of 46mi/73km – 1/2 - 1 day.*

▶ *From Birr take R 440 E.*

After the unvarying landscapes of the midlands, the plantations of pine and spruce, and mountains rising from the bog to 1728ft/527m (Arderin) are most refreshing A good way to enjoy the scenery is to walk sections of the 44mi/70km **Slieve Bloom Way**. Otherwise, the drive east from the village of Kinnitty, past Forelacka Glen to Drimmo, then north through The Cut to Clonaslee is recommended.

> ### American Connection
>
> One of the signatories of the American Declaration of Independence in 1776, Charles Carroll of Carrollton, was the grandson of Charles Carroll, who emigrated in 1688 from Letterluna in the Slieve Bloom mountains to the USA, where he was granted land in Maryland.

Kinnitty

The village itself has considerable charm, set in idyllic scenery. For details on walking trails, the flora and fauna of the area, contact the **Slieve Bloom Centre**. ◷ *Open Apr-Sep, daily.* ☎ *086 2789147 - www.slievebloom.ie*

The **Kinnitty Pyramid** in the churchyard south of the village (on the Roscrea road), is an extraordinary mausoleum modelled on the pyramid of Cheops in Egypt, honouring the Bernards of Kinnitty Castle.

Shannon Valley *Drive of 20mi/32km.*

▶ *From Birr take R 439 N.*

Banagher (Beannchar)

The town on the **Shannon** was an important crossing point, defended on the Connacht bank by Cromwell's Castle. A tower house with bastions was added c 1650. The Revd Arthur Nicholls came from Banagher, and when he married **Charlotte Brontë**, the couple spent their honeymoon nearby. Another literary resident was Anthony Trollope.

Anthony Trollope (1815–82) in Ireland

Having been in the employ of the Post Office since 1834, Trollope was appointed a Surveyor's Clerk in1841 and went to Ireland. His first appointment, to which he travelled from Dublin by canal boat, was in **Banagher**, where he took up hunting, and visited Sir William Gregory of Coole Park, a contemporary at Harrow School. In 1843 during a visit to Drumsna he was inspired to begin his first novel, *The Macdermots of Ballycloran*, published in 1847.

On 11 June 1844 he married Rose Heseltine. Later that year they moved to **Clonmel**, renting rooms on the first floor of a house in O'Connell Street (then High Street) where two sons were born - Henry Merivale (March 1846) and Frederic James (September 1847). In 1845 Anthony began his second novel *The Kellys and the O'Kellys*, which was published in 1848. The family then moved to **Mallow** (1848-51) and Anthony was able to indulge his passion for hunting with various great hunts including the Duhallow, the oldest in Ireland. While on secondment in the Channel Islands in 1853, Trollope implemented the idea of the first **post boxes**, which were painted sage green. In 1854, after a year in Belfast as Acting Surveyor, he was appointed Surveyor of the Northern District of Ireland but obtained permission to reside in Dublin, where he lived at 5 Seaview Terrace, Donnybrook. As his work involved a good deal of travelling, he created a portable desk so that he could write on the train.

He began his third Irish novel, *Castle Richmond* which takes place during the Great Famine, in 1859, the year in which he was transferred permanently to England. At the end of his life he began a fourth Irish novel, *The Landleaguers*, about agrarian reform but died in December 1882 before it was finished.

▶ *From Banagher take R 356 E ; turn left to Shannon Harbour.*

Shannon Harbour

The junction of the **Grand Canal** and the Shannon is now a popular mooring for river cruisers. In its commercial heyday, a dry dock, warehousing, a customs post and hotel (now in ruins) served the lock and canal basin; the local population numbering 1 000, saw the trans-shipment of some 300 000 tons of produce and over 250 000 people on the barges, many of them emigrants on their way via Limerick and Cobh to Australia, Canada and America.

The area provides excellent coarse fishing and birdwatching when rare birds, including the corncrake, visit the wet grasslands known as the Shannon Callows.

▶ *Beyond Shannon Harbour in Clonony turn left into R 357 to Shannonbridge.*

Clonmacnoise and West Offaly Railway

♿ *Train excursions on the hour: Apr, May, Sep, Mon-Fri; Jun to Aug, daily,10am-5pm.* €6.50. ☎ 090 9674450 - www.bnm.ie

The narrow-gauge railway takes passengers on a guided tour (45min – 5.5mi/8km) of the **Blackwater Bog**, part of the Bog of Allen (20 000 acres/8 090ha) which is one of the largest unbroken raised bogs in Ireland. The tour includes a view of the various stages in the process of harvesting the peat to fuel the electricity power station at Shannonbridge; there is a half-way halt to see the bog.

BOYLE

POPULATION 1 695

On the River Boyle at the foot of the Curlew Mountains (867ft/264m), this pleasant little town (Mainistir Na Búille) has one of the lovliest set of abbey ruins in Ireland and fascinating reminders of one of the most ruthless and ambitious Anglo-Irish landowning dynasties, the King family. The river and the nearby loughs give excellent fishing. *King House, Boyle.* *Open May-Sep,* *closed for lunch.* ☎ 071 9662145

▶ **Orient Yourself:** Boyle lies on N 4, the Dublin to Sligo road, south of the Curlew Mountains between Lough Key and Lough Gara.
◔ **Also See:** CARRICK-ON-SHANNON, KILLALA, KNOCK, SLIGO, STROKESTOWN.

Visit

Boyle Abbey★

2mi/3.2km E of Boyle by N 4. (Dúchas) ♿ *Open Apr-Oct, daily 10am-6pm (5.15pm last admission).* ☞ *€1.30.* P ☎ *071 9662606; www.heritageireland.ie*

The **Cistercian** house was founded in 1161 by monks from Mellifont. The church, built over several decades, shows the transition from the Romanesque to the Gothic style. Normally frowning on exuberance of any kind, here at Boyle the austere Cistercians gave free rein to their masons, who endowed the capitals with carvings of men, beasts and foliage. The abbey buildings were occupied by the Cromwellians who showed them their usual disrespect; thereafter they served as barracks until the 18C. Information on the monastic life is provided in the **gatehouse**.

> **EVENTS AND FESTIVALS**
>
> **O'Carolan Harp Festival** – Performance of O'Carolan's works, music, song and dancing, many open-air events – *Late-Jul or early-Aug. Information from the Secretary, Keadew, Co Roscommon.* ☎ *071 9647247; www. ocarolanharpfestival.ie*
>
> **Boyle Arts** – *King House.* Summer *(July)* festival of contemporary art, drama, jazz and classical music recitals. *www.boylearts.com*

King House★

Open May to Sep, 10am-6pm; last admission 5pm. ☞ *€7.* ✗ P ☎ *071 9663242 - www.kinghouse.ie - www. boylearts.com*

The Palladian mansion of the King family stands at the east end of the main street. It was built around 1730, probably by an assistant to Sir Edward Lovett Pearce. The first King was Sir John, a Staffordshire gentleman sent here a century earlier, charged with subjugating the native Irish and rewarded with the lands confiscated from the local ruling clan, the MacDermots. The Kings became increasingly powerful, eventually acquiring the title of Earls of Kingston, and moving to a more splendid residence in the vast Rockingham estate.

King House, Boyle

King House has been carefully restored to accommodate descriptions of the old rulers – O'Connors, Kings of Connaught and MacDermots of Moylurg – and the exploits of the King family who displaced them. For many years, the Connaught Rangers were billeted here: they served the Crown well but eventually mutinied in 1920 in protest against government repression during the struggle for independence. The **Boyle Civic Art Collection** is considered to be among the finest collections of contemporary Irish painting and sculpture, anywhere.

Excursion

Lough Key Forest Park★

2mi/3.2km E of Boyle by N 4. 🅿 👷 *Visitor centre undergoing redevelopment.*

With its woodlands, bog garden, ornamental trees and estate buildings, this vast forest park (865 acres/350ha) looks out over Lough Key and its islands. Until 1959 it formed part of the Rockingham estate, the desmesne of the Earls of Kingston, who built themselves a great house here on the site of a MacDermot castle. In the early 19C, the house was remodelled by John Nash and the estate was landscaped by Humphry Repton. In 1959 the house was destroyed by fire. A modern structure, the **Moylurg Tower** (132 steps) gives visitors panoramic views over the woods, lakes and hills which formed the setting of one of Ireland's grandest country houses.

> **Woodbrook**
>
> The name of the house, situated between Lough Key and the main road, which was once the home of the Kirkwood family, is also the name of a charming book by David Thomson, an 18 year old Oxford student who took a summer job as tutor to Phoebe Kirkwood in 1932 and wrote about the experience.

Driving Tour

Mountains and Lakes of Moylurg★ *Round-trip of 50mi/80km.*

▷ *From Boyle take N 4 N.*

As it climbs over the **Curlew Mountains** (867ft/264m) the road provides splendid **views**★ of the lakes *(east)*.

Ballinafad

The Castle of the Curlews, now in ruins, was built in 1590 to protect the Curlew Mountain pass. It had four round corner towers with square interiors.

▷ *Continue N on N 4. In Castlebaldwin turn left signed to Carrowkeel Cemetery; at the fork bear left. Park at the gate if locked; 1hr on foot there and back.*

Carrowkeel Megalithic Cemetery

The bleak hilltop in the **Bricklieve Mountains** (1 057ft/321m), provides a fine **view**★★ of the surrounding country. The stone mounds contain passage graves dating from the Late Stone Age (2500 to 2000 BC). On a lower ridge (east) are about 50 round huts, probably dwellings.

▷ *From Castlebaldwin take the road along the shore of Lough Arrow. At the end of the lake turn left. In Ballyfarnan turn left into a steep minor road to Altgowlan.*

Arigna Scenic Drive (Slí)★

From the **viewpoint,** you see Lough Skean and Lough Meelagh. As the road crosses the watershed, more fine views extend over the steep Arigna Valley cleared of its trees and then blighted by coal mining for fuel to power the iron industry and, until 1990, a local electricity generating plant.

▶ *At the T-junction turn right; after 2.5mi/4km turn left into Arigna. In Arigna cross the river and turn left uphill; after 1.5mi/2.4km turn right (sign) onto a very steep and narrow road. At the next junction turn right.*

As the road descends from the bare and rugged heights there is an extensive **view**⋆ of **Lough Allen**, the most northerly of the great Shannon lakes. Nearby, the river rises in a bog at Shannon Pot *(9mi/14.5km north)*, running past Slieve Anierin (1 927ft/586m), the highest point in the Iron Mountains.

▶ *At the bottom of the hill turn right onto R 280 to Drumshanbo.*

Drumshanbo (Droim Seanbho)
The town at the southern end of Lough Allen is a haven for anglers who flock to fish the Shannon and drumlin lakes beyond Ballinamore, or the Ballinamore and Ballyconnell Canals.

▶ *From Drumshanbo return N on R 280; turn left onto R 285 and drive through Keadew (Keadue).*

O'Carolan's Grave
The tombstones mark the site of **Kilronan Abbey**, founded in the 6C between Lough Meelagh and the Arigna Mountains: the doorway is 12C–13C; in the transept is the tombstone of **Turlough O'Carolan.**

▶ *Return to the last junction; turn right. In Knockvicar turn right to Corrigeenroe; in Corrigeenroe turn left to return to Boyle, past Lough Key.*

Turlough O'Carolan (1670–1738)

The blind harpist who wrote poetry and music, including the melody of *The Star-Spangled Banner,* was born in **Nobber** in Co Meath. In 1684 his family moved to Carrick-on-Shannon, where Mrs MacDermot Roe became his patron and provided for his education and musical studies. She even gave him a horse so that he could perform his compositions at the big houses. After his marriage in 1720 he lived several years in Mohill. His death in **Keadew** (Keadue) was marked by a 4 day wake. Annual harp festivals are held in his honour in Keadew and Nobber.

BOYNE VALLEY⋆⋆

Upstream from Drogheda, the River Boyne winds through a fertile and well-wooded landscape with an extraordinary concentration of ancient and pre-historic sites. Huge grave mounds, laboriously constructed and enigmatically decorated, testify to the skill and sophistication of the people who thrived here long before work started on the pyramids of Egypt. Much later, in the pre-Christian era, the High Kings of Ireland held court at the Hill of Tara. Christianity was brought to the region by St Patrick himself; the early monastic site at Monasterboice evokes the Irish church before its 12C romanisation, in contrast to the later, European style of monastery at Mellifont. The clash of arms on the banks of the river in 1690 was an event of European as well as local importance, and the outcome of the Battle of the Boyne is still a factor in contemporary Irish politics.
🛈 *Bru na Boinne Visitor Centre, Donore.* 🕐 *Open daily.* ☎ *041 988 0300*

▶ **Orient Yourself:** The Boyne Valley runs inland from Drogheda; the sights can be reached from N 51 on the north bank of the River Boyne, from M 1 which passes just west of Drogheda or from N 2 which passes through Slane.

🕓 **Organizing Your Time:** Allow half a day at least for a visit.

😊 **Don't Miss:** Newgrange - a UNESCO World Heritage Site, and Monasterboice.

👓 **Also See:** DROGHEDA, FINGAL, KELLS, TRIM.

Visit

Prehistoric Sites

The prehistoric burial sites at Knowth, Dowth and Newgrange are the oldest in the British Isles. They were built by a farming and stock-raising community in the Neolithic era (3 500-2 700 BC), overlooking the Boyne, then a main through route.

> **WALKING PATHS**
>
> River Boyne towpath, Oldbridge Estate, Townley Hall grounds (nature trail)

Present knowledge suggests that Dowth was built first to align with the setting sun. It was followed by Newgrange where the rising sun penetrates the inner chamber at the winter solstice. Knowth was built later facing east–west to align with the rising sun in March and the setting sun in September.

Altogether, there are some 40 graves, consisting of three major graves and many satellites: only the major graves have been systematically excavated.

Brú na Bóinne Visitor Centre

(Dúchas) &🔥🔹 *All visits by guided tour.* 🕓 *Open May-Sep, daily, 9am-6.30pm (7pm Jun to mid-Sep); Mar-Apr and Oct-Feb, daily, 9.30am-5.30pm (5pm Nov-Feb).* 🕓 *Closed 25-26 Dec. Tour price includes shuttle-bus service.* 😊 *Arrive early in high season as tours sell out quickly.* ☎ *Visitor Centre only* €2.90; *Centre and Newgrange (2hr)* €5.80; *Centre and Knowth (Easter to Oct), 2hr,* €4.50. 🔲📁☎ *041 988 0300 - www. heritageireland.ie*

Informative displays with replicas of the monuments provide an excellent introduction to the archaeological sites: details of the people, their clothing, food and Neolithic dwellings are integrated into descriptions of their expertise and ability to move stones on rollers: 500 years before the pyramids of Egypt.

Newgrange★★★

Newgrange is one of the best examples of a passage grave in western Europe, its dimensions imposing, the enigmatic stone carving a marvel of imagination. The **mound** (1.25 acres/0.5ha, 260ft/79m–280ft/85m in diameter and 37ft/11m high) consists of a cairn of medium-sized stones enclosed within a circle of 97 kerbstones, some of which are decorated, set on their long edges, ends touching, surmounted by a facing of round granite boulders. Excavations in 1963 made it possible to reconstruct the original south front **revetment** of white quartz stones, except where the entrance has been enlarged to accommodate visitors. Above the entrance, which was originally closed by an upright slab *(right)*, is the **roof box**, a unique structure with a finely decorated lintel, through which the rays of

Newgrange

the rising sun penetrate to the inner chamber for 17 minutes at the winter solstice (21 December).

The passage, which is lined with large standing stones, some decorated and all dressed, leads into a corbelled **chamber** a third of the way into the mound. The three decorated recesses contain stone **basins**, which held the bones of the dead together with funeral offerings of stone and bone beads and pendants, bone pins and small stone balls resembling marbles. The corbelled vaulted roof, completed by a central capstone (4 tonnes), is quite waterproof as the outer faces of the stones are grooved to drain off water.

The mound was surrounded at a distance (39x49ft/12x15m) by a **great circle** of standing stones. The four opposite the entrance are among the largest.

South of the mound are traces of a late-Neolithic – early-Bronze Age **pit circle**.

Knowth★

The mound (40ft/12m high, 220ft/67m in diameter) probably dates from 2500 to 2000 BC. It contains two decorated passage graves discovered in 1967 and 1968; one is simply an enlargement of the passageway but the other is circular and corbelled with side chambers. It is aligned east–west and is surrounded by smaller tombs facing the large central mound. In the early centuries AD the central mound was surrounded by deep defensive ditches. In about 8C AD the settlement expanded and several souterrains and rectangular houses were built. From the 12C to 14C the site was occupied by the Normans who constructed a rectangular stone structure on the top of the mound.

Excavations conducted since 1962 have made it possible to reconstruct the smaller tombs which had collapsed owing to the passage of time and conversion of the material to other uses.

Dowth

The mound (⚲ *closed for excavation),* which was raised by man in 3000 BC (1 acre/0.4ha, 280ft/85m in diameter, 50ft/15.24m high), contains two tombs and a souterrain connecting with the north tomb. The base of the mound was enclosed by about 100 kerb stones, many ornamented, although most are covered by landslip.

Other Prehistoric Sites

Tara★
5mi/8km S of Navan by N 3. (Dúchas) &. ⊘ *Site: Open all year. Visitor Centre and guided tour: mid-May to late-mid-Sep, 10am-6pm (5.15pm last admission).* ◎ €2.10. ☎ 046 9025903

The name of Tara conjures up the spirit of Irish Celtic greatness; the Hill of Tara, also known as Tara of the Kings, played a significant part in Irish legends. Its origin as a religious site is lost in prehistory; it achieved its greatest prestige under the pagan High Kings of Ireland, and even after the introduction of Christianity it retained its significance as the nominal seat of the High King until it was abandoned in 1022. During the 1798 rebellion a skirmish took place on the hill. In the 19C O'Connell chose it as the site of one of his monster meetings in the cause of Roman Catholic emancipation; 250 000 people came to hear him speak.

The **bare hill** pockmarked with earthworks does not readily suggest a royal palace. An effort of the imagination is required to envisage the many small buildings, of wood or wattle and daub, where the king held his court.

The history of Tara is recounted in an audio-visual presentation in the early-19C **St Patrick's Church**, which incorporates a medieval window.

In the churchyard stands a red sandstone pillar stone, known as **St Adamnán's Cross,** which bears a carved figure which may be the ancient Celtic god **Cernunnos**.

West of the graveyard is the **Rath of the Synods**, a ringfort with three banks. Farther south is an Iron-Age ringfort, enclosed by a bank and a ditch, known as the **Royal Enclosure.** Within it is the **Mound of the Hostages**, a small passage grave which dates from about 1800 BC. In the centre of the enclosure are two ringforts, known as the **Royal Seat** and **Cormac's House;** beside the statue of St Patrick, is a standing stone known as the **Lia Fáil,** which was moved from its original position near the Mound of the Hostages to be a memorial to those who died in 1798.

South of the Royal Enclosure is part of another earthwork known as **King Laoghaire's Rath.** To the north of the churchyard is a hollow flanked by two long parallel banks, which may have been the grand entrance but which is known as the Banqueting Hall. On the west side are three circular earthworks; the first is known as Gráinne's Fort, the other two as the Sloping Trenches.

South of the hill *(0.5mi/0.8km – visible from the road)* is part of another ringfort, known as **Rath Maeve**, surrounded by a bank and ditch.

Fourknocks
11mi/18km S of Drogheda by R 108; after 10mi/16km turn right.

The **passage grave**, which dates from c 1500 BC, is unusually large compared with the size of the mound. The interior contains stones decorated with zigzags and other prehistoric designs and a human face. It contained over 60 burials. *Key available from Mr White* ☎ 0419809950

Battle Site

Battle of the Boyne Centre
(Dúchas) &. ⤳ *Guided outdoor tour (30-45min) May-Sep, 10am-6pm; last admission at 5.15pm. Living History activities at weekends.* ◎*Rainproof clothing and stout shoes for uneven ground adviseable.* 🅿 ☎ 041 9809950 - www.battleoftheboyne.ie

The battlefield site, now part of the Oldbridge estate, granted to the Williamite commander Coddington, is being developed to contain a museum and interpretive centre. The guided tour includes an account of the battle and demonstrations of the cannons and guns used by the opposing armies. There are walks on the estate and beside the river from the Obelisk Bridge.

Battle of the Boyne

The battle fought on 12 July 1690 was the decisive engagement in the War of the Two Kings *(Cogadh an Dá Rí)* as **King James II** of England, supported by Louis XIV of France, fought King William III of England (**William of Orange**) and his allies united in a struggle for the domination of Europe. British, Danish, Dutch, Finnish, French, German, Irish, Polish, Prussian and Swiss men were numbered among the 36 000 Williamites and 25 000 Jacobites troops.

While the French Jacobites were under orders to delay William, the latter was keen for a speedy victory. As he surveyed his troops the morning of the battle, a bullet tore his coat and grazed his shoulder, so he despatched troops upstream to attack the French left flank, they forded the Boyne at Oldbridge and attacked the Jacobite army on the south bank; five crossings were made between 10am and 2pm.

William lost 500 men; James lost about 1 000. On hearing that William had crossed the river, James left for Dublin and rode on to Duncannon near Waterford and sailed to Kinsale and France. In the hope of reversing the Cromwellian land settlement, the Irish fought on until the following year when they suffered defeats at Athlone, Aughrim and Limerick. The Williamite victory brought about the definitive defeat of the **Stuart** cause and determined the balance of power in Europe.

Monastic Sites

Monasterboice★★
8mi/13km N of Drogheda by N 1.

Overlooked by a half-ruined **round tower**, three **high crosses** of outstanding beauty and interest mark the site of the famous 6C monastery founded by **St Buithe** (**Boethius**), an important centre of learning closely connected with Armagh.

The **South Cross** was erected by Muiredach in the 9C. The west face shows the Crucifixion, Christ with Peter and Paul, the raised Christ flanked by Apostles and the Mocking of Jesus; on the east face are the Last Judgement, the Adoration of the Magi, Moses striking the Rock, David and Goliath, the Fall of Man, and Cain slaying Abel.

The **West Cross** *(between the two ruined churches)* is unusually tall (23ft/7m) and the subjects of the carvings are unusual: the Crucifixion, the Arrest of Christ, Christ surrounded by Apostles, the Resurrection of the Dead, the Soldiers at the Tomb; Christ Militans, Christ walking on the water, Simon Magus and the Fiery Furnace, Goliath, Samuel anointing David, the Golden Calf, the Sacrifice of Isaac, David killing a lion.

The **North Cross** *(NE corner of the graveyard)* also shows the Crucifixion. The original shaft is contained in the same enclosure as well as a monastic sundial indicating the hours of the Divine Office.

Behind the north church lies an early **grave slab** bearing the name Ruarcan. The **tower** and its treasures were burned in 1097.

High Cross, Monasterboice

B Kaufmann/MICHELIN

Mellifont Old Abbey★

6mi/10km W of Drogheda by N 51, R 168 and a minor road west of Tullyallen. (Dúchas)
🚫🕐 *Visitor Centre: open May-Sep, 10am-5.30pm (4.45pm last admission).* 📷 *€4.45.*
Guided tour (40min) by appointment. 🅿*Access by stone stairway.* ☎ *041 982 6459*
- www.heritageireland.ie

The first Cistercian house in Ireland was founded on the banks of the **River Mattock** by St Malachy in 1142 with four Irish and nine French monks. it no doubt owed its name ("Honey fountain" in Latin) to the beauty of its surroundings.

Still standing are the ruined **gatehouse**, the vaulted **Chapter House** (14C) and four faces of the two-storey **octagonal lavabo** (12C).The 12C church, which was consecrated in 1157, was designed by one of the Frenchmen; it had a crypt at the west end and three transept chapels. In 1225 the chancel and transepts were extended. In 1556 the abbey became a private house which was abandoned in 1727.

Hill of Slane

This hilltop with its wide-ranging views is one of the key sites in the story of Irish Christianity. In 433 St Patrick travelled from Saul (in Co Down) by sea and on foot to Slane, where he lit a fire on the hilltop on Easter Eve to challenge the druids who were holding a festival at Tara. As anyone who kindled a fire within sight of Tara did so on pain of death, Patrick was brought before Laoghaire, the High King, to whom he preached the Gospel. Although the king remained a pagan, he allowed his subjects freedom of conscience. One of them, Erc, converted and founded a monastery at Slane; he is said to be buried in the ruined mortuary house in the graveyard.

The church, which was in use until 1723, was part of **Slane Friary**, a Franciscan house, founded in 1512 by Sir Christopher Flemyng, whose arms are on the west wall of the courtyard. The friary, which housed four priests, four lay-brothers and four choristers, was suppressed in 1540, occupied by Capuchins in 1631 and abandoned under Cromwell. On the west face of the hill is a motte raised by Richard le Flemyng of Flanders, who arrived in Ireland in 1175.

Termonfeckin★

6mi/10km N of Drogheda by R 167 E or R 166 and a minor road E. (Dúchas) Key available from the cottage opposite.

In the graveyard of St Fechin's Church stands a 10C **high cross** depicting the Crucifixion and Christ in Glory; it marks the site of a monastery founded by St Fechin of Fore. Close to the shore stands a 15C or 16C three-storey **tower house** which has an unusual corbelled roof *(45 steps)*: **view** of the coast from Drogheda *(S)* to Clogher Head *(N)*.

Slane

The "square" at centre of the village was laid out by Viscount Conyngham in the late 18C; it is lit by oil lamps and bordered by four nearly identical Georgian houses, each flanked by two smaller houses. The Gothic Gate *(S of the crossroads)* was designed by **Francis Johnston** c 1795 as an entrance to Slane Castle. From the bridge over the Boyne there is a **view** of Slane Castle, Slane Mill (1766), the weir and the canal; the towpath goes upstream to Navan and downstream to Drogheda.

Slane Castle

0.25mi/0.5km W of Slane by N 51. 🥄 *Guided tour May to early-Aug, Sun-Thu noon-5pm.* 📷 *€7.* ☎ *041 988400- www.slanecastle.ie*

The impressive raised **site** overlooking the **River Boyne** is surmounted by an elegant assembly of square turrets, crenellations and artificial machicolations. The present house was built between 1785 and 1821 on the site of a confiscated **Fleming** fortress purchased by the Conynghams in 1641. Only the best architects were employed, among them James Gandon, James Wyatt, Francis Johnston and Thomas Hopper, while Capability Brown designed the stables and landscaped the grounds. Many of the rooms had to be restored after a disastrous fire in 1991.

Ledwidge Cottage Museum
0.5mi/0.8km E of Slane by N 51. ⚙🕐*Open daily, 10am-1pm and 2-5.30pm.* ⊜ €3.
🅿☏ *041 982 4544 - www.francisledwidge.com*
The four-roomed semi-detached cottage built under the Labourers' Dwellings Act (1886) was the childhood home of the poet, **Francis Ledwidge** (1887–1917), who wrote about his love of the Meath countryside. Today, it displays some of his manuscripts.

BUNCRANA

POPULATION 3 112

With its long sandy beach facing west across Lough Swilly to the mountains of Donegal, Buncrana (Bun Cranncha) is a busy seaside resort and the largest town on the Inishowen Peninsula, crowded in summer with holidaymakers from Londonderry, a mere dozen miles away on the far side of the border. Approached by a six-arched bridge spanning the Crana River, O'Docherty's Keep is all that remains of the castle built by the Anglo-Normans and later held by the local lords, the "O'Dochertys tall from dark Donegal" (Benedict Kiely). ▯ *Buncrana. Open Jun-Aug, Mon-Sat.* ☏ *074 9362600; The Diamond, Inishowen* ☏ *074 9374933 - www.visitinishowen.com*

▶ **Orient Yourself:** Buncrana is set on the east shore of Lough Swilly, NW of Londonderry. It is a good place to start a tour of the Inishowen Peninsula.
🙊 **Don't Miss:** the Inshowen Peninsula, Malin Head and Grianán of Aileach.
🕯 **Also See:** DONEGAL, DONEGAL COAST, DONEGAL GLENS, LONDONDERRY, SPERRIN MOUNTAINS.

Driving Tour

Inishowen (Inis Eoghain) Scenic Drive★★
100mi/160km – 1 day

The drive follows the coast of the Inishowen Peninsula to Malin Head, the most northerly point in Ireland. The landscape is composed of rugged mountains covered in blanket bog, fringed by steep cliffs or broad sweeps of sand. The peninsula is named after Eoghain, a 5C ruler who was a contemporary of St Patrick. By the 15C the powerful clan of the O'Dochertys held sway, but when their chief was killed in 1608, the land passed into the possession of the Elizabethan adventurer Sir Arthur Chichester, whose family eventually became the largest landowners in Ireland.

▶ *Take the coast road N to Dunree Head.*

Fort Dunree Military Museum★
🕐 *Open May-Sep,10.30am (1pm Sun) to 6pm; Oct-Apr, Mon-Sat10.30am-4.30pm, Sun 1-5pm .* ⊜ €5. ⊑🅿 *in the military compound.* ☏ *074 9361817 - www.dunree.pro.ie*
A drawbridge spans the narrow defile which separates this late 18C fort from the desolate headland of Dunree Head. The fort itself has been converted into a **military museum** containing the original guns; modern interactive technology and a video explain their role in a coastal defence battery and escribe the evolution of the

H Champollion/MICHELIN

Dunagree Point

fort from a fortified earthen embankment, built in 1798 under the threat of French invasion, to an important element in a chain of forts on the shores of Lough Swilly defending a Royal Navy base at Buncrana. In 1914 the entire British Grand Fleet sheltered behind a boom in the Lough. Knockalla Fort is visible across the narrow channel on the opposite shore.

▷ *Return to the junction and turn left; at the crossroads turn left.*

Gap of Mamore★
The road climbs past rocky outcrops to the **viewpoint** and sights of Dunaff Head.

▷ *Turn left past Lenan Strand to Lenan Head, through Dunaff to Clonmany and continue N on R 238*

Ballyliffin (Baile Lifin)
Beyond Lenon Head where a gun battery (1895) used to command the entrance to Lough Swilly, lies this attractive holiday village, slightly set back from Pollan Bay and Pollan Strand.

▷ *Continue E on R 238.*

Carndonagh High Cross★
At the top of the hill next to the Anglican church stands an 8C **high cross**, decorated with an interlaced cross and a Crucifixion and flanked by two **pillars**: one shows David with his harp. In the graveyard stands a **cross pillar**, known as the Marigold Stone, decorated with a seven-pointed star on one side and the Crucifixion on the other.

▷ *Continue N on R 238 and R 242.*

Malin
The 17C Plantation village retains its original layout, including its triangular green.

ⓘ *For coin ranges, see the Legend on the cover flap.*

WHERE TO STAY
⊖ **Carrickabraghey House** – *Shore Rd, Ballyliffin.* ☎ *074 9376977.*
⊖ **Castlelawn House** – *Shore Rd, Ballyliffin -* ☎ *074 9376600*

WHERE TO EAT
⊖ **The Niche and Taj Restaurant** – *Churchtown, Carndonagh. Dinner Tue-Sun -* ☎ *074 9374137 -* ⊙ *Closed Mon. Informal restaurant offering Indian dishes and local seasonal fare.*
⊖ **McGrory's of Culdaff** – *Inishowen -* ☎*074 9379104 - www.mcgrorys. ie Family-run business since 1924, known for locally-sourced seasonal seafood, beef and lamb. Live gigs in Backroom Bar.*

Lag Sand Dunes★

Massive sand dunes line the north shore of Trawbreaga Bay, the estuary of the Donagh River.

Malin Head★★

The tiny fishing village shelters in the lee of the great headland. On the cliffs stands a tower, originally built in 1805 by the British Admiralty to monitor shipping and later used as a signal tower by Lloyds. North across the sound *(1.5mi/2.4km)* lies Inishtrahull Island, once the site of a hermitage but now deserted. The road circles the headland providing dramatic **views★★** *(southwest)* to Pollan Strand and Dunaff Head.

▶ *Take the coast road S via Portaleen to Culdaff. Take R 238 S; turn left into minor road.*

Bocan Stone Circle

In a field *(left)* are the traces of a stone circle which may have comprised 30 standing stones.

▶ *Return to last junction; turn right into R 238 ; drive towards Culdaff; turn left into minor road.*

Clonca Church and Cross

In the 6C St Buodán founded a monastery at Clonca. The ruined church dates from the 17C/18C but the carved lintel is earlier. Inside is the 16C tombstone of Magnus MacOrristin, who probably came from the Hebrides, showing a sword and a hurley stick and bearing a rare Irish inscription. In the field opposite the church door is **St Buodán's high cross** depicting the miracle of the loaves and fishes.

▶ *Continue to the next junction, turn left and then right.*

Carrowmore High Crosses

The monastery founded by Chionais, St Patrick's brother-in-law, is now marked by two **high crosses**, a decorated slab and a boulder inscribed with a cross.

▶ *Return to the last junction; turn right; in Gleneely take R 238 S; after 3.5mi/4km turn left to Leckemy and take the minor road NE to Kinnagoe Bay.*

Kinnagoe Bay

The sandy beach is sheltered by steep headlands. A map *(at the road junction)* plots the sites of the Spanish Armada ships wrecked off the Irish coast; many military relics have been recovered from *La Duquesa St Anna* and *La Trinidad Valencia*, which foundered in the bay. *Clifftop footpath to Inishowen Head.*

▶ *Take the minor road S to Greencastle, turn left to Inishowen Head.*

Inishowen Head★

The headland (295ft/90m) above the tiny harbour next to the lighthouse on Dunagree Point commands a fine view east along the Antrim coast to the Giant's Causeway. *Clifftop footpath to Kinnagoe Bay.*

▶ *Take the coast road S past the golf course.*

Greencastle

The beach makes this a popular resort. North of the town, on the cliffs opposite Magilligan Point, commanding the narrow entrance to Lough Foyle. stand the overgrown ruins of a castle built in 1305 by Richard de Burgo, the Red Earl of Ulster, so-called because of his florid complexion. It was captured by Edward Bruce in 1316, fell into the possession of the O'Donnells in the 14C and was granted to Sir Arthur Chichester in 1608; the adjoining fort (1812) was used in the defence of Lough Foyle until the end of the 19C.

▶ *From Greencastle take R 241 S.*

Moville (Bun an Phobail)
Moville (pronounced with the accent on the second syllable), once a bustling port where emigrant ships set sail for the United States, is now a seaside resort. The granite mass of **St Pius' Roman Catholic Church** (1953) masks its handsome mahogany interior. The cliffs and beaches overlooking Lough Foyle have been incorporated into a landscaped coastal walk, **Moville Green**.

▶ *From Moville take R 241 S; after 2mi/3.2km turn right.*

In **Cooley** at the graveyard gate stands a **high cross** (10ft/3m) with a hole in its head through which people clasped hands to seal an undertaking. The graveyard contains a **mortuary house**, a tomb shrine known as the Skull House, a delightful little drystone structure thought to be associated with St Finian, the abbot of the monastery, founded by St Patrick, which survived until the 12C.

▶ *Continue S on R 241. In Muff turn right to Burnfoot; take the minor road to Spee-noge.*

Grianán of Aileach★★
The pre-Christian circular stone fort crowning the exposed hilltop ranks among the most spectacular of its kind in the country, though its present form is a late 19C reconstruction. It served as the seat of the O'Neill clan from the 5C–11C but even before then was sufficiently famous to have been included in Ptolemy's map of the world as a "royal residence". It was destroyed in 1101 by the King of Munster, Murtogh O'Brien, in retaliation for the destruction of his own royal seat at Kincora. A tunnel pierces the stone wall (13ft/4m thick) which contains small chambers and steps to the ramparts and encloses a circle (77ft/23m in diameter). From the ramparts there is an extensive **view**★★ *(east)* of Londonderry and the Sperrin Mountains, *(northeast)* of Lough Foyle, *(north)* of the Inishowen Peninsula, and *(west)* of Inch Island, Lough Swilly and Knockalla Mountain.

The circular shape of the stone fort is tellingly echoed at the foot of the hill in **St Aengus Church**, a magnificent modern building designed by Liam McCormick.

The Warrior Coirrgend
This fierce fighter had committed the terrible crime of murdering the son of the king. As punishment, he was ordered to carry the body and a burial stone to Grianán Mountain. The burden killed him and he died crying "Á, leac!" ("Alas, stone!") – the origin of the name of the site.

▶ *Return downhill to Burnfoot. Take R 238 N to Fahan.*

Fahan Cross-Slab
On the south side of the village in the old graveyard beside the Anglican church stands a 7C **cross-slab**, decorated with a cross formed of interlaced bands, one flanked by two figures. It marks the site of a monastery which was founded by St Mura in the 7C and survived until at least 1098.

▶ *Take R 238 N to Buncrana.*

THE BURREN★★

Covering much of County Clare, the austere limestone plateau of the Burren (Boireann - Place of Rock) is one of Ireland's strangest but most compelling landscapes. Six thousand years of human occupation have largely denuded the Burren of its trees, but in spring and early summer, the bleak scenery is coloured by extraordinary carpets of diverse flowers, with Mediterranean and Alpine species flourishing side by side. ▯ Cliffs of Moher, Liscannor, Co Clare. ◐ Open Apr-Oct. ☏ 065 708 1171 - www.shannon~dev.ie/touris.

▶ **Orient Yourself:** The Burren covers the northern part of Co Clare extending south from Ballyvaughan to Ennistimon and Corofin.
▧ **Don't Miss:** the Cliffs of Moher are a must!
▧ **Also See:** ARAN ISLANDS, ATHENRY, CONNEMARA, ENNIS, GALWAY.

A Bit of History

The Burren gently inclines south, its outer limits generally marked by steep escarpments. The classic karstic features of limestone pavements and underground drainage

Address Book

SIGHTSEEING

Aran Islands – From Doolin there is a ferry to the Aran Islands. ☏ 065 7074455 - www.doolinferries.com

For coin ranges, see the Legend on the cover flap.

WHERE TO EAT

◖**Linnane's bar** – *Opposite Burren Centre.* ☏ 065 7088157 - ◐ *Closed lunch Mon and Tue* - ▣ Perched on the rocks, above Galway Bay. Pews and pine tables and a menu that makes the most of local seafood; from chowder to mussels, crab cakes and fresh lobster.
◖**Vaughan's** – *Kilfenora* ☏ 065 708 8004 - *Closed 25 Dec* - ▣ Live music most nights and set dancing (Thu, Sun); menu ranges from sandwiches to beef and Guinness casserole.

ENTERTAINMENT / NIGHT-LIFE

Irish Traditional Music – **Doolin** has an international reputation both for the audience and for the quality of the musicianship. Other places for sessions in summer are Ballyvaughan, Kilfenora, Lisdoonvarna and Ennistimon.

SHOPPING

The **Burren Smokehouse** in Lisdoonvarna sells fish, cheese and other gourmet items. *Visitor Centre open 9am-5pm (6pm Jun-Sep; 4pm at weekends Jan-Mar)* - ☏ 065 7074432; *mail order service* - www.burrensmokehouse.ie.
National Knitting Centre and Crana Knits – *St Orans Road, Buncrana. Traditional hand-knits to suit all* ☏ 074 936 2355
Burren Perfumery *(see below).*

SPORTS AND LEISURE

Seaside Resorts – To the south at **Liscannor**, **Lahinch** (long sand beach with lifeguard) and **Milltown Malbay**; also to the north at **Fanore** *(S of Black Head)* and at **Finavarra** *(NE of Ballyvaughan).*
Burren Way – Walking trails between Ballyvaughan and Liscannor *(26mi/42km)* in the Caher Valley, mostly on Green Roads, through Doolin and along the Cliffs of Moher before turning inland to Liscannor. Good walk from Lisdoonvarna south across the bog at Cnoc na Madre.

FESTIVALS

The **Willie Clancy Summer School** *(July)* Milltown Malbay: major festival for all music, song and dance, particularly of the elbow *(uilleann)* pipes. An annual summer school is held in **Ennistimon** to celebrate the work of Brian Merriman (b 1749 in Ennistimon), whose poem *The Midnight Court* is unique in Irish Literature.

systems are accompanied by sink holes, which, when filled by a rise in the water table, become temporary lakes known as *turlach*. Fissures (grykes) between the slabs (clints) forming the limestone pavements contain enough soil to support a remarkably rich flora. The human impact has been considerable; drystone walls define field patterns and enclosures of immense variety, some dating back to neolithic times, and there are a multitude of tombs, forts and traces of ancient settlements.

The old Celtic practice of booleying is practised in reverse: in winter, the cattle are kept on the higher ground, where it remains relatively dry partly due to the Gulf Stream, partly because the limestone absorbs heat and releases it later; then , in summer, when the uplands may suffer from drought, the animals are kept near the homesteads, where they can be tended and watered.

Driving Tour *Round trip of 80mi/128km*

Ennistimon (Inis Díomáin)

The **waterfalls** on the River Cullenagh are visible from the seven-arch bridge, the river bank *(through arched entry in the Main Street)* and from the grounds of the Falls Hotel. The town itself is noted for its traditional shop fronts with Irish writing.

▶ *Take N 67 and R 481 N.*

Kilfenora

Kilfenora was once an important episcopal see. Its cathedral, now in partial ruin, has superb carved capitals, crude effigies, and an elegant east window. Outside stand three 12C **high crosses**★. The famous Doorty's Cross, despite its eroded condition, is carved with figures of Christ, a bishop, and Celtic decoration. A fourth cross *(100yd/90m W in a field)* shows the Crucifixion.

Brides for Bachelors

Lisdoonvarna is the scene in September of a famous – or notorious – Matchmaking Festival, whose original function was to provide partners for lonely lads living on isolated farms deep in the countryside. For several days the little spa town is filled with hordes of merrymakers, less intent nowadays on the serious business of finding a bride than of having a raucously good time. The Match-making Festival takes place from late August to early October with dancing, singsongs, evening pub sessions and walks.

The Burren Centre★

♿⏱ *Open Jun-Sep, 9.30am-6pm; Mar-May and Oct, 10am-5pm.* ◎ €6. ✗ P ☎ *065 708 8030 - www.theburrencentre.ie*
Excellent displays provide a clear insight into the unique natural history of the Burren, and the human impact on it.

▶ *Take R 476 NW.*

Lisdoonvarna (Lios Dúin Bhearna)

Ireland's only operating spa developed in the 19C round three mineral springs; naturally sulphurous water is served by the glass or the bottle at the Spa Wells; the health centre provides sulphur baths and other treatments.

▶ *Take N 67 N.*

Cliffs of Moher H Champollion/MICHELIN

Corkscrew Hill

There is a fine **view** of the terraced limestone landscape from Corkscrew Hill on the road between Ballyvaughan and Lisdoonvarna *(N 67)*.

Newtown Castle and Trail

🕐 *Open May to Sep, Mon-Fri, 10am-5.30pm.* 🅿 ☎ *065 707 7200 - www.burrenlawschool.org*

The stone spiral staircase of this fine 16C defensive tower house leads to a series of exhibits illustrating the recent restoration of the building and the importance of the region in medieval times as a centre for the study of law. A trail on the hillside behind the tower leads to a variety of natural and historic man-made features including an early lime kiln and a Victorian gazebo.

▶ *Take R 480 SE.*

Aillwee Cave★

&. ♨ *Guided tour (35min), 10am-6pm.* ☜ *€10.* ⌛ ✗ 🅿 ☎ *065 707 7036 - www. aillweecave.ie*

Fluctuating water levels make the underground Burren perilous. This cavern has a single tunnel (0.75mi/1km) with stalactites, stalagmites and a **waterfall**★ which is impressively floodlit from below. At the back of the Highway, the largest chamber, there is a vertical drop. The **visitor centre** explains the formation of the cave and its discovery in 1940 by a local herdsman, Jack McCann.

Poulnabrone Portal Tomb★

In a magnificently stony setting on the road between Aillwee and Leamaneh Castle *(R 480)* stands this **dolmen**, the most famous megalithic tomb in the Burren.

Leamaneh Castle

For permission to view ask at the modern house beside the castle (left).

Only the shell remains of a four-storey Elizabethan-style fortified house with mullioned windows which was built in the 17C by Conor O'Brien, killed in 1651 during the Cromwellian wars.

▶ *Return N on R 480 SE ; bear right into a minor road to Carran.*

Burren Perfumery

🕐 *Open 9am-7pm (5pm Oct to Apr).* ✗ 🅿 ☎ *065 708 9102 - www.burrenperfumery.com*

The astonishing diversity of Mediterranean and Alpine flowers in this seemingly inhospitable landscape are the inspiration for a range of perfumes and soaps made here by traditional methods of distilling and blending.

▶ *Turn right into N 67.*

Corcomroe Abbey★

The ruins of this Cistercian abbey founded around 1180 blend harmoniously with the limestone of the surrounding Burren. The monks dedicated their

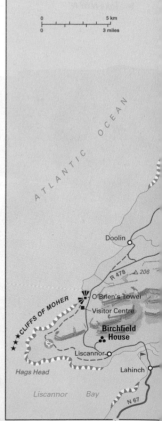

Botanising

The best months to view the 1000 or so species of flowering plants and ferns in the Burren are May or June but there is something to enjoy in every season. The rarer plants favour the more extreme habitats – the sunniest, shadiest, driest or wettest – look for cracks (grikes) shallow enough to admit light but deep enough to give shelter. Keep to naked limestone or grassy hill slopes, avoiding the cultivated farmland.

abbey to St Mary of the Fertile Rock, perhaps in response to abundance of flowers in the stony countryside. There are carved capitals and fine vaulting in the choir and transept chapels. It was here that William Butler Yeats set his verse play *The Dreaming of the Bones*. On Turlough Hill (925ft/282m) are the ruins of three 12C churches.

▶ *Take N 67 W to Ballyvaughan. Turn R 477 W.*

Scenic Route★★
The coast road south of Black Head provides a fine view of the huge boulders, deposited at the end of the Ice Age, resting on the bare limestone pavement; in fine weather the Aran Islands, of similar geological formation, are clearly visible offshore.

▶ *W of Lisdoonvarna take N 67 and R 478 S.*

Cliffs of Moher★★★

 ♿⏱ *Site: Open daily.* ⚭*Visitor Centre closed for major renovation.* ☎ *065 708 1171*
These great dark sandstone cliffs (600ft/182m high – nearly 5mi/8km long) are among the country's most stunning natural sights. Rising sheer from the Atlantic, they are inhabited by scores of sea birds. The best view is from **O'Brien's Tower**, built in 1853 by Cornelius O'Brien. The **Visitor Centre** provides information on the flora and fauna (birds) of the area.

Birchfield House

The ruins of the vast house, built by Cornelius O'Brien, local MP for over 20 years, are dominated by a tall column erected in his honour in 1853.

CAHER

POPULATION 2 236

In a fine location on the River Suir at the foot of the Galty Mountains, Caher (An Cathair) is a busy little crossroads town. The designated Heritage Town now benefits from a bypass carrying the main Dublin-Cork highway. Dominating the place is its formidable castle, built on a rocky islet in the river, in the 10C/11C the site of a residence of Brian Ború, High King of Ireland. The present stronghold was begun in the 13C, then greatly modified and extended by one of the greatest of Ireland's Anglo-Norman dynasties, the Butlers, who retained possession until it passed into State care in 1961. ⚑ *Castle Street, Caher.* ⏱ *Open Jul-Aug, Mon-Sat, 9.15am-6pm; May-Jun and Sep, Mon-Sat. 9.30am-5pm.* ☎ *052 41453*

▷ **Orient Yourself:** Caher, or Cahir and pronounced Care, marks the junction of N 8 and N 24, S of Cashel and NW of Clonmel
☺ **Don't Miss:** Caher (Cahir) Castle
♨ **Also See:** CASHEL, CLONMEL, LISMORE

Walking Tour

Caher Castle★★

(Dúchas) ♿⏱ *Open mid-Jun to mid-Sep, daily, 9am-7pm; mid-Mar to mid-Jun and mid-Sep to mid-Mar, daily, 9.30am-5.30pm (4.30pm mid-Oct to mid-Mar); last admission 45min before closing.* ⏱ *Closed 24-30 Dec.* ⚭ *€2.90.* ☎ *052 41011*
Though much restored, the castle is one of the largest and finest examples of a late medieval stronghold, with high outer walls embracing outer, middle and inner wards, a barbican, sturdy towers and a splendid keep. The whole ensemble expresses the power and pride of the Anglo-Norman Butlers, Earls of Ormond, who held sway over much of southeastern Ireland, though the castle's defences failed to save it from falling to an assault by troops led by Queen Elizabeth I's favourite, the Earl of Essex. More recently, the castle has featured in varous films - like Stanley Kubrick's *Barry Lyndon*. The guided tour explores its passageways, spiral staircases, sentry walks and great hall.

▷ *Walk along Castle Street to the Square.*

The **Cahir House Hotel**, formerly the family seat of the Butlers after the castle had fallen into disrepair, and the Market House (now the library) are part of the 18C transformation of the town centre by the Butlers; the mills also date from this period.

▷ *Walk along Old Church Street (N 24 to Clonmel).*

The ruined church, last used in the 1820s, had a curtain wall, which allowed Roman Catholics and Protestants to worship simultaneously; in the 19C, when Caher was an important garrison town, part of the adjoining cemetery was reserved for military burials. Many Caher men fell in the First World War; they are commemmorated by the Great War Memorial, a rarity in an Irish town.

▶ *Return to the Square and turn right into Church Street (N 8 north towards Cushel).*

The Anglican **St Paul's Church** was designed in 1820 by John Nash, the famous Regency architect .

Excursions

Swiss Cottage★
1mi/2km S of Caher by R 670 or on foot along the riverbank. (Dúchas) ◔◔ *Guided tour (40min) mid-Apr to mid Oct, 10am-6pm; last admission 5.45pm.* ◔ *€2.90. No photography.* ☎ *052 41144*
While in Caher, John Nash turned his hand to the design of this wonderfully light-hearted example of a *cottage orné*. The deliciously elaborate two-storeyed thatched cottage was built in 1812-14 as a fishing and hunting lodge for Lord Caher. In one of the two ground-floor rooms, the hand-painted French wallpaper shows views of the Bosporus.

Burncourt House
8mi/13km W by N 8; in Boolakennedy turn left. Access through farmyard and field.
The ruined house, with its 26 gables and many chimneys, was built in 1640. A mere ten years later the wife of its owner, Sir Richard Everard, set it on fire rather than let it fall intact into the hands of the hated Cromwellian army.

Mitchelstown Cave
9mi/14.5km W by N 8; in Boolakennedy turn left. ◔ *Open 10am-6pm.* ◔ *€5.* ▣☎ *052 67246*
A flight of 88 steep steps leads into three massive caverns (1mi/2km) containing dripstone formations – stalactites and stalagmites, curtains and pipes: the most impressive being the Tower of Babel, a huge calcite column, in the Kingston Gallery (250ft/76m long).

Swiss Cottage, Caher

CARRICK-ON-SHANNON★

POPULATION 1 868

On the main road and railway between Dublin and Sligo, the county town of Co Leitrim – (Cora Droma Rúisc) – is a major crossing point on the River Shannon. In recent years its status as a busy centre for boating and cruising has been boosted by the reopening of the Ballyconnell-Ballinamore Canal, completing the **Shannon-Erne Waterway.** 🅸 *The Old Barrel Store, The Marina.* 🕐 *Open Jul-Aug, daily; Apr-May and Sep, Mon-Sat.* ☎ *071 9620170 - www.irelandnorthwest.travel.ie*

▶ **Orient Yourself:** Carrick-on-Shannon lies on N 4, the Dublin to Sligo road, on the east bank of the River Shannon, close to Lough Allen and Lough Key.
👍 **Also See:** BOYLE, CAVAN, KNOCK, LONGFORD, STROKESTOWN.

Visit

The most remarkable thing about the **Costello Chapel** on Bridge Street is its size. The mortuary chapel built by Edward Costello as a memorial to his wife who died young (1877), a mere 16ft/5m x 12ft/4m. 🕐 *Open Mar-Oct, daily.* ☎ *078 20251*

At the east end of **St George's Terrace** stands the Town Clock (1905). The **Market House** and yard *(south side)* were built in 1839 by the local landlord, CM St George, whose elegant house, **Hatley Manor** *(north side)*, was built in the 1830s and named after his ancestral home in Cambridgeshire. Next to it stands the Courthouse of 1821, once linked by underground passage to the neighbouring County Gaol, the site of which is now occupied by a modern **marina**.

Cruising on the River Shannon

Driving Tour

Shannon Valley *Drive of 25mi/40km.*

▶ *From Carrick-on-Shannon take N 4 southeast.*

Shannon–Erne Waterway

This canal was built (1847–58) as the **Ballinamore–Ballyconnell Navigation** by the engineer John McMahon to join the River Shannon with Lough Erne: the final link in a waterway system devised to enable barges to travel between Dublin, Belfast, Limerick and Waterford. Competition from the railway and a lack of industry meant that the scheme failed and the canal was abandoned in 1869. By 1880 it was derelict. The course (40mi/65km) includes 16 locks and 34 stone bridges as it runs through Lough Scur, St John's Lough, Garadice Lough, and along Woodford River. It joins the River Shannon in **Leitrim** *(4mi/8km north of Carrick by R 280)*.

SIGHTSEEING

Moon River, Main St, Carrickon Shannon – Short (1hr) cruises on the Shannon. Weekdays at 3.15pm and 4.30pm; weekends at 2pm, 3.15pm, 4.30pm.⊗ €12. ☎ 071 9621777 - www.moon-river.net

Cavan and Leitrim Railway, Dromod – 🈺 Narrow gauge steam railway and tour of engine and work sheds – ⏱ Open Sat-Mon, 10am (1pm Sun) to 5.30pm. ⊗ €8. Train ride (20min). 🚃 ☎ 071 9638599 - www.irish-railway.com

Leitrim Way – Map guide published by Leitrim County Council. Low lying sections between Lough Allen and Carrick , linking up with the Cavan Way promoted by Inland Waterways Association of Ireland www.iwai.ie

Jamestown

The fortified settlement established in 1622 to guard the river crossing downstream from Carrick is named after James I. The stone arch through which the road enters from the north is all that is left of the **defensive wall** .

Drumsna

It was here that **Anthony Trollope** was inspired by the ruins of the Jones family mansion and the history of their downfall to write his first novel.

John McGahern

The author of *Amongst Women*, which won the Booker prize in 1991, was brought up in Cootehall, went to school in Carrick-on-Shannon and now lives near Mohill. He is a master at describing provincial life and examining the effect of people's interest in or indifference to their neighbours' lives.

▶ *South of Drumsna turn left onto R 201 to Mohill.*

At the centre of **Mohill** there is a statue of **Turlough O'Carolan (Carolan)** *(see BOYLE)* seated at his harp, having lived in the village for several years.

▶ *Leave Mohill by R 201 which bears right at the end of the main street; at the fork bear right onto L 112; at the next fork bear right; after 0.75mi/1.2km turn left onto a narrow road (sign).*

Lough Rynn Castle Hotel★

☎ 071 9632710 - www.loughrynn.ie

This extensive domain was acquired by the **Clements** family in 1750 but its picturesque estate buildings and lavish landscaping date largely from Victorian times to fit with the privileged lifestyle of the Clements, ennobled as the Earls of Leitrim. There are lakes, walled gardens ascending in a series of terraces and an arboretum planted with exotic species including a monkey puzzle said to be the oldest in Ireland.

▶ *On leaving the demesne turn right. At the T-junction turn right; after two side turnings and two crossroads bear right to Dromod.*

Dromod and **Roosky** are attractive Shannonside villages popular for cruising.

▶ *From Roosky continue south on N 4; after 3mi/4.8km turn left (sign) to Cloonmorris Abbey (1mi/1.6km).*

Beside the entrance to the graveyard of the ruined 12C **Cloonmorris church** stands an **Ogham stone** bearing the name Qenuven.

▶ *Return to N 4 and continue south; in Newtown Forbes bear right onto a minor road (direction Killashee); turn right onto N 4 and then bear left to Cloondara. Rejoin N 5 west of the village and continue to Termonbarry.*

CASHEL★★★

POPULATION 2 346

Rising like a mirage over the vastness of the Tipperary plain, the Rock of Cashel (Caiseal) is Ireland's Acropolis, its ruined buildings wonderfully evocative of the spirit of Celtic Christianity and Irish kingship. From the limestone outcrop (200ft/60m) rises a cluster of structures – castle and fortress, chapel, cathedral and round tower – forming the country's greatest landmark. At close quarters, the Rock reveals a wealth of pattern and texture, the primordial geometry of triangular gable, high-pitched roof, cubes, cones and cylindrical tower set off by battlements, blind arcades, slender window openings, and ornate carving.

City Hall, Main Street, Cashel. *Open Jul-Aug, daily; Apr-Jun and Sep, Mon-Sat.* *062 61333*

- ▶ **Orient Yourself:** Cashel, a designated Heritage Town, stands on the main road (N 8) between Cork and Portlaoise
- **P** **Parking:** Public car park beside the rock
- **Don't Miss:** Cormac's Chapel, and an excursion to Holy Cross Abbey
- **Also See:** ABBEYLEIX, CAHER, CLONMEL, KILKENNY, ROSCREA

A Bit of History

Royal Seat – Between c 370 and 1101, the rock was the seat of the kings of Munster, and therefore the provincial capital, comparable in regal stature to Tara, home of the High Kings of Ireland. St Patrick visited Cashel in 450 when he baptised King Aengus; there is a legend that during the ceremony, St Patrick accidentally pierced the king's foot with the point of his staff but the king, believing it to be part of the ritual, remained composed. Cashel was a place of great importance during the 10C when it was the stronghold of the holy Cormac MacCullinan, king and bishop.

Ecclesiastical Site – In 1101 the site was given to the ecclesiastical authorities whose first building, Cormac's chapel, was consecrated in 1134. The first cathedral

Rock of Cashel

was founded in 1169. Three years later it was at Cashel that the country's clergy assembled to honour the claim of Henry II to rule all Ireland.

In 1494 the cathedral was burned down by Gerald Mor, the Great Earl of Kildare. A greater act of desecration came in 1647, when Lord Inchiquin, seeking the presidency of Munster under the Cromwellian regime, attacked the town of Cashel; hundreds fled to the rock, so Lord Inchiquin ordered turf to be piled against the walls of the cathedral; in the subsequent fire, many were roasted to death. By the end of that terrible day, most of the population of 3 000 had perished.

In 1749 the Anglican Archbishop of Cashel, tiring of the climb from his palace to the cathedral, decided to move the cathedral into town. The great storm of 1847 did much damage to the abandoned building.

Visit

Rock of Cashel★★★

(Dúchas) ♿ ⏰ *Open, 9am-7pm (5.30pm mid-Mar to mid-Jun; 4.30pm mid-Sep to mid-Mar); last admission 45min before closing.* ⏰ *Closed 25-26 Dec.* ☞ *€5.30.* ☎ *062 61437 - www.heritageireland.ie*

Cormac's Chapel★★
Cashel's greatest treasure is the chapel started by Cormac MacCarthy in 1127 and consecrated in 1134. It is a highly ornate Romanesque building with twin towers, decorated with some of the earliest frescoes in Ireland and array of carvings, the most elaborate of their date. The human heads and animals are Celtic in style, while the interlace carving on a sarcophagus is of Viking inspiration. A centaur aiming his bow at a lion graces the tympanum of the north door.

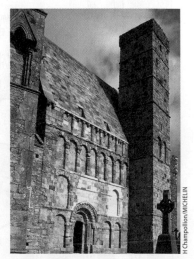

Cormac's Chapel

H Champollion/MICHELIN

161

Round Tower★

In perfect condition, the round tower is built from irregularly coursed sandstone (92ft/28m high). The round-headed doorway (12ft/3.5m above ground-level) has an architrave and the four top-storey windows are pointed.

Cathedral

Most of the ruin dates from the 13C, the central tower from the 14C. The transepts have two east chapels each. In the south wall of the choir is the tomb (1) of Archbishop Miler MacGrath, the Scoundrel of Cashel, who changed his religious beliefs several times and served as both Anglican and Roman Catholic bishop of Cashel during the reign of Elizabeth I; he died in 1621 at the age of 100. The west tower (91ft/28m), also called the **castle**, was built as a fortified residence by Archbishop O'Hedigan in 1450.

Museum★

The museum in the undercroft of the 15C Hall of the Vicars Choral, displays articles associated with the Rock – the stone cross of St Patrick (12C) , an evil eye stone and replicas of the 9C Cashel bell and brooch (originals in the Hunt Museum in Limerick).

Hall of the Vicars Choral

The building (extensively renovated in the 1970s) was the clergy residence. The main hall *(upstairs)* contains a huge 17C stone fireplace and fine items of medieval-style furniture made by modern craftsmen. The kitchen has been restored to its original state: butter churns and three-legged stools. A video presentation in the Dormitory sets Cashel in the context of Irish history.

ROCK OF CASHEL

12 C   13 C   15 C

Brú Ború

 ♿⏱ *Open May-Sep, 9am-5pm. Genealogy service. Folk Theatre (music, song, dance): mid-Jun to mid-Sep, Tue-Sat at 9pm.* ⚄ *Theatre show €18; theatre show and dinner €48.* ☎ *062 61122- www.comhaltas.com*

A modern village green is a fitting focal point for this cultural centre, which presents performances of native Irish music, song and dance, story-telling and folk theatre. The subterranean exhibition is entitled Sounds of History.

Walking Tour

▸ *From the Rock take Bishop's Walk down through Cashel Palace Hotel Gardens into Main St.*

Cashel Palace Hotel Gardens★

□ ☎ *062 7027- www.cashel-palace.ie*

The gardens contain a 1702 mulberry tree and hop plants, descendants of those used in 1759 to brew the first Guinness dark beer, invented by Richard Guinis, agent to the Archbishop of Cashel, and first brewed in Dublin by his son Arthur.

The Palladian mansion, now a luxury hotel, was built in 1730 as the archbishop's palace, designed by Edward Lovett Pearce for Archbishop Theophilus Bolton.

Cashel Heritage Centre

⏱ *Open Mar-Oct, 9.30am-5.30pm (Mon-Fri, Nov-Feb).* ☎ *062 62511 - www.heritagetowns.com*

The display traces the history of Cashel, its royal heirlooms and charters, and relics of the house of McCarthy Mor.

▸ *From Main St walk up John St.*

Cathedral and Library

The austere Anglican cathedral dedicated jointly to St John and to St Patrick of the Rock (1749- 84), has a fine panelled ceiling and stalls for Dean and Chapte. In the graveyard a number of 13C carved stone coffin lids have been placed against the walls, which are part of 14C town defences.

Bolton Library★ built in 1836 contains some 12 000 books. Among its treasures is a monk's encyclopedia (1168), two leaves from Chaucer's *The Book of Fame* printed by William Caxton at Westminster in London in 1483, a note signed by Jonathan Swift and a collection of ecclesiastical silver. ⏱ *Open Mon-Wed, 9.30am-5.30pm (circumstances permitting).* □☎ *062 61944 - www.heritagetowns.com.*

▸ *Walk through to Friar St.*

Parish Church

The Roman Catholic church of St John the Baptist, the oldest RC church in use in Ireland, was opened in 1795, screened by a row of cottages. The mosaics on the façade were added to commemorate the Eucharistic Congress in Ireland (1932). The interior is unusual in that two galleries run the full length of the building and the ceiling resembles the upturned hull of a ship.

▸ *Walk down to the end of Friar St; turn left into Main St and right into Dominic St.*

Folk Village

♿⏱ *Open Easter to mid-Oct, 10am-6pm.* ⚄ *€3.50.* □☎ *062 62525*

The folk village is a small reconstruction of 18C Irish rural life.

Dominican Friary

The friary was founded by Archbishop David MacKelly *(Dáibhí Mac Ceallaigh)*, a Cork Dominican, in 1243 and suppressed in 1540. The church, which was rebuilt after a fire in 1480, has a long narrow nave and choir.

Excursions

Holy Cross Abbey★★

9mi/16km north of Cashel by R 660. Open 10am-6pm. Guided tour: Jun-Sep. ☎ 0504 43241 or 43124

For long a roofless ruin, Holy Cross is one of the finest examples of 15C church architecture in the country; now restored, it serves as a flourishing parish church. It was originally founded for the Benedictines by Donal O'Brien, King of Munster (1168). Fourteen years later it was transferred to the Cistercians and became a major place of pilgrimage, as it was reputed to contain a relic of the True Cross. After the Dissolution it passed to the Earls of Ormond, under whose benevolent dispensation the monks were able to continue in residence into the 17C. The popularity of the abbey as a centre of pilgrimage made it rich, allowing the 15C rebuilding to be completed to the highest standard. There are windows with stained glass, fine original stonework, and a rare **wall-painting** , showing hunters about to kill a stag beneath an oak tree. The **grounds** contain a replica of the Vatican gardens, including the Stations of the Cross and an altar, commemorating the Italian stigmatist Padre Pio.

The eight-arch **bridge** spanning the River Suir, a copy of the original, was constructed in 1626 by James Butler, Baron of Dunboyne, and his wife, Margaret O'Brien; it is ornamented with their arms and carries a short prayer: "May the two who built it escape the pit of hell".

Lár na Páirce

14mi/23km north of Cashel by R 660 to Thurles; Slievenamon Road.
Open Apr to Sep, Mon-Fri, 10am-5pm. €3. ☎ 0504 22702; www.tipperarygaa.ie

An elegant 19C building now houses a display on the history of the Gaelic Games. The GAA *(Gaelic Athletic Association)* was formed at a meeting on 1 November 1884 in Miss Hayes' Commercial Hotel in Liberty Square in Thurles, with two objectives: to revive Gaelic games and to boost support for the Irish language, traditional dancing, music and song.

Hore Abbey

0.5mi/0.8km west of Cashel by N 74.

The last Cistercian house to be founded in medieval Ireland, Hore Abbey was established by monks from Mellifont in 1272. Most of the present extensive ruins date from the late 13C. The church was built in cruciform shape, with a chancel, two eastern chapels to each transept and an aisled nave.

Athassel Priory★

5mi/8km west of Cashel by N 74 and minor road S from Golden; across two fields.

This was one of the most extensive and prosperous establishments of its kind in Ireland, surrounded by a town. The priory was destroyed in 1447 but parts of the main church survive. In the church is a tomb, believed to be that of the Norman, William de Burgh, the founder of the priory.

Tipperary

10m/16km west of Cashel by N 74.

This pleasant small county town, with enough old buildings and 19C shop-fronts to merit Heritage Town status, was a centre of Land League agitation and later the headquarters of the 3rd Tipperary Brigade of the IRA which fought many battles in the War of Independence. It owes much of its fame, however, to what was probably the most popular of all the marching songs of the First World War:

> *It's a long way to Tipperary, it's a long way to go*
> *It's a long way to Tipperary, to the sweetest girl I know*
> *Goodbye Piccadilly, Goodbye Leicester Square,*
> *It's a long, long way to Tipperary but my heart lies there.*

Glen of Aherlow★
2m/3.2km S of Tipperary by R 664.
This lovely vale runs for 16m/26km between the conifer forests of the Slievenamuck ridge and the Galty Mountains, Ireland's highest inland range. The glen was once occupied by the great Wood of Aherlow, now it is lush farmland. A great perspective is available from the **viewpoint**★★ above Newtown. A gleaming white statue of Christ the King looks to the Galtees, their splendid swooping ridgeline reaching its highest point (3018ft/919m) at the summit of Galtymore.

CAVAN

POPULATION 3 509

The little capital of Co Cavan –(An Cabhán) – lies in drumlin country – a tranquil, undulating, well-wooded landscape, scattered with countless small lakes. Nearby is Lough Oughter, the largest lake in Co Cavan, fed by the River Erne. ▯ *Johnston Central Library, Farnham Street, Cavan. Open Mon-Fri, 9.30am to 5pm. ☎ 049 433 1942 - www.cavan.tourism.com*

▶ **Orient Yourself:** Cavan is set at the junction of N 3 with N 54 and N 55, in the heart of angling country.

  Also See: CARRICK-ON-SHANNON, ENNISKILLEN, LONGFORD, MONAGHAN

Walking Tour

Points of reference include the Roman Catholic **Cathedral** (1942) designed by **Ralph Byrnes** and sculptures by **Albert Power** (1883-1945), variously described as "sham Renaissance" or "the last flamboyant fling of historicism" and the crenellated **Anglican Church** with west tower and steeple by John Bowden, who also designed the Classical **Courthouse**.

Literary Associations

Several famous penmen are connected with County Cavan: the playwright **Richard Brinsley Sheridan** was the grandson of Dr Thomas Sheridan, the headmaster of Cavan Royal School and a good friend of Jonathan Swift, who lived at Quilcagh House near Mullagh. An ancestor of **Edgar Allan Poe** (1809–49) emigrated to America from Killeshandra in the mid 18C. William James, a Presbyterian from Baillieborough who settled in America, was the grandfather of **Henry James** (1843–1916). The song-writer and painter **Percy French** (1854–1920), born at Cloonyquin (west of Strokestown), worked in Cavan for 7 years as an inspector of loans to tenants. He began penning lyrics while studying at Trinity College, Dublin.

Address Book

& _For coin ranges, see the Legend on the cover flap._

WHERE TO STAY

Rockwood House – _Cloverhill, Belturbet. N3 to Monaghan, turn right on N54 -_ ☎ _047 55351 - jbmac@eircom.net_ ▣ _4 rm._ Lovely B&B set among woods with a bright conservatory, attractive garden. Bedrooms simply, yet pleasantly furnished. Hospitable owners and good value.

Eonish Lodge Farm Guesthouse – _Killeshandra - 5 mi SW of Cavan on N 55 and 2.5mi W of Bellinagh by N 55 off Arva road._ ☎ _049 433 4487 - eonishlodge@ eircom.net_ ▣ Peaceful location, convenient for boating, lake fishing, horse riding, exploring Killykeen Forest Park and 8 local pubs!

WHERE TO EAT

The Olde Post Inn – _Cloverhill_ ☎ _047 55555 - info@theoldepostinn.com Tue-Sun dinner, Sun lunch._ Guesthouse and award winning restaurant (2006) for use of locally-sourced ingredients; vegetarian menu. Check for special deals on dinner/bed/breakfast.

SHOPPING

Cavan Crystal – _Dublin Rd._ & _Open Mon-Fri, 9.30am-6pm; Sat-Sun and Bank Hols, noon (10am Sat) to 5pm_ ☎ _049 433 1800 - www.cavancrystal.com_ ▣ The second-oldest lead-crystal glass factory in Ireland.

Carraig Craft Centre – _Cavan._ Museum/shop for hand-made baskets, mainly crafted from rushes gathered each summer from Lough Sheelin.

Bear Essentials – _Tiernawannagh, Bawnboy. Mon-Sat, 9.30am-6pm, Sun 11am-6pm_ ☎ _049 952 3461 - www. irishbears.com._ Makers of teddy bears - may be closed if exhibiting at a fair, so call before going.

SPORTS AND LEISURE

Lough Oughter, a collection of many small lakes interlinked by short slow moving rivers, provides sport for **boating** and **canoeists**.

Coarse fishing on the lake and along stretches of the Annalee, a tributary of the Erne, for roach, bream, hybrids, pike, perch; **trout fishing** on Lough Annagh for trout; **game angling** for salmon and trout.

Watersport facilities: swimming, canoeing, windsurfing and waterskiing.

EVENTS AND FESTIVALS

Belturbet Festival of the Erne – Coarse and trout angling festival, outdoor music, activities for all age groups incorporating the annual huzzar Lady of The Erne pageant _(late Jul to early Aug)_

TRACING ANCESTORS

Cavan Genealogy Research Centre – _Cana House, Farnham St._ ⌚ _Open Mon-Fri, 9.30am-4.30pm_ ☎ _049 436 1094 - gen@cavangenealogy.com - www. cavangenealogy.com_

Excursions

Ballyjamesduff
10mi/16km S of Cavan by N 3, N 55 and a minor road via Cross Keys.
The town, named after Sir James Duff, the commander of British troops in the 1798 uprising, clusters around the Market House (1813). During the 18C, it became a lively place on the main coach road between Cavan and Kells with a weekly market, nine fairs a year and a reputation for selling black cattle.

Cavan County Museum
& ⌚ _Open Tue-Sat, 10am-5pm; also Jun-Oct, Sun, 2-6pm._ €3. ▣ ☎ _049 85 44070 - www.cavanmuseum.ie_
Archaeological artefacts trace the heritage of County Cavan, including a rare three-faced pre-Christian Corleck Head and Stone Age dug-out; other galleries for 1950s rural life; art; famine; costume; sport.

Carraig Craft Centre and Basketry Museum

15mi/24km S of Cavan by N 3, N 55 and R 154 to Mount Nugent. ⏰*Open Apr-Oct, Mon-Fri, 10am-6pm; Sun, 2-6pm; Nov-Mar, by appointment.* ⌖ €3.50. ⌣ P ☎ *049 8540179*

The great art of basket-making, old and new, is celebrated with donkey creels, pigeon panniers; bee skeps; straw, reed and willow containers for eggs, turf, potatoes, fish, poultry, flowers and more.

Basketry

In days of yore, a willow tree – there are 260 sorts of willow – grew outside each house, especially in Donegal, Mayo and Galway, for basket-making. The trees were coppiced to produce long straight shoots or withies. Withies with bark are dark, stripped ones are white; boiled and stripped withies have a red tinge. Different traditional designs come from different regions.

Kilmore Cathedral

2mi/3.2km W of Cavan by R 198. ⏰ *By appointment, see Tourist Information.*
The neo-Gothic Anglican cathedral known as the Bedell Memorial Church is dedicated to **St Felim** *(Fethlimidh)*, who brought Christianity to the region in the 6C. The fine 12C Romanesque north doorway may have belonged to an earlier church or to the abbey on Trinity Island in Lough Oughter.

Killykeen Forest Park★

5mi/8km W of Cavan by R 198.
The Forest Park (600 acres/243ha) replicates the patchwork of land and water so characteristic of the River Erne in counties Cavan and Fermanagh. Marked nature trails thread through the park, and there is a wildfowl sanctuary by the Sally Lake.

On Trinity Island at the southern end of **Lough Oughter** stands the ruin of a Premonstratensian Priory, established in 1250 by monks from Lough Key.

William Bedell (1571–1642)

William Bedell was born in Sussex, studied at Cambridge and travelled widely in Europe, before being appointed Provost of Trinity College in Dublin in 1627. In 1629 he became Bishop of Kilmore and tried to introduce reforms. During the 1641 Rebellion he was imprisoned for two years by the Confederates in Clogh Oughter Castle.

CLONMACNOISE★★★

POPULATION 1 695

Founded in 545 by St Kieran (Ciarán), Clonmacnoise (Cluain Mhic Nóis) was once a pre-eminent monastic site, second only to Armagh, where the Kings of Connaught and Tara are interred. With its churches, cathedral, high crosses, ancient grave slabs and round towers, it draws thousands of visitors, tourists and pilgrims, notably on 9 September (St Kieran's Day). 🛈 *via Shannonbridge, Athlone. Open Mar-Oct, daily.* ☎ *090 9674134 - www.eastcoastmidlands.ie*

▶ **Orient Yourself:** Clonmacnoise is situated on the east bank of the River Shannon 13mi/21km S of Athlone by N 6 and N 62 or 13mi/20km from Ballinasloe along R357.

⏰ **Organizing Your Time:** Allow 1-2 hours for your visit

⌖ **Also See:** ATHENRY, ATHLONE, BIRR, PORTUMNA, TULLAMORE.

A Bit of History

The monastery's position beside the Shannon now seems remote but in earlier centuries transport was easier by water than over land. The old Pilgrims' Road approached from the north along the esker (or ridge). As its reputation grew the settlement expanded from an original wooden oratory to a cluster of stone churches, numerous monks' dwellings and a round tower within an earth or stone enclosure. None of the surviving ruins predate the 9C, having been successively plundered by the Irish, Vikings and Anglo-Normans, until it was finally reduced to ruin in 1552 by the English garrison from Athlone. A castle built by the Normans in 1212 on the river was slighted in the Cromwellian period.

> ## St Kieran
>
> St Kieran was born at Roscommon, trained by St Finnian at Clonard before going to Inishmore, among the Aran Islands. His vision of a great tree growing in the heart of Ireland was interpreted by his tutor St Enda as a church growing on the banks of the Shannon. After a stay on Hare Island in Lough Ree, St Kieran and seven companions settled at Clonmacnoise, the field of the sons of Nos. He died months later of the plague, aged 33.

Walking Tour

Visitor Centre

(Dúchas) &. ⊙ *Open mid-May to early Sep, daily, 9am-7pm; mid-Mar to mid-May and mid-Sep to mid-Mar, 10am-6pm (5.30pm Nov to mid-Mar); last admission 45min before closing.* ⊙ *Closed 25 Dec.* ⊛ *€5.30.* ✗ ▣ ☎ *090 96 74195; www.heritageireland.ie*
The **Visitor Centre** displays the original **high crosses** and a collection of **grave slabs**★ (those on site are replicas), confirming Cloncmanoise's status as an important stone-carving centre from the 8C to 12C.

Monuments

The most important monuments include the early 9C **South Cross** (12ft/3.6m) with a carving of the Crucifixion, decorative spirals and interlacing recall designs on crosses at Kells, on Iona and Kildalton in Scotland. **Temple Doolin** is the pre-12C

Clonmacnoise

H Champollion/MICHELIN

Temple Finghin

Mass Shelter

Temple Connor

CEMETERY

Nun's Church

North Cross Shaft

Temple Kelly

Temple Kieran

Round Tower

CATHEDRAL

Temple Meaghlin

Cross of
the Scriptures

Temple Horpan

South Cross

Temple Doolin

Visitor Centre

CLONMACNOISE

0   30 m
0   50   100 feet

church named after Edward Dowling when he restored it (1689) as a mausoleum; **Temple Meaghlin or Temple Rí** has special windows that echo those at Clonfert and O'Heyne's Church at Kilmacduagh. **Temple Kieran** is the tiny church said to contain the grave of St Kieran. The **North Cross Shaft** (c 800) is decorated with lions biting their tail and a cross-legged figure thought by some to be the Celtic god Cernunnos. The sandstone **Cross of the Scriptures**★, related to the crosses at Monasterboice, was erected in the 10C possibly by King Flann (d 916); unusually, its arms protrude upwards from the circle - note scenes of the Crucifixion, the Last Judgement, the Passion (soldiers resting on their spears), and one showing Abbot Colman and King Flann founding the monastery.

Cathedral

The simple rectangular building has been modified many times. The oldest parts may date from the 10C when the original wooden church was replaced with a stone structure. The Romanesque west doorway dates from the 12C; the sacristy may be 13C. The elaborate north doorway with three plaques depicting St Dominic, St Patrick and St Francis, was added by Dean Odo in the 15C at the same time that the chancel was divided into three vaulted chapels.

Round Tower

This is a typical round tower despite having lost its conical cap, possibly built in the 10C by Fergal O'Rourke and repaired in 1120 by Abbot O'Malone. The arched doorway is most likely 12C.

Temple Connor

The Anglican church may date from 1010 when it was endowed by Cathal O'Connor.

Temple Finghin and Nun's Church

The 12C church, modified in the 17C, comprises a nave and chancel. Unusual features include the south door and mini round tower incorporated into the chancel.

▶ *From the centre of the enclosure follow the old path E across the extended graveyard and along the road.*

The ruined Nun's Church with nave and chancel was completed according to the Annals of the Four Masters in 1167 by Dervorgilla. The west doorway and chancel arch have striking Irish Romanesque style decoration.

Excursion

Clonfinlough Stone

2mi/3km E by the minor road and 0.5mi/0.8km S by the minor road; park by the church; 10min there and back on foot up the path and over the stile.
A large boulder bearing symbols similar to the Bronze Age rock art of Galicia in Spain are suggestive of human figures. To the south there is a **view** of the Brosna and Shannon.

CLONMEL ★

POPULATION 15 215

The principal town of Co Tipperary – (Cluain Meala) – stands in a lovely fertile valley. To the south rise the Comeragh Mountains in Co Waterford: a fine backdrop to the many historic buildings of the town which recall its great period of prosperity in the 18C and 19C. ⚑ *St Mary's Church ☎052 22960 - www.clonmel.ie;* ⚑ *Heritage Centre, Carrick-on-Suir ☎ 051 640 200;* ⚑ *Tierry Centre, Fethard ☎ 052 31000*

▶ **Orient Yourself:** Clonmel lies on N 24 between Waterford and Limerick, on the boundary between Co Tipperary and Co Waterford
☺ **Don't Miss:** the scenic drive through the Nier Valley
Kids Especially for Kids: Fethard Folk Farm and Museum
☺ **Also See:** CAHER, CASHEL, KILKENNY, YOUGHAL

A Bit of History

The town is said to pre-date the Vikings. The name comes from the Irish words for "a meadow of honey" - an Early Christian reference to the great fertility of the Suir valley. Viking longships sailed up the River Suir from Waterford and, according to tradition, fought at Clonmel in 916 or 917 against the local O'Neill clan. Edward I granted the town a charter and the **walls** were built in the early 14C. Later, it became an important stronghold of the Butler family, the Earls of Ormond. In the 17C, the garrison put up more resistance to Cromwell than any other Irish town.
Four English novelists had close links with Clonmel: **Anthony Trollope** wrote his first two novels here (1844-48); **George Borrow** who attended a local school refers to Clonmel in *Lavengro*; **Marguerite Power**, the Countess of Blessington, a noted early-19C literary figure, was born at Suir Island in 1789; **Laurence Sterne** (1713–68), author of *Tristram Shandy*, was born in Mary Street and his family lived at Suir Island.

Visit

Town Landmarks

The Anglican **St Mary's Church**★, with its unusual octagonal tower, was built in the 19C incorporating parts of earlier 14C buildings: it now accommodates an information centre. Prosperous Clonmel's mock-Tudor gateway (1831) was built on the site of the medieval **Westgate** separating the Anglo-Norman borough from its suburb, Irishtown. Cromwell's troops destroyed Clonmel's original courthouse during the 1650 siege. Its 1674 three-storeyed replacement, **Main Guard** with the town's coat of arms, is one of Ireland's earliest public classical buildings, inspired by the architecture of Sir Christopher Wren.

Riverside

The 17C **Old Bridge** links Little Island, Suir Island and Stretches Island (named after 16C Italian immigrants called Stroccio).The north bank between the Old Bridge and the 18C **Gashouse Bridge** forms the town **quay**, where ships used to unload their cargoes. Note the memorial to the Manchester Martyrs, the elegant **Georgian** terraces of houses and tall warehouses.

Museums

The **Tipperary County Museum**★ displays artefacts from the Stone Age to the 20C: rare early coins confirm links with the Roman Empire; fascinating documents relating to a famous trial of rebels (1848) and to the Royal Irish Regiment, based here until its demise in 1922 after the signing of the Anglo-Irish Treaty. There is also a good selection of paintings by Irish artists. ⓒ *Open Tue-Sat, 10am-5pm.* ⓒ *Closed Bank Hols.* ☎ *052 34550*

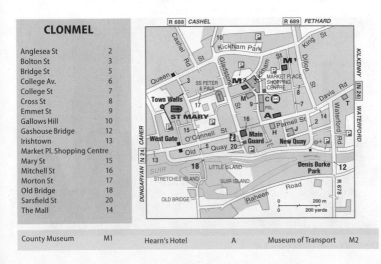

CLONMEL	
Anglesea St	2
Bolton St	3
Bridge St	5
College Av.	6
College St	7
Cross St	8
Emmet St	9
Gallows Hill	10
Gashouse Bridge	12
Irishtown	13
Market Pl. Shopping Centre	
Mary St	15
Mitchell St	16
Morton St	17
Old Bridge	18
Sarsfield St	20
The Mall	14

County Museum	M1	Hearn's Hotel	A	Museum of Transport	M2

Bianconi Cars

Charles Bianconi (1786–1875), son of an Italian immigrant from Lombardy and twice Mayor of Clonmel, began a horse-drawn car service in 1815 linking Clonmel to Limerick and Thurles. After the battle of Waterloo, thr price of horses fell to £10; by 1844 he had over 100 in his stables. In 1851 his open long cars, known as Bians, operated in 22 counties with central depots in Clonmel, Galway and Sligo. At its peak the service employed 1 400 horses and 100 vehicles painted crimson and yellow, ceating a nation-wide revolution in the carrying of mail, freight and passengers that was only superseded by the advent of railways in the late 19C.

One of the old mail cars ran between Clonmel and Dungarvan well into the 1920s, long after Bianconi retired in 1865. A mail coach horn and the clock (now handless) by which the departures were timed are preserved in the foyer of Hearn's Hotel.

Two floors of a stately six-storey mill house the **Museum of Transport** and its collection of motoring memorabilia; vintage, veteran and classic cars. *Manned by volunteers so telephone first.* ⊛ €4. ☎ 052 29727

Excursions

Nier Valley Scenic Route★★ *Round tour of 40mi/64km.*

▶ *From Clonmel take R 678 S. After 5mi/8km turn right; after 4mi/6km make a detour left to a viewpoint. In Ballymacarbry turn right onto R 671 to return to Clonmel.*

The road goes through the dark green forests, moorland and imposing escarpments of the **Comeragh Mountains** which culminate in Knockanaffrin at 2478ft/753m.

Carrick-on-Suir

3mi/21km E by N 24.
The bustling town enjoys a prime location on the tidal Suir between Slievenamon *(NW)* and the Comeragh foothills *(S)*. The 15C Old Bridge is the lowest river crossing before the estuary, built when the wool trade was at its height. The **Heritage Centre** traces local history. ♿🕐 *Open May-Aug, daily 10am-5pm; Sep-Apr, Mon-Fri, 10am-5pm.* 🅿 ☎ 051 640 200 - www.carrickonsuir.ie

Ormond Castle, Carrick-on-Suir

Duchas, Dublin

Ormond Castle★ consists of a partially ruined 15C castle with a most elegant Eliza-bethan mansion attached. The house was built around 1568 by the 10th **Earl of Ormond**, known as Black Tom, to receive his cousin Queen Elizabeth, who never in fact visited Ireland. Highlights include fine **ornamental plasterwork,** a long gallery hung with Elizabethan portraits, and a fascinating collection of charters tracing the rise in status of the Ormond family. *(Dúchas)* &. *Guided tour (40min) mid-Jun to early Sep, daily 9.30am-6.30pm (5.45pm last admission).* 🅿 ☎ *051 640 787*

Kilkeeran High Crosses
17mi/27km E by N 24 and R 697.
Three crosses, probably from the 9C, mark the site of an early monastery. The **West Cross** has eight horsemen and an unusual cap, like the plainer, possibly unfinished, East Cross. The Long Shaft Cross is the only one of its type in Ireland.

Ahenny High Crosses★
19mi/3a1km E by N 24 and R 697.
The decorative interlacing and spirals so characteristic of the Book of Kells are here repeated in stone, which may mean that the two crosses with their unusual caps may date from as early as the 8C. The figures on the base represent seven clergy carrying croziers, led by a clerical cross-bearer.

Fethard★
8mi/13km N by R 689.
Fethard, once an Anglo-Norman town of some importance, has late-14C **town walls** and a 15C **Castle** in one of three keeps. The **church** with a late-15C crenellated tower, has a huge roof-span; the east window is copied from Kilcooley Abbey.16C and 17C tombs lie among the ruins of the 12C Augustinian priory.
The **Fethard Folk Farm and Museum** is dedicated to the rural and domestic life of earlier centuries, including bicycles, washing machines and hearses! 🄺🄸🄳🅂 &. ⊘ *Open Sun and Bank Hol Mon, 11.30am-5pm.* ☜ €3 to €5. *Sunday car boot sale.* 🅿 ☕ ☎ *052 31516*

COBH★

POPULATION 6 468

Facing the sheltered water of Cork Harbour, Cobh (An Cóbh) has been an impor-tant naval base for generation. Expansion came in the late 18C, when Royal Navy ships assembled here for operations in the American War of Independence and later against France. A period as a health resort in the 19C left a fine legacy of Italianate buildings and neo-Gothic villas, which merit the title Heritage Town, sometimes known as Queenstown after Queen Victoria disembarked here in 1849 on her first visit to Ireland. 🄸 *Old Yacht Club, Cobh.* ☎ *021 4813 301 - www. cobhharbourchamber.ie*

▸ **Orient Yourself:** Cobh lies on the south side of Great Island, linked by road and rail to Fota Island and the mainland, where R 624 joins N 25.

⊙ **Don't Miss:** an excursion to Fota Island

🄺🄸🄳🅂 **Especially for Kids:** lots to do at Fota Wildlife Park.

🜂 **Also See:** CORK, KINSALE, MIDLETON, YOUGHAL

P Thebault/MICHELIN

Cobh Harbour and Cathedral

A Bit of History

The world's first yachting fraternity, the Water Club, was founded in Cobh (pronounced Cove) in 1720. Its successor, the Royal Cork Yacht Club, is now based at Crosshaven *(see CORK)*, but its old headquarters still stands, an elegant waterfront pavilion designed in 1854 by the architect Anthony Salvin. The Royal Navy continued to operate from here well after Independence (1922) until Cobh was handed back to the Free State with the other "Treaty Ports" (1938). Until the 1960s, large transatlantic cruise liners like the *Queen Mary* and the *Queen Elizabeth* would stop here: an era recorded in period photographs and paintings hanging in the bar of the Commodore Hotel.

Cobh witnessed the departure of Irish emigrants who left in their hundreds of thousands for North America or Australia in the late 19C and early 20C - commemorated in the statue of Annie Moore, the first emigrant to pass through the Ellis Island immigration reception centre in New York.

Visit

St Colman's Cathedral★

The neo-Gothic Catholic cathedral designed by Pugin and Ashlin (1868-1915) was clearly modelled on the French medieval cathedrals of Amiens, Chartre and Laon; the sculpture echoes Rheims. The tall **spire** houses a carillon of 47 bells. The interior is typically Victorian in style.

Lusitania Memorial★

The 1 500 lives lost when the *Lusitania* was torpedoed in 1915 are commemorated by an elaborate sculpture in Casement Square, designed by Jerome Connor (1876–1943) who was born in Cork; it was completed posthumously by Seamus Murphy.

Nearby in Pierce Square, a more modest memorial recalls the demise of the *Titanic* which docked at Cobh on 11 April 1912 before sailing on her fateful maiden voyage.

Museums

At the **Cobh Heritage Centre**, the exhibit **The Queenstown Story** explains how convicts were expelled to Australia and thousands emigrated to America; a separate

Address Book

GETTING AROUND

Cork Harbour Car Ferry across the River Lee between Carrigaloe *(east bank)* and Glenbrook *(west bank)* – Operates daily, 7am-12.15am. Capacity 28 cars. There and back ⮐ €3.50 (car), €1 (pedestrian). ☎ 021 481 1549

Cork Harbour Cruises – *Operate from Kennedy Pier (1hr – harbour forts, Spike Island, Naval base and major harbour industries) May to Sep, daily at noon, 2pm, 3pm, and 4pm; otherwise by appointment. €5.50.* ⓟ *(5-10min walk).* ☎ 021 481 1485 (Marine Transport Services Ltd).

Rail Service – *Operates between Cobh and Cork via Fota Island, daily.* ☎ 021 481 1655 (Cobh Railway Station); www.irishrail.ie

For coin ranges, see the Legend on the cover flap.

WHERE TO STAY / EAT

⮐ **Robin Hill House** – *Rushbrooke - 1 mi NE by R 624 -* ☎ 021 481 1395; www.robinhillhouse.com - Closed 25 to 27 Dec, 7 Jan to 7 Feb and Bank Hols ⓟ Converted 19C rectory with contemporary feel; work by local artists; seasonal menu.

---

display is dedicated to *RMS Titanic*. ♿ *Open daily, 10am-6pm (5pm Nov-Mar); last admission 1hr before closing.* ⮐ €6 ⌂ ☎ 021 481 3591 - www.cobhheritage.com
The **Cobh Museum** displays historical material relating to Cobh and the Great Island.
🕐 *Open Easter-Oct, Mon-Sat, 11am-1pm and 2-5.30pm; Sun, 2.30-5pm.* ⮐ €1.50. ☎ 021 481 4240 - www.cobhmuseum.com.

Excursion

Fota Island★★

4mi/6km N by R 624.
Until 1975, the 780 acre/316ha island in Cork Harbour belonged to the descendants of its 12C Anglo-Norman Lord Philip de Barri. In the early 19C the family's hunting lodge was converted by John Smith Barry into a fine neo-Classical gentleman's residence to plans by the leading architects Richard and William Vitruvius Morrison; other additions included sea defences, walls, lodges, workers' cottages and outbuildings, a landscaped parkland and a famous arboretum. Much of the island is now given over to one of the country's finest wildlife parks, and the house has been saved from near-dereliction.

Fota House and Gardens★★

♿🕐 *Open Apr-Sep, Mon-Sat, 10am to 5pm and 11am-5pm Sun and Bank Hols; Oct-Mar, daily 11am-4pm.* 🕐 *Closed at Christmas.* ⮐ €5.50. ☎ 021 481 5543 - www.fotahouse.com
Inside the Regency mansion are a series of exquisite interiors set off by fine furniture. The Morrisons' masterly manipulation of space is particularly evident in the entrance hall, while below stairs, the servery, kitchen and scullery are models of their kind. A short distance from the house is a delightful little **orangery**, and a walled garden.
The great **arboretum**★ was laid out by John Barry Smith, a prominent plant collector, and sustained by his successors into the 20C. Brown earth soils and mild climate favour rare species from North America, Chile, Australasia, Japan and China.

Wildlife Park★

🧒♿🕐 *Open daily, 10am (11am Sun) to 5pm.* ⮐ €11.50. ✗ⓟ☎ 021 481 2678 - www.fotawildlife.ie

The park (70 acres/28ha) was established by the Zoological Society of Ireland in 1983 to breed endangered species like cheetah, Oryx, Macaque. Zebra, antelope and kangaroo roam freely while giraffe, monkeys, flamingoes, pelicans, penguins and other waterfowl thrive in designated areas. A "train" ferries visitors around the grounds.

CONG

POPULATION 197

Once the seat of the kings of Connaught, attractive little Cong (Conga) sits close to the ruins of a famous abbey, on the narrow neck of land (conga in Irish) separating **Lough Corrib** and **Lough Mask**. It is a popular place for exploring the lakes, the mountains of Connemara and Joyce Country to the west. The famous Wilde family had a holiday house on the shore of Lough Corrib; in 1867 Oscar's father Sir William Wilde wrote an antiquarian guidebook Lough Corrib, its Shores and Islands, still in print today. Cong was put on the map in 1952 when the film The Quiet Man starring John Wayne was made. ⓘ Cong. ◷ *Open Jun-Aug, 9.30am-6.30pm.* ☎ *094 9546542*

▸ **Orient Yourself:** Cong lies on the N 84 and R 334 from Galway, Castlebar and Westport.
☾ **Also See:** ATHENRY, CONNEMARA, GALWAY, KNOCK, WESTPORT.

Walking Tour

Cong Abbey
The Augustinian abbey beautifully set by the river was founded in the 12C, probably by Turlough O'Conor, King of Connaught and High King of Ireland, on the site of an earlier monastic foundation (6C/7C). Ruins of the chancel, a lovely Romanesque doorway, **cloisters** (c 1200), sculpted **chapter house**, and the Guest Refectory with a twisted chimney stack remain. West of the abbey grounds on an island in the river is the **monks' fishing house** (12C) with a hole in the floor through which a net could be lowered, and when a fish was caught, a bell rang in the kitchen.

SIGHTSEEING
Lough Corrib Cruises – *Operate daily. Daytime/evening sailings* ☎ *092 46029 - www.corribcruises.com* Excursions to Inchagoil Island's 5C / 12C ruins, or Asford Castle for dinner.

For coin ranges, see the Legend on the cover flap.

WHERE TO EAT
John J Burke & Sons – *Clonbur* ☎ *094 9546175; www.burkes-clonbur.com. Mon-Sat 1-5pm; Apr -Sep 6-9pm daily.* House special: Irish stew.

Ashord Castle – ☎ *094 9546003 (see below).* Luxurious dining in sumptuous context.

Dry Canal

Lough Mask and Lough Corrib are linked by the River Cong, which runs mainly through caves and underground channels in the limestone. The idea of creating a navigable waterway between the two great lakes seemed about to coe to fruitiion, when men doing relief work during the famine laboured for six years to dig a canal (4mi/7km) with three locks. In March 1854 work was suspended; costs had risen, new railways threatened competition and attempts to fill the canal came to nothing when the water drained away into the porous limestone rock. No vessel has ever floated on Cong's dry canal.

Quiet Man Cottage Museum
Open Apr to mid-Oct, 10am-5pm. €4 094 95 4089 - www.museumsofmayo. com
The interior is furnished as a replica of the cottage used in the film. Upstairs, a local collection of historic artefacts from 7000BC-19C AD is displayed.

Ashford Castle
Pedestrian entrance south of the Abbey; vehicle entrance on R 346 east of Cong. Open 9am-6pm (grounds and gardens). €5. 094 95 46003 - www.ashford.ie
The Guinness family transformed the 13C castle, built by the de Burgos into a huge baronial residence of great sumptuousness in the 19C. It is now a luxury hotel with formal gardens, tennis courts, golfcourse, falconry centre and fishing facilities.

Excursion

Ross Errilly Abbey★
10mi/16km SE of Cong by R 346 and R 344.
Although in ruins, Ross Abbey, on the banks of the Black River, is one of the best-preserved Franciscan friaries in Ireland, founded around 1351 and extended in 1496 at a time when the Franciscans felt the need to take control of an idle and corrupt official church. In 1596 the complex was requisitioned by the English for use as barracks, in 1656 it was looted by the Cromwellians, in 1753 the last monks moved away.

Among its fascinating features, note the **cloister buildings**, a second courtyard with a postern gate for entry after dark, the **kitchen** with its big round **fish tank** and huge fireplace backing onto a large circular oven in the adjoining **bakery**. The **central tower** (70ft/21.5m), probably added in 1498, provides good **views**★.

> ## Captain Boycott
>
> From Lough Mask House (on the eastern shore of the lake) Captain Charles Boycott administered the estates of Lord Erne with a severity that made him extremely unpopular with his tenants. In 1880, after evicting a number for non-payment of rent, Parnell's Land League made him the first victim of the process that subsequently bore his name. The wretched man and his family were shunned and ostracised, and the land could only be worked by Ulstermen protected by troops. Boycott fled to England, securing lexicographical immortality.

Ross Errilly Abbey

CONNEMARA★★★

The largest Gaeltacht in Ireland, with many road-signs in Gaelic only, Connemara is a wild and beautiful region of mountains, lakes, tumbling streams, undulating bog, sea-girt promontories, unspoilt beaches and panoramic views. Its beauty and remoteness, together with its traces of a traditional way of life, have attracted craftsmen who are happy to introduce visitors to their handweaving, knitting, screen printing and carving, marble inlay, jewellery and pottery. *Galway Road, Clifden.* *Open Mar-Sep, Mon-Sat.* *095 21163; www.irelandwest.ie*

▶ **Orient Yourself:** Connemara is a sparsely inhabited area, bisected by the Galway–Clifden road (N 59) and a few minor roads which should be taken slowly.

Don't Miss: the scenery along the cliffs north of Clifden Bay and around Lough Corrib

Especially for Kids: Connemara National Park

Also See: ARAN ISLANDS, CONG, GALWAY, WESTPORT

A Bit of History

The mountains at the heart of Connemara are the **Twelve Bens** or **Pins**, that culminate with Benbaun (2 388ft/728m). The sharp grey peaks of quartzite rock resistant to weathering rise sharply out of the blanket-bog. The Bens are drained by mountain streams and ringed by a chain of lakes where trout are plentiful. Between the foot of the Twelve Pins and the southern coastline extends the level **Connemara Bog** dotted with innumerable tiny lakes. On a bright day the stretches of water act like mirrors reflecting the sun; in the rain, it all turns to water.

Connemara Pony

R Holzbachova, Ph Benet/MICHELIN

In this remote region with unyielding soils and harsh climate, the people of Connemara lived in settlements dotted along the coast, resisting invaders and colonisation. For centuries the ferocious O'Flaherty clan held sway until dislodged by Cromwell, whose ruthless men stayed on in their stronghold on Inishbofin. The population was decimated by the Famine but its Irish-speaking, peasant culture survived, exercising great fascination on Gaelic revivalists and on nationalists like Patrick Pearse.

Throughout Connemara's history, enterprising individuals have doggedly tried to implement improvements: John D'Arcy, a member of a long-established Galway family which had originally settled in Ireland in the reign of Elizabeth I, moved to the estate he inherited in 1815 and set about developing the new harbour town of Clifden, constantly importuning the authorities for funds to build roads to link his new settlement to Galway and Westport. The Galway road was completed in the 1820s, running through miles of uninhabited countryside between the Twelve Bens and the Connemara bog, built by labourers who had to be supplied with tents and cooking utensils. Although a railway line to the area was eventually opened in 1895, it closed in 1935. Another reformer nurtured in this wild land was Richard Martin, also known as "Humanity Dick", who founded the Society for the Prevention of Cruelty to Animals; his family home, **Ballynahinch Castle** on the south shore of Ballynahinch Lake, is now a hotel.

Address Book

GETTING AROUND

Ferries from Cleggan to Inishbofin - *Operate (weather permitting) Apr-Oct, daily, from Cleggan at 11.30am, 6.45pm (also 2pm Jul-Aug), from Inishbofin at 9.15am, 5pm (also 12.30pm Jul-Aug); winter times by phone.* €15 ☎ 095 45903 - www.inishbofinferry.com.

Ferry to St MacDara's Island - *Passage offered (weather permitting) by local fishermen on Festival Day (16 July) and other days by appointment. Check locally for details.*

SIGHTSEEING

Maritime Wildlife cruises and sea angling cruises from Letterfrack.

ぐ *For coin ranges, see the Legend on the cover flap.*

WHERE TO STAY

Letterfrack Lodge – *Letterfrack -* ☎ 095 41222; www.letterfracklodge.com - *11 rm* Self-catering B&B in beautiful rural setting.

Dolphin Beach Country House – *Lower Sky Rd, Clifden -* ☎ 095 21204; www.dolphinbeachhouse.com. *Mid-Mar to mid-Nov. 9 rm.* Modernised farmhouse in secluded location overlooking the bay; sandy beach; fishing; horse-riding available. Comfortable and welcoming; home-cooked dinners featuring local produce.

The Quay House – *Beach Rd, Clifden -* ☎ 095 21369 - www.thequayhouse.com. *Mid-Mar to Oct - 14 rm.* Elegant harbour master's house restored as stylish townhouse hotel.

Ballynahinch Castle Hotel – *Ballynahinch -* ☎ 095 31006; www.ballynahinch-castle.com. *37 rm/3 suites* The castle lies in a vast estate of 350 acres/142ha: scenic walks, salmon and trout fishing, sailing, shooting, horse-riding, golf. Log fires, quiet reading rooms, hearty dinners.

Inishbofin accommodation - contact Northwest Tourism, Sligo. ☎ 071 916 1201; www.irelandnorthwest.ie.

WHERE TO EAT

O'Dowds – *Roundstone* ☎ 095 35923; www.odowdsbar.com. Popular locally-sourced seafood, especially busy at weekends for family lunches.

SHOPPING

For crafts try the IDA craft village at **Roundstone**, the craft shop at **Kylemore Abbey** and, for woollen goods, the **Leenane Cultural Centre**.

SPORTS AND LEISURE

BEACHES

There is a long sandy beach on the north shore of Clifden Bay west of the harbour P.

Scubadive West, Renvyle – ⏰ *Open daily, 10am and 2pm*☎ 095 43922; www.scubadivewest.com

SEA ANGLING

In Clifden, at Letterfrack and at the **Roundstone Sea Angling Centre**.

FRESHWATER FISHING

In Lough Corrib, Lough Mask, Lough Nafooey, in the Joyce River, at Maam Cross and Recess.

RAMBLING

Visitors intending to walk in the hills should be properly equipped (map and compass, stout waterproof footwear, warm clothes and food) and should notify someone, preferably at the **National Park Visitor Centre**, of their route and expected time of return; no one should walk alone.

Information about guided walks up to *(2hr)* and through *(2–4hr)* the **Pass of the Birds** from Recess northeast up Owentooe River Valley, southeast of Maumeen Peak, through the Pass of the Birds, past St Patrick's Bed and Holy Well, down into Failmore and Joyce River valleys.

EVENTS AND FESTIVALS

Connemara Pony Show, Clifden *(August)*

Galway International Oyster Festival *(September)*

Driving Tours

North Connemara *Round trip of 60mi/96km – 1 day*

Clifden

Well-sited at the head of a long sea-inlet and still consisting mainly of John d'Arcy's original triangle of broad streets, Clifden is the unofficial capital of Connemara. In August, people flock to the Clifden Connemara Pony Show, a major event in the local calendar. Ireland's native pony breed is celebrated at the **Station House Museum**, together with local history and two happenings that put Connemara "in the forefront of communications technology": the opening of the Marconi radio station in 1905 at nearby Derryginlagh and the first transatlantic flight, which concluded with Alcock and Brown's crash-landing in Derryginlagh bog. &🕐 *Open May-Oct, Mon-Sat 10am-5pm, Sun, noon-6pm.* ⊗ *€2.* ☎ *095 21494*

▶ *From Clifden take the cliff road W.*

Sky Road★★

A steep and narrow road climbs along the cliffs on the north side of Clifden Bay past the site of Clifden Castle, John D'Arcy's house; looking south across Clifden Bay you see the round hump of Errisbeg (987ft/300m). As the road bears north-west over the ridge, a magnificent **view**★★ stretches *(NW)* along the coastline and offshore islands. The road descends in a curve to the head of Kingstown Bay and then continues inland along the south shore of Streamstown Bay.

▶ *At the T-junction turn left onto N 59. To visit Inishbofin go W to Cleggan (4mi/6.5km).*

Inishbofin

Ferry from Cleggan (see Address Book).
The island of the White Cow, where St Colman of Lindisfarne founded a monastery in the 7C, is inhabited by farmers and fishermen. The fort was used by Grace O'Malley, whose ancestors seized the island from the O'Flahertys in the 14C, then by Cromwell, who expelled the monks and interned Catholic priests there.

Connemara National Park (Páirc Náisiúnta Chonamara)★

(Dúchas). 🧒 *Visitor Centre:* &🕐 *Open Mar to mid-Oct, daily, 10am (9.30am Jul-Aug) to 5.30pm (6.30pm Jun-Aug); last admission 45min before closing.* ⊗ *€2.90.* 🚻 🅿️☎ *095 41054/41006*
The park (4 942 acres/2 000ha) preserves some of the finest scenery in the Twelve Bens range of mountains with areas of heath, blanket bog, grassland and natural oak and birch woodland. The flora includes Mediterranean, alpine and arctic species. The **red deer** and the **Connemara pony**, Ireland's only native pony, roam the park. From Diamond Hill (1 460ft/445m) there is a good view of the Polladirk River.

▶ *Continue N on N 59. In Letterfrack make a detour left to Rinvyle.*

Rinvyle Peninsula

From **Rinvyle (Currath) Castle**, a ruined tower house belonging to the O'Flaherty clan with a spiral stair and huge fireplace, there is a good view of the Mweelrea (Muilrea) Mountains *(northeast)* and offshore islands – Inishbofin *(west)*, Inishturk and Clare Island *(north)*. Rinvyle House, nearby, was once home to the Dublin wit and socialite, Oliver St John Gogarty, who loved his "long, long house in the ultimate land of the undiscovered West".

▶ *Return to N 59 and continue E.*

B Perousse/MICHELIN

Kylemore Abbey

Kylemore Abbey★

♿ *Abbey, Church & Gardens:* 🕓 *Open daily, 9am-6pm.* 🕓 *Closed Good Fri and Christmas.* 👓 *€11.* 🅿 ✕☎ *095 41146 - www.kylemoreabbey.com*

The Irish name *Coill Mhór* refers to the "big wood" on the north shore of Lough Pollacappul at the foot of Doughrough Mountain. The turreted and crenellated neo-Gothic castle, built (1860–67) of Dalkey granite, now houses a community of Irish Benedictine nuns and a convent school. The lavish mansion was built for the Manchester financier, MP and socialite, Mitchell Henry (1826–1901). The history of the castle and convent is retold with photographs and a short film. The **Gothic church** (1878 - *5min walk*) is a replica of Norwich Cathedral.

The magnificent 6acre/2.5ha **Victorian walled garden**★ (*shuttle bus*) is restored to its late 19C state when it was one of the most admired in Ireland. A stream and belt of trees divide the flower garden and geometrical parterres from the vegetable garden with in exemplary lazy-beds. The buildings comprise a castellated bothy, a head gardener's house and spectacular glasshouses.

▶ *Continue E on N 59.*

Killary

Killary harbour★ has a fine view of the deep fjord and Erriff River estuary.
The **Leenane Cultural Centre** shows how fleece is transformed into woollen cloth.
🕓 *Open Apr-Oct, 9.30am(9am, Aug-Jul) -7pm.* 👓 *€3* 🍵 ☎ *095 42323*

▶ *Take R 336 south; after 4.5mi/8km turn left onto a steep, narrow mountain road.*

Joyce Country★

This beautiful area takes its name from a Welsh family which settled in the mountains between Lough Mask and Lough Corrib after the Anglo-Norman invasion in the 12C.
Lough Nafooey★ lies at the foot of Maumtrasna (2 207ft/671m), while **Lough Mask** stretches towards the Parry Mountains (*west*).

▶ *At the T-junction turn left; in Clonbur turn right onto R 345.*

Lough Corrib★★

The second largest lake in Ireland, almost 30mi/48km long, is dotted with countless islands. On one stands the ruin of **Hen's Castle**, an O'Flaherty stronghold that was twice defended by Grace O'Malley.

▶ *At the T-junction turn left onto R 336. In Maam Cross turn right onto N 59.*

Galway – Clifden Road

Maam Cross (An Teach Dóite) and **Recess** (Sraith Salach) are two popular angling villages; beyond lie the many islands of **Derryclare Lough**. In the glaciated valley between the Maumturk Mountains *(east)* and two of the Twelve Pins, Bencorr and Derryclare *(west)*, lies **Lough Inagh**.

Lettershear

The **Connemara Heritage and History Centre** introduces visitors to the history and landscapes of the region; the **Dan O'Hara homestead** re-creates a farmholding typical of a Connemara family with seven children before the potato famine. ◐ *Open Apr to late-Oct, 10am-6pm.* ✆ *€7.50.* ✆☎ *095 21808*

South Connemara *Round trip of 75mi/121km – 1 day*

On the way to Roundstone

South of Clifden, the Owenglin River tumbles down a great waterfall towards Ardbear Harbour. After 2mi/3,2km, you see the **Alcock and Brown Monument** up on the hill commemorating the first non-stop transatlantic flight by Alcock and Brown who crash-landed in Derryginlagh Bog on 15 June 1919. At **Errisbeg**, outcrops of dense gabbro rock (987ft/300m) shelter two lovely sand beaches.

Roundstone (Cloch na Rón)★

The delightful harbour village created by Alexander Nimmo was originally populated with fisherfolk from Scotland. On the south side of the town is a **craft village**, established by the Industrial Development Authority, where Malachy Kearns has his workshop making traditional goatskin drums *(bodhrán)*.

▶ *In Toombeola turn right onto R 342.*

Cashel★

At the foot of a hill overlooking Bertraghboy Bay sits Cashel, good for angling.

▶ *Turn right onto R 340.*

Carna Peninsula

Offshore *(south)* lies **St MacDara's Island** where the 6C saint founded a monastery. The little church (c 10C, restored) built of huge stone blocks, has distinctive projections on the gable ends known as *antae* bend inwards that meet at the roof ridge,

---

Alexander Nimmo (1783–1832)

Alexander Nimmo was a Scot who came to Ireland in 1809 to assist in surveys into the economic potential of bogland. Fortunately for the natural beauty of the area, his elaborate scheme for converting the bogs of Connemara into productive farmland with an elaborate system of canals was never implemented. In 1822 he was appointed engineer of the Western District and his great legacy to the area is its highway network and a number of piers and harbours. While work was in progress on the Galway to Clifden road Nimmo lived at Corrib Lodge at Maam Cross.

possibly aping timber cruck construction. The island can be reached by boat from **Carna**, a lobster fishing village, which holds celebrations on the saint's feast day (16 July), sailing over to St MacDara's island for Mass, followed by a series of regattas.

Kilkieran (Cill Chiaráin)

Patrick Pearse's Cottage, 7mi/11.3km North of Kilkieran, on the west shore of Lough Aroolagh is the tiny thatched holiday cottage built by Patrick Pearse where he studied the Irish language. *(Dúchas)* &🕐 *Open mid-Jun to mid-Sep, 9.30am-6.30pm; Easter Sat-Mon, 10am-5pm; mid-Sep to late-Sep, Sat-Sun, 10am-6pm; last admission 45min before closing.*⊛ *€1.* 🅿⊛ *091 574292*

▶ *Return to R 340; continue east. At the T-junction EITHER turn left onto R 386 and left again in Maam Cross onto N 59 to return to Clifden OR turn right onto R 386 to take the coast road to Galway.*

CORK★★

POPULATION 127 187

The Republic of Ireland's second city, Cork (Corcaigh) is a major port and commercial centre, with a university, a distinct historical and cultural identity, and a vibrant and welcoming atmosphere. The city centre is built on reclaimed marshland between two arms of the River Lee, whose estuary, Cork Harbour, forms the largest natural harbour in Europe. Until the 19C many of the streets were open waterways where ships moored - likened in 1780, by Arthur Young, to the towns of the Netherlands. North of the river the land rises steeply, this is now covered by **Montenotte**, the city's most exclusive residential district. 🚹 *Grand Parade. Open Jul-Aug, daily; Sep-Jun, Mon-Sat.* ⊛ *021 425 5100; www.corkkerry.ie,* 🚹 *Blarney. Open daily.* ⊛ *021 438 1624;* 🚹 *Castle Gates, The Square, Macroom.* 🕐 *Open Jun-Sep, Mon-Sat.* ⊛ *028 43280*

▶ **Orient Yourself:** Cork sits at a major cross-roads: N 25 east to Waterford, N 8 northeast to Cashel, N 20 northwest to Limerick and N 22 west to Killarney

🅿 **Parking:** Multi-storey car parks and disc parking in the street; parking discs available at the Tourist Office and other outlets in Cork.

⊛ **Don't Miss:** a pint or two of local beer; the Anglican Cathedral, the Shandon Bells carillon, and an excursion to Blarney Castle.

Kids **Especially for Kids:** Lewis Glucksman Gallery, Cork City Gaol

Also See: COBH, KINSALE, MALLOW, MIDLETON, YOUGHAL

A Bit of History

"A Marshy Place" – Cork derives its name from the Irish for a "marshy place", where St Finbar founded a church in 650 on the banks of the River Lee near the present site of University College. Its early development was disrupted in 860 by Viking raids, and in 1172 by the invasion of the Anglo-Normans who eventually broke the Danish hold on the city.

Artistic Cork

Among those sons of Cork who made their mark in the world are **John Hogan** (1800-58), a sculptor whose work is found not only in Cork but elsewhere in Ireland, **Frank O'Connor**, who penned short stories, and **Frank Browne**, a Jesuit and photographer extraordinaire of life in Ireland at the beginning of the 20C but especially of the first stages of the fatal maiden voyage of the *Titanic*.

"Rebel Cork" – Cork's political independence is rooted in its long-standing commercial success. In 1492 **Perkin Warbeck**, the pretender to the English throne, arrived and soon won the support of the mayor and other leading citizens who accompanied him to England, where he proclaimed himself Richard IV, King of England and Lord of Ireland. They were all later hanged at Tyburn.

In the 1640s Cork supported the royal cause; when Cromwell entered the city in 1649, he inflicted great damage on it; then, in 1690 the city endured a five-day siege, until the army of William III breached the walls and destroyed fortifications.

In the early 18C Cork accommodated many Huguenots fleeing from religious persecution in France – hence the name of French Church Street.

In the 19C, the city lived up to its reputation of rebelliousness by being a stronghold of Fenian agitation. The daily *Cork Examiner* was founded in 1841.

The War of Independence and the subsequent Civil War were bitterly fought in and around Cork. In 1920 the Black and Tans set fire to a substantial portion of the city centre, which was later rebuilt in an anonymous modern style. The political unrest was aggravated by the deaths of two Lord Mayors of Cork: Terence McSwiney on hunger strike in Brixton Prison; Tomás McCurtain shot in his bed by Crown Forces in the presence of his wife and children.

South Mall, Cork

H Champollion/MICHELIN

Address Book

GETTING AROUND

Cork International Airport – ☎ 021 431 3131

Bus Travel – *Bus Éireann Travel Centre, Parnell Place* ☎ *021 50 8188; www. buseirann.ie.* Bus around the city and outskirts between early morning and midnight. Check for travel passes.

Rail Travel – *Iarnród Éireann, Travel Centre* ☎ *01850 366 222; Kent Station* ☎ *021 45 06766 www.irishrail.ie*

Car Ferry across **Cork Harbour** from Glenbrook *(southeast of the city centre)* to Carrigaloe near Cobh on Great Island – *Operates daily, 7am-12.15am. €3.50 (car), €1 (pedestrian).* ☎ *021 481 1549*

Taxis – Taxis for hire from the centre of the main street.

SIGHTSEEING

Day Coach Tours by Easy Tours Cork – *Apr to Sep. Depart from customer's Cork address. €30* ☎ *021 454 5328; www. easytourscork.com*

Walk Cork – 90min tours of central Cork. *Jun- Aug, Mon-Fri at 8pm from Cork Tourist Office in Grand Parade. €7* – ☎*021 4885405 - olgacork@eircom.net*

Cork Lough – A large grass-fringed lake, and thriving bird sanctuary, attracting wildfowl.
Railway buffs will be interested in a splendid example of an early Irish steam **locomotive**, a 2-2-2 built in 1848 and withdrawn in 1874 after 30 years of service, which stands In the railway station entrance hall.

For coin ranges, see the Legend on the cover flap.

WHERE TO STAY

⌒**Achill House B&B** – *Western Rd. 6 rm* 🅿 ☎ *021 427 9447; www.achil-lhouse.com.* Guest house with discernibly contemporary feel: spacious with basic mod-cons.

⌒⌒**Acorn House** – *14 St Patrick's Hill. 9 rm* – ☎ *021 450 2474; www.acorn-house-cork.com. Closed 22 Dec to 16 Jan.* Georgian house in the heart of the city decorated with sympathetic period charm; high ceilinged bedrooms, modern touches and facilities complement the comfort.

⌒⌒**Crawford House** – *Western Rd. 13 rm* 🅿 ☎ *021 427 9000; www.crawford-guesthouse.com. Closed 22 Dec to 2 Jan.* Bright and comfortable accommodation. home-baked selection at buffet breakfast. Bedrooms decidedly modern in feel, many with king size beds.

⌒⌒**Garnish House** – *Western Rd 14 rm* 🅿 ☎ *021 427 5111; www.garnish. ie.* Victorian-style guest house; tea and scones on arrival; generous breakfasts; some larger rooms with jacuzzi.

WHERE TO EAT

⌒⌒**Jacobs on the Mall** – *30A South Mall. Lunch 12.30-2.30pm; dinnner 6.30-10pm.* 🕐 *Closed Sun - Booking essential.* ☎ *021 425 1530; www.jacobsonthemall. com.* Former 19C Turkish baths converted into one of the city's most stylish restaurants, showcasing modern Irish art. Attentive service, modern cooking using the best local ingredients and some original combinations.

⌒⌒**Jacques** – *Phoenix St. Lunch, Mon-Fri; dinner Mon-Sat. Booking essential.* ☎ *021 427 7387 - jacquesrestaurant@ eircom.net - www.jacquesrestaurant. ie* Well-established restaurant located in a colourful little side street in the city centre. Always busy with locals yet retaining an intimate atmosphere. Modern menu with the emphasis on locally sourced ingredients from small producers.

⌒⌒**No 5 Fenn's Quay** – *Sheares St.* 🕐 *Open Mon-Sat, 10am til late -* ☎ *021 427 9527 - www.fennsquay.ie* Converted mews house, bright and informally run. Open all day for snacks, light lunches,

Busker in Cork City

SLIDE FILE, Dublin

more substantial dinner all freshly prepared and correctly priced.

◉◉**Blair's Inn** – *Cloghroe, Blarney – 3.5mi from Blarney via R 617 to Tower, then via R 579 -* ☎ *021 4381 470; www. blairsinn.ie.* Friendly pub in a charming and secluded wooded setting by the Owennageara river. Traditional fayre during the day, more elaborate evening menu. Live music Monday nights.

◉◉**Cafe Paradiso** – *16 Lancaster Quay, Western Rd.* 🕐 *Open Tue-Sat, lunch 12-3pm; dinner 6.30-10.30pm. Booking essential.* ☎ *021 427 7939; www. cafeparadiso.ie* Scrubbed pine tables, vivid colours and cherubs; pleasant and efficient service; popular well-priced vegetarian food so booking essential. Accommodation also available.

ENTERTAINMENT

Everyman Palace Theatre – *15 MacCurtain Street -* ☎ *021 4501 673; www. everymanpalace.com*

Kino Cinema – *Washington Street - Open daily.* ☎ *021 427 1571; www. kinocinema.net*

Opera House – *Emmet Place -* ☎ *021 427 4308; www.corkoperahouse.ie.* Opera, dance, drama, musicals, concerts and family entertainment.

The Half Moon Theatre – *Emmet Place, at the back of the Opera House* ☎ *021 427 0022 - www.halfmoontheatre.ie – Open daily 8.30am-11.30pm.* Variety of jazz, blues and rock music acts.

UCC Granary Theatre – *Mardyke -* ☎ *021 490 4275 - www.granary.ie* New and experimental work by artists across the disciplines.

Triskel is an artspace, funded by the Arts Council of Ireland, to host public art projects, exhibitions, performances and events across the city. *www. triskelarts.com*

SHOPPING

The main shopping street is **Patrick Street**. **North Main Street** is one of the oldest shopping areas. The **English Market** (*just off Patrick Street*) offers market-lovers a wide range of fresh produce.

The **Huguenot Quarter** is a bohemian district dotted with cafés, boutiques, antique shops; the **Shandon Crafts Centre**, housed in the old **Butter Exchange** (1750), is fun for crystal, jewellery and textiles – 🕐 *Open Mon-Sat, 9am-5pm.* ☎ *021 427 3251*

For woollen goods visit the **Blarney Woollen Mills**.

Merchant's Quay Shopping Centre – *1 Patrick Street -* 🕐 *Open Mon-Sat, 9am-6pm (9pm Thu & Fri), Sun 2pm-6pm.*

EVENTS AND FESTIVALS

Cork International Choral and Folk Dance Festival (April/May)

Cork Folk Festival (September)

Cork Jazz Festival (October) – *www. corkjazzfestival.com*

Cork Film Festival (October) – *www. corkfilmfest.org*

TRACING ANCESTORS

Cork City and County Archives, *Great William O'Brien Street, Blackpool* – 🕐 *Open by appointment Tue-Fri, 10am-1pm and 2.30-5pm.* 🕐 *Closed Bank Hols.* ☎ *021 4505886; www.corkcity.ie/ourservices/rac/archives/*

Commercial and Industrial Centre – Cork began trading in the 12C exporting hides and cloth, and importing wine from Bordeaux. By the 18C the city had become a major producer of butter, shipping it to Britain, Europe and America.

In 1852 Cork staged Ireland's first national Industrial Exhibition, modelled on the Great Exhibition in London. In 1917 the Ford car company set up its first overseas factory at the Marina; **Henry Ford**, the founder of the American firm, was born at Ballinascarty, north of Clonakilty. Dunlop started its plant in the 1930s – both Ford and Dunlop ceased operations in 1980; shipbuilding died shortly after. The principal commercial activity is now related to computer manufacturing.

CORK					
		Infirmary Rd	Z 24	Parnell Pl.	Z 38
		John Redmond St	Y 26	Pembroke St	Z 39
Baker's Rd	X 4	Lancaster Quay	Z 28	Proby's Quay	Z 40
Camden Pl.	Y 5	Langford Row	Z 29	Roman St	Y 42
Coburg St	Y 10	Lower Glanmire Rd	Y 30	South Link	Z 46
Commons Rd	X 12	Lower Mayfield Rd	X 31	South Main St	Z 47
Corn Market St	X 13	Merchant Quay		Southern Rd	Z 45
Curragh Rd	X 14	Shopping Centre	Y	St Patrick's Quay	Y 44
Dominic St	Y 15	Merchant's Quay	Y 32	St Patrick's St	Z
Eason Hill	Y 17	Middle Glanmire Rd	X 33	Summer Hill	Y 48
Emmet Pl.	Y 18	Newsom's Quay	Y 34	Thomas Davis St	X 49
Gardiner's Hill	X 20	North Main Street	YZ	Victoria Cross Rd	X 50
Gerald Griffin St	Y 21	North Mall	Y 35	Western Rd	X 53
Great William O'Brien St	X 22	O'Connell's Square	Y 36	Wilton Rd	X 55
Horgan Quay	X 23	Olivier Plunkett St	Z	Wolfe Tone St	Y 56

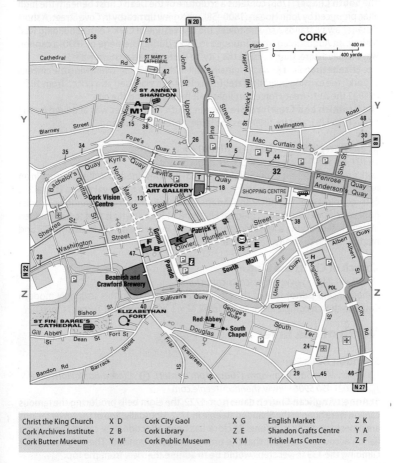

Christ the King Church	X D	Cork City Gaol	X G	English Market	Z K
Cork Archives Institute	Z B	Cork Library	Z E	Shandon Crafts Centre	Y A
Cork Butter Museum	Y M¹	Cork Public Museum	X M	Triskel Arts Centre	Z F

Visit

Historic landmarks

St Patrick's Street and Grand Parade★

St Patrick's Street★, Cork's main thoroughfare lined with shops, leads to the Merchant's Quay Shopping Centre. On the way, seek out the covered **English Market** (1610), the main aisle of which remained a waterway until the early 19C to allow merchandise to be brought in by boat. **Grand Parade**★ has been the principal commercial street since the 18C when the handsome bow-fronted buildings hung with grey slates were built with steps down to an open water channel draining into the River Lee, where merchants would have tethered their boats. those responsible for running the Butter Exchange, meanwhile, lived at the east end of **South Mall**★, in the Commercial Rooms (now part of the Imperial Hotel).

> ### Road Bowls
>
> The ancient Irish sport of road bowling is still played on Sundays in Co Cork and Co Armagh. A heavy iron ball (28oz/794g; 7in/18cm) is hurled along a stretch of quiet winding country road in as few throws as possible; the ball may hurtle through the air at shoulder height. Betting is heavy.

The **South Chapel** (1766) contains a sculpture of the Dead Christ beneath the high altar, produced by John Hogan (1800–58), who grew up nearby in Cove Street. A short distance away, stands a square tower, the last vestige of Cork's oldest building **Red Abbey**, an Augustinian friary founded in 1300; during the siege of 1690, a cannon was installed here, then outside the city, to batter Cork's eastern walls.

The **Elizabethan Fort**★ was originally built in the 1590s for "overawing the citizens of Cork"; the existing building dates from c1624 and was used as a prison from 1835. In 1922 the Anti-Treaty forces set light to it before fleeing the city.

The **Beamish and Crawford Brewery** in South Main Street was acquired by the brewers in 1791, and by 1809 was the largest brewery in Ireland.

St Fin Barre's Cathedral (Anglican)★★

☎ *021 496 3387 - www.cathedral.cork.anglican.org*

Cork's most exuberant church building (1865) was designed by William Burges in an early pointed French Gothic style on the site used since medieval times. The tallest of three spires rises to 240ft/73m; the apse is lit by 18 stained glass windows. A brass floor plate marks the resting place of Elizabeth Aldworth who is said to have hidden in a clock-case during a Masonic lodge meeting in her husband's house in 1712 and made a Mason to secure her silence.

Church of Christ the King★

☎ *021 431 2465 - www.turnerscross.com/church*

A magnificent **panorama** of the city can be enjoyed from this strikingly modern Catholic church completed in 1937 (*1mi/1.6km S of city centre at Turner's Cross*).

North of the River

Shandon Bells★★

🕐 *Open Mon-Sat, 9am-6pm (10am-4pm winter).* 🕐 *Closed Bank Hols.* ⊜ *€5.* 🅿 ☎ *021 450 5906 - www.shandonsteeple.com*

St Anne's Anglican Church dates from 1722, the eight bells producing the famous carillon were hung in the Shandon steeple in 1752. Unusually, two of the tower facings are limestone, two sandstone; its clock has been affectionately called the 4-faced liar on account of the fact that the time is rare synchronised. The only reason for climbing the 133 tower steps would be to admire the view from the top.

Cork Butter Museum

🕐 *Open Mar-Oct, 10am-5pm (6pm Jul-Aug).* ⊜ *€3.* ☎ *021 430 0600 - www.corkbutter.museum/index.php*

Displays present the vital history of Cork's butter production for export.

Cork City Gaol

🄺🄸🄳🄼 ♿ 🕐 *Open Mar-Oct, 9.30am-6pm; Nov-Feb, 10am-5pm; last admission 1hr before closing.* ⊜ *€6.* ☎ *021 4305022 - www.corkcitygaol.com*

The fortress-like prison in Convent Avenue, designed by Sir Thomas Deane, was in use from 1825 to 1923. Descriptions of the felonies committed by prisoners, their diet (porridge) and regime (oakum picking, treadmill, solitary confinement) are provided, and the role of the school (1856–79), the hospital and 20C graffiti are explained. The **Radio Museum** explains how Marconi made early transmissions from Ireland, and how Cork Radio was first broadcast from the prison governor's house in 1927.

South of the river

Crawford Art Gallery★
🕭🕐 *Open Mon-Sat, 10am-5pm.* 🕐 *Closed Christmas-New Year.* ✕☎ *021 49 07855 - www.crawfordartgallery.com.*
Named after its founding benefactor, WH Crawford, the gallery is housed in the Custom House of 1724 (later extended) and has a representative collection of 19C and 20C works by Irish artists such as William Conor, John Keating, Sir William Orpen and Seán O'Sullivan,and by John Hogan and Daniel Maclise from Cork. There are frequent touring exhibitions of contemporary art.

Cork Public Museum★
🕐 *Open Mon-Fri, 11am-1pm and 2.15-5pm (6pm Jun-Aug); Sun, 3-5pm.* 🕐 *Closed Bank Hols.* 🅿☎ *021 42 70679*
The Georgian house in Fitzgerald Park, houses historical artefacts relating to Cork from prehistoric to modern times including Civic Regalia, and displays relating to19C-20C crafts and trades; notable collections of 18C Cork silver, Cork glass, needlepoint lace from Youghal. Temporary exhibitions on local social history.

Cork Vision Centre
🕐 *Open Tue-Sat, 10am-5pm.* ☎ *021 427 9925 - www.corkvisioncentre.com*
St Peter's Church on North Main Street, is a venue for temporary exhibitions; 1:500 scale model of Cork.

University College Lewis Glucksman Gallery
Kids 🕭🕐 *Open Tue-Sat, 10am-5pm (8pm Thu), Sun 12noon-5pm.* ✉☎ *021 4901844 - www.glucksman.org*
University College Cork (UCC), now part of the National University, was founded by charter in 1845 as one of three Queens Colleges alongside Galway and Belfast. The original buildings were designed by Benjamin Woodward (1816–61). The striking **Lewis Glucksman Gallery** exhibits contemporary art and offers daily programs of lectures and activities.

Excursions

Blarney Castle★★
5mi/8km NW by N 20 and W by a minor road. 🕭🕐 *Open Mon-Sat, 9am-6.30pm (7pm Jun-Aug; dusk, Oct-Apr); Sun, 9.30am-5.30pm/dusk.* 🕐 *Closed 24-25 Dec.* ⚲ *€8.* 🅿⚲ ☎ *021 4385252 - www.blarneycastle.ie*
The central feature of the castle is the massive keep, a fine example of a tower house. In addition there are halls and dungeons, but the main reason why the castle attracts so many visitors is the presence here of the **Blarney Stone**, said to bestow the gift of eloquent speech on all those who kiss it. This is harder than it sounds since the famous piece of rock is set inside the parapet at the top of the castle and can be reached only by lying upside-down with a guide holding one's legs. The stone is believed to have been brought to Ireland during the Crusades.
In the 16C Queen Elizabeth I commanded the Earl of Leicester to take the castle from the head of the McCarthy clan. The Earl was frustrated in his mission but he sent

back numerous progress reports which so irritated the Queen that she referred to them as "all Blarney".

Blarney Castle House★ *(private)* was built in the 1870s in the Scottish baronial style with fine corner turrets and conical-roofed bartizans.

On a druidic site beside the Blarney River is the romantically landscaped dell known as **Rock Close**. Laid out in the 19C, the gardens contain wishing steps - ideally negotiated up and down with eyes closed. Two dolmens are sited in the close, which has a Fairy Glade with a sacrificial rock, also said to have druidic connotations. The **Blarney Woollen Mills** were established in the 19C, the successor to the thirteen mills developed around the castle as an industrial enterprise in the

Kissing the Blarney Stone

18C. Its enormous shop is almost as popular as the Blarney Stone. ♿🕐 *Open daily, 9.30am (10am Sun) - 6pm.* 🕐 *Closed 25-26 Dec, 1 Jan.* ✕☎ *021 451 6111.*

Crosshaven
15mi/24km SE of Cork by N 28, R 611 and R 612.
This popular little resort, located at the point where the Owenabue River widens to form a sheltered inlet of Cork Harbour, a perfect natural marina where, since 1969, the Royal Cork Yacht Club is based. It was here that the *Brendan* and *Gypsy Moth V* in which Sir Francis Chichester sailed round the world in 1971 were built. **Crosshaven House** (mid-18C) looks down on the activity of the waterfront while **Fort Meagher**, a fine coastal artillery fort, commands the approach from the sea.

Macroom
38km from Cork by N22 along the Lee Valley
This little town at the confluence of the River Sullane and the Laney River is famed for its trout fishing and its flour/oat mill.
The Gearagh, an unique area of post-glacial alluvial oak forest is protected as a National Nature Reserve. In the distant past, its many-branched stream, treacherous reed-beds, mud-banks and countless islands provided a refuge for fugutives from the law, notably distillers of illicit whiskey *(potheen)*. Today despite its forlorn appearance, with blackened tree-stumps protruding from the surface of the water, it is home to an extraordinary variety of flora and fauna.

DINGLE PENINSULA★★

The Dingle Peninsula is extreme western Ireland at its most spectacular and atmospheric, a Gaelic-speaking area with sheer cliffs, harsh mountainsides, an intricate network of tiny stone-walled fields, and an extraordinary concentration of ancient stone monuments – ring-forts, beehive huts, and inscribed stones. Brandon Mountain (3 121ft/951m) on the north coast, the second-highest in Ireland, is clothed in blanket bog and takes its name from St Brendan of Clonfert, a 6C monk, who is reputed to have set out on a transatlantic voyage from Brandon Creek, the narrow sea-inlet at the west foot of the mountain.

🚹 *Strand Street, Dingle.* 🕐 *Open May-Sep, 10am-1pm, 2.15-6pm, Apr and Oct, Mon-Sat.*
☎ *066 9151188 - www.dingle-pensinsula.ie*

▶ **Orient Yourself:** Dingle is the main town on the Dingle Peninsula reached by N 86 the main road from Tralee either via Anascaul or via a detour over the dramatic Connor Pass.

🅰 **Don't Miss:** a plate of local seafood; Slea Head, Gallarus Oratory, the view from Connor Pass before walking along Stadbally Strand

Kids **Especially for Kids:** Dingle Oceanworld Aquarium

🅱 **Also See:** KILLARNEY, TRALEE

A Bit of History

Extensive Bronze Age monuments have been recorded on the northern side of the Conor Pass near Cochlane. Later, the possibilities of the great natural harbour of Dingle were quickly realised by the Anglo-Normans; in 1257 Henry III of England imposed customs duties on exports. The peak of its commercial importance was reached in the 16C when Dingle had particularly strong trading links with Spain; in 1583 the town received permission to build a wall of enclosure.

In the same year a long period of local rule by the house of Desmond came to an end when Gearóid, the rebel Earl, was killed. Three years earlier 600 Spanish and Italian troops sent to aid the Desmond Rebellion had been massacred by government forces at Dún an Óir on tshe west side of Smerwick Harbour. Following the rebellion of 1641 and the Cromwellian wars Dingle declined significantly as a port for nearly a century, although during the late 18C it had a substantial linen industry.

Driving Tour

Dingle (An Daingean)★

Dingle, the principal centre of population, is the home port of one of Ireland's largest fishing fleets; when the catch is unloaded, the pier (0.25mi/0.4km long) is a scene of frantic activity. The town has developed as a popular tourist resort, with brightly painted houses and numerous pubs, restaurants, and places to stay.

As well as plenty of eye-level displays of marine life, the **Oceanworld Aquarium** has a perspex tunnel through the largest tank. **Kids** 🅱 🕐 *Open daily, 10am-6pm.* 🅰 €10.50. 💬 🅿 ☎ *066 91 52111 - www.dingle-oceanworld.ie*

The institute of Education and Celtic Culture , known as **Diseart**, actively promotes the Celtic culture: language courses, traditional festivals, art, poetry, music and storytelling. Attached to the former Convent of the Presentation Sisters designed by the architect J J McCarthy is the **Chapel**★ containing outstanding stained glass by Harry Clarke. ☎ *066 915 2476 - www.diseart.ie*

J J McCarthy, the successor to Pugin, also designed the adjacent **St Mary's Church**★ (1862); although the steel girders and copper sheet roof is modern. **Dingle Library** and the Thomas Ashe Museum displays material relating to the local hero **Thomas Ashe** (1885–1917), who took a leading role in the 1916 Easter Rising, born at Lispole *(5mi/8km*

Dingle

B Perousse/MICHELIN

east). ⏰ *Open Mon-Sat, 10am-5pm (8pm Thu).* ☎ *066 91 51499 - www.kerrycountyli-brary.com.*

▶ *From Dingle take R 559 W (signed Ceann Sléibhe).*

Address Book

GETTING AROUND

Blasket Islands Ferry – *Several services operate from Dunquin Pier (weather permitting). Prices vary.* ☎ *066 915 6422/915 1344/9154864; www.blasketislands.ie*

👍 *For coin ranges, see the Legend on the cover flap.*

WHERE TO STAY

⊜⊜**Captains House** – *The Mall, Dingle -* ☎ *066 915 1531 - captigh@eircom.net - 16 Mar to Nov - 9 rm.* A warm welcome is guaranteed at this B&B with a distinctive homely feel; well-tended garden.

⊜⊜**Greenmount House** – *Upper John St, Gortonora -* ☎ *066 915 1414 - www.greenmount-house.com - Closed 20 to 27 Dec.* 🅿*12 rm.* Request one of the superior rooms at the top of the B&B overlooking the town. A highlight is the sumptuous breakfast served in the conservatory.

⊜⊜**Heatons** – *The Wood - .05mi W on R 559 -* ☎ *066 915 2288 - heatons@iol.ie - www.heatonsdingle.com -* ⏰ *Closed 1 to 26 Dec.* 🅿*16 rm.* Excellent position by the water; elegant bedrooms decorated to a high standard. Extensive breakfast menu.

⊜⊜⊜⊜**Emlagh House** – *Off N 86 -* ☎ *066 915 2345 - info@emlagh-house.com - www.emlaghhouse.com.* ⏰ *Closed 6 Jan to 1 Mar and 15-28 Dec.* 🅿*10 rm.* Spacious and individually themed bedrooms with antique furniture; wonderful Bay views; some rooms with private patio. Internet access, home baking - an excellent option!

⊜⊜⊜⊜**Milltown House** – *0.75mi W by R 559 (Slea Head Drive) -* ☎ *066 915 1372 - info@milltownhousedingle.com. Late Apr to mid Nov.* 🅿*10 rm.* Wonderful view of the harbour; light menu offered from midday to 7pm, Mon-Sat. Hearty Irish breakfast.

⊜⊜⊜⊜**Pax House** – *Upper John St -* ☎ *066 915 1518 - paxhouse@iol.ie - www.pax-house.com.* ⏰ *Closed Dec and Jan.*

🅿*12 rm.* Terrific views of Dingle Bay from B&Bs elevated position a short walk from the town centre. Clean and roomy accommodation.

WHERE TO EAT

⊜⊜**Doyle's Seafood Restaurant** – *4 John St -* ☎ *066 915 1174 - cdoyles@iol.ie, www.doylesofdingle.com.* ⏰ *Open Mid-Feb to mid-Dec, Mon-Sat.* Choose your lobster, the house speciality, from the tank in the bar, then pick one of the kitchen tables. Stone floors and an old kitchen range add to the rustic feel of this renowned seafood bar. Accommodation available in the adjacent town house.

SHOPPING

John Weldon – *Green Street -* ☎ *066 915 2522 - www.johnweldonjewellers.com.* ⏰ *Open Mon-Sat, 9am-6pm.* John Weldon is a jewellery designer who takes his inspiration from Celtic traditions, mythology and heritage. This makes an ideal stop for those looking for an original gift or souvenir of their stay in Ireland and visitors are welcome to see the workshop.

The Weavers Shop / Siopana bhFiodoiri – weavings, hangings and tapestries by the Danish-born Lisbeth Mulcahy. ☎ *066 915 1688 - www.lisbeth-mulcahy.com*

Louis Mulcahy Pottery Workshop – *Clogher, Ballyferriter* ☎ *066 915 6229 - www.louismulcahy.com. Visitor centre open Easter to Sep, daily; Oct-Easter, Mon-Fri, 10am-5pm.*

SPORTS AND LEISURE

Beaches – At Ventry Harbour, Smerwick Harbour, Stradbally Strand.
Rambling – Make the pilgrimage up the **Saint's Road** *(7mi/12km)* from Kilmalkedar up the southwest face of Mount Brandon to the oratory and shrine dedicated to St Brendon on the summit.

Slea Head (Ceann Sléibhe)★★

On the steep south-facing slopes of Mount Eagle (1 696ft/516m), both east and west of the ford at Glenfahan, the agricultural landscape of Early Christian – possibly even prehistoric – times has been largely preserved in all its multi-layered complexity. Though some have been unthinkingly cleared, drystone walls define a filligree pattern of tiny fields, among which are more than 400 **clocháin** or **beehive huts**★ *(privately owned)*, some set within ringforts like **Cathair na gConchúireach** *(admission charge may be requested)*, where their superb workmanship can be admired.

Dunbeg Promontory Fort *(2mi/3.2km east of Slea Head)* seems to have been in use from c800 to Celtic times. *Visitor Centre* ☎ *066 915 9970*

Blasket Islands★

Accessible by boat from Dunquin (& see Address Book).

Uninhabited since 1953 when the last 22 residents abandoned a harsh and demanding life. The largest island, **Great Blasket** (4mix0.75mi/6kmx1.2km), is now a national historic park with buildings restored as holiday accommodation. In Blasket Sound, two Spanish Armada ships, *San Juan* and *Santa Maria de la Rosa*, founded in 1586.

Blasket Island Authors

The early 20C Blasket islanders were literate in both Irish and English, and were encouraged by their visitors to develop their literary talents and evoke their elemental way of life before it vanished. Among the better-known works are three novels translated from Irish: *Twenty Years A-Growing* by Maurice O'Sullivan, *Peig* by Peig Sayers, and *The Islandman* by Tomás Ó'Criomhthain, described by E M Forster as "an account of Neolithic life from the inside." Another fine account, albeit from the point of view of an outsider, is *Western Island* by the Englishman Robin Flower.

Dunquin

It was here that David Lean filmed *Ryan's Daughter:* although the fictional village of Kirrary was actually built in the mountains above Carhoo.

The starkly modern **Great Blasket Centre** celebrates the unique heritage and fine Gaelic literary tradition of the Blasket Islands, their folktales and traditional way of life until 1953. *(Dúchas)* & ☉ *Open Easter-Oct, 10am-6pm (7pm Jul-Aug); last admission 45min before closing; in winter by appointment* ☜ *€3.70.* ☁ ☐ ☎ *066 915 6444 - www.heritageireland.ie*

▶ *Take R 550 N to Ballyferriter.*

Ballyferriter

The **Corca Dhuibhne Regional Museum**★ describes life on the Dingle peninsula: ancient monuments, Blasket Island literature, 190 folk scenes. ☉ *Open Apr-Oct,10am-6pm and by request.* ☜ *€2.50.* ☎ *066 91 56333 - www.corca-dhuibhne. com/museum.html*

Gallarus Oratory★★

Ireland has several examples of Early Christian oratories built like beehive huts with dry stone walls corbelled inwards but none is so complete as this one, built with exceptional care in the 9C in the shape of an inverted boat. Unlike other beehive huts it is rectangular rather then circular in plan, a feature which in every other example has led to collapse, since the resulting walls are inherently unstable.

The **visitor centre** shows a video about the oratory and the local natural history. ☉ *Open daily, 10am (9am Jun to Aug) to 7pm.* ☜ *€3.* ☁ ☐ ☎ *066 91 55333*

Kilmalkedar★

The ruined Romanesque church, probably built in the 12C as part of a medieval religious complex echoes Cormac's Chapel at Cashel: inside there is an alphabet stone and fine stone carving and an Ogham stone. The chancellor's house *(404yd/369m*

Gallarus Oratory

H Champollion/MICHELIN

south) would have served the chancellor of the diocese of Ardfert. From here an old track, the **Saint's Road** *(7mi/12km)*, runs up the southwest face of Brandon Mountain to an oratory and shrine dedicated to St Brendan.

▷ *Return to Dingle and take the minor road NE (sign) to the Connor Pass.*

Connor Pass★★
Enjoy great **views** from the highest pass in Ireland (1 496ft/456m)of Dingle Harbour, Brandon Mountain, Brandon Bay , the Castlegregory Peninsula and Tralee Bay.

Stradbally Strand★★
Nestling in the beautiful horseshoe-shaped **Brandon Bay** is Ireland's longest sandy beach (12mi/19km); at the north end sit the **Magharee Islands** or The Seven Hogs. At low tide, Illauntannig, the largest island (early-Christian monastery) is linked to Reennafardarrig Island.

▷ *Continue E to Camp; turn right into N 86 towards Dingle; turn left (sign).*

Minard Castle
The great square fortress built by the Knight of Kerry in the 15C and largely destroyed by Cromwellian forces in the 17C occupies an excellent vantage point overlooking Dingle Bay.

DONEGAL

POPULATION 2 296

Donegal (Dún na nGall) **is an attractive small town at the mouth of the River Eske, a perfect spot from which to explore glens and mountains (north), dramatic coastal scenery (west) and seaside resorts on Donegal Bay (south).** ⓘ *Quay Street, Donegal. Mon-Sat.* ☎ *073 21148; www.ireland-northwest.travel.ie;* ⓘ *Main Street, Bundoran. Open Jul-Aug, daily; Jun and Sep, Mon-Sat.* ☎ *072 41350; www.ireland-northwest.travel.ie*

▶ **Orient Yourself:** Donegal is situated on the south side of the Blue Stack Mountains, overlooking Donegal Bay on N 15 which links Sligo with Strabane on the border with Northern Ireland

🔗 **Don't Miss:** a stroll along Rossnowlagh Strand

Kids **Especially for Kids:** a trip to Waterworld, Bundoran *(see Address Book)*

👁 **Also See:** BUNCRANA, DONEGAL GLENS, ENNISKILLEN, LONDONDERRY.

A Bit of History

Dún na nGall (the fort of the foreigners) was first established by the Vikings; for 400 years the O'Donnell clan ruled the area until the flight of the Earl of Tyrconnell in 1607. In 1610 it was granted by the English crown to Sir Basil Brooke who rebuilt the castle and laid out the new Plantation town round the triangular Diamond 'square'.

The Irish mounted an unsuccessful attack during the 1641 rebellion; during the Williamite war the town was burned by the Jacobite Duke of Berwick, but the castle held out. In 1798 two French ships, carrying reinforcements for General Humbert's army, anchored in Donegal Bay but cut their cables on learning of his defeat. The anchor abandoned by the *Romaine* is now displayed on the quay.

Visit

Donegal Castle★

(Dúchas) 🔗🕐 *Open mid-Mar to Sep, 10am (2pm Sun) to 6pm (5.15pm last admission).* 🕐 *Closed 25-26 Dec.* 💶€3.70. 🎟 *Tours (30min) also available.* 🅿 ☎ *074 9722405* Perched up on a bluff on the south bank of the River Eske, the O'Donnell stronghold was largely destroyed by Hugh Roe O'Donnell in 1604 to prevent it falling into English hands. The remains were incorporated into the splendid five-gabled Jacobean mansion with a great hall, furnished in the style of the 1650s.

Donegal Railway Heritage Centre

🕐 *Open Mon-Fri, 10am-5pm, also Sat-Sun in Summer.* 💶 *€3.50.* ☎ *074 97 22655* The old station museum is dedicated to the narrowgauge County Donegal Railway (1900-59); 7 1/4inch gauge miniature railway and vintage rolling stock.

SLIDE FILE, Dublin

Donegal Castle

Donegal Friary (Abbey)

On the south bank of the estuary overlooking Donegal Bay are the ruins of a **Franciscan house**, once a famous centre for learning founded by Red Hugh O'Donnell

Four Masters

Michael O'Cleary (b 1580), a Franciscan from Donegal Abbey, and three lay Gaelic scholars, compiled the *Annals of the Kingdom of Ireland*, an account of Irish history known as the Annals of the Four Masters in the 17C while the authors were in refuge at a Franciscan house by the River Drowes south of Bundoran *(see below)*. They are commemorated by the obelisk (1967) in the Diamond, and in the dedication of the Roman Catholic church built in 1935 of local red granite in the Irish Romanesque style.

and his wife Nuala (1474). Substantial damage was caused by an explosion during the English occupation in 1601.

Driving Tour

South of Donegal *22mi/36km – half a day.*

▷ *From Donegal take N 15 S. After 4mi/6.4km in Ballintra turn right onto R 231 to Rossnowlagh.*

Rossnowlagh Strand★★
A small village with a large hotel overlook a wonderful beach (2.5mi/4km) - swimming, surfing, horse riding - across Donegal Bay rises Slieve League.

▷ *Continue S on R 231.*

Address Book

GETTING AROUND
Donegal Airport – ☎ 074 954 8284

SIGHTSEEING
The Waterbus offers 90min tours of Donegal Bay – *Sailing times depend on time and weather.* ☎074 9723666 - www. donegalbaywaterbus.com

♿ *For coin ranges, see the Legend on the cover flap.*

WHERE TO STAY
⌂**Ardeevin** – *Lough Eske, Barnesmore - 5.5mi NE by N 15 following signs for Lough Eske Drive -* ☎ *074 9721790 - sean-mcginty@eircom.net - 18 Mar to Nov - 6 rm* 🅿 Peaceful location with stunning views of Lough Eske. Antique furniture; traditional Irish breakfast.

⌂⌂**Island View House** – *Ballyshannon Rd - 0.75mi SW on N 15 -* ☎ *074 9722411 - dowdsb@indigo.ie - Closed 25-26 Dec - 4 rm* 🅿 A grey hued purpose-built guest house with views of the surrounding countryside and lough. Simply decorated with the emphasis on value for money. The owners provide genuine Irish hospitality.

SHOPPING
The famous woollen **Donegal tweed** is made and sold locally. Magee of Donegal - one of 4 members of the Donegal Handweavers Association - is now a leading manfacturer of clothing. Magees, The Diamond – 🕐 *Open Mon-*

Sat, 9.45am-6pm. ☎ *074 9722660- www. mageeclothing.com*

The **Craft Village** on the southern outskirts of the town, provides workshops to craftsmen.

Donegal Parian China, *Ballyshannon –* 🕐 *Open Mon-Fri, 9am-5.30pm; daily in summer* ☎ *072 51826; www. donegalchina.ie*

SPORTS AND LEISURE
Drumcliffe Walk – A pleasant wooded walk from the river bridge in Donegal downstream along the north bank of the River Eske overlooking the estuary.

Rossnowlagh Strand is ideal for bathing, surfing and horse riding.

Bundoran town beach can be dangerous but there are sandy beaches for bathing (up and down the coast).

Indoor facilities at **Waterworld** *(Bundoran)* – tidal wave, aqua volcano, tornado slide, water rapids, sea-based treatments; sea baths and health suite.

🧒🕐 *Open Jun-Aug, daily, 10am-7pm; Apr-May and Sep, Sat-Sun; also Easter week.* ♿ €*9.50 (including sauna/steam rooms)* ⌂. ☎ *071 9841172; www.water-worldbundorran.com*

EVENTS AND FESTIVALS
Ballyshannon Folk and Traditional Music Festival – Irish music in marquee; open air oncerts; busking competition and workshops *(early August)*

Abbey Assaroe

In the late 12C **Cistercian monks** from Boyle Abbey settled by the Erne estuary. The history of their monastery is retold in the restored **Mill**. ○ *Open Jun-Sep, 11am-7pm; Oct-May, Sun, 2.30-7pm.*

Ballyshannon

The town, created a Borough by Royal Charter in 1613, guards an important crossing point on the **River Erne**. In 1597 the English under Sir Conyers Clifford were defeated here by Red Hugh O'Donnell. Today, it is known for its popular Folk and Traditional Music Festival.

The poet William Allingham (1824–89), born in the Mall, is buried in St Anne's churchyard at the top of the hill. Another famous native was "Speaker" Conolly.

▶ *From Ballyshannon take N 15 S.*

Bundoran (Bun Dobhráin)

Bundoran is a major seaside resort with fine views across Donegal Bay to Slieve League, and the great square mass of Benbulben north of Sligo.

DONEGAL COAST★★

Facing the full force of Atlantic gales in winter, this remote and rugged coastline of deep sea-inlets, jagged cliffs and sandy beaches is backed by spectacular mountains and blanket bog. Its pristine landscapes are largely unaffected by modern development; on the north coast the land is divided into fields by walls of huge round stones and dotted with tiny white houses with thatched roofs roped down against the furious winter weather. ▤ *Dunglow.* ○ *Open Jun-Sep, Mon-Fri, 9.30am-5.30pm, Sat 11am-3pm.* ☎ *074 95 21297 - www.ireland-northwest.travel.ie*

▶ **Orient Yourself:** Take care driving the narrow and winding coastal roads while enjoying the spectacular views

◉ **Don't Miss:** Cliffs of Bunglass, Glencolmcille Folk Village and the views from Glengesh Pass

◔ **Also See:** BUNCRANA, DONEGAL, DONEGAL GLENS, LONDONDERRY

Driving Tours

Donegal to Naran *70mi/113km – 1 day*

▶ *From Donegal take N 56 W of Dunkineely, turn to St John's Point, then left again.*

Killaghtee Cross

In the graveyard of the ivy-covered 12C Killaghtee Church stands a 7C **cross-slab**.

▶ *Return to N 56 and continue W. After 3mi/4.8km turn left.*

Killybegs

This bustling little harbour town on the River Strager is one of the country's foremost fishing ports. In the mid 19C it became a centre for hand-tufted carpets, celebrated in the local Heritage Centre. Within the gates of St Catherine's Church, which was designed by JB Papworth c1840, *(turn right uphill)* stands the **tomb slab** *(left)* of Niall Mor MacSweeney; allies of the O'Neills, the MacSweeneys originally came to Ireland as gallowglasses, and the slab shows several of these hardy Scottish mercenaries.

▶ *Continue W on R 263; after 3mi/4.8km turn left onto the Coast Road.*

Kilcar (Cill Cárthaigh)

A major centre for tweed (*see Address Book*) at the confluence of two rivers. Several sandy beaches nearby are ideal for swimming.

▶ *Continue W. In Carrick turn left to Teelin (Teileann); take the second right to Bunglass.*

Cliffs of Bunglass★★

The road leads to one of the most spectacular sights in the whole country, an awe-inspiring prospect of ocean, mountain, and great tall cliffs. After climbing steeply (over 1 000ft/305m) and skirting Lough O'Mulligan, stop at the top to contemplate

---

Address Book

GETTING AROUND

Arranmore Ferry – *Operates from Burtonport to Leadgarrow: Passenger / car ferry. 30min crossing, up to 8 sailings per day in Summer to Arranmore.* ☎ 074 9520532; www.arranmoreferry.com
Tory Island Ferry – *Operates (weather permitting) Bunbeg to Tory Island (1hr 30min). Magheroarty to Tory Island (45min) up to 3 times/day.* ☎ 074 9531991
Donegal Coastal Cruises. *Coastal Cruises from Bunbeg/Magheroarty (Meenlaragh)* ☎074 9531320 - www.toryislandferry.com
For coin ranges, see the Legend on the cover flap.

WHERE TO STAY

⌒**Atlantic House** – *Main St, Dunglow* - ☎ 074 9521061 - jcannon@iol.ie - www.atlantichousedungloe.com - ⏲ *Closed 20-30 Dec - 10 rm.* Clean and affordable accommodation in central location.

⌒⌒⌒⌒ **Ostan Gweedore** – *Bunbeg* - ☎ 074 9531177 - reservations@ostangweedore.com - *Restricted opening in winter. 33 rm, 3 suites. Discounts available for online bookings.* ✗ 🅿
Well equipped hotel with comprehensive leisure facilities; comfortable, modern bedrooms and great views over Gweedore. Seafood restaurant.

Arranmore and **Tory Island Accommodation** - check with North West Tourism, Sligo. ☎071 916 1201 - www.irelandnorthwest.ie

WHERE TO EAT

⌒**The Mill Restaurant** – *Dunfanaghy* - 0.5mi SW on N 56 - ☎ 074 36985 - www.

themillrestaurant .com- Tues-Sun 7-9pm. *Restricted opening in winter* 🅿 A converted flax mill in a super location on New Lake, with terrific views of Mount Muckish. Pleasant bedrooms and a pretty restaurant with modern Irish cooking. *6rm* ⌒. Delightful rooms with ensuite facilities.

SHOPPING

The famous **Donegal tweed** is on sale in several centres – Donegal, Kilcar, Ardara and Downies.
Studio Donegal, Kilcar, sells hand-woven tweed: throws, clothing, hats.
Doogan Donegal Factory Shop, Kilcar, sells knitted woolllens.

SPORTS AND LEISURE

Beaches at Naran and Portnoo. Angling in Glenties at the confluence of the Owenea and Stracashel Rivers.
Walking: 4 long-distance waymarked coastal paths - Bealach na Gaeltachta, Dun na nGall - details from North West Tourism Office Letterkenny ☎074 9121160

EVENTS AND FESTIVALS

International Mary from Dungloe Festival – *Dungloe. One week late-Jul to early-Aug. Music, dancing and craic.*

TRACING ANCESTORS

Donegal Ancestry Centre – *The Quay, Rathmelton – Genealogy research* - ⏲ *Open Mon-Fri, 9.30am-4.30pm (3.30pm Fri).* ☎ 074 9151266 - info@donegalancestry.com - www.donegalancestry.com

the view of the cliffs of Bunglass rising 300m from the sea, and the sheer south flank of Slieve League (1 972ft/601m).

▶ *Return to Carrick and turn left onto R 263. After 2mi/3.2km bear left to Malin Beg (Málainn Bhig).*

Glenmalin Court Cairn

In marshy ground beside a small stream are the substantial remains of a court tomb, known locally as Cloghanmore, meaning the Big Stone.

▶ *Continue to the crossroads; turn left along the coast.*

Trabane Strand★

The sheltered sandy bay faces south across Donegal Bay to Benbulben *(see SLIGO)*.

▶ *Return to the crossroads and go straight ahead to Glencolumbkille.*

Glencolmcille Folk Village★★

&✆⏱ *Open Easter Sat to Sep, daily 10am (noon Sun) to 6pm.* ⊜ €2.75. ⌑🅿✆ *074 97 30017 - www.glenfolkvillage.com*

The folk village was one of the many initiatives undertaken by **Father James McDyer** (d 1987) who resolved to put a stop to the traumatic exodus of emigrants from this poor and remote area. He helped build a community centre, had electricity connected and roads improved. In 1967 he initiated the idea of preserving traditional practises by building a folk village with a cottage for each century, furnished with artefacts donated by his parishioners. The school, shebeen, craftshop were added later.

The actual village of **Glencolumbkille** *(Gleann Cholm Cille)* lies inland from its sandy beaches guarded by a Martello tower on Glen Head (745ft/227m). In this remote and rugged valley St Columba *(Colmcille)* built himself a house of retreat for quiet prayer. On his feast day (9 June), pilgrims make a penitential tour (3mi/5km) of the glen between midnight and 3am, stopping at Stations of the Cross marked by cairns, boulders, pagan standing stones and early-Christian cross-slabs.

The **Ulster Cultural Institute** *(Foras Cutúir Uladh)*, a centre for Gaelic studies, offers a variety of activities and language courses. ✆ *074 97 30248; www.oideas-gael.com*

▶ *Take the road to Ardara. After 10mi/16km viewing point (left).*

Glengesh Pass★★

Stop at the head of the pass to view the glaciated, green valley, enclosed by steep and rugged mountains. Hairpin bends carry the road down to join the river.

Ardara (Ard an Rátha)

Ardara (pronounced with the accent on the last syllable) is an attractive market town on the Owentocker River at the head of a deep sea-inlet, famous for its production of Donegal Tweed. The **Ardara Heritage Centre** celebrates the local tweed industry; weaving demonstrations and Aran knitting tradition. ⏱ *Open Easter-Sep, daily 10am (2pm Sun) to 6pm.* ⌑✆ *074 95 541473*

▶ *Take N 56 E.*

Glenties (na Gleannta)

Glenties is the home town of Patrick MacGill (1890-1963), the "Navvy Poet" because of his uncompromising depictions of the hard life led by migrant labourers; he is honoured in a festival each summer*(July/August)*.

Glengesh Pass

St Connall's Church (Roman Catholic), one of Liam McCormick's masterpieces of modern architecture echoes the landscape between Big Glen and Wee Glen; marvellous use of natural light and collection of rainwater for the water gardens.

▶ *Take N 56 west. In Maas take R 261 west; after 3mi/5km turn right.*

The twin resorts of **Naran** and **Portnoo**, which face Inishkeel in Gweebarra Bay, have broad sandy beaches: great places for cliff walks, surfing, sailing, fishing and golf.

Naran to Dunfanaghy *70mi/113km – 1 day*

▶ *E of Naran take R 261 E. In Maas take N 56 N.*

The Rosses★
After the beautiful **Gweebarra Estuary**★ comes **Dunglow** *(An Clochán Liath)* an attractive small town regarded as the capital of The Rosses – a bleak flat rocky Gaelic-speaking region (100sq mi/259km²) dotted with tiny lakes.

▶ *Take R 259 NW.*

Burtonport (Ailt an Chorráin)
The tiny harbour provides regular ferry services *(2mi/3.2km)* to Arranmore Island *(& see Address Book).*

Arranmore Island
The scenic attractions are rugged cliffs on the northern and western shores, and several lakes. There are six pubs which hold regular traditional music sessions.

▶ *Continue N on R 259. In Crolly turn left onto N 56. After 1mi/1.6km turn left onto R 258; turn left to Bunbeg.*

Bunbeg (An Bun Beag)
Beyond the signal tower on the narrow winding Clady estuary is this lovely little harbour, well protected from the Atlantic storms. Boats sail from here to Tory Island.

▶ *Take R 257 N.*

Bloody Foreland Head

The headland owes its name to the reddish colour of the rocks, exaggerated in the evening sun. Offshore: Inishbofin and its islands point north towards Tory Island.

Tory Island (Toraigh)

Access by boat from Meenlaragh (Magheroarty) and Gortahork (see Address Book); from Gortahork follow the signs (Bloody Foreshore) and turn right down to the pier.
Frequently cut off from the mainland, bleak and windswept Tory Island *(7mi/11km from the mainland)* was largely inhabited by Gaelic-speaking fishermen ruled since time immemorial by their "king". Little is left of the monastery founded in the 6C by St Columba (Colmcille) other than a round tower, Tau cross and two ruined churches. At the Tory School of Primitive Art, islanders produce striking paintings in a naive folk style; examples are on show at Glebe House.

▷ *Turn left onto N 56.*

Ballyness Bay

The sheltered sea-inlet is overlooked by two Gaelic-speaking villages, **Gortahork** *(Gort an Choirce)* and **Falcarragh** *(An Fál Carrach)*.

Dunfanaghy

In the lee of Horn Head, this picturesque former fishing port was transformed into a resort when the harbour silted up. The mock-Tudor **Workhouse**, one of many built across Ireland in the 1840s, explains how the Famine devastated the area, highlighting the plight of one Hannah Harraty, who survived hunger, a wicked stepmother, a life of beggary, and reached the age of 90. ♿ ⏱ *Open Easter-Sep,Mon-Sat, 11am -5pm.* ⚀ €4. 50 ☎ 074 9136540

Horn Head Scenic Route★– 30min

The headland, a breeding colony for seabirds, rises to high cliffs (over 600ft/183m) on the north coast; the blow-hole is known as McSwyne's Gun *(SW)*. Magnificent **views** extend *(W)* to Inishbofin, Inishdooey and Inishbeg and Bloody Foreland Head; *(NW)* Tory Island; *(E)* Sheep Haven Bay and Rosguill Peninsula; *(NE)* Melmore Head, Malin Head and Scotland on a clear day; *(inland)* Muckish Mountain, Errigal Mountain.

Dunfanaghy to Letterkenny 80mi/130km – 1 day

▷ *From Dunfanaghy take N 56 E.*

Portnablagh

The fishermen's hamlet was transformed when the Portnablagh Hotel was opened in 1923. The golf course is a links course designed in 1905 by Harry Vardon.

Ards Forest Park

The park (1 188 acres/481ha), once part of an extensive estate owned by the prominent Stewart family of Scottish descent, includes the north shore of the Ards Peninsula, the Binnagorm headland, Sheep Haven Bay (bathing beaches). Broad variety of woodland, fenland, sand dunes, salt-marsh, a dolmen, ringforts, Lough Lilly; waymarked footpaths and viewpoints; children's playground.

▷ *Continue S on N 56.*

Creeslough

Muckish Mountain (2 197ft/670m) stands guard over the village, lending its profile to **St Michael's Church** (Roman Catholic), another of Liam McCormick's outstanding modern churches (1971). Frequent past visitors include artists and writers such as W B Yeats, AE Russell, Percy French and G K Chesterton.

The ruins of **Doe Castle**★ stand in a strategic position on a promontory in Sheep Haven Bay protected by the sea, a rock-cut moat and drawbridge. Built in the 1500s by Scottish mercenaries, the MacSweenys, the stronghold played an important role in local history until after the Battle of the Boyne (1690). In the late18C, it was made habitable by General George Vaughan Harte, who had served with distinction in India and who mounted several cannon from the Siege of Serringapatam on the turrets and sea front. A **tomb slab** carved with an elaborate cross may have belonged to one of the Scottish McSweeneys, sometime lords of the castle, moved here from the ruins of the neighbouring Franciscan monastery. *(Dúchas)* ⊶ *Closed for restoration.* ☎ *074 9138445*

▷ *On leaving the castle turn left over a hump-backed bridge; turn left onto R 245. At Carrigart (Carraig Airt), follow R 248 NW.*

Rosguill Peninsula Atlantic Drive★ *9mi/14.5km*

This scenic route follows the great curve of sand dunes alongside the Rosapenna golf links, before climbing up to **Downies** *(Na Dúnaibh)*, a resort renown for tweed from where it stretches past the deep inlet of Sheep Haven Bay backed by Horn Head, providing glorious views of the sheltered beach of Tranarossan Bay, Melmore Head and sandy coves and islands in Mulroy Bay.

▷ *In Carrigart take R 245 E to Mulroy Bay and Millford. Turn left onto R 246. 2mi/3.2km N of Carrowkeel fork left onto the coast road.*

Fanad Peninsula

A string of hamlets lines the east shore of Mulroy Bay and Broad Water. North of Kindrum where iodine was extracted from seaweed in the 19C, grass-covered dunes, dotted with white cottages and small lakes, extend to the sandy shore. The lighthouse on Fanad Head *(no access)* marks the entrance to Lough Swilly. Dunaff Head, the Urris Hills and Dunree Head come into view on the opposite shore. **Portsalon** is a small resort at the north end of Warden Beach.

▷ *From Portsalon take R 246; after 1mi/1.6km turn left onto the coast road.*

Knockalla Viewpoint★

The north end of Knockalla Mountain (1 194ft/364m) provides panoramic **views**.

▷ *At the junction bear left onto R 247.*

Rathmullan (Ráth Maoláin)

This pretty little place facing Lough Swilly has an eventful history. In 1587, at a time when the old Gaelic order still prevailed here in the north, "Red" Hugh O'Donnell, the future Earl of Tyrconnell, was trapped and spirited off to imprisonment in Dublin, a treacherous act which helped precipate years of unrest. In 1607 Hugh O'Neill and Rory O'Donnell fled to the Continent with friends and family from here, paving the way for the Plantation of Ulster when Irish lands were confiscated and reassigned to settlers from England and Scotland. In 1798 Wolfe Tone was brought ashore near Rathmullan a prisoner after his attempts to overthrow British rule.

The old Napoleonic battery beside the pier is now a heritage centre displaying the **Flight of the Earls' Exhibition**. ♿ *Re-opening 2007.* ☎ *074 9158178 - www. theflightoftheearls.com*

▷ *Continue SW on R 247.*

H Champollion/MICHELIN

Rathmelton Bridge

Rathmelton (Ráth Mealtain)★

This typical Plantation town stands on a salmon river flowing into Lough Swilly. The ruined 17C church at the top of the hill contains an interesting Perpendicular window and a Romanesque carving brought from Aughnish Island farther down the creek. The Revd Francis Mackemie, Rector in Rathmelton until he emigrated in 1683 to Virginia in America and founded the first Presbyterian church, is commemorated by **Mackemie Hall** *(Back Lane)*, a former meeting house which now houses the library. Among the 18C warehouses along the quay is the old Steamboat Store housing the **Donegal Ancestry Centre** and **Rathmelton Story** exhibition. *(Exhibition)* ◷ *Open Mon-Fri (Sat-Sun, Jun-Aug) 9.30am-5pm.* ☎ *074 9151266 - www. donegalancestry.com*

▶ *Take R 245 S to Letterkenny.*

DONEGAL GLENS

The centre of County Donegal is mountainous country interrupted by long and sometimes serpentine glens: the Barnesmore Gap running south of the Blue Stack Mountains (2 205ft/672m) to Donegal, the Barnes Gap north of Kilmacrenan to the east of Muckish Mountain (2 197ft/670m), and Muckish Gap at the foot of the south face. The most spectacular of the high peaks is Errigal (2 466ft/752m), a cone of white quartzite, towering over Dunlewy. Although Lifford is the county town, Letterkenny is larger and more conveniently situated for touring the county. ◪ *Neil T Blaney Rd, Letterkenny.* ◷ *Open Jun-Sep, Mon-Sat (daily Jun-Aug); Oct-May, Mon-Fri, 9am-5pm.* ☎ *074 9121160; www.donegaldirect.com*

▶ **Orient Yourself:** Most of the roads follow the course of the rivers through the glens. N 15 runs between Donegal and Letterkenny which is linked by N 13 to Londonderry over the border.

⊙ **Don't Miss:** Glenveagh National Park

Kids **Especially for Kids:** Seat of Power exhibition, Lifford

◔ **Also See:** BUNCRANA, DONEGAL, DONEGAL COAST, LONDONDERRY

Visit

Sites listed in rough clockwise order from Letterkenny.

Letterkenny

Large by local standards, and with a good range of local facilities, this otherwise undistinguished town on the River Swilly has the longest main street in Ireland and is the seat of the bishop of the Roman Catholic diocese of Raphoe. The vast Gothic Revival **Cathedral** has an interior with a somewhat uneasy mixture of neo-Celtic carving and Italianate decor.

The **County Museum**, housed in the old 19C workhouse, traces the folk life and traditions of Donegal, its history, archaeology and geology. ♿ ⏰ *Open Mon-Fri, 10am-12.30pm and 1-4.30pm, Sat, 1-4.30pm.* ☎ *074 24613*

Newmills

(Dúchas) ⏰ *Open mid-Jun to late-Sep, daily 10am-6.30pm (last admission 5.15pm).* 🅿 ☎ *074 9125155*

A tour of the water-powered corn and flax mill with the largest waterwheel in working order explains how the corn was dried and milled, the flax was treated by retting, rolling, scutching and buffering to produce linen thread.

Lake Finn

4mi/6km N by R 624. 19mi/31km west of Letterkenny by R 250 to Fintown.

Fintown's attractions include paddle boats for hire from the pier, and the restored narrow-gauge **Fintown Railway** (An Mhuc Dhubh) maintained by the Central Gaeltacht

---

St Columba

St Columba (known in Irish as St Colmcille) (521–597), a native of Donegal, was active during the transition from pagan to Christian Ireland. He was born an O'Neill in Gartan of a noble family, and was fostered at Kilmacrenan as a boy as was customary then.

Over a period of 15 years he founded monasteries at Tory, Drumcliffe, Kilmore, Swords, Moon and Durrow (553). In c 560 he embraced the white martyrdom by giving up all he loved, leaving Ireland for Iona off the coast of Scotland, where he established a famous monastic community. He died in 597, the year in which Augustine landed in Kent.

Address Book

WHERE TO STAY

🛏**Ballyraine Guesthouse** – *Ramelton Rd, Letterkenny - 1.75mi E by N 14 on R 245 -* ☎ *074 9124460 - ballyraineguesthouse@eircom.net - 8 rm* 🅿 Purpose-built guesthouse in the suburbs; well-equipped and generously proportioned bedrooms.

🛏**Dergfield House** – *Donegal Rd, Ballybofey - 1mi S of Ballybofey -* ☎ *074 9132775 - derghouse@eircom.net - 5 rm.* Family-run B&B set back from the main road out of Ballybofey.

SPORTS AND LEISURE

Fishing – Cod and pollack in Lough Swilly; Salmon, sea trout and brown trout in Crana River.

Rambling – Errigal, the highest mountain in Donegal offers extensive views over almost all of Donegal and its neighbouring counties. The tourist route to the summit starts off the R 251 at the layby before a sign to Altan Farm. There is no regular track in the first section; walkers must climb the lowest part of the southeast ridge and bear left; on reaching the lower screes, follow a faint track winding steeply upwards. Approx 4hr 30min to the summit and back.

GREYHOUND RACING

At Lifford.

TRACING ANCESTORS

Seat of Power Visitor Centre – *Lifford.* Genealogical service within the Visitor Centre.

Train Society. ♿ 🕐 *Open mid-Jun to mid-Sep, Mon-Fri, 11-4pm, Sun 1-5pm.* 👝 €6. ☎ *074 9546280*

Colmcille
St Columba (**Colmcille** in Irish), born by Gartan Lough, is remembered in a detailed exhibition in the **Heritage Centre**. ♿ 🕐 *Open Easter and May to early-Oct, 10.30am (1pm Sun) to 6.30pm; otherwise by appointment.* 👝 €3. 🅿 🛒 ☎ *074 9137306*

The **Glebe House and Gallery**★ was bought by the artist, collector and theatre designer Derek Hill, in 1953. The **gallery** (1982) houses the **Derek Hill Collection** of paintings by 20C artists (Braque, Corot, Degas, Picasso, Renoir, Graham Sutherland), notable Irish artists (J B Yeats) and by the inhabitants of Tory Island who paint in a primitive style producing striking "folk" works. The Regency **house** is richly furnished with Oriental prints, William Morris fabrics, William de Morgan tiles and Wemyss ware pottery; artworks by John Sherlock, Victor Pasmore, Basil Blackshaw, Augustus John, Evie and Nathaniel Hone, Sir William Orpen, Oskar Kokoshka, Cecil Beaton and John Bratby. *(Dúchas)* ♿ 🕐 *Open at Easter, mid-May to late-Sep, Sat-Thu, 11am-6.30pm (5.30pm last admission).* 👝 €2.90. 🅿 🛒 *(summer).* ☎ *0/4 9137071.*

On the hillside facing southeast over Lough Akibbon are the scanty remains of **St Colmcille's Oratory,** a monastery associated with St Colmcille: a holy well, two crosses and the ruins of a church in a graveyard.

Glenveagh National Park★★
(Dúchas) ♿🕐 *Open mid-Mar to early-Nov, 10am-6.30pm (5pm last admission). Castle* 👝 €2.60. Minibus between Visitor Centre and Castle. 👝 €2. 🅿 ✕ 🛒 ☎ *074 91 37090 - www.heritageireland.ie*

The park (23 887 acres/9 667ha) consists of Lough Beagh and the surrounding wild landscape of bogs, moorland, and rugged moutain clad in natural woodlands of oak and birch; luxuriant gardens surrounding a romantic granite castle on a promontory beside the lake. The estate was created by John George Adair by the amalgamation of several smaller holdings from which he evicted all the tenants in 1861. In 1937 it was bought by the Irish-American millionaire Henry McIlhenny, who sold the land to the Irish National Parks Service in 1975, he later donated the castle and gardens.

The **Visitor Centre** provides information about the park; video about the conservation of the flora and fauna, including the largest herd of **red deer** in Ireland.

Glenveagh Castle

The beautiful **gardens**★★, begun by Mrs Adair, is designed to provide colour and interest through the seasons. Stone statuary provides a formal note to the **Terrace** (1966) and in the **Italian Garden** (1958). From the long lawn at the centre of the **Pleasure Grounds**, paths lead up to the **Belgian Walk**, which was constructed during the First World War by convalescing Belgian soldiers billeted at the house. Within the **walled garden** is an Orangery (1958) designed by Philippe Jullian. From the south end of the gardens there is a long **view** up Lough Beagh to the head of the glen below the peak of Slieve Snaght (2 441ft/683m).

The castellated façade of the **castle** conceals a large Victorian house, designed in 1870 by John Adair's cousin, John Townsend Trench, that was lit by oil lamps until 1957. The sumptuous furnishings, left by the last American owners, include a carpet woven in Killybegs to match the **drawing room** furnishings; in the Library there are paintings by George Russell, better known as the poet AE. *Visit by guided tour.*

Dunlewy Centre (Ionad Cois Locha)

🕓 *Open Easter to early-Nov, daily10.30am Sun 11am)-6pm.* 🚗 *€5.50 (homestead); €5.50 (boat trip). Irish music night: Tue, Jul-Aug.* ✕☎ *074 9531699 - www.dunlewy-centre.com*

On the shore of the lake stands an old weaver's homestead coverted into a family-oriented visitor centre providing tweed weaving demonstrations, a guided tour of the cottage, pony treks, boat trips *(narrated stories)*.

The road from Dunlewy east to Letterkenny (R 251) offers wonderful **views** of the lake and its valley, known as the **Poisoned Glen**.

Doon Well and Rock

The rags on the bush show that people still believe in the curative properties long attributed to the well . Until the 16C the **Doon Rock** was the place of inauguration of the O'Donnells, the chiefs of Tirconail. Its flattened top *(5min there and back on foot)* provides a fine **view** of the surrounding country. It was near here that Sir Cahir O'Docherty was shot dead in 1608.

Kilmacrenan

St Columba built the first church here, on a site between the road to Millford and the Leannan River now marked by the ruins of a 17C church and the remains of Kilmacrenan Friary, which was founded in 1537 by the local chieftain, Manus O'Donnell.

Raphoe

The village of Raphoe (pronounced with the stress on the second syllable) is grouped around its Diamond, an attractive triangular green. In the south corner stands **Raphoe Cathedral**, a Gothic building with 18C tower and transepts, incorporating several carved fragments dating from the 10C to 17C. The gaunt ruin south of the church was the Bishop's Palace, built in 1636 by Dr John Leslie with flanking towers similar to Kanturk and Rathfarnham: this was damaged during the 1641 Rebellion and the Williamite Wars, repaired and then destroyed by fire in 1839.

Due south of Raphoe stands the **Beltany Stone Circle** *(west up a track - sign Stone Circle. 10min there and back on foot)* commanding fine views of the surrounding countryside. The Bronze Age stone circle which is about 4ft/1m high, consists of 64 stones (150yd/137m circumference) although there were originally many more.

Lifford

The county town's lovely old **courthouse** (1746) has been converted into the **Seat of Power Visitor Centre** (Chieftains of Ireland video; courtroom re-enactment), jail and genealogical centre. Kids ♿ 🕐 *Open Mon-Fri, 9am-4.30pm, Sun, 12.30-4pm.* ∞ €6 ✗ ☎ 074 9141733 - www.finnvalley.ie/places/seatofpower/index.html

Cavanacor House (*2mi/3km west of Lifford by N 14*), one of the oldest inhabited 17C houses in the province reprieved by James II after dining under a sycamore in the garden, was briefly home to 11th US President James Knox Polk: contemporary art gallery. ♿ 🕐 *Gallery: Open Tue-Sat, noon-6pm.* ☎ 074 9141143

DROGHEDA★

POPULATION 24 460

Straddling the River Boyne close to its mouth, Drogheda (Droichead Átha) was one of the most important towns of medieval Ireland, with a long and eventful history. It is still a place of some consequence, well located on the Dublin-Belfast road and railway, with varied industries and a harbour. There is an attractive coastline to the north and inland lies the **Boyne Valley**, with its superlative megalithic tombs and echoes of battle. 🕐 *Open May-Sep, daily; Oct, Mon-Sat; 9.30pm-5.30pm* ☎ 041 9837070 - www.drogheda-tourism.com

▶ **Orient Yourself:** Drogheda, now bypassed by M 1, is an important bridging point over the River Boyne

🖒 **Also See:** BOYNE VALLEY, DUNDALK, FINGAL, KELLS, TRIM

A Bit of History

The town was founded in 911 by Norsemen under the Dane Thorgestr. In the late 12C Hugh de Lacy, Lord of Meath, made it an important Norman stronghold with two separate parishes, Armagh and Meath. Little remains of the many monasteries which flourished in Drogheda in the Middle Ages and only the **Butter Gate** on Millmount and St Laurence Gate remain of the town walls built in 1234.

Parliament often met in Drogheda and it was during one of these sittings that Poynings' Law was enacted in 1494. During the Confederate Rebellion Drogheda was twice besieged: in 1641 Sir Henry Tichborne and Lord Moore withstood the forces of Sir Phelim O'Neill until the Earl of Ormond brought relief and in 1649 it was stoutly defended from **Oliver Cromwell** by Sir Arthur Aston and 3 000 men. During this second siege, many people took refuge in St Peter's Church and perished when the wooden steeple was set alight; eventually the city wall was breached on the southeast side of Millmount near St Mary's Church and, according to Cromwell's own estimate, 2 000 died by the sword; most of the survivors were transported to Barbados.

Walking Tour

Town Centre

Much of the town is set on the steep north bank of the river with narrow lanes and flights of steps linking the different levels.

St Peter's Roman Catholic Church, a neo-Gothic building (1881) on West Street contains the shrine of Oliver Plunkett (1625–81), the Roman Catholic Archbishop of Armagh. ♿🕐 *Open 8.30am-6pm.* ☎ *041 983 8537 - www.armagharchdiocese.org*

▶ *On leaving the church turn right along West Street; turn left into Old Abbey Lane.*

The roofless nave and crossing tower of **St Mary's Abbey** stand on the oldest monastic site in Drogheda, where, according to tradition, a monastery was founded after St Patrick's visit in 452. In 1206 a Norman settler, Ursus de Swemele and his wife, founded a hospital which was later administered by the Augustinian Friars until the Dissolution in 1543.

▶ *From West Street turn right uphill into Fair Street.*

Oliver Plunkett (1629-81)

Oliver Plunkett was a member of a notable Anglo-Irish family from Loughcrew in Co Meath. Educated in Rome and mentored by his kinsman Patrick, later Bishop of Meath, Plunkett was appointed Archbishop of Armagh and Primate of Ireland in 1670. Using family connections with the establishment, notably Viceroy Berkeley, he used his authority to reverse years of neglect following the Cromwellian era and the Penal Laws, travelling extensively in the north of Ireland administering the Sacrament of confirmation. In his wake, a school for pupils of all ages was set up, priests were ordained and bishops annointed.

Repression following the marriage of Charles II's bother, James Duke of York, to the Roman Catholic Mary of Modena, prompted Plunkett to go into hiding. Anti-monarchists in London accused him of complicity in the «Popish Plot» fabricated by Titus Oates and implicated in the organisation of an invasion of 40 000 men in Carlingford. He was arrested in 1679 and brought to trial in Dundalk but no one would give evidence against him. Convicted of treason in London, he was condemned to be hung, drawn and quartered at Tyburn. He was canonised in 1975.

Address Book

WHERE TO STAY

Boyne Haven House – *Dublin Rd – 2.5mi SE of Drogheda on N 1* ☎ *041 983 6700 - taramcd@ireland.com - 4 rm* 🅿
A bungalow surrounded by a mature garden, just off the main Dublin road. Welcoming fire, impressive Irish breakfast, attractively decorated bedrooms.

Windsor Lodge B&B – ☎*041 9841966; www.barwindsorlodge.com* 🅿
Centrally located, practical guesthouse with all required amenities for a comfortable stay.

WHERE TO EAT

Buttergate Restaurant – *Millmount Sq.* 🕓 *Open Tue, Wed, Sun, 12.30-2.30pm; Thu-Sat, 7-11pm. Booking* advisable. ☎ *041 9834759.* Good variety of dishes and vegetarian options.

The Boiled Onion – *32 Shop St* ☎ *041 9875566 - www.theboiledonion.com.* Dinner only - popular with the locals, Mexican influence.

The Black Bull Inn – *Dublin Rd* ☎ *041 983 7139.* Traditional local pub serving lunch and dinner for foodies.

SHOPPING

Millmount Craft Centre – *by Martello Tower* ☎ *041 984 1960 - Tue-Fri, 10am-5pm.* Designers and craftsmen working from their studios: jewellery, hand-painted silks, ceramics and knitwear.

SPORTS AND LEISURE

Extensive beaches at Bettystown (south)

The **Courthouse,** with its distinctive weather vane on the corner of Fair Street and Bolton Street, was designed by Francis Johnston and completed in 1790.

▶ *Walk E along Fair Street and turn left into Magdalene Street.*

St Peter's Anglican Church (1753) 🕓 *Open on request.* ☎ *041 9827345 (Rector) - www.drogheda.armagh.anglican.org.* Replacing the medieval one burnt by the Cromwellians in the siege of 1649, this church gained a porch and spire in 1793, added by Francis Johnston. The three rows of Georgian houses (c 1730) beyond the graveyard, with its cadaver tombstone, (at the east gate) were built for clergy widows.

▶ *Continue up Magdalene Street and turn right into Upper Magdalene Street.*

Magdalene Tower (14C) marks the site of a Dominican monastery founded in 1224 by Lucas de Netterville, Archbishop of Armagh, where in 1395 four Irish princes submitted to Richard II.

▶ *Continue along Upper Magdalene Street and turn right into King Street; continue into Palace Street and turn left.*

St Laurence Gate★ is unique in Ireland: the well-preserved three-storey barbican is an integral part of the 13C gate, built by the Normans using stone from the walls erected by the Vikings. A section of the town wall still stands on the south side.

SLIDE FILE, Dublin

Cadaver tombstone

▶ *Walk west along Laurence Street to Shop Street.*

The **Tholsel** stands at the crossroads in the town centre; a clock tower and a lantern surmount the limestone building (1770) where Corporation meetings and law courts were held until 1889.

Millmount *South Bank*

Generations of rulers left their mark on the eminence dominating the south bank of the Boyne, possibly the site of a passage grave and subsequently crowned by an Anglo-Norman motte, then by 18C fortifications. From the Martello Tower there is a fine **view** of the town centre and of Drogheda's most imposing individual structure, the **railway viaduct** built in 1855 across the Boyne estuary. Until the completion of this structure, passengers travelling between Dublin and Belfast by rail had to leave the train on the south bank and take a coach over the river bridge to join another train on the north side.

Drogheda Museum★
Located in the old Officers' quarters (1820), this museum is dedicated to local history and the importance of local industries, notably textiles, ironworks and shipbuilding. (♿ *to ground floor*) ⊙ *Open Mon-Sat, 10am-6pm; Sun, 2.30-5.30pm; last tour at 5.30pm.* ∞ *€4.50.* 🅿☎ *041 983 3097 - www.millmount.net*

Excursion

Whiteriver Mills
4mi/6km N by R 624. Dunleer; 9mi/14.5km north of Drogheda by N 1 and R 132. ⊙ *Open Apr-Sep, 10am (2pm Sun) to 6pm.* ∞ *€4.* ☎ *041 685 1141*
On the southern edge of Dunleer stands a three-storey 18C working flour mill *(restored)*.

DUBLIN★★★

POPULATION 481 854

Ireland's famous capital – the fair city – bestrides the River Liffey and looks seawards to its port and the broad waters of Dublin Bay. The unforgettable outline of the Wicklow Mountains forms a magnificent backdrop to the south, while suburbs stretch far inland as well as north to the Ben of Howth and south to Dalkey Headland. Something like a third of the country's population lives in the greater Dublin area, and a disproportionate amount of the country's business is carried out here. Georgian architectural elegance and the increasingly cosmopolitan life of street, cafe, restaurant and bar make the city an irresistible destination, not just for a weekend, but for longer periods of exploration.

🛈 *Dublin Tourism Centre, Suffolk St.* 🛈 *14 Upper O'Connell St.* 🛈 *Dublin Airport* 🛈 *Dun Laoghaire Ferry Terminal.* 🛈*Baggot Street Bridge* ☎ *01 605 7700;* ☎ *0800 0397000 (from UK);* ☎ *66 979 2083 (Fáilte Ireland)* 🛈 *Temple Bar Cultural Info Centre, 12 East Essex St* ☎ *01 677 2255 - www.templebar.ie; www.visitdublin.ie*

▶ **Orient Yourself:** Dublin is set on the east coast, on the estuary of the River Liffey and the shores of Dublin Bay. It forms the hub of the road and rail network and has direct connections with all the major provincial towns. It is served by an international airport (north of the city centre) and by shipping lines from Liverpool, Holyhead and the Isle of Man.

🅿 **Parking:** there are carparks throughout the city (👤 *see Address Book*)

🐾 **Don't Miss:** there are many things to see and do in Dublin - Trinity College, a stroll round Phoenix Park, Dublin Castle and Kilmainham Gaol are special, although there are several fabulous museums to appeal to every sensitivity.

🕐 **Organizing Your Time:** don't try to do too much - you will want to come back so reserve something for your next visit

Kids **Especially for Kids:** Dublinia and the zoo

👤 **Also See:** BOYNE VALLEY, FINGAL, KILDARE, MAYNOOTH, TRIM, WICKLOW MOUNTAINS.

A Bit of History

Viking Settlement – The name Dublin (Baile Átha Cliath) is derived from *Dubh Linn*, the Dark Pool at the confluence of the Poddle and the Liffey; the Irish name, *Baile Átha Cliath*, means the city by the hurdle ford. The first permanent settlement beside the Liffey was established at Wood Quay in the 9C by the Vikings, who then spread north of the river where their settlement was known as Oxmantown; at the Battle of Clontarf on the north shore of Dublin Bay in 1014 their power was curbed by Brian Ború.

Anglo-Norman Stronghold – After the Anglo-Norman invasion late in the 12C Dublin was granted to the port of Bristol as a trading post by Henry II in 1172. Under constant harassment by the Irish tribes and an unsuccessful attack in 1316 by Edward Bruce of Scotland, the extent of the Anglo-Normans' influence waxed and waned but they never lost control of Dublin, which gradually became the seat of Parliament and the centre of government. Early Lord Deputies operated from their own power bases in the Pale – Trim, Maynooth and Kilkenny – but in the 16C Sir Henry Sidney, who was four times Lord Deputy, took up residence in the castle and put it in good repair. Gradually the medieval fortress evolved into an administrative centre and vice-regal court.

Kildare Revolt – The most serious incident occurred in 1534 when Thomas Fitzgerald, known as "Silken Thomas" because of the silk embroidery on his men's apparel, was acting as Vice Deputy during his father's absence in London. On hearing a false report that his father had been beheaded, he renounced his allegiance to Henry VIII in St Mary's Abbey and launched a rebellion which became known as the Kildare or Geraldine Revolt. He laid siege to the Castle into which the Constable and his retinue had barricaded themselves, but the citizenry turned against Thomas; the besieged proclaimed the arrival of the king's army and made a sortie, whereupon the besiegers took fright and scattered. Fitzgerald himself escaped but he was forced to surrender some months later and was executed in London together with his five uncles.

Dublin Waterways

The urban landscape of Dublin is greatly enhanced by the five waterways which traverse the city – **River Liffey**, personified as Anna Livia Pluribella, which flows through the city centre before entering the sea in Dublin Bay; two tributaries, the **River Dodder** on the south bank and the **River Tolka** on the north bank; and two canals, the **Grand Canal** (1757–1803), which passes through the southern suburbs to join the Shannon at Shannon Harbour, north of Birr, and the **Royal Canal** (1790–1817), which passes through the Northside to join the Shannon west of Longford.

Georgian Dublin – In the relative peace of the 18C, restrictions eased and trade flourished. Buildings were constructed to house public bodies; terraces of fine houses were erected first north and then south of the river; men of property, drawn to the capital on parliamentary and other business, commissioned fine mansions. Under the activities of the Wide Streets Commissioners, established in 1758, Dublin developed into an elegant city, embraced by the Royal and Grand Canals and bisected by the Liffey, now embanked between quays and spanned by several bridges. With the Act of Union (1800) political affairs removed to London and, although known as the "second city of the Empire", Dublin stagnated. Despite many grievous losses, Dublin can still claim to be the finest Georgian city in the British Isles.

> ## Literary Dublin
>
> Several Nobel Prize winners figure among the Dublin-born writers who achieved international fame – Swift, Mangan, Wilde, Shaw, Yeats, Synge, O'Casey, Joyce, Behan, Beckett. Their former homes are marked with plaques or converted into museums. The major figures are celebrated in a literary parade in St Patrick's Park., while their literary works are marked in the Dublin Writers Museum.

Capital of the Republic – There was much destruction during the Easter Rising and the Civil War but key buildings like the Four Courts, the GPO and the Custom House were eventually restored to something like their former glory. The refurbishment projects carried out in the last decades of the 20C meant that Dublin well deserved the title European City of Culture in 1991. Temple Bar has been transformed from a dilapidated district into a network of pedestrian streets, vibrant with pubs, restaurants, hotels, craftshops and cafés. The district of Smithfield west of O'Connell Street has been regenerated under the Harp Project.

Walking Tour

The three walks covering the city centre start and finish at O'Connell Bridge or Ha'penny Bridge.

South Bank

This is perhaps city's youngest quarter, as it was vulnerable to Irish raiding parties swooping down from the Wicklow Mountains: until the construction of the Old

SLIDE FILE, Dublin

Grand Canal

Address Book

GETTING ABOUT

Dublin International Airport – ☎ *01 814 1111; www.dublinairport.com*
Aerdart is a bus service from Dublin Airport to the Dart Railway, ☎ *01 849 3016.*
Dublin city is served by a bus network and a railway line along the coast.
The **DART** (Dublin Area Rapid Transport) is a **rail service** along the coast (25mi/40km) from Howth in the north to Bray in the south. It serves three stations in central Dublin – Connolly, Tara Street and Pearse. The service operates daily between 6am (9am Sunday) and 11.45pm with trains running every 5–10min during peak times and every 15min off-peak. All-day tickets available at any station – rail only within the short hop zone €7; rail and bus €8.50. *Further details from 35 Lower Abbey Street; ☎ 01 836 6222 (Passenger information).*
The **Dublin LUAS System** is a **light rail transit** system with several routes radiating from the city centre – Abbey Street southwest via Drimnagh to Tallaght; St Stephen's Green south via Ranelagh and Dundrum to Sandyford – interlinked with Park and Ride facilities. Trams run Mon-Sat 5.30am (6.30am Sat) to 12.30; Sun 7am-11.30pm, every 5-10min (every 15min, 10.30pm onward). Travel on the Green or the Red line starts at €1.25 (single), €2.50 (return). ☎ *01 646 3400; www.luas.ie.*
Air Link is a bus service operated by Dublin Bus *(see below)* between Dublin Airport and central Dublin; pick-up points – O'Connell Street, Central Bus Station (Store Street); Connolly Railway Station; Heuston Rail Station.
Dublin Bus (CIE) operates the **bus network** which covers the whole city from the Central Bus Station (Busáras) in Store Street (behind the Custom House); any bus bearing the direction *An Lár* is going to the city centre. The price of a single ticket varies according to the number of stages from €0.95 to €1.90 (up to €4.10 for outer suburbs). All-day tickets available either exclusively for bus travel, for bus and rail travel combined or for bus and LUAS: bus only €5; bus and rail €8.50; bus and LUAS

€6.20. All-day tours are available north along the coast to Howth and Malahide; south along the coast to Bray and Grey-stones returning inland via Enniskerry. *Further details from Dublin Bus, 59 Upper O'Connell Street, Dublin 1; ☎ 01 873 4222; www.dublinbus.ie*
Nitelink buses run from the City Centre to the suburbs, every Fri-Sat on the half hour 12.30am-4am.
In the city centre there are **paying car parks**, **parking meters**, **pay and display machines** and **disc parking areas**; an electronic panel, advertising parking spaces, is visible from the west side of St Stephen's Green.
There is **no parking** on double yellow lines at any time; no parking on **single yellow lines** during the hours indicated on the time plate; no parking in **clear-ways and bus lanes** during the hours indicated on the time plate.
Parking bays for the **disabled** may be used only if a disabled parking permit is displayed. Cars parked illegally may be **clamped**; declamping costs €80 payable by phone by credit card only or at the Parking shop *(16 Bachelor's Walk, Dublin 1; ☎ 01 602 2500) by credit card, cash or cheque (with cheque card).*
A system of numbered car parks linked to numbered road junctions on the outskirts of Dublin makes it much easier to find the right route into the city centre.
The major **toll roads** are the Dublin East-Link (€1.45), which spans the Liffey estuary, and the Dublin West-Link (€1.80), which runs north south on the western edge of the city. ☎ *01 668 2888 (East-Link); 01 820 2000 (West-Link).* The M1 Drogheda bypass (€1.60) and M4 motorway, just west of Lucan to west of Kinnegad (€2.50, toll plaza at Enfield), also collect a toll.

SIGHTSEEING

The **Dublin Pass** can be purchased on the Web (at a discount) or at any of the five Dublin tourist information offices. Pass includes priority admission to 33 visitor attractions, 26 special offers and an airport transfer with AirCoach from the airport into the city. Passes start at €31 and may be purchased for

1, 2, 3, or 6 days. ☎ *01 605 7756; www. dublinpass.ie.*

Several companies organise **circular bus tours** of the city centre on an open-top bus comprehensive tour (2hr 45min) including all the famous sights and a running commentary given by an approved guide; **hop-on-hop-off bus tours** giving unlimited travel throughout the day, with the flexibility of stopping off and visiting various sights and then catching a later bus for no extra charge.

Dublin Bus City Tour – *Operates daily, 9.30am-3pm, every 10min; 3-5pm, every 15min; 5-6.30pm, every 30min. Hop-on-hop-off circular tour (20 stops; minimum 1hr 15min) starting from 59 Upper O'Connell Street. €14. b 01 703 3028;www.dublinbus.ie*

City-Sightseeing Dublin – *Bus tours operate every 6-15min (according to season), daily 9.30am-5.30pm (4pm Dec-Jan, 4.30pm Nov and Feb, 5pm Mar-Jun and Oct).* ◷ *Closed 17 Mar, 30 Oct and 18-26 Dec. All-day ticket ☞ €15. ☎ 01 458 0054. www.grayline.com.*

Gray Line Tours Ireland – *Operates Apr-Oct, daily at 10am (9.45am for Wicklow Mountains; 10.15am for Powerscourt and Glendalough). Half- or whole-day tours from Dublin to Howth and Malahide Castle (year-round), Glendalough and Wicklow Mountains (year-round), Newgrange, Powerscourt and Glendalough.* ◷ *Closed 17 Mar, 30 Oct and 18-26 Dec. ☞ €24-38. ☎ 01 458 0054. www.grayline.com.*

More active sightseers may consider a **bicycle tour** (bicycles provided) of Dublin, accompanied by a guide, who will point out the cultural and historical sights and avoid the busier roads.

For sightseers prepared to go farther afield, **steam train excursions** start from Dublin and travel to various provincial towns. (Contact any Dublin TIC for information.)

Viking Splash Tours – Sightseeing tour of Dublin by land and water in an amphibious military vehicle starting from Bull Alley Street beside St Patrick's Cathedral and entering the waer at the Grand Canal Basin in Ringsend. ☎ *01 707 6000; www.vikingsplashtours.com* Full-day and half-day tours to attractions in the Dublin area are organised

by various bus companies: **Dublin Bus** *(see above);* Irish City Tours *(see Dublin Tourism).*

Three different **heritage trails**, walking tours with historical themes, are organised by Dublin Tourism; further details from the Dublin Tourism Centre or from the website *(see above).*

To see the famous Dublin landmarks while learning about key events in Irish history, join a specialised walking tour.

Dublin Historical Walking Tour - *Operates May-Sep, daily 11am and 3pm; Apr and Oct, daily 11am; Nov-Mar, Fri-Sun 11am. ☞ €12. ☎ 87 830 3523*

1916 Rebellion Walking Tour - *Operates mid-Apr to early-Oct, Mon-Sat 11.30pm; Sun, 1pm. ☞ €12. ☎ 86 858 3847*

Literary Tour - *Operates daily 7.30pm and Sun noon.* ◷ *Closed Dec-Mar, Mon-Wed. ☞ €12. ☎ 01 670 5602/087 263 0270.*

Musical Pub Crawl – Details from Dublin Tourism.

For coin ranges, see the Legend on the cover flap

WHERE TO STAY

◔◔◉ **Pembroke Townhouse** – *90 Pembroke Rd - ☎ 01 660 0277 - Fax 01 660 0291; www.pembroketownhouse. ie. Closed 21 Dec to 2 Jan - P ⇔ - 48 rm ⇌.* A quieter location in a smart suburb for those wishing to avoid the bustle of the city centre. Thoughtfully furnished and faithful to its Georgian origins yet with all the necessary conveniences of modern living.

◔◔◉ **Trinity Lodge** – *12 South Frederick St - ☎ 01 679 5044; www.trinity-lodge.com. Closed 22 to 27 Dec. 16 rm ⇌.* Benefits not only from its city centre location but by being in one of the quieter streets. A modernised Georgian townhouse with clean, comfortable and well-furnished bedrooms.

◔◔◉◉ **Brownes Townhouse** – *22 St Stephen's Green - ☎ 01 638 3939; www.brownesdublin.com. Closed 25-27 Dec. ⇔⇖ 12 rm ⇌ - Restaurant ☞◉.* It would be hard to beat the location of this sympathetically restored Georgian house which overlooks Stephen's Green in the heart of the city. The original staircase and numerous four-poster beds add to the period atmosphere.

The Clarence – *6-8 Wellington Quay* - ☎ *01 407 0800; www.theclarence.ie.* ✕⊠🅿️♿ *Booking essential* - *43 rm, 5 suites* - ⌷ *€28* - *Restaurant* ⊜⊜🗐. Its stylish interior, merging the contemporary with the traditional, has made The Clarence popular with the cognoscenti and is owned by two members of the famous rock group U2. Staff are alert to every guests's need and bedrooms have every mod-con.

Harrington Hall – *70 Harcourt St* - ☎ *01 475 3497; www.harringtonhall.com.* 🅿️✕⊘ *28 rm* ⌷. Standing in an elegant terrace of classic Georgian properties and offering modern levels of comfort and service. All the bedrooms are a generous size, especially the three junior suites which have ornate ceilings and huge windows.

The Mercer – *Mercer Street Lower* - ☎ *01 478 2179; www.mercerhotel.ie. Closed 23 to 29 Dec.* ✕⊘♿ *41 rm* ⌷ *€5 - Restaurant* ⊜⊜. Keen shoppers will like this location, next to Grafton Street in the middle of the city. The hotel offers pleasantly furnished and air-conditioned bedrooms, decorated with a certain amount of individuality.

The Merrion – *Upper Merrion St* - ☎ *01 603 0600; www.merrionhotel.com.* ✕⊘ *122 rm, 20 suites* - ⌷ *€27- Restaurant* ⊜⊜. Those looking for sumptuous surroundings and pampering services will be more than satisfied at this elegant hotel, consisting of a row of carefully restored Georgian townhouses arranged around a private garden. Ornately decorated throughout.

WHERE TO EAT

The Bad Ass Café – *Crown Alley* - ☎ *01 671 2596* - ✄. Those after a flavour of Temple Bar and sensory overload should make this their first stop. It's loud, it's brash and it offers an undemanding menu of assorted grilled dishes and pizza.

MacGowans – *16-18 Phibsborough Rd* - ☎ *01 830 6606; michael@macgowans.ie.* A very busy pub blending Irish exuberance with American food and perhaps not for those watching the calories. Known for its exceptionally long bar and its late opening hours.

Bang Café – *11 Merrion Row* - ☎ *01 676 089; www.bangrestaurant.com.* 🕐 *Closed 1 week Christmas, Sun and Bank Holiday Mon - Booking essential.* Captures the zeitgeist, with a suitably unstuffy atmosphere that matches the bustle of the surrounding streets. Service is chatty and the open plan kitchen produces a mix of the classical and the more creative.

Bistro One – *3 Brighton Rd* - ☎ *01 289 7711 - bistroone@eircom.ie.* 🕐 *Closed 25-27 and 31 Dec, 1 Jan, Sun and Mon. Booking essential.* Gingham tablecloths and a blackboard menu contribute to the relaxed, informal feel. Somewhat hidden in a residential area to the south of the city. Modern cooking with the occasional added Asian influence.

Brownes Brasserie – *22 St Stephen's Green (at Brownes Townhouse)* - ☎ *01 638 3939; www.brownesdublin.com.* 🕐 *Closed 24 Dec to 4 Jan and Sat lunch. Booking essential.* It is essential to book before arriving at this ever-popular brasserie with its distinctive continental atmosphere and its 'belle époque' feel. The strength of the European-influenced menu lies in its seafood.

Bruno's – *30 East Sussex St, St, Temple Bar* - ☎ *01 670 6767; www.brunos.ie.* 🕐 *Closed 25 Dec to 2 Jan, Sat lunch and Sun. Booking essential.* Its Temple Bar location, wood flooring, mirrors and moody lighting make this another example of the city's new wave of contemporary, yet informal, establishments. The menu features some original touches and the wine list is well-priced.

Cafe Mao – *2-3 Chatham Row* - ☎ *01 670 4899; www.cafemao.com.* ⊶ *Closed for renovations. Estimated re-opening Nov 2006.* Those looking for a culinary change of pace should head for this authentic South East Asian restaurant. Spread over two floors in a clean, fairly minimalist style with vivid, ersatz Warhol prints. Helpful and attentive service assured.

The Cellar Bar – *Upper Merrion St (at The Merrion H)* - ☎ *01 603 0631 - info@merrionhotel.com.* It's best to book for the very popular lunch at this restored Georgian cellar with its vaulted ceiling and exposed brick walls, and a menu that features classic Irish dishes. At night it reverts to a popular bar, with live music on Tuesday nights.

Chapter One – *18-19 The Dublin Writers Museum, Parnell Sq -* ☎ *01 873 2266; www.chapteronerestaurant.com.* Closed 24 Dec to 9 Jan, Sun, Sat lunch and Bank Hols. Cavernous room beneath the Dublin Writers's Museum. Contemporary art hangs on the thick granite walls. The cooking is innovative and the service careful. There is an arched alcove available for larger groups.

Dobbin's – *15 Stephen's Lane, off Lower Mount St -* ☎ *01 676 4679 - dobbinswinebistro@eircom.net -* Closed 1 week Christmas-New Year, Sun, Mon dinner, Sat lunch and Bank Hols. - *Booking essential.* Almost surreal in its incongruity. A imported Nissen hut with sawdust on the floor plonked in the middle of the financial district. The lively and convivial atmosphere bears testament to its reputation as one of the city's institutions.

La Stampa – *35 Dawson St (at La Stampa H.) -* ☎ *01 677 8611; www. lastampa.ie.* Closed 25 Dec. Booking essential. Look no further if you're after a true flavour of Dublin's buzzing restaurant scene. The atmosphere reverberates around this converted 19C ballroom with its large mirrors, original artwork and ornate mosaic ceiling. Appropriately modern cuisine.

Nancy Hands Pub & Restaurant – *30-32 Parkgate St -* ☎ *01 677 0149 -* . Famed for its vast collection of Irish whiskeys and its mildly schizophrenic décor which lends it a certain Victorian charm. Fairly typical pub fare but generously portioned.

Roly's Bistro – *7 Ballsbridge Terr -* ☎ *01 668 2611 - ireland@rolysbistro.ie.* Closed 25-27 Dec. Booking essential. A veritable institution and one of the city's most celebrated restaurants. Tables set close together so you virtually rub shoulders with your neighbour but that's all part of its charm. Modern menu; particularly good value lunch.

Jacobs Ladder – *4-5 Nassau St -* ☎ *01 670 3865; www.jacobsladder. ie -* Closed 17 March, Good Fri, first week of August, 25 Dec to Jan 7.

Booking essential. A particularly good value lunch is offered at this first-floor restaurant overlooking Trinity College park. The chef owner provides modern Irish cooking in appropriately modern surroundings, complemented by a well-chosen wine list.

Mermaid Café – *69-70 Dame St -* ☎ *01 670 8236; www.mermaid. ie.* Closed Good Fri , 24-26 and 31 Dec, 1 Jan. Booking essential. Draws in the young and fashionable with its effervescent atmosphere as well as its sensibly priced menu. The food here has an eclectic hue, drawing influences from all over the world and also offers daily-changing blackboard specials.

The Tea Room – *6-8 Wellington Quay (at The Clarence H) -* ☎ *01 670 7766; www. theclarence.ie.* Closed lunch Sat. Booking essential. Double height windows ensure that this fashionable restaurant is flooded with light during the day. Cool, pastel shades add to the understated, airy feel and the menu offers modern Irish cooking using top quality ingredients.

The Commons – *85-86 Newman House, St Stephen's Green -* ☎ *01 478 0530; www.thecommons.ie.* Closed first 2 weeks Aug, 24 Dec to 5 Jan, Sat, Sun and Bank Hols. Newman House, former University College, boasts James Joyce as a student and the great man is celebrated through assorted paintings in this basement restaurant. A discreet and comfortable room, with detailed and accomplished cooking.

Patrick Guilbaud – *21 Upper Merrion St -* ☎ *01 676 4192; www. restaurantpatrickguilbaud.ie.* Closed Good Fri, first week Jan, 25 Dec, Sun and Mon. The city's most renowned restaurant occupies a Georgian townhouse adjacent to the Merrion hotel. The superlative cooking, cosmopolitan surroundings and courteous service all help to make this one of the ultimate dining experiences.

TAKING A BREAK

Abbey Tavern – *Howth -* ☎ *01 832 20 06; www.abbeytavern.ie.* Open daily from 10.30am. This charming 1879 pub north of the city exudes a genuine sense of authenticity and a very convivial atmos phere. Known for its traditional Irish concerts every evening from 8.30 with the 'Abbey Singers and Musicians'.

Brazen Head – *20 Lower Bridge St - ☎ 01 679 5186; www.brazenhead. com - Mon-Sat from 10.30am, Sun, 12am-12pm.* Claims to be the oldest pub in the city, being on the site of a 12C tavern. Although popular with tourists this doesn't seem to detract from the atmosphere. Worth getting there early to get a seat for the music. Has a pleasant terrace.

Butlers Chocolate Café – *24 Wicklow St - ☎ 01 671 0599; www.butlerschocolates.com.* ⏱ *Open daily, 8am-7pm.* The best place to buy chocolates and for a taste of Ireland try the Jameson Truffle, filled with Irish Whiskey. A useful place to stop for a mid morning break but instead of a tea or coffee try the house speciality, a hot chocolate.

Bewley's Cafe (1) – *Grafton St ☎ 635 5470; www.bewleyscafe.com. Daily 7.30am (coffee only until 8am) to 11.30am.* The essence of café society. Whether for a coffee and cake or a full breakfast, it's worth making a stop here. Particularly worth seeing the Harry Clarke room as well as gettting tickets for the Café Theatre in the evenings.

Café-en-Seine – *40 Dawson Street - ☎ 01 677 4369; www.capitalbars.com. Mon-Sat 9am-2.30pm (12.30pm Mon).* With its fin-de-siecle Parisian decor, this café represents the new wave of establishments which combine the café, bar and brasserie. It's a magnet for the young and hip with its fashionably long bar.

Cleary's – *36 Amiens St - ☎ 01 855 2952.* ⏱ *Open daily from 11.30am.* This is an authentic old dive, imbued with years of smoke, fumes, exhortations and the oaths of working men. Michael Collins roused such men here and not much has changed since his day.

Davy Byrne's – *21 Duke Street - ☎ 01 677 5217; www.davybyrnes.com. Daily 10.30am (11.30am Sun) to 11pm (1am Thu-Fri).* This may be the most famous of the many pubs associated with James Joyce. Despite the changes made over the years, Davy Byrne's is still a pleasant bar with a few remaining Art Deco touches.

Dohenny & Nesbitt – *5 Lower Baggot St - ☎ 01 676 2945.* ⏱ *Open daily from 10.30am.* A classic pub popular with government workers from the neighbourhood, especially civil servants from the Ministry of Finance. Dubliners like to refer to the Dohenny & Nesbitt School of Economics.

Johnnie Fox Pub – *Glencullen - ☎ 01 295 5647; www.jfp.ie. Mon-Sat, 10.30am-11.30pm, Sun, 12am-11.30pm.* The Fox may look as if it were built for a film set but it has been in business since 1798. Everything is Irish down to the brass tacks. Not only is this place for real but you can enjoy traditional music here every evening.

Kish Fish – *40-42 Bow St - ☎ 01 872 8211; www.kishfish.ie. Tue-Sat, 9am-4.30pm (1pm Sat).* 100m on the left as you come out of the Old Jameson Distillery is this sweet little fishmongers shop. Salmon is a particularly popular purchase and much of the produce comes from Galway.

Knightsbridge Bar – *23-25 Bachelor Walk - O'Connell Bridge. ☎ 01 804 9100; www.arlington.ie.* ⏱ *Open daily from 11am.* In the evenings this vast bar in the heart of the city really comes alive. There's entertainment every night of the week, be it song or dance, and it's all free. Although rather touristy, it's an experience not to be missed.

Messrs Maguire – *1-2 Burgh Quay – ⏱ Open daily from 10.30am-11.30pm; messrsmaguire7@hotmail.com.* This 19C building facing the Liffey is a good example of the fusion of the old and the new. It has cosy little nooks and crannies, a library bar, restaurant and brasserie. From Wednesday to Sunday a DJ pounds out the music from 9pm.

Mitchell & Son – *21 Kildare St - ☎ 01 676 0766; www.mitchellandson.com. Mon-Fri 9am-5.45pm, Sat 10am-5pm.* This wine merchants was founded in 1805 and the sixth generation of the family is now at the helm. Celebrated for its famous 'Green Spot' whiskey, aged in sherry casks. They also offer a vast range of wines, rare malts, spirits and cigars.

Mulligan's – *8 Poolbeg St - ☎ 01 677 5582; www.mulligans.ie. Mon-Sat 10.30am-11.30pm (12.30am Fri-Sat); Sun, 12.30-11pm.* One can't help feeling that this celebrated old pub is the genuine article. The Victorian interior with its mahogany and screens is ideal for those looking for more intimacy and is regularly frequented by journalists and those who take their drinking seriously.

Oliver St John Gogarty – *58-9 Temple Bar -* ☎ *01 671 1822; www.gogartys.ie.* 🕐 *Open daily from 10.30am.* Located in the heart of Temple Bar, this is always a very popular bar with visitors to the city. There's a first floor restaurant, live music every night until the wee small hours and it acts as the starting point for the 'Musical Pub Crawl'.

O'Donoghue's – *14-15 Merrion Row -* ☎ *01 660 7194 .* 🕐 *Open daily from 10.30am.* Although it is a bit touristy, this pub has excellent traditional Irish music nightly and all day Sunday. The famous group the Dubliners came roaring on the music scene here in 1962. Often crowded, especially weekends.

Temple Bar – *48 Temple Bar -* ☎ *01 671 2324 - www.temple-bar.ie -* 🕐 *Open daily from 10.30am.* A very agreeable pub and a popular choice for a good night out. The musical programme is varied, the acoustics are good and on a summer's day it all moves into the garden. There's even a small shop selling caps and T shirts.

The Auld Dubliner – *Fleet St -* ☎ *01 677 0527 –* 🕐 *Open daily from 10.30am.* Despite its name, this is a relatively recent arrival on the pub scene, and it already has a good reputation for traditional music, Thursday to Sunday nights.

The Long Hall – *51 South Great George St -* ☎ *01 475 1590.* 🕐 *Open Sun-Wed 4-11.30pm; Thu-Sat 1pm-12.30am.* This Victorian bar has remained largely unchanged since 1880 and is noted for its very long counter which appears to go on for miles. It's a welcoming and sociable place, attracting visitors from all parts of the globe.

The Porter House – *16 Parliament St -* ☎ *01 679 8847; www.porterhouse. ie.* 🕐 *Open daily from 11.30am (noon Sat, 12.30pm Sun).* The city's first micro-brewery has rapidly become a fashionable hangout. It offers a large range of modern beers and thus makes an ideal stop for those wanting a break

from the 'black stuff'. Traditional music at weekends, modern during the week.

Zanzibar – *Lower Ormond Quay -* ☎ *01 878 7212; zanzibar@capitalbars.com.* 🕐 *Open daily, 4pm-3am.* A classic example of the Dublin theme pub with its eccentric Arabic decoration as imagined by Walt Disney. Geared unashamedly to groups out for the night. Queues begin to form later in the evening when it turns into a night-club.

ENTERTAINMENT

Abbey Theatre – *26 Lower Abbey St -* ☎ *01 878 7222; www.abbeytheatre.ie. Mon-Sun, 10.30am-7pm.* The building is not very splendid, nonetheless it is a proud symbol of Irish culture. Works by Ireland's best-known authors are performed here regularly (Shaw, Synge, Yeats, O'Casey) as are works by less famous dramatists. The Peacock Theatre, in the same building, specialises in contemporary and experimental work.

Gaiety Theatre – ☎ *01 677 1717; www. gaietytheatre.com. Mon-Sat 10am-8pm.* Opera and musicals.

Gate Theatre – *1 Cavendish Row -* ☎ *01 874 4045; www.gate-theatre.ie. Mon-Sat, 10.30am-7pm.* 🕐 *Closed Sun.* Another Dublin institution, founded in the 1920s, this theatre includes non-Irish works in its repertoire.

Irish Film Institute – *Eustace St, Temple Bar -* ☎ *01 677 8788; www.irishfilm.ie.* 🕐 *Open Mon-Fri 10am-6pm.* Film buffs are catered for all year round here. The programme ensures that Irish films as well as the well-known classics are always being shown.

Jurys Irish Cabaret – ☎ *01 660 5000; www.jurysdoyle.com. May-Oct : Wed-Sun from 11am.* It began in 1960 and today they put on 2000 shows a year. These 2hr 30min spectaculars incorporate music, singing and dancing in both modern and traditional styles. There are also facilities to have a drink or meal.

National Concert Hall – *Earlsfort Terrace -* ☎ *417 0077; www.nch.ie. Mon-Sat, 10am-7am.*

Olympia Theatre – *72 Dame Street -* ☎ *016 77 7744; www.mcd.ie. Mon-Sat from 10.30am.* Mainly local bands and comedy shows.

The Burlington Cabaret – *The Burlington Hotel, Upper Leeson Street -* ☎ *01*

617 2743; www.jurysdoyle.com. May-Oct: Mon, Wed-Sat 6.45pm, Sun show from 8pm; 🕐 closed Thu and Sun. Part of the Burlington hotel, this cabaret venue describes itself as being ' a celebration of everything Irish in comedy, music, song and dance'. Two ticket prices; with or without dinner.

Taylor's Three Rock – *Grange Road, Rathfarnham* – ☎ 01 494 2999; www.taylorsirishnight.com. Mar-Dec daily. Venue changing locations in 2007. Prepare for audience participation and frenetic music and dance at this large thatched pub. You have a choice of three bars but what draws the crowds is the Music Room where live bands and dance troupes perform virtually nightly.

NIGHTLIFE

La Cave – *28 South Anne Street* - ☎ 01 679 4409; www.lacavewinebar.com. Just off Grafton Street is Dublin's oldest French wine bar serving French food and wine.

Rí-Rá – *11 Dame Court* – ☎ 01 671 1220; www.rira.ie. 🕐 Open daily, 11pm-2am. Spread over two floors, this night-club is loud, funky and popular with the 'in crowd' despite, or because of, being slightly more expensive than others in the city. It's next door to The Globe for those wanting a drink away from the music.

SHOPPING

There is a Post Office in Suffolk Street opposite the Tourist Information Centre.

The **central shopping** area extends from Grafton Street *(south bank)* to O'Connell Street *(north bank)*. Nassau Street *(parallel with the south side of Trinity College)* contains several good shops selling a range of **Irish goods** from high fashion to modest souvenirs – clothing, craftwork, pottery, Irish music and instruments, family crests. Bookshops congregate at the north end of Dawson Street. **Cobblestones** *(Smithfield Village)* offers examples of Irish craftsmanship.

The **Temple Bar** area offers an eclectic mix of individual little shops and outdoor stalls.

Market-lovers should visit the **Moore Street market** *(Mon-Sat)*, where barrow boys sell fresh fruit and vegetables; **Dublin Corporation Fruit and Vegetable Market** under a cast-iron roof *(Mary's Lane; Sat am)*, **Temple Bar Market** *(Meeting House Square; Sat am)* selling local produce (cheeses, sauces, bread, chocolates, vegetable drinks, pizzas, pies and sausages). For **antiques** go to Francis Street.

Avoca Mills, *Suffolk Street* – ☎ 01 677 4215; www.avoca.ie. 🕐 Open daily from 10am (11am Sun). A 7-level mini-department store filled with quirky gifts and fashionable design items.

Blarney Woollen Mills – *21-23 Nassau St* - ☎ 01 671 0068; www.blarneywoollenmills.com. Mon-Sat from 9am. There's a huge choice of knitted items and classic Aran sweaters as well as knitwear with more imaginative patterns and designs. They also offer for sale a large choice of crystal, from Waterford, Galway and Tipperary.

Brown Thomas – *Grafton Street* – Dublin's smartest department store.

Celtic Note – *14 Nassau Street* - www.celticnote.com. Fri-Sat, 9am-7pm, Sun noon-6pm. No trip to Ireland is complete without hearing some traditional Celtic music and this is the number one shop for those wishing to take home a musical reminder. There's a vast selection of CDs and cassettes, as well as traditional musical instruments.

Claddagh Records – *2 Cecilia Street, Dublin 2;* ☎ 01 677 0262; www.claddaghrecords.com. Specialist folk, traditional and ethnic music.

Dublin Woollen Mills – *41 Lr Ormond Quay* - ☎ 01 677 5014 - www.woollenmills.com; call for opening times. This family firm can lay claim to having once employed James Joyce as an agent during his sojourn in Trieste. A wide selection of authentic knitwear is available, as well as accessories such as scarves, caps and ties.

House of Ireland – *Nassau Street* - ☎ 01 671 1111 - Mon-Wed, Fri, 9am-6pm, Thu, 9am-8pm, Sat, 9am-6pm, Sun, 11am-6pm. If it's made in Ireland then it is probably available in this well known shop. Although perhaps a little expensive the range is vast; from woollens to crystal, porcelain to jewellery.

Kevin & Howlin – *31 Nassau St* - ☎ 01 677 0257; www.kevinandhowlin.com.

Mon-Sat, 9am-5.30pm. Call for Sun opening times. The definitive temple of Donegal tweed in all its forms. The range available at this family firm includes jackets, suits, waistcoats and ties. Alternatively, fabric can be bought by the metre and fashioned into garments by your own tailor.

Kilkenny Shop – *6 Nassau St* - ☎ *01 677 7066; www.kilkennyshop.com. Mon-Wed, Fri, 8.30am-6pm, Thu, 8.30am-8pm, Sat, 9am-6pm, Sun, 11am-6pm*. Tweeds, Aran sweaters, lace and Celtic jewellery are just some of the products for sale in this veritable supermarket of traditional Irish products. Wilting shoppers or uninterested partners can refuel in the cafeteria.

National Museum Shop – *Kildare Street, Dublin 2*. Items based on exhibits.

National Museum Shop – *Benburb Street, Dublin 7*. Items based on exhibits.

Market Arcades – *South Great George St*. This covered passage is home to twenty-odd shops, some offering second-hand clothing. There are some real bargains to be found, especially for tweed jackets.

Mother's Redcaps Market – *Back Lane - Fri-Sun, 10am-5.30pm*. This emporium has a little bit of everything: old records and second-hand clothes, Aran Island sweaters, lucky charms, dishes, knick-knacks, incense and patchouli.

The **Powerscourt Centre** – *South William Street, Dublin 2*. An 18C town house converted into a most attractive shopping centre with a great range of individual shops.

Rory's (Fishing Tackle) – *17A Temple Bar - Fleet St* - ☎ *01 677 2351. Mon-Sat 9.30am-6pm*. A Dublin institution and a must for fishermen. All the equipment you could ever need is here, including a huge range of flies made at the shop. They are more than willing to help with advice on what to buy and where to fish.

SPORTS AND LEISURE

Croke Park – *Drumcondra* - ☎ *01 819 2300; www.crokepark.ie*. The stadium where the national finals of home of Gaelic games – hurling and football – are held.

Horse Racing at **Leopardstown** (south) and **Fairy House** (north).

Greyhound Racing at Shelbourne Park (*Wed, Thu and Sat, first race at 7.55pm; ✆ €8 admission; ☎ 01 202 6601; www.igb.ie*); Harold's Cross (*Mon, Tue and Fri; first race at 7.55pm; €10 admission— including race card— ☎ 01 497 1081; www.igb.ie*).

EVENTS AND FESTIVALS

Bloomsday – Annual celebration (16 June) of James Joyce's great novel *Ulysses* – readings, re-enactments, music, theatre, street theatre.

Parliament in 1728 there was little building east of the old town except for Trinity College.

The district began to develop into a fashionable suburb in the 1750s when the Duke of Leinster erected the first nobleman's house south of the river; his prediction that fashionable society would follow soon proved true. Some of the most elegant Georgian terraces are to be found east and south of his mansion. In 1815 the Leinster property was bought by the Royal Dublin Society, and the National Museum, the National Library and the National Gallery were built in the grounds. After 1922 the mansion was converted to serve as the Parliament of the newly established Free State.

▶ *From O'Connell Bridge walk south along Westmoreland Street passing (right) the Bank of Ireland*.

College Green

At the centre stands a statue of **Henry Grattan** by John Foley (1879) and a modern iron sculpture designed by Edward Delaney in memory of **Thomas Davis** (1814–45), poet, leader of the Young Ireland movement and founder of *The Nation*. This triangu-

Trinity College

lar open space, formerly known as Hoggen Green, was an old Viking burial ground *(haugen)* and meeting place *(thengmote)*.

Trinity College★★

Trinity College, Dublin, sometimes known as TCD, was founded in 1592 by Elizabeth I on the site of All Hallows, an Augustinian monastery suppressed at the Dissolution. It developed according to the tradition of the Oxford and Cambridge colleges and long remained an Anglican preserve. Roman Catholics were excluded until 1873, while the Roman Catholic Church for its part strongly disapproved of the faithful studying here well into the 1960s. Women were first admitted in 1903. The College stands in its own grounds, **College Park**: an open space set aside for sport – cricket, rugby, running and hurling – although this has been encroached upon by the science and medical faculties. The film *Educating Rita*, starring Michael Caine and Julie Walters, was filmed here.

Beside the entrance gates stands an elegant Georgian house built for the Provost in 1758. Statues by Foley of Oliver Goldsmith and Edmund Burke flank the main gate. The buildings in **Front Court** date from the mid 18C; the wings terminate in the **Theatre** *(south)* and the **Chapel** *(north)*, both designed by Sir William Chambers with stuccowork by Michael Stapleton. The chapel is mainly lit by high semi-circular windows. The theatre (1777–91) is used for degree ceremonies, Senate meetings, musical and theatrical events; it is hung with portraits of Elizabeth I, Edmund Burke, George Berkeley, Jonathan Swift.

Library Court is dominated by the **Campanile** (1853) designed by Charles Lanyon. Among the trees in the centre is *Reclining Connected Forms* (1969), a sculpture by Henry Moore. The area behind the north range is called **Botany Bay**, after the Australian penal colony (possibly because of unruly student antics). The red-brick range on the east side, known as Rubrics, is the oldest building in the college: the south side is closed by the Old Library and Treasury.

The **Museum** (1850) *(south side of New Square)* was designed by Sir Thomas Deane and Benjamin Woodward in the Venetian style promoted by Ruskin; the delightful stone carving of flowers, leaves and animals is by the O'Shea brothers from Cork.

▷ *Turn left into Nassau St.*

On the corner with Kildare Street stands the former home of the **Kildare Street Club**, the oldest and most staunchly Unionist of Dublin's gentleman's clubs.

▶ *Continue along Nassau St and Clare St to Merrion Sq.*

Merrion Square★

The jewel of Georgian Dublin was laid out in 1762 by John Ensor for the 6th Viscount Fitzwilliam under the policy of the Wide Streets Commissioners. Delicate fanlights surmount the elegant doorways of the perfectly proportioned red-brick houses; commemorative plaques mark the homes of famous people – Oscar Wilde's father, Sir William Wilde, at no 1, William Butler Yeats at no 82. The west side is graced by the gardens of Leinster House, flanked by the Natural History Museum and the National Gallery. The southeast vista is closed by **St Stephen's Church**, designed in 1821 by John Bowden and completed by Joseph Welland: its domed tower, known as the "Pepper Canister", was inspired by three Athenian buildings – the Erechtheum, the Tower of the Winds and the Monument of Lysicrates. ☎ *01 2880663 (vicarage)*

▶ *Walk south up Merrion St past the Natural History Museum and Government Buildings (see below).*

Among the many handsome Georgian houses are the town house of the Wellesley family, where the Duke of Wellington spent some of his childhood, and the Merrion Street Hotel, with its splendidly restored interior.

▶ *Turn right into the north side of St Stephen's Green.*

The **Shelbourne Hotel** (1867), still a centre of Dublin's social life, was built by Martin Burke on the site of Kerry House, residence of the Earl of Shelburne, in 1824.

▶ *Turn right into Kildare St.*

Half way down, set back from the street, is the front of **Leinster House** – now seat of the *Dáil,* the Irish Parliament (*see below*) – flanked by the **National Museum** (right) and the **National Library** (left).

▶ *Turn left into Molesworth St and left into Dawson St.*

St Ann's Church

🕐 *Open Mon-Fri 10am-4pm. Lunch time, evening and weekend concerts ☎ 01 676 7727*

St Ann's was one of the earliest Georgian churches in Dublin, an elegant and fashionable place of worship designed by Isaac Wills and not really improved by the addition of a Victorian neo-Romanesque west front and stained glass. The bread shelf in the chancel was established in 1723 by a charitable bequest to provide 120 loaves of bread each week for the poor.

Mansion House

The house was built in 1705 by Joshua Dawson, a builder, and bought by the City of Dublin in 1715 as the residence of the Lord Mayor. The spacious Round Room was added for the visit of George IV in 1821; it was here that the first Irish parliament met in 1919 to adopt the Declaration of Independence.

▶ *At the top of Dawson St cross the road into the gardens of St Stephen's Green.*

St Stephen's Green

(Dúchas) 🕐 *Open daily 8am (9.30am Sun and Bank Hols) to dusk. ☎ 01 475 7816*

Formerly common land first enclosed in 1663, the beautifully landscaped and well-maintained **gardens** (22 acres/9ha) are a wonderful asset in this densely built-up part of the city. They were laid out in 1880 by Lord Ardilaun, a member of the Guinness

B Perousse/MICHELIN

St Stephen's Green

family, who is honoured with a statue on the west side. The bronze sculpture by Henry Moore was erected in memory of **William Butler Yeats** in 1967. The **Fusiliers' Arch** (*northwest entrance*) commemorates those who died in the Boer War and the **German Monument** (*southeast entrance*) expresses the gratitude of the people of the Federal Republic of Germany for help it received after the Second World War.

The **Royal College of Surgeons** (*west side*), designed by Edward Parke in 1806, was captured during the Easter Rising in 1916 by a party of insurgents led by Constance Markievicz.

On the south side are **Newman House**, **Iveagh House** (designed by Richard Castle and now the Department of Foreign Affairs) and the **University Church** (1854), designed at the behest of Cardinal Newman by John Pollen in the highly ornate Byzantine and Italian early-Christian style advocated by John Ruskin.

▶ *From the SE corner of the square turn left into Harcourt St then left into Clonmel St.*

Iveagh Gardens
Entrances in Clonmel St and Earlsfort Terrace. (Dúchas) 🕐 *Open 8am (10am Sun and Bank Hols) to dusk (5pm Feb and Nov; 6pm Mar-Oct; 4pm Dec-Jan).* ☎ *01 475 7816*
The gardens of lawns and tree-lined walks, enhanced by statuesque fountains, a rosarium and a maze, provide respite. The main axis is terminated by a massive rock-work cascade based on the Bains d'Apollon at Versailles.

▶ *Return to St Stephen's Green; walk south and into Grafton St.*

Grafton Street★
Dublin's finest shopping street is now a bustling pedestrian precinct and a favourite haunt of street musicians; in the 19C it was paved with pine blocks to deaden the sound of carriage wheels. **Bewley's Oriental Café** with its distinctive mosaic façade and stained-glass windows by Harry Clarke started in the 1840s but was re-opened in 1927; the previous building there was Whytes School, attended by Robert Emmet, Thomas Moore, Richard Sheridan and the Duke of Wellington.

▶ *Turn left into Johnson Ct.*

Powerscourt Centre★

◷ Open Mon-Fri 10am-6pm (8pm Thu), Sat 9am-6pm, Sun noon-6pm. ☎ 01 671 7000; www.powerscourtcentre.com

This 18C town house with fine stucco ceilings was designed in 1771 by Robert Mack for Viscount Powerscourt; it is now a shopping centre.

▶ *Return to Grafton St and continue north to College Green and O'Connell Bridge.*

Old Dublin

The heart of old Dublin occupies the ridge between the Liffey and its southern tributary, the Poddle River, which now flows underground. Excavations (1974–81) at **Wood Quay**, where the modern Civic Offices of Dublin Corporation now stand, revealed the remains of 150 Viking buildings at 13 different levels (AD 920–1100). The town expanded eastwards along Dame Street to meet the development taking place around Leinster House, and also westwards along the **High Street** into the **Cornmarket**, where vast quantities of grain were sold for export in the Middle Ages. Little remains of the old buildings in **Fishamble Street**, where Molly Malone was born and Handel conducted the first performance of *Messiah* to raise funds for the Rotunda Hospital. The **Liberties** was the name given to the area farther south and west, which lay outside the jurisdiction of the medieval city; here the buildings vary from 17C high-gable houses built by French Huguenot refugees to 19C mansion flats and 20C housing estates.

▶ *From the south side of O'Connell Bridge walk upstream along Aston Quay.*

DUBLIN

Adelaïde Rd	BT	3
Alfie Byrne Rd	CS	5
Bath Ave	CT	9
Benburb St	BS	15
Berkeley Rd	BS	16
Botanic Rd	BS	19
Canal Rd	BT	30
Clanbrassil St	BT	40
Conyngham Rd	AS	48
Denmark St	BS	52
Donnybrook Rd	CT	54
Dorset St	BS	55
Drimnagh Rd	AT	57
Eglinton Rd	CT	63
Grand Parade	BT	72
Inchicore Rd	AT	79
Infirmary Rd	AS	81
James St	BT	84
Leeson St Upper	BT	94
Macken St	BST	99
Morehampton Rd	BT	108
Mount St Upper	BT	112
Palmerston Park	BT	123
Phibsborough Rd	BS	132
Rathmines Rd Upper	BT	135
Ringsend Rd	CT	139
Sandford Rd	BT	151
Shelbourne Rd	CT	157
Shrewsbury Rd	CT	159
South Circular Rd	AS	162
St Agnes Rd	AT	141
St Alphonsus Rd	BS	144
St John's Rd West	AS	147
Suir Rd	AT	168
Terenure Rd East	BT	172
Thomas St West	BT	174
Victoria Quay	BS	178
Western Way	BS	184
Wolfe Ione Quay	BS	195

Ceol	BS	V
Guinness Storehouse	BT	M⁷
Kilmainham Gaol Museum	AT	M⁶
National Concert Hall	BT	T
Phoenix Monument	AS	L
Portobello Hotel	BT	Q
Shaw Birthplace	BT	W
St Stephen's Church	BT	X
Waterways Visitor Centre	CT	K
Wellington Monument	AS	N

Liffey Footbridges

The popular name for the delicate cast-iron footbridge, opened in 1816 as the Wellington Bridge, is the **Ha'penny Bridge**★, so-called because of the ½d toll levied until 1919. It now has a companion, the **Millennium Bridge**.

Liffey Bridge

▶ *Opposite the Ha'penny Bridge turn away from the river through the arch.*

Merchants' Hall *(Wellington Quay)* was designed by Frederick Darley for the Merchants' Guild, also known as the Fraternity of the Holy Trinity, the first of Dublin's 25 guilds; the arched passage through the building leads into Temple Bar.

Temple Bar

The area between the river and Dame Street, now known as Temple Bar (28 acres/ 11ha) takes its name from Sir William Temple, Provost of Trinity (1628–99), who owned land which included a sand bar on the south bank of the river. A stroll through its medieval network of narrow streets and courts reveals a variety of old buildings – Georgian houses, warehouses and chapels – restored and converted to new uses, interspersed with new purpose-built property. Derelict sites have been converted into open spaces – Temple Bar Square, Meeting House Square and Central Bank Plaza among the banks and insurance offices of Dame Street. This astonishingly successful case of urban renewal, has produced a **cultural district** with venues for entertainment and "alternative" shops, restaurants, hotels and residential areas. Eustace Street is now home to two national institutions – the Irish Film Centre and the National Photographic Archive; the **Temple Bar Information Centre** (*18 Eustace St*) provides details of what's on and when.

▶ *Walk west up Dame Street. Either walk past City Hall into Lord Edward St and turn left into Werburgh St. Or turn left into Dame Lane, walk past Dublin Castle, past Dubh Linn Garden and the Chester Beatty Library; continue west along Ship Street and turn right into Werburgh Street.*

St Werburgh's Church

🕐 *Open by appointment, Mon-Fri 10am-4pm. Key from 8 Castle St.* ☎ *01 4783710*
The 1715 church replaced an early 12C one; it was remodelled in 1759 after a fire and has one of the city's most elegant Georgian interiors. The British authorities, nervous after the 1798 rebellion, insisted on the removal of the spire overlooking the Castle courtyard. One of the most distinguished of the rebels, Lord Edward Fitzgerald, was secretly buried in the vaults; his captor, Major Henry Sirr, is buried in the churchyard.

▶ *Walk south down Werburgh St into Bride St; turn right into Kevin St Upper, right into St Patrick Close, passing Marsh's Library and the Cathedral (see below); turn right again into Patrick St.*

The arches on the east side of **St Patrick's Park** form a literary parade of Dublin-born writers, with their dates and major works; three won a Nobel Prize for Literature.

▶ *Continue north up St Patrick St; turn left into Back Lane.*

Tailors' Hall★

The Tailors' Hall (1703-07) is the only surviving guild-hall in Dublin. The Great Hall has a stage, a handsome marble fireplace and a minute gallery with a wrought-iron railing: the building is now used by *An Taisce*, the Irish National Trust.

▶ *Return to St Patrick St and continue to the south end.*

There is a fine view of **Christ Church Cathedral** (*see below*) and the covered bridge linking it to the old Synod Hall which now houses Dublinia.

▶ *Walk west along High St.*

St Audoen's Church

(*Dúchas*) ♿ 🕐 *Open Jun to Sep, 9.30am-5.30pm (4.45pm last admission).* ☎ *01 6770088*
The old church (now Anglican) was founded by the Anglo-Normans and dedicated to St Audoen of Rouen in France. The west doorway is 12C, the nave is 13C. **St Audoen's Gate** (1275), leading to the river, is one of 32 gates in the Norman city walls.

▶ *Turn right into Cook St and left into Winetavern St; walk down to the river and look across to Inns Quay.*

Four Courts

The building (1785) accommodating four major courts – Chancery, King's Bench, Exchequer and Common Pleas – was begun by Thomas Cooley and completed by James Gandon. It was seized by the rebels in 1916 and again by anti-Treaty forces. On the first occasion it escaped serious damage but in 1921, it was shelled by the Free

Sunlight Chambers

B Juge/MICHELIN

State army from across the river and mined by the insurgents; the building and the irreplacable national archives from 1174 it contained, were virtually destroyed.

▶ *Turn right and walk along Wood Quay and Essex Quay.*

On the corner of Essex Quay and Parliament Street stand **Sunlight Chambers**, built as the headquarters of Lever Brothers with coloured terracotta friezes telling the story of soap.

▶ *Continue along the quays to return to Ha'penny Bridge.*

North Bank

In the Middle Ages, the Viking settlement by the Liffey known as Oxmantown, was dominated by **St Mary's Abbey**. In the 17C it was built up on a grid plan around Oxmantown Green, now Smithfield. The Hospital and Free School of King Charles II was founded in 1670 for the education of poor boys who wore military-style blue uniforms; in 1773 the **Bluecoat School** was housed in Blackhall Place in a building designed by Thomas Ivory, now occupied by the Incorporated Law Society.

By the 18C, the north bank had become the most fashionable residential district of Dublin, centred on O'Connell Street, then known as Gardiner's Mall. No-one today would describe O'Connell Street as fashionable but it retains its generous dimensions and remains a vital part of the city centre. Farther north, the site of Parnell Square was developed by Bartholomew Mosse to raise money for his maternity hospital, which occupied the south side. Many of the once-elegant Georgian terraces in the neighbourhood, particularly **Mountjoy Square**, have passed through neglect and decay to demolition or restoration and conversion. **St George's Church** (1802–14), where the Duke of Wellington married Kitty Pakenham in 1806, was designed by Francis Johnston with a marked similarity to St Martin's-in-the-Fields in London.

Two of Dublin's major theatres are located on the north bank. The **Gate Theatre** was founded in 1928 by Hilton Edwards and Micheál MacLiammóir. The earlier **Abbey Theatre**, now a national institution, was founded in 1904 by Lady Gregory and W B Yeats as part of the Irish literary revival. In 1924 it became the first state-subsidised theatre in the English-speaking world, and for a while its productions continued to cause controversy, even riots, notably with the plays of Sean O'Casey. The original theatre building was destroyed by fire in 1951.

▶ *From the north side of O'Connell Bridge walk up O'Connell St.*

O'Connell Street★

This broad, elegant thoroughfare was laid out by Luke Gardiner in the 18C as a tree-lined mall and later converted into a narrow residential square. Renamed Sackville Street, it developed into the most important street in 18C Dublin; later it was extended south to Carlisle Bridge (1794) and renamed after O'Connell in 1922.

Down the centre of the street stands a row of **monuments** by John Foley of *(south to north)* Daniel O'Connell; William Smith O'Brien (1803–64), the leader of the Young Ireland Movement sentenced to death for treason in 1848; Sir John Gray, who organised Dublin's water supply; James Larkin (1876–1947), founder of the Irish Transport and General Workers' Union (1909); Father Theobald Mathew of the 19C temperance movement.

The **GPO building**★ with its Ionic portico was designed by Francis Johnston in 1814. It was the headquarters of the rebels in the Easter Rising in 1916 and still bears scars of the fighting.

The **Anna Livia Fountain**, a female personification of the Liffey, soon nicknamed the Floozie in the Jacuzzi, was erected to commemorate Dublin's Millennium in 1988; it occupies the site of Nelson's Pillar (1808), which was damaged by a bomb in 1966 and demolished. It was James Joyce who coined the term Anna Livia out of the Irish for the River Liffey *(Abhainn na Life)*.

▶ *Turn right into Talbot Street.*

Pro-Cathedral★

🕐 *Open Mon-Sat, 7.30am-6.45pm (Sat 7.15pm), Sun 9am-1.45pm, 5.30-7.30pm ☎ 01 8745441 - www.procathedral.ie*

Dublin's most important Roman Catholic church was built in 1821 in the style of a Greek temple with a Doric portico and a dome. Its monumentality contrasts with its rather cramped setting, but Protestant interests kept it away from its intended site on O'Connell Street. In 1851 John Newman made his profession of faith to Cardinal Cullen in this church. The Palestrina Choir was endowed in 1902 by Edward Marty; one of its early members was John McCormack.

Opposite, stands **Tyrone House**, an elegant mansion, designed by Richard Castle in 1741 and now occupied by the Department of Education.

▶ *Return to O'Connell St.*

Parnell Square

Rutland Square was renamed in honour of **Charles Stewart Parnell**, whose statue stands at the road intersection. The south side of the square is taken up by the elegant lying-in hospital designed by Richard Castle In 1752 for Dr Bartholomew Mosse (1712–59). The **Rotunda Hospital Chapel**★ is an exuberant Rococo creation, decorated with superb stuccowork by Bartholomew Cramillion and carved mahogany woodwork by John Kelly. 🕐 *Open Wed, 10am-noon; on application in writing.* ☎ *01 8730700*

Funds for the hospital were raised from entertainments given in the **Rotunda** (1764), designed by John Ensor – now

Charles Stewart Parnell

R Holzbachova, Ph Benet/MICHELIN

a cinema, or in the **Assembly Rooms** (1786), designed by Richard Johnston – now the Gate Theatre. Yet more fundraising was done in the walled **pleasure gardens** in the centre of the square, laid out with a wilderness, temples of refreshment and a terrace where music was played - known as the Orchestra. The surrounding houses were completed in the 1770s and inhabited by peers, bishops and members of Parliament. *(Dúchas)* &⏱ *Open May to Sep, 9.30am-8pm; Oct to Apr, 11am-7pm (4.pm, Nov-Feb).* ☎ *01 647 2498 (office); 01 874 3074 (garden)*

The north end of the square has been converted into a **Garden of Remembrance** designed by Daithí P Hanly; the gates incorporate Celtic motifs, the central sculpture by Oisín Kelly echoes Yeats' poem *Easter 1916* and the mythological transformation of the Children of Lir into swans. The broken spears in the mosaic reflect the Celtic custom of throwing weapons into water after a battle.

The site is significant because it was here that plans for the Easter Rising (1916) were hatched *(plaque on the north side)* and the rebels were held overnight.

▷ *On the north side of the square are the Dublin Writers' Museum and the Hugh Lane Gallery. Turn right into Granby St and pass the Wax Museum. Turn left into Dorset St and right into Henrietta St.*

King's Inns

The building where barristers used to live and study was started in 1795 and completed in 1827. It is the last great public building designed by James Gandon and the dining room is the only Gandon interior to survive.

▷ *Return to Dorset St; turn left and right into Dominick St Lower; turn left into Parnell St and right into Moore St.*

A lively **street market** is held here at the heart of a busy shoppping district.

▷ *Turn right into Henry St and left into Liffey St to return to the Ha'penny Bridge.*

Phoenix Park★★

The largest enclosed urban park in Europe (1 752 acres/709ha) derives its name from the Gaelic for clear water *(Fionn Uisce)*. The land, confiscated from Kilmainham Priory in 1543 by the Crown, was enclosed in 1662 by the Duke of Ormond who introduced a herd of fallow deer which still roam the Fifteen Acres (actually approximately 300 acres/121ha).

The southeast gate is flanked by the **Wellington Monument**, designed by Sir William Smirke in 1817, and the **Peoples' Garden** sloping to a small lake. From here Chesterfield Avenue, lit by gas lamps, leads to the **Phoenix Monument**, erected by Lord Chesterfield in 1745. To the south stands the residence of the Ambassador of the USA and the **Papal Cross** marking the visit of Pope John Paul II in 1979.

In 1882, at the height of agitation over the Land Act, the newly appointed Chief Secretary, Lord Frederick Cavendish, and the Under-Secretary, Thomas H Burke, the intended victim, were stabbed to death while walking in the park near the Vice-Regal Lodge by the "Invincibles", members of an extremist Fenian sect. All this and more besides, is told in the **Phoenix Park Visitor Centre**. *(Dúchas)* &⏱ *Open Apr to Sep, 10am-6pm (5.30pm mid-end Oct); Nov to mid-Mar, Sat-Sun 10am-5pm. Last admission 45min before closing; Sun 1hr before closing.* ☞ *€2.90* ☎ *016770095; www.heritageireland.com*

Zoological Gardens★
🄺🄸🄳🅂 ⏱*9.30am (10.30am Sun) to 6.30pm (dusk Oct to Feb). Last admission 1hr before closing.* ☞ *€13.50.* ✕☎*01 474 8900 - www.dublinzoo.ie*

The Zoo, founded in 1830, is set in attractive parkland (30 acres/12ha). Besides the animals on show, the zoo is actively involved in breeding programmes with other zoos and is under constant development. The **World of Cats** has snow leopards, lions and other felines; the **World of Primates** has vivacious monkeys and sad-faced orang-utans. Arctic foxes and snowy owls inhabit **Fringes of the Arctic**, while the lakes and their banks provides a habitat for water fowl, flamingoes, penguins and sea-lions. **City Farm** and **Pets Corner** are especially popular with children.

Aras an Uachtaráin

Tour (1hr) Sat 10.15am-4.30pm (3.30pm in winter). ◷ *Closed 24-26 Dec. Tickets available from Phoenix Park Visitor Centre.* ☎ *01 677 0095 - www.president.ie*

The **official residence** of the President of Ireland, formerly Vice-Regal Lodge, was built (1751–54) as a private house by Nathaniel Clements and in 1815 acquired its Ionic portico by Francis Johnston.

Sights

Inner Dublin

Trinity College Old Library★★★

Entrances in College Green and Nassau St. ♿◷*Open Mon-Sat, 9.30am-5pm; May to Sep, Sun 9.30am-4.30pm; Oct to Apr noon-4.30pm.* ◷ *Closed 21 Dec to 2 Jan.* ⊚ *€8* *College tour (30min, including the Colonnades and Book of Kells): mid-May to Sep 10.15am-3.40pm, every 40min from the Front Arch.* ⊚ *€5.* ☎ *01 896 1661; www. tcd.ie/library*

The austere building (1712–32) was designed by Thomas Burgh, Chief Engineer and Surveyor-General of Her Majesty's Fortifications in Ireland. The library acquired its books by purchase or donation until 1801, when it became a copyright library, receiving copies of every book published in the Commonwealth. Since then the increased pace of acquisition has required new buildings: the Reading Room built in 1937 and the Berkeley Library designed by Paul Koralek in 1967. Until 1892 the ground floor was an open colonnade designed to protect the books from damp; in 1992 part of it was converted to provide two galleries: The Colonnades for annual themed exhibitions, and the Treasury.

Long Room, Old Library, Trinity College

Treasury★★★

This gallery displays the great treasures of Trinity College Library. The **Book of Kells**, the most famous of them, is an illuminated manuscript of the four Gospels in Latin on vellum, produced c 800 and kept at Kells until the 17C. The **Book of Durrow** (c 700) is another illustrated manuscript of the Gospels in a simpler style. The **Book of Armagh** (c 807) contains the complete text of the New Testament in Latin, as used by the Celtic Church, as well as the lives of St Patrick and St Martin and the Confession of St Patrick. The **Book of Dimma** contains both the Gospels and some liturgical text; its silver shrine dates from c 1150.

Long Room★★

Above the entrance door at the top of the stairs are the **arms of Elizabeth I**, a relic of the original college. The **Long Room** (209ft/64m x 40ft/12m) is lined with bookcases. The original flat ceiling was replaced in the mid 19C by the present higher wooden barrel vault to provide more shelving. The 29-string **Irish harp** (c 15C, restored) made of willow, is the oldest in Ireland; it was found in Limerick in the 18C.

Chester Beatty Library★★★

Dublin Castle Precinct, Dubh Linn Garden; entrance in Dame Lane or Ship St. ♿🕐 *Open May to Sep, 10am(11am Sat, 1pm Sun) - 5pm; Oct to Apr, Tue-Sun, 10am (11am Sat, 1pm Sun) - 5pm.* 🕐 *Closed 1 Jan, Bank Hol Mon, Good Fri, 14-26 Dec.* ☎ *01 4070750*
This fabulous collection of Islamic and Far Eastern manuscripts and artworks was bequeathed to the nation by Sir Alfred Chester Beatty (1875-1968), an American businessman who was made the country's first honorary citizen. Among the **Arabic, Persian and Turkish manuscripts** are over 270 copies of the **Koran**, some with illuminations by great master calligraphers. The **Biblical material** consists of Syriac, Armenian, Ethiopian and Coptic texts, also early Western Bibles and Books of Hours. Of international importance are the biblical papyri dating from the early 2C to 4C. The **Japanese and Chinese collection** includes paintings and prints of the highest quality, including Japanese woodblock prints which influenced 19C European art. In addition, there is a large collection of snuff bottles, *netsuke*, jade books and rhinoceros-horn cups. The **Western European collection** contains many important printed books as well as prints by Dürer, Holbein, Piranesi, Bartolozzi and many others.

Dublin Castle★★

Entrances in Dame Lane and Ship St. (Dúchas) ♿🔊*Tour (45min including State Appartments, Chapel Royal and Undercroft), 10am (2pm Sat-Sun, Bank Hols) - 4.45pm.* 🕐 *Closed 1 Jan, Good Fri, 25-26 Dec.* ⊛ *€4.50* ✗☎*01 677 7129 - www.dublincastle.ie*
Between 1204 and 1922 Dublin Castle represented British rule in Ireland. People under suspicion languished in its prisons; traitors' heads were exhibited on spikes over the gate. Embedded within the tight-knit urban fabric of the city, the Castle changed over the centuries from a formidable fortress to an administrative complex of almost domestic character. By the 19C the Lord Deputy usually resided at Vice-Regal Lodge in Phoenix Park, staying at the Castle only for the few winter weeks of the Castle Season, which was a glittering round of levées, balls and receptions. The Castle is now one of the symbols of Irish statehood, its sumptuous State Apartments used to receive foreign dignitaries and other important ceremonial occasions.
Its construction began 30 years after the Anglo-Norman landing in Ireland, when King John ordered a castle to be built on the high ground southeast of the existing town, a site protected on two sides by the River Poddle. The original structure expanded into a rough quadrangle with a round tower at each corner on the site of the present Upper Yard. In 1684 much of the medieval castle was destroyed by fire. New apartments designed by Sir William Robinson were completed in 1688 but most of them were replaced in the middle of the 18C. The Castle's two courtyards now have an essentially Georgian appearance, with the Powder Tower as the most visible reminder of its medieval origin, even though it too was much altered in the early 19C.

Wedgwood Room, Dublin Castle

State Apartments

Upper Yard. The upper floor on the south side was built between 1750 and 1780 but the interiors have been much modified subsequently. The **Grand Staircase** and the **Battleaxe Landing** lead to a suite of sumptuously furnished and decorated interiors overlooking Castle Green and the wall named after Queen Victoria, built to protect the royal gaze from the sight of the adjoining stables. In 1916, one room served as a prison for James Connolly, one of the leaders of the Uprising. There is Sheraton, Regency and Louis XIX furniture, fine plaster or painted ceilings, and modern, colourful carpets from Killybegs. The **Throne Room** has ovals and roundels with deities probably painted by the Venetian Giambattista Bellucci in the early 18C, portraits of Viceroys in the **Picture Gallery** are set off by superb Venetian chandeliers, and the **Wedgwood Room** has paintings attributed to Angelica Kauffmann (1741-1807) and black Wedgwood plaques.

Many glittering balls were held in Ascendancy times in St Patrick's Hall built in the mid-18C and named after the Order of the Knights of St Patrick, an order instituted by George III in 1783. Crests, helmets and banners hang above the stallplates recording the names of the members of the Order, while the ceiling is a glorification of the relationship between Britain and Ireland, painted by Vincenzo Valdré (1742–1814), an Italian who came to Ireland in 1774 with the Viceroy, the Marquess of Buckingham, for whom he had worked at Stowe.

Castle Hall

The dignified two-storey building *(closed)* on the north side of the upper yard was designed c 1750 by Thomas Ivory for the Master of Ceremonies. It incorporates the **Bedford Tower**, named after John Russell, Duke of Bedford and Lord Lieutenant, and built on the base of the west tower of the original castle gate. Four days before the state visit of Edward VII and Queen Alexandra in 1907 the Crown Jewels were stolen from the Office of Arms in the Bedford Tower; they have never been recovered.

Flanking Castle Hall are two gates surmounted by statues by Van Nost: *Fortitude* on the west gate and *Justice* on the east gate, which was the sole entrance until the west gate was opened in 1988 and a new bridge built; the fountain and pool recall the old moat. A figure of Justice stands atop the Tower; Dublin wags liked to point out that her back is turned to the city and that her scales dipped unevenly in wet weather; holes were eventually bored in the outer pan to allow the rainwater to drain away.

Powder Tower Undercroft

Lower Yard. Excavations beneath the Powder Tower have revealed parts of the Viking and Norman defences – a 13C arch and relieving arch in the **Old City Wall** which enabled boatmen to enter the moat to deliver goods to the postern gate.

Church of the Most Holy Trinity

This fine example of a Regency Gothick building was designed by Francis Johnston and consecrated in 1814. Before reconsecration as a Roman Catholic sanctuary (1943) the building served as the Chapel Royal, on the site of an earlier, smaller church. The exterior is decorated with over 100 heads carved in Tullamore limestone by Edward Smyth and his son John; the interior plasterwork is by George Stapleton and the woodwork by Richard Stewart. The Passion of Christ panels in the east window are composed of old Continental stained glass. The arms of all the Viceroys from 1172 to 1922 are represented in the galleries, gallery windows, and on the chancel walls.

National Museum★★

Kildare St. (see below). &⏱ *Open Tue-Sun 10am (2pm Sun) to 5pm.* ⏱ *Closed Good Fri, 25 Dec.* ⟟*Guided tour (30-45min) at frequent intervals.* ⊚ €2. ⫢☎ *01 66 15133; www.nationalgallery.ie*

The National Museum off Kildare Street, was purpose-built in 1890 to display treasures from the national archaeological collections. A short video contextualises the masterpieces of Irish art now on show in **The Treasury★★**. Precious objects range in date from the Bronze Age to the 15C and include: a model boat in gold from the Broighter Hoard (1C); the Loughnashade Trumpet (1C BC); the Ardagh Chalice (8C); the Tara Brooch (8C); the Shrine of St Patrick's Bell in bronze, gold and silver (c 1100); the "Cathach", a book shrine made to contain the Psalter of St Columba (Colmcille) (12C–15C); the Kavanagh Charter Horn of ivory and brass, the only surviving object associated with Irish kingship (12C–15C).

The section on **Prehistoric Ireland** has a reconstruction of a passage tomb as well as the huge Lurgan Longboat from around 2500 BC. **Ireland's Gold** displays a gleaming array of artefacts, some from hoards preserved for millenia in the Irish boglands. The **Road to Independence** commemorates those involved in the Easter Rising in 1916 through photos, MSS, documents, uniforms and death-masks.

Among the objects shown in **Viking Ireland** are items from the Viking settlement at Wood Quay in Old Dublin: iron, bone, wood utensils, clothing and ornaments. St Manchan's Shrine, a spectacular reliquary, is one of several ecclesiastical treasures on display in the section entitled **The Church.**

The small but exquisite objects from **Ancient Egypt** are dramatically lit. **Irish Glass** has an excellent range of this craft in which the country has long excelled.

National Gallery★★

Kildare St, Merrion St or Clare St. (Dúchas) &⏱ *Open daily 9.30am (noon Sun) to 5.30pm (8.30pm Thu).* ⏱ *Closed Good Fri, 24-26 Dec.* ⟟ *Guided tour: Jul-Aug, daily 3pm; rest of year, Sat 3pm, Sun 2pm, 3pm, 4pm.* ⫢☎ *01 661 5133; www.nationalgallery.ie.*

Ireland's National Gallery, inaugurated in 1864, has one of the finest collections of art in Europe. By the Merrion Street entrance stands the statue of William Dargan (1799-1867), a railway magnate and the promoter of the Irish Industrial Exhibition of 1853 which included a Fine Art Hall, and it is these works that formed the founding collection. Other benefactors have included Sir Hugh Lane, Sir Henry Vaughan, and G B Shaw, whose donation included royalties from *My Fair Lady.* The Milltown Rooms were built to house the Milltown Collection. The latest addition is the controversial Millenium Wing, a striking stone-clad edifice providing a spacious new entrance area and space for loaned exhibitions from abroad.

Understandably, the gallery's collection of Irish art is outstanding, with examples by the country's major painters and sculptors from the 17C to the 20C, displayed alongside select items of furniture. There are fascinating topographical pictures, portraits, and a whole room devoted to the work of Jack B Yeats (1871-1957), who ably captured the colour and spirit of contemporary life in Ireland and its landscapes, as did, of course, his brother, W B Yeats. The gallery's British paintings include works by Hogarth, Wilson, Gainsborough, Reynolds and Romney; lovely watercolours by Bonington and Crome. There is an important Italian collection ranging from early altarpieces to paintings by Fra Angelico, Mantegna and Titian and a superbly dramatic Caravaggio, *The Taking of Christ*. French art is represented by Claude and Poussin, by several artists of the Rococo, and a number of Impressionists. Outstanding among the Dutch paintings is the tranquil *Woman Reading a Letter* by Gabriel Metsu, matched by works by Vermeer, Ruisdael and Hobbema. The Spanish collection is substantial, with pictures by El Greco, Velazquez, Murillo, Zurbaran, and Goya.

Christ Church Cathedral★★

&🕐 *Open Jun-Aug, Mon-Fri 9am-6pm; rest of year, Mon-Fri 9.45am-5pm; Sat 10am-4.30pm, Sun 12.45-2.45pm.* 🕐 *Closed 26 Dec.* ⊜ €5. *Self-guided tour with numbered leaflet.* ☎ 01 677 8099; www.cccdub.ie.

Like the Castle, Christ Church Cathedral became a symbol of the Ascendancy, and the Romanesque/Early English building is still the seat of the Anglican Bishop of Dublin and Glendalough and the Metropolitan Cathedral of the Southern Province of the Church of Ireland, second only to Armagh. Largely rebuilt in the 19C by George Scott, it is nevertheless an important link to the city's very earliest days, being the successor to the wooden church built in 1038 by Dunan, the first Bishop of Dublin, on land provided by Sitric, the Viking King of Dublin. Soon after 1170 this building was replaced by a stone church built on the orders of Strongbow, Richard de Clare, Earl of Pembroke. A number of medieval features survived the 19C rebuilding: the elegant **Romanesque south door** overlooking the ruins of the Chapter House, the **brass eagle lectern**, and some of the original encaustic tiles in the Chapel of St Laud. Hanging on the chapel wall *(right)* is a casket containing the heart of St Laurence O'Toole, the second Archbishop of Dublin. In the south aisle is the **"Strongbow" monument;** though the effigy in chainmail is certainly not the great Anglo-Norman commander, the half figure beside it may well belong to the original tomb. "Strongbow's tomb" was frequently specified in legal contracts as the place of payment. Of all the Cathedral interiors, the 12C Norman **crypt** *(access in the south aisle)* is perhaps the most evocative. It has been used for services, has been let to shopkeepers and used for burials until the mid 19C.

St Patrick's Cathedral★★

&🕐 *Open daily 9am-6pm (5pm Sat, Nov-Feb; 3pm Sun, Nov-Feb).* 🕐 *Closed 1 Jan and 25-26 Dec.* ⊜ €5. 🅿 ☎01 475 39472 *(office)*, 475 4817 *(cathedral); www.stpatrick-scathedral.ie*

John Comyn, appointed Archbishop of Dublin in 1181, objected to being subject to the laws and regulations of the City Provosts. He moved his seat out of the city jurisdiction to the site of a holy well used, according to tradition, by St Patrick to baptise converts. His church was promoted to a cathedral and rebuilt in the Early English style in the mid-13C, with a tower added a century later.

The cathedral is forever associated with **Jonathan Swift**, its Dean from 1713 to 1745. His tomb is marked by a bronze plaque in the floor near the main door, beside it that of his friend "Stella". Swiftian memorabilia includes his death-mask and a replica of his skull (in the bookcase). Swift wrote his own epitaph; he also composed an epitaph for the black marble tomb of the **Duke of Schomberg** *(north choir aisle)*, and put up a plaque *(south transept)* to his faithful servant Alexander McGee.

The vaulted **baptistery** in the southwest corner of the nave was probably the entrance to the original church. The 13C floor tiles, transferred from the south tran-

Jonathan Swift (1667–1745)

The famous Dean of St Patrick's Cathedral was born in Dublin in 1667 and educated at Kilkenny and Trinity College, Dublin. In 1689 he became Secretary to Sir William Temple of Moor Park in England but failed to secure advancement. Back in Ireland he was ordained (1694) and appointed as prebendary of Kilroot, near Carrickfergus, where he wrote his first book, *A Tale of a Tub*, a satire on "corruptions in religion and learning", published in 1704 together with *The Battle of the Books*. He went back England but, on Temple's death in 1699, returned to Ireland. He became Vicar of Laracor, south of Trim (1701) and appointed Dean of St Patrick's in 1713.

Swift is best remembered for *Gulliver's Travels* despite all that he wrote on church matters, politics and Ireland – including the delightfully satirical *A Modest Proposal* (1729) for disposing of unwanted babies. His *Journal to Stella*, a collection of intimate letters, was addressed to Esther Johnson; according to some she and Swift were married in the Deanery garden but they never lived together.

Swift spent one-third of his income on the poor and saved another third which he bequeathed for the founding of a hospital for the insane. At the end of his life he suffered from Ménière's disease and lost the use of many of his faculties.

sept in the 19C restoration, have been copied throughout the cathedral. The huge and splendid **Boyle Monument** (1632), erected by the great Earl of Cork in memory of his second wife Catherine, is adorned with no fewer than 16 polychrome figures.

In the north aisle stands a fine statue by Edward Smyth of the Marquess of Buckingham, Viceroy and first Grand Master of the **Order of St Patrick;** until 1871 the cathedral was the chapel of the Order, hence the banners and escutcheons.

In the north transept stands the old door of the Chapter House; the hole was cut in 1492 so that the Earl of Kildare could "chance his arm" in a conciliatory gesture to Black James Ormond who had taken refuge in the Chapter House; they had quarrelled because Ormond had been appointed Lord Deputy in place of Kildare.

R Holzbachova, Ph Benet/MICHELIN

Saint Patrick's Cathedral

Marsh's Library★★

St Patrick's Close. 🕒 *Open Mon, Wed-Fri, 10am-1pm, 2-5pm, Sat 10.30am-1pm.* 💶 *€2.50.* ☎ *01 454 3511; www.marshlibrary.ie*

The building in St Patrick's Close was designed in 1701 by Sir William Robinson to house the first public library in Ireland. A portrait of the founder, Archbishop Narcissus Marsh, hangs above the stairs. The dark oak bookcases, surmounted by a mitre, divide the long room into seven bays. Beyond the office are three "cages" where precious books can be consulted. The total of 25 000 books is composed of four individual collections.

Bank of Ireland★★

Foster Place. ♿ ⏰ *Open Tue-Fri 10am-4pm (5pm Thu).* 🔊 *Tour: Tue 10.30am, 11.30am, 1.45pm.* ⏰ *Closed Bank Hols.* ☎ *01 677 6801*

Ireland was governed from this elegant building in Foster Place from when it was completed (1728) until 1800, when the Act of Union abolished the country's jurisdiction and transferred it to Westminster. Several eminent architects contributed to its appearance – Sir Edward Lovett Pearce, James Gandon, and Francis Johnston, who converted it for use by the Bank of Ireland in 1803. The old House of Commons is now the banking hall. The **House of Lords** is still largely intact, with a magnificent coffered ceiling, a great chandelier of Irish glass, an oak mantlepiece to a design by Inigo Jones, and splendid 17C Flemish tapestries depicting the Battle of the Boyne and the siege of Londonderry.

In the **Story of Banking** a short video and display of currency, bank notes and an old money cart form part of an excellent interpretation of the role of the Bank of Ireland in the commercial development of the country, since its establishment in 1783.

Newman House★★

St Stephen's Green South. 🔊 *Tour (40min) Jul to Aug, Tue-Fri, 2-4pm on the hour; otherwise by appointment.* 💶 €5. ☎ *01 716 7422 / 475 7255*

The two 18C town houses named after Cardinal Newman honour the memory of the first Rector of University College, which started here in 1854. Almost intact, they provide an insight into the 18C city. The smaller house was designed by Richard Castle in 1738 and retains many original features like the glazing bars he devised. The splendid stucco figures of Apollo and the Muses are by the Lafranchini brothers. The larger house dates from 1765; the Bishops' Room has a portrait of Cardinal Newman and his Rector's Chair, while the staircase is decorated with lovely Rococo plasterwork by Richard West.

B Juge/MICHELIN

Newman House

Custom House★★

Custom House Quay; entrance in south front. The Custom House, with its long façade and central dome, is one of the great landmarks of Dublin. It was designed by James Gandon, completed in 1791, and restored after being set on fire by anti-Treaty forces at the beginning of the Civil War in 1921. The **Visitor Centre** in the ceremonial vestibules behind the south portico, offers a detailed and fascinating history of the building, Gandon's career and the work of the government offices which were housed there. ⏰ *Call for opening times and charges -* ☎ *01 888 2375.*

Outside on the quay beside the River Liffey stands the **Famine Memorial**: six bronze figures by Rowan Gillespie personify the mixed emotions – ranging from despair through suffering to hope – of the many victims of the Great Famine.

Hugh Lane Gallery of Modern Art★

Parnell Sq. North. ♿ ⏰ *Tue-Sun 10am (11am Sun) to 6pm (5pm Fri-Sun).* ⏰ *Closed Good Fri, 25 Dec.* 📷 *Francis Bacon Studio* 💶 €7 (€3.50 Tue, 9.30am-noon). 🍴 ☎ *01 222 5550 - www.hughlane.ie*

The extensive collection of late-19C and 20C works by Irish and Continental artists supplement the works acquired by **Sir Hugh Lane** (1875–1915), who drowned on the *Lusitania*. The building, a three-storey mansion of Portland stone and granite, flanked by curved screen walls, was designed in 1762 by Sir William Chambers for an earlier connoisseur, **James Caulfield**, 1st Earl of Charlemont, who also built the Marino Casino.

There are works by several Impressionists, Corot and Courbet, and contemporary pieces by the likes of Christo who swathed the pathways of St Stephen's Green. The most interesting room, however, is probably the one reserved for works by Irish artists. *Lakeside Cottage* (c 1929) is a landscape by Paul Henry; *The Rescue of the Prison Van at Manchester* by Maurice MacGonical dramtically portrays a famous Fenian incident from 1867. One room is devoted to Roderic O'Conor (1860–1940), a friend of Gauguin, who reflects the influence of colleagues, like Seurat and Van Gogh.

City Hall★

Dame St ◷ *Open 10am(2pm Sun) - 5.15pm (5pm Sun).* ◷ *Closed Good Fri, 25-26 Dec.* ☞ *€4.* ☎ *01 672 2204; www.dublincity.ie*

This magnificent edifice, one of the finest public buildings in Dublin, built in 1769-79 by Thomas Cooley as the Royal Exchange, marked the arrival in Ireland of the neo-Classical style. When economic activity declined after the 1800 Act of Union, the building lost much of its purpose, and in 1852 it was bought by the City Corporation. During the **Easter Rising** of 1916 it was occupied by the insurgents; from the roof they commanded the approaches and main gate of Dublin Castle but after about three hours the regular soldiers regained command of the Upper Yard.

The splendid domed **rotunda** has early 20C frescoes illustrating aspects of city history. **The Story of the Capital**, a lively introduction to Dublin's past, is housed in the vaulted basement: this excellent multi-media exhibition complements Dublinia, exploring the post-medieval history with plans, photographs, old film, artworks and precious objects like the Civic Sword presented by Henry IV around 1409.

Number Twenty-Nine★

Tour Tue-Sun,10am (1pm Sun) to 5pm. ◷ *Closed Good Fri, 2 weeks at Christmas.* ☞ *€4.50.* ✗ ☎ *01 702 6165 - www.esb.ie/numbertwentynine*

No 29 Lower Fitzwilliam Street was occupied from 1794 to 1806 by a widow and her three children: today, the 18C terrace house evocatively recreates domestic life in Dublin in the Georgian era. It is decorated throughout with appropriate furniture, carpets, curtains and paintings, and is crammed with the paraphernalia of everyday living. Among the wealth of objects a wine cistern designed by Francis Johnston and a curved belly-warmer.

Dublin Writers' Museum

Parnell Sq North - ◷ *Open daily 10am (11am Sun, Bank Hols) - 5pm (6pm Mon-Fri, Jun-Aug).* ☞ *€6.70.* ✗ ☎ *01 872 2077; www.writersmuseum.com*

The Irish writers associated with the city of Dublin are remembered with personal items, photos, portraits, busts, manuscripts and copies of their major works. The museum also traces the written tradition in Ireland from the illuminated manuscripts of the Celtic Christian church such as the Book of Kells to the present day. This therefore includes Jonathan Swift and his contemporaries, writers who left ireland like Oscar Wilde and Bernard Shaw, James Joyce and Samuel Beckett, writers who promoted the 19C interest in Irish folklore such as WB Yeats, Synge and O'Casey, as well as Flann O'Brien, Brendan Behan and Patrick Kavanagh. Temporary exhibitions are held in the elegant reception rooms, readings and workshops in the children's section. The museum occupies two Georgian terrace houses with **elegant stucco ceilings**★; the one in the library is by Michael Stapleton. Alterations made in 1891–95 by Alfred Darbyshire for George Jameson include the addition of stained-glass windows bearing the Jameson monogram, four female figures representing Music, Literature, Art and Science, and, in the first-floor saloon, a series of painted door panels by Gibson and an ornamental colonnade and gilded frieze.

James Joyce Centre

35 North Great George's St. ⏱ *Open Tue-Sat, 10am-5pm.* ⏱ *Closed Bank Hols.* ⚓ *€5.* 🚶 *Tour of Joyce's Dublin Tue, Thu, Sat at 11am, 2pm.* ⚓ *€10.* 🍴⚓*01 878 8547 - www.jamesjoyce.ie*

The centre promotes the life and work of James Joyce by hosting talks, tours of the house and walks through the north inner city. As a boy, Joyce lived nearby in Fitzgibbon Street and attended Belvedere College *(Denmark St)*. The restored terrace house, built in 1784 by Francis Ryan, once served as the town house of Valentine Brown, Earl of Kenmare; the very fine **plasterwork**★ is mostly by Michael Stapleton. Joyce family portraits line the staircase.

Statue of James Joyce

Dublinia

High St. 🎒 ♿⏱ *Open Apr to Sep 10am-5pm; Oct to Mar 11am (10am Sat-Sun, Bank Hols) - 4pm (last admission 3.15pm)* ⏱ *Closed 17 Mar, 23-26 Dec.* ⚓ *€6.* ⚓ *01 679 4611; www.dublinia.ie*

This entertaining interactive exhibition provides a sensory experience of the medieval city. There are tableaux, live costumed figures, a superb model of the Dublin of around 1500, a mock-up of part of an important archeological excavation along the Liffey and key finds, and a reconstruction of the face of a medieval Dubliner, whose skeleton was found nearby. It is housed in part of the Synod Hall of Christ Church Cathedral *(High Street)* to which it is linked by an arch.

Civic Museum

William St South. 🔑 *Closed until further notice. A database with most of the museum's holdings can be found at the Dublin City Library and Archive, 138-144 Pearse St.* ⚓ *01 674 4999/4998 - www.dublincity.ie*

The history of Dublin can be traced in the old City Assembly House displays of maps, prints, postcards, photographs, relics of old buildings and a set of Malton's views of Dublin (1792–99).

St Michan's Church

Church St. ♿⏱ *Open Mon-Fri 10am-12.45pm, 2-4.45pm, Sat 10am-12.45pm.* ⏱ *Closed Bank Hols.* ⚓ *€3.50.* ⚓ *01 872 4154*

The first church on the site was probably built by the Danes as St Michan is thought to be a Danish saint. The present church dates from 1095 but gained its present appearance in 1686. While the **Interior** boasts the early 18C organ played by Handel and **vaults** containing their **mummified corpses** preserved for over 300 years by the dry air and constant temperature.

St Mary's Abbey

(Dúchas) ⏱ *Open mid-May to mid-Sep, Wed and Fri, 10am-5pm (4.15pm last admission).* ⚓ *01 872 1490; wwwheritageireland.ie*

Founded by Benedictines but taken over by Cistercians, St Mary's was the richest monastery in the Pale and the meeting place for the Council of Ireland. It was here in 1534 that Silken Thomas renounced his allegiance to Henry VIII, thereby setting off the Kildare Revolt. All that remains of the abbey are the **Slype** and the rib-vaulted **Chapter House**, which now contains a reconstruction of the 15C cloister arcade (recovered in 1975 from a 17C building in Cork Street) and information about the foundation, architecture and history of the abbey and the Cistercian way of life.

Parliament

Tour (30min) Mon-Fri, 10.30am-3.30pm by arrangement through your embassy. Contact Events Desk for more information. ☎ *01 618 3781 - www.oireachtas.ie*

The two houses (**Dáil Éireann and Seanad Éireann**) meet in **Leinster House**, which was designed in 1745 by Richard Castle for the Duke of Leinster and converted to house the republican parliament in 1922. The public are admitted to the public gallery which overlooks the chamber of the lower house *(Dáil).*

Government Buildings

Marrion St Upper. Tour (40mins) Sat 10.30am-1.30pm. Tickets (no charge) available from National Gallery, Merrion Sq West. ☎ *01 619 4116 - www.taoiseach.gov.ie*

This imposing structure in Edwardian Baroque, opened in 1911 by George V, was the last major public building project completed in Dublin under British rule. Until 1989 parts of the building were occupied by Trinity College. Modern furniture and a fascinating range of contemporary art provide a fitting workplace for government committees and the Prime Minister *(Taoiseach).*

Natural History Museum

Merrion Street Upper. ♿🕑 *Open Tue-Sun, 10am (2pm Sun) to 5pm.* 🕑 *Closed Good Fri, 25 Dec.* ☎ *01 677 7444 - www.museum.ie*

A barely altered example of a Victorian museum, the building's pillared hall and galleries are as fascinating as their contents, which include three skeletons of the Great Irish Deer, now extinct. The specimens, still exhibited in the original display cabinets cover` complete range of creatures ever to have lived in Ireland.

Heraldic Museum

Kildare Street. ♿🕑 *Open Mon-Sat, 10am-4.30pm (12.30pm Sat).* 🕑 *Closed Bank Hols, Good Fri, 22 Dec-2 Jan.* ☎ *01 603 0311 - www.nli.ie*

The colourful collections include the banners of recognised heads of Irish families; the arms of the provinces, counties, cities and towns; the colours of Irish Regiments which served in France in the 17C and 18C; various heraldic artefacts.

National Wax Museum

Granby Row. 🕑 *Open 10am (noon Sun) to 5.30pm.* ‣ *€3.50.* ☎ *01 872 6340*

The display of waxwork figures combines fantasy and reality. Tableaux illustrate traditional fairy tales; while the ground floor is peopled by national figures such as O'Connell, the heroes of the Easter Rising, the Presidents of Ireland, theatrical stars, church leaders, poets and writers, politicians, sportsmen and pop stars.

Northside

National Museum★★

Collins Barracks, Benburb Street. Other collections of the National Museum are displayed at Kildare St. 🕑 *Open Tue-Sat, 10am (2pm Sun) - 5pm.* 🕑 *Closed Good Fri, 25 Dec.* 🍽🅿 ☎ *01 677 7444 - www.museum.ie*

The great barracks which once housed 3 000 men and 1 000 horses, was commissioned in 1700 by King William III. Thomas Burgh designed a "plain and useful, without any unnecessary ornament" complex which, in its day, was the largest institution of its kind in the British Isles, a progressive alternative to the contentious practice of billeting soldiers on the population. Today, the buildings have been converted for use by the National Museum for displays of decorative arts, folklife, history and geology.

The **West Block** shows an enthralling array of special treasures – 25 highly varied pieces grouped together under the heading of **Curators' Choice**; these might be a rare astrolabe from Prague, an elongated late-13C or early-14C wood statue of St Molaise and Bow figurines made by Thomas Frye, or modelled by his fellow London Irishmen.

The **South Block** displays Irish country furniture and woodcraft *(third floor)* from the Baroque to Modern era, including fascinating examples of late-19C Neo-Celtic pieces inspired by objects like the Tara Brooch discovered in 1850; scientific instruments *(second floor)*; Irish silver from the early 17C to today *(first floor)*.

Marino Casino★★

Off Malahide Rd, Marino. (Dúchas) ⌖ *Tour May to Oct, 10am-5pm (6pm Jun to Sep); Nov to Apr, Sat-Sun noon-4pm (5pm Apr). Last admission 45min before closing.* ⏱ *Closed 1 Jan, 25-26 Dec.* €2.90. ⌖ *01 833 1618 - www.heritageireland.ie*

The charming Palladian villa, designed by Sir William Chambers in 1765, was built in the grounds of Marino House (demolished 1921), the country seat of James Caulfield, Earl of Charlemont, who had met Chambers on the Grand Tour (1746–54). The centrally-planned French neo-Classical casino is built of Portland stone; 12 Doric columns support a frieze and cornice topped by pediments, statues and urn-shaped chimneys. The sculpture is by Simon Vierpyl and Joseph Wilton.

The interior contains four state rooms, decorated with elaborate plaster ceilings and inlaid floors using eight different kinds of wood, and four small bedrooms on the upper floor; plans of the building are displayed in the basement service rooms.

National Botanic Gardens★★

Botanic Rd, Glasnevin. (Dúchas) ⌖ *Gardens: open Apr to Sep, 9am (10am Sun) to 6pm; Oct to Mar, 10am-4.30pm. Glasshouses: open Apr to Sep, 9am (10am Sun) to 5pm (5.45pm Sat-Sun); Oct to Mar, 10am-4.15pm.* €2. ⌖ *01 837 7596 - www.botanicgardens.ie*

The gardens were started in 1795 on a 48acre/19ha site beside the Tolka River. The splendid Victorian glasshouses include the **Curvilinear Range** (1843–69), designed by Richard Turner, and the **Great Palm House** (1884). There is a delightful **walk** along the river from the **rose garden,** through the **peat garden** and the **bog garden** beside the ornamental pond to the **arboretum.** Further specimens in the rock garden, cactus house and fern house account for the 20 000 species grown here.

Glasnevin Cemetery★

Finglas Rd, Glasnevin. ⌖ *Tour (90min) from main gate, Wed and Fri at 2.30pm.* ⌖ *01 830 1133 - www.glasnevin-cemetery,ie*

Europe's largest cemetery (120acres/49ha) is the resting place of over a million people, nearly all Roman Catholics: anonymous paupers, cholera victims, and historical figures of every particular political persuasion – President De Valera, Daniel O'Connell. The guided tour becomes a fascinating walk through Irish history.

Old Jameson Distillery

Bow St, Smithfield Village. ⌖ *Tour (1hr) 9.30am-5.30pm.* ⏱ *Closed Good Fri, 25 Dec.* €8.75. ⌖ *01 807 2355 - www.jamesonwhiskey.com*

Part of the old distillery has been converted to show current and earlier methods of production of whiskey. A video *(8min)* is followed by a tour of a kiln and barley store; the mystery of worts and wash-backs in the process is explained. The tour ends in the bar where visitors are invited to take part in a whiskey tasting.

Chimney Viewing Tower

Smithfield Village. ⌖ *Tour 10am (10.30am Sun, Bank Hols) to noon, 1.15-5pm.* €5. ⌖ *01 817 3838*

The chimney (175ft/60m), constructed in 1895 as part of the Jameson Distillery, is now flanked by a glass-walled lift and crowned by a glass observation platform – fine views of the city, the bay and the mountains to the south.

GAA Museum

Off Clonliffe Rd. Open Mon-Sat, 9.30am (noon Sun) - 5pm (6pm Jul to Aug); match days, open to Cusack stand ticket holders only. Closed 1 Jan and 24-28, 31 Dec. Museum and stadium €9.50; museum €5.50. 01 819 2323 - http://museum.gaa.ie
Croke Park is the home of the national games of Ireland – hurling and Irish football. The museum traces the development of the **Gaelic Athletic Association** and its influence on the sporting, cultural and social traditions of Ireland. Computers provide highlights of past games; visitors can test their speed of reaction and high-jumping ability or try hitting the *sliothar* with a *camán* in the practice nets.

Southside

Kilmainham Gaol Museum★★

Inchicore Rd, Kilmainham. (Dúchas) Tour (1hr) Apr to Sep, 9.30am-5pm; Oct to Mar, 9.30am (10am Sun) to 5pm; last tour 1hr before closing. Closed 24-26 Dec. €5.30. 01 453 5984 - www.heritageireland.com

Duchas, Dublin

Kilmainham Gaol

The struggle for political independence is excellently presented in the prison where so many Irishmen were incarcerated for offences against the Crown – United Irishmen, Young Irelanders, Fenians, Invincibles, and participants in the Easter Rising. Collections of souvenirs, photographs, letters and press cuttings illustrate the many incidents and rebellions from 1796 to 1924 and their socio-political contexts. The **tour** includes the Central Hall (1862) containing 100 cells, the chapel, individual cells in the 1798 corridor, and the exercise yards also used for executions. The New Gaol, erected in 1792, consisted of a central range flanked by an east and a west courtyard divided into exercise yards; one contains Erskine Childers' boat the *Asgard*. In 1862, when the east wing was rebuilt, a high outer wall was constructed.

Irish Museum of Modern Art

Military Rd, Kilmainham. Open Tue-Sun, 10am (noon Sun, Bank Hols) to 5.30pm (5.15pm last admission). Closed 29 Mar. 01 612 9900 - www.imma.ie
The museum presents 20C Irish and international art, and allied theatrical and musical performances. Its exciting and wide-ranging programme includes exhibitions of major 20C art and promising contemporary talent.
The museum is housed in **Royal Kilmainham Hospital**★★, the earliest-surviving Classical building in Ireland. It was commissioned by the Duke of Ormond, James Butler of Kilkenny, who was appointed Viceroy in 1669 on his return from exile in France, and modelled on Les Invalides in Paris. The architect was William Robinson, Surveyor-General, who designed four ranges of buildings (1680–84) to provide accommodation for 300 old soldiers, the last of whom left in 1929.

The **Great Hall**, now hosts concerts and government receptions; the ceiling of the **Chapel**, is of papier maché. *(Dúchas)* &.*Heritage tour early Jul - mid Sep, Tue-Sun (1pm Sun, Bank Hols) to 4pm.* X@ *01 612 9900 - www.imma.ie*

Rathfarnham Castle★
3mi/5km south of Dublin by N 81 and R 115. (Dúchas) &.*Tour May to Oct, 9.30am-5.30pm; or by appointment. Last tour 1hr before closing.* @ *€2.* X@ *01 493 9462*

The magnificent but forbidding exterior gives no hint of the elegant 18C interior designed by Sir William Chambers and James "Athenian" Stuart. The rectangular central keep with four flanker towers was built c 1593 by Adam Loftus, a Yorkshireman who became Archbishop of Dublin . The castle was abandoned in the early 20C, then used as a Jesuit seminary; its splendid interiors, remodelled in the 1770s for Henry Loftus, are currently undergoing painstaking restoration.

Guinness Storehouse★
Crane Market St, off Thomas St. &.*Tour (1hr) 9.30am-5pm (8pm Jul to Aug).* ©*Closed Good Fri, 24-26 Dec.* @ *€14.* ⊞@ *01 408 4800 - www.guinness-storegouse.com*

The tour provides a complete survey of the Guinness production process and the 140 year history of the family firm.

In Thomas Street, next to the main brewery gate, is the house built by Arthur Guinness in the 18C. The brewery takes its name from St James' Gate, which pierced the old city wall at this point.

Drimnagh Castle
Long Mile Rd. &.* Tour Wed and Sun noon (2pm Sun) to 5pm. Last tour at 4pm.* @ *€4.* @ *01 450 2530*

Drimnagh is a 13C moated castle with a medieval Great Hall and vaulted undercroft, flanked by a battlemented tower; there is a formal 17C garden – box hedges, lavender bushes and herbs – at the rear.

GB Shaw Birthplace
33 Synge St. © *Open May to Sep, 10am-1pm, 2-5pm; Sat-Sun, Bank Hols, 2-5pm.* @ *€6.70.* @ *01 475 0854 - www.visitdublin.com*

The modest house, where **George Bernard Shaw** (1856–1950) was born and spent his early years, is furnished in the style of the mid 19C.

Waterways Visitor Centre
Grand Canal Quay. (Dúchas) o—*Closed until Jul 2007 for refurbishment.* @ *019650787 - www.waterwaysireland.org*

Modern displays explain canal engineering and the history of the countrywide network of canals established in the 18C.

Jewish Museum
Walworth Rd. © *Open May to Sep, Sun, Tue, Thu, 11am-3.30pm; Oct to Apr, Sun 10.30am-2.30pm or by appointment.* @ *Donation.* @ *01 490 1857 - www.visitdublin.com*

The museum in the old Walworth Road Synagogue (1917–c 75), opened by Chaim Herzog, President of Israel and son of the first Chief Rabbi of Ireland, displays material on the history of Irish Jews from the 11C. In the kosher kitchen, the table is laid for the Sabbath evening service. The **synagogue** upstairs retains all its ritual fittings.

Pearse Museum
4.5mi/7.2km S of Dublin by N 81. In Terenure fork left. In Rathfarnham bear left to Bray; turn first right onto Grange Rd; after 0.5 mile/0.8km turn right onto Sarah Curran Ave. 10min there and back on foot from the car park by the footpath parallel with the road. (Dúchas) o—*Closed until 2008 for renovation.* @ *01 493 4208*

Patrick Pearse (1879–1914)

James Pearse, a stone carver from England, kindled his son's love of English literature while his maternal great-aunt, Margaret, stimulated an interest in the Irish language. Patrick joined the **Gaelic League** aged sixteen and became editor of the League's newspaper. In 1905 he went to Belgium to study bilingualism in school; he wrote articles proposing the same policy for Ireland and set up his own boy's school. Great names - WB Yeats, Patrick MacDonagh and Padraic Colum - attended pupils' theatrical productions. Pearse holidayed in Rosmuc to study Gaelic. Over the years his original intention to promote a pride in things Irish evolved into more active political engagement. In November 1913 he joined the Irish Volunteers to campaign for Home Rule and in February 1914 he joined the IRB. He took a prominent part in the Easter Rising and was executed at Kilmainham Gaol on 2nd May 1916, not knowing that his brother was to be executed the following day.

Through pictures and manuscripts the museum traces the life of Patrick and William Pearse, founder members of the Irish Volunteers (1913), who were executed in 1916 for their leading role in the Easter Rising.

The house (1797) was acquired by the Pearse brothers in 1910 for their boys' school, named after St Enda of Aran, to encourage Irish culture and develop talents free from the pressure of exams. The curriculum included Gaelic language, literature and history, theatrical performances, nature study and games.

The **grounds** contain an avenue of trees, called Emmet's Walk in memory of Robert Emmet who courted Sarah Curran in the grounds, a walled garden, where the pupils grew vegetables, and a nature walk, called *The Wayfarer*, which follows the river from the lake where the pupils used to swim.

Excursions

The Ben of Howth★

North side of Dublin Bay by the DART (Raheny Station for North Bull Island) or by the coast road and R 105.

The Ben of Howth on the north side of Dublin Bay shelters North Bull Island, originally a mere sandbank covered at high tide, which has grown to its present size (3mi/4.5km long) and continues to increase in width seawards, since the Bull Wall was built in the late 18C to protect Dublin harbour from silting up.

North Bull Island Interpretive Centre

At the end of the central causeway. 🕐 *Open Mon-Thu, 10.15am-1pm, 1.30-4.30pm, Fri 10.15am-1.30pm, Sat-Sun 10am-1pm, 1.30pm-5pm (4.30pm Oct-Mar).* 🕐 *Closed one week at Easter and at Christmas.* 🅿 ☏ *01 833 8341*

The exhibition on the wildlife and natural habitats of the island underline the significance of the **nature reserve** where wildfowl and wading birds spend the winter, and where some 30 000 shore birds take daily refuge from the high tide covering their feeding grounds in Dublin Bay. The island has two golf courses and several lovley beaches.

▶ *Continue by road or rail to Howth.*

Howth

The picturesque village clings to the steep north face of the headland. At its heart are the ruins of **Howth Abbey** (St Mary's) and the splendid tomb of a late-15C knight and his lady. *St Mary's Abbey: key from Mrs O'Rourke, 13 Church St.*

B Perousse/MICHELIN

Howth Harbour

The harbour (1807–09), which now shelters sailing and fishing boats, was the packet boat station from 1813 until Dún Laoghaire (then Kingstown) took over in 1833.

Offshore lies **Ireland's Eye**, a bird sanctuary, where 6C Christians built a church (ruin). *Boats operate from East Pier, May to Sep,10.30am-6pm on demand.* €10. 086 8459154 - www.islandferries.net

West of the village is Howth Castle Demesne *(private)*, a medieval keep with a 15C gatehouse. Legend has it that when Grace O'Malley was refused hospitality on her return journey from visiting Elizabeth I in London, she abducted the Earl of Howth's son and returned him only when the Earl promised always to keep his door open to her family at mealtimes.

Guns for Independence

In July 1914, 900 German rifles and 25 000 rounds of ammunition for the Irish Volunteers were landed at Howth from the *Asgard*, the yacht belonging to Erskine Childers a committed Republican, influenced by the time he had spent at Glendalough, his mother's childhood home, which he loved passionately. Strongly opposed to the Anglo-Irish Treaty which partitioned the country, he was arrested in 1922 by the Free State government for possessing a revolver, and executed; his novel *The Riddle of the Sands* has been made into a film.

The **National Transport Museum**, a varied and comprehensively labelled collection of horse-drawn or motorised, commercial and military vehicles. *Open Jun to Aug, Mon-Fri 10am-5pm, Sat-Sun 2-5pm; Sep to May, Sat-Sun 2-5pm* *Closed Bank Hols.* €3. 01 832 0427 - www.national transportmuseum.org

Dún Laoghaire

South side of Dublin Bay by the DART or by N 31.

Dún Laoghaire, the main port of entry to Ireland from Great Britain, is now an attractive residential area in the greater Dublin region, with the amenities of a seaside and boating resort. It grew from a small fishing village into a busy port through the growth of trade with Britain in the 18C and is named after Laoghaire (pronounced Leary), the High King of Ireland in the 5C, who built a fort here. The **harbour** (251 acres/101ha), designed by John Rennie and dating from 1817-42, is largely built of Dalkey stone.

For 100 years the port was known as **Kingstown** in honour of **George IV**, who landed here in September 1821; an **Obelisk**, erected in memory of the king's visit to Ireland, stands on the waterfront south of the harbour.

National Maritime Museum of Ireland

Haigh Terrace, Dún Laoghaire. ♿🕐 *Open May to mid-Sep Sat-Sun, Bank Hols 1-5pm* ☎ *01 280 0969 - www.visitdublin.com*

The museum is housed in the Mariners' Church (1835–60) on the south side of Moran Park. The exhibits include a cannon from the Spanish Armada; a French longboat, painted red, white and blue, captured during an attempted landing in Bantry Bay in 1796; the lamp from the Baily lighthouse in working order; the chart used by the Commander of the German U-boat which landed Roger Casement on Banna Strand; models of a Guinness barge, Irish coastal curraghs, a Rosslare cot (a sea-going flat-bottomed boat), Galway and Donegal hookers (sailing ships), an Arklow schooner, racing skiffs, ferries, cargo ships, the first transatlantic steam ship *Sirius* (1838); the Halpin Collection, including a model of the *Great Eastern*, and the Cornelissen Collection of model ships showing the evolution from a Greek trireme to the fighting ships of the Second World War.

James Joyce Museum

0.5mi/0.8km east of Dún Laoghaire by the coast road to Sandycove. 🕐 *Open Mar to Oct 10am-1pm, 2-5pm(6pm Sun, Bank Hols); or by appointment.* ☞ *€6.70.* ☎ *01 280 9265*

The Martello Tower (1804) on the point at Sandycove now houses a **Joyce Museum:** first editions, letters, photos, his death-mask, piano, guitar, cabin trunk, walking stick, wallet and cigar case. Joyce stayed there for six days in 1904 as the guest of the writer Oliver Gogarty, who had rented the tower from the government. The upper room, the location of the breakfast scene in *Ulysses*, is furnished appropriately, while the **view** from the roof embraces Dún Laoghaire Harbour *(northwest)*, the coast to Dalkey Island *(southeast)* and the Wicklow Mountains *(southwest)*.

Dalkey Village

1mi/1.6km south of Dún Laoghaire by the coast road

Dalkey (pronounced Dawkey), now designated a Heritage Town, was once a walled town with seven fortified buildings. **Bulloch Castle** by the shore was built in the 12C by the monks of St Mary's Abbey in Dublin to protect the harbour. Two late-medieval tower houses survive in the heart of the village. **Archbold's Castle** stands opposite the graveyard of the ruined **St Genet's Church**, which may date from the 8C. **Dalkey Castle and Heritage Centre** has excellent displays on local history and a splendid all-round view from the battlements. ♿🕐 *Open Apr to Dec Mon-Fri, 9.30am (11am Sat-Sun, Bank Hols) to 5pm.* ☞ *€6.* 🅿 ☎ *01 285 8366 - www.dalkeycastle.com*

Dalkey Island and Vico Road

Bord Fáilte, Dublin

Many writers, among them LAG Strong, Lennox Robinson, James Joyce and Hugh Leonard, have associations with Dalkey; as a child (1866-74) George Bernard Shaw (1856–1950) lived in Torca Cottage on Dalkey Hill and learnt to swim at Killiney beach. Offshore lies **Dalkey Island**, which is now a bird sanctuary.

From the coast road south of Sorrento Point there is a magnificent **view**★★ of Killiney Bay extending south to Bray Head.

Killiney Hill Park
Northwest side of Dalkey Hill.
The park covering the south end of Dalkey Hill, was once the property of Col John Mapas who lived in Killiney Castle(now a hotel). It was opened to the public in 1887 to celebrate Queen Victoria's Jubilee. A **nature trail** winds through trees and over the heath to the **obelisk,** built by John Mapas in 1742 to provide work for his tenants: panoramic **view**.

DUNDALK

POPULATION 25 762

At the head of Dundalk Bay, midway between Dublin and Belfast, the old county town of Louth is one of the country's largest urban centres, with a harbour and a range of industries. In medieval times Dundalk (Dún Dealgan) was fortified by the Anglo-Normans, who used it as a base for incursions into the Gaelic strongholds of Ulster; subsequent repeated attacks and sieges have left little of its early heritage intact. Nevertheless it makes a good centre for exploring the many attractions of the nearby coast and countryside. 🅘 *Jocelyn St* ☎*042 933 5484 - www.eastcoastmidlands.ie*

▶ **Orient Yourself:** Dundalk is served by the main road (N 1) north up the coast to the border with Northern Ireland, and bypassed by the motorway (M 1)

⛿ **Also See:** BOYNE VALLEY, DROGHEDA, KELLS, MOURNE MOUNTAINS, NEWRY

Walking Tour

Dundalk was comprehensively replanned in Georgian times by its then owner, James, 1st Earl of Clanbrassil. To the south of the bridge over the Castletown River *(Church St)* stands one of the few reminders of the place's medieval past, the 14C

Address Book

SIGHTSEEING
Historical walking tour – Dundalk has a marked heritage trail for visitors to follow - details from Tourist Office.

SPORTS AND LEISURE
Táin Trail – Long-distance footpath *(19mi/30km)* encircling the Cooley Peninsula starting and finishing in Carlingford.
Sailing – Dundalk and Carlingford Sailing Club ☎ *042 937 3238*
Riding – Ravensdale Lodge offers tuition, trails and hacking ☎*042 937 1034 - www.ravensdalelodge.com*

Beaches – South at **Blackrock**, north at **Clogherhead** (Long Strand) and northeast on the Cooley Peninsula at **Giles Quay**, facing south, and at **Omeath**, on the shore of Carlingford Lough.
The salt-marshes and mud-flats *(east)* are a vast **bird sanctuary**.

EVENTS AND FESTIVALS
Annual Patrick Kavanagh Weekend – A celebration of the poet Patrick Kavanagh, held at the Patrick Kavanagh Centre in Inniskeen *(late November* – ☎ *042 937 8560)*

tower of **St Nicholas' Church** (Anglican); the church was rebuilt in 1707 and later given a spire by Francis Johnston.

The **Courthouse** *(south)* is a formidably austere neo-Classical structure with a Doric portico, designed by Park and Bowden in 1813. An elaborate porch-screen *(Roden Place – east)* leads to **St Patrick's RC Cathedral**, modelled on King's College Chapel in Cambridge; the sanctuary and the side chapels are richly decorated with mosaics.

County Museum

Jocelyn St ○ *Open May to Sep, Mon-Sat 10.30am-5.30pm, Sun, Bank Hols 2-6pm.* ○ *Oct to Apr, closed Mon.* ⊛ *€3.80* ☎*042 932 7056 - www.louthcoco.ie*

A restored 18C warehouse houses a clear and comprehensive review of local history (archaeological finds, farming and industry, the port and railway) through audio-visual presentations, touch-screens, films and graphics.

Driving Tours

Cooley Peninsula

The Cooley Peninsula is a mountainous granite promontory, providing magnificent land- and seascapes – *(south)* over Dundalk Bay and – *(north)* over Carlingford Lough to the glorious outline of the Mourne Mountains in Northern Ireland. Excellent walking country, it features in many a legend, in particular some associated with Cuchulain, the hero of the epic tale *The Cattle Raid of Cooley (Táin bo Cuainlge)*. Fine sandy beaches stud the edge of Carlingford Lough.

▷ *From Dundalk take N 1 N and R 173 E.*

Proleek Dolmen★

Ballymascanlon Hotel ▣*; 20min there and back on foot through the yard and along the tarmac path between the fields.*

The massive capstone (40 tons/47 tonnes) on its two supports dates from 3000 BC; according to legend the wish will be granted of anyone who can make three pebbles land on the top. Nearby is a wedge-shaped gallery grave.

▷ *Continue E and turn left into the mountain road north to Omeath.*

Windy Gap★

The road climbs towards Carlingford Mountain (1 932ft/587m). Beyond the site of the Long Woman's Grave *(plaque)* the road enters the aptly named **Windy Gap**, a narrow pass between rocky crags; fine view south over Dundalk Bay. Farther north there is a **viewpoint** overlooking the mouth of Newry River at Warrenpoint and the Mourne Mountains rising from the eastern shore.

Omeath

Once a Gaelic-speaking fishing village, Omeath is now a little resort with a rocky shoreline, where one can savour freshly caught seafood. In summer jaunting cars carry fares to the outdoor Stations of the Cross at the monastery of the Rosminian Fathers, and the Carlingford Lough Ferry plies across the border to Warrenpoint.

▷ *From Omeath take the coast road R 173 S.*

Carlingford★

Viking and Norman monuments add to the charm of this attractive resort at the foot of the Cooley Mountains, facing the Mourne Mountains across Carlingford Lough (marina and boat trips). Carlingford Oysters are a local delicacy with a more than local reputation.

Local history is traced on great triptychs in the **Carlingford Heritage Centre**, housed in the deconsecrated Anglican church, which is the starting point for a guided tour of the town centre. ◷ *Open Mon-Fri 9.30am-1pm, 2-4.30pm (last admission).* ◷ *Closed Bank Hols.* ⊗ *€2.* ☎ *042 9373888 - www.carlingfordheritagecentre.com*

Spanning the main street is the **Tholsel,** a gateway, once three storeys high, where Parliament is said to have promulgated laws for the Pale.

South of the town square stands a 15C fortified house *(right)* decorated with Celtic mouldings; although it is known as the **Mint**, there is no proof that the local mint, founded in 1467, ever operated there. Overlooking the harbour is **Taaffe's Castle**, a late-15C square tower fortified with machicolations, crenellations, arrow slits and murder holes; the vaulted basement may have been a boat-house since the tide used to reach the foundations. It was built by the Taaffe family, created Earls of Carlingford in 1661. The ruins of **King John's Castle** stand on a bluff north of the harbour commanding the entrance to Carlingford Lough; the western bailey was probably built by Hugh de Lacy, before King John's visit in 1210; the eastern apartments were added in 1261.

Between the Fane and the Dee

▶ *From Dundalk take R 171 SW to Louth.*

St Mochta's House★

It is hard to believe that little Louth was once the centre of the 11C/12C Kingdom of Oriel. In a field behind the ruins of a Franciscan friary (14C–15C) stands a stone oratory with a **corbelled roof**, which has been much restored; it is said to have been built in a night as a resting place for St Mochta who died in 534.

▶ *From Louth take the minor road N via Chanonrock to Inniskeen.*

Inniskeen

The village is the birthplace of Patrick Kavanagh (1904–67), poet, author and journalist, who is buried in the old churchyard; his life and work are sympathetically presented in the **Patrick Kavanagh Centre**, alongside information about the local history. The remains of a round tower mark the site of a 6C monastery founded by St Daig beside the Fane River. ◷ *Open Tue-Fri 11am-4.30pm, Sat-Sun 2-6pm.* ⊗ *€5.* ☎ *042 937 8560 - www.patrickkavanaghcountry. com*

Patrick Kavanagh Centre

▶ *From Inniskeen take the road W to Carrickmacross.*

Patrick Kavanagh

Carrickmacross

The town, a good angling centre, grew up round a castle built by the Earl of Essex, to whom the land was granted by Elizabeth I. For two centuries it has enjoyed a reputation for hand-made lace: the **Carrickmacross Lace Gallery** *(Market Square at the north end of the main street)* displays examples of the local "mixed lace", composed of cambric patterns applied to machine net and embellished with point stitches and loops. ◷ *Open Mon-Fri 9.30am-5.30pm (4.30pm Fri).* ◷ *Closed Bank Hols, 25 Dec-1 Jan.* ☎ *042 966 4176 - www.carrickmacrosslace.ie*

The Roman Catholic church (1866) was designed by JJ McCarthy, with stained glass (1925) by Harry Clarke.

▶ *From Carrickmacross take R 179 SW to Kingscourt.*

Dún A' Rí Forest Park★

The forest park, until 1959 part of the Cabra estate, is set in a valley beside the Cabra River. A **nature trail** and four sign-posted **walks** provide access to the red deer enclosure, a waterfall downstream from Cromwell's Bridge, a wishing well, Cabra Cottage – the Pratt family mansion until Cabra Castle *(east)* was built in 1814 – a ruined flax mill, an ice house and the ruins of Fleming's Castle (1607), – named after an Anglo-Norman family who lost their land for supporting James II.

▶ *From Kingscourt take R 165 SE via Drumcondra; at the crossroads turn left into N 52.*

Ardee (Baile Átha Fhirdhia)

The name means the Ford of Ferdia. On the east side of the main street stand two fortified buildings: **Hatch's Castle**, a late-medieval fortified house, and **Ardee Castle**, built in 1207 by Roger de Peppard, although much of the present building dates from the 15C. In the 17C the castle was granted to Theobald Taaffe, Earl of Carlingford.

ENNIS

POPULATION 15 333

Known as the "Banner County", Co Clare has a long history of dogged nationalism, the veritable heartland of Irish traditional music. There is evidence of both in the little county town of Ennis with its narrow winding streets and colourful shopfronts. Harriet Smithson, the wife of Hector Berlioz, was born in Ennis; her father was the manager of the first theatre built in the town in the late 18C. 🔲
Arthurs Row ☎ 065 682 8366 - www.shannon.ie

▶ **Orient Yourself:** Ennis (Inis) bestrides the junction of N 8, N 85 and N 68 midway between Limerick and the Burren
⚲ **Also See:** ADARE, THE BURREN, KILLALOE, KILRUSH, LIMERICK, TRALEE

A Bit of History

Royal Origins – Ennis is proud of its distinguished beginnings. Its origin can be traced back to the 13C, when the O'Brien family, kings of Thomond and descendants of the great Brian Ború, built their royal residence nearby. Because of its central position Ennis became the county town of Clare during the shiring of Ireland in the reign of Elizabeth I. In 1610 the town was granted permission to hold fairs and markets; two years later it received a corporation charter from James I.

Famous Statesmen – Two of the outstanding figures in Irish political history are commemorated in the town. In 1828, the election by an overwhelming majority of **Daniel O'Connell** as MP for Clare led directly to Catholic emancipation the following year. Nearly a century later, **Eamon de Valera** was elected to Parliament in 1917; he served as Member for the county until 1959. A modern statue to him stands before the old Courthouse (1850), a neo-Classical building with a pedimented Ionic portico *(Galway Road N18).*

Visit

Ennis Friary★
(Dúchas) ♿⏱*Open Apr-Oct 10am-5pm (6pm May to Sep).*♿ €1.60. 🅿 ☎ 065 682 9100

The Friary was founded by an O'Brien in the 13C, and by the 14C had become one of Ireland's foremost institutions of learning, with over 600 students as well as hundreds of friars. Now a lovely ruin, it has a superb east window but is most noteworthy for its sculpture. An **Ecce Homo** shows Christ with the Instruments of the Passion. St Francis is depicted the stigmata. The Creagh tomb (1843) in the chancel consists of five carved panels showing the Passion, taken from the MacMahon tomb (1475), and figures of Christ and the Apostles from another tomb.

ENTERTAINMENT

For a taste of Ireland in the Middle Ages, book a **medieval banquet** in **Knappogue Castle** accompanied by a pageant on the role of women in Irish history or head out to Bunratty Folk Park to attend an evening of **Traditional Folk Music and Dancing** in **Cois na h'Abhna**.

TRACING ANCESTORS

Clare Heritage Centre – *See below.*

Clare County Museum
♿⏱ *Open Jun to Sep 9.30am-5.30pm (1pm Sun); Oct to May, Mon-St 9.30am-1pm, 2-5.30pm. Last admission 1hr before closing.* ☎ 065 682 3382 - www.clarelibrary.ie

Housed in an imaginatively redesigned former convent school, the *Riches of Clare Exhibition* traces the history of this particularly distinctive county via four themes – Earth, Power, Faith and Water – using a variety of state-of-the-art techniques to interpret the carefully selected range of items on display. Among them is a *shelagh-na-gig*, a gorgeously carved panel from the wreck of an Armada galleon, and a striking banner of 1917 celebrating the election victory which confirmed Sinn Fein as a force to be reckoned with and De Valera as a major political player.

Cathedral
The Roman Catholic Cathedral, dedicated to St Peter and St Paul, was built between 1831 and 1843 in a Tau-cross shape; the tower with its spire was added 1871-74.

Railway Locomotive
One of the steam engines from the West Clare railway recalls the Percy French song *Are You Right There, Michael, Are You Right?* The railway, which rambled round the county to Kilkee *(see KILRUSH)* closed down in 1961.

Excursions

Dromore Wood
8mi/13km north by N 18 (signed) to Barefield. (Dúchas) ♿⏱ *Forest Park: Open daylight hours. Visitor Centre: 10am-6pm (last admission at 5pm).* ☎ 065 6837166 - www.heritageireland.ie

This nature reserve (1 000 acres/400ha) provides various animal habitats, including lakes, limestone pavement and turloughs, river, fen and semi-natural woodland; among the examples of human habitation are ruins of the 17C O'Brien castle.

Dysert O'Dea★
6mi/10km N by N 85, R 476; after 4mi/6.4km turn left; after 1mi/1.6km turn right. ⏱ *Open May to Sep 10am-6pm.* ♿ €4. ✗ 🅿 ☎ 065 683 7401 (065 683 7794 - off season)

This monastery was founded by St Tola in the 8C, and the site has a number of evocative remains, albeit of later date. A great battle raged here in 1318, when an O'Briens routed the Anglo-Norman Richard de Clare, thereby delaying

English control of Clare for two hundred years. There is an **Archaeology Centre** and a small **museum** devoted to the prehistoric and later culture of the neighbourhood, housed in a 15C tower house with a murder hole above the entrance.

In a neighbouring field *(access on foot or by car)* stands the late-12C **White Cross of Tola**: by this date, large figures carved in high relief had replaced the exuberant organic ornamentation; this example shows the Crucifixion and a bishop. The site also has the stump of an 11C **round tower,** and fragments of an 11C **church**.

Clare Heritage Centre★

8.5mi/14km north by N 85 and R 476 at Corrofin. Museum: Open May to Sep 10am-5pm. €4. Genealogy Centre: 9am-5pm. Closed Good Fri, 25 Dec. 065 683 7955 - www.clareroots.com

The centre, housed in the former Anglican church, illustrates life and work in Co Clare in the 19C, highlighting the exodus of some 100 000 inhabitants after the Famine. An intriguing section of oak trunk is marked with the dates of historic events. The centre also provides access to its extensive genealogical records.

Clare Abbey

1mi/1.6km southeast by R 469; turn right before the railway station, then left; park at the corner; 0.5mi/0.8km on foot over the level crossing and right.

Down by the River Fergus stand the substantial ruins of an Augustinian friary founded in 1189 by Dónall Mór O'Brien, last king of Munster.

Quin Franciscan Friary★

6.5mi/10.5km southeast by R 469; in Quin turn left. (Dúchas) Open late-May to late Sep, daily 10.30am (11.30am Sat-Sun) to 6pm. Closed Tue. 091 844084

The extensive ruins of the friary, built c 1430 by Sioda McNamara, include the **cloisters**, the tower and the south transept. The remains of an earlier ruined Norman castle (1280–86) include three round towers, erected over of an even earlier monastery.

Knappogue Castle★

8mi/13km southeast by R 469. Open Apr to Sep 9.30am-5.30pm (4.15 last admission - subject to change). €6.25. 061 368103. Medieval banquets: Apr to Oct at 6.30pm €49.95. 061 360 788 - www.shannonheritage.com

This massive tower house, the seat of the McNamara family from 1467 to 1815 has been beautifully restored and furnished, and the gardens and orchards replanted.

Craçaunowen, Shannon Heritage

The Brendan

Craggaunowen Centre★

11mi/18km southeast by R 469 (sign). ⚙🕐 *Open Apr to Oct 10am-6pm (4.45pm last admission - subject to change).* ⛽ *€7.85.* 🍴🅿☎ *061 367 178 - www.shannonheritage.com*

Aiming to re-create the ambience of ancient Ireland, the medievalist John Hunt set out to reconstruct various prehistoric structures based on archeological material. There is a ringfort, a *togher* (wooden marsh track), the artificial island of a *crannóg*. The *Brendan* is a replica wood and leather *curragh* aboard which St Brendan may have made his crossing of the Atlantic, and which itself was sailed across the ocean in 1976 by Tim Severin; the patch where the leather hull was holed by an ice floe is clearly visible. The **tower house** is used to display items from Hunt's extensive antiquarian collection not in the Hunt Museum in Limerick. There are also Wild Boar *(Porcus sylveticus)* and early breeds of Soay sheep on the estate.

The Brendan Voyage

St Brendan of Clonfert, known as Brendan the Navigator, was a seafaring monk, who in the 6C set sail from Brandon Creek, the narrow sea-inlet at the west foot of Brandon Mountain on the Dingle Peninsula. His account of the voyage, *Navigatio*, written in medieval Latin, was long thought to be fanciful until Tim Severin built the *Brendan* and proved that the earlier voyagers could have reached America several hundred years before Christopher Columbus. The 20C adventure, which substantiate the 6C narrative, are retold in *The Brendan Voyage*.

ENNISCORTHY

POPULATION 3 788

The market town of Enniscorthy (Inis Córthaidh) occupies an attractive site on the steep slopes of the River Slaney at its tidal limit. Historically, the town played a key role in the 1798 rebellion. Castle and cathedral dominate a townscape that has scarcely changed since the 19C. Local events are commemorated in the 1798 memorial *(Market Square)* showing Fr Murphy leading the uprising, while the 1916 Easter Rising is marked by Seamus Rafter, a local commander *(Abbey Square)*. The surrounding country is well suited to the growing of soft fruit, celebrated at the Strawberry Fair in early July. 🛈 *1798 Visitor Centre, Mill Park Rd* ☎ *053 92 37596*

Address Book

POTTERIES

Carley's Bridge Potteries – Ireland's oldest pottery is now leased to Paul Malone. Call ☎ 054 35149 for more information.

Hillview Pottery, 🕐 *Open Mon-Sat 9am-5.30pm, Sun 2-5.30pm* ☎ *053 923 5443*

Badger Hill Pottery, Enniscorthy – now produces Jack o'Patsy hand-thrown stoneware, ovenware, tablewear and ornamental pots. 🕐 *Open Wed-Sun, Bank Hols 10am-1pm, 2-5pm*

Kiltrea Pottery – *Off R 890 to Kiltealy.* Handthrown pottery and terracotta. 🕐 *Open Mon-Sat, 10am-1pm, 2-5.30pm; Call to confirm Bank Hol openings.* ☎ *053 923 5107; www.kiltreapottery.com*

SPORTS AND LEISURE

Greyhound racing - Show Grounds, Enniscorthy - ☎ *053 92 33172. Most Mon and Thu €6.* 🅿

▶ **Orient Yourself:** Enniscorthy sits on the junction of the N 11, running between Dublin and Wexford, and the N 30 to Enniscorthy and New Ross
⚲ **Also See:** NEW ROSS, WEXFORD, WICKLOW MOUNTAINS

A Bit of History

Monastic Foundation – The origins of Enniscorthy go back to the 6C, when St Senan arrived from Scattery Island to found a monastic settlement at Templeshannon, on the east bank of the Slaney River. From the 12C the monastery's fortunes were controlled by the Normans, who ruled from their castle until the 15C when the MacMurrough Kavanaghs clan gained control. In the late 16C, Queen Elizabeth I appointed Sir Henry Wallop and Philip Stamp to put an end to local rule.

Commercial Development – Commercial exploitation in Elizabethan times: trees were felled and the timber was exported to France and Spain through Wexford; Philip Stamp set up an ironworks, which survived until the 1940s, and brought many English families to settle in Enniscorthy, which expanded across the River Slaney. At the close of the 18C, several distillery and brewery businesses were launched; by 1796 Enniscorthy had 23 malthouses. Today, the main concerns revolve around bacon curing, fruit growing, cutlery and potteries.

Visit

National 1798 Visitor Centre
S of town centre. ⚲ ⏰ *Open Apr to Sep 9.30am(2pm Sat-Sun) - 5pm (last admission); Oct to Mar, Mon-Fri 9.30am-4pm.* ⊛ *€6.* ✗ 🅿 ☎ *053 923 7596; www.iol.ie/~98com*
The visitor centre was opened to mark the bicentenary of the 1798 uprising and to study the birth of popular democracy in Ireland. The rebellion, particularly the three weeks of disruption in Co Wexford, is presented in vivid detail; parallels are made with contemporary events in France and America and the emergence of modern political parties are reviewed. The highlight is the stirring virtual re-creation of the battle of Vinegar Hill.

Enniscorthy Castle★
With its four corner towers, the castle owes its present formidable appearance to a 1586 rebuilding of the original stronghold probably erected by Raymond le Gros, who led the first Anglo-Norman soldiers into the town in 1169. After many years in

Enniscorthy Castle and Bridge

Bord Fáilte, Dublin

Vinegar Hill

21 June 1798 is the most famous date in the history of Enniscorthy. Following the rebellion that year, centred mostly in Co Wexford and Co Wicklow, the insurgents, known as the pikemen after their weapons, made their last stand on Vinegar Hill, which they held for nearly a month. The 20 000 insurgents, accompanied by many women and children, were faced by an equivalent number of government troops led by General Lake; the armed men killed in the battle were far outnumbered by the defenceless people killed by the army. The defeat at Vinegar Hill marked the end of the 1798 rebellion.

the hands of the MacMurrough clan, the castle became Crown property; Elizabeth I granted it to her favourite poet, Edmund Spenser, who spent a mere three days here before escaping its chilly walls. The **Wexford County Museum**★ displays items relating to the 1798 rebellion, the 1916 Easter Rising and aspects of local history.
⚭ *Closed for renovation by Dúchas from Sep 2006.* ☎ *053 923 5926.*

St Aidan's Cathedral
This fine Gothic Revival Roman Catholic church is one of several built by Pugin (1843-46); much of the stone came from the ruined Franciscan friary in Abbey Square.

Excursions

Ferns★
8mi/13km NE of Enniscorthy by N 11.
The modest village was once capital of the province of Leinster and the royal seat of the MacMurroughs: as the significant **ruins** will testify. The tower and part of the north wall are vestiges of the abbey founded in the 12C by the King of Leinster, Dermot MacMurrough Kavanagh. The 13C **castle**, one of the best of its kind in Ireland, has a rectangular keep and circular towers; the first-floor **chapel** has a fine vaulted ceiling. (*Dúchas*) ♿🕐 *Grounds: open throughout the year. Castle: open May to Sep 10am-6pm.* 🍴 🅿☎ *053 936 6411.*

Bunclody
12mi/19km N of Enniscorthy by N 11 and N 80.
The town is attractively sited on the River Clody, a tributary of the Slaney, at the north end of the Blackstairs Mountains. The broad central mall is bisected by a stream that falls in steps. The Church of the Most Holy Trinity, consecrated in 1970, was designed by E N Smith. Bunclody was the last bastion in Co Wexford of the Irish language, commonly used until a century ago.

Mount Leinster★
17mi/28km N of Enniscorthy by N 11 and N 80. In Bunclody take the minor road W; after 4mi/6.4km turn left onto the summit road; it is 0.25 mi/0.4km to the peak.
From the summit (2 602ft/793m) on a clear day, there are great views over southeast Ireland: Wexford and Wicklow; the Welsh mountains across St George's Channel.

Altamont Gardens
25mi/40km north by N 11 and N 81; turn right (sign) into minor road. (Dúchas) ♿🕐 *Open 10am-5.30pm; phone to confirm.* 🅿☎ *059 914 9444 - www.altamontgarden.com*
The formal and informal gardens have many specimen trees, an arboretum and a small garden with species of flowers normally found growing in Ireland's marshy bogs. The lake was dug out by hand to provide employment during the Famine. On the horizon rise Mount Leinster (*south*) in the Blackstairs Mountains, and the Wicklow Mountains (*northeast*) across the River Slaney.

FINGAL★

The area north of Dublin, which re-adopted the ancient name of Fingal in 1994, consists of rich farmland fringed by a long coastline. The seaside resort of **Skerries** has several beaches, a colony of grey seals and a fishing harbour where famous Dublin Bay prawns are landed. **Portmarnock**, another popular resort, is known for its long sandy Velvet Strand and its championship golf course. In the Middle Ages Fingal formed part of **The Pale** *(see TRIM)* and contains several historic sites, elegant parks surrounding old stately homes and the charming dormitory town and seaside resort of Malahide. *Main St ☎ 01 840 0077- www.fingal-dublin.com*

▶ **Orient Yourself:** Fingal is the northern sub-division of County Dublin, which includes the city of Dublin and the adjacent suburbs from Balbriggan in the north to Lucan and Brittas in the west and Killiney in the south

👁 **Also See:** BOYNE VALLEY, DROGHEDA, DUBLIN, KELLS, TRIM

Visit

Malahide Castle★★
8.5mi/13km north of Dublin by R 107 or by M 1 and R 106. 🕐 *Open Apr to Sep, Mon-Sat 10am-5pm, sun, Bank Hols 11am-6pm; Oct to Mar, Mon-Sat 10am-12.45pm, 2-5pm, Sun, Bank Hols 2-5pm.* ⊛ *€7.* ✗ 🅿 *Banquets on request ☎ 01 846 2184 / 846 2516 - www.malahidecastle.com*

The castle was the home of the Talbot family for nearly 800 years, the great demesne was the prize awarded to Richard Talbot who came to Ireland with Henry II in 1177. Built around the original 14C tower, the castle has been picturesquely extended: the Great Hall dates from the 15C, the reception rooms, some furniture and wonderful **Rococo plasterwork** date from the 18C. It is still highly atmospheric, hung with portraits from the National Portrait Collection. The *Battle of the Boyne* by Jan Wyck in the **Great Hall** recalls the story that 14 Talbot cousins, all Jacobites, breakfasted at Malahide on the morning of the battle, and were killed in the fighting.

The **Talbot Botanic Gardens** (19 acres/7.5ha with 4 acres/1.5ha of walled garden) were largely created by Milo, the last Lord Talbot, between 1948 and 1973, who

Malahide Castle

indulged his passion for plants from the southern hemisphere. The result is a superb collection of trees and shrubs arranged around luscious lawns.

The **Fry Model Railway Museum** displays model engines and rolling stock made by Cyril Fry of Dublin; there is also information on the development of railways in Ireland and a huge O-gauge model railway incorporating replicas of various railway stations. *Open Apr to Sep, Mon-Thu, Sat 10am-1pm, 2-5pm, Sun, Bank Hols 2-6pm. €5.50; combined ticket with 5 Dublin attractions. 01 846 3779 - www.visitdublin.ie*

Tara's Palace re-creates the grandeur and elegance of three great 18C Irish mansions in miniature in this magnificent dolls' house. *Open Mon-Fri 10.45am-4.45pm, Sun Bank Hols 11.30am-5.30pm. Donation.*

Newbridge House★

10mi/16km north of Dublin by M 1 and a minor road east to Donabate.
Tour (45min) Apr to Sep, Tue-Sat 10am-1pm, 2-5pm, Sun, Bank Hols noon-6pm; Oct to Mar, Sat-Sun, Bank Hols noon-5pm. €7 (House); €3.80 (Farm). 01 843 6534/6530 - www.fingalcoco.ie

George Semple's early-18C Georgian country house, on the edge of Donabate, is set in extensive grounds, one of the finest remaining examples in Ireland of a landscape park. It has been the home of the Cobbe family since c 1740 when it was built for Charles Cobbe, who came to Ireland in 1717 as Chaplain to the Lord Lieutenant, and rose to become Archbishop of Dublin (portrait in the hall). Much of the interior has remained unchanged for centuries: some original furniture was made by Dublin craftsmen; the 18C- early 19C **stucco** and **plasterwork** is superb. The **Red Drawing Room**, added c 1760, preserves the wallpaper, curtains and carpet fitted in 1820. The family **museum** (1790), decorated in Chinese style is intriguing, crammed with souvenirs, trophies, and exotica brought back from foreign travels.

Traditional Farm – A museum of traditional rural life is presented in the outbuildings – dairy (19C), dwelling, carpenter's shop, forge, stables and coach house. Domestic animals live in the paddocks; the large walled garden was converted to an orchard during the Second World War.

Ardgillan Castle

22mi/35km north of Dublin by M 1 and a minor road east to Balbriggan. Open Apr to Sep, Tue-Sun (daily, Jul to Aug), Bank Hols 11am-6pm; Oct to Mar 11am-4.30pm Tour €6. 01 849 2212

On the coast north of Skerries stands the Georgian country house acquired in 1737 by the Taylor family, descendants of Thomas Taylor, a professional surveyor, who had come to Ireland from Sussex in 1650 to work on the Down Survey.

The elegant interiors contain mementoes and furniture of the Taylor family. Kitchens, larder and scullery occupy the extensive basement, and on the upper floor there is a excellent exhibition on the **Down Survey** .

Beyond the rose gardens are the walled gardens, laid out with lawns, flowers and vegetables in geometric plots. The west front is screened by 21 Irish yew trees.

Down Survey

The confiscation and redistribution of almost half the land in Ireland during the Cromwellian Settlement involved the preparation of accurate maps: these were provided Sir William Petty and his team of surveyors over 13 months (1655-6). This exercise, known as the Down Survey, has no connection with Co Down, but was so called because the results were set down on maps rather than in the more usual tabulated form. Several sets of maps were individually drawn and coloured; while at sea between Dublin and London in 1707 the Petty set was captured by the French.

Skerries Mills

20mi/32km north of Dublin by M 1 and R 127. ○ *Open 10.30am-5.30pm (4.30pm Oct to Mar.* ○ *Closed Good Fri, 20 Dec-1 Jan.* ⚲ *€6.* ☎ *01 849 5208 - www.skerriesmills.org*
The first 16C mill has been developed into a complex with a watermill, two windmills (one with five sails and one with four), mill races, a mill pond and wetlands. This rare survival of 17C-19C industrial technology has been restored to working order.

Swords (Sord)

8mi/14km north of Dublin by M 1.
The bustling county town has a history going back to the 6C when St Columba founded a monastery on a low hilltop now marked by the Anglican church, a 9C **round tower** and a 12C **Norman tower**. At the northern end of the town stand the substantial remains of **Swords Castle**, the summer palace of the Archbishops of Dublin. ♿⚷ *Closed for renovation until further notice.* ☎ *01 890 5629; www. fingalcoco.ie.*

Lusk Heritage Centre

13mi/21km north of Dublin by M 1 and R 127 to Lusk.
(Dúchas) ○ *Open mid-Jun to mid-Sep, Fri 10am-5pm (4.15pm last admission).* ⚲ *€1.20.* ☎ *01 843 7683/647 2461 - www.heritageireland.ie*
The tower of an Anglican church, which incorporates an earlier round tower, houses a display about the 5C monastery founded here and its star feature, the magnificent Renaissance effigy tomb of Sir Christopher Barnewall and his wife Marion Sharl, almost unique in Ireland at this early date (1589).

GALWAY★★

The largest town in the west of Ireland bestrides the Corrib River as it enters Galway Bay. Galway (Gaillimh) has grown from a medieval core of narrow streets into an exceptionally lively cathedral and university city sustained by modern industries and a thriving port, and is well placed as a centre for excursions westwards into the wild mountainous country of Connemara; east and south lies the fertile Galway plain. This location, together with the city's own dynamic character, draws cosmopolitan crowds of visitors to its busy streets, which take on an almost Mediterranean air when the summer sun contrives to shine. 🛈 *Forster St* ☎ *092 537 700* 🛈 *Salthill (summer)* ☎ *091 520 500* 🛈 *Oughterard* ☎ *091 552 808* 🛈 *Tuam (summer)* ☎ *093 25486.*

▶ **Orient Yourself:** Galway is located on the north shore of Galway Bay at the junction of N 17 from the north, N 6 from the east, N 18 from the south. It is a good centre from which to explore Connemara (R 336 along the north shore of Galway Bay, N 59 and N 84 along the lake shore) and to visit the Aran Islands
⊘ **Don't Miss:** a trip to Lough Corrib and a view of its setting from Curran
◔ **Also See:** ARAN ISLANDS, ATHENRY, THE BURREN, CONG, CONNEMARA.

A Bit of History

City of the Tribes – The Anglo-Normans were attracted by the sheltered anchorage strategically located midway along Ireland's western coast. The city was founded on the east bank of the river in the 12C by the de Burgo (later Burke) family, who encouraged immigration from England and Wales. Defensive walls were built and Galway prospered on trade with France, Spain and the West Indies. As an English enclave in the midst of an often hostile region, the city excluded the native Irish who had their own settlement outside the walls. Prosperity did not, however, survive the religious disputes of the Reformation and their political consequences. After two lengthy sieges – by the Cromwellians in 1652 and by William of Orange's forces in 1691 – Galway went into decline.

The Claddagh – Long before the arrival of the Normans, an Irish-speaking community with its own traditions and elected leader, known as the King, thrived in a fishing village on the west bank of the Corrib River. Its name - the Claddagh - derived from the Gaelic *cladach* meaning a rocky or pebbly shore. The men fished by night, and the women sold the catch on the Spanish Parade. The picturesque scattered whitewashed thatched cottages were replaced in the 1930s by a modern housing scheme. The Claddagh finger ring, formed by a heart held by two clasped hands, is popular throughout Ireland.

Gaelic Galway – The city adjoins the most extensive Gaelic-speaking region in Ireland: the Aran Islands, Connemara and the Joyce Country. The 19C revival of interest in the language drew many visitors to the region; two of the oldest Gaelic summer schools were founded at the turn of the century at Spiddal *(west)* and Tormakeady on the west shore of Lough Mask. Since the establishment of the Republic, the Gaelic character of the region has been reinforced: University College, Galway, founded in 1849 as Queen's College, was made a bilingual institution in 1929. Today it is an important centre for Gaelic culture with a state-sponsored Irish Theatre *(Taibhdhearc na Gaillimhe)* launched by Micheál Mac Liammóir and his partner Hilton Edwards. In 1969 the offices of the Gaelic Development Authority were moved to Furbogh (Na Forbacha – *5mi/8km west of Galway by R 336)* and in 1972 Gaelic Radio began operating from Costelloe (Casla – *further west by R 336)*.

Literary Galway – Galway city and its environs have produced or fostered several literary personalities: Patrick O'Connor (1882–1928) wrote short stories in Gaelic, Nora Barnacle (1884–1951) lived in Bowling Green and married James Joyce, who with Frank Harris (1856–1931) were natives of the city. Violet Martin, the second half of the Somerville and Ross partnership, lived at Ross House on the west shore of Lough Corrib. In 1896 Edward Martyn, who lived at Tullira Castle in south Galway, introduced William Butler Yeats to Lady Gregory; they co-founded the Irish Literary Theatre, which later became the Abbey Theatre in Dublin.

Walking Tour

Eyre Square
The focal point of the modern city centres on a small park named after John F Kennedy, President of the USA, who visited Galway in 1963. There are several monuments: the **Browne doorway** removed from the family house in 1906; cannons from the Crimean War presented to the Connaught Rangers; a statue of **Liam Mellows** who took part in the 1916 Easter Rising and was executed by the Free State army during the Civil War.

▶ *From Eyre Square turn left into William Street.*

Lynch's Castle

This splendid 16C mansion belonged to the most powerful of the 14 tribes. The grey stone façade has some fine carved gargoyles, hood mouldings over the windows, and medallions with the family crest (the lynx) and one with the arms of Henry VII.

▶ *Continue into Shop Street.*

St Nicholas' Church★

The medieval church dedicated to St Nicholas of Myra, the patron saint of sailors, was used by Christopher Columbus, or so it is said. The **exterior** has gargoyles

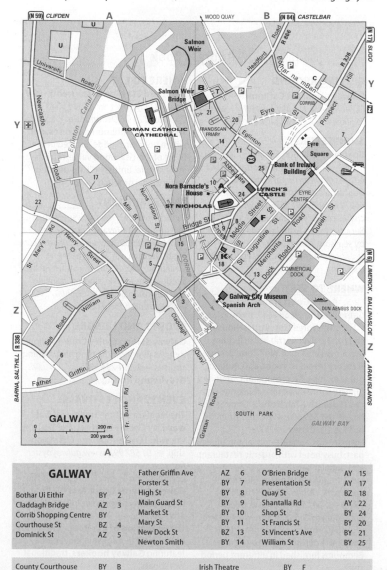

GALWAY			Father Griffin Ave	AZ	6	O'Brien Bridge	AY	15
			Forster St	BY	7	Presentation St	AY	17
Bothar Ui Eithir	BY	2	High St	BY	8	Quay St	BZ	18
Claddagh Bridge	AZ	3	Main Guard St	BY	9	Shantalla Rd	AY	22
Corrib Shopping Centre	BY		Market St	BY	10	Shop St	BY	24
Courthouse St	BZ	4	Mary St	BY	11	St Francis St	BY	20
Dominick St	AZ	5	New Dock St	BZ	13	St Vincent's Ave	BY	21
			Newton Smith	BY	14	William St	BY	25

County Courthouse	BY	B		Irish Theatre	BY	F
Druid Theatre	BZ	K		Lynch Memorial	BY	A

and carved mouldings; the **interior** includes a medieval water stoup, a font and numerous tombstones. The **Lynch Memorial** honours the 15C Judge James Lynch who condemned his son Walter to death for murder and acted as hangman when no one else would carry out the sentence.

▶ *Walk round to the north side of the Church and into Mary Street.*

Nora Barnacle's House

🕐 *Open Jun to mid-Sep, Mon-Sat 10am-1pm, 2-5pm (in general) or by appointment.*
✎ *€2.50.* ☎ *091 64743 (no phone in the house); www.norabarnacle.com*
Nora Barnacle, the wife of James Joyce, lived in this Cottage before she moved to wok in Dublin, where she met and married Joyce; letters, souvenirs, photos.

Address Book

GETTING AROUND

Galway Airport at Carnmore
(3.7mi/6km SE of Galway by N17) – ☎ *091 75 5569; www.galwayairport.com.*

SIGHTSEEING

Boat trips to Lough Corrib (🕐 *see below*) – *Corrib Cruises operates various options between Cong, Inchagoill Island, Oughterard and Ashford Castle -* ☎ *092 46029 / 46292; 091 552808 - www.corrib-cruises.com or www.lakedistrict.ie. €14.*
Services to the **Aran Islands** by air and by sea from Wood Quay.
🕐 *For coin ranges, see the Legend on the cover flap.*

WHERE TO STAY

☺☺ **Adare Guest House**- *9 Father Griffin Place.* ☎ *91 58 2638; www.iol.ie.* 🅿✎. This three storey guesthouse west of the river Corrib lies in a quiet residential area near Wolf Tone Bridge. A cheery breakfast room, and modern guest rooms with orthopaedic beds and pine furniture make for a relaxing stay.
☺☺**Spanish Arch Hotel** – *Quay St - 20 rm -* ☎ *091 569 600; www.spanisharch-hotel.ie.* 🕐 *Closed 24-25 Dec -* ✗🅿 Former 16C Carmelite convent in times past: busy hotel with organic restaurant and popular bar.
☺☺☺ **Killeen House** – *Killeen Bushypark, Dublin - 4mi NW by N 59 - 5 rm -* ☎ *091 524 179; www.killeen-housegalway.com.* 🕐 *Closed 23-27 Dec -* 🅿 1840's house with country feel and pretty garden down to the lake. Bedrooms furnished in different period style.

WHERE TO EAT

☺☺ **Ard Bia (The Restaurant)** - *First floor, 2 Quay Street.* ☎ *87 236 8648.*
🕐 *Closed 25-26 Dec and Sun.* ✗✗ - Personally run neighbourhood restaurant with a bohemian edge, located in the heart of the city. Good value, refreshingly simple, unfussy dishes utilising quality local produce.

ENTERTAINMENT

Druid Theatre, *Flood St* – Specialises in experimental/avant-garde works – ☎ *091 568660 - www.druidtheatre.com*
Irish Theatre (An Taibhdhearc na Gaillimhe), *Middle Street* – Stages Irish productions (music, singing, dancing and folk drama) - ☎ *091 563600 / 562024 - www.antaibhdhearc.com*

SPORTS AND LEISURE

Galway Sailing Club – Cruiser sailing, dingly sailing, windsurfing and training courses – ☎ *091 794 527*
Greyhound Racing

EVENTS AND FESTIVALS

The highlights of the traditional **Galway City Oyster Festival** *(late Sep)* are the World Oyster-opening Championship. ☎ *91 587 992; www.galwayoyster-fest.com.*
Commanding as much attention is the **Galway International Arts Festival**, held annually *(2 weeks in Jul);* ☎ *91 509 700.*
The **Gathering of the Boats** (*Crinniú na mBád*), held in August in Kinvarra Bay, featuring **Galway hookers**, traditional workboats.

R Holzbachova, Ph Benet/MICHELIN

Spanish Arch, Galway

▷ *Walk south along Mary Street; continue into Cross Street; turn right into Quay Street and left at the end.*

Spanish Arch

The arch, recalling the city's links with Spain, may have been part of a bastion, incorporating four blind arches, one of which was opened in the 18C to give access to a new dock beside Eyre's Long Walk. Part of the medieval **town wall** (20yd/20m long) is visible on the south side, as are the tidal quays of 1270.

Galway City Museum

♾ ⏱ *Opening times to be confirmed.* ✆ *091 532460*

In June 2006, this striking new modern complex was opened for imaginative exhibitions relating to the history of Galway City (historical material; interactive displays), including the city corporation Irish-made **sword and mace**★, and temporary shows from elsewhere. One special attraction is the statue by Albert Power RHA of **Patrick O'Connor** (Padraic O Conaire 1882–1928) from Eyre Square.

▷ *Return to the south end of Quay Street; turn left into a narrow lane; turn left into Bridge Street; turn right into Nuns Island Street.*

Roman Catholic Cathedral★

The huge neo-Romanesque cathedral, dedicated to Our Lady Assumed into Heaven and St Nicholas, was designed by John J Robinson in 1957 and defies all the precepts of architectural modernism. It is built of black Galway "marble", the local limestone. Above the altar in St Nicholas' Chapel *(east transept)* are the early-17C carved stone plaques rescued during the Cromwellian troubles from St Nicholas' Church.

Salmon Weir Bridge

This bridge (1818) was built to link the old prison (1802–1939) on the cathedral site, with the **County Courthouse** (1812–15) where Franciscan Abbey stood. Upstream is the **salmon weir**; beyond are the pontoons of the viaduct (1890–1935) of the old Galway-Clifden railway.

Excursions

Annaghdown Church and Priory

12mi/20km N of Galway by N 84; in Cloonboo turn left to Annaghdown.

St Brendan of Clonfert founded this convent for his sister: the extant 15C Cathedral incorporates earlier decorated stonework – a fine doorway and window (c 1200). The middle church is the oldest (11C or 12C). The ruined priory *(west of the graveyard)* is a good example of a fortified monastery (c 1195).

Tuam
20mi/32km NE of Galway by N 17.
The tiny city of Tuam, with its two cathedrals, is the ecclesiastical capital of Connaught and the market centre for north Co Galway. In the 12C, when the O'Connor kings of Connaught were High Kings of Ireland, it was virtually the capital of the whole country. Its present layout, with all the streets converging on the central diamond, dates from 1613, when it was given borough status by King James I.
St Mary's Cathedral★ stands in a walled enclosure, on the site of a monastery founded late in the 5C by Jarlath. The original cathedral dates from 1130, most of the present building however, including the hexagonal spire (200ft/61m), is the result of a neo-Gothic rebuild by Sir Thomas Deane (1860) around parts of the 12C Irish-Romanesque red sandstone chancel. The shaft of a high cross in the north aisle is inscribed with prayers for an O'Connor king.
The 14C building east of the cathedral, badly damaged by the Cromwellians, has been restored to its original castellated style to serve as a Synod Hall.
West of the town centre, Irish yews grow among the tombstones of **St Jarlath's Churchyard** and ruins of the 13C parish church dedicated to Tuam's patron saint.
The 17C corn mill on a tributary of the Clare River *(west of North Bridge)* houses the **Mill Museum** with three sets of mill-wheels driven by an undershot spur wheel. A video provides an insight into the history of Tuam and its locality. ◷ *Open Mon-Fri 10am-5.30pm.* ✆ *Donation.* ☏ *093 24141; www.tuam-guide.com*
The cruciform neo-Gothic **RC Cathedral of the Assumption** was one of the first major Roman Catholic places of worship to be built in the 19C, initiated in 1827, a year before the Emancipation Act set off a wave of church construction. Funds were subscribed by the local inhabitants regardless of denomination: its profusion of spikes and spires prompted one 19C tourist (C Otway) to describe the sight of the cathedral as putting him "in mind of a centipede or a scorpion thrown on its back and clawing at the sky". The Stations of the Cross are 17C, the modern stained glass is from the Harry Clarke Studios.

Knockmoy Abbey★
20mi/32km NE of Galway by N 17 and N 63. In Knockmoy village turn left. After crossing the river turn right and park by the cemetery 15min there and back on foot.
In fields on the north bank of the River Abbert are the substantial ruins of an abbey founded in 1189 for the Cistercians of Boyle by Cathal O'Connor, king of Connaught. The church, with nave, a transept with two chapels and **chancel**, has some fine stone carving and a 13C tomb niche. A grill protects a rare **fresco** (1400) of the medieval legend of the Three Live Kings (dressed for hawking), and the Three Dead Kings (the inscription reads "We have been as you are, you shall be as we were").

Driving Tour

Lough Corrib★★
17mi/27.5km NW of Galway by N 59.

Lough Corrib, the second-largest lake in Ireland (36mi/58km long), is dotted with islands and **drumlins**, including Inchagoill island, the site of a 5C monastery.

▷ *From Galway take N 59 ; after 16mi/26km turn right (sign).*

Aughnanure Castle★
From car park 5min there and back on foot. (Dúchas) ♿ ☞ *Tour Jun to Oct, 9.30am-6pm (last admission 5.15pm).* ✆ *€2.90.* 🅿 ☏ *091 552214. www.heritageireland.ie*

The formidable ruins of a tower house and bawn probably built by Walter de Burgo, defended but also undermined by the Drimneen River. The circular **watch tower** is all that remains of the original bawn wall. Most of the **Banqueting Hall** has collapsed into the river leaving the east wall with its Decorated windows. The **keep** rises through six storeys from a battered base to Irish-style crenellations with a machicolation on each side. From the roof there is a fine view of Lough Corrib.

▶ *Continue NW on N 59 .*

Oughterard (Uachtar Ard)★

This attractive town on the west shore is famed for its excellent fishing.

The road north runs parallel to the shore to **Curraun** *(8mi/13km there and back)* where the **view★★** of the lake and its backdrop of mountains is truly spectacular.

Beyond Oughterard *(on N59)* you come to **Glengowla Mine** – a silver and lead mine reaching down 70ft/20m, complete with its original timbers, which closed in 1865. *Tour Mar to Nov 10am-6pm (5.30pm in low season), every 20min in high season.* €8. 091 552021/087 2132236

GLENDALOUGH★★★

POPULATION 1 695

This once-remote valley among the Wicklow Mountains where St Kevin sought solitude and later founded a great monastery has long been a place of pilgrimage and continues to attract innumerable visitors. The "Glen of the Two Lakes" (Gleann Dá Locha) is one of the most evocative of all Irish monastic sites, both for the beauty of its setting and for the array of buildings left over from the early days of Christianity in Ireland. *Glendalough* ☎ *0404 45688*

▶ **Orient Yourself:** Glendalough stands S of Dublin in the Wicklow Mountains and can be reached by the coast route (M 11 and N 11 S to Ashford and R 763 to Annamoe, R 755 S to Laragh and R 756 W or by the inland route (N 7, N 81 and R 756); slower but more scenic routes take the road through the Sally Gap (R 115) or via Enniskerry, Roundwood and Annamore (R 117, R 760, R 755and R 756)

⊛ **Don't Miss:** a tour of the monastic site

⚲ **Also See:** ATHY, KILDARE, WICKLOW MOUNTAINS

A Bit of History

The monastery founded by St Kevin flourished long after his death (c 617), drawing pilgrims deterred from journeying to Rome by war and conflict: seven pilgrimages to Glendalough were said to be the equivalent of one to Rome. Despite repeated raids and destruction by the Vikings and Irish, the monastery enjoyed a golden age in the 10C and 11C, a period of Celtic revival. Glendalough also prospered under St Laurence O'Toole (1128–80), who became abbot in 1153 and Archbishop of Dublin in 1163. Decline began in the 13C and an English attack in 1398 caused much destruction. Dissolution followed during the reign of Henry VIII but the pilgrimages continued until disorderly behaviour caused their suppression in the 1860s.

The two lakes at Glendalough, once one stretch of water, are set in a beautiful valley shaped by an Ice Age glacier descending from the Wicklow Mountains. The splendidly-wooded southern shore of the Upper Lake, associated with St Kevin, is particularly striking, with cliffs (100ft/30m) dropping precipitously into the dark waters of the lake. For many years the area was mined, so the woods were cut to

St Kevin

Probably born sometime in the mid-6C, the young Kevin soon attracted attention for his ability to work miracles. Entrusted to the care of three clerics, he escaped seeking solace from Nature, living in the hollow of a tree above the Upper Lake at Glendalough. Although he returned to his studies, he remained bewitched by Glendalough. The monastery in the lower part of the valley he started flourished under his leadership, until he retreated once more to the wilderness, living in complete solitude probably somewhere above the Upper Lake (Temple-na-Skellig). One story tells how a blackbird laid her egg in his hand as he stood in ascetic contemplation, his arms outstretched in the shape of the Cross.

"in the sun and rain for weeks, until the young are hatched and fledged and flown."
(Seamus Heaney)

smelt the lead, zinc, iron, copper and silver ores. The Miners' Road, which runs along the northern shore of the lake to a deserted mining village at the top of the valley, provides the best view of St Kevin's Bed and the ruins of Temple-na-Skellig.

Walking Tour

The spacious modern **visitor centre** presents various displays including a fine model, based on Glendalough, of a typical medieval monastery complex. Old photographs show the site before and after restoration; a video narrates the history of monastic Ireland. *(Dúchas)* 🖐🕙 *Open 9.30am-6pm (5pm mid-Oct to mid-Mar). Last admission 45min before closing.* 🕙 *Closed 24-27 Dec.* ✎ *€2.90.* 🅿 ✆ *0404 45688*

Monastic Site★★★
The ruins of the later monastic settlement, east of the Lower Lake, form the most important part of the Glendalough site, approached through the gateway, an unique example to a monastic enclosure. Set in the wall just beyond the first of two arches is a great slab of mica schist with an incised cross, probably marking the point at which sanctuary would be granted to those seeking it.
The **Round Tower**★★ (100ft/30m high) is a major landmark, probably constructed in the early 10C. It would have served as a six-storeyed storehouse, bell-tower, lookout and refuge: note how its entrance is some way above the ground (12ft/4m), and how the thick walls (3ft/1m at the base) taper slightly towards the top.

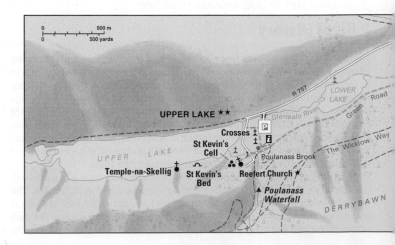

The roofless **Cathedral** ★★, once the focal point of the community, continues to be a substantial presence on the site, its nave one of the widest of early Irish churches. Built in stages, perhaps from the late 10C, it consists of a nave and chancel with a small sacristy. Note the nave pilasters, the west doorway and south windows. A gravestone against the north chancel wall bears is carved with crosses and inscriptions in Irish; an adjacent slab has outstanding scroll designs.

Bus Tours

St Kevin's Bus Service - *Originates in Dublin (Dawson St. on the north side of St Stephen's Green) and Bray via Roundwood. Operates from Glendalough visitor's centre, daily 7.15am (9.45am Sat-Sun and Bank Hols) and 4.30pm (5.40pm Sat in Jul-Aug, Sun and Bank Hols). Glendalough to Dublin, single €11; there and back €18;* ☎ *01 281 8119; www.glendaloughbus.com.*

St Kevin's Cross, the early, undecorated Celtic high cross (12ft/3.5m high) is the best preserved.

St Kevin's Church★★ is an early 11C Irish oratory with a high-pitched roof of overlapping stones. Its alternative popular name – St Kevin's Kitchen – was perhaps prompted by its unusual circular chimney-like tower or the scullery-like sacristy.

St Saviour's Priory★

The Priory *(east of the Lower Lake by the Green Road)* is said to have been founded by St Laurence O'Toole, Abbot of Glendalough, but may be earlier in origin. The buildings (reconstructed in 1875), now enclosed in a forestry area, include a church nave and chancel with fine carving typical of the Irish Romanesque style.

Upper Lake★★

1.5mi/2.5km on foot west of the Visitor Centre by the Green Road – or 0.5mi/0.8km on foot from the Upper Lake car park. ☺ *The way up to St Kevin's Cell is steep in places.*

The **crosses**, which originally marked the boundary of the monastic site on the east shore, were later used by pilgrims as Stations of the Cross.

Reefert Church★, set above the lake. among oaks and hazels, is deemed to be the traditional burial place of kings, and maybe of St Kevin. The roofless late 10C church has a plain but beautiful chancel arch, nave windows and an imposing granite doorway with sloping jambs.

Nothing remains of **St Kevin's Cell** save for a ring of foundation stones, colonised by three oak trees. His lonely abode was probably built with corbelled stones on the pattern of the beehive dwellings on Skellig Michael.

Glendalough

St Kevin's Bed and Temple-na-Skellig (⌐ *No access.*)
The tiny cave known as **St Kevin's Bed** (30ft/9m above the lake) was probably a Bronze Age tomb. For as long as it was believed to be where St Kevin would come to pray and fast, it attracted pilgrims to Glendalough; after landing at Temple-na-Skellig by boat, they would walk along the lake shore and up the steps hewn in the cliff, to be helped, one by one, into the "bone-rock bed of the austere saint" (Richard Hills).
The first church at **Temple-na-Skellig** (about 20ft/6m above the lake) may date from the time of St Kevin, though the present ruins are probably 12C. The huts of the earliest monastic community are thought to have been in the raised enclosure west of the church.

Poulanass Waterfall
From close to the cottage housing the National Park Information Centre, a path follows the Lugduff Brook steeply upstream to a lovely waterfall in the woods.

KELLS ★

POPULATION 2 183

This little market town, a designated Heritage Town, in the valley of the River Blackwater owes its fame to the wonderful Illuminated manuscript now in the library of Trinity College. Of the monastery from which the Book of Kells was taken there remain some fascinating relics, while the town itself boasts a courthouse and a church designed by the Georgian architect Francis Johnston. *Kells Heritage Centre ☎046 9247840 - www.meathtourism.ie*

▶ **Orient Yourself:** Kells is situated in the Irish Midlands, NW of Dublin on N 3
☺ **Don't Miss:** the Round Tower and carved High Crosses
⏾ **Also See:** BOYNE VALLEY, CAVAN, DROGHEDA, DUNDALK, MULLINGAR, TRIM

A Bit of History

The Book of Kells – The monastery at Kells (Ceanannas Mór) was founded by St Columba in the 6C. In the 9C his relics were brought here by monks fleeing the Viking raids on Iona. Even here they were not secure and Kells itself was attacked by the Vikings, by the native Irish in the 12C, and by the Scotsman Edward Bruce in the 14C. The great illuminated manuscript may have been produced at Kells or brought here from Iona. In 1007 it was stolen from the sacristy but found two months later minus its gold ornament. During Cromwell's campaigns, it was taken to Dublin for safe keeping, and presented to Trinity College in 1661.

SHOPPING

Loughcrew Studio, Loughcrew Gardens *(see below)* – Furnishings, carpets, fabrics; showrooms and workshop

EVENTS AND FESTIVALS

Opera in Loughcrew Gardens – Two performances under canvas in late July, and **Jazz** in late June. ☎ *49 85 41356; www.loughcrew.com.*
O'Carolan Harp Festival – This festival of traditional music is held annually at Nobber *(9mi/15km NE by N 52 and R 162) – Fri-Sun in late-Sep/early-Oct.* ☎ *46 905 2115; www. nobberfest.com.*

Visit

Round Tower and High Crosses★★

Market Street. ♿🕐 *Open daily outside service times.* 👄 *Tours by arrangement with TIC.* 🅿☎*046 9247840*

Parts of the monastery survive in the grounds of **St Columba's Anglican Church**. The **round tower**, built before 1076, has lost its conical cap, but still rises to an impressive height (100ft/30m). A number of well-weathered heads adorn the doorway. Next to the tower stands the **South Cross**, considered to be from the 9C. The lively biblical scenes, among the interlacing, foliage, birds and animals include Daniel in the Lions' Den, the Three Children in the Fiery Furnace, Cain and Abel and Adam and Eve; the Sacrifice of Isaac, St Paul and St Antony in the desert, David with his harp, the miracle of the loaves and fishes, the Crucifixion and Christ in Judgement. South of the church stands an unfinished cross with raised panels ready to be carved and the Crucifixion.

Detailed information about the monastery, the crosses, the Kells crozier *(in the British Museum)* and the Book of Kells is displayed in the gallery of the church.

St Columba's House★

🕐 *Keys available at the house in the lane beside the east churchyard gate.*
Higher up the lane stands an ancient stone oratory with a steep corbelled stone roof, probably from the 11C/12C. The original entrance is visible in the west wall; the intervening floor is missing; between the ceiling vault and the steep roof there is a tiny chamber *(access by ladder).*

Kells Heritage Centre

Old Courthouse. 🕐 *Open May to Sep Mon-Sat 10am-5.30pm, Sun, Bank Hols noon-6pm; Oct to Apr Mon-Sat 10am-5pm.* 👛*€4.* ☎ *046 9247840*

The Board of Trinity College, Dublin

Book of Kells

Artefacts on loan from the National Museum, touch screens, models and a video shed light on the monastery and history of the locality.

Excursions

St Kilian's Heritage Centre, Mullagh

8mi/13km north of Kells by R 164. ○ *Open Easter to Oct Tue-Fri 10am-6pm, Sat-Sun, Bank Hol Mon 2-6pm.* ⊜ €3. ⊡ ℗ ⊛ 046 9242433

The centre celebrates the life of St Kilian (640–689), the "Apostle of the Franks" and patron saint of Würzburg. North of Mullagh stands a ruined church known as Kilian's church *(Teampall Ceallaigh)*. People still pray at his holy well, although formal observances ended early in the 19C.

St Kilian

Kilian was born in the 7C in Mullagh, Co Cavan and was educated at the monastic school in Rosscarbery in Co Cork. As a pilgrim for Christ, he went to Würzburg in Franconia to make Christian converts. Legend has it that he disapproved of the local ruler, Gozbert, one of his converts, marrying his brother's wife, so she had St Kilian beheaded. In 782 his remains were moved to Marienberg.

Castlekeeran High Crosses

▷ *5mi/8km west of Kells by R 163; after 3mi/5km turn right at the crossroads. Through the farmyard and across the field and stile.*

The graveyard has three undecorated early crosses which pre-date the scriptural crosses at Kells; beside the yew tree stands an Ogham Stone. They mark the site of an early monastery which grew up around the hermitage of Kieran, a monk from Kells.

Ballinlough Castle Gardens

3mi/5km W of Kells by R 163 to Ballinlough. ♿○ *Open May to Sep Sat-Sun noon-6pm by arrangement.* ⊜ €6. ℗ ⊛ 046 9433268

Set in extensive parkland, Ballinlough Castle *(not open)* has been continuously inhabited by the O'Reilly/Nugent family since the Middle Ages. Its present appearance reflects the late 18C idea of what a castle should look like. its complex of walled gardens, rescued from dereliction, are expertly planted for maximum contrast.

Loughcrew Historic Gardens

15mi/24km from Kells by R 163 and R 154 and a minor road west to Millbrook. ○ *Open mid-Mar to Sep 12.30-5pm; Oct to Mar Sun, Bank Hols 1-4pm or by arrangement.* ⊜ €6. ⊡ ℗ ⊛ 049 8541060 *(Visitor Centre); www.loughcrew.com*

The gardens are an extraordinary palimpsest of ruins, earthworks, and ancient avenues, once owned by the Plunkett family – including Saint Oliver Plunkett. Around the church (roofless) extends the skeleton of an early 17C formal garden with an avenue of venerable yew trees leading to a medieval motte. Close by are the foundations of the original Loughcrew House, replaced in the early 19C by an imposing neo-Classical mansion

Loughcrew Historic Gardens

Mercury Gate, Loughcrew Gardens

devised by Charles Cockerell, which has also disappeared, although its portico survives as a folly beyond the gardens.

Loughcrew Passage Graves★

15mi/24km west of Kells by R 163. Beyond Ballinlough bear right onto R 154. After 3mi/4.6km turn left; after 0.5mi/0.8km turn left again onto narrow rough road. (Dúchas) ⏰ *Carnbaen East: open 10am-4pm. Key kept at Loughcrew Gardens Visitor Centre. Contact Loughcrew House to make alternative arrangements when the centre is closed (☎ 049 85 41356). The deposit of a passport, driving license or €50 is required. Access to Carnbane West with permission from Dúchas National Monuments ☎ 01 647 6916/6915*

Far less famous than the Neolithic tombs of the Boyne valley, the passage graves prominently sited on the Loughcrew Mountains, are almost as impressive. The cemetery covers the adjoining peaks, Cairnbane East and Cairnbane West, and Slieve na Calliagh (908ft/277m). There are at least 30 graves, some of which have been excavated, most dating from 2500–2000 BC. In 1943, however, excavations in Cairn H on Cairnbane West uncovered objects bearing Iron Age La Tène style decoration. **Cairn T** (120ft/37m in diameter), the largest grave on Cairnbane East, is decorated with concentric circles, zigzag lines and flower motifs.

KENMARE★

POPULATION 1 420

The small market town, a designated Heritage Town, is charmingly set in a horse-shoe of mountains at the point where the Roughty River widens into the long sea-inlet known as the Kenmare River. Kenmare (Neidín) is a popular tourist centre, with a wide range of hotels and restaurants and elegant shops (jewellery, linen, delicatessen, books) catering for visitors from many countries, many of whom use it as a starting point for explorations of the Beara and Iveragh peninsulas. 🛈*Kenmare* ☎ *064 41233 (seasonal).* 🛈 *Glengarriff* ☎ *027 63084 (seasonal); www.corkkerry.ie*

▶ **Orient Yourself:** Kenmare is located on N 71, a scenic road between Killarney and Glengarriff, and is a good place to stay while exploring Co Kerry
◈ **Don't Miss:** Glen Inchaquin Park and the Ring of Beara
◐ **Also See:** BANTRY, CORK, KILLARNEY

Visit

Town Centre

Kenmare is an 18C planned town shaped like a cross, sponsored by the first Marquess of Lansdowne. Its two streets, lined with neat stone houses, meet at a triangular space intended to serve as a market-place and now a park. The town's real origin, however, goes back to the energetic Sir William Petty (1623-87), organiser of the Down Survey who encouraged immigration from England

Kenmare Lace

Kenmare lace is needlepoint lace introduced from Italy in the 17C. It is particulalr difficult because it is worked in needle and thread (linen rather than cotton), according to designs drawn on parchment or glazed calico and outlined with skeleton threads: these are later removed, as is the backing. Raised point is created by using buttonhole stitches over cords or horsehair.

and Wales, founded ironworks, and astutely acquired property to the extent that he owned of a quarter of Kerry.

Address Book

GETTING AROUND

Garnish Island Ferry – Ferries *operate from Glengariff Mar-Oct (times vary seasonally). Blue Pool Ferry: €10.* ☎ *027 63333; www.bluepoolferry.com; Harbour Queen Ferry:* ☎ *27 63116; www. harbourqueenferry.com. €12.50 (ferry); €3.70 (gardens).*

Dursey Island Cable Car - *Operates from Ballaghboy year-round, Mon-Sat 9-11am, 2.30-5pm, 7-8pm; Sun 9-10.30am, 1-2.30pm, 4-5pm (Jun-Aug only), 7pm-8pm. Arrive 30min before departure.*

Bere Island Ferry – *Operates from Castletownbere and Bere Island mid-Jun to Sep. Call for price and times.* ☎ *27 75009; www.bereislandferries.com.*

Driving tours – Kenmare Coach and Cab Co offer day trips round the Rink of Kerry and Beara. *Jun-Aug 10am-5pm €25* ☎ *087 248 0800 - www.kenmare-coachandcab.com*

For coin ranges, see the Legend on the cover flap.

WHERE TO STAY

⊖⊜ **The Rosegarden** – *0.75mi W by N 71 on N 70 (Sneem rd) -* ☎ *064 42288; www.iol.ie/~rosegard. Mar to Oct - 8 rm - Meals* ⊖⊜. It would be hard to find more immaculately kept accommodation. The Dutch owners provide old school hospitality; the bedrooms are colourful, bright and cheerful. A simple dinner menu is also provided.

⊖⊜ **Sea Shore Farm** – *Tubrid - 1mi. W by 71 on N 70 (Sneem rd) - 6 rm -* ☎ *064 41270; www.neidin.net/seashore. Mar to mid-Nov.* ♿ 🅿 With its 32 acres/13ha and views of the river and Caha mountains, one would be hard pressed to find a better spot than this farmhouse B&B. Comfortable bedrooms come in different colour schemes and bathrooms have power-showers.

⊖⊜⊜ **Sallyport House** – *0.25mi S on N 71 -* ☎ *064 42066; www.sallyport-house.com. Apr-Oct.* 🚭 🅿 ⊱ ⊟ *5 rm.* Here guests are assured of a warm welcome, an impressive breakfast and a particularly comfortable bedroom. Nicely decorated with antique pieces; there's a veritable mountain of local tourist information.

WHERE TO EAT

⊖⊜ **An Leath Phingin** – *35 Main St -* ☎ *064 41559 - Closed Tue, Wed and mid-Nov to mid-Jan.* ⊱ Hard to resist the winning combination of this high street restaurant; authentic Italian home cooking, sweet-natured service and rustic surroundings juxtaposed with modern art. Always, and understandably, busy.

⊖⊜ **Packies** – *Henry St -* ☎ *064 41508 -* 🕐 *Closed Sun and Feb-Mar; restricted opening in winter.* One of the town's most established dinner spots, with its flagstone flooring adding to the character. The tried and tested menu features traditional Irish country cooking complemented by relaxed and welcoming service.

⊖⊜ **Mulcahys** – *16 Henry St -* ☎ *064 42383; www.kenmarerestaurants.com.* 🕐 *Closed Nov-May: Tue-Wed.* The decoration of this modern restaurant testifies to a well travelled owner. Asia is the theme with an assortment of banners and sculptures. This fusion, particularly Japanese, is further reflected in the eclectic menu.

⊖⊜ **The Lime Tree** – *Shelburne St -* ☎ *064 41225; www.limetreerestaurant.com. Apr-Oct* 🅿 Converted from a former schoolhouse but with such warm hospitality and confident modern cooking, it means that truancy will never be a problem here. Local artists' work is for sale in the upstairs gallery.

SPORTS AND LEISURE

The Beara Way – Rarely rising above 1115ft/340m, these old roads and tracks form a loop (122mi/196km) round the Beara Peninsula that may be walked with moderate ease.

EVENTS AND FESTIVALS

Queen of the Sea Festival – Held in Castletownbere *(early August)*

H Champollion/MICHELIN

Kenmare

Kenmare Heritage Centre

&⏰ *Open Easter to Oct, 9.15am-5pm (9am-7pm mid-Jun to Aug)* ☎ *064 41233*
The centre traces the history of Kenmare, originally called Nedeen (*Neidín* in Irish),
the local impact of the Famine and the story of the Nun of Kenmare, one of the
community which established the lace-making industry in the 19C.

Lace and Design Centre

⏰ *Open mid-Apr to Oct, 10am-1.15pm, 2.15-5.30pm; Nov to Apr, Mon-Sat 10.30am-
1.30pm. Lace-making demonstrations.* ☎ *064 41491/42636; www.kenmarelace.ie*
Displays of lace and lace-making demonstrations are provided by a local cooperative
to designs created by the nuns.

Stone Circle

The prehistoric circle comprises one central stone and a ring of 15 upright stones.

Excursion

Glen Inchaquin Park★★

8mi/14km SW by R 571 and left turn into a single-track lane (5mi/8km).⏰ *Open
year round to dusk.* ⬟ *€4.* 🚻🅿 ☎ *064 84235*
The lane leads into a remote landscape of mountains and lakes, clear streams, glorious
sessile oak woodland and wildflowers (laid footpaths). At the head of the glen there
is a farmhouse by a spectacular braided waterfall. The views down to the Kenmare
River and McGillycuddy Reeks are spectacular.

Driving Tour

Ring of Beara★★ *Round trip of 85mi/137km – 1 day*

The Beara peninsula projecting some 30mi/48km into the Atlantic, has some wild
and beautiful mountain, moorland and coastal scenery.

▸ *From Kenmare take N 71 S and turn left beyond the Kenmare River.*

Caha Pass

Work on the Kenmare-Glengarriff road began around 1839, cutting across the Caha Mountains, providing great **views** of Glengarriff and Bantry Bay.

Glengarriff (An Gleann Garbh)★

Little more than a high street, Glengarriff has been a resort of international renown since the mid 19C, famed for its mild climate and exotic flora. The **Eccles Hotel**, built in 1833 as a coaching stage, accommodated Queen Victoria on her visit to south western Cork, and George Bernard Shaw wrote part of his play *St Joan* in the dining room on his way to Garinish Island: it retains its original façade.

There are pleasant walks along the wooded shore of the Blue Pool (*poll gorm*) in the northwest corner of Glengarriff Harbour. The best view of Glengarriff is from the top of **Shrone Hill** (919ft/280m – *southwest*).

Ilnacullin★★

Access by Garinish Island Ferry. (Dúchas) & ⏰ *Open Jun to Aug, 9.30am (10am Jun) - 5.30pm; May and Sep, 10am (noon Sun)-5.30pm; Mar and Oct, Mon-Sat 10am-4pm, Sun 1-5pm* 🚶 *Hiking trail (1hr 45min).* ◉ *€3.70.* ▭☎ *027 63040; www.heritageireland.ie*
Garinish Island (37 acres/15ha), also known as **Ilnacullin**, lies in Glengarriff Harbour. It was turned by the English landscape designer Harold Peto into a meticulously planned garden for the Belfast-born MP Annan Bryce. Italianate formality and Classical pavilions contrast well with the austere mountain backdrop and with the lush planting of exotic species. A path leads to the **Martello Tower** (135ft/41m above sea-level), the highest point on the island.

Bamboo Garden

Glengarriff. & ⏰ *Open 9am-7pm.* ◉ *€5.* ▭ 🅿 ☎ *027 63975/635070*
The bamboo is ideally suited to the climate, so 30 different species and 12 types of palm thrive here. There are fine views of Glengarriff Harbour and Bantry Bay from the Tower and from the waterfront, which is embellished with 13 stone pillars.

▷ *From Glengarriff take R 572 west; in Adrigole turn right (sign) to the Healy Pass.*

Healy Pass★★

⊕ *The road is particularly steep near Glanmore Lake.*
Opened in 1931, the road climbs through a series of tortuous hairpin bends *(7mi/11km)* to the summit; on a clear day there are **views**★★ of both shores of the peninsula.
The **Healy Pass** was named after Tim Healy, who was born in Bantry in 1855. Healy was a Nationalist MP at Westminster (1880- 1916) before being appointed the first Governor-General of the Irish Free State (1922): at a presentation in the Anchor Bar, Bantry, on his retirement as Lord Chief Justice of Ireland, he was invited to choose a leaving present – he requested the bridleway over the mountains between Adrigole to Lauragh be improved.

Derreen Gardens★

⏰ *Open Apr to Oct, Fri-Sun 10am-6pm or by appointment.* ◉ *€6.* ▭ 🅿 ☎ *064 83588*
These lush mature gardens were planted by the fifth Lord Lansdowne beside Kilmakilloge Harbour, an inlet on the south shore of the Kenmare River. The woodland is richly underplanted with azaleas and rhododendrons, and rare New Zealand tree ferns.

▷ *Take R 571 W for 8mi/12.9km to the Ballycrovane junction.*

Ballycrovane Ogham Pillar Stone

Donation to enter the field. In a field stands the tallest pillar stone in Ireland (15ft/5m high); the Ogham inscription - MAQI-DECCEDDAS AVI TURANIAS - of the son of Deich descendant of Torainn - was probably added later.

▶ *Continue W to Eyeries.*

Eyeries

This typical Irish mountain settlement is renown for its soft tangy cow's cheese.

▶ *Take R 575 W along the coast to Allihies.*

Allihies

The peninsula became known for its rich **copper mines** ★, worked by a predomonantly Cornish workforce, and bestowing prosperity on 19C Allihies. Old engine houses and spoil heaps are visible among the many invisible but dangerous abandoned mine-shafts. **Ballydonegan Strand** *(1mi/1.6km south)* is a magnificent beach composed of crushed stone from the mines.

▶ *Continue S on R 575; after 2.5mi/4.2km turn right onto R 572.*

Garnish Bay

At low tide, one can walk from the tiny hamlet of six houses and a post office to **Garnish Island**, a good vantage-point for **views** ★ *(north)* of the Iveragh Peninsula and *(northwest)* of the Skellig Islands.

▶ *Continue W to Dursey Island.*

Dursey Island

Access by cable-car (see Address Book).

The island's isolation was broken when Ireland's only cable railway was strung across the strait in 1970, capable of carrying six passengers or a cow and its minder. Cliff-girt Dursey, 4mi/6km long, has one village, Kilmichael, and one road, large nesting colonies of birds and superlative.

▶ *Return E; after 1.5mi/2.4km turn right to Crow Head.*

Crow Head

The bleak headland provides a fine view of Mizen Head *(south)* and the Skellig Islands. On 23 July 1943 a German bomber plane crashed in fog killing all four crew.

▶ *Continue E on R 572; after 6mi/9.7km turn left.*

Slieve Miskish Mountains

After 2mi/3km the road becomes a track suitable only for climbers.

The high climb into the mountains is rewarded with splendid **views** ★; the summit commands the entire length of Bantry Bay.

▶ *Return to R 572 and continue E; after 1mi/1.6km turn right to Dunboy Castle (0.5mi/0.8km).*

Dunboy Castle

Surrounded by Dunboy woods are the remains of this star-shaped castle, the last O'Sullivan stronghold to resist the English in 1602. Nearby is the vast shell of Puxley's Castle, part French château, part Italian villa, burned down by the IRA in 1921. It was built by the Puxley family with the huge revenues generated by the Beara copper mines. The history of the family and the mines inspired Daphne du Maurier to write her novel *Hungry Hill*.

▶ *Continue east on R 572 to Castletownbere.*

Castletownbere

This town was developed in the early 19C when rich copper deposits were discovered at Allihies; and was particularly badly affected by the potato famine. By the late 19C, it had become an important fishing port: today fish processing is a substantial industry.

Bere Island

Access by Bere Island Ferry.

The island was an important Royal Navy base, one of the three Treaty Ports relinquished to the Free State in 1938. It is now home to a sailing school.

▶ *Take R 572 east to return to Glengarriff and N 71 north to return to Kenmare.*

KILDARE★

POPULATION 4 278

The name of Kildare (Cill Dara) is intimately associated with the nearby Curragh, the extensive plain covered in short springy turf and clumps of yellow gorse famous for horse racing and breeding. Neat little Kildare itself is a county and cathedral town and designated Heritage Town, tracing its origins to the 5C religious community founded by St Brigid and St Conleth, which was one of the few convents for women in the Celtic period. *Market House* ☎ *045 521240 - www.eastcoastmidlands.ie*

▶ **Orient Yourself:** Kildare is situated on the main road (N 7) leading SW from Dublin to Limerick.
Don't Miss: a visit to the Irish National Stud
Also See: ABBEYLEIX, ATHY, MAYNOOTH, MULLINGAR, ROSCREA, TULLAMORE, WICKLOW MOUNTAINS

Visit

Cathedral★

🕐 *Open May to Sep Mon-Sat 10am-1pm, 2-5pm, Sun 2-5pm. (Cathedral)* ⊛ *Donation. (Round Tower)* ⊛ *€4*

Kildare Cathedral is a late-19C building incorporating 13C sections. Inside there is a medieval stone font, stained-glass windows, and a number of tombs with effigies, including the superb figure of Bishop Wellesy dating from around 1539. Beside it stands a **round tower** (108ft/30m high - the tallest scaleable tower in Ireland) which has been

SIGHTSEEING

Canal Barge trips in summer from the **Old Canal Hotel**, Robertstown (*Operates on demand; call for information,* ☎ *045 890 450*); cruisers for hire from **Lowtown Marina**- *(see below)*

SPORTS AND LEISURE

The **Curragh Racecourse** hosts all five Classic **horse races** including The Budweiser Irish Derby and 19 other racedays. ☎ *045 441205; www. curragh.ie.*

substantially restored in recent years. Opposite, a small road leads to **St Brigid's shrine** and **well**.

Kildare Heritage Centre

&⏰ *Open May to Sep Mon-sat 9am-1pm, 2-5pm; Oct to Apr: call in advance.* ☜ €1.
☎ *045 521240/045 530672 (answerphone)*
The history and heritage of Kildare are clearly described (video and story boards).

Excursions

Irish National Stud and Japanese Gardens★★

1mi/1.5km SE of Kildare (sign) at Tully. &⏰ *Open mid-Feb to Oct 9.30am-5pm.* 🗣Tours *(35min) of Stud.* ☜ €9. 🅿☎*045 52 1617/52 2963 - www.irish-national-stud.ie*
Lord Wavertree, a wealthy Scotsman from a brewing family, began breeding horses at Tully in 1900; in 1915 he gave his stud to the British Crown and it continued as the British National Stud until it was handed over to the Irish Government in 1943.
The stallion boxes, with their lantern roofs, were built in the 1960s. In the Sun Chariot yard, finished in 1975, pregnant mares are stabled during the stud season and yearlings are housed from July to October. Mares and foals can be seen in the paddocks from the Tully Walk *(2mi/3km long)*. In the **Irish Horse Museum** traces the story of horseracing in Ireland and contains the skeleton of Arkle, an outstandingly successful racehorse whose career ended in a fall at Kempton Park in England on 27 December 1966. The other exhibits, which include a 13C horse skull found at Christchurch Place in Dublin trace the history of the horse, horse racing and steeple-chasing.
The grounds contain a large lake, created by Eida *(see below)*, and the ruins of the **Black Abbey**, founded as a preceptory of the Knights Hospitaller of St John after the Anglo-Norman invasion of Ireland in 1169. According to tradition it is connected by a tunnel (1mi/1.5km) to Kildare Cathedral. When the abbey was suppressed in the mid 16C, it passed into the possession of the Sarsfield family and it was here c 1650 that **Patrick Sarsfield**, leader of the Irish at the Siege of Limerick, was born.
Among the most ambitious of their kind outside Japan, the **Japanese Gardens** were created for Lord Wavertree between 1906 and 1910 by the Japanese gardener Eida and his son Minoru. The main garden depicts the story of the life of man, beginning with the **Gate of Oblivion** and the **Cave of Birth,** continuing across the bridges of engagement and marriage to the **Hill of Ambition** and the **Well of Wisdom.** Formerly the concluding feature, the **Gateway to Eternity** now leads into the **Garden**

One of the horses at the Irish National Stud

of **Eternity** (1974) depicting the conflict of human nature. The **Zen meditation garden** (1976) encourages contemplation.

Bog of Allen Nature Centre
12mi/19km N by R 401 and R 414 at Lullymore. &⊙*Open Mon-Fri, 10am-5pm. (under development until 2013).* ⊜€5. ⌹ 🅿 ☏ *045 860133; www.ipcc.ie*
Bog Allen is the largest complex of raised bog in Ireland; as 90% of the fragile eco-systems have been lost through drainage and mining over the past four centuries, the Irish Peatland Conservation Council is campaigning for conservation initiatives: all this is encapsulted in their visitor centre.

Hill of Allen
6mi/10km N by R 415.
The summit of the 19C tower (676ft/206m) provides **views** of the vast Bog of Allen stretching westward to the Shannon.

Robertstown (Inis Robertaig)
10mi/16km N by R 415.
The village is strategically located where the Grand Canal divides bound for Waterford and the Shannon. The waterfront is dominated by the stately red-brick Grand **Canal Hotel**, built in 1803 to serve the passengers on the flyboats .

Punchestown Standing Stone
15mi/24km E by N 7 to Naas and R 411.
North of the famous racecourse *(Woolpack Road)* stands a granite long stone (20ft/6m high) which is thought to date from the early Bronze Age.

Kilcullen
7mi/11km east by R 413.
The **Hide Out Bar** has a bizarre relic: the black and withered right arm of prize-fighter Dan Donnelly (1786–1820), who won a spectacular bout on the The Curragh on 13 December 1815.

KILKENNY★★

POPULATION 8 507

Kilkenny (Cill Chainnigh) is Ireland's outstanding medieval city, set on the banks of the River Nore and dominated by the castle and cathedral. Narrow alleys, known locally as slips, recall the medieval street pattern. The city's historical legacy, splendidly expressed in any number of well-restored ancient buildings, is matched by a strong cultural and artistic tradition. 🛈 *Shee Alms House, Rose Inn St* ☏ *056 7751500 - www.southeastireland.com*

▸ **Orient Yourself:** Kilkenny is a good base for exploring the south-east corner of Ireland, well served by good roads in all directions
⊙ **Don't Miss:** Kilkenny Castle and the Design Centre, St Canice's Cathedral and Jerpoint Abbey
⚭ **Also See:** ABBEYLEIX, CAHER, CASHEL, CLONMEL, ENNISCORTHY, NEW ROSS, ROSCREA

A Bit of History

Capital of the Kingdom of Ossory – The city is named after St Canice, the 6C founder of a church here, in what was, from the 2C to the 12C, the capital of the Gaelic Kingdom of Ossory, mainly ruled by the MacGiolla Phadruig family who constantly struggled for the kingship of Leinster.

Statutes of Kilkenny – Following the Anglo-Norman invasion (12C), Kilkenny quickly assumed strategic and political importance as a major venue for Anglo-

Address Book

SIGHTSEEING

Guided walking tour of the medieval town. *Operates 4 times daily May-Oct (twice Sun). €6. Call TIC for details.*

For coin ranges, see the Legend on the cover flap.

WHERE TO STAY

🍽 **Shillogher House** - *Callan Rd, Southwest.* ☎ *056 776 3249; www. shillogherhouse.com.* 6rm. More modern than its gables at first suggest, this is a redbrick guesthouse facing a landscaped lawn and includes modern en suite bedrooms kept spotless by affable hosts.

🍽 **Blanchville House** - *Dunbell, Maddoxtown, Southeast. 6rm Mar-Oct.* ☎ *056 772 7197; www.blanchville. ie.* Follow the tree-lined drive to this restored Georgian country house in quiet farmland. A firelit drawing room and charming bedrooms furnished with antiques and family heirlooms make this experience complete.

🍽 **The Hibernian** - *1 Ormonde St - Closed 24-26 Dec. 43rm, 3 suites.* ☎ *056 777 1888; www.kilkennyhibernian-hotel.com.* Part Georgian hotel, set in a former bank within sight of Kilkenny Castle, this classically proportioned haven houses understated, modern bedrooms, a spacious bar in dark wood with long tan sofas and a comfortable restaurant with traditional appeal (🍽).

WHERE TO EAT

🍽 **Zuni** – *26 Patrick St -* ☎ *056 772 3999; www.zuni.ie. Closed 23-27 Dec.* Its origins as Kilkenny's first cinema are reflected in the original façade and contrast with the stylish and modern interior, following its conversion

in early 2000 into the city's trendiest restaurant. Cooking from the open-plan kitchen is equally à la mode.

SHOPPING

The **Kilkenny Design Centre** *(Castle Stables;* ☎ *056 772 2118; www. kilkennydesign.com)*, housed in the monumental 18C stable buildings of the Castle, is a major retail outlet for high-quality souvenirs and provides accommodation for a variety of craftspeople; it was set up in the 1960s as a focal point for improvement in the design of ceramics, textiles, furniture and jewellery.

A number of craft studios are grouped in **Bennettsbridge** *(7mi/11km south)*, including **Nicholas Mosse**, housed in an old flour mill, which offers a variety of craft work, including pottery made on the premises.

For hand-blown glass, where the craftsmen can be seen at work, visit **Jerpoint Glass Studio** *(south of Stoneyford on the Thomastown road; www.jerpointglass. com)*.

SPORTS AND LEISURE

The magnificent estate of **Mount Juliet** (1 400 acres/567ha) offers many sporting facilities including a golf course designed by Jack Nicklaus; the house (c 1780) is a luxury hotel, open only to residents. ☎ *056 777 3000; www. mountjuliet.ie.*

Greyhound racing.

EVENTS AND FESTIVALS

Kilkenny Arts Festival – One of the most important arts events in Ireland, featuring classical music, visual art, theatre, literature, children's arts and outdoor events *(mid-Aug; www.kilkennyarts.ie)*.

Irish parliaments. Under Anglo-Norman rule, the native clans and the invaders lived alongside each other in relative harmony despite frequent incomprehension. Over the centuries, the Anglo-Norman families, led by the dominant Butler clan, integrated into the native Gaelic culture, adopting their dress and language, and intermarrying. Not unnaturally, this process displeased the authorities in Dublin and England:so in 1366, the **Statutes of Kilkenny** were passed by Parliament to prohibit the Anglo-Normans from intermingling with the Irish; but it was too late, and the new laws were ignored .

Confederation of Kilkenny – The height of Kilkenny's authority (1642-48) came when the Confederation of Kilkenny functioned as an independent Irish parliament, representing both the old Irish and the Anglo-Irish Roman Catholics. When this body split, the Anglo-Irish sided with the English Viceroy, and the Old Irish looked to Pope Innocent X for support. The Old Irish, led by Owen Roe O'Neill, were eventually defeated; following Cromwell's siege of Kilkenny in 1650, the Irish army was permitted to march out of the city.

Nationalist Tradition – Kilkenny has always had a strongly nationalistic tradition and played a key role in the movement for independence early in the 20C. **William**

KILKENNY		The Parade	Z 10	Abbey St	Y 2
		Kenny's Well St	Y 7	Upper New St	Z 15
Parliament St	Y 13	John St Upper	Y 6	Vicar St	Y 17
Water Barrack St	Y 18	John's Bridge	Y 5	Ormonde Rd	Z 9
Rose Inn St	Z 14	Castlecomer New Rd	Y 3		

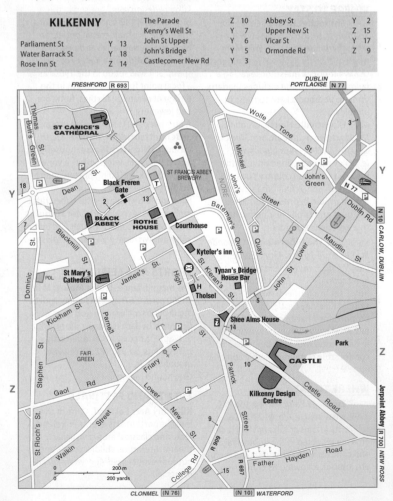

T Cosgrave, the first president of the Executive Council, was a steadfast leader in the young Free State, acting as Sinn Féin member for Kilkenny at Westminster and then in the Irish Parliament *(Dáil)*.

Walking Tour

Among the vestiges of the old town, there is the 16C **Shee Alms House**, once used as a hospice and the **Tholsel**, built in 1761 (restored), used for exhibitions. *(Almhouse TIC)* ◷ *Open Mon-Fri 9.30am-6pm, Sat 10am-6pm.* ☏ *056 7751500*

The **courthouse**, above Grace's Castle (1210), served as a prison in 1568, and the Hole in the Wall - a 'supper house' renown from 1750-1850 when the Kilkenny breweries thrived.

R Holzbachova, Ph Benet/MICHELIN

▸ *Walk up Rose Inn Street and turn right into High Street.*

Irish pipers

Rothe House★

◷ *Open Apr to Oct 10.30am (3pm Sun)-5pm; Nov to Mar Mon-Sat 10.30am-4.30pm.* ◷ *Closed 24 Dec-3 Jan.* ⊜ *€3. Combined ticket with St Canice Cathedral* ⊜ *€5. Genealogy service.* ☏ *056 7722893; www.rothehouse.com*

With its splendid Tudor facade, this is the only remaining town house of the Renaissance period in Ireland. Built in 1594 by a local merchant, John Rothe, it was used in the 17C as a meeting place by religious and political leaders during the Kilkenny Confederation, then in the 19C by the nationalist Gaelic League. It now houses the local museum for local historical curiosities: letters written by Daniel O'Connell when he was MP for Kilkenny City in 1836–37, an 18C penal cross, the Carlingford Screw, and a small costume collection.

▸ *Continue N along Parliament Street over the bridge; cross Dean Street and take the steps up to the Cathedral.*

St Canice's Cathedral★★

♿◷ *Open Jun to Aug, 9am (2pm Sun) to 6pm; May and Sep, Mon-Sat 10am-1pm, 2-5pm, Sun 2-6pm; Oct to Mar, Mon-Sat 10am-1pm, 2-4pm (incl Sun).* ☞*Tours by arrangement.* ⊜ *€3 (Cathedral); €2 (Round Tower).* ☏ *056 7764971; www.cashel.anglican.org*

The 13C Early Gothic cathedral may stand on the raised site of St Canice's 6C church. It is best approached by St Canice's Steps *(SE)* laid out in the early 17C when damage inflicted by Cromwell needed repair – having stabled horses in the long nave.

There are many fine tombs: the best-known is that in black Kilkenny marble of Piers Butler, Earl of Ormond and Ossory (died 1539) and his wife Margaret Fitzgerald; her effigy has a finely jewelled and embroidered girdle. The oldest tomb (13C) bears part of the original dog-tooth ornament. The oldest slab, found under the High Street in 1894, is the **Kyteler slab**, inscribed in Norman French in memory of Jose Kyteler, probably the father of Dame Alice Kyteler, who was tried for witchcraft in 1323.

In the graveyard stands a **round tower** (100ft/30m high), built between 700 and 1000, which gives an overall view of Kilkenny and its surrounding countryside.

▸ *From Parliament St turn left into Abbey St, through the medieval **Black Freren Gate**.*

Duchas, Dublin

Kilkenny Castle

Black Abbey★

The **medieval church**, founded c 1225 for the Dominicans and repressed in 1543, served as the city's courthouse from the 17C. It was re-consecrated in the 19C. The interior is lit by fine early-14C traceried windows and a lovely alabaster carving of the Most Holy Trinity beside the altar from c 1400 despite the inscription. In the graveyard are 10 stone coffins dating from the 13C and 14C.

Visit

Kilkenny Castle and Park★★

(Dúchas) &. ⟲ Tours (45min) Jun-Aug 9.30am-7pm; Sep 10am-6.30pm; Apr to May 10.30am-5pm; Oct to Mar 10.30am-12.45pm, 2-5pm. ○ Closed 25-26 Dec. ⊕ €5. P ☏ 056 77 21450

The castle, built by William the Earl Marshal (1192-1207) overlooks the River Nore. Uniquely among Irish castles, it was a nobleman's residence: the seat of the Butler family, Earls and Dukes of Ormond, who dominated the southeast of Ireland. Much of the medieval fabric remains, including three of the four corner towers; it was acquired by the state in 1967 to save it from dereliction. Today, after much restoration, the great stronghold provides a window on the lifestyle of the Anglo-Irish aristocracy. The most imposing interior is the 19C Long Gallery hung with Gobelin tapestries and family portraits (on loan), with a hammerbeam roof decorated with pre-Raphaelite neo-Celtic motifs. The **Butler Gallery** displays 19C-20C Irish art and visiting contemporary art exhibitions.

The extensive **park** (50 acres/20ha) has formal gardens and woodlands.

Excursions

Thomastown

11mi/18km S of Kilkenny by R 700.

Little twisting streets converge on the main street close to the old bridge over the Nore, half-obliterated by its modern concrete deck. The **Ladywell Water Garden** is an intricate mixture of trees, shrubs and aquatic plants. &. ○ Open May to Sep 10am-5pm; Oct-Apr, Mon-Fri 10am-4.30pm. ○ Closed Public Hols. ♿ Facilities being redeveloped 2006/7. ⊕ Donation to Camphill. ⊃ P ☏ 056 7724690

Kilfane Glen and Waterfall★

14mi/23km S of Kilkenny by R 700 and N 9 N from Thomastown. ○ *Open Jul to Aug 11am-6pm; Apr to Jun, Sep Sun 2-6pm.* ● *€6.* ▣◐ *056 7724558*

This wonderful, unusual Romantic creation from the late 18C nestles in a wooded ravine, with more formal contemporary gardens and modern sculpture added later – including an installation by the American artist, James Turrell, inviting visitors to contemplate the sky. Precipitous walks, steps and bridges, a waterfall and, a delightful thatched cottage orné set in a grassy glen, testify to the Power family's interest and love of the landscape since the 1790s.

The ruined church in the village contains a famous effigy, the **Cantwell Knight**★, a fine carving of a Norman nobleman, placed upright in the roofless nave.

Jerpoint Abbey★★

12mi/19km S of Kilkenny by R 700 and N 9 S from Thomastown. (Dúchas) ♿○ *Open Jun to mid-Sep, 10am-6pm; mid-Sep to May 10am-5pm (4.30pm Nov to Mar).* ● *Tours by appointment.* ○ *Closed Christmas week.* ● *€2.90.* ▣◐*056 7724623*

The sturdy tower with its stepped Irish battlements rising over the Little Arrigle River is a landmark for one of the country's foremost Cistercian monasteries.

Cistercian monks from Baltinglass in Co Wicklow (♿ *see ATHY*) arrived here in 1180, and constructed their own complex on an earlier Benedictine house. In the mid-13C there were 36 monks and 50 lay-brothers; after the Dissolution (1540), the monastery, its farm buildings, fisheries, and considerable estates, passed to the Earl of Ormond.

Jerpoint is of sufficient importance to warrant a **visitor centre**, with a small exhibition devoted to medieval stone carving in the region.

The abbey **church** has the classic Cistercian cruciform plan. The transepts, which belong to the original late-12C construction, have two chapels each. In the **chancel** are splendid effigies of two bishops, one believed to be Felix O'Dulany, first abbot of Jerpoint and bishop of Ossory (1178–1202). On the north wall are remains of a 15C–16C wall painting showing the heraldic shields of Jerpoint's main benefactors.

The columns of the 14C or 15C **cloisters** (restored) bear remarkable carvings of animals, saints, knights and ladies in contemporary attire and armour.

Bord Fáilte, Dublin

Jerpoint Abbey Cloisters

Kells Priory★

8mi/13km S of Kilkenny by R 697.

The tranquil remains of this priory by the Kings River are some of the most extraordinary ruins in Ireland. Founded in 1193 by Geoffrey de Marisco with four Augustinian canons from Bodmin in Cornwall, the priory suffered repeated attacks, which perhaps explains why it was fortified so impressively; the extensive (5 acres/2ha) site is enclosed by a curtain wall with towers and a gateway.

Edmund Rice Centre

Callan; 10mi/16km SW of Kilkenny by N 76. ♿○ *Open, in principle, Apr-Sep 10am-6pm.* ○ *Closed Good Fri, 25 Dec.* ◐ *056 77 25993.*

Run by the Christian Brothers, the complex with its visitor centre and chapel is built around the the cottage **birthplace** of Edmund Ignatius Rice (1762–1844), founder of this teaching order which has played an important role in Irish education. The kitchen has a stone-flagged floor, open hearth and spinning wheel, as in Rice's day: the other rooms are similarly preserved with furniture of the period.

In the town of Callan there are substantial remains of a 15C Augustinian priory.

Bród Tullaroan

10mi/16km W of Kilkenny by a minor road. ◷ *Open Jun to Aug Mon-Fri 10am-4pm; otherwise call to confirm. Irish story telling/ music nights.* ⊚ *€4.* ☎ *056 77 69202/ 087 66 88881; www.brodtullaroan.com*

This heritage centre, the "Pride of Tullaroan", set in deep countryside, is devoted to the memory of **Lory Meagher**, the "prince of hurlers" who dominated the sport in Co Kilkenny in the 1920s and 1930s. The thatched farmhouse where he was born and lived has been restored and furnished to evoke the period around 1884, the year in which the Gaelic Athletic Association was founded by Lory's father among others. The **Museum of Hurling** presents the fascinating local history of the sport, and demonstrations by local school children can be organised by arrangement.

Kilcooly Abbey

21mi/32km NW of Kilkenny by R 693; from Urlingford take R 689 S for 3.5mi/5.5km; 500yd/0.5km on foot from parish church car park.

The substantial ruins of this Cistercian abbey, founded c 1200, include a massive tower and a cloister; note the carved effigy of a knight. The abbey is protected by a ha-ha and formidably buttressed. In the field stands a large dovecot.

Dunmore Cave★

7mi/11km N of Kilkenny by N 77 and N 78. (Dúchas)⬝⬝*Tours (45min) mid Jun to mid-Sep, 9.30am-6.30pm; mid-Mar to mid-Jun, mid-Sep to Oct 10am-5pm; Oct to mid-Mar Sat-Sun, Bank Hols 10am-4.30pm (last admission 45min before closing).* ⊚ *€2.90.* Ⓟ ☎ *056 7767726 - www.heritageireland.ie*

Beneath the isolated Castlecomer limestone outcrop is this large cave encrusted with stalagmites and stalactites. The visitor centre explains the site's geology and history. The 10C tale of a horrible massacre by Vikings seemed confirmed when coins and human skeletons were found (1973), adding to the Viking remains, coins, brass buckles and delicate silverwork of North African origin recovered in the 1880.

Castlecomer

11.5mi/19km N of Kilkenny by N 77 and N 78.

The village was laid out like an Italian village by Sir Christopher Wandesforde in 1635; his family mined coal in the region for three centuries. There is now no more coal-mining, but plenty of mementoes are preserved at Reddy's Coal Mine Lounge.

KILLALA★

POPULATION 713

Killala (Cill Ala) is a quiet seaside resort overlooking Killala Bay at the mouth of the River Moy, and Bartragh Island, a narrow sandbank. It has a sandy beach, and plenty of sports facilities. The harbour warehouses are a reminder of its importance in the past, most notably as it was here that the French first halted when they invaded in 1798. To the west of the town lies North Mayo, one of the most remote and least inhabited regions of Ireland. In fine weather the bog gleams gold in the sun but when the sky is overcast the prospect is bleak like the entrance to the underworld. This apparently unwelcoming land was nevertheless an important human habitat in Neolithic times, and fascinating traces of its occupation are still to be seen. *Ballina 096 70848 (seasonal)*

▶ **Orient Yourself:** Killala lies on R 314 north of Ballina (N 59 west of Sligo)
Kids Especially for Kids: plenty to do at the beach and the Waterpoint complex
🔥 **Also See:** KNOCK, SLIGO, WESTPORT

Sight

St Patrick's Cathedral

The present Anglican **cathedral** was erected in 1670 by Thomas Ottway, Bishop of Killala, using stone from the ruined medieval cathedral, including the south doorway and Gothic east window. The great 12C **round tower**, built of limestone (84ft/25m high) and recapped in the 19C, is all that remains of the monastery founded by Muiredach, the first bishop of Killala, who was appointed by St Patrick in the 5C. There is also a 9C **souterrain** with many chambers *(unfenced)*.

Driving Tours

North Mayo Coast *25mi/40km*

The northern coast of Co Mayo confronts the Atlantic with a line of dramatic sea cliffs, broken only by **Broad Haven**, a wide bay of sandy coves, narrow sea-inlets and tiny habitations, enclosed by **Benwee Head** (829ft/253m – *east*) and **Erris Head** (285ft/87m – *west on the Belmullet Peninsula*). Inland the country is largely covered in

---

The Year of the French

In August 1798 a force of 1 067 French revolutionaries under General Humbert landed at Kilcummin in Killala Bay and Humbert appointed John Moore as President of the Provisional Government of Connaught in Killala; as the French advanced inland they were joined by enthusiastic but ill-equipped Irishmen.

Their first success was at Ballina; then they met General Lake and his vastly superior force of militia and yeomanry. Although outnumbered, General Humbert routed his opponent and the ignominious retreat of General Lake's cavalry became known as the **Races of Castlebar.** At Carrignagat, they had their third victory. Humbert moved southeast hoping to avoid the English army and join up with the United Irishmen but the latter had been defeated; he was defeated at Ballinamuck, near Longford. The French were taken prisoner; the Irish were hanged as traitors.

The 1798 Rebellion was re-enacted in Killala in 1981 for the film version of Thomas Flanagan's historical novel, *The Year of the French.*

SLIDE FILE, Dublin

Killala Harbour

Atlantic blanket bog (400sq mi/1 036km²): its turf is extensively harvested by machine to fuel the power station at Bellacorick, which is supplemented by wind turbines.

▷ *From Killala take R 314 N; after crossing the river turn right; climb the stile into the field (left).*

Breastagh Ogham Stone
The stone (8ft/2.5m high), probably a Bronze Age standing stone, is marked with the linear Ogham script that is only partially legible.

▷ *Continue to the crossroads; turn right.*

Rathfran Abbey
The 13C Dominican friary by the shore was burned down in 1590 by Sir Richard Bingham, the English Governor of Connaught, in the course of one of his destructive forays. Little remains of the cloisters and out-buildings but the long rectangular church is still largely intact. Note the panel over the west door depicting the Crucifixion.

▷ *Return to the crossroads; turn right; continue N via Carrowmore, Killogeary and Rathlackan. Turn right to Downpatrick Head.*

Downpatrick Head
The projecting headland is undermined by the sea which comes up through a **blow hole** *(fenced off)*. Just offshore stands Dunbriste, a rock stack surmounted by a prehistoric earthwork, probably detached from the mainland in 1393. The views are superb, taking in *(E)* Benbulben and the Dartry Mountains north of Sligo, *(SE)* the Ox Mountains (Slieve Gamph), *(SW)* the Nephin Beg Mountains, *(W)* the cliffs to Benwee Head and the Stags of Broadhaven offshore.

▷ *Continue to Ballycastle; take R 314 NW.*

Céide Fields★
(Dúchas) 🚶🕐 *Open Apr to Oct 10am-6pm (5pm Apr- May, Oct).* 😊 *Be sure to dress warmly and wear walking shoes as the site is outdoors.* 🚌€3.70. 🚾☎ *096 43325*

Most of North Mayo is covered by blanket bog, a desolate and seemingly unwelcoming landscape that conceals fascinating evidence of settled and productive prehistoric occupation. Using iron probes and bamboo markers, archeologists have mapped several square miles of fields laid out by the Neolithic people who lived near the Céide Cliffs over 50 centuries ago and who were contemporaries of the tomb builders of the Boyne Valley.

The centrepiece of the strikingly modern **visitor centre** is a large, twisted 4 400 year old Scots pine found in the vicinity; displays explain the geology and evolution of the bog reaching depths of 13ft/4m. Parts of a primitive plough and postholes suggest how the Stone Age farmers might have cleared the land of primeval forest and piled stones to create enclosed fields and houses.

For information about visits to Belderrig Prehistoric Farm Research Station, enquire at Céide Fields.

Moy Estuary *20mi/32km*

The coast road around the estuary of the salmon-rich River Moy passes close to the exceptionally picturesque ruins of two 15C Franciscan establishments, and continues to North Mayo's largest town, Ballina, and Inishcrone beyond.

▶ *From Killala take the coast road S.*

Moyne Abbey★

The extensive remains of the Franciscan friary at Moy include cloisters, sacristy, chapter-house, kitchen, refectory, church, and splendid six-storey tower. As elsewhere, Sir Richard Bingham, the English Governor of Connaught attempted to make the place uninhabitable; although some friars remained until the close of the 18C.

▶ *Continue S; on reaching the Rosserk River turn left.*

Rosserk Abbey★

The abbey on the Rosserk River, a tributary of the Moy, was the first Franciscan house to be built in Ireland, and its ruins are some of the best preserved in the country. Among the decorative features to survive, note the west door of the church and the carved piscina in the chancel, carved with a round tower, angels and the instruments of the Passion. From the cloisters, stairs lead up to the dormitories and refectory. Rosserk also suffered grievously at the hands of the ruthless Sir Richard Bingham.

▶ *Return to T-junction and turn left; continue S.*

Address Book

WHERE TO STAY

🍽️🍽️**Downhill Inn** – Sligo Rd, Ballina - 1mi E off N 59 - ☎ 096 73444; www.downhillinn.ie. Closed 1 week at Christmas. 🖥️👤 45 rm. 🍴 Restaurant 🍷. This family owned purpose-built hotel on the outskirts of town offers clean and comfortable accommodation. Bedrooms are warmly decorated and uniform in size.

SPORTS AND LEISURE

Surfing, waterskiing, wind surfing and sub-aqua in and around Killala Bay
Salmon fishing in the River Moy and in the Deel River at Crossmolina
Canoeing on the Moy River at Foxford
Boating on the lakes and rivers
Hot seaweed baths at Inishcrone.

TRACING ANCESTORS

Enniscoe House, Crossmolina

Ballina

Busy Ballina, the largest town in North Mayo and the seat of the bishop of the Roman Catholic diocese of Killala, straddles the River Moy. Lacking in distinction, it offers good salmon fishing on the Moy. The **Cathedral of St Muredach** on the east bank was built in the 19C next to the ruins of a late-14C Augustinian **friary** founded by the O'Dowd family; elements of the friary church date from the 15C.

▶ *From Ballina drive through Castleconor, for 9mi/14km.*

Inishcrone (Enniscrone)

This is a popular family seaside resort on the east coast of Killala Bay, with indoor water facilities at Waterpoint. The local speciality is a traditional Irish seaweed bath at the elegant Edwardian **Kilcullen Seaweed Baths**; the deliciously silky warm seawater is a fine way of relaxing and is said to relieve the symptoms of rheumatism and arthritis. ○ *Open 10am-8pm.* ⊛ *€17.* ⌒ P ☎ *096 3628*

KILLALOE ★

POPULATION 972

Killaloe (Cill Dalua) is delightfully sited on the west bank of the Shannon, at a point where the river, emerging from Lough Derg, is forced into a relatively narrow channel, constricted by the Arra Mountains to the east and Slieve Bernagh to the west. It is a pretty village and designated Heritage Town, with steep and narrow streets, a cathedral, and an ancient stone bridge. It is also a watersports centre of international importance. *The Bridge, Killaloe* ☎ *061 376866 (May to Sep) Connolly St, Nenagh* ☎ *067 31610 (Jul to Aug) - www.shannonregiontourism.ie*

▶ **Orient Yourself:** Killaloe is just off the main road (N 7) between Limerick and Nenagh, at the south end of Lough Derg

Kids **Especially for Kids:** plenty to do at the seaside

◔ **Also See:** BIRR, CASHEL, ENNIS, LIMERICK, ROSCREA

Visit

St Flannan's Cathedral ★

The Dónall Mór O'Brien's austere, aisle-less **cathedral** of 1185, on the site of a monastery founded in the 6C by St Molua and dedicated to his successor, was rebuilt in 1225 in the Romanesque/Gothic transitional style you see today. Its outstanding features include an elaborately carved 12C **Romanesque doorway**, a 12C High Cross from Kilfenora in the Burren, and a cross shaft carved c 1000 bearing a unique dual inscription in both **Ogham** and **Viking Runic script**.

Beside the cathedral stands the vaulted nave of **St Flannan's Oratory**, a little 12C Romanesque church incorporating a loft beneath its steeply sloping stone roof.

GETTING AROUND

Holy Island Ferry –Operates (weather permitting) from Mountshannon pier. ○ *Open May- Oct 9.30am-6pm.* ⊛ *€8 (boat and tour).* ☎ *086 87 49710*

SPORTS AND LEISURE

Killaloe is a watersports centre of international importance.

TRACING ANCESTORS

Tipperary North Genealogical Service is housed in the Governor's House in Nenagh. ○ *Open Mon-Fri 9.30am-5pm.* ☎ *067 33850; www.irish-roots.net/Ntipp.htm*

St Molua's Oratory

The oratory beside the Roman Catholic church at the top of the hill, was built c 1000 on Friar's Island in the Shannon; it was transferred here when its original location was submerged by the hydro-electric scheme in the 1920s.

Killaloe Brian Ború Heritage Centre

&⊙ *Open May to Sep 10am-6pm.* ⊕ *€3.15.* 🅿 ☎ *061 376866*

The display traces in pictures and text the history of Killaloe from the birth of Brian Ború, High King of Ireland (1002-14), through many years of fishing and cruising to the Civil War and the building of the Ardnacrusha dam to provide electricity.

Driving Tours

Lough Derg

▷ *From Killaloe take R 463 N; after 1mi/1.6km turn right into a track (0.5mi/0.8km).*

Béal Ború Earthwork

This large circular earthwork surrounded by a deep ditch and a grove of beech and pine trees is set immediately above the Lough Derg shoreline. From its name, which means "Pass of the Tributes", Brian Ború took his title.

▷ *Continue N on R 463.*

Tuamgraney

The village is known as the birthplace of the novelist, Edna O'Brien. At the south end of the village stands a 15C tower house and St Cronan's Church (Anglican), which is believed to be the oldest church in continuous use in Ireland or Great Britain. The west portion with its lintelled doorway dates from c 969; the east end of the building is 12C; note the Romanesque windows. It now houses the **East Clare Heritage Centre**, which documents the local history, including the life and times of Brian Boru. &⊙ *Open Jun to Oct 10am-5pm (closed for lunch 12.30-1.30pm).* ⟶ *Tour* ⊕ *€4.* ☎ *061 921351*

The **Memorial Park** *(330yd/300m W of the village),* is planted with indigenous trees and shrubs to commemorate the victims of the Great Famine of 1845-52.

▷ *Continue N on R 463 to Mountshannon.*

Holy Island★

The island with its extensive and evocative remains of a 7C monastery is a good excuse for a short trip on Lough Derg. As well as the remains of no fewer than six churches, there is a **round tower** (80ft/24m high) and a curious **bargaining stone** with a hollow channel through which men would shake hands to seal an agreement.

Mountain Drive

▷ *From Killaloe take R 463 S; in O'Briensbridge cross the river; in Montpelier turn right to Castleconnell.*

Castleconnell★

The well-kept small village by the Shannon offers excellent salmon fishing and riverside walks under the trees.

▷ *From Castleconnell drive E on a minor road (crossing N 7); turn left onto R 503; E of Newport turn right (sign); car parks both sides of the river.*

Clare Glens★

The Clare River descends in a series of lovely **waterfalls** through wooded glens.

▶ *Continue S on minor road to Murroe; turn in through the park gates.*

Glenstal Abbey

Impressive grounds and lakes surround the castle now used as a Benedictine monastery and school *(private)*. The modern **church** is known for its surrealistic decor and for the Ikon Chapel in the crypt. ◯ *Grounds open daily* ☎ *061 386103; www. glenstal.org*

▶ *Return to R 503 and continue E. At the crossroad near Inch turn left onto R 497. Drive N via Dolla to Nenagh.*

Nenagh

Little survives of the **Anglo-Norman castle**★ built c 1200 save the colossal circular keep (100ft/30m high), the finest in the country, and the 13C hall (restored). Nenagh, a substantial garrison town in the 19C, is now the county town and commercial centre of Tipperary North Riding. The 13C Franciscan friary, one of the most important in Ireland, was dissolved in Elizabethan times; only the church wall stands.

▶ *From Nenagh take R 494 W. Beyond Portroe turn left (sign) into minor road.*

Graves of the Leinstermen

The group of prehistoric stones on the west face of Tountinna (1 512ft/461m) may be one of the first inhabited places in Ireland. There are commanding **views**★ over much of Lough Derg to Slieve Bernagh.

▶ *Continue along minor road. Turn left into R 494. In Ballina turn right to Killaloe.*

KILLARNEY★★

POPULATION 8 809

Tourists have been coming to Killarney (Cill Airne), Ireland's foremost tourist town, for more than two hundred years, entranced by its glorious setting of lakes, luxuriant vegetation, romantic ruins and meticulously managed desmesnes. All around are rugged mountains including the Macgillycuddy's Reeks which culminate in the highest peak in Ireland, Carrauntoohill (3 414ft/1 041m). No visit to the area is complete without making the classic trip into the Gap of Dunloe, a formidable breach rammed by a glacier through the heart of the mountains.
🛈*Beech Rd* ☎ *064 31633* 🛈 *Kerry County Airport (freefone)* 🛈 *Waterville* ☎ *066 9474646 (Jun-Sep) - www.corkkerry.ie*

Cinematic History

The Dawn, a famous Irish film set in the War of Independence, was shot in Killarney between 1933 and 1934, with a cast of 250, mainly local amateurs; its initiator was Tom Cooper, a local cinema owner. Shooting usually took place on Thursdays, early closing day. Photographs of this production, of *The Quiet Man,* filmed in 1952 at Cong, and of *Ryan's Daughter*, shot at Banna Strand in 1968, can be seen in the bar of the Three Lakes Hotel.

▶ **Orient Yourself:** Killarney is an ideal touring centre on N 22 between Cork and Tralee, not far from Farranfore Airport *(north by N 22.*

🚗 **Don't Miss:** the Gap of Dunloe and Killarney National Park, the Ring of Kerry and Skellig Islands

🖐 **Also See:** DINGLE PENINSULA, KENMARE, TRALEE

A Bit of History

The monastery founded on the little island of Innisfallen in the 7C became a centre of learning, where the *Annals of Innisfallen*, one of Ireland's earliest historical chronicles, was composed. The area was subsequently governed by the O'Donoghues, McCarthys, and O'Sullivans, who were displaced by Elizabethan settlers like the Brownes and Herberts. It was in the 18C that Thomas Browne, the 4th Viscount Kenmare (1726-95), planned the present neat town of slated houses and shops. He also introduced linen and woollen manufacturing and beautified the surroundings by planting trees and providing seats and belvederes. Over time, streams of

R Holzbachova, Ph Benet/MICHELIN

Jaunting car

KILLARNEY		College Square	DX	7	Marian Terrace	DX	15
		College St	DX	9	O'Connell's Terrace	DX	18
Bohereen Na Goun	CX 3	Green Lawn	CX	10	O'Sullivan's Pl.	DX	19
Bohereencael	DX 4	Hillard's Lane	DX	12	Plunkett St	DX	21
Brewery Lane	DX 6	Mangerton	DX	13	St Anthony's Pl.	DX	22

Kerry Poets' Memorial	DX A

Address Book

GETTING AROUND

Valentia Island-Renard Point Car Ferry – ☎ 066 94 76141; www.corkkerry. ie. Operates Apr-Sep, daily 8.30am-10.30pm.

Skellig Islands Ferry - ☎ 066 94 72437/087 23 95470; www.skelligislands. com. From Portmagee Pier to the Skellig Islands (45min) daily at 10.30am (return at 3pm), weather permitting. ☎ €40. Reserve two days in advance.

Farranfore Airport – ☎ 066 976 4644; www.kerryairport.ie

SIGHTSEEING

There are **information centres** at Muckross House and at Torc Waterfall (*summer only*). The **National Park** may be explored on land or by water. There are many miles of **walks** to suit all tastes at Ross Castle, Muckross House and through the Gap of Dunloe.
There are **boat trips** on Lough Leane from Ross Castle to Innisfallen Island or as part of the trip through the Gap of Dunloe.
Trips in a **jaunting car** are available from the southern end of the Main Street or at Muckross House.

For coin ranges, see the Legend on the cover flap.

WHERE TO STAY

⊜ **Kingfisher Lodge** – *Lewis Rd* - ☎ 064 37131; www.kingfisherkillarney. com. Closed 12 Dec to 9 Feb. ▣ ⧏ 10 rm ☲. Friendly and comfortable guesthouse, three minutes walk from the centre. Bedrooms are clean and neat, in co-ordinated pastel colours, with the quieter ones at the back of the house. All have large showers.

⊜ **Hussey's Townhouse** – *43 High St* - ☎ 064 37454. Open Easter to Oct. ▣ ⧏ 5 rm ☲. Relax in the first floor lounge, with its quiet reading area, or mix with the locals in the snug bar at the front of this town house. Bedrooms are compact, cosy and well-kept and all have en-suite shower rooms.

⊜ **Naughton's Villa** – *Muckross Rd* - ☎ 064 36025 - 17 Mar to 15 Nov - ▣ - 5 rm €35/80 ☲. Guests can take advantage of the balcony terrace at this pink hued guesthouse, close to the centre.

Bedrooms have a certain cottagey feel and the ensuite bathrooms are all a decent size.

⊜ **Old Weir Lodge** – *Muckross Rd* - ☎ 064 35593; www.oldweirlodge.com. Closed 23-29 Dec. ▣ ⧏ 30 rm ☲. The emphasis is on comfort and space at this purpose-built town centre property. There are two comfortable lounges and a roomy breakfast room with conservatory extension. Immaculate bedrooms in warming hues.

⊜ **Redwood** – *Rockfield, Tralee Rd - 3mi N on N 22* - ☎ 064 34754; www.redwood-killarney.com. ▣ ⧏ 6 rm ☲. Comfortable and well priced bed & breakfast accommodation to the north of the town, surrounded by several acres of farmland. Spacious sitting room and conservatory, comfy bedrooms. A non-smoking house.

⊜⊜ **Fuchsia House** – *Muckross Rd* - ☎ 064 33743. Closed Jan-Feb. ▣ ⧏ 9 rm ☲. A small hotel with the feel of a country house, from its antique furnished and individually designed bedrooms to the comfortable sitting room and well-tended back garden. Home-made breakfast produce.

⊜⊜ **Kathleens Country House Hotel** ↝*Tralee Rd - 2mi N on N 22* - ☎ 064 32810; www.kathleens.net. Open Easter to Oct. ▣ ⧏ 17 rm ☲. Neat, comfortable and well-kept with pretty bedrooms overlooking the garden. The eponymous Kathleen, with her ebullient hospitality, is one of the main reasons why her guests keep returning each year.

⊜⊜⊜ **Coolclogher House** – *Mill Rd* - ☎ 064 35996; Closed Dec-Jan. ▣ 4 rm ☲. Play Lord of the Manor by staying at this imposing Victorian Italianate mansion standing proudly in 68 acres/27ha of parkland. Sympathetically restored yet retaining a period charm. Noted feature is the 180 year old camellia in its own conservatory.

WHERE TO EAT

⊜ **The Laurels** – *Main St* - ☎ 064 31149; www.thelaurelspub.com. Probably one of the best of the town's myriad pubs. Live music, a bustling atmosphere and palpable sense of tradition. The menu offers an extensive selection of favourites from Irish stew to home-made burgers.

 The Old Presbytery – *Cathedral Pl - ☎ 064 30555. Closed Tue (Mon-Wed Nov-Mar), Good Fri, 25 and 26 Dec, 2 weeks Jan.* 🅿 A more recent addition to the town's restaurant scene, opposite St Marys Cathedral. Spread over two floors with a pianist who belts out the classics. Menu adds some modern touches to its traditional base.

 The Granary Restaurant & Bar – *The Pound, Touhills Lane, Beech Rd - ☎ 064 20075; www.granarykillarney. com.* Black and white photos of filmstars adorn the walls of this contemporary spot. The bar is open all day for light snacks with a more formal upstairs restaurant open for dinner. Trendy and popular.

TAKING A BREAK

Killarney Pub – *7 High Street - ☎ 064 30 200 - Open daily from noon.* For those looking for that traditional Irish pub then head for the town centre and this recently restored family owned watering hole. There's a welcoming atmosphere and traditional music twice a week. They also organise tours from here in a 1926 bus.

SHOPPING

High Street – This is the main shopping district of the town and where to find the majority of pubs and restaurants. There are a number of shops ideal for those looking for souvenirs; from jewellery to linen and glassware.

Quills Woollen Market – *High Street - Market Cross - ☎ 064 32 277; www.quillsireland.com. Open daily 9am (11am Sun) to 6pm (9pm for the tourist items shop).* A family business established in 1939. Spread over two floors, with a large collection of authentic, and typically Irish, goods, ranging from Donegal tweeds and Aran handknits to linen and individually designed pieces of jewellery.

Avoca Weavers – *Moll's Gap - 15mi/24km S by N 7.1* Fashionable woollen clothing.

Kerry Woollen Mills – *Beaufort; 5mi/8km W by N 72; 4mi/6km turn right at sign; after 1mi/1.6km turn left and then right - ☎ 064 44122; www.kerrywoollenmills.ie. Open Mon-Sat, 9am-6pm. Closed Good Fri, 25 Dec.* Woollen goods have been produced here for over 200 years; showroom and retail shop - rugs and blankets for people and horses, tweeds for clothes and furnishings, scarves and shawls, knitwear and knitting yarn.

visitors came, including poets, painters and writers – Shelley found Killarney more impressive even than Switzerland, Macaulay thought Innisfallen "not a reflex of heaven, but a bit of heaven itself"; on the other hand, Charlotte Brontë had the misfortune to be thrown from her horse while exploring the Gap of Dunloe and Thackeray was dismayed by the throngs of touts and guides. Killarney's tourist vocation was confirmed with the visit of Queen Victoria in 1861. In 1932 the Muckross estate was presented by its American owners to the nation as the Bourn Vincent Memorial Park, becoming the core of the present National Park, Ireland's first.

Walking Tour

Killarney town is thronged with visitors crowding its streets, bars, hotels and shops. Focal points include Market Cross, the intersection of Main Street, High Street and New Street, and Kenmare Place, where the jaunting cars wait for passengers.

A prominent spire (285ft/87m high) marks **St Mary's RC Cathedral**★ designed by Augustus Pugin. Although work began in 1842, it was not consecrated until 1855 as the building was used to provide shelter to famine victims between 1848 and 1853. It was adapted for the new liturgy in 1972–73.

The Early-English **St Mary's Anglican Church**, built in 1870 contains a stained-glass window reproducing Holman Hunt's *Light of the World*. Among its memorials, there is one to the Revd Arthur Hyde, great-grandfather of Douglas Hyde, first president of Ireland.

Kerry Poets' Memorial

The personification of Ireland as a beautiful woman *(speir bhean)* was created in 1940 by Seamus Murphy to commemorate Co Kerry's four best-known Gaelic poets – **Pierce Ferriter**, a poet, soldier and musician from the Dingle Peninsula, who refused to submit to the Cromwellians in 1652 and was hanged in 1653 in Killarney; **Geoffrey O'Donoghue of the Glens** (1620-78), who was Chieftain of Glenflesk and lived in Killaha Castle, southeast of Killarney; **Egan O'Rahilly** (1670-1728), the greatest of the four poets, who was educated in the bardic tradition and gave his allegiance to the Brownes, as the McCarthys were unable to act as his patrons; **Owen Roe O'Sullivan** (1748-84), who led a roving life as a hedge schoolmaster in winter and an itinerant labourer in summer, as well as serving in the British army and navy; to the delight of Admiral Rodney he wrote a poem in English about the Admiral's victory over the French at Dominica in 1782.

Franciscan Friary

The friary, built in 1860 in a style similar to Muckross Friary *(see below)*, contains a stained-glass window *(entrance hall)* by Harry Clarke.

Excursions

Gap of Dunloe★★

There are various ways of exploring the Gap. Gap of Dunloe Tours operate 17 Mar to Oct. Depart by bus from Killarney at 10.30am to Kate Kearney's Cottage; either travel by pony trap (€20 extra) or walk (2.5hrs) through the Gap to Lower Brendans' Cottage (lunch extra); boat trip across the three lakes at 2pm; return by bus to Killarney at 4.pm. Tours must be booked in advance; take a rain jacket. Bus and boat €20 064 30200 - www.gapofdunloetours.com
By car: from Killarney take N 72 W; after 4mi/6km turn left and continue to Kate Kearney's Cottage, hire a pony and trap or continue on foot before returning to the car park. Boat trips only possible if booked as part of a tour with Dunloe Gap Tours.
By bicycle: make a round trip by hired cycle either via the lakes (cycles are carried aboard a special boat), via the Kerry Way (involving some pushing) or via Moll's Gap.
The jarvies plying for hire with their carriages throng the roadsides and the forecourt of **Kate Kearney's Cottage**, originally an old coaching inn kept by the beautiful Kate, who served *poteen* to 19C tourists. *Open daily 10am until late. Live music nights. Food served noon-8pm.* 064 44146; www.katekearneyscottage.com
The trip through the deep and narrow rock-strewn gorge is one of the highlights of a visit to Ireland, and deservedly so. The initial press of pony traps, riders, cyclists and walkers soon thins out; it is less crowded towards the end of the day, and can be entered from the Black Valley to the south. The U-shaped glacial breach (1 500ft/457m deep) is traversed by a narrow track which winds up a series of hairpin bends, past several mountain tarns, to cross a stream before reaching the ruins of a Royal Irish Constabulary strongpoint. Most traffic turns back on reaching the Head of the Gap (794ft/242m). As the track descends into the Gearhameen Valley, where red deer graze, there is a fine view of the Upper Lake, bordered by native oakwoods and backed by Mangerton Mountain (2 756ft/838m).

Killarney National Park★★★ 2 *Tour of 30mi/48km.*

S of Killarney by N 71. **Killarney National Park** (39sq mi/101km²) embraces the three lakes – Lower (Lough Leane), Middle (Muckross Lake) and Upper, which are linked by the Long Range River – the foreshore and the mountain slopes south and west. The original nucleus of the Muckross Estate is now complemented by Knockreer, Ross Island and Innisfallen, formerly part of the Kenmare Estate. Blanket bog on the higher land contrasts with Ireland's largest remaining area of ancient oak woodland, and examples

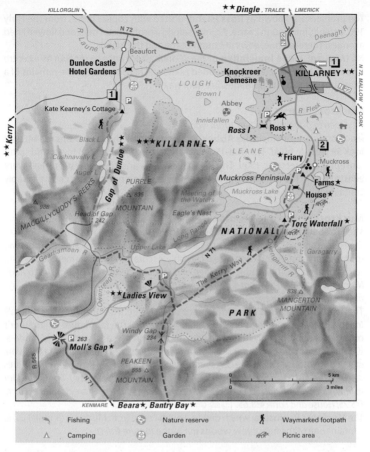

KILLORGLIN   ★★ **Dingle** , TRALEE ▸ LIMERICK

Dunloe Castle Hotel Gardens

Kate Kearney's Cottage

★★ **Kerry**

Black L.

Cushnavally L.

Auger L.

★★★ KILLARNEY

PURPLE

△ 835

△ 988   MOUNTAIN

MACGILLYCUDDY'S REEKS

Gap of Dunloe

Head of Gap 242

Knockreer Demesne

Brown I.

Abbey

Innisfallen

Ross I   **Ross ★**

L E A N E

★ Friary

Muckross Peninsula

Muckross Lake

Farms ★

House ★

Meeting of the Waters

Eagle's Nest

★ Torc Waterfall ★

N A T I O N A L

Long Range

L. Garagarry

838 △

MANGERTON MOUNTAIN

KILLARNEY ★★

Muckross

R. Flesk

R. Laune

N 72

R 563

Beaufort

L O U G H

Deenagh R.

N 72 , MALLOW ✦ CORK

The Kerry Way

Gearhameen R.

Upper Lake

Owenreagh R.

N 71

★★ Ladies View

P A R K

Windy Gap 234

P 263

Moll's Gap ★

PEAKEEN

555 △

MOUNTAIN

R 568

N 71

KENMARE   **Beara ★ , Bantry Bay ★**

	Fishing		Nature reserve		Waymarked footpath
Λ	Camping		Garden		Picnic area

of mature yews, alder carrs, and, arbutus (or strawberry tree) which flourishes in the exceptionally mild climate. The special character of the park was given international recognition in 1981 when it was designated as a UNESCO Biosphere Reserve. *(Dúchas)* 🕙 *Visitor Centre: open mid-Mar to Oct 9am-6pm (7pm Jul-Aug), Nov to mid-Mar on request. Last admission 1hr before closing.* 🌐 *No charge.* 🅿 ☎ *064 31440*

Knockreer Demesne

Footpath to Ross Castle. The grounds of Knockreer House extend westwards from Killarney to the shore of Lough Leane; the entrance from the town is marked by a thatched cottage, **Deenagh Lodge** *(tea room).*

Ross Castle★

1mi/1.6km S by N 71 and a minor road W (sign). Boat trips to Innisfallen Island. (Dúchas) *(40min) Jun to Aug, 9am-6.30pm; Apr to May, Sep to Oct 10am-6pm (5pm Apr, Oct). Last admission 45min before closing.* 🕙 *Closed 24-26 Dec.* 🌐 *€5.30.* ☎ *064 35851* The well-restored castle, the last in Munster to hold out against Cromwellian forces (1652) until attacks were mounted from armed boats, was built on the shore of Lough Leane in the 15C by one of the O'Donoghue Ross chieftains. A fortified bawn reinforced by circular flanking towers surrounded the rectangular keep. The four floors have been restored using medieval techniques and furnished in styles appropriate to the early-15C to late-16C period.

The promontory, known as **Ross Island**, dotted with copper mines from the early 19C, extends into Lough Leane. Access is along a profusion of tree- and flower-lined avenues. There are fine views of Lough Leane and the islands.

No trace remains on **Innisfallen** of the 7C monastery once so renown as a centre of learning, but the luxuriantly wooded island still harbours evocative remains of a later abbey with a fine Romanesque doorway.

Muckross Friary★

🕐 *Open mid-Jun to early Sep 10am-5pm.*

Muckross Friary (or **Muckross Abbey**), was founded for the Franciscans in 1448 and took 59 years to build. The mid-15C nave and choir, broad central tower and south ransept were erected c 1500. The 22-arch cloisters and the domestic offices were constructed in four phases. The three-storey building north of the choir probably contained the Sacristy and the Sacristan's lodging.

Muckross House and Farms★

The Elizabethan-style **Muckross House** in Portland stone was built in 1843 for the Herbert family. Many rooms are reflect the taste of the early 20C: the drawing room, library and dining room are all lavishly decorated. The basement is devoted to regional crafts. *(Dúchas)*🕐 *Open mid Mar to Oct 9am-6pm (7pm Jun to Aug); Nov to mid-Mar 9am-5.30pm. Last admission 45min before closing.* 🕐 *Closed 9 days at Christmas.* ⌦ *House: €5.75; house and farm €8.65.* 🖂✕🅿☎ *064 31440*

The **Traditional Farms** are a showpiece of early 20C Irish rural life. Live animals inhabit the yards and fields and the buildings, from large farmhouse to labourer's cottage, are appropriately furnished with dressers, presses and settle-beds. Indoors, turf fires burn in the hearths and the staff, in period costume, demonstrate the work of a country housewife in the days before electricity and other modern amenities came to the Irish countryside. 🕐 *Open Jun to Sep 10am-7pm; May 1-6pm; mid-Mar to May, Oct, Sat-Sun and Bank Hols 1-6pm. Last admission 1hr before closing.* ⌦*Farm: €5.75; House and Farm €8.65.* 🅿☎ *064 31440*

The **Muckross Peninsula**, which divides Lough Leane from Muckross (Middle) Lake, contains one of the finest yew woods in Europe *(nature trails)*.

Muckross Gardens

SLIDE FILE, Dublin

Torc Waterfall★

The **cascade** (60ft/18m) is one of the highest in Ireland. The viewpoint *(173 steps)* provides a fine view of the lakes.

Ladies View★★

Climbing over the hills to Kenmare, the N17 enables visitors to enjoy some of the finest panoramas over the Killarney landscape without the need to scale a mountain. Queen Victoria was particularly impressed by the prospect of Macgillycuddy's Reeks and the island-studded Upper Lake, little changed since she and her entourage came this way in 1861.

Moll's Gap★

The pass (863ft/263m) provides *(north)* a striking view of the Gap of Dunloe in Macgillycuddy's Reeks and *(south)* a glimpse of the Kenmare River.

Driving Tour

Ring of Kerry★★ *126mi/203km – 1 day*

The Iveragh peninsula is endowed with a spectacular high mountains, rocky bays, sandy beaches and dramatic seascapes. The **Ring of Kerry** is the road (N 70) that skirts the entire coastline between Killorglin and Kenmare. This great scenic drives can be completed in a single day but only a more measured trip of several days is sufficient to do justice to the wonderful, ever-changing succession of landscapes.

▶ *From Killarney take N 72 NW. Most coach tours on this route travel from north to south; passing is difficult as the coast road is narrow. After 4mi/6km turn left*

Dunloe Castle Hotel Gardens

🕐 *Open May to Sep.* 🅿 ☎ *064 44111; www.dunloecastlehotel.com*
From the modern hotel, the luxuriant gardens, partly enclosed by grey stone walls, extend to the 13C tower house overlooking the River Laune and the River Loe with a clear view of the Dunloe Gap. The botanic collection consists of exotic specimens including the Killarney Strawberry tree, South African lilies, Australian gums, New Zealand cabbage trees and cherries, Japanese maples, North American dogwood, Chilean fir trees, South American fuchsias, Chinese swamp cypress and the "Headache" tree with aromatic leaves.

▶ *Return to N 72 and continue NW to Killorglin.*

Killorglin (Cill Orglan)

The town is best known for the **Puck Fair** *(August)* when a large local billy-goat is enthroned on a chair in the town square during three days and nights of revelry.

▶ *Continue W on N 70; turn left to Caragh Lake, then right and left to Lickeen.*

Lough Caragh★

The road along the west shore affords views of the lake, renown for salmon and trout fishing; southeast rise the Macgillycuddy's Reeks (3 414ft/1 038m).

Lough Caragh, Ring of Kerry

B. Kaufmann/MICHELIN

▶ *Return to N 70 and continue W; in Caragh Bridge turn right.*

Cromane Strand
The long spit of sand shelters the shallow water known as Castlemaine Harbour.

▶ *Continue W on N 70; west of Glenbeigh take the minor road W across the bridge to Rossbeigh Strand.*

Rossbeigh Strand
The long strand (3mi/5km) is backed by a small hamlet; there are good walks in Rossbeigh Woods.

▶ *Continue W on N 70; in Kells turn right onto the minor road to Kells Bay (lovely beach) or continue W on N 70.*

Cahersiveen (Cathair Saidhbhín)
The native town of Daniel O'Connell by the Valentia River, dates from the early 19C. The **O'Connell Memorial Church**, built in 1888 of Newry granite with dressings of local black limestone, lacks the intended tower – rejected by the church authorities as too elaborate, but approved by Pope Leo XIII.

▶ *Take the minor road N towards Cooncrome harbour; after crossing the river turn left (2mi/3.2km).*

Cahergall Fort
The walls of this massive stone fort are stepped on the inside as at Staigue: within are two drystone buildings, a beehive hut and a rectangular house.

▶ *On foot continue W; turn right into a private road.*

Leacanabuaile Fort
This partly reconstructed prehistoric drystone fort was inhabited during the Bronze and Iron Ages; from the top ramparts there are excellent **views**★★ of the coast.

▶ *Return to Cahersiveen and continue W on N 70. To visit Valencia Island EITHER turn right to Renard Point and take the ferry to Knight's Town (seeAddress Book) OR continue on N 70, turn right onto R 657 to Portmagee and cross the bridge over the Portmagee Channel.*

Valentia Island
The island is a small (7mi/11.3km x 2mi/3.2km), but an important landmark in the radio shipping forecasts. In 1858, less than 2 000mi/3 219km from Newfoundland, Valentia was the eastern terminal for the first transatlantic telegraph cable.
Knight's Town, a quiet little harbour settlement, consists of a single street. A steep narrow road north of the church leads up to a disused slate quarry – good views of Beginish Island and Doulus Head extend from the hill.
The western extremity of island is marked by **Bray Tower**, a 16C stone watchtower with views *(south)* to the Skellig Islands and *(north)* to the Dingle Peninsula.
The stone-clad, grass-roofed building by the bridge linking Valencia to the mainland, houses the **Skellig Experience** – an imaginative display about the extraordinary character of the Skellig Islands: the monastery, lighthouses, wildlife and underwater sealife. ♿🕒 *Open May to Sep 10am-6pm (7pm Jun to Aug); Apr, Oct to Nov 5 days a week (provisionally Sun-Thu) 10am-5pm.* 🚫 €5 Boat trip (at 3pm, 2hrs) €25. ♿🅿 ☎ 066 9476306 - www.skelligexperience.com

Skellig Islands★★

These bare and rocky islands, 10m/16km offshore, rise dramatically above the Atlantic. Little Skellig *(no landing allowed)* is a nature reserve with bird colonies (kittiwakes, razorbills, guillemots, shearwaters and gannets). The larger island, Skellig Michael, now a World Heritage Site, can be accessed, weather permitting, by boat. Its remote position on the westernmost edge of the known world was chosen as a monastic site in the 6C by St Finian; in 11C/12C the remaining residents moved to more congenial quarters at Ballinskelligs on the mainland. The well-preserved ruins – church, two oratories and six beehive huts – survive, perched precipitously above the sea on a narrow platform.

▶ *From the island take the bridge over the Portmagee Channel to Portmagee (An Caladh); turn right to take the coast road S up behind Glanearagh (1 044ft/318m) to St Finan's Bay. Continue S on R 567.*

Ballinskelligs (Baile an Sceilg)

This Irish-speaking village has a minute harbour and long strand (4mi/6km).

▶ *Continue E on R 567; at the junction turn right onto N 70.*

Waterville (An Coireán)

The little resort, built on an isthmus between **Lough Currane** and the sea, has a long promenade (0.5mi/0.8km). Photographs of Charlie Chaplin's frequent visits hang in the foyer of the Butler Arms Hotel, once redolent of 1950s splendour.

Derrynane National Historic Park★★

(Dúchas)&⏰ *Open May to Sep Mon-Sat 9am-6pm, Sun 11am-7pm; Apr, Oct Tue-Sun 1-5pm; Nov to Mar Sat-Sun 1-5pm.* ✆ *€2.90.* 🅿✆ *066 9475113*
The demesne formerly belonged to **Daniel O'Connell** (1775–1847), the great champion of Catholic emancipation, known as the Liberator. The **park** (298 acres/121ha) which borders Derrynane Bay includes a bathing beach, a bird sanctuary and Abbey Island *(accessible at low tide)*. The south and east wings of the slate-fronted **house** are presented as they were when built by O'Connell in 1825 – there are family portraits, original furniture and mementoes. The centrepiece of the drawing room *(first floor)* is the elaborate **table** presented to O'Connell when he was an alderman of Dublin Corporation; the top is made of walnut and the base, made from Irish oak, features Irish wolfhounds and a harp. The chapel adjoining the house was built by O'Connell in 1844 in thanksgiving for his release from prison; the huge triumphal chariot, in which he was paraded through Dublin, has been restored.

▶ *From Derrynane take N 70 E; in Castlecove turn left at the Staigue Fort House hotel.*

Staigue Fort★

😊 *Narrow approach road;* ✆ *€0.20 donation "for trespass."*
This restored 2 000-year-old drystone fort is one of the finest in Ireland. It was built as a centre of communal refuge probably before the 5C. The walls (18ft/5m high and up to 13ft/4m thick) are stepped on their interior face to provide access to the parapets. The entire fort is surrounded by a bank and ditch.

▶ *Continue E on N 70.*

Sneem (An Snaidhm)★

This attractive village is set at the head of the Sneem Estuary. Monuments to Cearbhall O'Dálaigh (1899–1976), former President of Ireland, who lived in Sneem, have been erected in the two large grass-covered squares, linked by a narrow bridge.

The **Anglican Church** is a charming small building dating from 1810 with a tower and a small spire supporting a salmon-shaped weathervane.

▶ *Continue E on N 70 to Kenmare and then on N 71 N to return to Killarney.*

KILRUSH★

POPULATION 2 740

Overlooking the sheltered waters of the Shannon estuary, the second-largest town in Co Clare retains something of the character it had when laid out by the Vandeleur family in the 18C. In the 19C Kilrush (Cill Rois) prospered as a port, and became the favourite summer resort of prosperous people from Limerick. Today it is a designated Heritage Town and a gateway to the beaches and cliffs of the Loop Head peninsula. There is a modern marina and colourful horse fairs are often held in the main square. In summer families of bottle-nosed dolphins can be seen sporting in the Shannon Estuary. *Kilrush ☎ 065 905 1577 (mid-May–mid-Sep) Kilkee ☎ 065 9056112 (seasonal)*

▶ **Orient Yourself:** Kilrush is SW of Ennis by N 68 and a few miles W of Killimer on the north bank of the River Shannon (Shannon Ferry Terminal)

 Also See: ADARE, ENNIS, LIMERICK, TRALEE

Visit

Vandeleur Walled Garden

Ferry Road. ◯ *Open year-round 10am–5pm (6pm Apr–Oct).* ☎ *065 90 51760*
The magnificent woodlands (420 acres/168ha), the old walled garden and the stables (visitor centre), are all that remain of the Vandeleur family seat; the mansion (1803) was destroyed by fire in 1897. The Vandeleurs, a family of Dutch origin, settled in

SLIDE FILDE, Dublin

Kilkee Beach

Address Book

GETTING AROUND

Shannon Car Ferry - *From Killimer; 5.5mi/8.8km E of Kilrush.* ☎ *065 90 53124; www.shannonferries.com.* Carries vehicles and passengers to Tarbert on the south shore of the Shannon Estuary
Ferry to Scattery Island – *From Kilrush Creek Marina. Apr-Oct.* ☎ *065 90 51327.*

SIGHTSEEING

Dolphin watch trips departing from Kilrush Marina – *Apr-Oct (subject to demand and weather). €18.* ☎ *065 90 51327; www.discoverdolphins.ie.*

Dolphin watch trips departing from Carrigaholt – *Apr-Sep, daily. €20 (dolphin trips).* ☎ *065 90 58156; www. dolphinwatch.ie.*
Boat Trips – Cruises and deep-sea fishing expeditions.

SPORTS AND LEISURE

Beaches at Cappa and Brew's Bridge.
Marina at Merchant's Quay in Kilrush with 120 berths, a boatyard and yacht hire.
Fishing in the Shannon Estuary and off the Atlantic Coast.

Kilrush in 1688 and were responsible for building the town in the 18C but they acquired an unvenviable reputation as harsh landlords in the 19C.

Excursions

Scattery Island★
Accessible by boat from Kilrush (see Address Book).
In the 6C the island 2mi/3km out in the estuary was chosen as the site of a monastery by St Senan. Legend relates that the saint had first to rid it of a terrible monster; more certain is the monastery's fate at the hands of the Vikings, who raided it on more than one occasion. There are evocative ruins of five medieval churches, but the most imposing structure is the tall (115ft/33m) **round tower**, with its doorway, unusually, at ground level.

West Clare Railway
4mi/6.4km NW of Kilrush by N 67 opposite Clancy's pub in Moyasta. ○ *Open 17 Mar to Aug 10am-6pm; Sep to mid-Mar, Sat-Sun and Bank Hols noon-5pm.* ⊗ *€7.* ▱ P ☎ *065 9051284*
Visitors may take a ride on a restored section of the West Clare Railway, which once ran between Ennis and Kilkee.

Kilkee (Cill Chaoi)
8.5mi/13.5km NW of Kilrush by N 67.
This seaside resort is set deep in Moore Bay with a long promenade embracing a wide horseshoe-shaped sandy beach, where horse races are held at low tide *(last weekend in August)*. The Duggerna rocks at the entrance to the bay are accessible at low tide.

Loop Head Peninsula
West of Kilrush and Kilkee the land forms a peninsula, terminating in Loop Head. The treeless landscape is divided into fields by earthbanks rather than the hedges or flagstones found farther inland.
On the south coast, **Carrigaholt Tower House** stands beside the pier. It was built in the 16C by the McMahon family, who once controlled the peninsula, and was last besieged in 1649. From the top of the tower there are fine **views** south to the north Kerry coast *(3mi/5km)*.
The north coast is much wilder, with spectacular cliffs, stacks and puffing holes. Near Moneen a huge natural arch, the **Bridge of Ross**★ *(sign)*, formed by the action of the sea, is visible from the edge of the cliffs.

Loop Head is surmounted by the lighthouse (277ft/84m above sea-level) which was built on the headland in 1854. It is the third light on the site; the first, built in about 1670, was one of four stone-vaulted cottage lights which had a coal-burning brazier on a platform on the roof.

KINSALE★★

POPULATION 2 007

Pretty little Kinsale (Cionn Tsáile), a designated Heritage Town on the broad estuary of the River Bandon, has had a long history as a harbour town, then as a favoured resort, with charming narrow lanes and neat Georgian houses stepping up the hillside overlooking the water. In recent years Kinsale has become particularly fashionable, with a gastronomic reputation which is celebrated annually with a food festival. *Pier Rd ☎ 021 4772234 (provisionally closed Sep-Apr)* *Ashe St, Clonakilty ☎ 023 33226 - www.corkkerry.ie*

▶ **Orient Yourself:** Kinsale, situated south of Cork city and Cork Airport, is easily reached by N 27 and R 600

Kids Especially for Kids: the West Cork Model Railway Village at Clonakilty and a swim at one of the many local beaches

⌚ **Also See:** COBH, CORK, SKIBBEREEN

A Bit of History

Kinsale was founded in the late 12C by the Anglo-Normans, but only really enters the history books in 1601 when a Spanish force occupied the town, a long way from their ally Hugh O'Neill, fighting the English in far-off Ulster. Kinsale was besieged by an English army, who were besieged in their turn by O'Neill after an exhausting march from the north. The combined Irish/Spanish forces should have easily defeated their enemy but the Spaniards watched from the walls as O'Neill was routed. This defeat marked the beginning of the end of the old Gaelic order and clan system; until the end of the 18C no native Irish were to settle within its 13C walls. In 1641 the town declared for Cromwell and so was spared much damage.

Kinsale at night

B Perousse/MICHELIN

Similar lack of success attended James II who landed at Kinsale in March 1689 in an attempt to regain his kingdom; after the Battle of the Boyne he returned to exile in France from Duncannon in Waterford Harbour.

During the 17C Kinsale flourished as a shipbuilding port for the Royal Navy, which constructed *HMS Kinsale* here in 1700. The 18C trend towards larger ships rendered the docks obsolete.

Visit

Kinsale Regional Museum★
Call for opening times. ☎ 021 4777930

The museum in the late-17C town hall with distinctive Dutch gables, has many relics of old Kinsale, including several royal charters. The great hall is associated with the famous inquest on the victims of the *Lusitania*. The exhibition room displays a variety of items: Kinsale-made lace which, like the Kinsale cloak, was popular for over a century; footwear and cutlery belonging to the Kinsale giant, **Patrick Cotter O'Brien** (1706–1806), who made a lucrative career on the English stage – who lived in Giant's Cottage *(private)* in Chairman's Lane.

St Multose Church (Anglican)★

The original church was built about 1190 and dedicated to St Multose or Eltin, the patron saint of Kinsale, who lived in the 6C. The massive square tower has a 12C Romanesque doorway with zig-zag decoration; a statue of St Multose stands in a niche over the west door. Inside are various interesting 16C tombstones.

Desmond Castle

(Dúchas) ⊙ *Open mid-Apr to Oct 10am-6pm. Last admission at 5.15pm.* ⊷ €2.75. ☎ 021 4774855

The three-storey tower house was built in the late 15C or early 16C by the Earls of Desmond as a custom-house. During the siege of Kinsale it served as a magazine; in 1641, it served as a gaol for French and other foreign prisoners. It now houses a **Museum of Wine** reflecting the days when Kinsale was a port, and highlights several Irish families connected with winemaking in France, Spain, Australia and the USA.

Excursion

Kinsale Harbour★

There is a pleasant walk *(1.5mi/2.4km)* along the east bank of the Bandon estuary to **Summercove** where English ships landed guns and supplies for their army during the siege of Kinsale (1601–02). From the graveyard of St Catherine's Anglican Church there are extensive **views**★ across the harbour.

Charles Fort★ *(up the hill)*, was begun about 1670 and remained in use until 1922. The vast star-shaped stronghold is a typical example of Baroque fortification, and is the largest structure of its date in Ireland. Many of the buildings surrounding the quadrangle of greensward are derelict but the old ordnance-store houses a good interpretive exhibition. From the fort there are extensive **views** of Kinsale harbour.

Lusitania

On the seabed *(12mi/19km S)* lies the wreck of the great transatlantic liner *Lusitania*, torpedoed by a German submarine on 7 May 1915 on her way from New York to Liverpool; her sinking changed the climate of opinion in the United States and prepared the way for the American declaration of war on Germany two years later. Among the 1 500 who lost their lives was Sir Hugh Lane, the wealthy art collector who established the Hugh Lane Gallery of Modern Art in Dublin.

Address Book

SIGHTSEEING

Historic Kinsale Walking Tours
- *Guided tours (1hr) from Apr-Oct, daily 11.15am. €6. Start from outside the Tourist Office.* ☎ 021 77 2873.

Kinsale Harbour Scenic Cruises
☎ *021 77 3188; www.kinsaleharbourcruises.com. €12. Cruises operate daily downstream past Summer Cove and Charles Fort to James Fort and Ringrone Castle and under the road bridge, turning for home at the bend in the River Bandon.*

🖑 *For coin ranges, see the Legend on the cover flap.*

WHERE TO STAY

☺ **Chart House** – *6 Denis Quay -* ☎ *021 477 4568; www.charthouse-kinsale. com. Closed at Christmas.* ⇥ *4 rm* 🛏. An elegant, cream-painted Georgian guesthouse with cosy, quaint ambience. Look for the William IV dining suite at breakfast and bedrooms that boast antique beds with crisp white linens.

☺ **Glebe Country House** – *Ballinadee -* ☎ *021 477 8294; Closed Christmas and New Year.* 🅿 ⇥ *4 rm* 🛏 *- Meals by arrangement* ☺🍽. The spacious gardens of this ivy-covered 17C former rectory provide many of the ingredients for the kitchen. A peaceful setting with the church steeple peeping over the trees. Individually decorated bedrooms with antiques aplenty.

☺ **Kilcaw Guesthouse** – *1mi E on R 600 -* ☎ *021 477 4155.* 🅿 ⇥ *7 rm* 🛏. A custom-built guesthouse in seven acres/3ha of land. The breakfast room has a farmhouse feel while the sitting room, with its open fireplace, offers a restful sanctuary. The pine furnished bedrooms are uniform in size.

☺ **Rivermount House** – *Barrells Cross – 0.5mi NE -* ☎ *021 477 8033.* 🕐 *Open Feb-Nov.* 🅿 ⇥ *6 rm* 🛏. This bungalow guesthouse in a quiet hillside spot enjoys sweeping views over the garden and the River Bandon. The owner will gladly provide packed lunches for those off to the beach, just a short drive away.

☺☺🍽 **Desmond House** – *42 Cork St -* ☎ *021 477 3575; www.desmondhouse-kinsale.com.* ⇥ *4 rm* 🛏. The owners of this centrally located Georgian townhouse are justifiably proud of the extensive breakfasts they lay on for their guests. Bedrooms are a good size and all come in a different colour.

WHERE TO EAT

☺ **Dalton's** – *3 Market St -* ☎ *021 477 7597.* 🕐 *Closed Good Fri, 2 weeks in Aug, and 25 Dec.* 🍴 The purple painted exterior is the first clue that this is no ordinary pub. The emphasis is firmly on the food with a menu that blends international influences garnered from the owner's experiences abroad.

☺ **Kinsale Gourmet Store and Seafood Bar** - *Guardwell -* ☎ *021 477 4453 -* 🕐 *Closed Sun Oct-Mar.* 🍴 *Bookings not accepted.* Half shop, half restaurant, this friendly, informal and busy seafood spot is fresh and full of fish, but be sure to arrive early or be prepared to queue. Choose your fish from an impressive selection behind the counter or from the menu and grab a seat inside or on the pavement terrace.

☺ **Max's** – *Main St -* ☎ *021 477 2443 -* 🕐 *Closed Nov-Mar and Tue.* 🍴 Sweet and intimate with exposed beams, wood flooring and a small conservatory extension. The menu has a discernible French accent and features carefully sourced local produce with deft use of herbs.

☺🍽 **Toddie's** - *Kinsale Brew Co, The Glen.* 🕐 *Closed 15 Jan-Mar and 25-26 Dec.* Relocated in 2005; now in a modern extension to a local brewery. Delightful terrace leads to a relaxed restaurant with lots of glass and artwork. Comprehensive modern menus

☺🍽 **The Vintage** – *Main St -* ☎ *021 477 2502; www.vintagerestaurant.ie.* 🕐 *Closed 2 Jan to 11 Feb, and Mon.* The oak beams add to the palpable sense of history while the cosy bar and candlelight add to the intimate atmosphere. The traditional menu features local produce and oysters are something of a house speciality.

SHOPPING

There is a wide variety of shops, selling craftwork of all kinds.

SPORTS AND LEISURE

Good facilities for yachting and deep-sea fishing.

EVENTS AND FESTIVALS

A **good food festival** is held in October when visitors sample the delights created by the international chefs of the Kinsale Good Food Circle or buy a day ticket to enjoy the many other local restaurants and pubs; reservations are scarce but can be booked on the Web in advance.

(Dúchas) 🚶🕐 *Open 10am-6pm (5pm Nov to mid-Mar). Last admission at 5.15pm.* ✆ *€3.50.* 🅿️☎ *021 772263*

The harbour was guarded on the west side by **James Fort** of 1604 *(cross the bridge over the Bandon River and turn left; 0.5mi/0.8km on foot from the carpark)* which is less well preserved than Charles Fort; only the central tower, blockhouse and portions of the defensive walls are still partially intact.

The harbour entrance is protected by the **Old Head of Kinsale** *(from the river bridge take R 600 W and R 604 S)*. On the top of

Kinsale Harbour

the headland stand the ruins of a 15C de Courcy fort. The road stops just short of the modern lighthouse, which replaced one built in 1683.

Driving Tour

Carbery Coast★ *38mi/61km W of Kinsale by R 600*

Timoleague★

The village on the Argideen estuary is dominated by a ruined **Franciscan friary**★, founded in 1320 and plundered by Oliver Cromwell in 1642. The extensive ruins include the cloisters and the outer yard, and the ruins of a 12C leper hospital.

Courtmacsherry★

3mi/5km detour E by R 601. This attractive village is a fine base for walking and deep-sea fishing; footpaths lead through the trees to Wood Point, or to a pebble beach at Broadstrand Bay.

▶ *From Timoleague take R 600 W. Before the junction with N 71, turn left (sign).*

Lios na gCon

☞ *Tours noon-4pm.* ✆ *€5.* 🅿️☎ *023 32565 (voicemail) / 08 77852238*

The 10C Ringfort of the Hound has been restored using evidence uncovered by archaeological excavations (1987–88). The souterrain is intact; the enclosing ditch and bank are well preserved and give a wide **view** of the surrounding country.

Clonakilty (Cloich na Coillte)

The market town, founded in 1598, is renowned for its Gaelic traditions and its **black puddings**, which were first produced in the 1880s by Philip Harrington at 16 Sovereign Street (now Pearse Street). The celebrated water pump, known as the Wheel of Fortune *(at the junction of Connolly St and Lamb St Lower)*, was provided by the Earl of Shannon in 1890.

The town centre is distinguished by **Emmet Square**, with its central garden and tall Georgian houses. Many renovated shopfronts have attractive Gaelic lettering.

The **West Cork Regional Museum**★, in the converted schoolhouse, traces local history with special emphasis on the War of Independence and on Michael Collins, who was born at Sam's Cross *(3mi/5km west)*. *Knock at the house next door if the museum is closed.* *Donation.* 023 33115

The **West Cork Model Railway Village**, which is set in the 1940s, is a delight for young children interested in following the trains round the track and learning about each station on the circuit. *Open Feb to Sep 10am-5pm; Christmas hols - phone to confirm.* *Village: €6.50; Village and train ride: €10.* 023 33224

The peninsula known as Inchydoney Island *(3mi/5km S by the causeway road)*, has a series of lovely sandy beaches; the large grass-covered spit of land jutting south into the sea is known as the "Virgin's Bank".

▷ *From Clonakilty take N 71 W.*

Rosscarbery

This small village at the head of a narrow inlet has an enormous quadrangular square and a much-restored 12C Romanesque building, **St Fachtna's Cathedral** (Anglican), with an elaborately-carved west doorway. That great evangeliser of the Germans, St Kilian was educated here at the monastic school, founded in AD 590 by St Fachtna, bishop and abbot, before setting out on his mission to Würzburg; two centuries later, that city repaid the compliment by sending one of its monks, St James, to found a Benedictine community in Rosscarbery.

▷ *From Rosscarbery take R 597 W towards Glandore; after 4mi/6.4km turn left to the Drombeg Circle (sign).*

Drombeg Stone Circle★

This is probably the most impressive of the 60 stone circles built in prehistoric times in west Cork. It has 14 evenly-spaced stones which form an enclosed circle (30ft/9m in diameter); usually the number of stones was uneven. Of similar antiquity is the nearby cooking pit.

▷ *Continue W on R 597 to Glandore.*

Glandore★

The original Irish name for this small village, Cuan Dor meaning the "harbour of the oaks", alludes to the days when extensive woodland covered much of west Cork. The semicircular harbour faces two minute islands in the estuary called Adam and Eve; old sailing directions told sailors to "avoid Adam and hug Eve".

▷ *Cross the river to Union Hall; take the road via Rineen to Castletownshend.*

Castletownshend★

The steep Main Street of this tiny village descends to the water's edge where a small pier offers fine views across the lovely Castle Haven estuary. **St Barrahane's Church** (Anglican) is attractively set at the top of four flights of steps *(50)* at the foot of the Main Street; the colourful Nativity Window was designed by Harry Clarke.

Somerville and Ross

Castletownshend in West Cork was once a stronghold of the Anglo-Irish Ascendancy: a perfect subject for the novelists Edith Somerville and Violet Martin, second cousins, known as **Somerville and Ross.** The successful of *Some Experiences of an Irish RM* (1899) prompted *Further Experiences of an Irish RM* (1908) and *In Mr Knox's Country* (1915). More serious issues appear in *The Real Charlotte* (1894); but *The Big House at Inver* (1925), written by Edith after Violet's death, is perhaps the best. Both lie buried in St Barrahane's Church graveyard.

KNOCK

POPULATION 575

Until the late 19C Knock (An Cnoc) was a quiet little village set on a wind-swept ridge in the middle of a vast and inhospitable bog. Today, it has become one of the world's great Marian shrines, attracting up to a million pilgrims a year, many of them during Knock Novena week in August, when the Statue of the Virgin is carried in procession in the grounds to celebrate the anniversary of the Apparition. 🛈 Knock Shrine ☎ 094 9388193 🛈 Ireland West Airport Knock ☎ 094 9368100 - www.irelandwest.ie

▶ **Orient Yourself:** Knock straddles the crossroads of N 17 and R 323, between Galway and Sligo in Co Mayo
🚬 **Don't Miss:** Museum of Country Life, Turlough Park
♨ **Also See:** BOYLE, CONG, SLIGO, STROKESTOWN, WESTPORT

Visit

Apparition Church
The south gable of the church where the apparition was seen is protected by glass, as early pilgrims used to take away pieces of the wall plaster, believing it to have miraculous powers.

Basilica of Our Lady, Queen of Ireland★
The huge hexagonal church (48 687sq ft/ 4 524m²), designed by Dáithí P Hanly to hold 12 000 people, was consecrated in 1976. The external ambulatory has 12 pillars of red Mayo granite and 32 pillars of stone from each of the 32 counties of Ireland. Inside, hangs a large Donegal hand-knotted tapestry of the apparition designed by Ray Carroll. The central space accommodates the high altar; the rest is divided into five chapels dedicated to the Sacred Heart, St John the Evangelist, Our Lady of Knock, St Joseph and St Columba. The partition walls hold replica church windows from each of the four provinces of Ireland.

GETTING ABOUT

Ireland West Airport Knock, *Charlestown, Co Mayo. 9mi/14.5km northeast of Knock by N 17 – ☎ 094 9368100; www.knockairport.com.*

SHOPPING
Foxford Woollen Mill - *(see below).*

SPORTS AND LEISURE
Castlebar International 4 days Walks – *Held late Jun-early July; www.castlebar4dayswalks.com.*

Apparition at Knock

One wet August evening in 1879 two village women said they saw Mary, Joseph and St John bathed in light against the south gable of the church. Others were called to share the vision. A church commission examined the witnesses and accepted their account. Pilgrims came in droves, miracles happened. In 1957 the church was affiliated to the Basilica of St Mary Major in Rome and special indulgences are granted to pilgrims. On the centenary of the apparition, Pope John Paul II paid the first papal visit to Ireland.

Folk Museum

&🕐 *Open May to Oct 10am-6pm; Nov to Apr noon-4pm.* 🕐 *Closed 25-26 Dec.* ∞ *€4.* 🖼🅿☏ *094 9388100 - www.knock-shrine.ie*

A modern building, bearing the shields of the four provinces of Ireland – Ulster, Connaught, Leinster, Munster – houses a well-presented display illustrating life in the west of Ireland in the 19C; the development of the Knock shrine; the Papal visit in 1979 and the life and achievements of Mgr James Horan, parish priest (1963–87).

Driving Tour

Inland Mayo *Round trip of 86mi/139km*

▶ *From Knock take R 323 N via Kiltimagh; in Bohola turn left onto N 5 to Turlough.*

Museum of Country Life★★

🕐 *Open Tue- Sun 10am (2pm Sun)-5pm.* 🕐 *Closed Mon, Good Fri, 25 Dec.* 🖼🅿☏ *094 90 31773/64 86292 - www.museum.ie*

Some 50 000 items from the National Museum's collections are displayed in the Victorian Gothic mansion and a stunning, purpose-built structure cleverly blended with the terraced landscape of Turlough Park. The richly varied collections eschew any hint of sentimentality to present traditional life in the Irish countryside until the late 20C. The displays address the physical realities of the countryside, the unremitting cycle of work, the home, the role of women, the community, folklife and folklore. The imposing ruin of a medieval Fitzgerald stronghold guards the approach to the park. The hilltop on the far bank of the Castlebar River is marked by a fine round tower and a roofless church marking the site of a monastery founded by St Patrick.

▶ *Continue W on N 5.*

Castlebar

The county town and commercial centre of Mayo on the Castlebar River was the place where the French General Humbert and his Irish peasant allies put a far superior British force to ignominious flight (1798), an event gleefully referred to as the "Castlebar Races". John Moore, the leader of the short-lived "Republic of Connaught", died in prison; he is buried by the 1798 memorial in **The Mall**.

▶ *From Castlebar take L 134 N; on the outskirts of the town turn left onto the minor road towards Burren and Windy Gap. Continue N and turn left onto R 315; 3mi/5km beyond Lahardaun turn right.*

Errew Abbey★

20min there and back on foot across the fields.

The few ruins of an Augustinian abbey (1413) enjoy a picturesque **site** on a spit of land pointing into Lough Conn. A 13C church with trefoil windows pre-dates the cloister buildings.

▶ *Return through Lahardaun and continue S on R 315; turn left in Pontoon. Continue E to R 318, and turn right.*

Foxford

The **Woollen Mills** were set up by Mother Arsenius of the Irish Sisters of Charity in 1890 and established the thriving mill. The nuns are no more, but the famous Foxford blankets, rugs and tweeds continue to be commercial. An audio-visual presentation about the history of the mill is followed by a tour of the obsolete machinery (1930s) and a view of the carding, spinning, weaving, mending, washing and drying involved

Michael Davitt (1846–1906)

Davitt was born during the Great Famine. When aged four, his family was evicted for non-payment of rent and emigrated to Lancashire in England. Five years later, he was working in a woollen mill; a bad accident there meant his right arm had to be amputated. He went to a Wesleyan School; at 16 he was employed in a printing business, following evening classes in Irish history at the Mechanics' Institute. He joined the Fenian movement, rose to be secretary in Northern England and Scotland until he was arrested and imprisoned for seven years for smuggling arms.

He returned to Co Mayo (1878) and helped tenants to get better treatment from the landlords. Then he persuaded Parnell to join the movement, and the Mayo Land League was formed in Daly's Hotel in Castlebar on 16 August 1879. The Irish National Land League was formed in October. During the ensuing Land War, Davitt and others were arrested under the Coercion Act (1881). On his release, Davitt abandoned the spotlight to work as a reformer, teacher, writer and social thinker, defending the rights of agricultural labourers and trade unionism. He helped to form the GAA and travelled widely. His books – *Leaves from a Prison Diary* (1885), *The Fall of Feudalism in Ireland* (1904), and other writings examine working conditions in Australia and South Africa.

in production. 🐾 *Tour (self-guided) May to Oct 10am (noon Sun) to 6pm; Nov-Apr 10am (2pm Sun) -6pm. Last tour at 5.30pm.* 🎫 €9. ✕ 🅿 ☎ 094 925 6756

▶ *Take N 58 S.*

Strade

The Pre-penal church houses the **Michael Davitt Memorial Museum**, devoted to the life of the founder of the Land League, born and buried in Strade: on display are documents, memorabilia, books by and about Davitt who was elected to Parliament four times and used his position to advocate prison reform. ♿🕐 *Open 10am-6pm.* 🎫 €3.20. 🅿 ☎ 094 903 1022

▶ *Continue on N 58, turn left onto N 5; in Bohola turn right onto R 321; in Kiltimagh take R 323 to return to Knock.*

LIMERICK★★

POPULATION 52 039

Astride the River Shannon at its lowest fording point, Limerick (Luimneach) is the main administrative and commercial centre of the mid-west region and the fourth largest city in Ireland. Its three historic quarters are still quite distinct: medieval Englishtown on King's Island defending by one of the most formidable castles in Ireland, Irishtown, forming the modern city centre, and the Georgian district of Newtown Pery, laid out on a grid pattern during the 18C. The atmosphere created by a particularly turbulent past, with extremes of wealth and poverty, marked Limerick deeply but today the city, with its recently established (1972) university, modern industries and proximity to Shannon Airport is a much more welcoming place. 🛈 *Arthurs Quay* ☎ 061 317 522 🛈 *Shannon Airport* ☎ 061 471 664

▶ **Orient Yourself:** Limerick on the River Shannon stands at the junction of N 7 from Dublin, N 24 from Waterford, N 18 from Galway, N 20 from Cork, N 21 from Tralee and N 69 which leads along the south shore of the Shannon Estuary.

Don't Miss: the Hunt Museum and an excursion to Bunratty Castle

Also See: ADARE, ENNIS, KILLALOE, KILRUSH

A Bit of History

City of Sieges – In 922 Vikings from Denmark sailed up the Shannon, landed at Great Quay *(now Long Dock)*, and established a base on King's Island from which they plundered the rich agricultural hinterland. For over a century the town was repeatedly attacked by Irish forces until Brian Ború, High King of Ireland, sacked it and banished the settlers. In 1194, the Normans seized control of the region, raising the great fortress of King John's Castle, building city walls, and peppering the countryside with hundreds of strongholds.

In 1642 Limerick was besieged by the Cromwellians, followed by a more momentous one after the Battle of the Boyne in July 1690, when James II had fled to France and the defeated Jacobites withdrew to Limerick. Eventually, under the bold leadership of Patrick Sarsfeld, the Williamites abandoned their siege at the end of August. The following year another Williamite army led by General Ginkel returned to the attack while an English fleet blocaded the Shannon; Sarsfield sued for peace: this was granted on surprisingly generous terms by the **Treaty of Limerick**. The Irish were given safe conduct to France and Roman Catholics in general were guaranteed various rights and privileges, including the freedom to practise their religion. Ratification of the treaty by the Irish Parliament was, however, only partial and the Penal Laws enacted from 1695 were seen by Roman Catholics as a betrayal.

18C to 20C – Despite a considerable agrarian revolt in the region in the 18C, the City Corporation decided that Limerick no longer needed to be fortified, so most of the city walls were demolished (1760). The 18C also marked the last flowering of the old Irish culture: as the Great Famine and subsequent emigration, devastated the local population in the 1840s, Gaelic ceased to be the vernacular language of Limerick.

In the early 20C, the city and county became strongholds of nationalism and working-class radicalism. Three of the leaders of the 1916 Easter Rising came from the Limerick district, including **Eamon de Valera** (1882-1975), Prime Minister *(Taoiseach)* and President of the Republic. In 1919, at the start of the three-year War of Independence, a general strike took place to protest against British military rule. In more recent years, Limerick has been twinned with Slovenia.

Limerick Lace

The craft was introduced to Limerick in the 1820s by English lacemakers and reached its peak in the 19C when 900 girls were employed locally. The elaborate Celtic patterns were outlined on machine-made cotton net in thin or thick thread and filled in with decorative stitches

Walking Tour

As **King's Island** was almost encircled by the Shannon and the Abbey River, it was an obvious site for the Vikings and Normans to establish their settlements.

St Mary's Cathedral★
The transitional Romanesque Anglican cathedral, founded in 1168 by Dónall Mór O'Brien, King of Munster, is the oldest surviving building in Limerick, with parts of the king's palace incorporated in the original cruciform church.

The 15C black oak choir stalls and splendid carved misericords are unique in Ireland; the high altar reredos was carved by the English father of Patrick Pearse; the north transept contains the fine 15C **Arthur Memorial** *(below the window)* commemorating the cathedral Treasurer Geoffrey Arthur (d 1519), and a small rectangular lepers' squint *(right);* the south transept contains the 15C Galway-Bultingfort tomb.

Address Book

GETTING ABOUT

Shannon International Airport
– ☎ 061 712 000; www.shannonairport.
com.

SIGHTSEEING

Walking Tours – Historical tour
and *Angela's Ashes* tour, based on the
popular novel by Frank McCourt about
the wretched life of the poor in Limerick
during his childhood. Depart from
Arthur's Quay. €6. Call for times.☎ 061
327 108; www.visitlimerick.com.
*For coin ranges, see the Legend on the
cover flap.*

WHERE TO STAY

☻ **Carrig House** – *2 Meadowvale,
Raheen – 2.75mi SW by N 20* – ☎ 061
309 626; www.geocities.com/robertbra-
zil2004/index.htm. Closed 24-26 Dec. P
3 rm. This affordable and immaculately
kept, purpose-built guesthouse offers
compact but colourfully decorated
bedrooms, all with en-suite showers.
The welcoming owner runs a friendly
and welcoming house.

☻ **Clifton House** – *Ennis Rd – 1.25mi
NW on R 587* – ☎ 061 451 166. Closed
21 Dec to 2 Jan. P 16 rm. Simple but
well-priced accommodation in this uniformly decorated house perched on an
elevated position out of town. Guests
can make use of the large garden and
there are family rooms available.

☻ **Clonmacken House** – *Clonmacken
Rd, off Ennis Rd – 2.5mi NW by N 18* turning right at Clonmacken roundabout - ☎
061 327 007. P 10 rm. Five minutes from
the city centre and a useful modern
guesthouse. Pretty little garden, a fairly
quiet position and a well-kept house.
Family runs available.

☻☻ **Jurys Inn Limerick** – *Lower
Mallow St* - ☎ 061 207 000; http://limer-
ickhotels.jurysdoyle.com. Closed 24-26
Dec. ♿ 151 rm - Restaurant ☻☻. While
it may be a branded group hotel, it is in
an excellent location and bedrooms are
competitively priced and all a good size.
Some even overlook the River Shannon;
those at the rear are quietest.

WHERE TO EAT

☻ **Brûlées** – *Corner Mallow/Henry St*
- ☎ 061 319 931 - ⏰ *Closed Sun, Mon,
25 Dec to Jan 1*. Split between three
floors of a Georgian house, with the
aproned owner providing the attentive
service and his wife the cooking, which
emphasises local produce. Plenty of
daily specials and local fish.

TAKING A BREAK

Dolans – *Dock Road* - ☎ 061 314 483
- www.dolanpub.com – ⏰ *Open daily
from 8am*. Probably the best known pub
in the region. It offers a fairly comprehensive menu of assorted seafood but
what really draws the crowds is the live
music at the end of the week, a variety
of traditional and folk.

Schooners – *Steamboat Quay, Dock
Road* - ☎ 061 318 147 – ⏰ *Open
daily from 8am*. Boasts a super location
beside the Shannon; make use of the
terrace in summer to watch the boats
go by. The bar's a favourite with the
locals and live concerts are held at the
end of the week.

ENTERTAINMENT

Belltable Arts Centre – ☎ 061 319 866;
www.belltable.ie. ⏰ *Open daily, 9am-
6pm*. Host to various theatre productions.

Savoy Cineplex – *Bedford Row* - ☎ 061
311 900. Five screens.

SHOPPING

Arthur's Quay Shopping Centre
– *Arthur's Quay* - ☎ 061 419 888
- ⏰ *Open Mon-Sat, 8.30am-8pm (10pm
Thu-Fri) and Sun, 12am-6pm*. Housing
more than 30 stores, this centre has
several boutiques where you will find
hand-knit and machine-made sweaters
and clothing by Irish designers in linen,
tweed and cotton.

Limerick Lace is now rare, though a
few still hand-make the delicate fabric
on request. ☎ 061 303 871 (Eileen
Brown)

Irish Dresden – Factory tours of the
production of the porcelain figures and
a sales shop.

Sarsfield's Ride

A gentleman of Old English, Catholic descent, **Patrick Sarsfield** showed daring and effective generalship. In early August 1690, acting on information from a deserter, he slipped out of the city with 600 cavalry, and headed north, then east, fording the Shannon upstream of Killaloe Bridge, which was held by the Williamites. After travelling south through the Silvermine Mountains, he intercepted the Williamite siege train at Ballyneety *(18mi/30km south of Limerick);* the noise of its destruction reached the city. With this coup Sarsfield had bought time but not victory. After negotiating the Treaty of Limerick he and 10 000 Irish soldiers known as "Wild Geese", left for France. Sarsfield died in battle in 1693, fighting for Louis XIV.

Farther along Nicholas Street are the remains of the **Old Limerick Exchange**, built in 1673: seven Tuscan columns, bricked up to form a wall.

▶ *Turn down Bridge St and cross Mathew Bridge.*

Hunt Museum★★

 ⏱ *Open 10am (2pm Sun)-5pm.* ⌵ *€5.*
⛶✆ *061 312 833 - www.huntmuseum.com*
The 18C Custom House designed by Italian architect Davis Duchart provides a fitting home for this outstanding collection of art and antiquities amassed during the life of John and Gertrude Hunt. The expertly selected items span every age and include works of every scale. Highlights include the wooden carved *Apollo – Genius of the Arts*, a small bronze *Horse*, attributed to Leonardo da Vinci, and a startling self-portrait by Robert Fagan (c.1745–1816), a painter of the English school and dealer in antiquities in Rome. The archaeological collection is drawn from ancient civilisations in Egypt, Greece and Rome, and compared with Irish treasures such as the Cashel Bell and Antrim Cross; a Jewellery Gallery displays the Mary Queen of Scots Cross. Religious Art is dramatically exhibited in the Treasury: among the silver and precious stones is a Greek coin, traditionally thought to be one of the "Thirty Pieces of Silver".

17C Italian mould blown emerald green glass jug with gilt metal mounts

Hunt Museum

▶ *Walk over the pedestrian bridge, past the County Court House (1809) and back to Nicholas St.*

Limerick Museum/Jim Kemmy Municipal Museum★

 ⏱ *Open Tue-Sat 10am-1pm, 2.15pm-7pm.* ⏱ *Closed Bank Hols.* ✆ *061 417 826*
The museum in Castle Lane gives a comprehensive account of the city and its history. An excellent collection of 18C silver, tambour, needlepoint and tape **lace** recall important Limerick crafts. The brass-topped limestone **Nail** from the Old Exchange was used to settle commercial transactions - hence the expression "paying on the Nail". Finds from excavations in the Abbey River are also displayed.

King John's Castle

King John's Castle★

  Open Mar-Oct 9.30am-5.30pm; Nov-Feb 10am-4.30pm; Mar-Apr 9.30am-5pm. Last admission 1hr before closing. ◐ *Closed Good Fri, 24-26 Dec.* €8.35. ☎ 061 360788 - www.shannonheritage.com

The castle by Thomond Bridge, was once the most important Norman stronghold in the west. It remains a fine example of medieval fortification (1200-16): Instead of a keep, it has massive round towers protecting the gateway; the walls would have been taller to withstand contemporary siege machines, but in 1611, the towers and the wall-walks were lowered to accommodate cannon, and the diamond-shaped gun bastion was added. The repairs carried out after General Ginkel's assault (1691) are still visible from Thomond Bridge. The history of the castle and the city is retold in the modern **visitor centre**.

Reproductions of war engines are displayed in the courtyard. The sentry walk on the battlements provides good views of the Shannon, the city and its surroundings.

Bishop's Palace

The oldest-surviving dwelling in Limerick, was designed in the Palladian style by Francis Bindon (c 1690–1765), a native of Limerick. It now houses the Limerick Civic Trust. ◐ *Open by arrangement.* ☎ 061 313 399 - www.limerickcivictrust.ie

Limerick is unusual in having two sets of almshouses: the **Villiers Almshouses** (1826), north of the castle, were built in the Bishop's Palace garden by James Pain for 12 poor Protestant widows with an annual income of £24. The **Corporation Almshouses**, also known as the 40-shilling (£2) Almshouses for 20 widows were erected by the Limerick Corporation in 1691.

Thomond Bridge

The Gothic-style **Toll House** with castellated parapets dates from 1839 when the bridge was rebuilt.

The **Treaty Stone** *(on the west bank of the river)*, is a block of limestone on which the 1691 Treaty of Limerick is said to have been signed; it was moved here in 1865 from outside Black Bull Pub, where it had been used as a mounting-block.

Visit

The old Irish quarter on the south bank of Abbey River, outside the walls of the English town, now forms the **town centre** of modern Limerick. The district to the south is a fine example of 18C town planning with broad parallel streets lined with **red-brick terraces** – named **Newtown Pery** after Edmond Sexton Pery (1719–1806), Speaker of the Irish House of Commons.

People's Park

The focal point of the Newtown Pery district was built by the Pery Tontine Company in 1838. The **Georgian House**★ at No 2 Pery Square has been restored as a splendid example of Georgian architecture and décor. The **Ashes Exhibition** in recalls the filming of the popular novel *Angela's Ashes* by Frank McCourt portraying the wretched life led by the poor in Limerick during the 1950s. ♿⏱ *Open Mon-Fri 10am-4.30pm (last admission).* ⊛ *€5. Ashes Exhibit by arrangement.* ☎ *061 314130.*

The newly extended **Limerick City Gallery of Art**, once the Carnegie Library, now houses a growing collection of leading 18C-20C Irish art (Sean Keating, Jack B Yeats and Evie Hone) and visiting exhibitions. ♿⏱ *Open Mon-Fri 10am-6pm (7pm Fri), Sat 10am-1pm.* ☎ *061 310 633*

At **St Saviour's Dominican Church**, stands the 17C statue of Our Lady of Limerick, brought from Flanders in 1640 and presented to the Dominicans as a mark of atonement by a Limerick merchant, whose uncle had sentenced Sir John Burke to death for allowing a priest to say Mass during a time of severe religious persecution.

Milk Market

The open area, on the corner of Ellen Street and Wickham Street, accommodates a bustling Saturday market, where home-grown local produce has been traded since 1830: as a result it is the gourmet area of Limerick. **William Street** and **O'Connell Street** are prime shopping areas: the **Franciscan Church** (1876-86) with its fine Corinthian portico, was extended in 1930 with a richly decorated apse.

John Square★

The square, laid out in 1751, is bordered by terraces of three-storey houses once occupied by the wealthy citizens. On the fourth side, stands **St John's Church** (1843). The neo-Gothic Roman Catholic **St John's Cathedral**★ on the edge of what was the old Irish town dates from 1861. The spire (280ft/85m), completed in 1883, is the tallest in Ireland.

Excursions

Cratloe Woods House

5mi/8km W by N 18. ♿⏱ *Open Jun to mid-Sep 2-6pm by appointment.* ⊛ *€5.* ☎ *061 327 028*

The house (1600) is a rare example of the Irish long house, albeit altered. The interior displays furniture and fascinating souvenirs of the owners, direct descendants of Brian Ború and the O'Briens, the leading family of the region.

Cratloe Wood at the foot of Woodcock Hill incorporates a lake and forest walks.

Bunratty Castle★★

7mi/11km W by N 18. ♿☕ *Guided tours Apr to Oct 9am-5.30pm (6pm Jun-Aug); Dec to Jan 9.30am-5.30pm. Last admission 45min before closing; last tour at 4pm.* ⏱ *Closed Good Fri, 24-26 Dec.* ⊛ *€13; Medieval banquet €51.95; Irish nights €43.25.* ☎ *061 361 511 - www.shannonheritage.com*

The most splendid **tower house** in Ireland commands a formidable position on the main road between Limerick and Ennis, at the point where the Bunratty River flows into the Shannon Estuary. It was built in 1460 by the powerful O'Brien family on the site of earlier fortifications. In the 1950s, it was restored to its 16C state to display the superb Gort collection of furniture and tapestries from the 14C-17C. In the evenings medieval-style banquets are held in the Great Hall which has a fine **oak roof**.

The **Folk Park** is a wonderful and very convincing re-creation of country life at the turn of the century when traditional practices were dying out. There is a blacksmith's forge, flour mill and houses of different regional types - a mountain farmhouse and a more elaborate thatched Golden Vale farmhouse. The **village** contains 19C shops:

a pawnbroker, pub, post office, hardware shop, grocery store, draper's and printing workshop equiped with hand-set type and a hand-operated press.

Bunratty House, built in 1804, is a local adaptation of the Georgian box house so common in Ireland. In its farmyard is displayed the **Talbot Collection of agricultural machinery**.

Driving Tour

Maigue Valley

▶ *From Limerick take R 512 S; after 8.5mi/13.6km bear left.*

Lough Gur

Set among low hills, horseshoe-shaped Lough Gur is the largest water body in Co Limerick. The area around the lake is one of the longest-inhabited districts in Ireland, with an exceptional wealth of stone circles, standing stones, burial chambers and cairns. Artefacts, relics and models of stone circles and burial chambers, are on display in the thatched hut housing the **Lough Gur Interpretive Centre**★, which also screens a video illustrating the life of Neolithic people in this region. ⌖◷ *Open May to mid-Sep 10am-6pm.* ⬤ *€4.75.* ☎ *061 361 511 - www.shannonheritage.com*

▶ *Return to T-junction; turn left into R 512; continue S via Holycross and Bruff.*

Kilmallock★

Kilmallock developed around the 7C abbey founded by St Mocheallog, to become the seat of the Fitzgeralds and a pre-eminent town in the province of Munster, with town walls, a castle and four gates. In 1568 it was burnt down to prevent it from being taken by the English; a century later, after Cromwell's departure, its extensive walls had gone and many of its buildings lay in ruins; it suffered again in the Williamite wars and never regained its former status.

By the river stand the ruins of the 13C Dominican **Kilmallock Abbey**★. A fine transept window and part of the tower (90ft/27m high) survive. At the entrance to the abbey is a small town **museum**. ◷ *Open 11am-3pm.* ☎ *063 91300*

The walls and arches of the nave and south transept of the 13C Roman Catholic **Collegiate Church**★, dedicated to St Peter and St Paul, are largely intact; the

Kilmallock's Poet

In the 18C a rustic school of Gaelic poetry flourished along the banks of the River Maigue and its tributary the Loobagh. Aindrias Mac Craith, a hedge schoolmaster and versatile versifier who died in 1795 in the 15C house by the bridge in Kilmallock and is buried in the graveyard of the Collegiate Church, was possibly jointly responsible for the invention of the limerick; in playful poetic conflict with a fellow-poet and tavern-keeper, one Seán Ó Tuama, he wrote

O'Toomey! You boast yourself handy
At selling good ale and brandy,
But the fact is your liquor
Makes everyone sicker
I tell you that, I, your friend Andy.

tower is part of an ancient round tower. A substantial section of the medieval **Town Walls** can be seen between the Collegiate Church and **Blossom's Gate** - the only one of five still standing. The **King's Castle**, a 15C tower house, occupies the site of an earlier fortress built to guard the Loobagh valley. During the Parliamentary Wars (1645–51) it was used as an arsenal by the Irish and later as a hospital by the Cromwellians.

▶ *From Kilmallock take R 518 W to Bruree.*

Eamon de Valera

Eamon de Valera (1882-1975), born in New York to a Spanish father and Irish mother, was largely brought up by his uncle near Kilmallock. De Valera was imprisoned by the British, but escaped execution after the 1916 Rising because of his American birth; he was later spared by the Free State authorities after siding with the Republicans in the Civil War. He founded the Fianna Fáil party in 1926, became Prime Minister *(Taoiseach)* in 1932, and kept Ireland neutral in the Second World War. Between 1959 and 1973 he served as President of the Republic, steadfastly nationalist in his politics but conservative when deciding how Ireland should develop .

Bruree

The **De Valera Museum** in the old national school in between the ancient six-arch bridge over the River Maigue and the old mill celebrates the former President of the Republic with displays of his school copy-books and a desk carved with his initials.
&⚿🕐 *Open 10am (2pm Sun)-5pm. Confirm in advance.* ☎ *063 91300/90530*

▷ *From Bruree take the minor road N; in Athlacca bear left to Croom; take the minor road E to Monaster.*

Monasteranenagh Abbey★

The impressive ruins beside the River Camoge are those of a Cistercian monastery, colonised by monks from Mellifont, founded in the 12C by Turlough O'Brien, King of Thomond, as a mark of thanksgiving for defeating the Danes in the Battle of Rathmore in 1148.

"Crom Abu"

The battle cry of the Earls of Kildare derives from their castle at Croom on the River Maigue.

LISMORE★

POPULATION 715

No bigger than a village but a designated Heritage Town, this idyllic little place on the banks of the salmon-rich River Blackwater was once a great centre of medieval learning. It still has a cathedral, but the dominant landmark is the Romantic castle overlooking the lovely wooded valley. ⓘ *Lismore Heritage Centre* ☎ *058 54975 - www.discoverlismore.com*

▷ **Orient Yourself:** Lismore (Lios Mór) is situated on the south bank of the River Blackwater on N 72 between Dungarvan and Fermoy, in Co Waterford
⚿ **Also See:** CAHER, CLONMEL, COBH, CORK, MALLOW, MIDLETON, YOUGHAL

A Bit of History

The monastery founded by **St Carthach** in the 7C became one of Europe's most distinguished universities with some 20 seats of learning and religion until 978, when the Danish Vikings raided the town and burned the monasteries. Lismore was still sufficiently important, however, for Henry II to receive the submission of Irish chiefs here soon after his landing in Ireland in 1171. A prosperous town developed around the castle built by King John (1185), which passed to Sir Walter Ralegh in 1589, and sold to Richard Boyle, the "Great" Earl of Cork.

The present castle *(private)* was eventually rebuilt in spectacular style by Sir Joseph Paxton of Crystal Palace fame and gardener to the Duke of Devonshire, the castles's new proprietor. It is a theatrical neo-Tudor fantasy looking out over the park-like valley of the River Blackwater with a bridge by the Dublin architect Thomas Ivory. In the mid-20C thie castle was home to Adele Astaire, sister of the great dancer Fred, and wife to the then owner Lord Charles Cavendish. In 2000 the town was given a new park

Visit

Lismore Castle Gardens★
&⊙ *Open Apr-Sep 1.45pm (11am Jun-Aug) to 4.45pm.* ⊛ €6. ⌦ ⚹ 🅿 ☏ *058 54424*
The gardens, divided into two sections, comprise the 17C walled garden and the lower garden. Traditionally, it was here that Spenser may have composed part of *The Faerie Queene*. The lower garden, known as the Pleasure Grounds was laid out c 1850, although the Yew Walk is much older. Yew, beech and box hedges screen flower and vegetables beds; Paxton's greenhouses date from 1858. The Broghill Tower *(SW corner)* provides a fine view. Contemporary sculpture (Anthony Gormley, Emily Young, David Nash, Marzia Colonna) add a modern twist to these immaculate gardens owned by the Cavendish family.

St Carthage's Cathedral (Anglican)★
Surrounded by a picturesque graveyard shaded by yews and lime-trees, the parish church is somehow redolent of Lismore's long history. The existing building, the fourth on the site, is largely the result of a rebuild ordered by Sir Richard Boyle in 1633; the **ribbed ceilings** were added by Sir Richard Morrison (c 1820), and the fine **tower** and **ribbed spire** (1826) by the Payne brothers of Cork. Note the fine stained-glass window donated by Sir Edward Burne-Jones, the pebbles from the Isle of Iona (Scotland) in the floor of St Columba's Chapel; the elaborate **table-tomb** of 1548.

St Carthach's Church (Roman Catholic)
Designed by WG Doolin in 1881, this is one of the most outstanding Lombardo-Romanesque churches in Ireland, richly detailed and built of red sandstone with white limestone dressings and a detached bell-tower.
Facing the west entrance to the church is a fine row of 19C artisans' cottages.

Lismore Heritage Centre
⊙ *Open Mon-Fri 9.30am-5.30pm, Sat-Sun 10am (noon Sun)-5.30pm. Video show.* ⊛ €4. ☏ *058 54975*
The Old Courthouse provides a history of Lismore and the life and works of Robert Boyle, the father of modern chemistry, who was born in Lismore Castle.

Excursions

The Gap★
10mi/16km N by R 688.
Beyond the Blackwater valley, rise the Old Red Sandstone Knockmealdown Mountains (2608ft/795m). The Lismore-Caher road follows the lush valley before climbing to the scenic V Gap with its magnificent **views**★. On the north slopes of Sugar Loaf mountain (2 144ft/653m) stands **Grubb's Grave**, the burial cairn of a local Quaker called Samuel Grubb who died in the 1920s; the sugar-loaf construction enabled him to be buried upright overlooking his estates.

Mount Melleray Abbey

8mi/13km NE by N 72, R 669 and a minor road right. &🕐 *Open daily.* ✆ *Donation*
🅿 ✆ *058 54 404 - www.mountmellerayabbey.com*

The Cistercian monastery on the lower slopes of the Knockmealdowns facing the Blackwater valley, was founded in 1832 for Irish Trappist monks from Melleray in France; the community is devoted to prayer and pursues numerous crafts. Only part of the church is open to the public.

LONGFORD

POPULATION 6 393

The market centre for the surrounding agricultural area, Longford (An Longfort) lies on the Camlin River amid the pleasant but undistinguished scenery of its county, a few miles from where the Shannon broadens out into Lough Ree. Co Longford has important literary associations with Oliver Goldsmith (Lough Ree) and Maria Edgeworth (at Mostrim), and it was at Ballinamuck (10mi/16km north) that the last engagement of the 1798 rebellion was fought, when General Humbert's French troops and Irish volunteers were defeated by the English forces under General Lake. 🛈 *Dublin St* ✆ *043 46566 (seasonal) - www.longford-tourism.com*

▶ **Orient Yourself:** Longford stands on the road (N 4) between Dublin and Sligo
🔥 **Also See:** ATHLONE, CARRICK-ON-SHANNON, MULLINGAR, STROKESTOWN

Visit

St Mel's Cathedral

Longford's principle landmark is the monumental neo-Classical Roman Catholic cathedral with its vast Ionic portico supporting a richly sculpted pediment and tall octagonal bell-tower capped with a dome – designed by John Keane (1840).

The greatest treasure of the **Diocesan Museum** *(right transept)* is **St Mel's Crozier** (10C), a stick of yew encased in

---

LOCAL ART

Michael Casey, Barley Harbour, Newtowncashel – Artist in bog-woods, tree roots uncovered during peat-harvesting; several of his works stand round the village green in Newtown Cashel on the east bank of Lough Ree.

Maria Edgeworth

Maria Edgeworth (1767-1849) was the eldest daughter of Richard Lovell Edgeworth, a wealthy eccentric with an interest in science who had four wives and 22 children, and who installed heating in Tullynally Castle. She is best remembered as a pioneer of regional and historical novels: *Castle Rackrent* (1800), *The Absentee* (1812) and *Ormond* (1817) are about Irish life. In her day her influence was acknowledged by Jane Austen, Macaulay, Ruskin, Thackeray, Turgenev and Sir Walter Scott. Apart from a few school years in England, she spent her whole life at the family home in Mostrim, also known as Edgeworthstown *(8.5mi/14km east)*, where her circle included the Pakenhams of Tullynally and the Lefroys of Carrigglas.

Dúchas, Dublin

Corlea Trackway

bronze inset with studs and decorated with animal motifs, foliage and interlacing, found at old St Mel's Church in Ardagh in 1860.

Excursions

Carrigglas Manor Hotel
3mi/5km E of Longford by R 194.
The castellated neo-Gothic mansion was built in 1837 for Thomas Lefroy, Lord Chief Justice of Ireland and youthful admirer of Jane Austen, who may have used him as the model for the hero of *Pride and Prejudice,* Mr Darcy.
The woodland garden, planted with a rich variety of species, was inspired by the great Victorian designer, William Robinson.

Ardagh
7mi/11km SE of Longford by N 4 and R 393.

Goldsmith Country

The country around Lough Ree is where the poet, playwright, historian and naturalist **Oliver Goldsmith** (c 1731–74) spent the first 20 or so years of his life, visiting relatives and going to school in Elphin, Mostrim, Athlone and Lissoy.

In **Ardagh** he experienced the plot of his play *She Stoops to Conquer*, by mistaking the big house for the village inn. The site of his first boyhood home at **Pallas** is marked by a statue by Foley. Until 1731 his father was Rector of **Forgney** church, which contains a stained-glass window depicting "sweet Auburn".

After her husband's death in 1747, Goldsmith's mother lived in **Ballymahon** on the Inny River. It was in **Tang** that Goldsmith first went to school near the mill. The pub, known as **The Three Jolly Pigeons**, preserves the name of the inn in Goldsmith's play *She Stoops to Conquer.*

Lissoy Parsonage, now in ruins, was the house where the Goldsmith family lived from 1731 to 1747; **Lissoy** village is recalled as "sweet Auburn" in his poem *The Deserted Village.*

The charming little estate village was largely rebuilt in the 1860s by Lady Fetherstone, who lived at Ardagh House. The ruins of a simple stone church, St Mel's Cathedral, are said to stand on the site where the saint, a nephew of St Patrick, was buried. The **Ardagh Heritage Centre** traces the history of the locality from the pre-Christian era, through the internal rivalries of the local O'Farrell tribe and the 1619 Plantation to the present. 🕓 *Open Mon -Sat 9.30am-5.30pm* 🕓 *Closed Bank Hols* ☎043 42577

Corlea Trackway

10mi/16km S of Longford by N 63 and R 397; in Kenagh turn right (sign). (Dúchas)♿🕓 *Open Mon-Sat 10am-6pm. Last admission at 5.15pm.* ⊛ €4. ⌑ 🅿 ☎ *043 22386*
The ancient trackway *(togher)*, dating from 147-8 BC consists of a series of oak planks secured by pegs, wide enough to carry wheeled vehicles across the bog, sinking under the weight over time. A section of the preserved timber trackway is displayed under cover, while the story of its discovery in the 1980s and its preservation are the subject of a video; the accompanying exhibition sets it in its Iron-Age context.

MALLOW★

POPULATION 6 434

The busy market town of Mallow (Mala) in Co Cork is built at a major crossroads, attractively sited above the River Blackwater, sometimes described as the "Irish Rhine". A faint air of nostalgia still pervades, recalling the glory days when it was the foremost spa in Ireland, frequented by the notorious "Rakes of Mallow", who today would no doubt be keen patrons of the local racecourse. 🏛 *Bridge St* ☎ *022 42222 - www.mallow.ie*

▶ **Orient Yourself:** Mallow sits on N 20 between Cork and Limerick at the junction with N 72, the Dungarvan to Killarney road
👣 **Also See:** COBH, CORK, LISMORE, MIDLETON

A Bit of History

Mallow had a late 12C Anglo-Norman castle, built perhaps by King John, that was replaced by a 16C mansion *(in ruins just inside the gates of Mallow Castle)* as a seat for Sir John Norreys, Lord President of Munster. In 1688, the town was granted a charter by King James II. The spa developed in the 18C after the discovery of the natural hot

A Rakish Resort

The curative properties of Mallow water, said to be good for purifying the blood, were discovered in 1724. It was not long in becoming a popular spa with a fast reputation; its male patrons infamous as the **Rakes of Mallow**.

living short but merry lives,
Going where the devil drives,
Having sweethearts, but no wives…

From April to October, visitors would take the waters; in the evening, there was dancing and cards; balls, meetings and gatherings were held in the Long Room as was the fashion in Bath, Tunbridge Wells and Scarborough. By 1828, when the Spa House was completed Mallow had had its hey day.

Elizabeth Bowen

Until the age of seven, the author Elizabeth Bowen (1899–1973) used to spend the winter in Dublin, where she was born, and the summer at the family seat, Bowen's Court (demolished), built by Henry Bowen c 1775 near Kildorrery *(NE of Mallow)*. Despite moving to England, she continued to live and entertain at Bowen's Court in the summer until 1959 when she could no longer afford to run such a large house. She and her husband lie buried at Farahy Church.

In *Seven Winters* (1942) she describes her childhood; *Bowen's Court* (1942). retells the family's history; *The Last September* (1929) paints life in an Irish country house.

spring (66°F - 72F° depending on the season). As the spa declined in the early 19C, the town became a centre of great political activity, in part because two eminent Nationalists were born here: **Thomas Davis** (1814-45), the Protestant patriot and unchallenged leader of the Young Ireland movement at 73 Main Street; the noted MP **William O'Brien** (1852–1928) at Bank Place, Main Street. Meanwhile, Mallow has literary connections with **Anthony Trollope**, a resident for some years *(Davis St)*; with **Canon Patrick Sheehan**, the former parish priest at Doneraile (1895-1913) who became one of Ireland's most prolific and popular authors of the late 19C and early 20C *(born at 29 O'Brien St)* and with Elizabeth Bowen.

Visit

St James's Church★

Mallow's Anglican church is a fine example of Gothic Revival architecture, built in 1824 by the English-born Pain brothers from Cork. Substantial ruins remain of the former medieval church of St Anne's, badly damaged in the Williamite wars, in which Thomas Davis was baptized in 1814.

Spa House

 Tour (20min) Mon-Fri 9am-5pm.
☎ 022 43610

The Tudor-style complex housing the pump-room, reading room and baths,was built in 1828 by Charles Jephson, although George Pain's original designs were for something on the classical lines of a Greek temple. The exhibition relates to geo-thermal tecnology.

Clock House

The four-storey timber-framed building flanked by a clock tower was erected c 1855 by an amateur architect, supposedly enthused by an Alpine holiday.

Church of the Resurrection

J R Boyd Barratt's Catholic church (1966-9) is shaped like an open fan; the Stations of the Cross are of Tyrolean oak; the stained glass is by the Murphy Davitt Studios of Dublin.

P.Thebault/MICHELIN

Window, Church of the Résurrection

Excursions

Buttevant Friary★
7mi/11km N of Mallow by N 20.
The ruins of the Franciscan friary (1251), stand beside the River Awbeg next to St Mary's Roman Catholic Church. The building, used until recently as a place of burial, has two crypts, one above the other; the chancel walls are still largely intact.

Doneraile Wildlife Park★
6mi/10km NE of Mallow by N 20 and R 581.
&⊙ *Open mid-Apr to Oct, Mon-Sat 8am (10am Sat) to 8.30pm, Sun, Bank Hols 11am -7pm; Oct to mid-Apr 8am (10am Sat-Sun, Bank Hols) to 4.30pm.* ⊚ €1. ☎ 022 24244
The walled demesne (395 acres/160ha) is noted for its herds of red, fallow and sika deer. Wooded areas and ornamental lakes punctuate the gently rolling landscaped parkland around Doneraile Court *(private)*, built c 1700 and remodelled in the early 19C. A stone vault and

> ### Steeplechasing
>
> The **steeplechase** had its origin in Ireland, when huntsmen set wagers with each other on who would be the first to reach a prominent landmark. The first such contest took place from Buttevant in 1752, with the steeple of the Anglican Church as the starting point of a race to St Leger Church near Doneraile (4.5mi/7km).

spiral staircase are all that remains of **Kilcolman Castle**, once the residence of the English poet Edmund Spenser.

Annes Grove Gardens★
11mi/18km E of Mallow by N 72; in Castletownroche turn left onto the minor road.
&⊙ *Open 17 Mar to Sep, Mon-Sat 10am-5pm, Sun 1-6pm.* ⊚ €6. ℗☎ 022 47156
The woodland gardens surrounding an 18C house overlooking the River Awbeg include a fine collection of rhododendrons and magnolias, rare trees and shrubs. Winding paths lead to the cliff garden and an extensive river garden; 19C hedges in the walled garden enclose herbaceous borders and water gardens.

Longueville House
3mi/5km W of Mallow by N 72; turn right at sign.
This magnificent house (1720), now a hotel, with an imposing dual staircase is hung with political portraits: featuring many of the great men who fashioned the course of Irish history from the 18C to the 20C. In the courtyard at the rear there is a mature **maze**. The estate (500 acres/202ha) includes a **vineyard** (3 acres/1.2ha), the only one in Ireland, which produces grapes that make a Riesling-type wine.

> ## Edmund Spenser
>
> In 1586 a perpetual lease of the lands (3 028 acres) and castle of Kilcolman, a four-storey tower house near Doneraile, was granted to Edmund Spenser, who held a post in the Dublin Court of Chancery. During his years at Kilcolman Spenser received Sir Walter Raleigh (1589), and wrote poetry – the fourth, fifth and sixth books of *The Faerie Queen*, the *Amoretti* (love sonnets about his courtship of his second wife Elizabeth Boyle), the *Epithalamion* about their marriage on Midsummer's Day in 1594, his *Veue of the State of Ireland* (1596) and memoranda on the Irish situation. Although he had little sympathy for the Irish, his sensitivity to the beauty of the landscape pervades his work. During the Rising in 1598 the castle was burned by insurgents; some of Spenser's MSS may have perished, including a seventh book of *The Faerie Queen* of which only fragments are known.

Kanturk (Ceann Toirc)★

13mi/21km W of Mallow by N 72 and R 576.

This small market town has three great **bridges** spanning the River Dalua and River Allua erected in 1745, 1760 and 1748: the latter, a four-arch Metal Bridge built by Sir Edward Tierney. Its striking French Gothic church at the western end of the town is dedicated to the Immaculate Conception.

According to legend, the ruined **castle**★ *(south by R 579)* from 1609 was intended by the local chieftain, MacDonagh MacCarthy, to be the largest mansion ever to belong to an Irish chief; the English Privy Council ordered the work to stop on the grounds that "it was much too large for a subject"; MacCarthy was so enraged that he threw away the blue glass tiles destined for the roof.

MAYNOOTH

POPULATION 8 528

The name of this town on the Royal Canal is almost synonymous with the great seminary which for more than two hundred years has educated priests for the Roman Catholic Church. For far longer Maynooth (Maigh Nuad) was the seat of the Fitzgeralds, descendants of a Norman-Welsh adventurer who arrived in Ireland in 1169, and who became one of the country's most powerful families. Today it is a growing commuter and university town, with rail and motorway connections to Dublin.

▸ **Orient Yourself:** Maynooth is a mere 15 miles/24km from Dublin on the Grand Canal, and arteries out of the capital; it is now bypassed by M 4

◔ **Also See:** DUBLIN, FINGAL, KILDARE, MULLINGAR, TRIM

Visit

Maynooth Castle

The ruins of the 12C Fitzgerald castle predate the period when the Earls of Kildare reached pre-eminence serving as Lord Deputy from 1471 to 1534, when Maynooth was effectively the political capital of Ireland. In 1535, following the Silken Thomas rebellion the previous year, it was successfully besieged by the royal forces and Thomas was spirited to London to be executed. In 1656 the castle was abandonned in favour of a new residence at Carton House *(private)*, rebuilt by Richard Castle. Meanwhile, Maynooth was extensively remodelled to provide a fit setting for the new Great House and to accommodate the army of estate workers.

Maynooth College

The college, now part of the National University, is laid out around two spacious courtyards: the first dates from the early 19C, the second is one of Pugin's finest Gothic Revival projects, completed in mid-century despite the Great Famine and inadequate funding. The Chapel with its tall spire and splendid oak choir stalls are by Pugin's pupil, JJ McCarthy.

The preceding College of the Blessed Virgin Mary, founded by a Fitzgerald in 1518, was suppressed a mere 17 years later after town and castle were seized by royal forces. During the Penal period, Roman Catholic priests had to be educated abroad; this changed during the French Revolution as continental seminaries were suppressed and the government became anxious to propritiate local Catholic opinion by opening a seminary in Ireland. St Patrick's College was founded in 1795 with some refugee French priests on the academic staff. Since then, it has educated countless churchmen who have served congregations throughout the British Empire where Roman Catholics far outnumbered Protestants notably across India, China and Africa. In 1966, the first lay students were admitted.

The history of the college, the town and district is presented in the **Visitor Centre**, which organises guided tours of the Chapel, Stoyte House, the Pugin building and the gardens. The museum dispalys scientific and ecclisiastical artefacts.
🕐 *Open May to Sep 11am-5pm, Sat-Sun 2-6pm. Self-guided tour booklet ☜ €4.* ☕ 🍴 🅿 ☎ *01 708 3576 - www.maynoothcollege.ie*

Excursion

Castletown House★★
Celbridge; 4mi/6.4km SE of Maynooth by a minor road
At the time of its completion (1722), this great Palladian mansion was the largest private house in Ireland, setting a precedent for scores of other palatial residences. The final result, facing south over the Liffey valley to the Wicklow Mountains, consists of a 13-bay central block by the Italian architect Alessandrio Galilei linked by curving colonnades to two pavilions designed by Sir Edward Lovett Pearce: all built for William "Speaker" Connolly, reputedly the richest commoner in Ireland.

House
(Dúchas) ♿ 🚶 *Tour (1hr) 10am (1pm Sat-Sun)-6pm (5pm Apr to Oct). Last tour at 4.45pm.* ☜ *€3.70.* ☕ 🅿 ☎ *01 6288252* Work on Castletown's sumptuous interiors spanned two generations. The original decorative scheme, using only local wood and stone, is preserved in the **Brown Study** (tall and narrow oak doors and pine panelling). But in 1758, at the age of 15, Lady Louisa Lennox married into the family

Long Gallery, Castletown House

Irish Picture Library

and her touch is evident throughout the house: the Lafranchini brothers transformed the stairwell with exuberant stuccowork, Sir William Chambers gave the ground-floor rooms a neo-Classical decor, the **print room** was hung with Old Master prints, and the magnificent **Long Gallery** was modelled on Pompeii and provide with hand-blown chandeliers from Venice.

Castletown Follies

The extraordinary **Castletown Obelisk**, also known as the **Conolly Folly** *(visible from the windows of the Long Gallery and from the Maynooth–Castletown road)*, north of the house, comprises two tiers of arches designed by Richard Castle; it was erected in memory of Speaker Conolly by his wife, in part to provide employment during the severe winter of 1739.

The **Wonderful Barn** *(private)* which closes the north-east vista *(3mi/5km east by R 403 and R 404)* was built in 1743; the conical structure, with an external spiral staircase and four diminishing brick domes, was used for drying and storing grain.

Lodge Park Walled Garden and Straffan Steam Museum

5mi/8km S of Maynooth by R 406. ⏱ *Open Jun-Aug, Wed-Sun, Bank Hols 2-6pm.* ⌨ *€7.50.* ♿ 🅿🚻 *01 6273155(Summer)/6288412 - www.steam-museum.ie*

Restored 18C garden attached to a Palladian house *(private)* built in 1773 provides a strong contrast to the Gothic Revival church used by the engineers of the old Great Southern & Western Railway, transferred from Inchicore near Dublin: today, it holds the **Model Hall** in which a fascinating collection of more than 20 18C-20C locomotives are displayed and the **Power Hall** housing an array of engines that once powered mills, distilleries and breweries, and a triple-expansion marine engine from SS Divis of Belfast.

Coolcarrigan Gardens

10mi/16km SW of Maynooth by R 408 via Donadea to Timahoe; 1mi/1.6km S of Timahoe turn right (sign). ♿⏱ *Limited opening, phone to check.* ⌨ *€8.* 🚻 *045 863527 - www.coolcarrigan.ie*

The parkland laid out in the 19C has been enriched by subsequent planting. Roses and herbaceous borders add colour to the formal gardens near the handsome Victorian house. The **glasshouse** hosts a vine, a passion flower, peaches and nectarines. At the end of the **woodland walk** *(30min)* there is a fine view across the Bog of Allen. The **church** (1881), surrounded by a moat and approached through a lych gate, is in the Hiberno-Romanesque revival style and decorated with stained glass.

MIDLETON

POPULATION 3 266

Incorporated in 1670, Midleton (Mainistir An Corann) is a pleasant enough old market town, set in the rich fertile plain of East Cork. Its greatest draw, however, is the distillery where all the famous brands of Irish whiskey – except Bushmills – are produced. ℹ *Jameson Heritage Centre* 🕾 *021 461 3594*

▶ **Orient Yourself:** Midleton is situated on N 25, between Cork and Youghal
♿ **Also See:** COBH, CORK, KINSALE, YOUGHAL

SLIDE FILE, Dublin

Midleton Distillery

Visit

Old Midleton Distillery
&♿☕↖ *Tours Mar to Oct 10am-6pm (last tour at 4.30pm); Nov to Feb: at 11.30am, 2.30pm, 4pm.* ⊗ *€8.50.* ✗ 🅿 ⚭ *021 4613594- www.jameson.ie*
The Jameson Irish Whiskey distillery was built in 1975 alongside the old buildings that once accommodated a woollen mill and barracks. The tour begins with a video presentation on the history of the distillery, there follows a visit to the old buildings, the drying kiln, great storehouse, the water-wheel (1852) that drove five pairs of millstones, the **largest copper pot still** (1825) in the world (capacity 33 000 gallons/1 485hl), and the oak casks in which the spirit was matured. The tour concludes with a whiskey tasting.

Excursions

Cloyne
5mi/8km S by R 630 and R 629.
Three people are particularly associated with the cathedral village of Cloyne: Christy King, the greatest ever hurler; **George Berkeley** (1684-1753), the bishop of what

---

Address Book

SHOPPING
Stephen Pearce Pottery *(9mi/14.5km southeast by R 630 and R 629)* – finished articles and demonstrations.

SPORTS AND LEISURE
Safe beaches and coves dot the coast south of Midleton from Roche's Point eastwards to Knockadoon Head.
Trabolgan Leisure Complex *(at Roche's Point;* ☎ *21 466 1551; www. trabolgan.com)* has an indoor swimming pool, plunge pool, sauna, solarium, fitness centre, tennis, 10-pin bowling and an indoor sports hall.

Sailing opportunities in Ballycotton Bay, at Roche's Point and in Cork Harbour. Angling from the shore or on the lake. The area also boasts golf courses, pleasant walks notably in **Rostellan Wood** on the shore of Cork Harbour in what was once the demesne of Rostellan House (demolished) *(6mi/9.7km SE by R 630)* or along the **cliff-top** from Roche's Point to Ballycotton overlooking Ballycotton Bay and the lighthouse on Ballycotton Island *(11mi/18km SE by R 630 and R 629)*.

was once a vast diocese, and St Colman (522–604) who founded a local monastery, of which only a tiny oratory and 10C **round tower** (100ft/30m high) remain next to the restored 14C **Cathedral**★. Bishop Berkeley, a highly regarded and original philosopher, devoted himself to practical matters such as good farming practice and the benefits of drinking tar water; though his attempt to found a college in America came to nothing, he is honoured by Berkeley in California.

Barryscourt Castle
4mi/6.4km W by N 25 and R 624. (Dúchas) 🕭 ⛨ *Tours (1hr) Jun-Sep 10am-6pm.* 🖂
€2. 🍽 🅿 🖅 *021 488 2218*
The ruined medieval castle, surrounded by a bawn, is strategically sited on the main route from Cork to Waterford. Its name is derived from Philip de Barri of Manorbier in Wales, who arrived c 1180 in the early days of Anglo-Norman Ireland. A more famous descendent was **Gerald of Wales** (c 1146–1233), known as Giraldus Cambrensis, who travelled with Prince (later King) John and published accounts of the country and of its conquest by Henry II.

MONAGHAN

POPULATION 5 628

Monaghan (Muineachán) is the commercial centre and the county town of Co Monaghan, once part of the original province of Ulster projecting into Northern Ireland as far as the Blackwater River. Previously ruled by the McMahon clan, the area was settled by the British in the early 17C and Monaghan town was given its charter in 1613. Its mostly Scottish Presbyterian citizens established a thriving linen industry in the 18C; in the 19C the building of the Ulster Canal and the Ulster Railway brought further benefits, and the town still bears the imprint of these prosperous times, with dignified grey limestone buildings lining its narrow streets. 🄸 *Market House* 🖅*047 81122 - www.monaghantourism.com*

▶ **Orient Yourself:** Monaghan is situated on N 2, an important route north from Dublin, which runs close to the border before becoming the A 5 to Omagh
🕭 **Also See:** CAVAN, ENNISKILLEN, NEWRY

Visit

St Macartan's Cathedral
The landmark overlooking the town from the southeast stands the splendid Gothic Revival Roman Catholic cathedral of 1892. Built of local limestone, with a soaring spire (250ft/76m), it is an accomplished statement from Ruskin's prolific pupil JJ McCarthy. The exterior is extravagantly decorated with Carrara marble statues of

Charles Gavan Duffy (1816–1903)
Duffy, who was born in Monaghan *(no 10 Dublin Street)*, became a journalist and co-founded *The Nation*. He worked through the Young Ireland movement to repeal the Act of Union, formed the Tenant Right League and was elected as MP for New Ross. Disillusioned by the lack of response from Westminster, he emigrated to Australia where he became Prime Minister of the State of Victoria (1871) and worked for federation of the states.

saints and bishops; the spacious interior is contained by a splendid **hammerbeam roof** and ornamented by modern **tapestries** illustrating the Christian life and the life of St Macartan, one of the earliest Irish saints.

Town Centre

The elegant grey limestone **Market House** (1792) was designed by Samuel Hayes, an amateur architect. Church Square *(east)* forms a dignified ensemble, with the **Courthouse** (1830), a handsome Classical building still bearing the scars of the Civil War, and **St Patrick's Anglican Church** (1831), a charming example of Regency Gothic style. East of Church Square is the **Diamond**, the original market place against the north wall of the 17C castle (demolished); the **Rossmore Memorial**, an elaborate neo-Gothic drinking fountain (1875) honours the 4th Baron Rossmore.

Museums

Two elegant early 19C terrace houses in Hill Street accommodate the **County Museum** which has exceptional displays on the region and its history; linen and lace-making feature strongly, but the museum's greatest treasure is the 14C **Cross of Clogher**. ♿🕐 *Open Mon-Sat 11am (noon Sat)-5pm* ☎ *047 82928*

The **St Louis Heritage Centre** tells the story of the Order of St Louis, founded in France in 1842, and its nuns who came to Ireland in 1859. There is a **crannóg** in Spark's Lake in the convent grounds. 🕐*Open Apr to Oct Thu - Sun 2-4.30pm* ☎ *047 83529*

Excursions

Rossmore Forest Park

2mi/3.5km S of Monaghan by N 54 and R 189. ♿🕐 *Open 9am-8pm (6pm winter)* ☎ *047 81968*

Only the foundations of the Rossmore residence remain, though the Earls' mausoleum still stands in the grounds of the desmesne, now a Forest Park landscaped with woods and water.

Clones

12mi/19km SW of Monaghan by N 54.

Right on the border with Northern Ireland, Clones (pronounced as two syllables) is a pleasant market town renown for angling. A typical Ulster plantation settlement with a long history stretching back to a monastery founded by St Tighernach in the 6C, of which a **round tower**, **monolithic shrine** and a 12C **church** survive. The **high cross** (c 10C) standing in the central Diamond, below the Anglican church (1822), may also be contemporary with the monastery: one side depicts Daniel in the Lions' Den, Cain and Abel, Adam and Eve; the other shows the Crucifixion, the Last Supper and the Adoration of the Magi.

The **Ulster Canal Stores** now hosts a display of **Clones lace**, a crochet lace with individual motifs connected by areas of Clones knot.

Clones Lace

B Lynch/Bord Fáilte, Dublin

Lough Muckno Leisure Park
15mi/24km SE of Monaghan by N 2 to Castleblaney.

Lough Muckno, the largest and loveliest of the lakes in Co Monaghan is surrounded by a wooded park (91 acres/37ha) threaded with **nature trails.** The park was originally the desmesne of Sir Edward Blaney, King James I's Governor of Monaghan, whose name lives on in Castleblaney, the little town overlooking the lake's western shore. A later Blaney built the Georgian **Courthouse** and, in 1808, the Anglican church. In the late 19C Blaney Castle was bought by Thomas Hope, a London banker, who renamed it Hope Castle; his name too lives on as the owner of the ill-omened Hope Diamond, now in the Smithsonian Institution.

MULLINGAR

POPULATION 8 040

Mullingar (An Muileann Gcearr), the county town of Westmeath, is an important agricultural market in the middle of prime cattle country. *Dublin Rd* ☎ *044 93 48761*

▶ **Orient Yourself:** Mullingar is situated on N 4, the major road from Dublin to Sligo in the northwest

Just for Kids: Belvedere House adventure playground

Also See: ATHLONE, BIRR, KELLS, KILDARE, LONGFORD, TRIM, TULLAMORE

A Bit of History

In the 2C AD a royal residence topped **Uisneach Hill** *(6mi/9.6km W by R 390)*, an ancient druidic sanctuary where the Celts held their rituals. The **Catstone** marks the meeting point of the five provinces of ancient Ireland. When the Normans arrived in the 12C, they constructed stone castles and several mottes and baileys across the region; a Corporation was established in Mullingar. In the 16C under Henry VIII, Meath was divided in two: Mullingar became the county town of Westmeath, its prosperity assured by good communications with Dublin - the Royal Canal (1790s), the Midland & Great Western Railway (1848), and the main Dublin-Sligo road which ran through town until the bypass was built. In 1825 a prison and a handsome courthouse were erected in Mount Street, with the space between used for public hangings.

During his student days **James Joyce** came to Mullingar, where his father was reorganising the electoral rolls: hence the reason it features *Ulysses* and *Stephen Hero*.

SHOPPING

Mullingar Pewter Ltd. - *5mi/8km east of Mullingar by N 4; after 4mi/6km bear left towards Killucan to The Downs.* ⏲ *Open Mon-Fri 9.30am-6pm, Sat 10am-5.30pm. Last tour Fri 12.30pm.* ☎ *044 48791, www.mullingarpewter.com.* Here visitors may watch the moulding, soldering, turning, polishing and blackening, and admire and purchase the finished articles in the showroom.

SPORTS AND LEISURE

Fishing and sailing on Lough Ennell.
Greyhound Racing.

Visit

Cathedral of Christ the King

The main landmark is the Roman Catholic cathedral set in parkland that stretches down to the Royal Canal, with its tall twin towers (140ft/43m), designed by Ralph Byrne in a "last flamboyant fling … of Classicism" (J Sheehy), dedicated in 1939. The portico tympanum **sculptures** of Portland stone are by Albert Power, a pupil of Rodin. The chaple **mosaics** are by the Russian artist Boris Anrep.

The **museum** *(upstairs – ask the Verger)* displays a letter written by Oliver Plunkett, his vestments and other church-related artefacts.

Excursions

Belvedere House and Gardens★

3.5mi/5.6km S of Mullingar by N 52 – half a day. 🧒 ♿ 🕐 *Open May to Aug, Park: 9.30am-9pm, House: 10am-5pm; Mar to Apr, Sep Park: 10.30am-7pm, House: 10.30am-5pm; Nov to Feb, Park: 10.30am-4.30pm, House: 10.30am-3.30pm. Adventure playground* 🎟 *€8.75.* 📷🍴📶 *044 934 9060 - www.belvedere-house.ie*

The beautiful landscape park above Lough Ennell is graced by an elegant villa (1740) probably designed by Richard Castle as a fishing lodge for Robert Rochfort,

> ### Everest Expedition
>
> In 1921 Col Charles Howard-Bury led an expedition to Everest. Dressed in Donegal tweed his party came within 2 000ft/609m of the summit, took the first photos of the mountain and brought back stories told by the local porters of "abominable snowmen" clad in their own hair.

the Wicked Earl. The house has been restored to its original appearance, complete with finely-carved wood work and Rococo plasterwork ceilings; the furnishings are in period. The **visitor centre** gives a detailed history of the estate and owners, including the mountaineer Colonel Charles Howard-Bury who lived there(1912-60).

The **gardens** include three terraces overlooking the lake, added by Charles Brinsley Marly, Robert's great-great-grandson. The **woodland walk** *(2mi/3km)* is dotted with various follies inclusing an **octagonal gazebo**, a **Gothick arch**, an **ice house**, and two **stone bridges** over the stream. The **jealous wall** (148ft/45m high), designed

Detail from interior, Belvedere House

Belvedere House

The Wicked Earl

Robert Rochfort (1708–79), created 1st Earl of Belvedere in 1757, was a quarrelsome man. In 1736, following the death of his first wife, he married Mary Molesworth, then aged 16, despite her reluctance because her father considered it a good match; four children were born. As Robert spent ever more time at court, Mary turned to her brother-in-law Arthur and his wife for company. Rumours of an affair reached Robert and he brought an action against his brother for £20 000 damages. Unable to pay, Arthur emigrated; when he returned on a visit, Robert had him arrested and sent to prison. Mary was confined to Robert's gloomy residence at Gaulstown, seeing no one but the servants: following one escape, her parents in Dublin despatched her back to Gaulstown, a lonely prisoner until Robert's death in 1779 when she was released by her son.

as a mock-Gothic ruin, was erected c 1760 by Robert either to hide the stables or to blot out the view of Tudenham House (now in ruins) where his estranged brother George lived.

Multyfarnham Franciscan Friary★
8mi/13km N of Mullingar by N 4; in Ballynafid turn right.
The Stations of the Cross are represented by life-size figures among the trees.

Taghmon Church
7mi/11.5km N of Mullingar by N 4 and R 394; in Crookedwood turn right.
By the stream, on the site of a monastery founded by St Fintan Munna, stands a fortified church; the four-storey tower contains living accommodation. Note the two sculpted heads facing out from the north and west walls.

Tullynally★
15mi/24km N of Mullingar by R 394 to Castlepollard and R 395 west; ramped drive (0.75mi/1.2km) from gateway to house.
&. ⏱ *Gardens: open Jun to Aug 2-6pm. Concert details on Web site.* ⊖ *€6.* ⌂
✕ 🅿 ☎ *044 61159 - www.tullycastle.com*
Tullynally, the seat of the Pakenham family since 1655, bristles with turrets and crenellations above the treetops of the extensive grounds. The original fortress with massive walls (10ft/3m thick) was converted early in the 18C into a country house, Gothicised by Francis Johnston and extended by Sir Richard Morrison.

The Children of Lir

Tullynally is an old Irish place name meaing the Hill of Swans, and Tullynally Castle is set on high ground sloping south to Lough Darravaragh, where, according to Irish legend, the Children of Lir spent 300 years after they were changed into swans by their jealous stepmother.

The interiors reflect the 19C love of all things medieval: it has a **Great Hall** and an octagonal dining room covered with wallpaper designed by Pugin for the House of Lords. The fascinating service wings display all that was required to run a large country house. The family coach parked in the courtyard.

By 1760 the early-18C formal layout of canals and cascades had been replaced by naturally landscaped **gardens**; the terraces date from Victorian times when tennis and croquet were popular. Two Coad stone sphinxes (1780) guard the huge walled **kitchen garden** with its Regency glasshouses and avenue of Irish yews linked by a variegated hedges of box, yew and holly.

A **forest walk** leads past a waterfall to the lower lake and **views** of the castle.

Fore Abbey★

15mi/24km N of Mullingar by R 394 to Castlepollard and R 195 E; turn right.

This ancient monastic site is one of the loveliest in the country. The extensive ruins – church, cloisters, chapter house, refectory, kitchen and columbarium - belong mostly to the Benedictine abbey founded in 1200, but **St Fechin's Church**, named after the founder (d 665) of the earlier complex (11C- 12C). In 1436 the buildings were fortified to protect them from attack by the native Irish.

Various features have traditionally been known as the **"Seven Wonders of Fore"** and described in miraculous terms. They comprise the "monastery in a bog", the **abbey** itself, raised on firm ground in the middle of marshland; "water that will not boil" from **St Fechin's Well** in the shade of a "tree that will not burn", the three branches of which represented the Trinity; the "stream that flows uphill" to drive the "mill without a race" appeared when the saint beat his crozier on the ground; the "hermit in the stone" was Patrick Beglen, the last anchorite in Ireland, who in the 17C languished in a medieval watchtower, later incorporated into a **chapel mausoleum** for the Nugent family; the "stone raised by St Fechin's prayers" is the huge lintel over the west doorway of his church, which proved too heavy for the masons to lift into place and had to be wafted aloft by the power of prayer.

> ### A Literary Family
>
> The talented **Pakenham** family includes Lord Longford, a Socialist peer, his wife Elizabeth who writes biographies, their son, Thomas Pakenham, an author, and their daughters Antonia Fraser, another biographer, and Rachel Billington, a novelist.

NEW ROSS

POPULATION 5 012

Far inland on the tidal River Barrow, this thriving place was once the country's principal port; ocean-going ships still dock at the broad quayside opposite the substantial warehouses and tall houses remeniscent of the 19C. Its history, however, can be traced back to the 6C. Narrow streets, many linked by footpaths and flights of steps, rise steeply from the riverside to Irishtown, site of the ancient monastic settlement on the heights above. Very much a working town, New Ross (Ros Mhic Treoin) is an ideal place from which to explore the attractive scenery of the Barrow valley upstream to Nore, and downstream to the Hook Head Peninsula. ▯ *The Quay* ☎*051 421857 - www.newrosstourism.com* ▯ *Hook Head* ☎*051 421 857*

▶ **Orient Yourself:** New Ross is situated on the junction of several important routes: N25 to Wexford and Waterford; N 30 from Enniscorthy, R 705 from Graiguenamanagh on the River Barrow, R 700 from Thomastown and Kilkenny on the River Nore. R 733 and R 734 lead to the Hook Head peninsula.

Ȼ **Also See:** CLONMEL, ENNISCORTHY, KILKENNY, WATERFORD, WEXFORD

A Bit of History

New Ross itself was founded below the site of St Abban's late 6C-early 7C monastery, in about 1200 by William le Marshall, Earl Marshal of Ireland, and his wife, Countess Isabelle de Clare, daughter of Strongbow. The first bridge across the River Barrow was built in 1211 and in 1265 the first town walls were constructed. New Ross prospered but by the end of the 17C Ireland's premier harbour was Waterford. In 1649, mindful of the massacre suffered by Wexford, the Catholic garrison prudently surrendered the town to Cromwell. In the 1798 rebellion the town was successfully defended against the insurgents, who suffered thousands of casualties. In 1832, a cholera epidemic swept through the region claiming three thousand lives. By the mid 19C New Ross had re-established a substantial trading links, with ships sailing to the Baltic and across the Atlantic, some carrying emigrants fleeing the Famine.

Walking Tour

Dunbrody Famine Ship★

🕐 *Open Apr to Sep 9.45am-5pm; Oct-Mar 10am-4pm.* 🎫 *€7.50.* ☎ *051 425239 - www.dunbrody.com*

The *Dunbrody* is a splendid replica of a 458 tonne three-masted barque (176ft/54m long). The original freighter, built in Quebec by an Irish shipwright for a New Ross merchant, ferried emigrants mainly between 1845 and 1851. Visitors boarding her are met by "emigrants", who re-enact the terrible conditions endured on a trip to New York in 1849. A fascinating exhibition evokes the achievements of members of the Irish diaspora like John Fitzgerald Kennedy; a JFK Trust database lists records of more than two million emigrant passages.

▶ *From the bridge walk up Mary St.*

Tholsel

At the crossroads on the Corner of South St and Quay St (right). 🕐 *Open by appointment Mon-Fri 9am-5pm.* ☎ *051 421 284 -www.newrosstc.ie*

The neo-Classical building with a tower topped by a weather-vane, was erected in 1749 and rebuilt in 1806 after the ground subsided. The front façade is by William Kent, pupil of Sir Christopher Wren. It now houses the local council, its volumes of

---

Address Book

GETTING AROUND

Waterford Harbour Ferry – *Operates between Passage East and Ballyhack daily, 7am (9.30am Sun and Bank Hols) to 10pm (8pm Oct-Mar).* 🕐 *Closed 25-26 Dec. Single* 🎫 *€6.50 (car), there and back €9.50 (car); there and back €2 (pedestrian).* ☎ *051 382 480, 382 488, www.passageferry.com.*

ENTERTAINMENT

Galley Cruising Restaurants – Gourmet and ecological trips on the local rivers – *Cruises from New Ross and Waterford Apr-Oct, 11am-7pm; check time and price when booking. Cruise only prices*
from €8; cruise with lunch from €20; afternoon cruise €10 with afternoon tea; evening cruise with dinner from €38. ☎ *051 421 723, www.rivercruises.ie.*

SPORTS AND LEISURE

Beaches at Duncannon; scuba-diving at Slade; riverside walks in Inistioge; bird-watching In spring and autumn on the Hook Head Peninsula, where over 200 species have been recorded.

TRACING ANCESTORS

Dunbrody – Computer database with records of more than two million emigrant journeys between 1846 and 1886 *(see below).*

corporation minutes collected since the 17C, the mace of Charles II (1699) and the charter of James II (1688).

Opposite stands a statue of a **croppy boy**, a local term given to the insurgents in the 1798 rebellion because of their short hair, commemorating the uprising and subsequent battle of New Ross.

▶ *Continue up Mary St.*

St Mary's Church★

The early-19C Anglican church was built on the site of the nave and crossing of what was probably the largest parish church in medieval Ireland, part of the abbey founded by William le Marshall and his wife (1207-20). Besides the ruined chancel, there are a number of striking late-13C and early-14C effigies.

▶ *Walk back down Mary St; turn left into Bewley St and right into Michael St.*

Roman Catholic Parish Church

The building with its high ceiling and Corinthian columns echoes St Mary's Church *(adjacent)*; its completion was delayed by the cholera epidemic in 1832.

▶ *Leave by the rear entrance. Walk up Cross Lane; turn right into Neville St.*

Town Walls and Gates

At the junction stands the Three Bullet Gate *(left)*, through which Cromwell entered the town in 1649, and the Mural Tower erected in the 14C. The substantial remains of the Maiden Gate are 15C.

▶ *Walk down William St. Turn right into Priory St and left into Marsh Lane to return to the Quay.*

Excursions

Upstream from New Ross

Graiguenamanagh★
11mi/18km N of New Ross by N 30, R 700 and R 705.

The commercial quays of Graiguenamanagh ("granary of the monks") occupy a particularly attractive stretch of the River Barrow, overlooked by the heather-covered summit of Brandon Hill (1694ft/516m). The township is dominated by the restored ruins of Duiske (pronounced Dooishka) Abbey, established here in the early 13C by William le Marshall for the Cistercians.

Duiske Abbey★★

Despite having been suppressed in 1536, the abbey continued to function for years after. The tower collapsed in 1774 and most of the precincts were subsequently built over. The most outstanding feature of the restoration is the high-pitched church roof, constructed from unseasoned timbers of oak and elm secured with pegged wooden joints. The superb effigy of the Knight of Duiske, cross-legged, sword-seizing, is c 1300, although his identity remains a mystery.

The Abbey Centre houses a museum for examples of the Abbey plate and other items; a gallery shows works by contemporary artists on Christian themes. ⓒ *Open Mon-Fri 10am-5pm. Concerts.* ☎ *059 972 4238*

Inistioge★
10mi/16km N of New Ross by N 30 and R 700.

Inistioge (pronounced Inisteeg), a famously picturesque village , is set on the west bank of the Nore, spanned by a splendid 18C 10-arch bridge.

The ruins of the 13C **castle**, once the borough courthouse, flank the tree-lined **square**. On the west side next to the ruined Tholsel is a real curiosity, the **Armillary Sphere**, a device said to have been invented by Eratosthenes in 250 BC to demonstrate the movements of the earth and moon. The 19C almshouse was built by a member of the Tighe family, who resided at Woodstock. The Roman Catholic church contains early stone carvings, apparently illustrating the legend of the mermaid being taken from the River Nore in 1118. Up the lane is **St Colmcille's Well.**

Adjoining the Anglican Church are the tower, nave and Lady Chapel of the **Augustinian priory**, founded in 1210 and dedicated to St Mary and St Columba (*Colmcille*). In the graveyard is the elaborate tomb of Mrs Mary Tighe, a poet of local renown.

Woodstock Forest Park (*1mi/1.6km SW of Inistioge*) is the former Tighe family demesne, once claimed to be the finest 18C mansion in Co Kilkenny, which was burned down during the Civil War. In the grounds there are forest walks, an old tiled Japanese garden and a conical dovecot.

Downstream from New Ross

Dunganstown
4mi/6.4km S of New Ross by R 733 and the minor road W

The **Kennedy Homestead** where the great-grandfather of John F Kennedy, President of the USA (1961–63) was born in 1820 and still in family hands, now displays photographs and souvenirs of the President's visit in 1963, including the wreath he laid on the graves of the leaders of the 1916 Easter Rising at Arbour Hill in Dublin. ♿🕐 *Open Jul-Aug 10am-5pm; May to Jun, Sep Mon-Fri 11.30am-4.30pm.* ⊗€4. 🅿 ☎ *051 388264 - www.kennedyhomestead.com*

The **Kennedy Arboretum**★, opened in 1968 to honour John F Kennedy, is divided into the plant collection, forest plots and mountain heathland. Various lovely walks meander through the estate (667 acres/252ha), and a scenic road winds to the summit of Slieve Coillte from where extensive views extend over farmland, the Hook Peninsula and mountains. (*Dúchas*)♿🕐 *Open May to Aug 10am-8pm (6.30pm Apr, Sep; 5pm Oct to Mar).* 🕐 *Closed 25 Dec, Good Fri.* ⊗ €2.90. ⌨🅿 ☎ *051 388 171*

Kilmokea Gardens★
10mi/15km S of New Ross by R 733 and a minor road west. Guesthouse and spa: 🕐 *Open May to Oct.* ⊗ €6. ☎ *051 388109; www.kilmokea.com*

Within the earthern ramparts of what was probably an Early Christian monastic foundation stands a handsome Georgian glebe house (now a guesthouse); its assorted gardens, among the most exquiste in Ireland, were developed over half a century.

Dunbrody Abbey★
10mi/15km S of New Ross by R 733. Key at Furlong's Cottage by the main entrance. 🕐 *Open May to mid-Sep 10am-6pm.* ⊗ €2. ☎ *051 388 603*

Close to the village of Clonmines, a deserted medieval borough with remains of tower houses, a fortified church and Augustinian priory, are the handsome ruins of the abbey built in 1182 by Cistercian monks from St Mary's Abbey in Dublin. The roofless but well-preserved cruciform abbey church, pleasantly set above an inlet of the river Barrow, has a low turreted tower and six transept chapels with slender single-light windows. After the Dissolution, the abbey passed to the Etchingham family who erected a fortified dwelling (now ruined) around the Norman keep.

Ballyhack Castle
(*Dúchas*)🕐 *Open Jun-Sep 9.30am-6.30pm. Last admission 5.45pm.* ☎ *051 389 468*
Overlooking the ferry crossing to Passage East on the west bank of Waterford Harbour is an imposing tower house (15C or 16C); steep stairs in the thickness of the wall

link the five floors. The site originally belonged to the Knights Templar, then to the Knights Hospitaller before being acquired by the Earl of Donegall.

Duncannon

Duncannon Fort★ was first selected for defensive purposes by the Anglo-Normans in the 12C. In 1588, as part of the precautions against the Spanish Armada, the fortress was strengthened and assumed its present star-shaped form with a dry moat (3 acres/1.2ha). In 1690 both James II and William III took ship from Duncannon following the Battle of the Boyne. ♿🕐 *Open 9.30am-5.30pm.* 🚶 *Last guided tour 4.30pm (in winter by appointment).* 🎟 *€3 (€5 tour).* ☎ *051 389 454*

Tintern Abbey★

5mi/8km E of Duncannon by R 737, R 733 and R 374 to Saltmills. (Dúchas) ♿🕐 *Open mid-May to Oct 10am-6pm. Last admission 5.45pm.* 🎟 *€2.10* 🅿 ☎ *051 562650*
The ruined Cistercian abbey, a daughter house of Tintern Abbey in Monmouthshire, was founded in 1200 by William le Marshall in thanks for his safe crossing from England in a violent storm. At the Dissolution of the Monasteries in the 16C the abbey was granted to the Colclough family, who took up residence in the nave and tower.

Hook Head Peninsula

The remote beaches and distinctive landscapes have long drawn holiday-makers to this spot, bounded to the west by Waterford Harbour and to the east by Bannow Bay. The pleasant little resort of **Fethard** was originally founded by the Anglo-Normans, whose first expedition to Ireland landed in 1169 at Bannow Island.
Slade is a minute fishing village, with a small double harbour, popular for scuba-diving. On the pier are the remains of 18C salthouses where sea water was evaporated to make salt. Beside them stood **Slade Castle**, a tower house (15C–16C) and house (16C–17C) built by the Laffan family.
Hook Head Lighthouse is one of the oldest in Europe, where a light was maintained almost continuously for 1 500 years. The first cylindrical keep (82ft/25m) with its vaulted chambers was built by the Normans in the early 13C to aid navigation up Waterford Harbour to their port at New Ross. It is topped by a more conventional structure erected early in the 19C. 🚶 *Tour: Mar to Oct 9.30am-5.30pm; Nov to Feb 10am-5pm.* 🎟 *€5.50.* ☎ *051 397055/4 - www.thehook-wexford.com*

PORTUMNA★

POPULATION 984

The little township of Portumna (Port Omna), meaning the port of the oak, is a major crossing point on the River Shannon where it enters Lough Derg, the lowest and most attractive of the Shannon lakes. Occupying part of the shoreline, Portumna Forest Park has a deer herd, nature trails, a marina and an observation tower; the bird life, both migratory and resident, is abundant.

▶ **Orient Yourself:** Portumna is situated at the north end of Lough Derg on N 65 between Borrisokane and Loughrea and R 489 and R 353 between Birr and Gort. The road bridge over the Shannon is raised at regular intervals to allow the passage of vessels on the river (🌀 *see Address Book*)

🌀 **Also See:** ATHENRY, BIRR, CLONMACNOISE

Portumna Castle

Dúchas, Dublin

Visit

Portumna Castle★

(Dúchas) &⏱ *Ground floor and formal gardens only: open Apr to Oct, 10am-6pm (5pm early Apr). Last admission 45min before closing.* ⊗ *€2.* ☎ *090 974 1658*

The early 17C castle was for centuries the seat of the Burke family. Long derelict but now restored to its full splendour, it is a handsome example of the sophisticated, semi-fortified residence that replaced the tower houses and castles of medieval times. The first house was accidentally burnt out in 1826 and abandoned; its replacement, designed by Sir Thomas Deane, was burned down during the Civil War.

The approach passes through a series of formal gardens. The Gothic Gate houses an exhibition telling the story of the castle and its occupants; the 17C walled kitchen garden is planted with fruit trees, flowers, herbs and vegetables.

GETTING AROUND
Portumna Lifting Bridge
– *(Duchas)* ⏱ *Closed to road vehicles for 10-15min mid-Mar to early-Nov, Mon-Fri, 6 times daily, Sun, 4 times daily; early-Nov to mid-Mar, Mon-Fri, 3 times daily, Sun, twice daily.*

SPORTS AND LEISURE
Boating, coarse angling and game fishing on Lough Derg.

De Burgo – de Burgh – Burke

The origins of Burke can be traced to the Norman de Burgo. In 1193 William de Burgo, came to Ireland with Prince John and married the daughter of Donal Mor O'Brien, king of Thomond (1185); their son was made Lord of Connaught. In 1265, Walter de Burgo was created Earl of Ulster. In the 14C the property was owned by a descendant of Richard, Lord of Connaught, who adopted the name de Burgh by royal licence, and made Earl of Clanrickard (1543). John, the 9th Earl, fought with the Jacobites and was taken prisoner at Aughrim (1691); 12 years later he redeemed his property for £25 000. When Hubert de Burgh Canning (1832–1916) died, the title passed to the Marquess of Sligo and the land went to Henry Lascelles, 6th Lord Harewood who married the daughter of George V and Queen Mary.

South of the castle stand the ruins of **Portumna Priory**, originally a Cistercian chapel granted to the Dominicans by O'Madden, the local chieftain.

Excursions

Clonfert Cathedral★
17mi/27km NE of Portumna by N 65, R 355, R 356 via Eyrecourt and minor road E. *Key available from the house to the right of the cathedral.*

The 12C church was built on a monastery founded in 563 by St Brendan the Navigator. It is justly famous for its great **west doorway**★★, a masterpiece of Hiberno-Romanesque decoration in red sandstone, aptly described as "the apogee of the Irish Romanesque mason's love of ornamentation" (P Harbison). Friezes of heads and triangles, fantastical motifs and animal heads are contrived in one harmonious whole; the sixth order dates from the 15C, as do the tower, south transept and sacristy.

The grounds *(through the rear churchyard gate; turn left)* contain an ancient **yew walk**, probably planted by the monks in the shape of a cross. The ruined **Bishop's Palace** belonged to Sir Oswald Mosley from 1951 to 1954, when it was destroyed by fire. The charming circular oratory serves the Emmanuel Retreat House.

Meelick Franciscan Friary
7mi/11km NE of Portumna by N 65, R 355 and minor road E.

The friary, built in the 15C overlooking the Shannon, has been restored for worship. Most of the walls, the west door and two arches in the south wall are original. A short walk *(0.5mi/1km east)* leads to Meelick Weir and Victoria Lock, the largest lock on the Shannon.

Lorrha
6mi/10km E of Portumna by R 489 via Portumna Lifting Bridge and minor road S.

The tiny village contains no fewer than three ruined churches. The west front of the Anglican church has a 15C doorway carved with a pelican vulning (pecking at her breast); its predecessor was the monastery founded by St Ruadhán (d 845), a disciple of St Finian of Clonard. **St Ruadhan's Church** is the 15C building with an ornate west doorway, handsome east and west windows and a vaulted sacristy. By the Roman Catholic church, are the remains of a church that formed part of a Dominican priory founded by Walter de Burgo c 1269.

ROSCREA★

POPULATION 4 170

Laid out on the steep banks of the Bunnow River, this prosperous agricultural town (Ros Cré) nestles between the Slieve Bloom Mountains to the north and Devils Bit Mountain to the south. Ancient roadways converge on the 7C site of a monastery started by St Cronan, and where, in early 13C, the Anglo-Irish had a strategic castle built.

▶ **Orient Yourself:** Roscrea is situated at the junction of the N 7 to Dublin and Limerick and N 62 to Birr and Thurles

◉ **Also See:** ABBEYLEIX, ATHY, BIRR, KILKENNY

Visit

Roscrea Castle

(Dúchas) ⏱ *Open Apr to Oct 10am-6pm. Last admission 5.15pm.* ⊜ *€3.70.* ☎ *050 521 850. Restored period gardens open at all times.*

Dominating the centre of the town is the 13C **castle,** an irregular polygonal enclosure contained by curtain walls and two D-shaped towers. The medieval gatetower was embellished with gables and chimneys in the 17C.

Damer House★ is an elegant three-storey furnished house started in 1715 by Joseph Damer, a member of a Plantation family which came to Ireland in 1661; when he died in 1720, he was deemed to be the richest man in Ireland. On completion, the house was used by the Anglican Bishop of Killaloe. Today, the rooms display exhibitions relatind to local history.

Blackmill, the mill built in 1722, is dedicated to providing information about **St Cronan's Church and Round Tower**, the remains of the monastery sacked no fewer than four times in the course of the 12C, which was plundered for building stone in the 19C and further destroyed when the main Dublin-Limerick road was completed. Little survives other than the west façade of the 12C church, a 12C **high cross** and the 8C round tower (60ft/18m high) which lost its conical cap in 1135 and suffered further damage during fighting in 1798.

Franciscan Friary

The present Roman Catholic church of St Cronan is approached through the bell-tower of the original 15C friary. The east and north walls of the earlier chancel and part of the nave arcade have been incorporated into the modern church.

Excursion

Monaincha Abbey

1mi/1.6km W by N 7 and minor road from the roundabout.

An exquisite 12C ruin with its finely carved doorway and chancel arch stands on a raised isolated site, which was an island until the bog was drained in the late 18C. In Early Christian times this was a famous retreat associated with various saints, notably St Cronan, which grew to be a major pilgrimmage centre in the Middle Ages.

Devil's Bit Mountain

15mi/24km S of Roscrea by N 62.

Legend has it that the gap at Devil's Bit Mountain was scooped out by the devil to form the Rock of Cashel, in reality it was caused by glaciers. An easy climb to the summit (1 577ft/479m) is rewarded by extensive views over the Golden Vale.

SKIBBEREEN

POPULATION 1 926

This attractive and prosperous little market town owes its existence to Algerian pirates, who raided the neighbouring settlement of Baltimore in 1631, capturing some of the English settlers while others fled inland and set up two settlements: Skibbereen (Sciobairín) was one. The town suffered severely during the 19C famine (documented at the old gas works heritage centre). It is an excellent spot, with good restaurants, from which to explore the beautiful coastal scenery and Lough Hyne. 🛈 *North St* ☎ *028 21766*

▶ **Orient Yourself:** Skibbereen stands on the southwest Cork coast road (N 71) where it crosses the River Ilen a few miles inland

◔ **Also See:** BANTRY, CORK, KINSALE

Excursions

The Liss Ard Foundation

2mi/3km S of Skibbereen by R 596. ♿ ◷ *Open May to Oct, Mon-Fri, 10am-4.30pm.* ◷ *Closed Bank Hol. www.lissard.com; www.lissardresort.com*

The estate is managed to encourage the natural flora and fauna to flourish. A series of isolated contemplative areas allow the visitor to enjoy the peace and tranquility of the place, the sounds of the landscape, the colours of the flowers and an oval reflection of sky in the Crater, created by James Turrell. The 19C house is a private retreat.

Lough Hyne Nature Reserve

6mi/10km southwest of Skibbereen by R 595 and a minor road south. 🙂 *Beware of sea urchin spines if moving about barefoot.*

Set among low hills, this unpolluted saltwater lagoon is a marine nature reserve, with a unique ecosystem; over 60 species have been recorded, including the redmouth goby, otherwise found in Portugal.

Baltimore

8mi/13km SW of Skibbereen by R 595.

The picturesque fishing village faces a myriad of islands offshore in Roaring Water Bay, the most sheltered bay in these parts. There is always boat traffic animating the horizon. Overlooking the piers – one old, one new – are the ruins of the early-17C fortified house built by the local lord, Sir Fineen O'Driscoll. On the breezy headland *(1mi/1.6km south)* stands **Lot's wife**, a medieval beacon, shaped like a rocket and painted white.

Sherkin Island★

Access by ferry. 🙂 *A full day is needed to explore the island; if the weather turns stormy visitors may be marooned for a night or more.*

SLIDE FILE, Dublin

Baltimore

Address Book

SIGHTSEEING

Baltimore-Sherkin Island Passenger Ferry – *8 return journeys from 9am to 8.30pm from Baltimore; 9.45am to 8.45pm from Sherkin* ☎ *028 20125 - www.baltimore-ireland.com*

Baltimore-Cape Clear Island Ferry- *Operates daily (weather permitting); times available by phone or Web site. There and back €12.* ☎ *028 39159 (boat's phone), 086 3465110 (boat's mobile), 028 39126 (office) - www.capeclearferry.info.*

West Cork Coastal Cruises –*Operates from Baltimore to Cape Clear Island and from Cape Clear to Schull (Fastnet Rock) Jun-Aug, twice daily. Baltimore to Cape Clear (45min) 11.30am and 5.30pm, Cape Clear to Schull 3.30pm, Schull to Cape Clear 2.30pm, Cape Clear to Baltimore 10.30am and 4.30pm. There and back €12.50.* ☎ *028 39153, 087 268 0760 (mobile); www.westcorkcoastalcruises. com*

⚫ *For coin ranges, see the Legend on the cover flap.*

WHERE TO STAY

⌂ **Fastnet Guesthouse** – *4 rms - ☎ 028 20515 - www.baltimore-ireland. com/fastnet – Feb-Nov .* Old stone walls, open fireplaces and wooden floors bear out the history of this old Merchant's house, dating back to 1820 and located in the centre of town. Still very much a family home, with multilingual owners.

ENTERTAINMENT

West Cork Arts Centre *(North Street, Skibbereen)* – Regular arts events and contemporary art exhibitions –*Open Mon-Sat, 10am - 6pm.* ☎ *028 22090 - www.westcorkartscentre.com*

SPORTS AND LEISURE

Sailing at Baltimore (temporary marina in summer) and Schull.

As well as the remains of an O'Driscoll stronghold, a ruined friary, and some lovely beaches, little Sherkin has a **marine research station**, which monitors the marine environment and organises courses on pollution.

Cape Clear Island

Access by ferry. ⊕ *At least two days, more in bad weather, are needed to visit the island. Basic accommodation for visitors is provided by the bird observatory.*

Great colonies of guillemots, cormorants, shearwaters, petrels and choughs attract ornithologists to the remote, rocky Cape Clear Island, Ireland's southernmost inhabited island; in the waters around, whales, turtles, sharks, seals and dolphins can be seen. The tiny settlement of **Cummer** is the last bastion of Irish in west Cork. Many of the people living here are called O'Driscoll or Cadogan, which can be confusing.

Driving Tour

Mizen Peninsula *Tour of 35mi/56km W of Skibbereen – 1 day*

▸ *The spectacular scenery is particularly dramatic around the wave-shattered cliffs of Mizen Head. From Skibbereen take N 71 W. After 10mi/16km turn left.*

Ballydehob

The main street, lined with brightly painted houses slopes steeply down to Roaring Water Bay. The 12-arch railway bridge, part of the Schull and Skibbereen light railway which closed in 1947, has been converted into a **walkway.**

▸ *Take the minor road north uphill bearing W and S to Mount Gabriel and Schull.*

Mount Gabriel

It is a stiff climb to the aircraft tracking station (1 339ft/408m). During the Bronze Age, copper was mined here; in the 19C the production rivalled that of Cornwall.

▶ *Take the road S to Schull.*

Beyond the pass there is a fine **view**★★ of Roaring Water Bay and the pretty little market town of Schull.

Schull (Skull)★

Ferries to Baltimore and Cape Clear Island (& see Address Book).
Schull's name, meaning "school," dervies from the monastic centre of learning established here in the 10C. The

> ## "Keeping an eye on the Czar of Russia"
>
> In the 1890s a leader in the *Skibbereen Eagle* remarked that the paper was "keeping an eye on the Czar of Russia." The comment, outrageously bombastic for a small provincial newspaper, was picked up by the international wire services and went around the world. Still quoted today, it turned out to be the most famous line ever written in an Irish newspaper. The files of the old *Eagle* may be inspected by appointment at the offices of the *Southern Star* newspaper in Ilen Street.

planetarium holds exhibitions, regular astronomy shows *(60 seats)* and telescope viewing nights. & ③ *Starshow (45min): Mon and Thu at 8pm; Tue, Fri, Sat at 4pm.* ☞ €5. ☏ 028 28315

▶ *Continue W; in Toormore turn left into R 591 to Goleen and Crookhaven. Turn right (sign) at the entrance to the village of Goleen.*

Crookhaven

The little resort of Crookhaven was once a busy fishing harbour of some importance as mailboats stopped here en route to America and the West Indies, copper mined at nearby Brow Head was moved on, and Marconi's transatlantic telegraph station was put into operation in 1902.

▶ *Take the minor road along the east side of Barley Cove.*

Barley Cove

The deep inlet lined with **sandy beach** between the cliffs makes this a splendid holiday resort, especially popular with surfers.

▶ *After crossing the causeway at the head of Barley Cove turn left to Mizen Head.*

Mizen Head

10min steep descent on foot from car park.
The storm-battered cliffs of Mizen Head mark the southwesternmost tip of Ireland. In 1910 the Irish Lights fog signal station was built on Cloghnane Island, with access to it via a reinforced concrete footbridge constructed with some difficulty because of the extreme exposure. Crossing the chasm 150ft/46m above the Atlantic swell can be a thrilling experience in wild weather. The **Visitor Centre** presents the work of the station and of lighthouse keepers, local marine life – dolphins, seals, basking sharks and whales and seabirds – and wrecks, the Fastnet Race and the building of the Fastnet Rock Lighthouse *(SE – 9mi/14km).* ③ *Open Jun to sep 10am-6pm; mid-Mar to May, Oct 10.30am-5pm; Nov to mid-Mar Sat-Sun 11am-4pm.* ☞ €6. ☏ 028 35115/35225 - www.mizenhead.net

SLIGO★★

Sligo (Sligeach) is a busy market town, an important shopping and cultural centre for much of the northwest of Ireland. It stands on the River Garavogue which drains Lough Gill into the sea and one of its greatest assets is the beautiful and varied landscape all around – green and wooded valleys, lofty mountains, sandy seashores, and an exceptional wealth of prehistoric monuments. Sligo and its surroundings are intimately associatiated with the Yeats family: the portrait painter John B Yeats, the artist Jack B Yeats, and the poet William Butler Yeats (1865-1939). *Aras Reddan Temple St ☎ 071 916 1201 - www.irelandnorthwest.ie*

▸ **Orient Yourself:** Sligo is the hub of several major roads: N 4 east to Dublin ; N 59 west into Co Mayo; N 15 north into Donegal and N 16 over the border to Enniskillen

▢ **Don't Miss:** Lough Gill

◔ **Also See:** BOYLE, DONEGAL, ENNISKILLEN, KILLALA, KNOCK.

A Bit of History

A Turbulent History – In 807 Sligo was plundered by the Vikings; following the Norman invasion in the 13C it was granted to Maurice Fitzgerald. Over the following 200 years, its possession by the O'Conors was disputed by the O'Donnells. A fort was built by the Cromwellians; Patrick Sarsfield reinforced the defences so that Sligo was one of the last places to capitulate after the Battle of the Boyne (1690). The Battle of Carrignagat (1798) was fought south of the town.

A Prosperous Port – In the 18C and 19C Sligo developed into a busy trading port from which many emigrants set out for the New World. Buildings from that period include the warehouses by the docks, the Courthouse (1878), and the Italianate City Hall (1865). The stone look-out turret, known as the **Yeats Watch Tower** *(no public access)*, marks the warehouse owned by W B Yeats's mother's family, the Pollexfen dynasty of Sligo merchants and sea traders.

Sligo Today – Sligo has a lively cultural scene: theatre, music and high-profile art-installations at the Model Arts Centre; festivals stud the calendar; the Yeats Memorial Building hosts a famous summer school devoted to the work of the poet and his family. All this urban bustle contrasts strongly with the unspoilt countryside beyond, its fine sandy beaches at Strandhill and at Rosses Point, where there is also a championship golf course.

Yeats' Country

In their youth, the Yeats brothers spent many of their summer holidays with their Pollexfen cousings at Elsinore Lodge on Rosses Point, watching their grandfather's ships in the bay from the top of the warehouse now known as the Yeats Watch Tower. Jack Yeats once remarked that he never did a painting without putting a thought of Sligo in it. The countryside and its rich legendary associations, continued to inspire William throughout his life, recording in verse his visits to Lissadell House on Drumcliff Bay; he is buried at Drumcliff.

Visit

Sligo Abbey★

(Dúchas) ◷ *Open Apr to Oct 10am-6pm. Last admission 5.15pm; Nov to Mar Sat-Sun (call to confirm).* ⬤⬤ *€2.90.* 🅿 ☎*071 914 6406*

The ruins on the south bank of the Garavogue River occupy the site of a Dominican friary, founded by Maurice Fitzgerald c 1252, damaged by an accidental fire in 1414;

Address Book

GETTING AROUND

Sligo Airport – ☎ *071 9168280 - www. sligoairport.com.*

SIGHTSEEING

Walking Tour – *Operates Jun-Sep.* ☎ *071 9161201 .*

Wild Rose Water Bus – *Operates mid-Jun to Sep, from Doorly Park and Parke's Castle, particularly to the Isle of Innisfree (€6.35). Apr, May, Oct, limited sailings. Check Web site or call for details.* ✗ ☎ *071 9164266; 087 25988869 (mobile) - www.roseofinnisfree.com*

There are also boat trips offshore to **Inishmurray** from Mullaghmore *(north of Sligo). 15 passengers minimum.* ☎ *071 9166124 (Lomax Boats).*

For coin ranges, see the Legend on the cover flap.

WHERE TO STAY

⊜ **Ard Cuilinn Lodge** – *Drumiskabole - 3mi SE of Sligo by N 4 off R 284 -* ☎ *071 91 62925; www.littleireland.ie/ard-cuilinnlodge. Open 16 Mar to Oct.* 🅿*4 rm.* Noteable for its quiet, semi-rural location with views of the surrounding hills, yet five minutes drive from the town centre. The three well-kept bedrooms overlook the garden. Local smoked salmon and scrambled egg are a breakfast speciality.

⊜ **Benwiskin Lodge** – *Shannon Eighter – 1.25mi N of Sligo by N 15 -* ◷ *Closed 22 Dec to 7 Jan.* 🅿 *4 rm.* ☎ *071 9141088; www.benwiskin.com*

DIY enthusiasts can compare their handiwork with that of the owner; he handcrafted the majority of the furniture at this detached guesthouse. The décor is bright and cheery and the pitch n' putt close by.

⊜ **Tree Tops** – *Cleveragh Rd - 0.25mi S of Sligo by Dublin road -* ☎ *071 9160160; www.sligobandb.com.* ◷ *Closed*

one month at Christmas. 🅿 *5 rm.* An unassuming house in a residential area but made special by the warmth and hospitality of the owner. She also has an impressive collection of Irish art which adorns many of the walls. Bedrooms are cosy and comfortable.

WHERE TO EAT

⊜⊜ **Montmartre** – *Market Yard -* ☎ *071 9169901. Closed 9-27 Jan, 25 Dec and Mon.*

Broad range of styles but the atmosphere and style of the room have a strong Gallic accent, from the pictures of French landmarks on the walls to the helpful mesdemoiselles providing the service.

ENTERTAINMENT

The **Hawk's Well Theatre** – ☎ *071 9161526; www.hawkswell.com*

SHOPPING

Sligo Crystal– *10mi/16km north by N 15 at Grange –* ◷ *Open Jun-Sep, Mon-Fri, 9am-9pm, Sat-Sun, 10am to 7pm; Oct-May, Mon-Sat, 9am to 6pm.* ☎ *071 43440.* Factory and showrooms with guided tours; see craftsmen using the oldest traditions known for producing hand-cut crystal.

SPORTS AND LEISURE

Strandhill is good for wind-surfing but bathing can be dangerous.
Rosses Point *(An Ros),* a sandy peninsula projecting into Drumcliff Bay, provides a championship golf course and two beautiful sandy beaches for bathing and wind-surfing.

EVENTS AND FESTIVALS

Yeats Annual Winter School – Weekend in February of lectures and a tour of Yeats Country the refurbished buildings (1416), spared by Queen Elizabeth on condition that the friars became secular clergy, were deliberately set on fire in 1641 by the Parliamentary commander Sir Frederick Hamilton. The nave contains an elaborate altar tomb honouring the O'Creans (1506); a 15C rood screen across the 13C chancel containing the 17C O'Conor monument. North of the church are the 13C sacristy and chapterhouse and extant parts of the 15C **cloisters**.

Model Arts and the Niland Gallery★

♿🕐 *Open Tue-Sat 10am-5.30pm, Sun 11am-4pm.* 🅿 ☎*071 914 1405 - www. modelart.ie*

The somewhat forbidding Model School has been extended and transformed to provide an arts centre of more than regional importance with room for the **Niland Collection of Modern Irish Art** assembled by the former county librarian Nora Niland comprising some 200 paintings by Jack B Yeats, works by George Russell, Maurice McGonigal, Norah McGuiness, Estella Solomons, Paul Henry, Augustus John and Seán Keating.

County Museum

♿🕐 *Open Jun to Sep Tue-Sat 10am-noon, 2-4.50pm; Oct to May Tue-Sat 2-4.50pm* ☎ *071 9141623*

The old manse (1851) houses the **Yeats Memorial Collection** of manuscripts, photographs and letters; local antiquities and a large painting *"1916"*, showing Countess Markiewicz and fellow-insurgents surrendering outside Dublin's College of Surgeons.

St John's Cathedral

🕐 *Open Jul to Aug 10am-2pm.*

This unusual structure was designed in 1730 by Richard Castle, and altered in 1812. A brass tablet *(north transept)* commemorates the mother of WB Yeats, Susan, who was married here; the tomb of her father, William Pollexfen, lies near the main gates.

Cathedral of the Immaculate Conception

The highlight of this uninspired neo-Romanesque building (1874) are the 69 stained-glass by Loblin of Tours in France, best seen in the early morning or evening light.

Excursion

Sligo Peninsula

Strandhill marks the end the peninsula assaulted by Atlantic breakers (*good surfing but hazardous bathing*). Here too is Sligo's little airport, but the area's particular attraction are its outstanding prehistoric monuments.

Carrowmore Megalithic Cemetery★

3mi/5km SW of Sligo by a minor road. (Dúchas) ♿🕐 *Open Easter to Oct 10am-5.15pm.* 🎫 *€2.10.* ☎ *071 916 1534*

Carrowmore is the largest Stone Age cemetery in Ireland, having over 60 passage graves, dolmens, stone circles and one cairn marking the largest grave. The most ancient dates from 3200 BC, 700 years earlier than Newgrange. The **visitor centre** contains an exhibition about Stone Age man and the excavations.

Knocknarea★

▶ *7mi/11km W of Sligo by R 292. After 6mi/10km bear left; park after 1mi/1.6km; 1hr 30min there and back on foot to the summit.*

The approach road climbs up "The Glen", a natural fault in the limestone providing a haven for rare plants. On the summit of **Knocknarea** (1 076ft/328m) is a massive heap of stones (197yd/180m round), visible for miles and providing a fine **view**★★ on a clear day. According to tradition, and W B Yeats, this contains a passage grave and tomb of Medb/Maeve, Queen of Connaught in 1C AD; however, it is more likely that she was buried at **Rathcroghan** near TulskLimerick.

Driving Tours

Lough Gill★★ *Round tour of 30mi/48km E of Sligo – half a day*

Lough Gill is one of Ireland's loveliest lakes, dotted with islands, fringed by shoreline woodlands, picturesquely set against looming limestone mountains *(northwest)*.

▶ *From Sligo take N 4 S; after 0.25mi/ 0.4km bear left to Lough Gill.*

Tobernalt
The holy well shaded by trees marks an old Celtic assembly site where a summer festival (Lughnasa) was celebrated in August.

▶ *Continue on the shore road; at the T-junction turn left onto R 287.*

Dooney Rock Forest
The top of Dooney Rock offers superlative views of the lake and Benbulben.

▶ *At the crossroads turn left; after 2mi/3.2km turn left; 2mi/3.2km to car park.*

Innisfree
W B Yeats was especially drawn to this tiny island, immortalisedin his poem *Lake Isle of Innisfree.*

▶ *Return to R 287 and continue E.*

Parke's Castle

Dromahair

This attractive riverside village sits between the shell of Villiers Castle (17C) and a ruined abbey.

Creevelea Abbey

Park behind the Abbey Hotel (left); 6min there and back on foot across the bridge.
An avenue of evergreens beside the Bonet River leads to the ruins of a Franciscan friary which was founded by Owen O'Rourke in 1508. The church presents well-preserved east and west windows and west door. Carved pillars in the cloisters show St Francis with the stigmata and birds on a tree.

▷ *Continue on R 287.*

Parke's Castle★

(Dúchas) ♿ 🕐 *Open mid-Mar to Oct 10am-6pm. Last admission at 5.15pm.* 🗣 *Tour by appointment.* 💶 *€2.75.* ✉ 📞 *071 916 4149 - www.heritageireland.ie*
The extensively restored fortified plantation mansion, apparently sitting on the lough waters, was built in 1609 by the Englishman Capt Robert Parke on the site of Sir Brian O'Rourke former home. The bawn wall enclosing the yard once supported the less substantial thatched outbuildings; note how the water-level must have been higher (10ft/3m) in the 17C. A **sweat house** has been hollowed out in the wall by the shore. A video presentation provides an overview of the area's history.

▷ *Continue W on R 286 (car park and viewpoint); after 7mi/11.3km turn left.*

Hazelwood

Striking views of the lake are to be enjoyed from the trails through the woods; the Palladian house *(private)* was designed by Richard Castle in 1731.

▷ *Continue W on R 286 to return to Sligo.*

Benbulben *Round-trip of 44mi/71km N of Sligo – Allow 1 day*

The dramatic silhouette of Benbulben, a limestone table mountain with a west-facing escarpment like the prow of a dreadnought, dominates the country for miles.

H Champollion/MICHELIN

Yeats' Tomb

▶ *From Sligo take N 15 N.*

Drumcliff★

William Butler Yeats admirers come to the churchyard at Drumcliff, where his great-grandfather had been rector, to pay tributes to the poet. Yeats died in the south of France in 1939, and was buried here in accordance with his wishes. The gravestone carries an enigmatic epitaph he composed himself :

> *Cast a cold eye*
> *On life, on death.*
> *Horseman, pass by!*

The site beneath Benbulben (1 730ft/526m) by the Drumcliff River was also chosen by St Columba for the foundation of a monastery in c 575; the **round tower** was damaged by lightning in 1396; the **high cross** (c 1000) is carved with Adam and Eve, Cain killing Abel, Daniel in the Lions' Den and Christ in Glory; the Presentation in the Temple and the Crucifixion.

▶ *Make a detour left via Carney.*

Lissadell House

House tour(40min):16 Mar to Sep 10.30am-6pm. Last tour at 5pm. €6. Walled garden: open Jun to Sep 10.30am-4pm. €5. Alpine garden: open mid-Jul to late Sep 10.30am-4.30pm. €5. 071 916 3150 - www.lissadell-house.com

Standing on the north shore of Sligo Bay surrounded by woods, this austere neo-Classical house owned by the Gore-Booth family (until 2003), descended from the Englishman Captain Gore, who settled in the district in the reign of Elizabeth I. Sir Robert Gore-Booth, for whom the house was built in 1830, was almost bankrupted by efforts to relieve the distress of his tenants during the Famine. W B Yeats was a visitor here, enchanted by the house's atmosphere and entranced by Eva and Constance.

Countess Markievicz

The most remarkable member of the Gore-Booth family was Constance (1868–1927), the wife of the Polish artist, impresario and boulevardier Casimir Markievicz, who lived in Dublin and Paris. The couple drifted apart as Constance devoted herself to the Nationalist cause. While Casimir fought on the Allied side in World War I, Constance took part in the Easter Rising. Condemned to death and later reprieved, she was the first woman elected to the House of Commons in Westminster, though she never took her seat.

Since its latest acquisition, the house and garden are being carefully renovated.

▶ *Leave the grounds by the north gate; turn left; after 1mi/1.6km turn left to Raghly.*

Ardtermon Castle

Standing within its bawn wall is the restored fortified dwelling built by a member of the Gore family in the early 17C. The entrance is flanked by two round towers; the staircase is contained in a semicircular projection at the rear.

▶ *Return to N 15 and continue N.*

The road passes **Streedagh Point**, a sand bar (3mi/5km) lying parallel with the shore, where three ships from the Spanish Armada – *Juliana*, *La Levia* and *La Santa Maria de Vision* – went down; those that survived drowning were put to death by the English troops; together over 1 300 men perished.

▶ *In Cliffony turn left to Mullaghmore.*

Mullaghmore
The village shelters on the east side of the rocky headland pointing north into Donegal Bay, grouped around the stone-walled harbour, built in 1842 by Lord Palmerston before his splendidly picturesque neo-Gothic **Classiebawn Castle** (1856) was completed on the exposed west shore. The castle was later acquired by Lord Mountbatten, who, with several members of his family, was blown up in his boat in 1979, by the IRA.

Inishmurray
11mi/18km offshore; access by boat from Mullaghmore pier and from Rosses Point near Sligo.
St Molaise founded a settlement on this little island in the 6C. The remains of the monastery include the Women's Church *(Teampall na mBan)*; rectangular and "beehive"-style dwellings; the main or Men's Church; souterrains and stone altars. Elsewhere on the island are pillar stones which may be pre-Christian, 57 inscribed stone slabs and 16 Stations of the Cross, spaced around the rocky perimeter. The island has a long history of human habitation – one decorated container found here has been dated to 2000 BC – and not until 1948 did the last people leave, defeated by wartime fuel restrictions, which ended the regular supply-boat trips from Killybegs.

▶ *From Mullaghmore return inland bearing left at the first fork and right at the second. At the crossroads turn left onto N 15.*

Creevykeel Court Cairn★
The well-preserved Late Stone Age court tomb (c 2500 BC), consists of an open court and a double burial chamber surrounded by a wedge-shaped mound of stones. Two other chambers, entered from the side, are probably later.

▶ *At the crossroads turn left inland.*

Gleniff Horseshoe Scenic Drive
This short loop road *(6mi/10km)* makes a fascinating incursion into the upland landscapes of the Darty Mountains between **Truskmore** (2 120ft/644m), and Benbulben.

▶ *Turn left onto the minor road. After 6mi/9.5km turn left onto N 15; before reaching Drumcliff turn left onto a minor road.*

Glencar Waterfall★
Access path right; 5min there and back on foot.
The waterfall tumbles over the rocks to a sheer drop (50ft/15m). The wind howling in from the Atlantic sometimes blows up the spray - as described by W B Yeats:
…the cataract smokes upon the mountain side… that cold and vapour-turbaned steep.

▶ *Continue E. At the junction turn right into N 16 to return to Sligo.*

STROKESTOWN★

POPULATION 568

A particularly fine example of an estate village and now a Heritage Town, Strokestown (Béal Na Mbuillí) has a broad main street running up to the fanciful Gothic arches of the entrance to Strokestown Park House. Lived in by its founding family until 1979, the house gives an intriguing picture of the life led by a prominent family of the Anglo-Irish Ascendancy. The surrounding district is rich in relics of earlier Irish society. 🄸 *Abbey St, Roscommon* ☎ *090 662 6342 - www.irelandwest.ie*

▶ **Orient Yourself:** Strokestown is on N 5, the main road leading north-west from Longford, in the north part of Co Roscommon

👣 **Also See:** ATHLONE, BOYLE, CARRICK-ON-SHANNON, KNOCK, LONGFORD

A Bit of History

Confiscated from its original owner, O'Connor Roe, part of whose bawn survives in the building now housing the restaurant, land at Strokestown was granted to Capt Nicholas Mahon (d 1680), a Cromwellian officer; the

> **TRACING ANCESTORS**
> **County Roscommon Heritage & Genealogy** – *Mon-Fri* ☎ *071 963 3380 - www.roscommonroots.com*

estate was later extended to secure his support for Charles II. As they prospered, successive members of the Mahon family rebuilt or extended the house begun by Nicholas Mahon. In 1800, Maurice Mahon accepted a Union peerage, becoming Baron Hartland of Strokestown, despite his father having been a bitter opponent of the Act of Union. In 1845, as the Great Famine began, the property passed to Major Denis Mahon, who acquired an unenviable reputation as a heartless evictor of his destitute tenantry, more than 3 000 in total, many of whom perished aboard the notorious "coffin ships". On 2 November 1847 in broad daylight, while riding in an open carriage, he was shot dead by two assassins; that evening, bonfires were lit in celebration on the nearby hills.

Visit

Strokestown Park House and Famine Museum★

♿ 🍴 *House tour: 17 Mar to Oct 10.30am-5.30pm. House and garden* 🎫*€12.50; garden only* 🎫 *€8.* 🍽 🅿 ☎ *071 963 3013 - www.strokestownpark.ie*

The house, a fine Palladian mansion designed by Richard Castle in the 1730s, consists of a central three-storey block with a pillared portico, linked by curving corridors to the service wings. The well-preserved interiors give an impression of a comfortable and sociable rather than ostentatious life. As well as spits and a trio of ovens for baking, roasting and smoking, the great **kitchen** has a dresser filled

Famine pot, Strokestown Famine Museum

Strokestown Park

with Belleek pottery and is overlooked by a gallery from which the housekeeper could supervise her underlings.

The **Walled Gardens** have been restored; the larger pleasure garden (4 acres/1.6ha) is embellished with a magnificent Edwardian pergola and long herbaceous border; the smaller Georgian fruit and vegetable garden contains the original glasshouses used to cultivate grapes, peaches and figs.

The **Famine Museum** in the stable yard, presents a comprehensive, detailed and balanced account of the Great Famine , based on State archives and the Strokestown estate records, used by Cecil Woodham-Smith for her book *The Great Hunger*. References to the family, the estate and their history are put in their mid-19C context.

Driving Tour

Cruachan District

▷ *From Strokestown take R 368 N to Elphin and follow sign.*

Elphin Windmill

Tour Jul to Aug 10am-6pm, Sep-Jun Mon-Fri 2-6pm, Sat-Sun 10am-6pm. Phone to confirm. ☜ €5. ☎ 086 400 2765

The early 18C windmill (restored) is the only one of its kind in the west of Ireland: what is unusual about it, is its conical thatched roof and sails made to face the wind by means of cartwheels running on a circular track.

▷ *From Elphin take R 369 W ; turn left onto N 61 ; in Tulsk turn right onto N 5 to Rathcroghan.*

Cruachan Aí Visitor Centre

&⊙ *Open Jun to Sep Mon-Fri 9am-6pm, Sat-Sun 10am (1pm Sun)-6pm; Oct to May Mon-Sat 9am-5pm.* ☜ €5. ☎ 071 963 9268 - www.cruachanai.com

On the banks of the little Ogulla River, this sensitively designed structure hosts fascinating display about the area's extraordinary field monuments which have long fascinated archeologists and antiquarians but whose precise function and meaning is only now being unravelled.

The Centre abuts a ringfort and the motte of an Anglo-Norman style castle, but the majority of the monuments – Bronze Age tumuli, ring-barrows, souterrains, field systems and ceremonial avenues – are spread widely over a broad and fertile landscape which has been grazed since Neolithic times, featuring in the country's most compelling myths, legends and history. According to the *Táin Bó Cúailgne* saga, it was from here that Queen Medb/Maeve set out on the great Cattle Raid of Cooley; the kings of Ireland were buried here before Tara became the favoured royal cemetery in the first century AD. The kings of Connaught were inaugurated on the summit of the hill at Carnfree, the last such ceremony taking place as late as 1641.

▷ *Continue NW on N5 for 9mi/14km.*

Douglas Hyde Centre

&⊙ *Open May to Sep, afternoons only*

The Anglican Church in Portahard, Frenchpark, where his father was Rector, is now devoted to the life of Douglas Hyde (1860–1949), first President of the Irish Republic (1938–45). Unusually for one of Anglo-Irish origin, Dr Douglas Hyde was an Irish scholar and a passionate collector of Irish poetry and folk tales. As president of the Gaelic League, his efforts were directed to the preservation of Gaelic as the national language of Ireland and the promotion of Irish literature.

▶ *Take the minor road S via Cloonfad and Fairymount and R 361 to Castlerea. Turn right onto N60, then right again.*

Clonalis House★

♿ 🚭 *Tour (45min) Jun to Aug Mon-Sat 11am-4pm.* ♿ €7. 🛏*B&B accommodation.* 🅿 ☎ *094 962 0014 - www.clonalis.com*

Clonalis is the seat of the O'Connor Don (Don means king or leader), one of the most ancient of Irish dynasties with an ancestry leading back to Federach the Just in AD75. The Italianate house, overlooking the River Suck, was designed in 1878 by the English architect Pepys Cockerell.

Beside the front door *(left)* stands the inauguration stone of the O'Connor clan which was formerly at Rathcroghan.

The well-furnished house is a monument to the O'Connors in Ireland and abroad: one member founded the city of Tucson in Arizona. There is a great library of books and archived documents (correspondence from Louis XIV, Samuel Johnson, Daniel O'Connell, Gladstone, Douglas Hyde), portraits, costumes, uniforms, and the standard borne at the coronation of George V in 1911 by Denis O'Connor, the first member of an Irish Gaelic family to be so honoured. There is also the blind bard Turlough Carolan's harp, who often played for the O'Connors.

Two relics from the Penal Period are displayed in the **chapel:** an altar from a secret chapel, and a special chalice.

▶ *Take N 60 SE; after 2.5mi/4km turn left to Ballintober.*

Ballintober Castle

The ruined castle was inhabited well into the 19C. The high walls, fortified by a polygonal tower at each corner and originally surrounded by a moat, enclose a large rectangular courtyard. Two projecting turrets guard the entrance gate. In 1652 the castle was captured by the Cromwellians but in 1677 it was returned to the O'Connor Don, by whose ancestors it was built c 1300.

▶ *Take R 367 S ; turn right onto N 60. In Ballymoe turn left and left again onto the minor road to Glinsk.*

Glinsk Castle

The four-storey ruin suggest a fine fortified house, built by the Burkes c 1618-30.

▶ *Continue SE through Creggs and on R 362. Before joining N 63, turn left and left again onto a private drive.*

Castlestrange Stone★

In a field *(right)* is a rounded granite boulder decorated with a curvilinear La Tène from 250 BC.

▶ *Turn left onto N 63 towards Roscommon.*

Roscommon Dominican Friary

The ruined friary, established in 1253, still has an effigy of its founder, Felim O'Connor, his feet resting on a dog; below is a panel with vigorous carvings of mail-clad and well-armed gallow glasses the fearsome mercenary warriors imported from the west of Scotland in the 14C.

▶ *Continue on N 63 to Roscommon.*

Roscommon

The county town, an important market in the middle of rich cattle and sheep country, is named after St Comán, first Bishop of Roscommon and abbot of Clonmacnoise. He founded a monastery of Augustinian canons in Roscommon, elements of which may be incorporated into the Anglican church. The history of the monastery, the town and the district is illustrated in the endearing **Roscommon County Museum**, housed in a former Presbyterian chapel. &⃝ *Open Jun to Aug Mon-Sat 10am-5.30pm; Sep to May Mon-Fri 10am-4pm.* ☎ *090 6625613 - www.visitroscommon.ie*

▶ *North of the town on N 61 ; From the car park 2min on foot across a field.*

Roscommon Castle★

The impressive ruin of an enormous Norman castle, built in 1269 by Robert de Ufford and originally protected by a lake or swamp suggests it had massive walls, and round corner bastions. The mullion windows were inserted by Sir Nicholas Malby, Governor of Connaught; it was destroyed largely by Cromwellian troops.

TRALEE

POPULATION 19 056

At the head of its bay, the county town of Kerry is a flourishing, workaday place with a range of traditional and modern industries. Not particularly oriented to tourism, it is nevertheless an important gateway to the Dingle peninsula, treating its visitors to an ambitious and informative evocation to the "Kingdom of Kerry". It is also the home of the country's National Folk Theatre, which attracts hopefuls from the Irish diaspora for the annual "Rose of Tralee" festival. 🛈 *Ashe Memorial Hall* ☎ *066 7121288*

▶ **Orient Yourself:** Tralee is situated at the neck of the Dingle Peninsula on N 21 and N 69, between Dingle and Limerick; 20mi/32km north of Farranfore Airport

Kids **Especially for Kids:** Crag Cave

☝ **Also See:** ADARE, DINGLE PENINSULA, KENMARE, KILLARNEY

A Bit of History

Desmond Stronghold and Denny Fief – Tralee (Trá Lí) grew around the Anglo-Norman castle, built by John Fitzgerald in 1243; his descendants, the Earls of Desmond

Tralee Bay

Rose of Tralee

Every August the town is host to the International Rose of Tralee Festival which attracts visitors, particularly emigrants, from many parts of the world; all girls of Irish descent are eligible for the title. In the Town Park stands a statue of William Mulchinock (1820–64), who wrote the song *The Rose of Tralee*, of which this is the refrain:

> *"She was lovely and fair as the rose of the summer*
> *Yet t'was not her beauty alone that won me*
> *Oh no t'was the truth in her eye ever dawning*
> *That made me love Mary, the Rose of Tralee.*

became one of the most powerful Old English clans, "more Irish than the Irish" and deadly rivals of the Ormonds. The Geraldine (ie Fitzgerald) line came to an end in 1583 when the 15th Earl, who had rebelled with Spanish and Papal help, was betrayed and executed; his head was displayed on a spike at the Tower of London. Tralee and the Desmond estates were granted to Sir Hugh Denny, who had helped defeat the Spanish; the Denny family held sway here for 300 years.

The town suffered badly in the wars of the 17C and now has a mostly 18C and 19C character, its most distinguished edifice being the Greek Revival Courthouse designed by Sir Richard Morrison in the mid-19C. Strongly nationalistic in outlook, Tralee became an important centre of opposition to British rule in the late 19C/early 20C.

Visit

Kerry The Kingdom★

&⚙ ⏰ *Open 17 Mar to Oct 10am-6pm; Nov to 23 Dec noon-2.30pm* ⏰ *Closed 24-27 Dec* ☞ *€8* ☂ 🅿 ☎*066 712 7777*

This popular visitor attraction has three sections: **The Geraldine Experience** recreates the sights, sounds and smells of the medieval town; **Kerry in Colour** is an exciting multi-media presentation of the history of the region from Mesolithic times; the **Kerry County Museum** displays an array of artefacts and scale models.

Address Book

GETTING AROUND

Tarbert Pier is the departure point for the **Shannon Ferry**, which carries cars and passengers to Killimer on the north bank. ☎ *065 905 3124; www.shannonferries.com*

ENTERTAINMENT

National Folk Theatre of Ireland (Siamsa Tíre) – ☎ *066 712 3055; www.siamsatire.com.* Founded in 1974, this theatre company draws on the rich local Gaelic tradition to evoke the seasonal festivals and rural way of life in past centuries. The ultra-modern theatre building is shaped like a ringfort.

SHOPPING

Crafts – Visit the Blennerville craft workshops *(see below)*.

SPORTS AND LEISURE

Beaches – West and north in Tralee Bay. There are indoor water facilities at the **Aqua Dome** – ☎ *066 712 9150 (24hr info); www.discoverkerry.com/aquadome.*

Seaweed baths at Ballybunnion. Greyhound Racing.

EVENTS AND FESTIVALS

Listowel Writers' Week – Celebration of the exceptional literary reputation of Listowel held annually in May.

The surrounding **town park** contains a statue of William Mulchinock, the the ruins of the **Geraldine castle**.

Tralee & Dingle Railway

&♿⏰ *Open May to Sep.* ⚷ *Locomotive may be under repair, so phone to confirm trains are running.* ⊕ *€5 there and back.* ✗ *at Blennerville* 🅿 ☎ *066 712 1064 - www. tdlr.org.uk*

The Tralee & Dingle Railway, serving the disparate communities of the Dingle peninsula closed in 1953, but the centenary year of its construction was marked in 1991 by the re-opening to passenger traffic of the first stretch *(1.5mi/2.4km)* of the narrow-gauge (3ft/1m) line between Tralee and Blennerville. The train is composed of three original carriages drawn by No 5, last of the original steam locomotives.

Excursions

Blennerville Windmill★

2mi/3.2km S of Tralee by R 559. &♿⏰ *Open Apr to Oct 10am-6pm.* ⊕ *€5.* ✗ 🅿 ☎ *066 712 1064*

The exceptionally tall, white-painted five-storey windmill (60ft/18m high), built by the local landlord, Sir Rowland Blennerhassett, c 1800 and derelict by 1880, is again in working order; an electric engine takes over when the wind fails.

The **Emigration Exhibition** illustrates the experience of the many thousands who left Ireland for America in the 19C. The 540 ton replica of the emigrant ship *Jeannie Johnston*, shows what the conditions were like onboard.

Blennerville Windmill

Crag Cave★

11mi/18km E of Tralee by N 21 to Castleisland (Oileán Ciarraí); take the minor road N for 1mi/1.6km (sign). 👶&♿⚷ *Tour (30min): mid-Mar to Oct 10am-5.30pm (6pm Jul-Aug). Adventure playground 10am-6pm.* ⏰ *Closed Mon-Tue Jan to Feb.* ⊕ *€7.* ▭✗ 🅿 ☎ *066 714 1244*

The limestone caves (4 170yd/3 813m), discovered in 1983, are thought to be over a million years old. A short descent *(62 steps)* leads to the tunnels and chambers of the show cave (383yd/350m) with stalactites, stalagmites, columns, curtains, drip stones and flow stones. The myriad shimmering white straw stalactites in the **Crystal Gallery** provide a magical climax.

Driving Tour

North Kerry *Drive of 87mi/140km*

▸ *From Tralee take R 551 N and R 558 W; take a minor road N to Ardfert.*

Ardfert★

(Dúchas) &⏰ *Open May to Sep 9.30am-5.15pm.* ⊕ *€2.10.* ☎ *66 7134711*

Ardfert was established as a missionary base as early as the 5C. The stone church, founded in the 6C by St Brendan the Navigator as part of a monastery, was destroyed by fire in 1089. Under the Normans Ardfert became a borough, far more important than Tralee, though the lack of a harbour led to its eventual eclipse; two major ecclesiastical ruins have survived from this period.

The **cathedral** was built c 1150 and destroyed by fire in the 17C but its walls still rise to the eaves and its east end has a trio of elegant lancet windows. The south transept (15C) contains an exhibition on the history of the building and the two adjacent small churches, which are decorated with interesting sculptures.

Standing among the fields, **Ardfert Friary**, a Franciscan house, was founded in 1253 and substantially rebuilt in 1453; much of the tower and of the chancel with its nine lancets in the south wall and five-light lancet in the east wall are still intact.

▶ *Continue N on R 551.*

Banna Strand★

The vast stretch of sandy beach (5mi/8km) was used for the filming of *Ryan's Daughter* in 1968. A memorial at the entrance commemorates Sir Roger Casement (1864–1916), who landed on the beach on 21 April 1916 from a German submarine with a consignment of arms for the Easter Rising ; he was recognised and arrested almost at once and subsequently executed.

▶ *Continue N on R 551.*

Rattoo Round Tower★

The exceptionally well-preserved round tower and the ruined 15C church mark the site of an abbey founded in 1200 for the Knights Hospitaller of St John the Baptist. In 1202 it became an Augustinian house, which was burned in 1600.

▶ *Continue N on R 551 ; detour along the coast road via Kilcoly, Beal and Astee.*

Ballybunnion

This rather old-fashioned little seaside resort has amusement arcades and several fine beaches; it is also noted for its outdoor baths, where seaweed is used for therapeutic purposes.

▶ *Continue N and E on R 551; just before Ballylongford turn left into a minor road.*

Carrigafoyle Castle★

Once the principal seat of the O'Connor clan, who ruled most of north Kerry, the castle, originally on an island, was finally destroyed by Cromwellian forces in 1649. One of the flanker towers is fitted out as a dovecot. A spiral staircase leads to the top of the tower (80ft/29m high) for extensive **views** of the Shannon estuary.

▶ *Return to R 551 and continue E; in Ballylongford turn left to Saleen.*

Lislaughtin Abbey

This Franciscan foundation dates from the 15C; the church has an attractive west window and three well-preserved sedilia; traces of the refectory and dormitory remain on the east side of the cloisters; the lavatories were housed in the tower at the north end.

▶ *Continue E on minor road to Tarbert.*

Tarbert

Tarbert Bridewell has been converted into a museum describing, through wax tableaux in the courtroom and cells, the legal and penal systems in force in Ireland 1828–31. 🕐 *Open Mon-Fri 10am-5pm.* ✆ €5. ☎ 068 36500

The **woodland walk** *(starting from the car park)* leads through the grounds of **Tarbert House** (17C), which has seen such notable guests as Benjamin Franklin, Charlotte Brontë and Daniel O'Connell, and continues along the wooded shore to Tarbert Old Pier. *Tour by appointment May to mid-Aug.* €8. 068 36198

▶ *From Tarbert take N 69 S.*

Listowel (Lios Tuathail)
17mi/27km N of Tralee by N 69.
The literary reputation of the market town and Heritage Town of Listowel and of North Kerry is celebrated in **Writers' Week**, ireland's longest running literary festival held annually in May/June with an international reputation.

In the huge central square stands **St John's Theatre**, formerly the Anglican parish church, which offers live performances of music and theatre and the **Seanchai Kerry Literary and Cultural Centre** which honours the writers and story-tellers of Co Kerry: Eamon Kerry, John B Keane, Brian McMahon, Brendan Kennelly and other local writers with displays of texts and video screenings. *Open Jun to mid-Sep 9.30am-5.30pm; mid-Sep to May, Mon-Fri 9.30am-4.30pm.* €5. (Mon-Fri) 068 22212 - www.writersweek.ie

In the north-east corner of the square is the striking **plasterwork façade** of the Central Hotel.

▶ *Continue S on N 69 to Tralee.*

TRIM★

Straddling the Boyne by an ancient ford, little Trim (Baile Átha Troim), **a designated Heritage Town, is dominated by its ruins of its castle, the largest in Ireland, a medieval monument to match the great prehistoric structures farther down the valley. Other imposing remains recall Trim's important role as a stronghold and ecclesiastical centre on the outer edge of the Pale established by the Anglo-Normans.** Castle St 046 943 7227 - www.meathtourism.ie

▶ **Orient Yourself:** Trim is situated on the River Boyne, a little southwest of Navan, on a minor road (R 154) which forks off the N 3 Dublin-Navan road
Don't Miss: Trim Castle
Also See: BOYNE VALLEY, FINGAL, KELLS, MAYNOOTH, MULLINGAR

Visit

Trim Castle★★
South bank; access through the Town Gate or along the river bank from the bridge. (Dúchas) Open Jun to mid-Sep 9.30am-5.30pm; May Mon-Fri 9.30am-4.30pm; Nov to Easter open for group visits only €5; Castle and grounds only €1.60. *Keep tour (45min)* €3.70. *Site is extremely busy in summer so come early.* 046 943 8619
This magnificent medieval castle overlooks the meadows beside the Boyne, whose waters fed the now-dry moat. An outer curtain wall with gatehouses and several towers encloses a broad grassy space dominated by the formidable **keep** (1225) with its two great halls and sleeping accommodation above.
The first stronghold here was built in 1172, in the early days of the Anglo-Norman conquest by Hugh de Lacy, but was soon attacked and destroyed by the native Irish.

H Champollion/MICHELIN

Trim Castle

Rebuilt, it served as King John's headquarters on his sojurn in Ireland and is often called King John's Castle. Protected by two drawbridges and a barbican, the Dublin Gate served as a prison, where the young prince who was to become Henry IV was held prisoner by Richard II. The castle was attacked by Cromwell's troops, who left a breach in the river wall; an adjacent stretch of wall collapsed in 1839, in the course of a storm known as the Big Wind.

Across the river stands a stone arch, the medieval **Sheep Gate**, a fragment of the town's medieval walls; tolls were levied here on flocks bought and sold at the great sheep fairs.

Yellow Steeple

North bank; access from the High St.

The ruined late-14C tower, which gleams in the sun, marks the site of **St Mary's Abbey**, an Augustinian community, founded by St Malachy of Armagh in the 12C near the point where St Patrick landed in the 5C and converted Foitchern, the son of the local chieftain and later first Bishop of Trim. Many pilgrims were attracted to the abbey by Our Lady of Trim, a wooden statue with a reputation for effecting miracles, which disappeared in the Cromwellian period.

In 1425 the west cloisters of the abbey were converted by Lord Lieutenant Talbot into a fortified house, **Talbot's Castle**, which bears the Talbot coat of arms on the north wall. After the Reformation the house became a Latin School, later attended by the young Duke of Wellington, sometime MP for Trim, whose family home was at Dangan *(southeast).* Unlike many other members of the Ascendancy, the Iron Duke was not particularly proud of his origins, famously denigrating his Irishness by declaring "because a man is born in a stable, it does not make him a horse".

Cathedral

1mi/1.6km E at Newtown Trim.

Among the graves of Newtown Cemetery is a **tomb** bearing the recumbent figures of Sir Luke Dillon, in his Renaissance armour, and his wife, Lady Jane Bathe, in an Elizabethan gown. Separated by a sword, they are referred to as "the jealous man and woman", Lady Jane supposedly having deceived her husband with his

The Pale

In Medieval times the Irish living outside Anglo-Norman jurisdiction were "beyond the Pale", from the Latin *palus* for a stake. Its use to describe the part of Ireland under effective English rule dates from 1446. The settlement, under Henry II (1154–89), comprised Louth, Meath, Trim, Dublin, Kilkenny, Tipperary, Waterford and Wexford; by the late 15C, as English control weakened, the Pale included Louth, Meath, Dublin and Kildare.

brother. People leave pins on the tomb in the belief that their warts will disappear.

Farther west are the lovely ruins of a **cathedral**, built early in the 13C to replace the church at Clonard *(southwest)*, which was burned by the Irish at the end of the 12C. To the southwest, further remains are those of a priory, two walls of its refectory still standing next to the 14C kitchen.

Crutched Friary
1mi/1.6km E at Newtown Trim.
On the south bank of the Boyne are the ruins of a 13C hospital built by the Crutched Friars, an order of mendicant friars who wore a cross on their habits. The buildings consist of a keep with several fireplaces, a ruined chapel with a triple-light window and the hospital and stores beside the river.

Excursion

Bective Abbey★
5mi/8km NE by R161 (T26); after 4mi/6.4km turn right. Park beyond the abbey near the bridge.
The impressive and extensive ruins stand in a field on the west bank of the Knightsbrook River. The abbey, one of the earliest Cistercian houses in Ireland, was founded in 1150 by the King of Meath, Murcha Ó Maolsheachlainn, and dedicated to the Blessed Virgin; its abbot was a member of the Parliament of the Pale and Hugh de Lacy was buried here in 1195. Little remains of the 12C buildings. The **cloisters**, the tower and the great hall in the south wing date from the 15C when the buildings were altered and fortified.
The film *Braveheart* (1996) was shot among these ruins and at Dunsoghly Castle.

TULLAMORE

POPULATION 9 221

Once known as King's County after Mary Tudor's Spanish husband, Co Offaly forms the very heart of southern Ireland, with the Shannon to the west, the great Bog of Allen to the east, and the Slieve Bloom Mountains to the south. Bustling Tullamore (Tulach Mhór) has been the county town since 1833. Otherwise undistinguished, the place still has something of its late 18C/early 19C character, when much rebuilding took place and when the construction of the Grand Canal brought the town a measure of prosperity. ▯ *Tullamore Dew TIC* ☎ *057 9352617*

▶ **Orient Yourself:** Tullamore is due west of Dublin, on the Grand Canal, just south of the Dublin-Athlone road (N 6)
₺ **Also See:** ABBEYLEIX, ATHLONE, ATHY, BIRR, KILDARE, TRIM

Visit

Tullamore Dew Heritage Centre
₺⏱ *Open Apr to Sep Mon-Sat 9am-6pm, Sun noon-5pm; Oct to Mar 10am (noon Sun)-5pm.* ◉€6. ⏱ ▯ ☎ *057 9325015 - www.tullamore-dew.org*
A golden drop of *Tullamore Dew* or *Irish Mist* awaits in the bar but first it is worth

TRACING ANCESTORS
Irish Midlands Ancestry *Bury Quay, Offaly - Open Mon-Fri, 9am-1pm and 2-4pm.* ☎ *05 06 21421; www.offalyhistory.com.*

discovering the history of Tullamore, particularly of the distillery, founded in 1829 by Michael Molloy. In 1887 Daniel E Williams, who had been steeped in whiskey production since joining the staff at the age of 15, became general manager and gradually acquired overall control of the business. He used his own initials to provide a brand name – *Tullamore Dew* – for the distillery's pot still whiskey and from that flowed the advertising slogan – *Give every man his Dew*. In the 1950s, when sales were low, the distillery began to produce *Irish Mist*, a whiskey-based liqueur, inspired by a traditional Irish recipe for heather wine made with pot still whiskey, herbs and heather honey.

Excursions

Locke's Distillery Museum

Kilbeggan; 7.5mi/12km N of Tullamore by N 52. ♿ 🎧 *Tour (40min): Apr to Oct 9am-6pm; Nov to Mar 10am-4pm.* 🎧 *€5.50.* 🍴 🅿 ☎ *057 933 2134 - www.lockesdistillerymuseum.com*

Bord Fáilte, Dublin

On the west bank of the River Brosna stand the extensive buildings of the distillery (1757–1953) established by John Locke, possibly the oldest licensed pot distillery in Ireland. The process of distilling whiskey is explained and much of the original equipment is still in place: three sets of millstones for grinding barley; the mash tuns (known as kieves) for making wort; the huge wooden vats (washbacks) for fermentation; the hogsheads for maturing the whiskey; coopers' tools; the under-shot water-wheel, and the steam engine which replaced it when the water-level was too high or too low.

Locke's Distillery

Clara Bog

7mi/10km NW of Tullamore by N 80; in Clara take a minor road south; car park at the end of a short causeway. 🚫 *Visitors should not stray from this causeway unless accompanied by a knowledgeable guide.*

This raised bog (1 640 acres/665ha; 23ft/7km maximum depth) is one of the finest and largest of its kind remaining in Ireland and is of international interest. In 1987 it was designated a National Nature Reserve. It has a diverse flora, including at least 10 different bog mosses; in wet areas carnivorous plants, like sundews and bladderworts, entrap unwary insects.

Durrow High Cross

The *Book of Durrow*, an illuminated manuscript now in Trinity College Library, Dublin, was produced at the abbey founded in 556 by St Columba at Durrow *(4mi/7km N of Tullamore by N 52)*. In 1186 the abbey church was pulled down by the Anglo-Norman Hugh de Lacy, an act of sacrilege which so outraged a local man that he cut off the intruder's head. The *Book* survived despite being used by a farmer to cure his sick cattle, touching them with it after soaking it in water. The site of the abbey *(private property)* is a gloomily romantic place, with a ruined 18C church, a holy well, a cemetery with 9C to 11C grave slabs, and above all a fine 10C **high cross**. Its east face shows the Sacrifice of Isaac together with Christ in Glory flanked by David with his harp *(left)* and David killing the Lion *(right)*; the west face shows the Crucifixion and associated events.

WATERFORD ★

POPULATION 42 540

The harbour city of **Waterford** (Port Láirge) continues to benefit from its superb location on the tidal River Suir inland from its confluence with the River Barrow and the vast stretch of sheltered water known as Waterford Harbour. With glassware which has become a global brand, the city enjoys a prosperity which has deep roots in a mercantile and manufacturing tradition going back to its foundation by the Vikings in the 9C. Many memories of this long history are preserved in the mile-long quayside, the close-packed streets and the surviving sections of the once extensive City Walls★ which enclosed the town. The watchtower (35ft/10m high) surveys a well-preserved section on the south side near John's River. As well as the Norman extensions, which are mostly 13C, there are traces of the 9C and 10C Danish walls, including the sallyports in Reginald's Bar near Reginald's Tower. *The Granary, Merchant's Quay* ☎ 051 875 823 *Waterford Airport* ☎ 051 875589 *Waterford Crystal Visitor Centre* ☎ 051 332585 - www.southeastireland.com

▶ **Orient Yourself:** Waterford is situated on the country boundary with County Wexford on the major coast road between Wexford and Cork (N 25) and at the junction of N 9 to Carlow, N 24 to Limerick
⏱ **Also See:** CLONMEL, NEW ROSS, WEXFORD, YOUGHAL

A Bit of History

The Danish Vikings sailed up the Suir in 853, establishing a settlement which they called *Vadrefjord* (meaning weatherhaven). Despite constant warfare with the local Irish, the Danes retained control of Vadrefjord until 1169 when the Anglo-Norman Earl of Pembroke (Strongbow) fought his way into the town, subsequently marrying the King of Leinster's daughter in Reginald's Tower.

Under Anglo- Norman rule Waterford became the second most important town in Ireland after Dublin with a reputation of fierce loyalty to the English king. In 1649 Waterford was unsuccessfully besieged by Cromwell but it fell to his general, Ireton, the following year.

Terry Murphy Photography

Waterford Crystal

Famous Sons

Thomas Francis Meagher (1822–67) was a wealthy lawyer, who joined the Young Ireland Uprising. For his part in the rising at Ballingarry in Co Tipperary he received a death sentence, which was commuted to transportation to Tasmania. From there he escaped to the USA where he founded the Irish Brigade and fought in the American Civil War.

William Hobson (1783–1842), who was born in Lombard Street near The Mall, became the first Governor of New Zealand.

Thunderbird
BOOKSHOP CAFE

▼

OPEN 10 TO 9 DAILY

WE SHIP WORLDWIDE!
Special orders *most* welcome.

**Join our Reader's Club
& earn Book Bucks
toward future purchases.**

Pick up our newsletter at the
front desk, or subscribe for mail
delivery, for information on
events, lectures, book signings,
& workshops.

Specializing in children's
books, travel, cookbooks, &
metaphysical subjects.

The Thunderbird Café serves
homemade soups, sandwiches,
popovers, daily specials,
salads, & desserts.
Open for lunch & dinner.

**THANKYOU FOR SUPPORTING YOUR
LOCAL INDEPENDENT BOOKSHOP.**

PHONE: **831-624-1803**
FAX: **831-624-9034**
EMAIL: **info@thunderbirdbooks.com**
WEBSITE: **www.thunderbirdbooks.com**

1-800-94BOOKS

IN THE BARNYARD, OFF HIGHWAY ONE
AT CARMEL VALLEY ROAD

Walking Tour

Reginald Tower

The stone fortress in a commanding location overlooking the River Suir, was built by the Vikings in 1013 as part of the town's defences, then strengthened by the Anglo-Normans. Its four floors, linked by a spiral stair built within the thickness of the walls, contain displays about tower. (Dúchas) ♿🕐 *Open Easter to Oct 10am-6pm; Nov to Easter Wed-Sun 10am-5pm.* ∽ €2.10. ☎ 051 304220

French Church

(Dúchas) Access through Reginald Tower - on request

Address Book

GETTING AROUND

Passage East Car Ferry – There is a ferry across Waterford Harbour from Passage East *(southeast of Waterford by R 683)* to Ballyhack. ☎ *051 382 480, 382 488; http://homepage.eircom. net/~passferry.*

SIGHTSEEING

Walking Tours – Tours of the city are organised by the Tourist Board ☎ *051 873 711 (before 5pm), 051 851 043 (after 5pm).*

🪙 *For coin ranges, see the Legend on the cover flap.*

WHERE TO STAY

⊜ **Diamond Hill** – *Slieveroe* - ☎ *051 832 855; www.stayatdiamondhill.com.* 🄿 ✖ *18 rm* ⊑. Away from the town centre, Diamond Hill boasts delightful mature gardens for which the owners have won awards. As it is purpose-built, the bedrooms are bright and modern and the house is ideal for those happier in a village atmosphere.

⊜⊜ **The Anchorage** – *9 The Quay* - ☎ *051 854 302.* ✖ *14 rm* ⊑. Simple, clean and strightforward accommodation on the edge of the city and priced fairly. The rooms at the front have the views of the quay and the river while those at the back tend to be quieter.

⊜⊜ **Avondale** – *2 Parnell St, Dunmore East* - ☎ *051 852 267; www.staywithus. net.* 🕐 *Closed 23-29 Dec.* ⊑. Personally run, clean and friendly terraced town house, two minutes walk from the town centre. Bedrooms are tidy, come in a variety of shapes and sizes and are sensibly priced.

⊜⊜ **Coach House** – *Butlerstown Castle, Cork Rd* - ☎ *051 384 656; http:// homepages.iol.ie/~coachhse.* 🕐 *Closed 20 Dec to 5 Jan; restricted opening Feb and Nov.* 🄿 ✖ *7 rm* ⊑. Large stone built house of Victorian origins that lies in the grounds of the ruins of Butlerstown Castle. Attractive and warmly decorated with period furniture sitting alongside modern facilities.

⊜⊜ **Foxmount Country House** – *Passage East Rd* – *4.5mi SE by R 683, off Cheekpoint rd* - ☎ *051 874 308; www. foxmountcountryhouse.com.* 🕐 *mid-Mar to Oct* - ✖ 🄿 ✖ *5 rm* ⊑. Ideal for those escaping the pressures of modern metropolitan life, this charming Georgian house is surrounded by a working dairy farm. Bedrooms, named after flowers, look out over the mature gardens.

⊜⊜ **Three Rivers** – *Cheekpoint - 7mi E of Waterford by R 683* - ☎ *051 382 520.* 🕐 *Closed 20 Dec to 7 Jan.* 🄿 *14 rm* ⊑. If eating at McAlpin's Suir Inn *(see below)*, this purpose-built house offers worthy local accommodation. It has a peaceful setting, with the garden overlooking the estuary. Bedrooms are uniformly decorated and are all en-suite.

⊜⊜⊜⊜ **Waterford Castle Hotel and Golf Club** – *The Island, Ballinakill* – *2.5mi E by R 683, Ballinakill Rd and private ferry* - ☎ *051 878 203;* 🕐 *Closed 23-26 Dec* - 🄿 ✖ *14 rm, 5 suites* ⊑ *€22. Restaurant* ⊜⊜⊜⊜. Catch the private ferry to reach this imposing 15C castle on its own 300 acre/121ha island on the River Suir. Granite arches, gargoyles, oak panelling, log fires and tapestries all add to this authentic baronial experience. Plenty of outdoor activities available.

WHERE TO EAT

⊜ **McAlpin's Suir Inn** – *Cheekpoint* ☎ *051 382 220; www.mcalpins.com.* This pretty and immaculately kept inn on the harbour-front has served the local fishermen for almost 300 years. The hand-written daily changing menu may include mackerel salad or large seafood platters.

⊜⊜ **The Ship** – *Dock Rd, Dunmore East* - ☎ *051 383 141; www.theshiprestaurant. com.* 🕐 *Open May-Oct: daily; Nov-Apr: Wed-Sun.* With chairs fashioned from barrels, fishing nets covering the ceiling and local seafood on the menu it is little wonder this ivy-clad pub is the first port of call for hungry sea dogs in this picturesque fishing village.

⊜⊜ **Wine Vault** – *High St* - ☎ *051 853 444; www.waterfordwinevault. com.* 🕐 *Closed Good Fri, 25 Dec and Sun.* Amateur oenologists need look no further. Wine is the theme at this converted 15C warehouse and features weekly wine specials and an impressive number available by the glass. The menu mixes the classical with the more modern.

ENTERTAINMENT

Immigrant's Tale - *Dooley's Hotel on the Quay - May-Sep, Thu 8.30pm, €12. Show and dinner, €25.* ☎ *051 873 531.* Irish Music, story, song and dance in an historical setting.

Garter Lane Arts Centre – Regular art exhibitions, recitals and theatrical productions – ☎ *051 855 038; www. garterlane.ie.*

SHOPPING

The main shopping streets are Barronstrand Street, which runs inland from the Clock tower in the Quay, and the neighbouring streets.

SPORTS AND LEISURE

Beaches and bathing at Tramore and at Woodstown south of Passage East and south of Duncannon Fort on east shore of Waterford Harbour.
Splashworld – ☎ 051 390 176. Ireland's premier water leisure centre.
Greyhound Racing.

EVENTS AND FESTIVALS

Waterford International Festival of Light Opera – *Held annually in September.* ☎ *051 874402.*

TRACING ANCESTORS

Waterford Heritage Genealogical Service, *St Patrick's Church, Jenkin's Lane* – 🕐 *Open Mon-Fri, 9am-5pm (2pm Fri).* ☎ *051 876 123; www.iol. iel~mnoc.*

Many distinguished families of Waterford are buried within the precincts of the now ruined church. Originally a Franciscan foundation, built in 1240, then a hospital, this was where the Huguenots of Wexford worshipped between 1693 and 1815.

City Hall and Theatre Royal

The **City Hall**, originally the city exchange, is a stately edifice designed by John Roberts in 1788. The building incorporates the **Theatre Royal** (1876); its Victorian decor is rare in Ireland. The three-tier horse-shoe design (seating capacity 650) rises to an impressive dome; the specially designed Waterford Crystal chandelier was presented by Waterford Crystal in 1958 ☎051 874 402 - www.thetheatreroyalwaterford.com

Christ Church Cathedral

♿🕐 *Open Easter to Oct 10am (11am Sun) to 5pm.* 👥 *Tours at 11.30am, 3pm. Concerts* 🎫 *€3.* ☎ *051 858 958 - www.christchurchwaterford.com*
The present building was designed by John Roberts (1714–96) in the 18C English Classical style; it was completed in 1779. In 1891 the galleries and square pews were removed. Within is a model of the original Viking church, which stood on the site from 1050 to 1773; among the monuments from the medieval church, is one of James Rice, showing his body a year after his death with signs of decay and vermin; two monuments by John van Nost to the Fitzgeralds and to Susanna Mason.

Medieval Waterford

When the City Square Shopping Centre was built, 12 layers of housing were found resting on Viking foundations. Stones mark the site of St Peter's church (12C), the earliest example of an apsed church in Ireland. The mural depicts the area c 1100.

St Patrick's Church

As it was built during the Penal Period, the church was deliberately constructed to resemble a house from the outside.

Chamber of Commerce

The fine Georgian building (1795) was designed by John Roberts, a noted 18C Waterford architect.

Waterford Treasures

Visit

Waterford Crystal★

1.5mi/2.5km south by N25. ♿ 🚂 Tours (1hr): Mar to Oct 8.30am-4.15pm; Nov to Feb Mon-Fri 9am-3.15pm. ⊕€8. ⌇ 🅿 ☎ 051 332500 - www.waterfordvisitorcentre.com
Waterford Glass was first produced in 1783; the factory is now the largest glassworks in the world. Tours begin with a film about the story of glass in Ireland and continue through the different stages of production.

Waterford Treasures★

The Granary. ♿🕐 Open Apr to Sep 9.30am-6pm (9pm Jun to Aug); Oct to Mar 10am-5pm. ⊕€4. ☎ 051 30 4500 - www.waterfordtreasures.com.
The old grain store houses a fascinating display of Viking and medieval finds from local excavations: a plan of a Viking house, the city charters and regalia, interactive displays, video.

Driving Tour

Waterford Coast *From Waterford take R 683.*

Passage East

▷ *Take the car ferry across Waterford Harbour to Ballyhack.*

Formerly a fort, the fishing village is built beneath a high escarpment with small squares and streets and brightly painted houses; there are no fewer than three quays: Boathouse Quay, Hackett's Quay and Middle Quay.

▷ *Continue S on R 685.*

Geneva Barracks

On the west shore of Waterford Harbour stand the remains of an extraordinary project undertaken by the government in 1793. The four walls (each 0.25mi/0.4km long) enclosed a new town intended to house Swiss immigrants, who would set a good example with their metalworking skills and their Protestant work ethic. The project failed, and the buildings became a barracks, notorious in 1798 for the atrocities committed against the rebels held there.

▶ *Continue S on R 685; turn left into a minor road.*

Dunmore East★
The Breton-style fishing village comprises several thatched cottages clustered around attractive little coves, including Badger's Cove and Ladies' Cove. There are forest walks beside the Ballymacaw Road *(0.25mi/0.4km west)*.

▶ *Take R 684 and R 685 W via Clohernagh.*

Tramore (Trá Mhór)
9mi/14.5km S of Waterford by R 675.
Tramore is one of Ireland's main holiday resorts equipped with a large amusement park (50 acres/20ha) and a long sandy beach (3mi/5km) overlooking Tramore Bay. There are fine walks, with extensive sea views, along the Doneraile cliffs *(south)*. Great Newtown Head *(west)* across the bay, is marked by three early-19C navigational pillars; the **Tramore Metal Man** is an extraordinary cast-iron figure (14ft/4m high), with pale blue jacket and white trousers, erected in 1823 as a warning to shipping.

▶ *Take R 675 N to return to Waterford.*

WESTPORT★★

POPULATION 4 253

Westport (Cathair Na Mart), a designated Heritage Town, occupies an attractive site on the meandering Carrowbeg River and is an excellent centre for touring the west coast of Mayo. With more than a touch of Georgian elegance and charm, the town was planned and built c 1780 for the local landlord, John Denis Browne, of Westport House, one of Ireland's great country houses. Until the arrival of the railway in the 19C, Westport Quay on the estuary was a busy port lined with imposing 18C warehouses. 🛈 James St ☎ 098 25711 🛈 Achill ☎098 45384 (Jul-Aug).

▶ **Orient Yourself:** Westport is at the western extremity of N 5, part of the national road network, and about 30mi/48km from Knock International Airport

The Brownes of Westport
Twelve generations of Brownes have lived at Westport, all documented in the 400 year family archive. The family is descended from Sir Anthony Browne of Cowdray Castle in Sussex, whose younger son John came to Mayo in the reign of Elizabeth I. The first house was built by Col John Browne (1638–1711), a Jacobite bankrupted by the Williamite victory, married to the great-great-granddaughter of Grace O'Malley. Their grandson, John Browne (1709–76), was brought up an Anglican to avoid the Penal Law sanctions, ennobled as Earl of Altamont. John Denis (1756–1809) was made Marquess of Sligo at the time of the Act of Union in 1800. The 2nd Marquess, Howe Peter (1788–1845), a friend of Lord Byron, returned from a tour of Greece in 1812 with the two columns from the doorway of the Treasury of Atreus in Mycenae; in 1906 they were presented to the British Museum.

Address Book

SIGHTSEEING

Clare Island Ferry (☼ *see below*)
– *Operates from Roonagh Quay (20min) Jul-Aug, 6 times daily; May, Jun and Sep, 4 times daily. There and back €15.* ☎ *086 8515003; 098 25265/25212 (winter); www. clareislandferry.com*

☼ *For coin ranges, see the Legend on the cover flap.*

WHERE TO STAY

○ **Ashville House** – *Castlebar Rd - 2mi E on N 5 -* ☎ *098 27060 ; http:// homepage.eircom.net/~ashville. Mar-Oct* 🅿 *9 rm* ⌷. This guesthouse is a couple of miles outside of town but is worth it for the tennis court, large garden and suntrap terrace. Wood-floored throughout with two of the bedrooms on the ground floor. A warm welcome is assured.

○ **Augusta Lodge** – *Golf Links Rd – 0.5mi N off N 59 -* ☎ *098 28900; www. augustalodge.ie.* ☼ *Closed 1 week at Christmas -* 🅿 ✕ *10 rm* ⌷. There' a clue in the name. Not only is this guesthouse close to the local course but the owner has his golfing memorabilia displayed in the lounge along with a wall-mounted map highlighting all of Ireland's courses. He even has his own putting green next door.

○○ **The Wyatt Hotel** – *The Octagon -* ☎ *098 25027; www.wyatthotel.com.* ☼ *Closed 23-27 Dec.* ✕ & *49 rm* ⌷ *Restaurant* ○○. Contemporary comfort in the very centre of the town. Its busy bar is a popular local spot and the restaurant provides a menu featuring assorted influences from around the world. Bedrooms are modern and comfortable.

○○○○ **Atlantic Coast** – *The Quay - 1mi W by R 335 -* ☎ *098 29000; www. atlanticcoasthotel.com.* ☼ *Closed 24-25 Dec -* 🅿 ✕ & *- 84 rm, 1 suite* ⌷ *Restaurant* ○○. Originally an 18C mill, converted into a modern and well-equipped hotel and overlooking Clew Bay and Croagh Patrick. Bedrooms are roomy and stylish while the top floor restaurant offers contemporary cuisine. Up-to-the-minute leisure club.

○○○○ **Delphi Lodge** – *Leenane – 8.25mi NW by N 59 on Louisburgh rd -* ☎ *095 42222; www.delphilodge.ie.* ☼ *Closed 20 Dec to 6 Jan.* 🅿 *- 12 rm* ⌷ *- Restaurant* ○○○○. Dwarfed by the surrounding mountains and nestling by the lake, this Georgian sporting lodge boasts an unrivalled setting and is much loved by holidaying fishermen. Communal dinner around the large polished table allows guests the chance to discuss the one that got away.

WHERE TO EAT

○ **Matt Molloy's** – *Bridge St -* ☎ *098 26655; www.mattmalloy.com* ✕. The eponymous Matt Molloy is a member of the celebrated Irish folk band, The Chieftains, and live music plays a big part in this town centre pub. Its smoky, lively, noisy and the authentic Irish pub experience.

○○ **Lemon Peel** – *The Octagon, Leenane -* ☎ *098 26929; www.lemonpeel. ie.* ☼ *Closed 24-26 and 31 Dec and Mon - Booking essential.* Klimt prints and appropriately lemon hued walls decorate this narrow little restaurant in the town centre. The chef owner often comes out of his kitchen to greet the regulars. Lively, informal feel with an eclectic mix of influences on the menu.

○○ **Linenmill** – *The Demesne - Off Newport Rd -* ☎ *098 29500 - www. linenmill.ie -* ☼ *Closed Good Fri , 25-26 Dec, Mon, Tue, Sun dinner -* 🅿 . Part of a new development to the west of town, comprising of a museum of the textile industry, a shop selling fabrics and home decoration and a roomy, bright restaurant. Accomplished modern cooking; try the daily changing seafood dishes.

SHOPPING

Linen Mill & Museum – ☼ *See above.*

SPORTS AND LEISURE

Sailing, fishing, walking and horse riding; sandy beaches to the southwest (Silver Strand).

⊗ **Don't Miss:** Westport House, Ballintubber Abbey, and the scenic drive around the Murrisk Peninsula
⊗ **Also See:** CONG, CONNEMARA, KNOCK

Visit

Town Centre★

The focal point of the neat Georgian town is the **Octagon**, where the weekly market is held; the Doric pillar once bore a statue of George Glendinning, a local banker and benefactor. From here James Street descends to the river past the **Heritage and Genealogy Centre**, with informative displays and splendid models of the town and the nearby holy mountain of Croagh Patrick. ♿⊗ *Open when the Tourist Information centre is open 9am-6pm* ☎ *098 25711.*
The leafy North and South Malls follow the river, spanned by three bridges.
The most prominent building in South Mall is **St Mary's Church**, rebuilt in the 20C as a spacious, basilica-like structure, with stained glass by Harry Clarke and Patrick Pye. By contrast, **Holy Trinity Church** is a neo-Gothic building, with a pencil spire and an interior decorated with ornate mosaics illustrating scenes from the Gospels.

Westport House★★

⊗ *Open Apr to Sep 11.30am-5pm (6pm Jul-Aug); Mar, Oct to Nov Sun 11.30am-4pm . House attractions: Jul to Aug Sun-Fri; Jun Sun-Wed; May Sun, Bank Hols.* ⊗ *House: €9.50. House and attractions: €18.* ⊗🅿☎ *098 25430/27766 - www.westporthouse.ie*
The house is the work of several architects: Richard Castle designed the east front (1730), Thomas Ivory was responsible for the south elevation (1778), and James Wyatt added the west front c 1780; the columns on the south date from 1943. Before, stood an earlier house (1650) erected on the site of an O'Malley castle, lapped by the sea; the lake was created in the 18C by damming the Carrowbeg River. The garden terraces were built in the early 1900s.
The **tour** of the interior reveals an elegant decor with several distinctive features – the Pompeian frieze and cloud-painted ceiling in the drawing room commissioned by the 2nd Marquess in about 1825; a collection of **family portraits** in the Long Gallery; doors made of mahogany from the family estates in Jamaica; Waterford glass finger bowls; 18C silver dish rings and a unique **centrepiece** of bog oak and beaten silver; the **Mayo Legion Flag** brought to Mayo in 1798 by General Humbert; an **oak staircase** by James Wyatt and **marble staircase** installed by Italians; *The Holy Family*

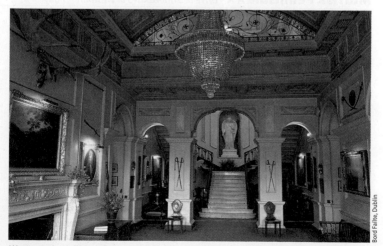

Westport House Staircase

by Rubens; 200-year-old wallpaper in the **Chinese Room**. The **basement** dungeons of the O'Malley castle, now pleasantly furnished for children.

The old **walled garden**, containing a mulberry tree planted in 1690, now houses a small zoo. A **craft shop** is located in the Farmyard Buildings Holiday Centre, there are fishing and rowing boats on the lake and a diesel train in the grounds.

Clew Bay Heritage Centre

🕐 *Open Apr to Oct Mon-Fri 10am-5pm (3pm Apr, Oct) Jun to Aug Sun 3-5pm.* 🐾 €3 ☎098 26852

The small museum on Westport Quay is endearingly cluttered with items relating to local history and colourful characters associated with the area: Grace O'Malley, John MacBride (1868–1916), executed in Kilmainham Gaol for his part in the Easter Rising, and William Joyce, who broadcast from Germany as Lord Haw-Haw during the Second World War. The Genealogical Service relies on an extensive database.

Excursion

Ballintubber Abbey★★

13mi/20km SE of Westport by R 330; after 11mi/18km turn left. 🚲🕐 *Open 9am-12midnight.* 🐾 *Donation.* 🚶 *Tours by arrangement.* 🐾 €4. 🅿 ☎ 094 9030934 - www. ballintubberabbey.ie.

The wonderful Romanesque abbey is one of the few medieval churches where mass has been celebrated continually for over 750 years. Founded in 1216 by Cathal O'Conor, king of Connaught, for a community of Augustinian canons, the abbey lost most of its conventual buildings when sacked in 1653 by the Cromwellians who destroyed its timber roof. Note, however, the 13C west door and window, and 13C piscina with a carved head in the Lady Chapel. The de Burgo chapel (now the Sacristy) contains the tomb of Theobald Burke, Viscount Mayo, who was murdered in the locality in 1629.

The **Cloisters** are in ruins but elements have survived of the 13C Treasury and Chapter House and of the warming room with under-floor heating ducts and an external fireplace. The abbey is the rallying point for the revived pilgrimage *(20mi/32km)* to Croagh Patrick, and caters for retreats and Faith Formation Programmes.

Driving Tours

Murrisk Peninsula★★   *Drive of 51mi/82km S of Westport – 1 day*

On leaving Westport Quay the road skirts the wooded shore, crossing the Owenee River at Belclare where the O'Malley chiefs *(see below)* had their seat.

▷ *From Westport take R 335 W; after 5.5mi/9km turn right.*

Murrisk Abbey

By the shore are the ruins of an Augustinian Friary founded by the O'Malleys in 1457 and suppressed in 1574, although a chalice was made for the monastery by Grace O'Malley's son Theobald in 1635.

▷ *Return to R 335.*

Croagh Patrick★

2hr on foot to the summit.

The distinctive conical mass of Ireland's sacred mountain (2 503ft/763m) dominates Clew Bay and its countless islands. According to legend all the snakes in Ireland plunged to their death when St Patrick rang his bell above the mountain's steep southern face. In his honour up to 100 000 pilgrims, some of them barefoot, climb the stony slopes to the summit on the last Sunday in July (Reek Sunday); in the past, the climb was completed by torchlight, possibly an echo of the old Celtic festival of Lughnasa. Recent excavations have shown that the narrow plateau at the top was occupied by a pre-Christian hillfort, then by a Early Christian oratory; the present one dates from 1905. The superlative panorama of sea and mountains is ample reward for the rigour of the climb, best begun from the attractively designed **Croagh Patrick Information Centre**, which gives essential background information on the mountain as well as useful tips on the ascent *(2hr).* 🚻🕐 *open Apr to Aug 10am-7pm (6pm Apr-May); Sep to Oct 11am-5pm; Nov to Mar limited times.* 🍴 🅿 ☎ *098 64114 - www.croagh-patrick.com.*

On the opposite side of the road to the Centre, John Behan's startling modern sculpture of a "coffin ship" constitutes the **National Famine Monument**, unveiled by former President Mary Robinson in 1997.

▶ *Continue W on R 335.*

Louisburgh

The central octagon of this charming little 18C town on the Bunowen River was laid out by the 1st Marquess of Sligo, whose uncle Henry had fought against the French at the Battle of Louisburgh in Canada.

The **Gronwaile Heritage Centre** traces the family tree of the O'Malleys, the history of the clan and their territory, and the life of Grace, the Pirate Queen (1530–1603). 🕐 *Open Jun to Sep 10am-6pm.* 👓 *€4.* 🅿☎ *098 66341*

▶ *Take the road south towards Killadoon. Make a detour W to Roonagh Quay for the ferry to Clare Island.*

Clare Island

Clare Island Ferry (🚴 see Address Book). Bicycles for hire at the island harbour.
Bounded by 300ft/90m cliffs and rising to 1512ft/461m at the summit of Mount Knockmore, the massive bulk of Clare Island commands the entrance to Clew Bay. Grace O'Malley spent her childhood in the castle by the quay; she may be buried in the Carmelite friary which was founded on the island by the O'Malleys in 1224, although the ruins are of later date. The sandy beach near the harbour is safe for bathing and water sports. Traditional Irish music is played in the island pubs.

▶ *Return to the road to Killadoon and continue S.*

Killeen

A cross-inscribed stone stands in the northwest corner of the graveyard.

Granuaile

Granuaile, better known as **Grace O'Malley** (1530–1603), resisted English rule as it undermined Gaelic traditional practice. From her strongholds in Clew Bay, where the many islands made pursuit difficult, she commanded a fleet of privateers who preyed upon ships in Galway Bay, imposing pilot charges or confiscating cargoes: for which she was imprisoned (1577-78). She had two sons and a daughter from her first marriage to Donal O'Flaherty, who owned castles at Ballynahinch and Bunowen in Connemara. Her brief marriage (1566) to Iron Richard Burke gave her Carrigahowley Castle, where she brought up her youngest son, Theobald Burke. In 1574 she successfully repelled an English attempt at besieging the castle. In 1593 she sailed to Greenwich to petition Elizabeth I for the release of her brother and son; Theobald Burke was later made Viscount Mayo by Charles I in 1627.

SLIDE FILE, Dublin

Bunlahinch Clapper Bridge

▶ *Turn right at the crossroads; after 0.5mi/0.8km turn right and park.*

Bunlahinch Clapper Bridge★
Beside a ford stands an ancient stone footbridge of 37 arches constructed by laying flat slabs on stone piles.

▶ *Return to the crossroads. Either go straight across or turn right to make a detour (10mi/16km there and back) to Silver Strand.*

Silver Strand
The vast sandy beach (2mi/3.2km) is sheltered by dunes.

▶ *Return to the crossroads and turn right.*

Altore Megalithic Tomb
Beside the road *(left)* overlooking Lough Nahaltora are the remains of a wedge-shaped gallery grave.

▶ *At the T-junction turn right onto R 335.*

Doo Lough Pass★
The road, which was constructed in 1896 by the Congested Districts Board, descends from the pass to **Doo Lough** (2mi/3.2km long), which is enclosed by the **Mweelrea (Muilrea) Mountains** (2 668ft/817m) *(W)* and the **Sheeffry Hills** (2 504ft/761m) *(E)*; at the southern end of the lake rises Ben Gorm (2 302ft/700m).

Delphi
The 2nd Marquess of Sligo renamed his fisheries on the Bundorragha River near Fin Lough after visiting Delphi in Greece.

Aasleagh Falls★
At the narrow head of the fjord the Erriff River gushes over a broad sill of rock.

▶ *Turn right onto N 59.*

Killary Harbour

Killary Harbour★

The harbour is a magnificent fjord, a narrow arm of the sea (13 fathoms deep) extending inland *(8mi/13km)* between high rock faces; it broadens out opposite Leenane on the south shore.

Clew Bay *Drive of 25mi/40km – half a day*

▶ *From Westport take N 59 N.*

Newport

The charming little angling resort is dominated by the disused railway viaduct (1892), converted into an unusual walkway across the Newport River. The broad main street climbs the north bank to the pink granite Irish-Romanesque St Patrick's Church (1914) containing a particularly spectacular **stained-glass window** by Harry Clarke.

▶ *Continue N on N 59; after 1mi/2.4km turn left.*

Burrishoole Abbey★

By a narrow inlet where the waters of Lough Furnace drain into the sea lie the ruins of a Dominican Friary, founded in 1486. A squat tower marks out the church. The east wall is all that remains of the cloisters. In 1580 the friary was fortified and garrisoned by the English under Sir Nicholas Malby.

Burrishoole had an important port before the Normans came, but it was abandoned when Westport harbour was developed.

▶ *Continue N on N 59; after 2.5mi/4km turn left.*

Carrigahowley (Rockfleet) Castle

The 15C/16C four-storey tower house is built on flat rocks beside a sea-inlet commanding Clew Bay. The living room was on the fourth floor separated from the lower storeys by a stone vault. In 1566, its owner, Richard Burke, married Grace O'Malley.

▶ *Take N 59 E; after 1mi/1.6km turn left.*

Furnace Lough★

A narrow switchback road loops north between Lough Furnace and Lough Feeagh. At the salmon leap where the waters of Lough Feeagh run over the rocks into Furnace Lough, the Salmon Research Trust of Ireland monitors the numbers of fish moving up and down stream. There is a **view** north to Nephin Beg (2 065ft/628m).

▶ *Continue W on N 59 and R 319.*

Achill Island★

The island approached by a bridge from the Corraun peninsula is Ireland's largest (36 223 acres/14 659ha), a wonderful mixture of sandy bays and spectacular cliffs dominated by two peaks – Slievemore (2 204ft/671m) and Croaghaun (2 192ft/667m). Once poor and remote, its economy dependent on emigrants' remittances, it attracted artists and writers like the painter Paul Henry and the German Nobel Prize winner Heinrich Böll; today, tourism has brough prosperity, stimulated by the excellent conditions for surfing, boating and sea angling.

On the shore of Achill Sound south of the bridge stand the ruins (restored) of **Kildavnet (Kildownet) Church** (c 1700), which contains Stations of the Cross in Gaelic, dedicated to Dympna, an Irish saint who sought shelter on Achill in the 7C.

Kildavnet (Kildownet) Castle, a square four-storey 15C **tower house**, commanding the southern entrance to Achill Sound, was one of the strongholds of the redoubtable Grace O'Malley; there are traces of a boat slip and the original bawn.

Trawmore Strand has a splendid sandy beach backed by cliffs. **Keel** is the main resort; at the southeastern end of its long beach the cliffs have been sculpted into bizarre forms. **Keem Strand** too has a lovely sandy shore, sheltered by the great mass of Croaghaun, whose northwestern face plunges spectacularly seaward forming one of the most awesome sea-cliffs in Europe, best viewed by boat.

Between Keel and the little north coast resort of **Doogort** are the remains of abandoned settlements. One was a 19C Anglican mission founded to woo the islanders from Roman Catholicism, the other consists of the ruins of summer dwellings known as booleyhouses; this seems to have been the last place in the British Isles where transhumance was practised until the 1930s.

WEXFORD★

POPULATION 9 533

The county town and the commercial centre of the southeast region, Wexford (Loch Garman) is a place of great antiquity and a designated Heritage Town – it was first granted a charter in 1317 – with narrow streets and alleyways, set on the south bank of the River Slaney where it enters Wexford Harbour. The town has a strong cultural tradition and is known internationally for its annual opera festival. *Crescent Quay* ☎ *053 9123111 - www.southeastireland.ie*

▶ **Orient Yourself:** Wexford, in the southeast corner of the country, is linked to Dublin by N 11 and to Waterford by N 25. The **ferry terminal** at Rosslare Harbour *(5mi/8km SE)* provides passenger and car ferry services from Ireland to South Wales and the ports of northern France

♿ **Also See:** ENNISCORTHY, NEW ROSS, WATERFORD, WICKLOW MOUNTAINS

A Bit of History

The site of Wexford was noted by Ptolemy in his 2C AD map but the town's history really began when the Vikings arrived in 950, naming their settlement *Waesfjord* (the harbour of the mud-flats). Following the Anglo-Normans invasion (1169) Wexford was captured and the first Anglo-Irish treaty was signed at Selskar Abbey. In the 13C the earthen ramparts of the Norse town were replaced by stone walls.

In 1649 Cromwell entered Wexford; Selskar Abbey was destroyed and hundreds, possibly thousands of citizens were massacred in the market place.

During the rebellion of the United Irishmen in 1798 Wexford was held for a month by the insurgents, some of whom treated their opponents with extreme cruelty. It was then recaptured with even more bloodshed by the Crown forces.

Address Book

GETTING AROUND

Environmental and sightseeing trips around the Saltee Islands from Kilmore Quay. Reef and wreck fishing. *Operates Apr-Oct (12 person maximum). Call for rates.* ☎ 053 9129704; Mobile 087 254 9111.

SIGHTSEEING

Walking Tours – Enquire at the Tourist Information Office.

For coin ranges, see the Legend on the cover flap.

WHERE TO STAY

⊜ **McMenamin's Townhouse** – *3 Auburn Terr, Redmond Rd -* ☎ *053 91 46442 www.wexford-bedandbreakfast. com Closed 20-29 Dec -* 🅿 🍴 *- 6 rm* 🛏. Sympathetic decoration, antiques and original fireplaces add to the charm and period feel of this late Victorian townhouse. The bedrooms have original washstands and wrought iron or half tester beds.

⊜ **Whitford House** – *New Line Rd - 2.25mi W on R 733 -* ☎ *053 91 43444; www.whitford.ie.* ◷ *Closed 23 Dec to 7 Jan -* 🅿 *- 36 rm.* 🛏 *- Restaurant* ⊜🍽. Particularly comfortable bedrooms, many with private balconies or patios, at this family owned and run purpose-built hotel. The spacious dining room often features live music and the menu makes good use of local seafood.

⊜🍽 **Ferrycarrig Hotel** – *Ferrycarrig - 4.5mi NW on N 11 -* ☎ *053 91 20999; www.ferrycarrighotel.com.* 🅿 🍴 ♿ *98rm* 🛏 *- Restaurant* ⊜🍽. This imposing hotel is idyllically set on River Slaney and its estuary. In addition to public areas on an enchanting waterfront curve, the hotel boasts modern rooms with super views and balconies and good leisure facilities.

ENTERTAINMENT

Wexford Arts Centre – Concerts, plays and art exhibitions are held throughout the year. ◷ *Open Mon-Sat 10am-6pm, Sun noon-4pm.* ◷ *Closed Bank Hols. Guided tour (15min) available.* ☎ *053 9123764; www.wexfordartscentre.ie.*

SHOPPING

The majority of shops are in Main Street – North and South.

SPORTS AND LEISURE

Beaches at Rosslare (south) and Curracloe (north)

EVENTS AND FESTIVALS

Wexford Festival Opera – *High Street -* ☎ *053 9122400; www.wexfordopera. com. Open Mid-Oct to early-Nov, Mon-Fri 9am-5pm; performances Sat-Sun.* The **Opera Festival** was inspired by a long-established love of opera in Ireland and provides many young singers with a opportunity to start a career. It is an annual event, lasting 18 days in late October; during this time it puts on three productions and over 50 events. It has gained an international reputation for the quality of its performances and for its policy of specialising in rare or unjustly neglected operas. The company of artists and the audiences are truly international, being drawn from all over the world. The productions are staged in the **Theatre Royal**.

In the 19C, led by local shipping companies, Wexford built up a strong maritime trade. Silting of the harbour and competition from Waterford led to its decline in the early 20C but the town's proximity to the harbour at Rosslare and its vibrant cultural life have more than compensated for this.

Walking Tour

Crescent Quay
Wexford's long quayside and promenade, facing the broad and tidal River Slaney, is relieved by the curve of Crescent Quay; a statue honours John Barry, a native of Co Wexford, who became senior commodore of the US Navy in 1794.

▶ *From Crescent Quay walk inland along Henrietta St and turn right into Main St.*

Main Street★
The commercial centre of Wexford is a long and narrow winding street (pedestrianised), fronted by grey slate building so typical of the area, and shops that retain the traditional 19C design and style of country town establishments.

St Iberius' Church★
🕐 *Open 10am-4pm (3pm in winter - dependent on volunteers).* ✉ *Donation.*
The Anglican church stands on an ancient Christian site, formerly at the water's edge. The present Georgian church dates from 1760. The Venetian façade is mid-19C.

Bull Ring
The scene of Cromwell's devastating massacre in 1649 is marked by the **Bull Ring** so called because it was used for bull baiting, a pastime popular in 12C/13C Wexford. The 1798 **memorial** shows the bronze figure of a pikeman, a dramatic work by Oliver Sheppard (1864-1941), designer of many patriotic monuments.

▶ *Continue along Main Street North.*

Selskar Abbey
Only the outer walls and square tower remain of the abbey, founded c 1190 by the Anglo-Norman nobleman Sir Alexander de la Roche on his return from the Crusades. In 1170-71 Henry II, king of England, spent time in Ireland, partly to assert his authority over the ambitious Strongbow, partly perhaps to escape the opprobrium following the murder of Thomas à Becket, and it was at Selskar that he passed the whole of Lent 1171 doing penance for the assassination of his archbishop.

West Gate Heritage Centre
♿🕐 *Open Feb to Dec Mon-Sat 10am-5.30pm.* 🚶 *Walking tours (1hr) of the city at 10.30am, 2.30pm (€5).* 📹*Video History of Wexford: €3. Craft shop.* 🅿️@*0539146506*
The West Gate is the only one of the five original fortified gates still standing; it was built by Sir Stephen Devereux c 1200 and closed to traffic in the late 16C. The Norman rooms in the tower give access to a battlement walk to Selskar Abbey.

▶ *Walk south along Abbey St and High St; turn right into Rowe St Upper.*

Twin Churches★
The **Church of the Immaculate Conception** (*Rowe St*) and the **Church of the Assumption** (*Bride St – farther south*) were both designed by Augustus Welby Pugin in an almost identical Gothic style; their towers are the same height (230ft/70m) and their foundation stones were laid on the same day in 1851.

▶ *From Rowe St Upper turn left into School St.*

Franciscan Friary★

🕐 *Open 9.30am-5.30pm (1.30pm Sun)* ⚲ *Due to close in 2008.* ☎ *053 9122758*
The church founded by the Franciscans in 1230 was confiscated in 1540 at the Dissolution of the Monasteries but returned in 1622. The present church (restored) has an attractive stucco ceiling and works by contemporary Irish artists, including **The Burning Bush Tabernacle** sculpted by Brother Benedict Tutty of Glenstal Abbey.

▶ *Continue south via School St and Roches Road; turn left into Bride St. From Bride St turn left into Main St South.*

Excursions

Rosslare (Ros Láir)
10mi/16km S of Wexford by N 25 and R 740.
The popular seaside resort / Ferry Port has a lovely long beach (6mi/9.5km) with ample sporting facilities. *Rosslare TIC* ☎ *053 9233232*

Lady's Island
11mi/18km S of Wexford by N 25 and minor road from Killinick.
The centre of pilgrimage developed around an Augustinian friary and Norman castle.

Tacumshane Windmill
11mi/18km S of Wexford by N 25 and minor road from Killinick. 🖐 *Key available from shop next door.* ⚲ *Donation*
The windmill, built in 1846, was restored complete with sails in the 1950s.
Tacumshin Lake attracts flocks of wintering wildfowl.

Kilmore Quay★
15mi/24km SW of Wexford by N 25 and R 739.
This fishing village retains some its 19C character, notably where the houses are thatched. The *Wooden House* pub has a great collection of historic photographs.
The **maritime museum** in the former *Guillemot* lightship, moored in the harbour, contains artefacts relating to Wexford seafaring: maps, antique compass and binnacle, a whale's backbone and a large-scale model of *HMS Africa*, sister ship to Nelson's *Victory*. 🕐 *Open Jun-Sep noon-6pm.* ⚲ *€4.* 🅿️☎*053 9121572.*

Saltee Islands★
Boat trips from Kilmore Quay; 3mi/4.8km offshore.
The Great and Little Saltee Islands (each about 0.5mi/0.8km long), normally uninhabited, form Ireland's largest bird sanctuary (gannets, guillemots, puffins).

Irish Agricultural Museum, Johnstown Castle★★
5mi/8km SW of Wexford by N 25; after 4mi/6.4km turn right (sign). ♿🕐 *Open Jun to Aug 9am (11am Sat-Sun)-5pm; Sep to Nov Sat-Sun 2-5pm; Dec to May Mon-Fri 9am-5pm. Closed 12.30-1.30pm for lunch.* ⚲ *€6.* 🍽️🅿️☎*053 9171200*
The Johnstown estate was donated to the Irish State in 1945. **Johnstown Castle** (⚲ *not open to the public*), designed by Daniel Robertson, now houses an agricultural research centre.
The park (50 acres/20ha) contains **ornamental grounds** with over 200 species of trees and shrubs, three ornamental lakes, walled gardens and hothouses.
The well-presented **Agricultural Museum** displays obsolete farming machinery. The transport section includes tub traps, widely used in rural Ireland until the arrival of the motor car in the 1920s, a jaunting car made in Gorey, Co Wexford, about 1880, carts, traps and harness; corn winnowing machines and old tractors which spearheaded the revolution in farming. There are sections on dairying, haymaking

and poultry keeping; reconstructions of a cooperage, a harness-maker's workshop, a blacksmith's forge and a carpenter's shop; a re-creation of 19C Irish rural living and a display of fine Irish country furniture. The **Famine Exhibition** is a thorough, science-based interpretation of the causes, effects and aftermath of the Great Famine (1845–49), with re-creations of a rural home and the lazy-beds in which potatoes were grown, a soup kitchen and a field laboratory showing how the fight against disease was conducted.

Irish National Heritage Park★

2.5mi/4km NW of Wexford by N 11 going N across the River Slaney to Ferrycarrig.
Open 9.30am-6.30pm (may change). €7.50. 053 9120733
Nine thousand years of Irish history are brought to life by 16 separate sites, linked by a trail. The **Stone Age**, 7000–2000 BC, is represented by a Mesolithic camp site, an early Irish farmstead and a portal dolmen. The **Bronze Age** is illustrated by a cist burial chamber and a stone circle. The Celtic and early-Christian ages are represented by an early-Christian monastery, an **Ogham stone** showing the earliest form of writing in Ireland, and a **crannóg**, an artificial island protected by a palisade. The horizontal watermill is a reconstruction of one dating from 833 in Co Cork. The round tower is a replica, built in 1857 to commemorate Wexford men killed in the Crimean War (1854–56). The only real historic relic is the Norman earthworks and fortifications, built by Robert FitzStephen in 1169. Other exhibitions cover the Great Potato Famine (1845-47) and Harry Ferguson and his system.

Wexford Wildfowl Reserve

3mi/4.8km N of Wexford by R 741; turn right along the coast.
(Dúchas) Open 9am-6pm (5pm Oct to Mar). Closed 25 Dec. 053 9123129
For eight months of the year most of the world's population of Greenland white-fronted geese winters on the north shore of Wexford Harbour.

Curracloe★

6mi/9km N of Wexford by R 741 and R 742.
Thatched cottages, glorious sand dunes and seemingly endless sandy beaches (7mi/12km) overlook Wexford Bay.

Curracloe Beach

WICKLOW MOUNTAINS★★

The Wicklow Mountains, south of Dublin, provide high peaks and spectacular views, lakes, reservoirs and waterfalls, open moorland and verdant valleys, some landscaped into elegant gardens. The rolling heights are covered in peat bog where the rivers form broad shallow treeless corridors; on the harder schist they create deep and narrow wooded gorges, like Dargle Glen, Glen of the Downs and Devil's Glen. In the past the mountains were even wilder and far less accessible than today and served as a refuge for outlaws and rebels; some of the 1798 insurgents found sanctuary here for several years, prompting the construction by the British of the Military Road. The mountains fall eastward to the shingle ridge and sand dunes of the coast, with its string of resorts: Bray, Greystones, Wicklow and Arklow. *Fitzwilliam Sq, Wicklow ☎ 0404 69117 Arklow ☎ 0402 32484 - www.wicklownationalpark.ie ; www.eastcoastmidlands.ie*

▶ **Orient Yourself:** The Wicklow Mountains extend south from Dublin for about 30m/48km as far as Arklow. Between the coast road (N 11) and the inland road (N 81) there is a network of steep and narrow country roads providing magnificent views of the lakes and moorland
◉ **Don't Miss:** Powerscourt, Russborough
◉ **Also See:** ATHY, DUBLIN, ENNISCORTHY, KILDARE, MAYNOOTH

Driving Tours

Inland *North to south*

Powerscourt★★
♿⊙ *House and gardens: open 9.30am-5.30pm* ⊙ *Closed 25-26 Dec* ⊛ *€9*
✗ℙ ☎ *01 2046000 - www.powerscourt.ie*
Restored after a terrible fire in 1974, the Palladian mansion designed by Richard Castle in 1730 looks out over a magnificent landscaped park with grassy terraces, stone stairways, antique statuary, fountains, woodland and specimen trees, set against the backdrop of mountains beyond, including the near-perfect cone of Great Sugar Loaf

Powerscourt Estate

Powerscourt Gardens

Address Book

GETTING AROUND

Bus Service from Dublin to Glendalough – *Operates daily 11.30am, 6pm, Sun and Bank Hols, 11.30am, 7pm from Dublin (north side of St Stephen's Green) via Bray and Roundwood. Single €11; there and back €18. www.glendalough-bus.com.*

SIGHTSEEING

Wicklow Mountains National Park Information Point by the Upper Lake (open May - Aug 10am-6pm; Apr -Sep Sat-Sun 10am-5pm) and Visitor Centre at Glendalough (see GLENDALOUGH) – 0404 45245; www.wicklownationalpark.ie

 For coin ranges, see the Legend on the cover flap.

WHERE TO STAY

 Keppel's Farmhouse – *Ballanagh - 2mi S of Avoca by unmarked road - 5 rm* - 0402 35168; www.keppelsfarmhouse.com. *May-Oct.* Farmhouse on a dairy farms dating back to 1880 with far-reaching views of countryside. The atmosphere is relaxed and tranquil and breakfast a predictably hearty affair.

 Ballyknocken House and Cookery School – *Glenealy - 3mi S of Ashford by N 11. Mar-Nov. 7 rm* 0404 44627; www.ballyknocken.com. *Restaurant* . A Victorian farmhouse providing home cooked meals (Irish modern). Sympathetically restored with homely charm. Menus feature home produce.

 Glendalough River House – *Rathdrum - 0.5mi S of Laragh off R 755 - 4 rm* - 0404 45577; www.glendaloughriverhouse.com. *Closed 15 Nov to 3 Jan.* Late 17C farmbuilding beside a meandering river provides quiet and cosy accommodation. Surrounded by 10 acres of woodland so plenty of choice for walkers. Simple but spotless pine-furnished bedrooms.

WHERE TO EAT

 Avoca Handweavers – *Avoca* - 0402 35105; www.avoca.ie. Learn the art of weaving at reputedly Ireland's oldest mill, see the finished article in the shop then stop for a light bite to eat. Simple formula; queue up at the serving counter then find a table.

Salad, quiches, even local wild salmon available.

 Ballymore Inn – *Ballymore Eustace.* 045 864 585; www.ballymoreinn.com. *Closed Sun and Bank Hols.* A characterful pub in the middle of town. On one side there's an informal café offering a range from coffees and salads to sausages and puddings. Adjacent is a more formal restaurant specialising in Wicklow lamb.

SHOPPING

Avoca Weavers – Fashionable woollen goods available at the mill in Avoca or at the shop in Kilmacanogue (see Where to Eat).

Glendalough Woollen Mills - *Laragh* - 040 445156.

Kildare Outlet Village - *Kildare* - 045 520 501; www.kildarevillage.com.

SPORTS AND LEISURE

Devils Glen Village - 0404 40637; www.devilsglen.ie. An equestrian centre with cross-country, show jumping and hunting in addition to riding lessons.

Clara Lara Fun Park, *Vale of Clara* – *Open Apr-Sep, daily 10.30am-6pm.* *€8 (some extra charges).* 0404 46164; www.claralara.com. Variety of activities for children – assault course, adventure playgrounds, radio-controlled boats, bathing, boating and fishing, picnic meadows.

Wicklow Way, a long-distance footpath (82mi/132km), starts in Marlay Park in Rathfarnham, in the southern suburbs of Dublin, passes near Powerscourt, Lough Tay and Lough Dan, Glenmacnass, Glendalough, Glenmalur and Aghavannagh and finishes in Clonegal in Co Carlow (access at Moyne, Bridgeland and Kilquiggin); the trail, consisting of forest tracks, bog roads and mountain paths, crosses mountains, switches back and forth through river valleys and presents glorious views.

Tiglin Adventure Centre, *Devil's Glen* – (see *Planning Your Trip: Outdoor Fun*).

TRACING ANCESTORS

Wicklow Family Heritage Centre- *Wicklow's Historic Gaol, Wicklow* 0404 20126; www.wicklow.ie.

(1 654ft/503m). An exhibition provides the history of the estate the house is often hired out for private functions.

The estate is named after Eustace le Poer, a Norman knight. In 1609 the land was granted to Sir Richard Wingfield by James I, who made him Viscount Powerscourt. In 1961 the estate was sold to Mr and Mrs Slazenger.

The **gardens** may have first been laid out by Richard Castle. They were then added to by successive viscounts, mostly in the course of the 19C. In 1843 the 6th Viscount employed the architect Daniel

Military Road

After the 1798 Rebellion the British Government built a military road running south from Dublin through some of the most rugged and isolated parts of the Wicklow Mountains. The original barracks in Glencree now house **St Kevin's**, an organisation which seeks to promote reconciliation between people of different religious traditions on both sides of the border.

Robertson to design the terraces; this gouty eccentric directed the work from a wheelbarrow, usually with a bottle of sherry to hand. The 7th Viscount added the superb wrought-iron gates and much of the statuary, some of it brought from Europe, some of it specially commissioned, like the Triton Fountain in the lake, which spews a 100ft/30m jet of water into the air. Many of the ornamental trees were planted at this time, among them numerous superb conifers. New features continued to be added in the early 20C, among them the Pepper Pot Tower and the jungle-like Japanese Gardens, created in 1908 on reclaimed bogland.

▶ *Take R 760 south; after 2mi/3.2km turn right (sign); at the crossroads drive straight on for 2mi/3.2km to Valclusa.*

Powerscourt Waterfall★★

Open 9.30am-7pm (10.30am - dusk in winter). Closed 2 weeks up to 26 Dec €4.50. Nature trails. 01 2046000 - www.powerscourt.ie 5min on foot from car park to waterfall; Climbing the rock face is dangerous.

The highest waterfall in Ireland is formed by the Dargle River which plunges (400ft/122m) in a spray of thick white spume down a jagged grey rock face in a horseshoe of hills. There are pleasant walks and nature trails by the river, and swings and slides for children at the visitor centre.

Killruddery★

Gardens: open May to Sep 1-5pm; Apr Sat-Sun 1-5pm. House May -Jun, Sep 1-5pm. Gardens: €5. House and gardens: €8. 01 2863405 - www.kilruddery.com

The **formal gardens** at Killruddery were designed by a Frenchman in 1682 for the Earl of Meath, whose descendants still inhabit the house. The gardens are a fascinating rarity, a particularly complete example of the kind of formality which went out of fashion in the following century, when most desmesnes were landscaped (or re-landscaped) in an informal, naturalistic manner.

The major features are a pair of parallel canals (550ft/168m long), the **Long Ponds**, prolonged by the **Lime Avenue** leading uphill to the 18C park. The **Angles** consists of a number of intersecting walks lined with high hedges; the wilderness of trees is bisected by broad walks; a bay hedge encloses the **sylvan theatre**, while the **beech hedge pond** consists of two concentric circular beech hedges, surrounding a round pond (60ft/18m in diameter) and a fountain.

The **house**, which dates from the 1650s, was considerably remodelled in the 1820s in neo-Tudor style by Richard and William Morrison. The west front is enhanced by a lovely conservatory with a domed roof and an ornamental octagonal dairy. Above the stableyard entrance is a clock and striking mechanism, both operated by water power and built by members of the family in 1906–09.

Kilmacanogue

Avoca Weavers stand on the site of a house, Glencormac, built in 1864 by James Jameson of the famous whiskey family. The grounds contain various rare species of tree – a weeping cypress, Blue Atlantic cedars, several Wellingtonias, various types of eucalyptus and pine and 13 yew trees which are said to be 700 to 800 years old and originally formed part of an avenue leading to Holybrook Abbey.

Russborough★★★

Drawing Room detail, Russborough

Kids 📷 *Tour May to Sep 10am-5.30pm; Oct, Apr Sat, Bank Hols 10am-5.30pm. Last admission at 5pm. €6. Children's playground.* ✗ 🅿 ☎ *045 865239*

This is one of the grandest country houses in Ireland, a Palladian palace in Wicklow granite facing a lake which mirrors the mountains rising to the east. Commissioned in 1742 by Joseph Leeson, heir to a brewing fortune, it is the masterpiece of the architect Richard Castle, its central block reaching far out into the landscape via curving colonnades, side pavilions, walls, archways and minor buildings.

Leeson – later Earl of Milltown – is depicted in stucco over the door linking the staircase and entrance halls; he was a great traveller and collector and, when his line died out at the end of the 19C, his paintings passed into the ownership of the National Gallery in Dublin.

Today Russborough is home to another fine collection, assembled by Alfred Beit (1853-1906), co-founder with Cecil Rhodes of the De Beers diamond mining company; in 1952 his heir, also an Alfred Beit, bought the great house in order to provide a home for his uncle's **Old Master paintings**★★ by Goya, Murillo, Velasquez, Gainsborough, Rubens, Vermeer and Frans Hals.

The setting in which the Old Masters are hung is superb – with ornate mantlepieces, extensive use of carved mahogany and satinwood inlay, fine furniture and displays of porcelain and silverware – but the outstanding features are the almost incredibly rich **stucco ceilings** by the Lafranchini brothers and their pupils. The thick and heavy stuccowork on the staircase is by a less accomplished hand. Gorgeous stucco panels frame exquisite seascapes by Vernet, now back in place after being sold in 1926.

Sally Gap★★

The crossroads on the Military Road offers splendid views of the surrounding blanket bog on the Wicklow Mountains.

Russborough's Stolen Treasures

Russborough's magnificent painting collection has proved too great a temptation to thieves not once, but twice. In 1974 a gang including the British heiress Rose Dugdale broke in and took 19 pictures worth £8m, using them in a vain attempt to get IRA prisoners in England transferred to Belfast. On this occasion all the paintings were swiftly found by the police. In 1986 another raid, this time by professional criminals, netted £30m worth of pictures. Their fame made them almost impossible to sell and most, but not all, have been subsequently recovered.

Loughs Tay and Dan★

Scree slopes plunge directly into the dark waters of Lough Tay, which is linked to Lough Dan by the Cloghgoge River.

Roundwood

The village (780ft/238m above sea-level) consists of little more than a broad main street lined with pubs and craft shops; a pub and a café both claim the honour of being the highest in Ireland.

Annamoe

There are pleasant walks beside the Annamoe River. It was here at the age of seven that Laurence Sterne fell into the mill race and emerged unscathed.

Glenmacnass Waterfall★

The mountain river streams dramatically down an inclined rock face.

Wicklow Gap★★

The road west from Glendalough to Hollywood follows the course of the medieval pilgrims' path, **St Kevin's Road**, through the Vale of Glendasan. Where the modern road loops northeast, hikers may follow the old direct route *(2mi/3km)* closer to Lough Nahanagan. The motor road rejoins the old route to pass through the Wicklow Gap between Tonelagee (2 686ft/816m *north*) and Table Mountain (2 302ft/700m *west*).

Devil's Glen★

The Vartry River makes a spectacular **waterfall** (100ft/30m) by cascading into the Devil's Punchbowl, a deep basin in the rock. There are **walks** in the immediate vicinity and good views of the coastline.

Mount Usher Gardens★

&♿ &🕐 *Open Mar to Oct 10.30am-5.30pm.* &⬡ €7. 🅿 ☎ *0404 40116 www.mountush-ergardens.ie*

Set on the outskirts of Ashford village, the natural-style gardens (20 acres/8ha), which are planted with over 5 000 species, many sub-tropical, are renowned for the collections of eucryphia and eucalyptus. They were laid out in 1868 by Edward Walpole, a member of a Dublin linen-manufacturing family, and totally restored following severe flood damage in 1986.

Glenmacnass

H Charr pollion/MICHELIN

Two suspension bridges lead to the woodland walks on the east bank of the River Vartry, which has been attractively developed with the addition of weirs.

Vale of Clara

The road, which follows the lushly wooded course of the Avonmore River, links Laragh, a natural junction of roads and glens, to the attractive village of Rathdrum.

Glenmalur★

The road beside the upper reaches of the Avonbeg River ends in a remote and desolate spot at the northeast foot of Lugnaquilla, Ireland's second-highest mountain (3 039ft/926m high).

Avondale★

🧒 ♿ 🕐 Park: Open to dusk. House mid-Mar to Oct 11am-6pm. Last admission at 5pm. 🕐 Closed Mon in Mar-Apr, Sep-Oct, Good Fri. Children's play area. 🍴 Car park: €5; House: €6. ✉ 🅿 ☎0404 46111

The Avondale estate was the home of the Parnells, a prosperous Protestant landlord family, and it was here that **Charles Stewart Parnell** (1846-91), the ill-fated Nationalist leader was born and lived. The two-storey neo-Classical **house** has been restored to its appearance during Parnell's lifetime when it was much used for social occasions. It was designed in 1759 by Samuel Hayes; there is Coade stone ornamentation by the **Lafranchini brothers** in the dining room. The life of Charles Parnell, the history of his family in Ireland, his role in 19C Irish politics, are traced by a video. Among the furniture and memorabilia are Parnell's stick and chair (he was 6ft 3in/1.9m tall), photos of Parnell and Kitty O'Shea, her wedding ring of Avonmore gold mined by Parnell, a set of folding library steps made of Irish bog oak.

The **forest park** (512 acres/207ha) covers a steep slope facing east across the Avondale River. The oldest surviving trees – two gigantic silver firs by the river as well as oaks, beeches and larches – were planted by Samuel Hayes in the 18C. The stump of a beech tree, planted nearly 250 years ago, has its rings delineated in relation to subsequent historical events. There are several trails and woodland walks ranging from the **Pine Trail** (0.5mi/0.8km), which is suitable for disabled people, to the **River Walk** (4mi/6.4km), which passes through the massed conifers on the banks of the Avonmore River and along the Great Ride.

Samuel Hayes

Avondale was inherited by the Parnell family from Samuel Hayes, a plantsman, whose Chippendale bureau is on display in the house. In 1788 Hayes presented a bill to Parliament "for encouraging the cultivation of trees" and in 1904 Avondale became the national forestry training centre.

Meeting of the Waters★

The confluence of the rivers Avonbeg and Avonmore is set amid the forests of south Co Wicklow; it was here, that Thomas Moore (1779–1852) is said to have celebrated the "valley so sweet" in his poem *The Meeting of the Waters* of 1807.

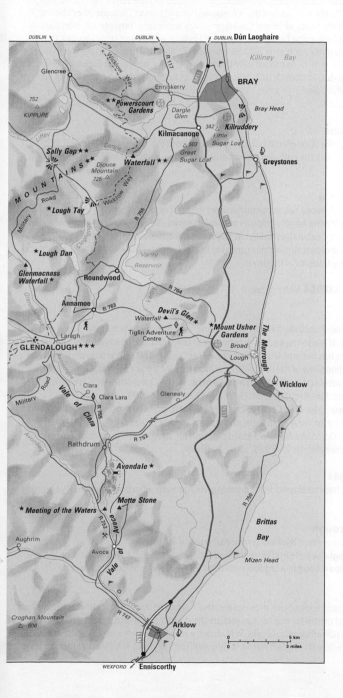

Charles Stewart Parnell (1846–91)

Despite an unpromising start, Parnell entered Parliament in 1875 and won Nationalist support: he became Vice-President of the Home Rule Confederation of Great Britain, and President of the Land League, campaigning for tenants' rights to their homesteads and travelling to America and Canada to raise funds. He was so well received that he was dubbed the "uncrowned king of Ireland". In September 1880 he proposed the policy of "moral Coventry" which advocated "boycotting", after Capt Boycott who was the first to feel its effect. His own newspaper *United Ireland* attacked government policy. In 1882 he founded the National League to campaign for Home Rule. In 1886 he moved in with Mrs Kitty O'Shea, prompting Captain O'Shea to win his case for divorce (1889); Parnell refused to resign; his party split. His career destroyed, he died in October 1891 four months after marrying Kitty.

Motte Stone

The name of the large glacial boulder is derived from the French word for half (*moitié*), as it used to mark the half-way point between Dublin and Wexford before the advent of mileposts.

Vale of Avoca

The village of Avoca has attracted visitors in great numbers, since it was chosen as the setting for the hugely popular television series, *Ballykissangel*. There are forest walks in the wooded river valley. At the **Avoca Weavers Mill**, founded in 1723 and therefore the oldest surviving business in Ireland, visitors may watch the production of textiles by traditional methods.

On the coast North to south

Bray

Bray is an old-established resort with a sand and shingle beach at the south end of Killiney Bay; it is also the southern terminus of the DART suburban railway line and in recent years has become a dormitory town for Dublin. The public park on Bray Head provides a fine **view** of the coastline. The local history is traced through photographs, maps and artefacts in the **Heritage Centre**. ♿ ◷ *Open Mon-Fri 9.30am-1pm, 2-4.30pm (5pm Jun-Aug), Sat 10am-3pm.* ⌚ *€3.* ☎ *01 286 6796*

The **National Sea-Life Centre**, on the sea-front, presents more than 30 displays populated by an array of marine and freshwater creatures. ♿ ◷ *Open Arp to Sep 10am-6pm; Oct to Mar Mon-Fri 11am-5pm, Sat-Sun, school hols 10am-6pm. Last admission 1hr before closing.* ⌚ *€9.75.* ☎ *01 286 6939*

Greystones

The resort has developed from a fishing village with a harbour flanked by shingle beaches.

The Murrough

0.5mi/0.8km north of Wicklow on the east bank of the estuary.
A long shingle beach (3mi/5km) backed by a broad grass bank is flanked by the sea and the **Broad Lough**, a lagoon noted for its wildfowl and golden plover.

Wicklow

At the eastern foot of the mountains, the harbour town of Wicklow is the main commercial centre for the area as well as the county town and a Heritage Town. Its Irish name (*Cill Mhantáin*) recalls St Mantan, a missionary who established a church in the 5C, while its English name is derived from *Wyking-alo*, Viking-meadow in

Danish; the Vikings came here in the 9C, establishing a port which developed into an important trading centre.

The statue of a pikeman in the Market Square represents all those who fought in nationalist uprisings. The **Halpin Memorial**, an obelisk of polished granite, commemorates Captain Robert C Halpin (1836–94), a native of the town, who commanded the *Great Eastern*, the ship built by Brunel which laid the first transatlantic telegraph cable; mementoes are displayed at his residence, Tinakilly House, now a hotel *(2mi/3km northwest by N 11)*.

Black Castle, which stands on a rocky promontory immediately south of the harbour, was built in 1176 by Maurice Fitzgerald, to whom the district had been granted after the 12C Anglo-Norman invasion, and was the subject of frequent attacks by local clansmen, the O'Byrnes and the O'Tooles, until the 16C. The ruins form a fine vantage point for **views** over the town and the coast of north Co Wicklow.

The 18C **Anglican Church** has an onion-shaped copper cupola, donated in 1777, and incorporates a 12C Irish-Romanesque doorway. The interior contains a fine king-post roof, a 12C font, an organ, transferred in the late 18C from the Anglican cathedral in Cashel, and a memorial tablet to Captain Halpin *(see above)*. The title "the Church of the Vineyard" recalls the vines planted by the Normans on the "Vineyard Banks" which descend to the River Vartry.

In the grounds of the parish priest's house are extensive ruins of a **Franciscan friary**, founded by the Fitzgerald family in the 13C.

Wicklow's Historic Gaol

&. ⊙ *Open mid-Mar to Oct 10am-6pm. Last admission at 5pm.* ⇔ €6.80. ⌤ ☎ *0404 61599 - www.wicklows historicgaol.com* The formidable stone-built prison dates from 1702, the time of the Penal Laws, and was used as a prison until 1924. It now houses elaborate exhibits which bring to life some of the more dramatic aspects of Ireland's history. A warder inducts visitors into the ghastly conditions suffered by prisoners in the 18C; British soldiers ponder how to crush the 1798 Rebellion (many of the participants were tried in this building); local gentleman-rebel Billy Byrne awaits his execution; the life of convicts in the 19C, both here and in Australia, is evoked; stern Captain Betts shows how to deal with recalcitrant prisoners on board the transportation vessel Hercules.

Brittas Bay

The long sandy beach (3mi/5km), backed by dunes, is one of the most popular resorts on the east coast.

Arklow

The seaside resort, founded by the Vikings on the Avoca estuary, is an important east-coast fishing harbour and a base for Ireland's main fleet of coastal trading ships. The most famous product of the local boatyards is **Gypsy Moth III**, the yacht in which Sir Francis Chichester sailed around the world in 1967. There are attractive walks by the harbour and along the south bank of the river.

The **Maritime Museum** displays about 200 exhibits connected with Ireland's maritime history and traces the development of local commercial shipping since the 1850s; a video *(15min) Eyes to the Sea* tells the maritime history of Arklow. &. ⊙ *Open Mon-Fri 10am-1pm, 2-5pm and Sat (May to Sep).* ⇔ €5. 🅿 ☎ *0402 32868*

Arklow Rock *(2mi/3.2km south)* provides a fine **view** of the coastline.

YOUGHAL★

POPULATION 5 630

Nowadays an attractive seaside resort with miles of fine beaches along the lovely estuary of the River Blackwater, this ancient harbour town looks back on a long and colourful history, attested to by a fine array of old buildings and the country's most extensive system of defensive walls, enough to merit the title Heritage Town. *Heritage Centre* ☎ *024 20170* *Dungarvan* ☎ *058 41741*

▸ **Orient Yourself:** Youghal lies on the coast road (N 25) to Cork and Waterford
Don't Miss: St Mary's Collegiate Church
Also See: COBH, CORK, CLONMEL, LISMORE, MIDLETON, WATERFORD

A Bit of History

The name Youghal (Eochaill – pronounced yawl) comes from the Irish for yew tree, a reminder that the town's hinterland was once richly wooded. In the 9C the site was occupied by the Danish Vikings, who used it as a base to plunder the rich lands along the River Blackwater and to raid other settlements along the south coast. The Anglo-Normans arrived at the end of the 12C; strategically placed for the landing of forces from England and always vulnerable to the threat of invasion from France and Spain, Youghal became one of Ireland's most strongly defended seaports, enclosed by impressive town walls.

In the late 16C, while mayor of Youghal, **Sir Walter Ralegh** introduced the tobacco and potato plants into Ireland. He later sold his extensive estates to another Englishman, Richard Boyle (1566-1643), an unscrupulous speculator in confiscated lands who became the richest individual in Ireland and was ennobled as the 1st «Great» Earl of Cork. In 1649 Youghal's garrison prudently went over to Cromwell, who overwintered here with his army. Despite its prosperity as one of Ireland's leading ports, for much of the 18C the town was riven by conflict between the dominant Protestant minority and the underprivileged Roman Catholic majority. In the latter part of the

---

Address Book

SIGHTSEEING

Guided walking tour of Youghal – Operates Jun-mid-Sep daily at 11am or by appointment (1hr). ☎ 024 92447.

For coin ranges, see the Legend on the cover flap.

WHERE TO STAY

Ardsallagh Lodge - *N25 toward Waterford; just past the Blackwater River Bridge.* ☎ *024 93496; www.waterfordhouseireland.com.* ✕ *Also known as the Waterford House, this is the place for comfort with river and sea views.*

Glenally House – *Copperalley - 1mi N by N 25 -* ☎ *024 91623; www. glenally.com. Mar to mid-Dec -* - *4 rm. - Meals* . *The owners have successfully combined contemporary*

styles and bold, rich colours with the original features of this peaceful Georgian house. Guests can enjoy carefully prepared meals 'en famille'.

WHERE TO EAT

Aherne's Seafood Restaurant and Bar (at Aherne's Hotel) – *163 North Main St -* ☎ *024 92424; www. ahernes.net. Closed at Christmas. 12rm* *Lovers of seafood have made this family-run business something of a landmark since its opening in the 1960's. The artwork in the dining room is available to buy and the bedrooms are all thoughtfully decorated.*

SPORTS AND LEISURE

Beaches at Ardmore.
Greyhound Racing.

Youghal Harbour

19C some 150 sail-powered schooners traded from here; sailors from Youghal could recognise one another throughout the ports of the world by their distinctive whistle. This once-strong tradition began to decline early in the 20C with the silting-up of the estuary and the building of steam-powered freight ships.

Walking Tour

Youghal Heritage Centre

&. ⏱ *Open Apr to Oct Mon-Fri 9am-5.30pm, Sat-Sun 9.30am-5pm; Nov to Mar by appointment.* 📷 *Walking tours by arrangement.* ☎024 20170

The old Market House now houses the Tourist Information Office and an exhibition on the history of the walled port of Youghal.

In the Market Square stands a memorial commemorating the *Nellie Fleming*, the last of the old Youghal sailing vessels.

The pub on the corner, **Moby Dick's**, displays many photographs taken during the filming of *Moby Dick* on location in Youghal during the summer of 1954.

▶ *Walk inland along one of the side streets; turn right into South Main Street.*

Clock Gate★

The unusual four-storey building straddling the Main Street was constructed by the corporation in 1777 to replace the Iron Gate, also known as Trinity Castle, part of the walls. The new tower was used as the town gaol until 1837; such was the state of insurrection in the late 18C that it soon became overcrowded; rebels were hanged from the windows as an example to the rest of the populace.

▶ *Walk though the Clock Gate and continue north along South Main Street.*

Benedictine Abbey

Left side of the street. All that remains of the abbey is the east gable wall pierced by a moulded Gothic doorway with ornamental spandrels; in the passageway are the arched piscina and square aumbry from the original church. The abbey was founded in 1350 and used by Cromwell as his winter headquarters in 1649–50.

The Red House
Left side of the street. This fine example of early-18C Dutch domestic architecture creates a marked contrast with its neighbours. The red brick façade with white stone quoins is surmounted by a triangular gable and a steep mansard roof. It was designed in 1710 for the Uniacke family by a Dutch architect-builder Claud Leuvethen.

Tynte's Castle
Right side of the street. This 15C battlemented building has a device over the front door for pouring boiling oil on rebels and other unwelcome visitors. Once on the waterfront, it is now some distance (200yd/182m) from the river.

Almshouses
Left side of the street. The Elizabethan almshouses, still used for residential purposes, were erected in 1610 by the Earl of Cork, who provided "five pounds apiece for each of ye six old decayed soldiers or Alms Men for ever".

▶ *Turn left into Church Street.*

Also used for residential purposes is the neighbouring former Protestant **asylum**, dated 1838 and now called Shalom House.

St Mary's Collegiate Church★★
It is probable that the first church on the site, a wooden building, was erected by followers of St Declan of Ardmore in c 400. The present early-13C edifice was pronounced "one of Ireland's most impressive churches" by the late Claud Cockburn, writer and long-time Youghal resident; it replaced an 11C Danish-built church destroyed in a great storm soon after its construction. During the late-15C wars, the forces of the Earl of Desmond occupied the building and removed the roof of the chancel. Large-scale restoration, including the re-modelling of the chancel, took place between 1851 and 1858. The church contains a large collection of **grave slabs** and **effigies,** including some from the 13C and 14C with Norman-French inscriptions. None remotely match the monument in the south transept erected to himself by the 1st Earl of Cork, a superbly pretentious house-size structure showing him reclining nonchalantly beneath his family tree, surrounded by his wives, children, and mother-in-law.

Town Walls★
Partially accessible from the churchyard. Youghal has the best-preserved town walls in Ireland, their extent even greater than the city walls of Londonderry. They were built in the 13C and extended in the 17C; large sections are still in excellent condition, although only three of the 13 medieval towers remain. The portion restored in the 19C with a turret and a cannon is accessible from the churchyard; the sentry walk provides a fine **view** of the town and the harbour. The full length of the walls is best seen from the outside *(Raheen Road).*

Excursion *30mi/48km*

▶ *From Youghal take N 25 E; beyond Kinsalebeg turn right into a minor road via Moord to Ardmore.*

Whiting Bay★
The bay, which is flanked by Cabin Point and Ardoginna Head, is very isolated but offers fine **views** *(SW)* across Youghal Bay to Knockadoon Head.

Master McGrath Monument

In a career of 37 races, Master McGrath, a locally-bred greyhound, was beaten only once. Between 1868 and 1871 he won the Waterloo Cup in England three times and is commemorated in the only monument in Ireland to a dog *(2mi/3.2km NW of Dungarvan by R 672).*

Ardmore★

The many attractions of this pleasant little resort include a lovely sandy beach, wonderful cliff walks, and a fascinating architectural heritage evoking the era of St Declan, a predecessor of St Patrick.

Declan, who died early in the 5C, seems to have studied in Wales and to have sailed across St George's Channel to Ardmore in the company of a large stone carrying his bell; the stone (in fact a glacial boulder) stands on the beach and offers a cure for rheumatism to anyone agile enough to crawl beneath it. There is also a holy well associated with the saint. The site of his original monastic foundation overlooking the sea is marked by the exceptionally fine **round tower**★ (97ft/29m) which is among the best preserved of its kind; probably dating from the 12C; it has a conical cap, projecting string courses marking each of its four storeys and corbels carved with human and other ornaments. The outstanding feature of the ruined **cathedral**★ (10C–14C) is the exterior **arcade**★ of sunken panels on the west gable; nearly all the panels are filled with vigorously carved but much weathered sculptures similar in style to those found on high crosses dating from the 10C, the best known being the one depicting the Weighing of Souls. Nearby, a small building probably dating from the 5C settlement of Ardmore by Declan is known as **St Declan's Oratory**.

The long distance footpath called St Declan's Way runs for almost 100km from here to Cashel, but a shorter local walk offering superb sea views, is from the Cliff House Hotel to Ram Head.

▶ *Take the coast road E to Mine Head and Helvick Head.*

Ringville (An Rinn)

This small village is the centre of an Irish-speaking area, the **West Waterford Gaeltacht**; excellent **views**★ across Dungarvan harbour.

Helvick Head★

1mi/1.6km E of Ringville. Helvick Harbour, a small but busy port backed by a row of fishermen's cottages, shelters below the headland which, despite its modest height (230ft/82m), provides outstanding **views**★ of the coastline.

Cunnigar Peninsula

1mi/1.6m W of Ringville. The sandy spit of land extending into Dungarvan harbour shelters a wealth of bird life and may be walked from end to end *(1.5mi/2.4km)*.

Dungarvan

18mi/29km E by N 25. The thriving seaside resort occupies an attractive **site** astride the Colligan estuary overlooking the broad bay known as Dungarvan Harbour and flanked by the Drum Hills *(S)* and the Monavullagh and Comeragh Mountains *(N)*.

King John's Castle, built by the king in 1185 not long after the Anglo-Norman invasion, consists of a large circular **keep** surrounded by fortified walls, much modified in subsequent centuries.

The **Waterford County Museum**, housed in the old Town Hall, has a nautical theme; local shipwrecks are well documented, especially the *Moresby* which went down in Dungarvan Bay on 24 December 1895 with the loss of 20 lives. ⏱ *Mon-Fri 9.30am-5pm ☎ 058 45960 - wwwwaterfordcountymuseum.org.*

On the east bank of the river are the ruins of a 13C **Augustinian priory** which was founded by the McGraths, who also built the 12C or 13C **castle**, of which only the west wall still stands. The walk on the seaward side of the graveyard provides fine **views**★ across Dungarvan Harbour south to Helvick Head.

Giant's Causeway

H Champollion/MICHELIN

Driving tours

For descriptions of these tours, turn to the Planning Your Trip section following.

1 Dublin and its Surroundings : 205mi/330km (one week)

2 Aspects of Ulster : 370mi/590km (one week)

3 Sights of the Southeast : 305mi/490km (one week)

4 The Southwest – Counties Cork, Kerry and Limerick : 505mi/813km (ten days)

5 Glories of Galway, Connemara and Sligo : 515mi/829km (one week)

6 The Heart of Ireland, the unknown Midlands : 320mi/515km (one week)

7 Ulster Odyssey : 590mi/950km (two weeks)

8 Irish Highlights, a grand tour : 1080mi/1738km (two weeks)

Signpost near Kilkenny

Ph Hurlin/MICHELIN

ANTRIM

POPULATION 20 878

The former county town of Co Antrim, traditionally known for its linen-spinning, is linked to Belfast by rail and motorway and was subjected to rapid expansion in the last decades of the 20C. Located on the Six Mile Water, a fine trout stream, the town's greatest asset is its proximity to the broad waters of Lough Neagh. Antrim (Aontroim) was attacked during the 1798 Rebellion by a force of 3 500 United Irishmen under Henry Joy McCracken, a Belfast cotton manufacturer, who was defeated and subsequently hanged. *16 High Street, Antrim ☎ 028 94428331 - www.antrim.gov.uk*

▶ **Orient Yourself:** Antrim is situated on the shore of Lough Neagh, 20mi/32km NW of Belfast by M2

◔ **Also See:** ANTRIM GLENS, BELFAST, CARRICKFERGUS, LOUGH NEAGH

Walking Tour

Pogue's Entry
East end of the main street. ♿◷ *Open Jul to mid Sep, Thu-Fri 2-5pm; Sat 10am-1pm and 2-5pm ☎ 028 94481338*
The simple cabin was where Alexander Irvine (1863–1941), the son of a cobbler, spent his childhood. Irvine became a missionary in the Bowery in New York; his book, *My Lady of the Chimney Corner*, is about his mother's struggle against poverty.

Antrim Castle Gardens
West end of the main street.
Beyond the Market Place and the Court House (1726), a magnificent Tudor gate leads to the former demesne of the Clotworthys, ennobled as Lords Massarene in the 17C. Their castle burned down in 1922 but the formal garden survives, best viewed from the Norman motte. The garden is a rare, and in Ulster unique, example of a Dutch-style landscape, with ornamental canals, a cascade, geometric parterres and high pleached hedges of lime and hornbeam.

Round Tower★
From the High Street 10min on foot north along Railway Street and Station Road.
Among the trees of Steeple Park stands a fine example of a round tower (90ft/27m), one of the best preserved in Ireland, probably built c 900 as part of an important 6C monastery, that was abandoned in 1147.

Excursions

Patterson's Spade Mill
5mi/8km SE by A 6 via Templepatrick. (NT) ♿ Tour: Jun to Aug, Tue-Sun 2-6pm; Apr, May, Sep, Sat-Sun, Bank Hols 2pm-6pm ☎ £3.90 ☎ 028 94433619 - www.naion-altrust.org.uk
The only surviving water-powered spade mill in Ireland was founded in 1919; five generations of Pattersons worked at the mill until 1990. The tour includes all the

---

ENTERTAINMENT

Clotworthy Arts Centre, *Antrim Castle Grounds* - Theatrical and musical performances, exhibitions of painting, photography and sculpture; talks and lectures; courses and workshops – ☎ *028 94481338 - www.antrim.gov.uk*

SPORTS AND LEISURE

Antrim Forum Leisure Centre – *Open 8.15am-10.30pm. Swimming pool, badminton, bowling, tennis.*
Allen Park / Antrim Golf Course – ☎ *028 94429001*

Finishing Shop, Patterson's Spade Mill

stages involved in producing spades in the traditional way completed by two men. Beside the mill are the ruins of associated industrial buildings.

Ballance House

11mi/17km S by B 101, A 26 and A 30 via Glenavy. ⏱ *Open Apr to Sep, Sun, Wed, Bank Hols, 2-5pm or by appointment.* ⏱ *Closed 12 Jul.* ✍£3 ☎ *028 92648492 - www.ballance.utvinternet.com*

This is the birthplace of John Ballance (1839–93), who emigrated to Birmingham and then to New Zealand, where he became a journalist and rose to be the first Liberal Prime Minister. Partly furnished in mid-19C style, the house is a fascinating museum devoted to the Ulster-New Zealand connection.

Templetown Mausoleum

Templepatrick; 5mi/8km E of Antrim by A 6. Park at the end of the drive. (NT) ⏱ *Open 11am-6pm.* ☎ *028 97510721*

A walled graveyard encloses the mausoleum, a triumphal arch designed by Robert Adam in the Palladian style c 1770 for Sarah Upton in memory of her husband Arthur. Tablets honour subsequent generations of Uptons entitled Viscount Templetown. The name Templepatrick derives from an earlier church dedicated to St Patrick who is supposed to have baptised converts at a nearby Holy Well in about 450.

Slemish

16mi/26km NE by A 26 to Ballymena, A 42 east and B 94; after 1mi/1.6km turn left; after 3mi/4.8km turn right (Carnstroan Road); after 0.25mi/0.4km turn right. From the car park 1hr there and back on foot.

The distinctive profile of the Slemish (1 437ft/438m) rises abruptly from the flat landscape of the Ballymena plain. On St Patrick's Day (17 March) it is a place of pilgrimage since tradition has it that **St Patrick** spent six years here in captivity herding swine for the local chieftain Miluic. The fine **view** takes in the ruins of Skerry Church *(northwest)*, the burial place of the O'Neills, supposed to be founded by St Patrick himself.

Arthur Cottage

17mi/27km NW by A 26 to Ballymena and B 62 to Cullybackey. Cross the river and turn sharp right onto a narrow lane. ◷ *Open Easter to Sep, Mon-Sat 10.30am-5pm (4pm Sat).* ◷ *Closed 12 Jul.* ⬠ *£2.30.* ☎ *028 25880781/25638494 (Oct-Apr) - www.ballymena.gov.uk.*

At the end of the lane stands an isolated one-storey cottage; from here the father of Chester Alan Arthur, 21st President of the USA, emigrated in 1816 to Vermont where he became a Baptist clergyman. His son was one of more than a dozen US Presidents with Ulster roots. Traditional crafts, local agricultural and domestic implements, a display on Chester Alan Arthur's family and 19C emigration from Ireland are on show in the summer; especially atmospheric on 'baking days' (high summer).

Gracehill

11mi/18km NW by A 26 to Ballymena and A 42.

This attractive Georgian village was laid out by a group of Moravian settlers from Bohemia fleeing religious persecution. Begun in 1759, the community built a central square, a church, the minister's house and communal houses for single men and women. The boarding schools for girls and boys acquired an enviable reputation far outside their locality. Men and women sat on separate sides in church and were buried in separate sections of the graveyard.

Randalstown Presbyterian Church

5mi/8km W by A 6.

The charming oval church dates from 1790, its porch was added in 1829 and the row of oval oculi was inserted in 1929 when the height of the walls was raised.

GLENS OF ANTRIM★★★

A drive up the Antrim Coast offers a great variety of scenery: seaward are attractive villages, long flat strands, steep basalt or limestone cliffs, and a distant prospect of the Mull of Kintyre in Scotland; inland are the glens created by the tumbling mountain streams which descend from the uplands of heath and bog, now punctuated by forestry plantations. In the glens, where the underlying sedimentary rocks are exposed, the farms are arranged like ladders climbing the valley sides so that each has a share of the good land near the river and of the poorer upland pasture. ⓘ *Ballycastle* ☎ *028 20762024;* ⓘ *Larne* ☎ *028 28260088 - www.larne.gov.uk*

▸ **Orient Yourself:** The A 2 runs along the Antrim coast between Larne and Ballycastle at the foot of the nine Glens of Antrim

🙂 **Don't Miss:** excursions to Glenariff Forest Park and its waterfall, and Murlough National Nature Reserve to admire the view from Benmore, and a hair-raising walk across the Carrick-a-rede Rope Bridge.

♿ **Also See:** CARRICKFERGUS, GIANT'S CAUSEWAY, PORTRUSH

A Bit of History

This once isolated area was the least anglicised part of the country, accessed by an old coastal track. The first road dates from 1832 when the Grand Military Road from Carrickfergus to Portrush runs along an ancient raised beach, or ledge blasted from the basalt and chalk rock.

Two narrow-gauge railway lines (3ft/1m) were laid in the 19C to carry the increasing output of the Glenariff mines in operation from the late 1860s. The Glenariff Iron Ore

& Holding Co line ran from Inverglen down Glenariff to the southeast end of Red Bay, where the bed of the track is still visible. The other, from Ballymena up the Clogh Valley to Retreat (1876) was never extended farther because of the steep gradient down Glenballyemon to the coast; it closed in 1930.

Driving Tour

Larne to Ballycastle *70mi/113km – 1 or 2 days*

Larne

The southern gateway to the Glens of Antrim is a busy port with a regular ferry service to Cairnryan in Scotland and Island Magee. Larne has been a regular landing point since the 9C when the Vikings arrived and Edward Bruce sailed here from Scotland to secure an Irish crown in 1315. In April 1914, in open defiance of British authority, 25 000 German rifles and 3 million rounds of ammunition were unloaded and rapidly distributed to the Ulster Volunteers, clear evidence of their determination to resist Home Rule by all possible means.

On Curran Point stand the ruins of **Old-erfleet Castle**, a square four-storey tower house, one of three built in the early 17C to protect the entrance to the lough.

The **Chaine Memorial Tower** honours James Chaine, a local MP and benefactor.

▶ *From Larne take A 2 N.*

> **ADDRESS BOOK**
>
> **Rathlin Island Ferry** – *Mar to Sep, departs Rathlin four sailings from 8.30am -5.30pm; departs Ballycastle four sailings from 10am-6.30pm; October, from Rathlin at 9am, 3pm; from Ballycastle at 10.30am, 4pm. £9 rtn. ☎ 028 20769299 - www.calmac. co.uk*
>
> *In bad weather, accommodation at Rathlin Guesthouse (☎ 028 20763917) Manor House (☎ 028 20763964).*
>
> **Larne Lough Ferry** to Island Magee *– operates (weather permitting) hourly* ☎ 028 28274085

Carnfunnock Country Park

🕐 *Open 9am-dusk (9pm Jul-Aug; 4.30pm winter). Maze and miniature railway: Easter to Oct* 🚻🅿☎ *028 28270541 (or Larne TIC ☎ 028 28260088) - www.larne.gov.uk*

In a lovely setting of green hills dropping down to the sea north of Drains Bay village, the Park (473 acres/190ha) was once a private demesne. The walled garden has 12 sundials showing GMT, Summer Time or local time; other features include a Northern Ireland-shaped **maze**, a 9-hole golf course and putting green.

▶ *Continue N on A 2.*

Ballygally Castle, now a hotel, was built in 1625 by James Shaw; the twin barti-zans are original but the sash windows were introduced later. Inland rises a natural amphitheatre, Sallagh Braes; the fine walk above the Braes along the plateau edge *(access via Carncastle and Ballycoose Road)* forms part of the Ulster Way.

▶ *Continue N on A 2.*

Glenarm Village

This attractive little port is the oldest village in the Glens. The main street runs inland past the 19C barbican gateway of **Glenarm Castle** *(private)*, the seat of the Earl of Antrim, which was begun in 1606 and re-modelled in the Elizabethan style by William Vitruvius Morrison early in the 19C.

The **Forest Park** at the top of the street provides a view of the castle, and there are pleasant walks by the stream in the upper woodlands beyond the belt of conifers.

▷ *Return to A 2; turn left onto B 97.*

The road runs up **Glenarm**, the southernmost of the Antrim Glens, passing through open farmland with views of Glenarm Forest on the far side of the valley. At the top of the glen, the unmistakable outline of Slemish can be seen due south.

▷ *At the T-junction turn right onto A 42. Turn left into A 2.*

Carnlough

The large sandy bay makes this an attractive resort. Until the 1960s, limestone was quarried above the town and was transported by rail to the tiny harbour (now full of pleasure-boats). The low bridge, former courthouse and adjoining clock tower, were built by the Marquess of Londonderry in 1854.

Beyond Garron Point lies **Red Bay**, backed by the distinctive steep-sided, flat-topped silhouette of Lurigethan (1 154ft/352m).

Glenariff (also Waterfoot)

The village lies at the mouth of the Glenariff River. On the headland, above the road tunnel, stand the ruins of Red Bay Castle, built by the Norman Bisset family.

In **Glenariff**★, justly named the **"Queen of the Glens"**, the broad lush pastures are enclosed between steep hanging crags.

▷ *From Glenariff take A 43 inland.*

Glenariff Forest Park★★

&🕭 *Open 10am-dusk.* ☞ *£4 car; £1.50 pedestrian.* ✕☎ *028 29556000*

The forest (2 298 acres/930ha) comprises areas of woodland, peat bog, rocky outcrops lakes and rivers. The visitor centre provides information about the Antrim Glens, and has excellent displays on local wildlife, the 19C iron ore and bauxite mines and their railways.

The **waterfall**★★ known as Ess na Larach *(1hr there and back on foot from the north side of the car park)* tumbles through a wooded gorge created by the Glenariff River.

B. Kaufmann/MICHELIN

▷ *Continue SW on A 43; at the junction turn right onto B 14.*

Waterfall, Glenariff Forest Park

Cushendall

Urbane little Cushendall stands at the meeting point of three glens. Its principal landmark is the red sandstone tower, known locally as the Curfew Tower, which was built as a watchhouse in 1809 by Francis Turnly of the East India Company.

▷ *Take Layde Road, the steep coast road going N to Cushendun.*

Layd Old Church

The ruins of the church stand in a graveyard romantically sited by a swiftly flowing stream which plunges directly into the sea. Between 1306-1790 it served as a parish church, hence the MacDonnell memorials in the graveyard.

▷ *At the T-junction in Knocknacarry turn left onto B92 and left onto A 2.*

The name of **Glencorp** translates as the glen of slaughter.

▶ *After 1.5mi/2.4km turn right onto Glenaan Road. Turn left onto a lane; 20min there and back on foot.*

Ossian's Grave

The figure of Ossian appears in a number of guises, one of them as an early Christian warrior-bard, the son of Finn McCool, whose legendary feats are recounted in the Ossianic Cycle. Revived in the work of the 18C poet James McPherson, Ossian became a hero to the Romantic writers of the late 18C/early 19C, particularly in continental Europe. Whoever he was, it was not here that he found his last resting place; Ossian's Grave is a Neolithic court tomb, enclosed in an oval cairn.

▶ *Continue W up the glen.*

In **Glenaan**, the Glenaan River flows down from the slopes of Tievebulliagh *(south)* where Neolithic men made axe heads from the hard porcellanite rock.

▶ *At the crossroads turn right onto Glendun Road to Cushendun.*

Glendun★, the Brown Glen, is the wildest of the nine glens; its river is noted for sea trout and salmon fishing. The viaduct was designed by Charles Lanyon in 1839.

Cushendun

The houses of this picturesque village, cluster at the southern end of a sandy beach flanked by tall cliffs. The village owes its distinctive and rather fey character to Sir Clough Williams-Ellis, the playful architect of Portmeirion in North Wales, who worked here for Ronald McNeill, the first (and last) Lord Cushenden. There are terraces of small white houses around a square, a number of slate-hung cottages, and a neo-Georgian mansion, Glenmona Lodge, which stands in a pine grove facing the sea.

▶ *Take the steep and narrow road N. After 5mi/8km fork right onto Torr Rd.*

Torr Head is a low promontory, crowned by a look-out post – the nearest point to the Scottish coast (12mi/19km).

▶ *Continue NW along the coast road; after 2.5mi/4km turn right.*

Murlough National Nature Reserve★★★

1mi/1.6km to the upper car park; smaller car park lower down the cliff face. Facilities 🕐*Open Jun to mid-Sep 10am-6pm; mid-Mar to May, Sat-Sun 10am-6pm.* 🐾 *£2.50 car* ☎ *028 43751467*

This is the most beautiful bay on the Antrim coast, set in the lee of **Fair Head** (Benmore) at the foot of steep and towering cliffs. The stone cross is a memorial to Sir Roger Casement. The waymarked footpaths from the lower car park lead north to some long-abandoned coal mines before returning along the shore past the remains of the miners' cottages and the ruins of Drumnakill Church; south past an old lime kiln, through a wood to avoid Murlough Cottage *(private)* and ends at Benvan farmhouse. A second path goes along the clifftop to windblown **Fair Head** (Benmore) from where there are glorious **views**★★★ of Rathlin Island *(north)* and the Mull of Kintyre *(northeast)*, before cutting across the rough and often wet ground of the plateau, past a **crannóg** in Lough na Cranagh *(right)*, farm buildings at Coolanlough, to reach Lough Fadden *(left)*.

▶ *Return to the coast road; turn right to Ballycastle.*

Bonamargy Friary

The remains of a Franciscan friary (c 1500) sit by a stream, surrounded by Ballycastle golf course. The ruined church has a vault containing remains of several MacDonnells, descended from the Scottish MacDonalds who engaged in bitter rivalry with the McQuillan clan for possession of this part of Ireland, and known for their treachery and lack of scruple, fighting now for, now against the English. By contrast, the McQuillans produced a nun, Julia, known for her piety; the round-headed cross in the nave is thought to mark her grave, placed here so that even in death she could practise humility, walked on by the feet of worshippers.

▷ *On the edge of Ballycastle turn left onto B 15; after 0.25mi/0.4km bear right uphill onto Dunamallaght Rd.*

Glenshesk

The road overlooks the Glenshesk River and skirts the southern edge of Ballycastle Forest. From Breen Bridge, at the foot of Knocklayd Mountain, runs the waymarked **Moyle Way**, a spur of the Ulster Way, leading north over Knocklayd (1 695ft/514m) to Ballycastle *(4mi/6.4km).*

▷ *From Breen Bridge take B 15 W.*

The base of the **Armoy Round Tower** (30ft/9m) sits in the graveyard of St Patrick's Church; built in 460 by the monastery founded by Olcan, a disciple of St Patrick.

▷ *From the crossroads take the minor road N. Turn right onto A 44 to Ballycastle.*

Ballycastle

This attractive little market town backed by Knocklayd Mountain, has many amenities – a long sandy beach, angling and golf; in June there is popular Irish Music and Dance Festival; in August the Ould Lammas Fair combines agricultural and holiday interests. Look out for **Yellowman**, a sort of toffee, and **Dulse**, a dried edible seaweed.

A stone memorial (aerials and radio waves) by the harbour, recalls the wireless link between Ballycastle and Rathlin Island set up in 1898 by Marconi and his assistant George Kemp. On the cliffs east of the town is the **Corrymeela Centre**, which works for reconciliation between the two cultural traditions in Northern Ireland.

▷ *From Ballycastle take B 15 W. After 5mi/8km turn right to Larry Bane Bay and Carrick-a-rede Rope Bridge.*

Carrick-a-rede Rope Bridge★★★

From the car park 30min there and back on foot. ♿ *Can be perilous in high wind. (NT)* ○ *Open Jun to Sep, 10am-7pm (6pm October).* ✆ *£2.50.* ☎ *028 20769839 - www.nationaltrust.ork.uk*

The bridge is put up every spring for the fishermen working at the salmon fishery. As the migrating salmon head for their spawning grounds in the River Bush or River Bann, they are deflected north by the island (*Carrick-a-rede* means Rock-in-the-Road) straight into the nets which

Carrick-a-rede Rope Bridge

H Champollion/MICHELIN

are always set in the same place. The bridge (66ft/20m long) sways with each footfall over the rock-strewn water (80ft/25m below).

Rathlin Island★

Access by boat from Ballycastle

The island is separated from Ballycastle by Rathlin Sound (5mi/8km). L-shaped, tree-less, pitted with shallow lakes and divided into fields by drystone walls, Rathlin is almost entirely surrounded by tall white cliffs where seabirds breed in late spring. From the sheltered harbour, three roads radiate to the outlying homesteads and lighthouses. The traditional occupations are fishing and farming, supplemented in the past by smuggling and now by tourism.

In the 6C St Columba nearly lost his life off Rathlin when his boat was trapped in a whirlpool. In 1306, according to tradition, it was while taking refuge in one of the island's many caves that Robert the Bruce received his famous lesson in perseverance from a spider *(accessible only by boat)*.

ARMAGH★★

POPULATION 14 265

Ireland's ecclesiastical capital stands on hills surrounded by pleasant countryside and prosperous fruit orchards, planted originally by English settlers come to populate the early 17C plantation of Ulster. The town with its many fine Georgian buildings is dominated by its two cathedrals, the seats of Ireland's Anglican and Roman Catholic archbishops. In 1994, Armagh (Ard Macha) was given city status, a tribute to its unique significance in the religious life of the whole country. *40 English St ☎ 028 37521800*

▶ **Orient Yourself:** Armagh lies between Lough Neagh and the border, 50mi/80km SW of Belfast by M 1

Kids Especially for Kids: Land of Liliput at St Patrick's Trian, Armagh Planetarium

�* **Also See:** DUNGANNON, MONAGHAN, LOUGH NEAGH, NEWRY, SPERRIN MOUN-TAINS

A Bit of History

Armagh, from *Ard Macha* meaning Macha's Height, alludes to the legendary pagan queen who built a fortress on the central hill. Although the major pre-Christian power centre of Ulster was nearby at Navan Fort, Armagh acquired new prominence after Navan's destruction in AD 332. St Patrick arrived in Armagh (c 445) and made it the centre of the new religion, declaring that his new church should take precedence

Architectural Elegance

During peaceful times in the 18C and early 19C, farming and commerce flourished; Armagh acquired some fine buildings under the patronage of its Anglican Primate: Richard Robinson, later Lord Rokeby, Archbishop form 1765. Robinson restored the cathedral, built himself a fine palace, commissioned a library and other public buildings, started the observatory, and beautified the Mall. He was the patron of Francis Johnston (1761-1829), a native of Armagh, helping him to become one of Ireland's leading architects. He did not manage, however, to make Armagh into a university city and the capital of Ulster.

over all other churches in Ireland. In the following centuries Armagh developed into a leading centre of learning: it was here that the famous 9C manuscript, the *Book of Armagh*, now in Trinity College Library was produced; in the 12C, the great Archbishop St Malachy was based here; its reputation grew such that an ecclesiastical Synod decreed (1162) that only those who had studied at Armagh could teach theology elsewhere in Ireland. The school was dissolved at the Reformation. Armagh's population today is largely Protestant in the north and Catholic in the south.

ARMAGH			Cathedral Close	Y	7	Russell St	Y	17
			College St	Z	10	Scotch St	Z	
Banbrook Hill	Y	2	Dobbin Lane	Z	12	Shopping Centre	Z	
Barrack Hill	Z	3	Gaol Square	Z	13	Upper English St	YZ	
Barrack St	Z	5	Lower English St	Y	14	Vicar's Hill	YZ	18
Castle St	YZ	6	Mac Crums Court	Z	15			

Armagh County Museum	Y	M¹	Royal Irish Fusiliers Museum		
Robinson Public Library	Y	A	(Sovereign's House)	Y	M²

Walking Tour

The Mall★

The distinctive long stretch of grass with a pavilion and cricket pitch bordered by elegant terraces is an unusual urban feature. In the 8C it was common grazing land used also for horse racing, bull-baiting and cock-fighting until such activities were stopped by Archbishop Robinson in 1773.

The Classical-style **Courthouse**, at the north end, was designed in 1809 by Francis Johnston. The former **Sovereign's House** now houses the **Royal Irish Fusiliers Museum**★, and its splendid collections of flags and standards, uniforms, medals, weapons, silver, portraits and paintings relating to the five units raised in 1793 to fight the French, and merged into one battalion in 1881. ○ *Open Mon-Fri, 10am-12.30pm and 1.30-4pm.* ☎ *028 37522911 - www.rirfus-museum.freeserve.co.uk*

Beresford Row was designed by John Quinn between 1810 and 1827 and named after Lord John George Beresford, appointed Archbishop in 1822. **Charlemont Place**, one of the finest Georgian terraces (1827), was designed by Francis Johnston as was the Ionic portico gracing the **Armagh County Museum**★ dedicated to the history of the area. ○ *Open Mon-Fri, 10am-5pm, Sat 10am-1pm and 2-5pm.* ☎ *028 37523070 - www.armaghcountymuseum.ork.uk*

Up the long tree-lined drive stands Johnston's **St Marks Church** (1811), while the small Savings Bank (1838) is the work of his nephew, William Murray. The old **gaol** at the end replaced former barracks

St Patrick's Fold

The house, which is thought to stand on the site of St Patrick's first church in Armagh, was designed in 1812 for Leonard Dobbin, MP for Armagh (1833-38), by Francis Johnston to whom the houses (1811) in nearby Dobbin Street are also attributed.

Old Market House

A technical school now occupies the former two-storey Market House, commissioned in 1815 by Archbishop Stuart from Francis Johnston.

St Patrick's Anglican Cathedral★

○ *Open 10am-5pm (4pm Nov-Mar).* ☎ *028 37523142*

SLIDE FILE, Dublin

Cricket in the Mall

The core of the cathedral on its hilltop site is medieval, although its present plain Perpendicular Gothic appearance is the result of works conducted by Archbishop Robinson in 1765, and by Archbishop Beresford (1834-37) when it was clad in sandstone and had its steeple demolished.

Inside, note the outstanding collection of 18C monuments by eminent masters such as Roubiliac, Rysbrack, Nollekens and Chantrey. Outside, note the grotesque medieval stone heads and sundial (1706). When King BrianBorú and his son, Murchard, were killed at the Battle of Clontarf (1014), on the north side of Dublin Bay, they were buried according to the king's wishes at Armagh *(north transept)*.

The terrace of small houses known as **Vicar's Row** on the west side of the cathedral close was begun in about 1720 to accommodatie female clergy dependants.

♦ *For coin ranges, see the Legend on the cover flap.*

WHERE TO STAY

Armagh City Hotel – *2 Friary Rd - 82 rm -* ☎ *028 3751 8888; www.armaghcityhotel.co.uk.* ⏱ *Closed 25 Dec* ♻ *Purpose-built group hotel with fully equipped leisure club.*

TRACING ANCESTORS

Armagh Ancestry – *38a English St. Mon-Fri, 11am-4pm* ☎ *028 37521802 - www.irish-roots.net*

Armagh (Robinson) Public Library

⏱ *Open Mon-Fri 10am-1pm and 2-4pm.* ☎ *028 37523142 - www.armaghrobinsonlibrary.org*

Thomas Cooley's library, founded by Archbishop Robinson (1771), bears a Greek inscription which translates as "the healing of the mind". Besides many ancient books and manuscripts, the library has a copy of *Gulliver's Travels* annotated by Swift, the Rokeby Collection of 18C engravings, and a range of historical maps, including a complete set of 1838 Ordnance Survey Maps of the 32 counties of Ireland.

George Ensor's 1774 **infirmary** opposite (still in use), was also founded by Archbishop Robinson.

▸ *Turn right into Abbey St.*

St Patrick's Trian

⏱ *Open Mon-Sat 10am-5pm; Sun 2 (1pm Jul-Aug)-5pm.* ⏱ *Closed 12 July.* ∓ *£4.50* ☎ *028 37521801*

This modern attraction offers interactive displays and dynamic activities to stimulate three colourful experiences of local history, St Patrick's Testament and *Land of Lilliput* about Jonathan Swift's *Gulliver's Travels*. Swift was a frequent visitor to Co Armagh, where he had several friends.

Shambles

Archbishop Beresford's meat market (1827) was designed by Francis Johnston.

▸ *From Dawson St turn left into Cathedral Rd*

St Patrick's RC Cathedral★

⏱ *Open 10am-5pm (4pm Nov to Mar).* ☞ *Guided tours Jun to Aug, Mon-Sat 11.30am-2.30pm*

The twin-spired 19C Roman Catholic cathedral stands up 44 steps, flanked by statues of Archbishop Crolly and Archbishop McGettigan, under whom it was built. It is a striking Gothic Revival structure, occupying the most prominent position available, an expression of growing Catholic confidence, built with the proceeds of countless collections and raffles, and contributions from royalty and the Pope.

Ceiling, St Patrick's Roman Catholic Cathedral

Construction began in 1840 in the Perpendicular style of Thomas J Duff but the Great Famine halted progress until 1854, delaying completion in 1873 but allowing a change to the Decorated style favoured by JJ McCarthy.

The **interior** is lavishly and colourfully decorated with a painted vaulted roof, stained-glass windows and wall mosaics; the spandrels honour Irish saints. The sanctuary was renovated in 1981–82 by the architect, Liam McCormick.

Visit

Palace Demesne

Friary Rd. ⏰ *Open Apr, May, Sep, Sat 10am-5pm, Sun noon-5pm; Jun to Aug, Mon-Sat 10am-5pm, Sun noon-5pm.* ⏰ *Closed 12 Jul.* ⏱ *£4.50.* ✕ 🅿 ☎ *028 27529629 - www. visitarmagh.com*

Between the 17C-20C the estate served as the state residence of the Anglican Archbishop of Armagh. The **Palace Stables Heritage Centre** re-enacts life in the palace on 23 July 1786 when Arthur Young, the famous agricultural improver, and other guests were entertained by Archbishop Richard Robinson. Costumed interpreters ensure visitors have a memorable experience.

The **Primate's Chapel** commissioned by Richard Robinson, is a superb example of Georgian neo-Classical architecture bgun by Thomas Cooley 1770 and completed in 1786 by Francis Johnston. It contains very fine carved oak panelling and an ornamental plaster ceiling. The long ruin of the 13C Franciscan **Armagh Friary** is typical.

Armagh Planetarium

College Hill. 🧒 ♿ ⏰ *Open Tue-Sat, 11am-5pm (6pm Sat), Sun 11.30am-5pm.* ⏱ *Exhibition £2.50. Show and exhibition £5. Booking essential.* ☎ *028 37523689 - www.armaghplanet.com*

The Planetarium on College Hill has a great dome (50ft/15m in diameter) and interactive technology to learn about the stars and planets. 360° projection theatre for showing videos.

Road Bowls

The ancient Irish sport of road bowling is still played on Sundays in Co Armagh and Co Cork. A heavy iron ball (28oz/794g; 7in/18cm) is hurled along a stretch of quiet winding country road in as few throws as possible; the ball may hurtle through the air at shoulder height. Betting is heavy.

In the grounds stands the **Observatory**, founded and endowed in 1789 by Archbishop Robinson: one of the oldest meteorological stations in the British Isles.

Excursions

Navan Fort★

2mi/3.2km W of Armagh by A 28. 👍🕐 *Open Jun to Aug, 10am (noon Sun) -5pm; Apr-May and Sep, Sat-Sun, 10am (noon Sun) -5pm.* 🕐 *Closed 12 Jul, Oct to Mar.* 🎟 *£4.50.* 🍴🅿☎ *028 37521801*

The fort is an impressive earthwork, surrounded by sacred places and settlement sites; in the late Bronze Age it was the most important place in Ulster, thought to be synonymous with Emain Macha, the capital of legendary Ulster, mentioned in the *Ulster Cycle (👁 see Myths and Lore in Introduction).* The multi-media displays in the **Visitor Centre** evoke the world of the Celts and pre-Christian Ireland; archaeological research about the fort and its associated Neolithic sites charts their evolution. The fort itself *(5min on foot from the Visitor Centre)* consists of a massive circular bank and inner ditch around a hill with a high mound on top, flanked by a low circular mound surrounded by an infilled ditch.

Navan Centre

NITB, Belfast

The Argory★

10mi/16km N of Armagh by A 29 and a minor road right. (NT) 👍*House:* 🔑 *closed for refurbishment 2007* 🍴🅿🕐 *Grounds: 10am-7pm (4pm Oct to Apr).* ☎ *028 87784753*
This handsome neo-Classical country house built around 1824 by the River Blackwater remained for many years in the ownership of the McGeough-Bonds, who eventually installed heating and lighting, delivered by an acetylene gas plant in the yard. Little has changed here since the early years of the 20C, and a tour of the house is a fascinating evocation of an ancient family home. The most extraordinary single object is the cabinet **barrel organ** of 1820, still in full working order.
The **Gardens**, which extend to the Blackwater River, comprise old roses set in box-lined beds, a sundial dated 1820, yew tree arbours, Pleasure Grounds, a Garden House, a Pump House and a lime tree walk.

Navan Fort Excavations

Excavations (1961-71) have revealed traces of human activity from 2 000 BC. The round wooden house and yard built c 400 BC was replaced many times over the ensuing three centuries. In c 100 BC a huge wooden structure (125ft/40m in diameter) comprising an outer timber wall and five concentric inner rings of large posts occupied the site. Soon after it seems to have been filled with limestone boulders and set on fire, covered with earth to form a mound at the heart of a religious complex. The four Iron Age bronze trumpets (one now in the National Museum in Dublin) found in the 18C at the edge of Lough na Shade *(NW of the Fort beyond the quarries)*, may have been deposited in the lake as an offering to the gods. Excavations carried out in 1975 show that the King's Stables *(NW of the Fort)* was an artificial pool used for ritual deposits in the Late Bronze Age.

Ardress House

7mi/11km NE of Armagh by B 77. (NT) ♿🕐 *Open Apr to Sep, Sat-Sun, 2-6pm.* 📷 *£3.40.*
📞 *028 87784753*

Ardress is a simple 17C manor house enlarged and embellished in the 18C. It was inherited by the architect, George Ensor, on his marriage in 1760.

The house displays glass from Dublin, Cork and Belfast, and some fine furniture, including Irish Chippendale chairs. The symmetry and proportions of the elegant **drawing room** are enhanced by the delightful stuccowork of Michael Stapleton.

The cobbled **farmyard** with its central pump is surrounded by farm buildings equipped with of antiquated implements including baskets and bee skeps.

Orange Order Museums

6mi/10km NE of Armagh by A 29 and B 77 to Loughgall. Dan Winter's House 🕐 *Open 10.30am (2pm Sun) to 8.30pm (5.30pm Sep-Mar). Jim Sloane: by appointment .* 📷 *Dona-tion.* 📞 *028 38851344 - www.orange.net.org/winter*

On 21 September 1795, following the affray later called the "Battle of the Diamond" at **Dan Winter's House** *(3mi/5km NE)*, the victorious Protestant Peep O'Day Boys retired to celebrate their triumph at **Jim Sloane's pub** *(half way up the main street)*. It was here that the Orange order was instituted, dedicated to sustaining the "glori-ous and immortal memory of King William III". The pub's long and narrow room is overflowing with mementoes of the Order: sashes, caps, waistcoats, banners, guns and pikes used in 1795.

Tayto Potato Crisp Factory

11mi/18km E of Armagh by A 51; factory entrance next to the police station on entering Tandragee. 🥔 *Tours (not suitable for children under 5), by appointment, Mon and Thur, 10.30am, 5pm, Fri 10.30am.* 📷 *£5.* 📞 *028 38840249; www.tayto.com*

The factory is installed in Tandragee Castle, overlooking the town, built in 1837 by the 6th Duke of Manchester. The factory tour *(1hr)* starts in the warehouse and follows the route of the potato on its journey of transformation into wavy golden crisps, flavoured and packed.

Gosford Forest Park

7mi/11km SE of Armagh by A 28 to Markethill.

The Forest Park was formerly the demesne of the Acheson family, the Earls of Gosford. The present castle *(private)*, a huge pseudo-Norman pile designed by Thomas Hopper in 1819, was built at the same time as the **arboretum** was planted with exotic trees. The **walled gardens** contain a brick **bee house** with niches to protect the straw skeps from damp. The **Gosford Heritage Poultry Collection** aims to preserve rare native poultry breeds once common in the 18C.

Jonathan Swift was a privileged but frequently irritating guest here, hence the waterfall called Swift's Well; the **Dean's Chair** is an artificial sun trap created by making a semicircular hollow protected by a yew hedge in a south-facing bank.

BANGOR

POPULATION 52 437

Looking out over Belfast Lough at the northern end of the Ards Peninsula, Bangor (Beannchar) is Northern Ireland's foremost seaside resort equipped Victorian hotels and guest houses. Its origins, however, can be traced through history to one of Ireland's most important monastic settlements, reformed as a 17C Plantation town. Today it serves as a dormitory for Belfast commuters. ⚏ *34 Quay St* ☎ *028 91270069 - www.northdown.gov.uk*

▶ **Orient Yourself:** Bangor is situated 15mi/24km E of Belfast by A 2
☺ **Don't Miss:** Ulster Folk and Transport Museum, and a trip to the beach
☝ **Also See:** BELFAST, MOUNT STEWART, STRANGFORD LOUGH

A Bit of History

Bangor Abbey, founded by St Comgall in 558, became one of the most famous abbeys in western Christendom, sending its missionary monks to found monasteries in Ireland and abroad. In the 9C Comgall's tomb was desecrated in Viking raids; Malachy, appointed abbot in 1124, built a stone church and introduced the Augustinian Order; in 1542 the abbey was dissolved.

Address Book

SIGHTSEEING

There are **boat trips** in Bangor Bay, cruises to the Copeland Islands in the afternoon and deep-sea fishing trips from Donaghadee.
Bangor Bay Cruise – *MV Blue Aquarius, Bangor Marina* ☎ *07779 600 607*
Belfast Lough Cruise – *146 Killaughey Rd.* Daily sea fishing trips, pleasure cruises, day trips to the Copeland Islands (Jun to Sep) from Donaghadee Harbour. ☎ *028 91883403 - www. nelsonsboats.co.uk*
☝ *For coin ranges, see the Legend on the cover flap.*

WHERE TO STAY

☕☕**Cairn Bay Lodge** – *278 Seacliffe Rd – 1.25 mi E by Quay St -* ☎ *028 9146 7636 - www.cairnbaylodge.com* ⊞ A detached Edwardian house, sympathetically decorated with plenty of wood panelling. The sitting room is particularly attractive while the dining room overlooks the garden. Listless guests can take advantage of the owners's beauty therapy business.
☕☕**Shelleven House** – *59-61 Princetown Rd - 11 rm -* ☎ *028 9127 1777 www.*

shellevenhouse.com ✗ ⊞ A large Victorian terraced house with the bedrooms at the top of the house enjoying views over the town. Clean, tidy and traditionally decorated bedrooms, with home-cooked meals available if booked in advance.

WHERE TO EAT

☕☕**Coyles**– *44 High St-* ☎ *028 9127 0362 - Restaurant: Tues-Sat 5-9pm, Sun 5-8pm.* Also open for bar meals
☕☕**Donegans** - *37 High St* ☎ *028 91463928 - Restaurant: Mon-Sat, noon-2.30pm, 5-9pm, Sun noon-8pm.* Also open for bar meals.
☕☕**Grace Neill's** - *33 High St, Domaghadee -* ☎ *028 91884595 - www.grace-neills.com - Restaurant: noon (12.30pm Sun) -2.30pm; 5.30-9pm (8.30pm Sun).* The oldest pub in Ireland (f 1611) serves up a rich array of tempting food.

SPORTS AND LEISURE

Safe sandy beaches, sea-water swimming pool, marina (560 berths), waterfront fun park, golf course.

On the accession of James I in 1603, Bangor was granted to Sir James Hamilton, later Viscount Clandeboye, who created a town with settlers from his native Ayrshire. In 1620 he was granted a warrant to establish a maritime port including the nearby creeks. In 1689 the Duke of Schomberg landed at Groomsport; his army of 10 000 men probably coming ashore at Bangor or Ballyholme; the Duke spent a night with the Hamiltons before setting off to the Battle of the Boyne, where he was killed.

In 1710 Sir James's estates passed by marriage to the Ward family of Castle Ward on Strangford Lough. Two generations later Col Robert Ward improved the harbour, promoted the textile industry and founded a boys' school. Bangor's role as a seaside resort, complete with pier, really started with the arrival of the railway in 1865.

Walking Tour

Old Custom House and Tower

The Custom House (Tourist Information Centre) was built by Sir James Hamilton in 1637 with financial assistance from the Crown, in the Scottish Baronial style with flank-ing watchtowers, a crow-stepped gable and a quarter-round corbelled turret.

Bangor Abbey Church

The 14C tower is the only section to survive Dissolution of Bangor Abbey in 1542.

North Down Heritage Centre★

🕒 *Open Tue-Sun 10am (2pm Sun)-4.30pm (5.30pm Jul-Aug).* 🖻 🅿 ☎ *028 91271200-www.northdown.gov.uk/heritage*

The Centre is housed in part of Bangor Castle, a fanciful mid-19C exercise in Eliza-bethan-Jacobean revival stylel. An exhibition of evocative artefacts and models celebrates Bangor's eventful past and development into a popular seaside resort. There is also an informative section promoting the 15mi/26km coastal walk.

Excursions

Crawfordsburn Country Park

7mi/11km W of Bangor by B 20. (HM) 🕒 *Open Mar to Aug, 9am-8pm (4.45pm Sep). Visitor centre: 1am-5pm.* 🍴 🅿 ☎ *02891853621 - www.ehsni.gov.uk*

The picturesque village and its coastal country park, are named after the Crawford family from Scotland who bought the estate in 1674.

The history of the estate and its flora and fauna are comprehensively illustrated in the **Park Centre**, equipped with interactive displays for children.

The **glen walk** *(30min there and back on foot)* passes the old salmon pool before dip-ping under the handsome railway viaduct of 1865. Upstream is the waterfall which was used to power corn, flax and saw mills, and from 1850 to generate electricity to light the glen.

Grey Point Fort *(accessible by footpath – 1hr there and back – within the Country Park or by residential roads (Coastguard Avenue)* commands the sea approaches to Belfast and was manned during both World Wars by the Royal Artillery. Panels outline its history (1907-63) and a solitary six-inch gun, a gift from the Government of the Republic of Ireland, is mounted in one of the massive reinforced concrete gun emplacements.

Ulster Folk and Transport Museum★★

8mi/13km W of Bangor by A 2. ♿🕒 *Open Mar to Jun, Mon-Fri 10am-5pm, Sat-Sun 10am (11am Sun)-6pm; Jul-Sep, 10am(11am Sun)-6pm; Oct to Feb, Mon-Fri 10-4pm Sat-Sun, 10am (11am Sun)-5pm. Last admission 1hr before closing.* 🎫 *£5.50 for each collection; £7 combined ticket.* ☎ *028 90428428 - www.uftm.org.uk*

This is one of the most extensive and interesting museums in the whole of Ireland: since the estate of Cultra Manor was bisected by the busy coast road *(A 2)*, one section is dedicated to the folk collection, the other (sea side) to transport.

Folk Museum

A vast open-air museum is installed in a series of old buildings transferred from the Ulster countryside where traditional trades, practices and crafts can be demonstrated. Costumed staff narrate the story of each structure and explain how the equipment was used for weaving, spinning, agricultural work and cooking.

Rectory and Church, Ulster Folk Museum

The dwellings, furnished as they would have been at the end of the 19C, range from a one-room farmhouse shared between the family and their cows, to a substantial 17C farmhouse with panelled walls. Working premises include a flax-scutching mill and a spade mill, a weaver's house and a bleach green watchman's hut. The **village** is composed of a school, a market-cum-courthouse, a church and a rectory, together with two terraces of urban cottages including a shoemaker's workshop and a bicycle repair shop.

In the **Gallery** *(three floors)* the traditional Ulster way of life is illustrated with original domestic, industrial and agricultural implements.

Transport Museum

With examples of virtually every kind of wheeled vehicle used in Ireland in the last two centuries, the museum has displays each in its social context, thereby enhancing the interest value of old hardware so beloved by enthusiasts.

In the **Irish Railway Collection**, fascinating wall panels evoke the sometimes idiosyncratic history of the railways powered by the beautifully restored engines and carriages; note the wonderful *Maeve (Maebh)*, named after an ancient Celtic deity, one of the 4-6-0 800 Class locomotives built in 1939 and the most powerful ever to run on Irish rails. The **Road Transport Galleries**, richly furnished with all types of transport memorabilia, display two-wheelers through the ages. Buses include a lovingly rebuilt 1973 Daimler Fleetline, and No 2 of the Bessbrook and Newry Tramway Co, built in 1885 and still carrying passengers in the 1940s. The final gallery is devoted to *The Car in Society*, and includes an 1898 Benz Velo Confortable, the oldest petrol vehicle in Ireland, and a glamourous model produced in 1981 by the short-lived De Lorean company. The **Dalchoolin Transport Galleries** present a miscellany of exhibits – shoulder creels and wooden sledges, carts and jaunting cars; horse-drawn vehicles and ships.

The **Flight Experience** is a hands-on exhibition on flight and the aerospace industry (archive film footage, CDRom, models, interactive displays), and the Short SC1, a pioneering VTOL (Vertical Take-off and Landing). The **Titanic Gallery** honours the great liner, built at the famous Harland and Wolff shipyard in Belfast, which sank on her maiden voyage, and photographed in 1985.

Somme Heritage Centre

3mi/5km S of Bangor by A 21. ⏱ *Open Apr to Sep, Mon-Thu 10am-4pm (5pm Jul-Aug), Sat noon-4pm (5pm Jul-Aug); Jul-Aug, Sun noon-5pm; Oct to Mar, Mon-Thu and 1st Sat of the month, 12 noon-4pm.* 🚶 *Last tour 1hr before closing.* ⊙ *£3.75.* ☎ *028 91823202 - www.irishsoldier.org*

With the outbreak of the First World War (1914), many Irishmen put aside their political differences and volunteered for service in the British army. Irish units suffered terrible losses in the Somme offensive of 1916: 5 000 men from the Ulster Division were killed in the first two days alone. The Centre commemmorates the sacrifices made in battle with a "time tunnel" and uncanny re-creation of the trenches complete with terrible sights and sounds.

Groomsport
1.5mi/2.5km E by coast road. Groomsport is an attractive little seaside resort complete with sandy beaches, modern bungalows and caravan parks. Fishing is still an important activity but only two fishermen's cottages overlooking the harbour filled with pleasure boats; they now house an **art gallery**.

Donaghadee
7mi/11km E of Bangor by B 21. The picturesque, winding streets lead to the **parish church** which dates from 1641. The huge harbour, now full of leisure craft, was built in 1820 to accommodate the mail ships, which were transferred to Larne in 1849. From the 16C to 19C Donaghadee–Portpatrick was the most popular route between Ireland and Scotland as it is the shortest crossing (21mi/34km). The Norman **motte** near the shore was probably raised by William Copeland, a retainer of John de Courcy; it is crowned by a stone building (1818) providing a fine **view** of the Copeland Islands and the coast of Galloway across the North Channel.

Copeland Islands
Accessible by boat from Groomsport or Donaghadee.
The nearest and largest island was inhabited until the 1940s. A modern lighthouse was built on Mew Island in 1884. Lighthouse Island is now a wildlife sanctuary in the care of the National Trust, populated by buzzards, golden eagles, resident seals, dolphins, porpoises, basking sharks, minke whales, killer whales.

Ballycopeland Windmill★
10mi/16km SE of Bangor by B 21 and A 2; in Millisle turn right. (HM) ⏱ *Open Tues-Sun, 10am (2pm Sun) -6pm.* ☎ *028 91861413- www.ehsni.gov.uk*
In the late 18C, when grain was grown extensively in the Ards Peninsula, the landscape was thickly dotted with windmills. The rare survivor at Ballycopeland was probably built between 1780-90 and worked until 1915. The complex includes the mill, back in working order; the miller's house with an explanatory display; a dusthouse and kiln where the grain was dried before being milled.

Ards Peninsula
The peninsula extending south from Bangor to Ballyquintin Point *(23mi/37km x 3–5mi/5–8km)* encloses the broad waters of Strangford Lough. Favourable soils and a relatively dry and warm climate make this low-lying land one of the best grain-producing regions of Ireland.
The **coast road**, fanned constantly by breezes, follows the contours of bare shoreline, past sandy beaches and occasional rocky outcrops. **Portavogie** shelters one of Northern Ireland's three fishing fleets. The southern end of the peninsula presents an austere landscape of marsh and heath.

SyndicationInternational

Ballycopeland Windmill

BELFAST★

POPULATION 279 237

Few cities have such a splendid natural setting; Belfast (Béal Feirste) stands at the mouth of the River Lagan at the point where it discharges into the great sea inlet of Belfast Lough which is sheltered on both sides by hills; to the west rises the formidable basalt escarpment of Cave Hill and Black Mountain. One of the great industrial and commercial cities of the Victorian era, the capital of Northern Ireland has survived thirty years of Troubles. Today's fragile peace has encouraged a wave of new building and a vibrant cultural life without equal in the rest of the province. Half a million people live within a few miles of the city centre, a third of Northern Ireland's population. 🖬 *Belfast Welcome Centre, 47 Donegall Pl ☎ 028 90246609 🖬Belfast City Airport, Sydenham Bypass ☎ 028 90939093 🖬Belfast Intl Airport ☎ 028 94422888 - www.gotobelfast.com*

▶ **Orient Yourself:** Belfast is set on the shores of Belfast Lough which opens into the North Channel a narrow strait between Ireland and Scotland. It is served by 2 motorways – M 1, running westwards via Craigavon and Dungannon to Enniskillen, and M2, running northwest via Antrim and Dungiven to Londonderry

🚳 **Don't Miss:** Belfast Zoo

🕯 **Also See:** ANTRIM, BANGOR, CARRICKFERGUS, LISBURN

A Bit of History

Norman Castle to Industrial City – Belfast takes its name from a ford by a sandbank (*bealfeirste* in Irish) where the Anglo-Norman John de Courcy built a castle after his invasion of Ulster in 1177. Development only came in the early 17C when a quay was built and trade diverted from Carrickfergus. The city was settled by hard-working Scottish Presbyterians, followed later by industrious Huguenot refugees who brought new techniques to the burgeoning linen industry. Cotton spinning was introduced in 1777, shipbuilding in 1791; by the early 19C, industry was booming; the population multiplied fifteenfold, from under 25 000 to 350 000 over to generations.

General engineering flourished, as did distilling, rope-making and tobacco products, but it was the great shipyards that gave the city its distinctive industrial character, with Harland and Wolff – builders of the *Titanic* - becoming the United Kingdom's largest construction and repair yard. In the 20C, Short Brothers produced the Sunderland flying boat and the first VTOL jet; their airstrip in the docks is now used by Belfast City Airport.

Dissent and Division – The predominance of the Presbyterian Church, its cultural links with Scotland and its commercial wealth, underpinned Belfast's early reputation as a centre for intellectual activity and articulated independence. Belfast had the first printing press in Ireland (c 1690) and published the first

Ph Hurlin/MICHELIN

Belfast City Hall

Address Book

GETTING AROUND

Public transport - ☎ 028 90666630
- www.tranlink.co.uk

Metro / Citybus – For travel within the city of Belfast – Citybus kiosk, Donegall Sq West, Mon-Sat 8am-6pm
Ulsterbus – For travel outside Belfast – Europa Bus Centre, Glengall St
Bus service between the Europa Bus Centre and Belfast International Airport.

SIGHTSEEING

City Sightseeing Belfast - Bus tours operate from Castle Place all year every 30mins ☎ 028 9062 6888
Black Taxi Service – Guided tours with commentary.
There are various **themed walking tours** of the city, including:
Belfast – Historic Belfast – Wed, Fri, Sat (Sun, Jun to Sep) at 2pm from the Belfast Welcome Centre £5 ☎ 028 9024 6609.
Bailey's Historical Pub Tour of Belfast – Sat at 4pm and Tue at 7pm from Crown's Dining Room (upstairs in the Crown Bar), Great Victoria Street ☎ 028 9268 3665 (Judy Crawford) or ☎ 028 9088 2596. £7
Coiste Political Tours – Republican West Belfast accompanied by a guide from the ex-prisoner community Mon-Sat 11am, Sun 2pm from Divis Tour £8 ☎ 028 90200770
Titanic Awakin Tour – www.awakin. com. Self-guided tour of Titanic Quarter with interactive terminal £8 from Belfast Welcome Centre.
For coin ranges, see the Legend on the cover flap.

WHERE TO STAY

☞☞**Ash Rowan Town House** – 12 Windsor Ave - 5 rm - ☎ 028 9066 1758 - ashrowan@hotmail.com - Closed 23 Dec- 7 Jan 🅿 Bed and breakfast with the emphasis on breakfast. Close to Ulster Museum and good range of restaurants. A Victorian house with a traditional feel and period charm. It was once home to Thomas Andrews, designer of the Titanic.

☞☞**Benedicts of Belfast** – 7-21 Bradbury Place - Shaftsbury Sq – ☎ 028 9059 1999; www.benedictshotel.co.uk

– 🕐 Open daily from 11.30am. Boutique hotel with themed bar hosting live music shows and popular restaurant.

☞☞**Madison's Hotel** – 59-63 Botanic Ave - ♿ 35 rm. ☎ 028 9050 9800; www.madisonshotel.com 🍴🅿 Its proximity to the university ensures a lively local atmosphere and this hotel contributes by having its own nightclub. Bright bedrooms with all facilities, bar and restaurant (7am-10pm).

☞☞**The Old Rectory** – 148 Malone Rd - 5 rm – ☎ 028 9066 7882; www.anoldrectory.co.uk. 🕐 Closed 24 Dec- 1 Jan, Easter 🅿 A very nice little place in what feels like the middle of nowhere. Nice garden.

☞☞**Roseleigh House** – 19 Rosetta Park 1 1/2mi S of Belfast by A 24 Ormeau Rd - 9 rm - ☎ 028 9064 4414; www.roseleighhouse.co.uk - 🕐 Closed 25 Dec - 🅿. A well-located guest house in a fairly quiet residential area close to Belvoir Park, with easy access to the city centre. Bedrooms are well-equipped and breakfasts delicious.

☞☞☞**The Crescent Townhouse** – 13 Lower Cres - 11 rm - ☎ 028 9032 3349; www.crescenttownhouse.com- 🕐 Closed 11-12 July, 25-26 Dec and 1 Jan. Regency house in a vibrant area of the city, has been converted into a stylish and comfortable hotel. The bar has a distinctive Gothic feel with oak panelling and the brasserie offers imaginative dishes in a lively atmosphere. Conference facilities.

WHERE TO EAT

☞**Cayenne** – 7 Lesley House, Shaftesbury Sq - ☎ 028 9033 1532; Mon-Fri 12-2pm; 6-10pm; Fri-Sun 6-11pm (8.45pm Sun). 🕐 Closed 12-13 Jul, 25-26 Dec, 1 Jan, Sun and lunch Sat - Booking essential. Emphatically stylish place with impressive modern artwork. Lively atmosphere, well-priced menu featuring contemporary cuisine with an Asian twist. Always busy so worth booking.

☞☞**Ginger** – 7-Hope St, Gt Victoria St - ☎ 028 9049 4421 - 🕐 Closed 2 weeks Jan, 2 weeks July, Sun and Mon - Booking essential. Busy and unpretentious little place, tucked away in a parade of shops.

Ample choice from the blackboard menu of daily specials, with influences from all around the world, and it's unlicensed so take your own wine.

Nick's Warehouse – *35-39 Hill St - ☎ 028 9043 9690 - www.nickswarehouse.co.uk.* Open Mon-Fri noon-2.30pm, Tue-Sat 6-9.30pm. Closed Easter Bank Hols, 1 May, 12 July, 25-26 Dec, 1 Jan. Former Bushmills warehouse on a cobbled street is one of the city's best known restaurants. Downstairs has the "buzz", upstairs slightly more formal. The eponymous Nick oversees a busy kitchen producing carefully prepared modern cooking. Excellent wine list.

Oxford Exchange – *First floor, St Georges Market, Oxford St - ☎ 028 9024 0014 - www.oxfordexchange.co.uk.* Open Mon-Sat noon-2.45pm, Set Menu 4-6.30pm, 5pm-9pm (10pm Fri-Sat) - Closed 1 week July, 25 Dec, 1 Jan. First floor location overlooking St George's market. The glass roof ensures the room is bright and airy. The open plan kitchen speciality is chargrilled fish and meats.

The Wok – *126 Great Victoria St - ☎ 028 9023 3828 -* Closed 25-26 Dec and 1 week July. In the vanguard of modern Chinese restaurants; stylish and contemporary interior with efficient service. Choice of the classics and more unusual dishes from various regions.

Restaurant Michael Deane – *36-40 Howard St - ☎ 028 9033 1134 - www.michaeldeane.co.uk .* Open Wed-Sat 7-9.30pm (last orders). Closed Easter, 1 week July, Christmas, New Year and Sun-Tue. The city's premier restaurant provides original and accomplished fusion cooking, discreet and professional service.

TAKING A BREAK

Bittle's Bar – *103 Victoria St - ☎ 028 903 11 088 –* Open daily from 11.30am. Well worth a drink here as it is something of an architectural oddity from 1861.

Kelly's Cellar – *30 Bank St - ☎ 028 9032 4835 –* Open daily from 11am. This 1720 pub in the financial district is a wonderful antidote to the homogeneous modernity of the city's development.

Kitchen Bar – *16-18 Victoria Street - ☎ 028 903 24 901 -* Open Mon-Sat from 11.30am. Reputedly opened in 1859, this bar is celebrated for its live traditional Irish music; it was once frequented by the music hall stars performing at neighbouring Empire Theatre. Comprehensive beer selection.

Madden's – *Berry St - ☎ 028 9024 4114 –* Open Mon-Sat, 11am-1am. Fits the bill for those looking for that authentic pub experience with live music: blues or folk.

Pats Bar – *19-22 Princes Dock St - ☎ 028 9074 4524 –* Open Mon-Sat from 11am. Century-old atmospheric pub set in a buzzing young cafe in the docklands. Wednesday is traditional music night.

Robinson's – *38-40 Great Victoria St - ☎ 028 902 47 447 –* Open Mon-Fri, 11.30am, Sat, 11.30am-2am. Worth making the effort to find this Victorian pub which was rebuilt in the 1990's. Individual rooms have various themes: there is an upstairs lounge decked out like an 18C ship, a library on the ground floor and a back bar resembling a country grocers.

Rotterdam Bar – *54 Pilot St - ☎ 028 907 46 021 –* Open daily from 11.30am. Daytime oasis of calm in docks area with open fires is transfomed at sundown with live music: blues, salsa, folk, jazz. Good choice of spirits.

The Crown Liquor Saloon – *46 Great Victoria St - ☎ 028 9024 9476 –* Open Mon-Sat, 11.30am-1am, Sun, 12.30am-10pm. Featured in the James Mason film *Odd Man Out* and rightly celebrated for its highly ornate Victorian style with original Italian influences.

The Empire – *40-42 Botanic Ave - ☎ 028 902 49 276 – www.belfastempire.com.* Open Mon-Fri, Sun, 11.30am-1am. Contemporary music and funky atmosphere at this once derelict Presbyterian Church with a resident ghost. It is also home to a popular comedy club.

The Garrick – *29 Chichester St - ☎ 028 903 33 875 –* Open daily from 11.30am. Apparently named after David Garrick, the Shakespearean actor, although there is some dispute as to whether he ever visited. Under new management.

The John Hewitt – *51 Donegall St - ☎ 028 902 33 768 – ◷ Open from 11.30am.* This pub in the Cathedral District has a genuine community feel. Good food, art gallery, live gigs (Jazz, Ulster Scots Folk, Cajun!) and, with its log fire and long counter, ensures that the art of conversation is alive and well.

Whites Tavern – *2-4 Winecellar Entry - ☎ 028 9024 3080 – ◷ Open daily from 11.30am.* Claims to be the oldest tavern in the city. Traditional folk music and honest "pub grub" on offer.

ENTERTAINMENT

Belfast Waterfront Hall – *2 Lanyon Place - ☎ 028 903 334455 - www.waterfront.co.uk.* ◷ Opened in the late '90's, the Waterfront plays host to a variety of art forms throughout the year

Cultúrlann Macadam Ó Fiaich – *Falls Rd - ☎ 028 9023 9303.* Irish Language arts centre featuring concerts and exhibitions.

The Crescent Arts Centre – *University Rd - ☎ 028 9024 2338 - www.crescentarts.org* Various work-shops in what was originally a Victorian school.

The Grand Opera House – *Great Victoria St - ☎ 028 9024 1919 - www.goh.co.uk* Recently endowed with a new extension. Theatre, musicals and opera.

The Odyssey – *2 Queen's Qay - ☎ 028 9045 0055 - www.theodyssey.co.uk.* This millennium project features a 10,000 seater stadium – home to the "Belfast Giants»"ice hockey team, IMAX

Crown Liquor Saloon

cinema,discovery centre for children bars and restaurants.

Ulster Hall – *Bedford Street - ☎ 028 9032 3900.* Pop concerts, sporting events and a regular venue for the Ulster Orchestra.

SHOPPING

St George's Market – *12-20 East Bridge St – Open Fri, 8am-2pm, Sat, 8am-2pm.* This covered market is over 100 years old and has been recently renovated. Market day is every Friday, where the atmosphere is colourful and the crowds considerable. On Saturday mornings there is a small farmers market.

EVENTS AND FESTIVALS

Belfast Festival at Queen's –*3 weeks Oct to Nov. Information from Festival House, 25 College Gardens ☎ 028 90667687 - www.belfastfestival.com*

Irish newspaper, the *Belfast News Letter* in 1737 – the oldest morning paper in the British Isles.

It was in Belfast in 1791 that Wolfe Tone helped to found the Society of United Irishmen; in 1792 they published the *Northern Star*, a newspaper which expressed radical opinion and first promoted the idea of the Irish nation, which, in Tone's words, would "substitute the common name of Irishman in place of ... Protestant, Catholic, and Dissenter". To the dismay of the United Irishmen, their ideals, which had sharpened existing divisions, did not survive the failed 1798 Rebellion. The overwhelmingly Presbyterian city of the late 18C changed as spectacular industrial growth began employing large numbers of Catholics drawn from all over Ireland in the 19C, settling in the Falls Road area of the city, between the predominantly Protestant working-class districts of Sandy Row and Shankill Road: names which resonate today as areas divided by sectarian loyalties.

Walking Tour

City Centre

Donegall Square★

The hub of Belfast is Donegall Square: a vast rectangle of grass and gardens peopled with statues, laid out around the City Hall.

Facing onto the square are a variety of buildings, notably **Yorkshire House** with roundels containing low-relief heads of famous men and deities *(south side)*; the elegant block commissioned for Scottish Provident (1899–1902) designed by the Belfast architects, Young and Mackenzie *(west side)*; an old pink stone linen warehouse

(1869) *(north side)*, and the **Linen Hall Library**, founded in 1788 as the Belfast Library and Society for Promoting Knowledge: its old-fashioned interior contains a good collection of material relating to the Troubles. ○ *Open Mon-Sat 9.30am-5.30pm (4pm Sat).* ○ *Closed Bank Hols.* ✉☎ *028 90321707 – www.linenhall.com*

City Hall★

♿☜ *Tour (1hr) Mon-Fri at 11am, 2pm, 3pm; Sat 2pm, 3pm – Sat from back entrance in Donegall Sq.* ☎ *028 90270456 – www.belfastcity.gov.uk*

The great neo-Renaissance Portland stone building with its copper-covered dome and corner towers was designed by Sir Brumwell Thomas and completed in 1906, at a time when Belfast was at its zenith of industrial and commercial might, to mark its city status granted by Queen Victoria in 1888.

Highlights of the **interior** include the grand staircase; a mural of the founding of the city and its principal industries painted by John Luke; a sculpture by Patrick Mac-Dowell (1790–1870), a native of Belfast, of the Marquess of Donegall (1827–53), who devoted the proceeds of his music and poetry to good works; the Council Chamber, panelled in hand-carved Austrian oak; the Reception Hall displaying the original Charter of Belfast granted by James I on 27 April 1613; the Banqueting Hall; and the shields of the Provinces of Ireland in the stained glass of the Great Hall.

▶ *From the NW corner walk west along Wellington Place.*

Royal Belfast Academical Institute

The inter-denominational boys' school commonly known as "Inst", on College Square, was probably designed by Sir John Soane and completed in 1814.

▶ *Turn left into Fisherwick Place.*

Church House

The headquarters of the Presbyterian Church in Ireland was designed by Young and Mackenzie (1905), Belfast architects, in the 15C Gothic style. The massive corner tower, inspired by St Giles' Cathedral in Edinburgh, contains a peal of bells.

The **Presbyterian Historical Society Museum** contains old communion plate, pitch pipes and communion tokens made of lead and card. The Society keeps records and information about the Presbyterian Church in Northern from the 19C on. ♿○ *Open Mon-Tue, Thu-Fri 10am-12.30pm, Wed 10am-12.30pm, 1-3.30pm.* ☎ *028 90322284*

Grand Opera House

Designed by the theatre architect Frank Matcham and opened in 1894, this gorgeous building has a gilt-and-red-plush interior to match its exuberant facade. It, and its famous neighbour, the Europa Hotel, were badly damaged during the Troubles.

Crown Liquor Saloon★

(NT) ♿○ *Open Mon-Sat 11.30am-11pm; Sun 12.30-10pm.* ☎ *028 90279901*

The Victorian interior is richly decorated with coloured glass, coloured and moulded tiles, arcaded mirrors and polished marble. Carved animals top the doorposts of the panelled snugs. The ornate ceiling is supported on hexagonal wooden columns with feathered ornament. Inspired by his travels in Spain and Italy, Patrick Flanagan built the public house as a railway hotel in 1885; it is now owned by the National Trust.

▶ *Turn left into Amelia Street and walk eastwards along Franklin Street. Turn right into Alfred Street.*

St Malachy's Church★

The austere fortified exterior of this red-brick crenelled Roman Catholic church (1844) gives no hint of the ornate interior enclosed by white stucco fan vaulting inspired by Henry VII's Chapel in Westminster Abbey.

▹ *Return to the junction; turn right into Sussex Place; walk along Hamilton Street and into East Bridge Street; turn left and walk north along Oxford Street past St George's Market (see Address Book).*

The massive Portland stone **Royal Courts of Justice** (1929-33) are by JG West.

▹ *Continue north along the waterfront.*

The area facing onto the River Lagan has been redeveloped in recent years: the glittering Postmodern **Waterfront Hall** is a vast circular structure used for all kinds of entertainments and for prestigious conferences.

Custom House

The building designed by Charles Lanyon was erected in 1857.

▹ *South of Custom House turn away from the river into Queen's Sq and continue along the High St.*

On the corner stands John Bowden's **St George's Church** (1816) fronted by a Classical portico from the palace at Ballyscullion (1787) intended for the Earl Bishop.

▹ *Turn right into Skipper St and left into Waring St.*

Royal Ulster Rifles Museum

🕐 *Open Mon-Fri 10am-12.30pm, 2-4pm (3pm Fri); or by appointment.* 👝 *£1.* ☎ *028 9023 2086*

The small museum at 5 Waring Street celebrates the military exploits of the regiment (weapons, trophies, medals, uniforms and drums including the Lambeg.

▹ *Continue from Waring St into Rosemary St.*

Oval Church (Rosemary Street First Presbyterian Church)

🕐 *Open Sun and Wed 10.30am-12.30pm; or by appointment* ☎ *028 90242854*

The First Presbyterian Church (1783), the oldest church in Belfast, was designed by Roger Mulholland. The Lewis organ (1907) retains its tubular pneumatic action and is of special interest to visiting musicians.

▹ *Turn left into Royal Ave to return to Donegall Sq.*

Visit

City Centre

St Anne's Cathedral★

🕐 *Open Mon-Fri 10am-4pm.* 🚫*Closed Sat-Sun except for services.* ☎ *028 9032 8332*

Belfast's Hiberno-Romanesque Anglican Cathedral (1899-1981) by Sir Thomas Drew, suffered many delays in construction, not least because, like much of the city, it is built on waterlogged and unstable ground. Unremarkable externally, it contains a fine Chapel of the Holy Spirit, consecrated in 1932 on the 1500th anniversary of St Patrick's mission to Ireland.

Botanic Gardens, Belfast

Sinclair Seamen's Church★

🕐 *Open Sun 11am-1pm, 6.30-8.30pm, also Mar to Oct, Wed 2-4pm.* ☎ *028 90232086*
The church's service to the maritime community is reflected in its position near Belfast docks and its unusual interior furnishings.

University District

The area south of the city centre is dominated by Queen's University and the "Golden Mile" lined with busy pubs, bars and eateries. In between, clustered around the university are pleasant Georgian and Victorian suburban streets, the Botanic Gardens and the province's most important museum.

Ulster Museum★★

🔑 *Closed 2006-2009.* ☎ *028 90383000 – www.ulstermuseum.org.uk*
The national museum and art gallery of Northern Ireland is housed in a modern building (1972) appended to premises built in 1929 in the Botanic Gardens. The varied and well-presented collections give an excellent overview of the province, its capital and their place in Ireland.
☺ *It is best to take the lift to the fourth floor and descend through the galleries.*

The **Art Galleries** enclose a small collection of pre-1900 British and Continental painting by JMW Turner (1775–1851) and portraits by Sir Joshua Reynolds (1723–92), George Stubbs (1724–1806) and Pompeo Batoni (1708–87). The two charming views of the Giant's Causeway by Susanna Drury (c 1740) were largely responsible for popularising the extraordinary natural landscape. Works by Irish artists – Hugh Douglas Hamilton (1740–1808), Joseph Peacock (c 1783–1837), Sir John Lavery (1856–1941), Roderic O'Conor (1860–1940), Sir William Orpen (1878–1931), Andrew Nicholl and Richard Dunscombe Parker – or on Irish subjects are periodically presented alongsige furniture in the **Irish Gallery**.

The **Craft Galleries** document developments in glass, ceramics (Belleek pottery, silver (17C to 19C), jewellery (16C to 20C), textiles and dress (18C to 20C) that include collections of lace, embroidery and household linen.

A skeleton of the extinct Giant Irish Deer dominates the excellent **Geology of Ireland** gallery dedicated to the Irish Flora and Fauna and Living Sea.

Human activity from the Prehistoric Era to the Middle Ages is traced through artefacts excavated from archaeological sites: the **Shrine of St Patrick's Hand**★, a 14C or

15C silver-gilt hand studded with glass and rock crystal and stamped with animal figures; a Bronze Age cauldron and a pair of horns which still produce a musical note; early Iron Age sword scabbards decorated in the "Celtic" style; an early Christian brooch. Pride of place goes to the **Spanish Armada treasure**★★, excavated from shipwrecks on the Irish coast: cannon and shot, a gold salamander set with rubies, gold chains, rings and crosses and coins.

The **Local History (16C-20C)** galleries have a "Made in Belfast" section devoted to industry in the northeast of Ireland; a section for coins minted up to 1690 and another on the Post Office displaying the portable desk used by **Anthony Trollope** to write his novels.

The **Textile Gallery** explores the process of turning flax into linen, the traditional industry most intimately associated with Ulster.

Botanic Gardens

🕐 *Open dawn to dusk.* ☎*028 90320202 - www.belfastcity.gov.uk*

At the entrance stands a statue of Lord Kelvin (1824–1907), a native of Belfast, who invented the absolute scale of thermodynamics, the Kelvin Scale.

The gardens (28 acres/11ha) slope gently to the River Lagan: they were originally laid out for the study of plants by the Botanic and Horticultural Society, founded in 1827, but many activities and entertainments have encroached on the space to meet the constant need for funds. In 1895 the Gardens became a public park.

The beautiful cast-iron and curvilinear glass **Palm House**★, one of the earliest of its type, was designed by Charles Lanyon and completed in 1840. It was constructed by Richard Turner, who later collaborated with Decimus Burton on the construction of the Great Palm House at Kew. The dome was added in 1852.

The **Tropical Ravine House** is an extension of the older Fernery established in 1887 by the curator, Charles McKimm. In 1900 a stove section was added; two years later the lily pond was created over the boiler house.

Queen's University

Queen's College, Belfast, was incorporated in 1845 and established as a university in 1908. The red-brick Tudor-style building by Charles Lanyon is reminiscent of

Queens University, Belfast

Magdalen College in Oxford. **Elmwood Hall**, now an examination hall, is the Italianate building with an arcaded façade in polychromatic freestone which was designed in 1862 by John Corry as a Presbyterian Church.

University Square is an attractive mid-Victorian terrace with fanlights over the front doors and magnolia trees in the gardens – now occupied by the Faculty of Arts.

Excursions

Belfast Zoological Gardens★★
5mi/8km N of Belfast by A 6. P *footpath to McArts Fort.* ◯ *Open 10am-5pm (2.30pm Oct to Mar).* ☞ *£6.* ☎ *028 90776277*

The Zoo, which opened in 1934, are set in the former Hazlewood Gardens, surrounded, where possible, by dry ditches or water-filled moats. There are spacious green areas for the big cats, various types of deer and kangaroos; an aquatic complex houses penguins, sea-lions and polar bears. A large walk-through aviary enables visitors to look for free-flying birds in the trees. The zoo is in a state of continuous development; recent additions include an otter park and buildings housing groups of chimpanzees and gorillas.

Belfast Castle
4mi/6.4km N of Belfast by A 6. Turn left into Innisfayle Park to Belfast Castle. ◯*Open (functions permitting) 9am-10pm (6pm Sun).* ☎ *028 90776925 – www.belfastcastle.com*

In a superb location on the lower slopes of Cave Hill, this great mansion in Scottish Baronial style was built for the Donegall family in 1867–70 by WH Lynn; the external Baroque staircase was added in 1894. The **Heritage Centre** has displays on the history of the castle and its surroundings. The castle has formal gardens and waymarked trails to the **Cave Hill Country Park**.

Cave Hill
4mi/6.4km N of Belfast by A 6. Accessible on foot from Belfast Castle, the Zoological Gardens and various other points across town.

North of Belfast rears the black basalt cliff with a profile likenend to Napoleon, known as Cave Hill (1 182ft/360m), which marks the southern end of the Antrim plateau. The headland, which is separated by a deep ditch from the rest of Cave Hill, is marked by an ancient earthwork, known as **McArts Fort** which has served as a watchtower providing refuge to the native Irish hounded by Vikings and Anglo-Normans. In 1795 Wolfe Tone and his fellow United Irishmen spent two days and nights in the fort planning the independence of Ireland. Fine views extend over Belfast and the lough to County Down and Strangford Lough *(southeast)*, Lough Neagh and the Sperrin Mountains *(west)*.

Stormont
4mi/6.4km E of Belfast by A 20.

The Northern Ireland Parliament, a plain white Classical building designed by A Thornley, stands prominently on a hill surrounded by rolling parkland. Parliament met regularly from 1932 until 1972 when direct rule from Westminster was imposed. In 1999 it became the meeting place of the new Northern Ireland Assembly. Stormont Castle *(right)* accommodates other government offices. ◯ *Grounds: Open dawn to dusk.*

CARRICKFERGUS

POPULATION 22 786

Atop its basalt promontory, the largest and best-preserved Norman castle in Ireland dominates this pleasant seaside town (Carraig Fhearghais) on the north shore of Belfast Lough. A broad promenade runs along the front, between the bathing beach and the Marine Gardens; and a marina packed with yachts and fishing boats now occupies the harbour where, until the development of Belfast, there was a thriving port. The district has nurtured three literary figures: Jonathan Swift wrote his first book at nearby Kilroot; William Congreve and Louis MacNeice lived in Carrickfergus as children. *11 Antrim St* ☎ *028 93358049 - www.carrickfergus.org*

▶ **Orient Yourself:** Carrickfergus is situated on the north shore of Belfast Lough, 10mi/15km from Belfast by A 2
- **Don't Miss: a visit to** the Castle
- **Also See:** ANTRIM, ANTRIM GLENS, BELFAST

A Bit of History

The name Carrickfergus (Rock of Fergus), refers to the ruler of the ancient kingdom of Dalriada, Fergus Mór, who was shipwrecked in c 531. The castle was built late in the 12C by the Anglo-Norman, John de Courcy, and completed by Hugh de Lacy c 1240. Its strength and strategic position conveyed the idea that it was the key to Ulster, indeed to Ireland. In 1315 it was captured after a year-long siege by Lord Edward Bruce from Scotland. The English recaptured it and held it for the next 300 years, withstanding many attacks by the local Irish and by invading Scots troops.

In 1688 the castle and the town were held for James II by Lord Iveagh but were captured in 1689 by Schomberg. On 14 June the following year William of Orange landed in Carrickfergus harbour *(plaque)* on his way to the Battle of the Boyne.

In February 1760 the town was briefly occupied by a French naval detachment, then in 1778 the American privateer John Paul Jones in his vessel *Ranger* attacked *HMS Drake* in an offshore engagement; Belfast folk, many of whom sympathised with the American Revolution, gathered in boats to watch the spectacle.

Visit

Castle★★

(HM) ♿ ⏰ *Open Apr to Sep, Mon-Sat 10am-6pm; Sun noon (2pm Apr-May, Sep)-6pm; Oct to Mar, Mon-Sat 10am-4pm, Sun 2-4pm.* ⊚ *£3.* 🅿 ☎ *028 93351273 - www.ehsni.gov.uk*

Commanding the seaward approach to Belfast, the great stronghold makes a splendid picture. Initially, it occupied just the tip of the basalt promontory but was extended over the years, protected by the sea on all sides but one.

The once circular **gatehouse towers** built at the same time as the Outer Ward, were cut back some time after the Elizabethan period. The **outer ward** was probably built by Hugh de Lacy between

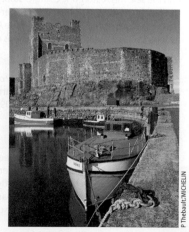

Carrickfergus Castle

P.Thebault/MICHELIN

423

1228 and 1242, to enclose the whole promontory and make the castle less vulnerable to attack. Originally it probably contained living quarters but these were replaced in the 19C by ordnance stores supporting gun platforms.

The wall enclosing the **middle ward**, now partly reduced to its foundations, was built to improve the castle's defences soon after it had been successfully besieged by King John in 1210. The northeast angle tower is a fine example of 13C defensive work with an impressive array of arrow slits.

The castle's nucleus was the **inner ward**, enclosed by a high curtain wall, built by de Courcy between 1180 and 1200. The **keep** provided living quarters. Life in the castle is recreated by a large model at the time of Schomberg's siege (1689), a video *Feasts and Fasts* in the Banqueting Hall, and with period costume on the top floor.

St Nicholas' Church★

John de Courcy provided Carrickfergus with a church as well as a castle. Centuries of turbulence left the building in a poor state; in 1614 it was heavily restored. The west tower, initiated in 1778, was completed in 1962 as a memorial to both World Wars. In the north transept is a fine marble and alabaster monument to Sir Arthur Chichester (1563–1625), an energetic Englishman who as Governor of Carrickfergus played a prominent and particularly ruthless role in the subjugation of Ulster, who fathered the great landowning Donegall dynasty.

North Gate and Town Walls

Between 1607 and 1610 Carrickfergus was enclosed with defensive walls and ditches by Sir Arthur Chichester, who by this time had been elevated to the rank of Lord Deputy of Ireland. The big arch of the North Gate is still largely 17C despite repairs and alterations; the pedestrian arch and crenellations are 19C. A good stretch of wall survives to the east in Shaftesbury Park.

Excursions

Andrew Jackson Centre

2mi/3.2km N of Carrickfergus by A 2; turn right onto Donaldsons Ave. ○ *Open Apr to Oct, Mon-Fri 10am-1pm, 2-6pm (4pm Apr-May, Oct), Sun 2-6pm (4pm Apr-May, Oct).* ☎ *028 93358049*

The Jackson family emigrated from Carrickfergus in 1765; their son, Andrew, born two years later, went on to become the 7th President of the United States. The Jackson homestead has long since disappeared but close to where it stood between the road and the sea, this restored 17C single-storey cottage with its earthern floor preserves the family memory and traces the Ulster-American connection. The adjoining **US Rangers Centre** presents the story of the American force, formed in Northern Ireland in June 1942, to spearhead the invasions of the Second World War.

Dalway's Bawn

6mi/10km N of Carrickfergus by A 2, B 149 and B 90.

By the side of the road south of Ballycarry *(left)* stand the remains of a bawn and three towers built by John Dalway c 1609.

Whitehead

5.5mi/9km NE of Carrickfergus by A 2.

The little seaside resort sheltered between the cliffs of White Head and Black Head has a pebble beach backed by a promenade and two golf courses. The **Railway Preservation Society of Ireland** is partly based here, organising its owns a unique collection of steam locomotives and coaches, and operating steam rail tours to all parts of Ireland during the summer season.

Island Magee

6mi/10km N of Carrickfergus by A 2.

Although not an island, the peninsula (7mi/11km long) separating Larne Lough from the North Channel seems detached from the mainland. The road *(B 90)* provides fine views across Larne Lough. At the northern end of the peninsula, standing incongruously in the front garden of a private house, is the **Ballylumford Dolmen★**, a Neolithic burial monument, consisting of four stones supporting a capstone. From the sandy shores of **Brown's Bay**, you can watch the maritime traffic to and from Larne. **Portmuck** is a small bay and harbour. Farther south are **The Gobbins**, precipitous cliffs (2mi/3.2km) from which the local inhabitants were flung into the sea in 1641 by the soldiers from the garrison in Carrickfergus.

Glenoe Waterfall

12mi/20km N of Carrickfergus by B 58 and B 99.

The gorge is so deep and so well screened by trees that this well-known waterfall can be heard long before it is seen. The double cascade pours into a deep pool before flowing on under an old stone bridge through the village.

DOWNPATRICK

POPULATION 10 113

Historic Downpatrick (Dún Pádraig) owes the first part of its name to a pre-Christian fort (*dún* in Irish), built on the prominent site now occupied by the cathedral, but the town is famous above all for its associations with the patron saint of Ireland. Traditionally held to be St Patrick's burial place, it developed into an ecclesiastical city with many religious foundations. Despite losing its status as a county town in 1973, Downpatrick is still a busy market centre serving the surrounding agricultural area, which to the south is known as the Lecale Peninsula. ▊ *53a Market St* ☎ *028 44612233*

▶ **Orient Yourself:** Downpatrick sits between the Mourne Mountains and Strangford Lough, 23mi/37km S of Belfast by A 7.

◔ **Also See:** LISBURN, MOURNE MOUNTAINS, STRANGFORD LOUGH

A Bit of History

As well as the hill now crowned by the cathedral, there is a second great Iron Age earthwork, known as the **Mound of Down**, which rises from the marshy levels north of the town. The tree-covered mound sheltered an urban settlement destroyed by the Norman knight de Courcy in 1177 as a first step in his conquest of east Ulster. In the 18C, when Downpatrick was the administrative centre for the whole county, great improvements were made to the physical appearance of the town by the Southwell family, who had acquired the demesne of Down through marriage to Lady Betty Cromwell, the last of the line to whom the land had been granted by James I in 1617. Until modern times Downpatrick was almost entirely surrounded by water and marshy ground, its narrow medieval thoroughfares – English, Irish and Scotch Streets – converging on the town centre where the market house once stood.

Walking Tour

Saint Patrick Centre

🕐 *Open Apr to Sep, Mon-Sat 9.30am-6pm (5.30pm Apr-May, Sep), Sun 1-6pm (5.30pm Apr-May, Sep); Oct to Mar, Mon-Sat 10am-5pm.* 👓 *£4.75.* 🍴 ☎ *028 44619000*

The great story of Ireland's the patron saint is retold and the impact of Irish missionaries in Europe is explored.

English Street

The red-brick Venetian Gothic Assembly Rooms (1882) were designed by William Batt of Belfast. The **Customs House** *(no 26)* was built in 1745 by Edward Southwell. The Clergy Widows' Houses *(nos 34-40)* date from 1730 and 1750, but were altered in the early 19C. The low two-storey edifice *(right)*, was originally conceived to hold prisoners, its vaulted cells were converted in 1798 into the **Downe Hunt Rooms:** they house records from 1757. The Courthouse (1834) is the sole section of the new prison complex to survive.

Down County Museum★

♿🕐 *Open Mon-Fri 10am-5pm, Sat-Sun 1-5pm* ☎ *028 44615218*

The old Down County prison, built between 1789-96 was where Thomas Russell, the United Irishman, was hanged in 1803. When the prison moved, these premises were taken over by the South Down Militia, then by the army until the mid 20C.

The **gatehouse** contains the **St Patrick Heritage Centre** which narrates the saint's history; a video traces his associations with the many local sites.

The display in the former **Governor's House** in the centre of the courtyard traces the history of Co Down from 7000 BC and describes the local wildlife.

The Mall

To avoid the deep dip between the Cathedral and English Street the road was raised (15ft/5m) in 1790. Well below road level stands the **Southwell Charity**, a school and almshouses founded in 1733 by Edward Southwell, the Secretary of State for Ireland, who by his marriage in 1703 became Lord of the Manor of Down. Opposite are the **Judges' Lodgings** *(nos 25 and 27)*, two late Regency houses built soon after 1835.

Down Cathedral★

♿🕐 *Open Mon-Sat 9.30am-5pm, Sun 2-5pm.* 👓 *Donation.* ☎*028 44614922*

No traces of the monastic complex founded by St Patrick survive, although a round tower stood on the site until 1780. In the 12C, John de Courcy replaced the incumbent Augustinians with a community of Benedictine monks from Chester, rebuilt

---

Address Book

♿ *For coin ranges, see the Legend on the cover flap.*

WHERE TO STAY

〰**The Mill at Ballydugan** – Drumcullen Rd -2.5mi SW by A 25 - 11 rm ☎ 028 4461 3654 – www.ballyduganmill.com - ♿🏊🍴❌🅿 1792 flourmill sympathetically converted into a well-equipped B&B in peaceful village, with cafe and restaurant.

〰**Pheasants' Hill Farm** – 37 Killyleagh Rd - 3mi N on A 22 - 5 rm ☎ 028 4461 7246 - www. pheasantshill.com 🅿 Organic farm bordering the Quoyle Pondage National Nature Reserve.

OTHER IDEAS

County Down Crafts – 11b Scotch St - ☎ 028 44617214 - www.countydown-crafts.com.

Downpatrick Railway Museum - *Open Mon-Fri 11am-2pm, trains steamed up most weekends, and 2-5pm Jul-Aug* ☎ 028 44615779

St Patrick's Tomb

P Thœault/MICHELIN

the abbey church and interred the supposed relics of St Patrick, St Colmcille and St Brigid there, changing the dedication to St Patrick and renaming the town Downpatrick to please the native Irish. This building was destroyed by Edward Bruce in 1316; its replacement by the English in 1538. The present building largely dates from the early 19C, built using the stone on site, and incorporating the chancel of the abbey church. The original dedication to the Holy and Undivided Trinity was restored in 1609 by James I.

Inside, there are various remarkable features: the granite font was once used as a watering trough, two unusual figures in ecclesiastical robes flank the Chapter Room door, the choir screen is unique in Ireland, the splendid Georgian Gothick organ was given by George III. Outside, in the graveyard south of the cathedral stood a stone bearing the names of the three saints said to be buried in the same plot; this was replaced in the early 20C by a great slab of granite inscribed with the name Patrick.

Excursions

▶ *From Downpatrick take a minor road E for 2mi/3.2km to Saul.*

St Patrick's Memorial Church
2mi/3.2km E of Downpatrick.
The hilltop site, where St Patrick is said to have made his first Irish convert, now accommodates a church, built of Mourne granite in 1932 to commemorate the 1 500th anniversary of St Patrick's landing near Saul, designed in the Celtic Revival style by Henry Seaver of Belfast with a characteristic Irish round tower incorporated.

There are few traces of the original medieval abbey, but its graveyards hold two cross-carved stones and two small **mortuary houses**.

St Patrick

When St Patrick returned to Ireland in 432 to convert the people to Christianity, his ship was carried by the wind and tide into Strangford Lough, and up the River Slaney, now a mere stream, to land near Saul. He converted the local chief, Dichu, who gave him a barn (*sabhal* in Irish, pronounced Saul) to use as a church. St Patrick grew attached to Saul and returned there to die in 461; some records even state he was buried there!, rather than in Downpatrick: but many strong associations live on.

427

Slieve Patrick

3mi/4.8km E of Downpatrick. 15min there and back on foot to the top of the hill.
A statue of St Patrick was erected on the top of the hill in 1932 to commemorate the 1 500th anniversary of St Patrick's landing near Saul. The path up to an open-air altar is marked by the Stations of the Cross. From the top there is a fine **view** over the surrounding countryside and the drumlin islands of Strangford Lough.

St Tassach's (Raholp) Church

4mi/6.4km E of Downpatrick.
The ruins of this 10C/11C church stand on the spot where Bishop Tassach is said to have administered the last sacrament to St Patrick.

Struell Wells★

2mi/3.2km SE of Downpatrick.
The site, in a secluded rocky hollow by a fast-flowing stream, comprises five buildings: an unfinished 18C church; a circular Drinking Well with a domed roof built on a wicker supporting arch; a rectangular Eye Well with a pyramidal corbelled roof; a Men's Bath-house, with a stone roof and a dressing room with seats next to the bath; and a Women's Bath-house without a roof – its dressing room is in the men's bath-house.
Although the oldest of these buildings dates only from c 1600, there is written reference to a chapel on the site in 1306. A strong tradition associates the site with St Patrick, although Struell has probably attracted pilgrims since pre-Christian times as streams and springs were important to the Celts.

Ardglass★

7mi/11km S of Downpatrick by B 1.
Little Ardglass is attractively located in a natural harbour, home to one of the province's fishing fleets. In the 15C it was an Anglo-Norman enclave, the busiest port in Ulster, protected from the native Irish by numerous fortified buildings. The finest of those standing is **Jordan's Castle**, an early-15C tower house overlooking the harbour, which, in the Elizabethan era, withstood a three-year siege under its owner, Simon Jordan, until relieved by Mountjoy in June 1601. It was restored in 1911 by FJ Bigger, a solicitor and antiquarian from Belfast, and now houses his collection

Ardglass Harbour

of antiquities.*(HM)* ◷ *Open Jul to Aug, Tue, Fri, Sat, Bank Hols 10am-1pm; Wed-Thu, 2-6pm.* ☎ *028 90543034*

King's Castle and Isabella's Tower are predominantly 19C. A row of fortified warehouses along the harbour front is now the clubhouse of the local golf course.

Killough
7mi/11km S of Downpatrick by B 176.

A broad central avenue runs through this peaceful village on the edge of a deep seainlet. In the 17C it was known as Port St Anne after Anne Hamilton, whose husband, Michael Ward of Castle Ward, developed the port to facilitate the export of lead and agricultural products from his estates.

St John's Point
10mi/16km S of Downpatrick by B 176, A 2 and a minor road.

The ruins of a 10C/11C pre-Romanesque church mark the site of an early monastery. A lighthouse stands on the southernmost point of the Lecale Peninsula.

Ballynoe Stone Circle

▶ *3mi/5km S of Downpatrick. Park opposite the old railway station (east); 6min there and back on foot by the track (west) between the fields.*

Low close-set stones encircle an oval mound which contained a stone cist at either end in which cremated bones were found (1937–38), probably built by the late-Neolithic Beaker people c 2000 BC.

Clough
6mi/10km SW of Downpatrick by A 25.

North of the crossroads stands a stone tower (13C with later additions) surmounting an Anglo-Norman earthwork castle, which was enclosed by a wooden palisade.

Loughinisland Churches
5mi/8km W of Downpatrick by A 2 and a minor road north.

Three ruined churches stand on what was originally an island overlooking the lake. The oldest (13C) is the middle one; the largest is 15C; the third bears the date 1636 over the door, but may be earlier; the initials PMC stand for Phelim MacCartan, whose family owned property in the area and are probably buried here.

Seaforde Garden
9mi/14.5km W of Downpatrick by A 25 and A 2 north.

◷ *Open Mon-Sat, 10am-5pm, Sun 11-6pm.* ⊕ *Garden: £3; Butterfly House and garden: £5.50.* ⊞ ☎ *028 4481 1225 - www.seafordegardens.com*

The old walled garden has been revived with a large hornbeam **maze** and a **tropical butterfly house.** The Pheasantry is a deep dell planted with great rhododendrons and exotic trees.

DUNGANNON

POPULATION 9 190

On its hilltop, Dungannon (Dún Geanainn) was for centuries a main residence of the O'Neill clan, one of the great families of Gaelic Ulster. Nowadays it is the busy hub of a rich dairying and fruit-growing district, and a manufacturing centre of some importance; one of its oldest industries, textiles, has brought international fame to the name of Moygashel (founded in 1875). 🔢 *Killymaddy Centre, Ballygawley Rd ☎ 028 87767529 - www.dungannon.gov.uk*

▸ **Orient Yourself:** Dungannon is situated not far from Lough Neagh, 11mi/18km N of Armagh on A 29
◔ **Also See:** ARMAGH, LOUGH NEAGH, SPERRIN MOUNTAINS

A Bit of History

Plantation Town
When ruled by the O'Neills, Dungannon was little more than a collection of huts grouped round Castle Hill; but early in the 17C English and Scottish settlers started on developing a modern town. A charter was granted in 1612; in 1614 the Royal School was founded. When the native Irish rebelled in 1641, the settlers' buildings were burned and their farms and orchards destroyed; the population dropped to 130. A new plantation followed the restoration of peace in 1653. After the Battle of the Boyne (1690) Dungannon expanded rapidly; in 1692 the town was purchased by Thomas Knox, whose expansionary regime coincided with the development of the coalfields at Drumglass and the digging of the local canal.

Visit

Tyrone Crystal
NE in Killybrackey Road (A 45)♿🚌 Factory tours: Mon-Fri 11am, noon, 2pm, 3pm (booking advisable). 🎫 £5. Shop: open 9am (1pm Sun)-5pm. 🍴 🅿 ☎ 02897725335 - www.tyronecrystal.com
Tyrone Crystal opened in 1971, exactly 200 years after an earlier glasshouse had started production under Benjamin Edwards at Drumreagh, Newmills *(north)*. The nascent enterprise faced closure in the late 1970s' recession but local financial support was found and the factory moved into its present premises in 1990.
The **tour** takes visitors through the various stages of production to the cut and polished product on sale in the shop.

Victorious O'Neill
Two important military engagements involving the O'Neills took place south of Dungannon. At the **Battle of the Yellow Ford** on the River Callan in 1598 Hugh O'Neill defeated the English forces under Sir Henry Bagnall; only about 1 500 Englishmen out of over 4 000 survived. In 1646 the **Battle of Benburb** at Derrycreevy, the Scottish army of General Monroe was outmaneuvered by Owen Roe O'Neill and 3 000 Scots were killed.

Excursions

Coalisland
4mi/7km NE of Dungannon by A 45.
The landscape around Coalisland is still scarred by the industries which once flourished here. Coal was dug from bellpits as early as the 17C but severe faulting problems led to the closure of the last mine in 1970. The other industries included weaving, milling and a fireclay works; the Coalisland Canal had the first inclined plane to be built in the British Isles.

Donaghmore
5mi/8km N of Dungannon by B 43.
In the centre of this quiet village stands an ancient sandstone cross (AD c 700–1000), associated with a former abbey, and composed of two different crosses. New and Old Testament scenes ornament the faces.

Castlecaulfield
5mi/8km NW of Dungannon by A 4 and a minor road N.
The stark ruins are those of a Jacobean **mansion** built (1611–19) by an ancestor of the Earls of Charlemont, Sir Toby Caulfield, who commanded Charlemont Fort and whose arms appear over the gatehouse, an earlier structure defended with murder holes above the main door. Although burned by the O'Donnells in 1641, the Caulfields continued in residents until the 1660s.

Moy
5.5mi/9km S of Dungannon by A 29.
"The Moy" is an attractive Plantation town laid out in the 1760s by James Caulfield, Earl of Charlemont, modelled on Marengo in Lombardy, which he had visit while on the Grand Tour. The broad central green was once the site of the great monthly horse fairs which lasted a whole week.
From here, the road slopes down to the Blackwater River past the screen and entrance gates to Roxborough Castle (destroyed by fire in 1921), the 19C seat of the Earl of Charlemont. The Blackwater marks the boundary between boundary between Armagh and Tyrone, and formed the front line in 1602 between territory held by the rebellious Hugh O'Neill and his English opponents, who fortified it with a great star-shaped stronghold. Most of the fort was burned down in 1922, though the gatehouse still stands at the end of a short avenue of trees.

Benburb
7mi/11km S of Dungannon by A 29 to Moy and W by B 106.
The ruins of **Benburb Castle** *(access on foot from priory grounds or just inside priory entrance)* occupy a dramatic site, a rocky ledge above the River Blackwater, which tumbles through the tree-lined gorge (120ft/37m below). The castle, which was built by Sir Richard Wingfield in 1611, replaces an earlier O'Neill stronghold.

Parkanaur Forest Park★
7mi/11km W of Dungannon by A 4.
The herd of **white fallow deer** are direct descendants of a white hart and doe given by Elizabeth I in 1595 to her goddaughter, Elizabeth Norreys, who married Sir John Jephson of Mallow Castle. The former Burgess family estate boasts several unusual specimen trees, notably two parasol beeches with branches like corkscrews. The woodland is being developed as an oak forest; walks and nature trail thread through the formal Victorian Garden, by the stone archway and stone bridge on the Torrent River. The farm buildings (1843) contain a display of forestry machinery.

Fallow Deer

Simpson-Grant Ancestral Home
11mi/18km W of Dungannon by A 4; before Ballygawley turn left to Dergenagh. *Open 10am-4pm.* ☎ *028 8775 0311*
The 17C homestead once belonged to the great-grandfather of Ulysses S Grant, 18th President of the USA (1869–77), who commanded the Union Army during the American Civil War.

Errigal Keerogue Cross
16mi/25km W of Dungannon by A 4; 1mi/1.6km W of the Ballygawley roundabout turn right to Errigal Keerogue (sign); at the crossroads in Ballynasaggart continue W; after 2mi/3.2km turn right.
In the graveyard stands a **high cross**. Two yew trees grow in the ruins of the medieval church, thought to be a Franciscan foundation (1489) replacing an earlier monastery associated with St Kieran.

Augher
18mi/29km W of Dungannon by A 4.
This beautiful stretch of the Blackwater River provides good fishing. On the north side of the lake stands Spur Royal, now a hotel, built on the site of a 1615 stronghold.

Clogher
20mi/32km W of Dungannon by A 4.
Clogher claims to be the oldest bishopric in Ireland, supposedly founded in the 5C by St Macartan or Macartin, a disciple of St Patrick. The present **Cathedral**★, is an austere mid-18C Classical structure with a squat tower, but it preserves some early relics: a 7C **stone cross** *(outer porch)*, thought to be a sundial for timing the services of the Celtic church; the **Golden Stone** *(inner porch)* – a famous oracle in pagan times, known in Irish as **Clogh-Oir**, which may be the origin of the name Clogher. *Open by appointment.* ☎ *028 6634 7879 (Diocesan Office)*

Knockmany Passage Grave★
21mi/34km W of Dungannon by A 4 and N by B 83; 1.5mi/2.4km N of the crossroads turn right onto a track. Car park; 20min there and back on foot.
The cairn on its hilltop site commands a superb view south over Knockmany Forest into the Clogher Valley. In 1959 a concrete bunker and skylight were built to protect it from the weather but the stones of the burial chamber are visible through the grill: the decoration of circles, spirals and zigzags is typical of passage grave art.

ENNISKILLEN

POPULATION 11 436

The principal town of Co Fermanagh (Inis Ceithleann) is a lively commercial and cultural centre, occupying a strategically important island site between Lower and Upper Lough Erne. In the 17C it was one of the main strongholds of the 17C Plantation of Ulster ; nowadays it makes an ideal base for exploring

Address Book

GETTING AROUND

Devenish Island Ferry – *Operates from Apr to Sep at 10am, 1pm, 3pm, 5pm. Check with TIC for additional times* ☎ *028 68621588*
White Island Ferry – *On the hour, between 11am-5pm*

SIGHTSEEING

Lough Erne Waterbus Cruises – From the **Round 'O' Jetty** in Brook Park on the west bank of the River Erne *(northwest of the town centre)* – MV Kestrel *operates May to Jun, Sun at 2.30pm; Jul to Aug, daily, 10.30am, 2.15pm, 4.15pm; Sep, Tue, Sat-Sun, 2.30pm. £7 morning tours; £8 afternoon tours. Public dinner cruise: mid-May to late Aug, Sat evening at 6.30pm-10pm* ☎ *028 66323110 - www. fermanaghlakelands.com*
Upper Lough Erne Cruises *(1hr 30min)* – From the Share Centre in Lisnakea *(east shore of Upper Lough Erne)* – The principal marinas are on Lower Lough Erne at **Kesh** *(east shore)* and on Upper Lough Erne at **Bellanaleck** *(west shore)* and **Carrybridge** *(east shore).*
For coin ranges, see the Legend on the cover flap.

WHERE TO STAY

◎◎**Rossahilly House** –*Enniskillen – 4.5mi N by A 32 off B 82 - 7 rm* ☎ *028 6632 2352 - info@rossahilly.com - www. rossahilly.com* ✗ 🅿 Built in 1930, a superbly located and personally run house in a quiet and elevated position with terrific views of Lower Lough Erne, where guests can fish. Dinner features local produce as well as specialties straight from the owners' garden.

WHERE TO EAT

◎◎**Ferndale Country House Restaurant** – *139 Irvinestown Rd, Cross, Ferndale – 2.5mi N by A 32* ☎ *028 6632 8374 -* 🕒 *Closed Sat and Mon lunch and Sun -* 🅿 Country restaurant where the chef owner combines robust Irish cooking with subtle modern influences picked up from his Antipodean travels.
Over the border is **MacNean Bistro**, Blacklion, Co Cavan – 🕒 *open Thu-Sun (also Wed in high season) 7-9.30pm; Sun 12.30-3.30pm* ☎ *071 985 3022*

SHOPPING

Belleek Pottery – *See below.*
Sheelin Irish Lace Museum & Shop – *Bellanaleck* ☎ *028 66348052 - www. irishlacemuseum.com*

SPORTS AND LEISURE

Fermanagh Lakeland Tourism – provide information on all amenities - boat hire, boat charters, fishing facilities and angling licences. ☎ *028 66323110 - www.fermanaghlakelands.com*
Melvin Angling Centre – ☎ *028 686 58194*
Belleek Angling Centre – ☎ *028 686 58181*
Lakeland Canoe Centre, Castle Island, Enniskillen.
Lakeland Forum – For swimming, squash, volley-ball, basket-ball, badminton, table tennis, bowls, archery, soccer, judo and keep-fit.
Share Village, established in 1981, is the largest activity centre in Ireland: canoeing, yaghtingarchery, long ship cruie - *www.sharevillage.org*

EVENTS AND FESTIVALS

Lady of the Lake Festival in Irvinestown in mid-July: drama, childrens' entertainment, fishing competition.

Lough Erne, the Shannon–Erne Waterway, the Fermanagh lakes and the Sperrin Mountains. Nearby are two of Ireland's most magnificent country houses, Castle Coole and Florence Court. 🛈 *Wellington Rd. Closed Nov to Easter ☎ 028 66323110 - www.fermanagh.gov.uk*

▶ **Orient Yourself:** Enniskillen is situated between Upper and Lower Lough Erne, 50mi/80km west of Dungannon by A 4 and 12mi/19km from the border
Don't Miss: Castle Coole, Florence Court , Marble Arch Caves and Lough Erne
Also See: CAVAN, DONEGAL, SLIGO, SPERRIN MOUNTAINS

Walking Tour

In 1688 the **East Bridge**, replaced the drawbridge built by the planters on the site of an old ford in 1614. The **Courthouse** *(left)*, with its Classical portico, was radically remodelled in 1821–22 by William Farrell of Dublin.
William Scott's **Town Hall** (1898) and splendid clock overlooks The Diamond.
In the **Buttermarket** *(turn right along Church Street)* the 19C courtyard buildings have been converted into a craft and design centre. **St Macartin's Anglican Cathedral** was completed in 1842 although the tower is earlier. The French Gothic Revival **St Michael's Roman Catholic Church** *(1875)* lacks a spire intended to crown the tower. Down by the **West Bridge** (completed in 1892) are the Old Militia Barracks (1790) and Enniskillen Castle.

Visit

Enniskillen Castle

🚻🕐 *Open Jul to Aug, Mon, Sat- Sun 2-5pm; Tue-Fri 10am-5pm: May to Jun, Sep, Mon, Sat 2-5pm, Tue-Fri 10am-5pm; Oct to Apr, Mon 2-5pm, Tue-Fri 10am-5pm; Bank Hols 10am-5pm. 🎟 £2.75. 📷☎ 028 66325000 - www.enniskillencastle.co.uk*
Until the 18C Enniskillen castle was surrounded by water from the Erne. Built in the 15C as a stronghold for the powerful Maguire family, the then rulers of Fermanagh, the castle defended the strategic route between Ulster and Connaught across the formidable Erne. In 1607 it was granted to the planter Captain William Cole, whose family later moved to nearby Florence Court. Cole laid out the town and made good damage to the castle; Enniskillen held out against the native Irish uprising in 1641 and against Jacobite attacks in 1689.
The castle exhibitions unravel the history of the region. The **Fermanagh Museum** has displays on the history, landscapes and wildlife of the county, while the keep, which incorporates parts of the original 15C fortress, deals with the evolution of the castle and the fortunes of the Maguires; it is also the home of the **Regimental Museum of the Royal Inniskilling Fusiliers**, the prestigious regiment formed in the late 17C at the same time as the Inniskilling Dragoons.
The **Curved Range** displays information about the ancient monuments and castles of Fermanagh, and the pilgrim's trail to Devenish Island.

Forthill Park

🕐 *Open Apr to Sep 1.30-3pm. 🎟 £1.*
Enniskillen's town park is named after the star-shaped fort built here in 1689 during the Williamite Wars. It has a delightful oriental-looking cast-iron Victorian **bandstand**. The centre of the fort is now occupied by **Cole's Monument**, erected between 1845-57, in memory of General the Hon Sir Galbraith Lowry Cole (1772–1842), brother of the 2nd Earl of

Portora Royal School

This famous school was founded in 1608 by James I at Lisnakea *(south)*. In 1643 it moved to Enniskillen and in 1777 to a site near **Portora Castle** *(17C)*, which was partially destroyed by an explosion caused by schoolboys in 1859. Among its pupils were Oscar Wilde and Samuel Beckett.

Enniskillen of Florence Court, and a close friend of the Duke of Wellington. Within the fluted Doric column a spiral stair *(180 steps)* climbs to a platform providing great **views** of the area.

Excursions

Castle Coole★★★

SE of the town centre by A 4. (NT) ♿🕐 *Grounds: open 10am-8pm (4pm Nov to Mar). House: Jul to Aug, noon-6pm; Sep, Sat-Sun 1-6pm.* 👝 *£4.50.* ☎ *028 66322690 - www. nationaltrust.org.uk*

Among great oaks and beeches and overlooking its lake, this superb neo-Classical house is perhaps the finest building of its kind in the whole country. It was completed to designs by James Wyatt in 1798 for the Corry family, Earls of Belmore, who lived here until the house passed into the hands of the National Trust in 1951. Built, decorated and furnished without apparent regard to expense, it has been comprehensively restored to something like its original glory.

The **exterior** consists of a central block containing the formal rooms, flanked by single storey colonnaded wings with the family accommodation. The pale Portland stone which lends the facade its particular distinction was imported from the far-off Dorset quarry via Ballyshannon, where a special quay had to be built. So as not to interfere with the harmony of the composition, the stable yards added in 1817 by Richard Morrison were built out of sight below the level of the house and linked by tunnel. Lord Belmore's coach, built in 1863 was used until the 1940s to fetch guests from the station.

The spacious feel and sense of proportion in the **entrance hall** are repeated throughout the house. **James Wyatt**'s scheme of decoration and furnishings is best seen in the **library** and in the **dining room**, where little has changed since Wyatt's day. The **oval Saloon**, the most important room in the house, is decorated with elaborate

The Corrys of Coole

John Corry, a Belfast merchant, originally from Dumfriesshire, purchased the manor of Coole in 1656 and in 1709 built a new house near the lake incorporating parts of an early-17C castle. In 1741 the estate passed to Armar Lowry-Corry, created 1st Earl of Belmore in 1797, who commissioned Wyatt to design the present house; his son, the 2nd Earl of Belmore, was responsible for the interior decoration and the Regency furnishings.

State Bedroom, Castle Coole

C Hill/National Trust Photographic Library

plasterwork; the curved mahogany doors veneered with satinwood, are hung on pivots. Wyatt specified the ceramic stoves which have the same decorative motif as the friezes.

Between 1807 and 1825 some interiors were refurbished by Preston, one of the leading upholsterers of the period ; his more flamboyant style is evident in the colours of the hall, staircase and first-floor landing; the hangings and furniture in the drawing room and the saloon and the **Bow Room.** The gold and scarlet decoration and furnishing of the **State Bedroom** were in anticipation of George IV's visit to Ireland in 1821.

Florence Court★★

8mi/13km S of Enniskillen by A 4, A 32 and W by a minor road. (NT) ⏱ *Grounds: 10am-8pm (4pm Nov to Mar).* ⚏ *£3 (car). House tours: Jul to Aug, noon-6pm, Sep 1-6pm. Last admission at 5pm.* ⚏ *£4.25.* ⛶❌🄿 ☎ *028 66348249 - www.nationaltrust.org.uk*

County Fermanagh's second great country house stands surrounded by parkland at the foot of Cuilcagh Mountain. Faced in attractive greyish-gold stone, the original three-storey house, probably designed in the 1740s, is flanked by seven-arched colonnades and canted pavilions, which were probably designed in the 1770s by Davis Ducart, a Sardinian, who spent most of his working life in Ireland. The property was transferred, largely unaltered, to the National Trust in 1955.

The interior is charmingly decorated with family portraits, photographs, drawings and other memorabilia, but the glory of Florence Court is the exuberant **Rococo plasterwork**, some of it restored after a fire in 1956.

The **Pleasure Grounds** were mostly planted by the 3rd Earl early in the 19C. The walled garden retains some of its original features, although lawn now replaces the vegetable plots.

Since 1975, the estate grounds have been developed as **Florence Court Forest Park**. In the woodlands southeast of the house stands the famous **Florence Court Yew**, also known as the Irish Yew, a columnar-shaped freak, which can be reproduced only by cuttings as seedlings revert to the common type. There are several trails signposted with coloured indicators; the most challenging extends to moorland *(9hr there and back on foot)* and the top of Cuilcagh Mountain (2 198ft/670m).

The Cole Family

The Coles came to Ireland from Devonshire in the reign of Elizabeth I. They lived first at Enniskillen Castle and then at Portora Castle. Sir John Cole (1680–1726) settled at Florence Court, named after his wife, Florence Wrey, a wealthy heiress from Cornwall. Their son, John Cole (1709–67), made Lord Mount Florence in 1760, built the present central block; the wings were added by his son, William Willoughby Cole (1736–1803), later Viscount and Earl of Enniskillen, who went on the Grand Tour in 1756–57.

Marble Arch Caves★★

11mi/18km S of Enniskillen by A 4, A 32 and W by a minor road. 🐾 *Tour: mid-Mar to Sep, 10am-4.30pm (5pm Jul to Aug); booking recommended in high season.* ⏱ *Closed after heavy rain.* ⚏ *£7.50.* ☎ *028 66348855 - www.marblearchcaves.net*

This spectacular cave system was formed in a bed of Dartry limestone by three streams on the northern slopes of Cuilcagh Mountain, converging underground to form the Cladagh River which emerges at the Marble Arch and flows into Lough Macnean Lower.

The **reception centre** presents an exhibition on caving and a video *(20min)*, covering the same ground as the tour. The **cave tour** includes a short boat trip on an underground lake into a fantastic subterranean decor of stalactites, stalagmites, columns, flow stones, cascades, draperies and curtains, with picturesque names such as the Porridge Pot, Streaky Bacon, Cauliflowers, Tusks and Organ Pipes. The

Lough Erne

longest stalactite (7ft/2m) is named after Edouard Martel, a famous French cave scientist who explored the caves in 1895.

The **nature reserve** consists of the wooded Cladagh gorge created by the collapse of caves eroded by the river. A path *(1hr there and back on foot)* along the east bank links the **Marble Arch** and the **Cascades**, where more water gushes forth.

Lough Erne★★

Wet and wooded, the Fermanagh Lakeland was once the remotest part of a remote province, described by an early 16C traveller as "full of robbers, woods, lakes and marshes". Nowadays it is more accessible, much frequented by fishermen and increasingly popular for water-based activities, though its vast extent is such that it rarely feels crowded. Fed by the River Erne (50mi/80km long), Lough Erne is divided into two by the narrows around Enniskillen; the Upper Lough is a watery labyrinth of islands and twisting channels, while the glorious expanse of Lower Lough Erne has a more orderly assemblage of islands and a greater share of attractions exploiting its maximum width of 5mi/8km.

In 1994, the Lough section of the **Shannon–Erne Waterway** was re-opened.

Lower Lough Erne *Round tour of 66mi/106km – 1 day*

▶ *From Enniskillen take A 32 N; after 3mi/5km turn left to Trory Point.*

Devenish Island★
Access by ferry (see Address Book).
Devenish was chosen as the site for a monastery in the 6C by St Molaise. Devastated by the Vikings, frequently caught up in local feuds, and burnt down in the 12C, it nevertheless survived until early in the 17C. The picturesque remains enjoy a lovely lakeside setting; while a **museum** traces the history of the monastery. ◐ *Open Apr to Sep 10am-5pm.* ◎ *£3 (including boat crossing).* ☎ *028 68621588*
Nearest to the jetty are the ruins of the **Lower Church** (Teampull Mór), begun in the early 13C and later extended. The mortuary chapel to the south was built for the Maguire family. The smallest and oldest building, **St Molaise's House**, dates from the 12C although it is based on an earlier wooden church.
St Mary's Priory dates from the 15C although the tower is later. A most unusual 15C **high cross** stands in the graveyard.

Devenish Island

▶ *Continue N by B 82 along the east shore of the lake.*

Castle Archdale Country Park★

🕐 *Park: open 9am - dusk. Museum and visitor centre: Jul to Aug, Tue-Sun 11am-7pm; Easter to Jun Sun noon-6pm, May Bank Hol 11am-6pm. ☎ 028 68621588*

The fortified residence built in the early 17C by the Archdales, an English planter family from East Anglia, has long since been abandoned, but their fine arboretum, 19C pleasure grounds, a cold bath and sweat house, and an old walled garden live on. The former outbuildings house a Visitor Centre with a display of agricultural implements. A caravan park occupies the site of the Second World War base used by the British and Canadian flying boats which patrolled the North Atlantic sea lanes, overflying neutral Ireland on the way.

The park has extensive and wonderfully diverse woodlands harbouring a variety of wildlife, while the ruins of **Old Castle Archdale** near the northeast entrance include the original gateway of the bawn.

White Island★

🕐 *Open Jul to Aug 10am-5pm; Jun, Sep Sat-Sun, Bank Hols. ☜ £3. ☎ 028 68621892*

Within a large pre-Norman monastic enclosure stand the remains of a 12C church with a handsome Romanesque doorway. Speculation continues to surround the eight 9C/10C **stone figures** set against the north wall: while definitely Christian, they have something of the pagan about them and include a particularly lewd example of a *sheilagh-na-gig*.

▶ *Continue N by the scenic route; N of Kesh bear left onto A 47. Near the W end of Boa Island park beside the road and follow sign to cemetery (about 550yd/500m there and back on foot).*

Janus Figure, Boa Island

Janus Figure★

In an overgrown graveyard, sits this squat and ancient stone figure with two faces, staring eyes and crossed arms, possibly from the Iron Age.

▶ *Continue W on A 47.*

Castle Caldwell Forest Park

An important bird sanctuary, the forest covers two long fingers of land at the western end of Lough Erne The ruined planter's castle (1612) was once owned by the Caldwells. In 1770, family members were being entertained aboard a boat by a fiddler whose inebriated state caused him to fall overboard and drown. He is commemmorated by the **Fiddler's Stone** at the park entrance.

▶ *Continue W on A 47.*

Belleek

◷ *Open Apr to Sep, Mon-Fri, 9am-6pm (8pm Jul-Aug), Sat 10am-6pm, Sun 2pm(11am Jul-Aug) -6pm; Oct to Mar, Mon-Fri 9am-5.30pm, Sat in Oct 10am-5.30pm, Sun in Oct 2-6pm. Pottery tours (30min) every 30min, Mon-Fri between 9.30am-12.15pm, 2.15-4.15pm (last tour on Fri at 3.30pm); Jun to Aug, Sat between 10.30am-4.15pm.* ◷ *Closed 1 Jan, 17 Mar; no tours on Bank Hols.* ⬚ *£4.* ⬚ P ⬚ *028 68659300 - www.belleek.ie*

The village stands at the point where the waters of the Erne flow swiftly westward in a narrow channel to enter the sea in Donegal Bay.

The **Belleek Pottery**, and its distinctive Parian ware, has an international reputation. The **tour** begins where the slip is moulded and trimmed and continues through the stages to completion and sale in the Visitor Centre.

The Erne Gateway Centre exhibition **ExplorErne** introduces visitors to the history, landscapes and ecology of the Lough, from legendary beginnings to the harnessing of its waters to generate hydroelectric power.

Belleek Parian Ware

The pottery was founded in 1857 by John Caldwell Bloomfield, shortly after he inherited Castle Caldwell and felt the need for more income. Being a keen amateur mineralogist, he discovered all the ingredients to make pottery – feldspar, kaolin, flint, clay, shale, peat and water power were avaiable on the estate. At first only earthenware was produced; Parian ware was refined over 10 years and won a Gold Medal in Dublin in 1865.

▶ *Leave Belleek by A 46 going E.   After 10mi/16km turn left to Tully Castle.*

Tully Castle★

(HM) ◷ *Open Jun to Aug, Wed-Sun 10am-6pm; Apr, Sep, Sat-Sun, Bank Hols 10am-6pm* ☎ *028 68621588; www.ehsni.gov.uk*

The ruins of a fortified planter's house, built in 1613 by Sir John Hume from Berwickshire were left when the castle was captured and abandoned in the rising of 1641. The partially paved bawn is protected by walls and corner towers with musket loops; the rest has been transfrmed into a17C-style garden. The three-storey house has a vaulted room on the ground floor containing the kitchen fireplace, an unusually large staircase leading to a reception room on the first floor and a turret stair to the floor above.

▶ *Return to A 46 and immediately turn right onto B 81 and then second right to the Lough Navar Scenic Drive. After 3mi/5km turn right opposite Correl Glen.*

Cliffs of Magho Viewpoint★★★

A scenic drive *(one way - ⊛ £3 car)* winds for 7mi/11km through the trees of **Lough Navar Forest** to a viewpoint on the top of the Cliffs of Magho. The panorama is immense, taking in the whole of the north end of Lower Lough Erne and extending to the far-off Blue Stack Mountains in Donegal.

▷ *Return to A 46 and continue S. on A 46; turn right to Monea Castle.*

Monea Castle

▷ *Proceed up the drive; after 0.25mi/0.3km turn right at the gates of the house.*

The ruined castle, one of the largest and best-preserved of the 17C tower houses, was built on a rocky bluff in 1618 by the planter Malcolm Hamilton, Bishop of Cashel. Crow-stepped gables and corbelling on towers and turrets lend a Scottish look, but despite everything, it fell to rebels(1641) and Jacobite forces (1689).

▷ *On leaving turn left; in Monea turn left onto B 81 to return to Enniskillen.*

Upper Lough Erne

Crom Estate

21mi/34km S of Enniskillen by A 4 and A 34; in Newtownbutler turn right. (NT)🕐 *Grounds: open Jul to Sep, 10am-7pm (6pm Sep); 1-15 Oct, Sat-Sun, noon-6pm. Visitor Centre: open May to Sep 10am-6pm. Last admission 1hr before closing.* ⊛ *£4.80 (car or boat).* 🖵 🅿 ☎ *028 67738118*

A visit to this estate, now a National Nature Reserve with oak woodland, reed beds, meadows and heronry, gives an opportunity to experience something of the less accessible Upper Lough. The desmesne and its planter's castle once belonged to the Creighton family from Scotland, who were later ennobled as the Earls of Erne: their story and that of the estate is told in the **visitor centre**. Trails lead through through woodland and along the lake shore, taking in the old castle, remains of a formal garden, and features like the boat house, summer house, riding school and stable yards.

GIANT'S CAUSEWAY★★★

Perhaps the strangest of Ireland's scenic attractions, the 40 000 basalt columns of the Giant's Causeway have inspired legend, intense scientific debate and endless wonder. Today the Causeway is a World Heritage Site, the annual destination of hundreds of thousands of visitors. It is the focal point, but by no means the only

Early Tourism

In the early days visitors to the Causeway travelled by boat or on horseback. Numbers greatly increased with the advent of the railway line from Belfast to Portrush. In 1883 a hydroelectric narrow-gauge tramway, powered by the River Bushmills, was built from Portrush to Bushmills and extended to the Causeway in 1887; it closed in 1949 unable to compete with road transport.

The Causeway swarmed with unofficial guides who repeated fantastic legends about the formation of the Causeway and invented fanciful names for the different features.

attraction, of the "Causeway Coast" which stretches eastward from the resort of Portrush. 🏛 *44 Causeway Rd, Bushmills* ☎ *028 20731855 - www.moyle-council.org*

▸ **Orient Yourself:** The Giant's Causeway is on the coast road, A 2, between Portrush and Ballycastle on the north Antrim coast

👓 **Also See:** ANTRIM, GLENS OF ANTRIM, LOUGH NEAGH, PORTRUSH

A Bit of History

The Giant's Causeway is the most dramatic geological feature along this coastline: the result of a great volcanic eruption some 60 million years ago that impacted on this part of northeast Ireland, western Scotland (Fingal's Cave) the Faroe Islands, Iceland and Greenland, when lava exuded through cracks in the chalk mantle, solidifying into layers of hard basalt. The distinctive mass of geometric forms caused during cooling has created a variety of four, five, six, seven, eight and even nine sided columns. The Causeway was first publicised in 1693 by the Royal Society; then, in the mid-18C, the Dublin artist Susanna Drury painted a pair of topographical view (now in the Ulster Museum) that were made into engravings and circulated widely abroad, provoking great speculation among geologists.

ACCESS AND CLIFF WALKS

From the Visitor Centre to the Causeway takes 10min on foot: in summer there is a shuttle bus service.

Observe the warning signs: freak waves can break over the rocks.

To view the Causeway from above, walk through the Giant's Gate into Port Noffer and climb up the Shepherd's Path (1hr – 2mi/3km) and continue along the top to the Visitor Centre. Alternatively, from Port Noffer, go up the path (steep steps) to Benbane Head and walk back along the cliff top path (5mi/8km – 2hr). If you have time, it is worth continuing east along the cliffs (2hr) to Dunseverick Castle (B 146).

🥾 *Proper walking shoes are recommended.*

The Giant's Causeway painted c 1740 by S Drury

Ulster Museum, Belfast

Many legends relating to the Causeway describe it as the work of giants, often in the form of the Ulster warrior Finn McCool. One story relates how he fell madly in love with a Scottish giantess and constructed a landbridge to reach her. In another he builds the causeway to facilitate a trial of strength with another giant from the far side of the water, the fierce Benandonner; Finn soon defeats his rival, and as the latter flees home, the causeway sinks beneath him.

Walking Tour

Giant's Causeway★★★ 1

The Visitor Centre has an excellent video and exhibition about the area. *(NT)* &
Causeway: open daily; shuttlebus. ∞ £0.80 each way. Visitor Centre: 10am-5pm.
P☎ *028 20731855 - www.nationaltrust.org.uk*

The Causeway proper extends from the foot of the cliffs into the sea like a sloping pavement, divided into sections by the sea: the Little Causeway, the Middle Causeway and the Grand Causeway. The columns themselves are split horizontally, forming concave and convex surfaces. Certain features have acquired fanciful references: the **Wishing Well** is a natural freshwater spring in the Little Causeway, and the **Giant's Gate** carries the coastal path through the **Tilted Columns**. East across Port Noffer the columns (40ft/12m) of the **Organ** are visible in the cliff face.

Causeway Coast Way 2

The headland known as Aird Snout gives a bird's-eye view of the Causeway, while from Weir's Snout to the west, there is a view across Port Ganny *(east)* to the Causeway and down into Portnaboe *(west)* where a volcanic dyke, known as the Camel's Back, is visible.

It is well worth escaping the crowds by walking to the headland. After Port Noffer comes Port Reostan, where the curved columns of the **Harp** are set in a natural **amphitheatre**. The next headland has the **Chimney Tops**, three rock stacks formed by the second lava flow. The path enters Port Na Spaniagh where the *Gerona*, a gal-leass of the Spanish Armada, was wrecked in 1588 with no survivors. Beyond the next headland, the Horse Back, lies Port na Callian; the farther promontory is the **King and his Nobles**, with its file of figures apparently riding in from the sea. After skirting two bays, the path climbs up past the **Horseshoe** *(left)* to Benbane Head. **Hamilton's Seat** recalls Dr William Hamilton who published his *Letters concerning the Northern Coast of Antrim* in 1786. The spectacular **view**★★ extends over the rocks to the mountains of Donegal *(west)*, Rathlin Island and the Mull of Kintyre in Scotland *(east)*.

Excursion

Dunseverick Castle

Accessible by road (B 146) from Bushmills or on foot by the narrow cliff top path from the Visitor Centre at Causeway Head (5mi8km).

On their craggy promontory, separated from the mainland by two defiles, the scanty ruins of Dunseverick recall the ancient kingdom of Dalriada which included Antrim and Argyll in Scotland. This, therefore, was a strategic spot on the road from the Hill of Tara to the sea, and lands beyond.

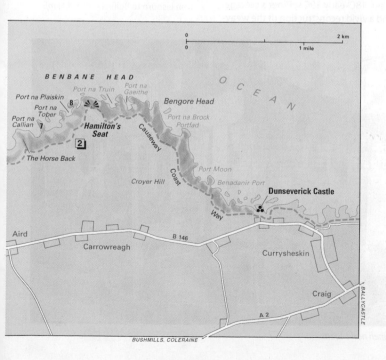

LISBURN

POPULATION 42 110

Lisburn (Lios Na Gcearrbhach) is a sizeable industrial and commercial town, now conjoined with Belfast's southwestern urban sprawl. It stands on the River Lagan at the very heart of Ulster's linen-manufacturing district, and in the 19C produced half the linen woven in the province. The Huguenot Louis Crommelin made Lisburn his headquarters when he was appointed Linen Overseer of Ireland by William III. In 1707 most of the town was destroyed by fire, save for the Assembly Rooms at the top of the market square. 🏛15 Lisburn Sq ☎ 028 92660038 🏛 The Square, Hillsborough ☎ 028 92689717 - www.visitlisburn.com

▶ **Orient Yourself:** Lisburn is situated on the Belfast to Armagh road, A 3, and skirted to the south by M 1
🕭 **Also See:** BELFAST, NEWRY, DOWNPATRICK, STRANGFORD LOUGH

Visit

Irish Linen Centre and Lisburn Museum★

🕭🕓 *Open Mon-Sat, 9.30am-5pm.* 🖵 🅿 ☎ *028 92663377*

Lisburn's Market House now displays exhibitions about the local linen industry, past and present. In the Middle Ages Irish flax was exported to England to be woven; in the 17C English and Scottish weavers helped establish looms in Ireland, largely under the direction of Crommelin, whose portrait hangs in the main hall. There are live demonstrations of spinning and weaving, a re-creation of a family at work in a late-18C–early-19C spinner's cottage, and a vivid reconstruction of the weav-

---

SIGHTSEEING

Irish Linen Tour – Tour of linen factories. Contact TIC in advance ☎028 40623322 - www.banbridge.com
Walks – Lagan Canal towpath walk from Lisburn to Belfast *(9mi/14.5km).*

Linen hand-loom

Irish Linen Centre

ers' toil in "Webster's," a hypothetical 19C mill, where conditions were tough.

Christchurch Cathedral
The cathedral is a fine example of the Gothic style adopted by the Planters (1623, reconstructed in 1708); in the graveyard *(south side)* is the Crommelin tomb.

Lisburn Castle Park
North of the cathedral is the site of the **castle**, now a small public park enclosed within the surviving walls; from the parapet there is a good view of the Lagan below.

Excursions

Hillsborough★
2.5mi/5km S of Lisburn by minor roads
This charming little town famous for its September Oyster Festival, acquired its Georgian aspect under Wills Hill (1718-92), Marquess of Downshire (from 1789).
Hillsborough Castle is a neo-Classical red-brick building with a magnificent 18C wrought-iron screen and gates from Richill Castle in Co Armagh. Today, former residence of the Governor of Northern Ireland is used mainly for state functions, most importantly, for discussions on the Anglo-Irish Agreement (1985). *Tours: May to Jun, Sat, every half hour between 10.30am-4pm.* £5. ☎ 028 92681308 .
The 18C **Courthouse** southern wing hosts a country market; the north wing contains an exhibition on Irish law, provocatively comparing ancient Brehon Law with modern penal policy. ⏰ *Open Mon-Sat 9am-5.30pm, Sun 2-6pm (Jul to Aug).* ☎ 028 90235000 - www.ehsni.gov.uk
Hillsborough Fort★ was built c 1630 to command the chief roads in Co Down, on instructions from Col Arthur Hill, who gave his name to the town. The fort is laid out as a square (270ft/82m x 270ft/82m) with a spear-shaped bastion at each corner to provide flanking fire from heavy cannon. Wills Hill later added the delightful gazebo over the northeast entrance and miniature Gothick fort in the northwest rampart. The central ditch is part of a circular trench revealed by excavations (1966–69) that

Walled Garden, Rowallane

prove the site was occupied from c 500–1000. ○ *Open Tues-Sat, 10am-7pm (4pm Mar-Oct), Sun, 2-7pm (4pm Mar-Oct).* ☎ *028 92683285*

St Malachy's Anglican Church (1662) was endowed with its towers and spire, Irish oak furnishings and box pews by Wills Hill in 1760–73.

Rowallane Gardens★

10mi/16km E of Hillsborough by B 178 to Carryduff, B 6 to Saintfield and A 7 S. (NT) ○ *Open 10am-8pm (4pm mid-Sep to mid-Apr).* ☜ *£3.80.* ☎ *028 97510131*

The gardens (52 acres/21ha) renown for their azaleas and rhododendrons, were planted by Hugh Armitage Moore, who inherited the estate in 1903. Over the years, he turned the drumlins with their light acid soil into a series of natural gardens, seeding wild flowers to attract butterflies. The pleasure grounds behind the house (National Trust headquarters) extend in a great grass sweep to a small pond.

Driving Tour

Lagan Valley *9mi/14.5km – half a day*

The River Lagan meanders between Lisburn and Belfast, through highly fertile country, before discharging into Belfast Lough. A succesion of woods and landscaped estates now form the magnificent **Regional Park**. The **Lagan Canal** built to bring coal from Coalisland via Lough Neagh to Belfast, ironically was used to transport coal imported through Belfast. Under the Lagan Navigation Company, founded in 1843, it became Ulster's most successful waterway; it declined in the 1930s and was closed in 1958; the section from Lisburn to Moira is now a motorway.

▶ *From Lisburn take A 1 N; in Hilden turn right (sign).*

Hilden Brewery Visitor Centre

○ *Open Tue-Sat 10am-5pm* ◜◝ *Tours (40min): 11.30am, 2.30pm.* ☜*£4.50.* ✕ 🅿
☎ *028 92663863*

The brewery, one of the last real-ale establishments in Ireland, occupies a Georgian house once visited by William Wordsworth. An exhibition in the restaurant covers the history of beer-drinking and brewing, Hilden Village and the brewery building. Guided tours of the brewery take place before and after lunch.

▶ *Continue N on A 1 and turn right under the railway bridge onto B 103 to Lambeg.*

Lambeg

This attractive village and delightful suspension bridge has given its name to the huge painted drums (over 30lb/14kg) introduced to Ireland from the Netherlands by William III's army, which are played in the Orange Day parades.

▶ *Continue on B 103 to Drumbeg.*

Drumbeg Church

Picturesque little Drumbeg has a church on a knoll, reached via a magnificent lych gate and path shaded by yews. The present cruciform church (1870) with a shallow apsidal chancel has an interesting wooden roof. The entrance porch contains a stone, marked "A Free Howse 1675", with a touching story.

▶ *Continue N on B 103.*

Dixon Park

The most famous rose trial grounds (11 acres/4ha) containing some 30 000 roses are set in a park with woods, meadows and a tranquil Japanese garden. The final judging of the trial roses takes place during **Belfast Rose Week** (mid July).

▶ *Continue N on B 103. At the roundabout turn right onto the dual carriageway and right again.*

Malone House

   Open 9am(noon Sun) -5pm. ☐ ☎ *028 90681246 - www.malonehouse.co.uk*
In 1603 James I granted the Barnett demesne to Sir Arthur Chichester, whose descendants became the Earls of Donegall, one of the country's great landed families which once owned Belfast itself. Since Sir Arthur's day, three houses have occupied the hilltop overlooking the Lagan crossing: the present one was probably designed by William Wallace Legge, who later bought the lease of the whole demesne. It is now owned by the City of Belfast, and used for meetings, conferences and lectures. Spanning the Ladan is the **Shaw's Bridge** (1711), which replaced an oak bridge built by Captain Shaw in 1655 to enable Cromwell's cannon to cross the river.

▶ *On leaving the park turn right; after crossing the bridge turn right; take the road along the south bank to Edenderry (sign).*

Edenderry

Five terraces of red-brick cottages and a chapel down by the river form part of a fascinating 19C industrial village built for the workers of the local weaving mill.

▶ *Return to the last T-junction; turn right onto Ballynahatty Rd; after 1mi/1.6km turn right (sign "Giant's Ring").*

Giant's Ring

The Ring is a huge circular bank of gravel and boulders (600ft/183m in diameter) around a megalithic chambered grave. Its true purpose is unknown; in the 18C it was used as a racecourse.

LONDONDERRY★

POPULATION 72 334

Northern Ireland's second city, close to the border with the Republic, is pleasantly sited on the River Foyle, surrounded by the Sperrin Mountains (southeast) and the wild heights of Donegal (west and north). Almost uniquely in the British Isles, it has kept its defensive walls, erected in the early 17C when the ancient Irish settlement of Derry became a key stronghold in the English Plantation of Ulster and was renamed Londonderry (Doire). One of the flashpoints of the North's Troubles, the scene of the "Bloody Sunday" events of 1972, the city has since undergone something of a revival, with renewed economic growth, vibrant commercial activity, and original visitor attractions. ⧉ *44 Foyle St* ☎ *028 71267284 - www.derryvisitor.com*

▶ **Orient Yourself:** Londonderry is situated at the junction of A 2, A 5 and A 6, close to the border and Co Donegal
   Don't Miss: a tour of the city walls
   Also See: BUNCRANA, DONEGAL COAST, DONEGAL GLENS, PORTRUSH, SPERRIN MOUNTAIN

A Bit of History

Monastic Foundation – According to tradition, the monastery at Derry (from *Doire* meaning "oak grove") was founded in 546 by St Columba. Between 1565-1600, Derry was occupied by the English. During the four-month rebellion of Sir Cahir O'Doherty in 1608, his forces attacked and captured Derry but could not sustain their momentum after his death at Kilmacrenan in Donegal.

The Irish Society – Under the scheme for the colonisation of Ulster with settlers from Britain, The Honourable The Irish Society was constituted by Royal Charter in 1613 to plant the County of Coleraine, now known as County Londonderry. Most of the land was parcelled out to the 12 main livery companies of London but the towns of Derry and Coleraine were retained by the Society, which still uses its income from fisheries and property to support projects of general benefit to the community.

> ## Lundy
>
> When the Scottish Col Lundy advised the citizens of Londonderry to avoid bloodshed and destruction and surrender to the superior Jacobite army, he utterly underestimated their fighting spirit. In his stead, Major Henry Baker and the Reverend George Walker rallied their fellow-Protestants and organised their brave resistance. Ever after, the term "Lundy" has been synonymous with cowardice and treachery, and the wretched colonel's effigy is ceremoniously burned during the Apprentice Boys' annual parade in August.

Siege of Londonderry – In the uncertainty created by James II's flight to France and William of Orange's landing in Devon, 13 Derry apprentices locked the city gates against the Jacobite regiment led by the Earl of Antrim sent to garrison the town in December 1688. The citizens declared for William and received an influx of supporters although food supplies were low. In March James II landed in Ireland with an army of 20 000 and in April besieged the city, erecting a boom across the river which held the relief ships at bay for seven weeks. The Scottish commander of the city, Robert Lundy, favoured capitulation to what seemed an overwhelming force but advocates of resistance deposed him and took command. On 10 July a shell bearing terms for surrender was fired into the town by the besiegers; the defenders raised a crimson flag on the Royal Bastion to signify "No surrender", a slogan which continues to

Ferryquay Gate

resonate with Northern Ireland's Protestant population. The siege lasted 15 weeks during which the 30 000 people crammed within the walls were reduced to eating cats, dogs, mice, rats and leather; thousands died of starvation. On 28 July 1689 the boom was broken and the relief ships sailed through to the quay. Three days later the Jacobite army retreated.

Sectors of the City – The character of the Plantation city changed drastically in the 19C. Migrants flocked here from all over Catholic Ireland, and by 1900 Protestants were a minority, though careful management of the boundaries of electoral districts and the allocation of public housing continued to deny Catholics control of the city council. While the traditional industry of shirt-making employed many women, male unemployment was rife, and housing conditions – notably in the Catholic Bogside district - were among the worst in the United Kingdom. The city erupted into riot in 1968, the "Battle of the Bogside" erupted in 1969, and on 30 January 1972 – Bloody Sunday, paratroopers shot dead 14 civilians in the violent aftermath of a banned protest march. In the years since, despite relative calm, sectarian boundaries have become more pronounced, with Protestants tending to withdraw from the west bank of the Foyle and settle in the Waterside district on the east bank.

Walking Tour

City Walls and Gates★★

   Walls open daily. Tour: (90min) from TIC: Jul to Aug, Mon-Fri 11.15am, 3.15pm; Sep to Jun, Mon-Fri, 2.30pm. £5. ☎ 028 71377577

The walls (1mi/1.6km long) enclosing the Plantation town were erected between 1613-18 by the Irish Society. Their near-perfect preservation is remarkable, for having sustained more than one siege, they would be potentially vulnerable to gunfire from warships in the Foyle. A walk around the walls past gateways, bastions, watch-towers and artillery pieces imparts a great impression of the city.

▶ *Join the wall walk on the east side by Newmarket St: walk clockwise.*

Ferryquay Gate was slammed shut by the 13 Apprentice Boys in the face of the Jacobite troops at the start of the 1688/89 siege.

The present triumphal arch replacing the original **Bishop's Gate** was erected to mark the centenary anniversary of the siege in 1789: it provides a good view down **Bishop's Street Within**, the city's most distinguished thoroughfare with its cluster of fine late 18C/early 19C buildings including the red-brick Bishop's Palace (Freemasons' Hall) built by the Earl Bishop, the Greek Revival Courthouse, the Irish Society's headquarters (1764) and elegant Deanery.

The Royal Bastion, overlooking Bogside, is the point where Col Michelburn hoisted the crimson "No Surrender" flag at the beginning of the great siege. The **Apprentice Boys' Hall** stands on the site of the original Shambles.

From **Butcher's Gate**, Butcher Street leads into **The Diamond**, the characteristic focal point of a Plantation town where four main thoroughfares meet in front of the Town Hall, in this case replaced by a war memorial. Beyond Butcher's Gate on the right is the **Fifth Province**.

The northernmost corner is marked by the entrance to the **Tower Museum**.

The **Shipquay Gate**, surmounted by five cannon used to defend the city during the siege, straddles another main thoroughfare up towards the Diamond.

Visit

Within the Walls

St Columb's Cathedral★

   Open Jun to Aug, Mon-Fri 9am-5pm; Sep to May 9am-1pm, 2-4pm – Sun for services only. £2. ☎ 028 71267313

The fortified Plantation city was speedily provided with a formidable battlemented late-Perpendicular cathedral, planned in 1613, started in 1628 and completed in 1634. It was the first cathedral to be built in the British Isles since the Reformation. The 191ft/58m spire was added in the early 19C. Probably its most striking feature

Children's Street Parade

is the superb open-timbered **nave roof** supported on corbels carved to represent the Bishops of Derry from 1634 to 1867, and the Revd George Walker, city governor during the Siege. In the porch stands the **mortar shell** containing terms for surrender which was fired into the city during the Siege; windows in the Choir Vestry *(right)* depict the Closing of the Gates (1688), the Relief of the City (1689) and the Centenary Celebrations (1789). The splendid 18C mahogany Chinese Chippendale **bishop's throne** was probably given by the flamboyant Earl Bishop. On the chancel arch above the pulpit is a **Cross of Nails**, a gift from Coventry Cathedral signifying peace and reconciliation. The **chapter house** dates from 1910 and houses a miscellany of historical objects *(for access ask the Verger)*.

Tower Museum★
🕐 *Open Tue-Sat 10am-4.30pm.* 👓 *£3.* ☎ *028 7137 2411 - www.derrycity.gov.uk*
Excellent displays of artefacts, wall panels and video deal comprehensively with the An Armada Shipwreck , following the work completed by the Derry Sub-Aqua Club in 1971 on the wreck of La Trinidad Valencera in Kinnagoe Bay. Elsewhere, there are comprehensive displays relating to the **Story of Derry**. From the top, there is an extensive view over the inner city and the Foyle.

Fifth Province
Butcher St. ♿🕐 *open Mon-Fri 9.30am-4pm.* 👓 *£3.* ☎ *028 7137 3177*
Embedded in the modern Calgach development in Butcher Street, is this ambitious and imaginative evocation of the history and culture of the Celts and its relevance to present-day people of Irish descent.

Beyond the Walls

Long Tower Church★
🕐 *Open summer 9am-9pm; winter 9am-8.30pm.* ☎ *028 7126 2301*
The oldest Roman Catholic church in Derry (1784–86) has an lovely Rococo interior with extensive steeply sloping galleries. It stands on the site of Templemore, a great medieval church built in 1164 alongside the Long Tower (10C) which survived an explosion in 1567. From the churchyard there is a fine view of the Royal Bastion.

Guildhall★

&⌚ *Open Mon-Fri 9am-5pm.* ⌚ *Closed Bank Hol Mon.* ☎ *028 71377335*

The late-Gothic Guildhall with the corner clocktower was erected in 1890 with a loan from the Irish Society. It was severely damaged by fire in 1908 and by bombs in 1972. A reproduction of Follingby's painting of the Relief of Derry graces the marble-faced vestibule. The numerous stained-glass windows by Ulster craftsmen, make up a visual history of the city, with London scenes on the stairs and early views of Derry in the Great Hall.

Harbour Museum

⌚ *Open Mon-Fri 10am-1pm, 2 -4.30pm.* ☎ *028 7137 7331 - www.derrycity.gov.uk*

The grandiose 19C building, which once hosted meetings of the Londonderry Port and Harbour Commissioners, is

The Guildhall from the City walls

now a museum with paintings, models and maritime memorabilia. The dominant exhibit is the largest curragh ever built, constructed in 1963 to recreate the legendary voyage of St Columba to Iona.

St Eugene's Cathedral

⌚ *Open summer, 9am-9pm; winter 9am-8.30pm.* ☎ *028 7126 2894*

Northwest of the city centre, between a district of elegant Georgian terraces and the green peace of Brooke Park, stands the Roman Catholic Cathedral dedicated to St Eugene in 1873 by Bishop Keely. The building was designed in the Gothic revival style by JJ McCarthy in 1853 and completed with a cross on the top of the spire in 1903.

Foyle Valley Railway Centre

⊶ *Closed until further notice*

Londonderry was once the focal point of no fewer than four railway companies, including the Londonderry and Enniskillen, "possibly the least efficient if not the most dangerous railway ever to operate in Ireland" and the County Donegal Railway, the most extensive of all the Irish narrow-gauge systems (125mi/200km). The Centre has steam engines, coaches, an old goods wagon, signals, signs and luggage. Excursion trains drawn by diesel car (1934) operate beside the Foyle.

Workhouse Museum★

⌚ *Open Mon-Thu, (Fri in Jul-Aug), Sat, 10am-4.30pm*

The city workhouse at 23 Glendermott Road, designed by George Wilkinson, opened in 1840 with 800 inmates. Today it servers as a library and museum acknowledging the important role played by the city in the Second World War, notably in the Battle of the Atlantic; upstairs recreates the grim 19C workhouse conditions.

Free Derry Museum

55-61 Glenfada Park. ⌚ *Open Mon -Fri 9.30am-4.30pm (3pm Fri), Sat-Sun 1-4pm.* ⊜ *Donation.* ☎ *028 71360880 - www.museumoffreederry.org.* The Museum is an archive focusing on the civil rights era of the 1960s and the Troubles during the 1970s; artefacts and documents explain the unrest in the Bogside area, the repercussions of Bloody Sunday and the effects on the local community.

MOUNT STEWART★★★

The combination on the eastern shore of Strangford Lough of superb formal gardens, extensive parkland, and the palatial mansion which was the home of one of the most eminent and politically influential families of the Ascendancy, make Mount Stewart one of Ireland's premier visitor attractions. ▯ *31 Regent St, Newtownards* ☎ *028 9182 6846*

▶ **Orient Yourself:** Mount Stewart on the eastern shore of Strangford Lough is 5mi/8km SE of Newtownards by A 20
◔ **Also See:** BANGOR, DOWNPATRICK, STRANGFORD LOUGH

Walking Tour

(NT)&.◔ *Formal gardens: open Apr-Oct 10am-6pm (8pm May-Sep); mid-end Mar Sat-Sun 10am-4pm.* ☞ *£4.50. House:* ☞ *tour: Jul-Aug, noon-6pm; May, Jun, Sep 1pm (noon Sat-Sun)- 6pm.* ◔ *Closed Tue in May, Sep; mid-Mar to Apr, Oct Sat-Sun noon-6pm. Last admission at 5pm.* ☞ *£5.50.* ◔ *Temple of the Winds: open Apr-Oct, Sun 2-5pm.* ◔ *Closed Nov to mid-Mar.* ⌘ 🄿 ☎ *028 42788387 - www.ntni.org.uk*

Gardens

The old desmesne acquired by the Stewarts was soon landscaped with fine parkland trees, including a number of exotic species planted by Edith, Lady Londonderry. Having consulted Sir Edwin Lutyens and Gertrude Jekyll, she laid out a series of formal gardens that effectively link the house with its surroundings. Work began in 1921, in part motivated by the need to provide work for the unemployed in the aftermath of the First World War.

The huge Irish yews by the house overlook the geometrical **Italian Garden** planted with herbaceous plants; the **Dodo Terrace** is ornamented with droll stone animals bearing nicknames that allude to Lady Edith's London set. The **Spanish Garden** echo the ceiling pattern in the Temple of the Winds *(see below)*. The **Sunk Garden** honours Gertrude Jekyll with its orange, blue and yellow-flowering plants. The **Shamrock Garden** celebrates Ireland with a topiary harp and Red Hand of Ulster bed.

The parkland beyond the formal gardens, is planted with exotic trees and shrubs, notably from Australasia (fine collection of eucalyptus). The hill overlooking the artificial **lake** (1846–48), provides a superb **view** over Strangford Lough. A genuine but miniature Japanese pagoda stands beside the **Ladies' Walk**, an old path to the dairy and kitchen gardens.

Soldiers and Statesmen

Mount Stewart owes its name to the Stewarts: a Scottish family granted land in the Inishowen peninsula at the time of the Ulster Plantation, who settled on the banks of Strangford Lough in 1774. They acquired vast fortunes from substantial property holdings, including their immensely profitable coal mines in northern England. Robert Stewart was made Marquess of Londonderry in 1816, but his elder son, Lord Castlereagh (1769-1822), is better known having served as leader of the House of Commons and attended the Congress of Vienna in 1815 as Foreign Secretary. The family's eminence was maintained in part by entertaining the British Establishment in London, across England and at Mount Stewart, rallying support for the Unionist cause. Mount Stewart's incomparable gardens are the work of Edith, the 7th Marchioness, one of the great hostesses of the interwar period.

J.Cornish/National Trust Photographic Library

Italian Garden

The Londonderrys' sumptuous **residence** was built in two stages. George Dance's west wing was completed in 1805, while the main part of the house was devised by William Vitruvius Morrison (1825-35).

The interior is richly furnished with family portraits, Irish and English furniture, a collection of porcelain and Classical sculpture. Perhaps its greatest treasure is George Stubbs' *Hambletonian* which shows the prize-winning racehorse being rubbed down after a triumph at Newmarket. Historical items include the portraits of William of Orange and his general, Schomberg (Dining Room) and 22 Empire-style chairs used by delegates at the 1815 Congress of Vienna, presented to Lord Castlereagh.

Temple of the Winds

30min there and back on foot from the house; 4min there and back from the carpark.
Inspired by the Temple of the Winds in Athens, this pleasure pavilion, designed by James "Athenian" Stuart in 1783, stands on a mound with a fine prospect of Strangford Lough and Scrabo Hill (topped by a tower commemorating the 3rd Marquess of Londonderry). The elegant banqueting room has a superb inlaid floor echoing designs in the ceiling. The gloomy servants' quarters, unusually, are underground.

MOURNE MOUNTAINS★★

The highest granite peaks in Northern Ireland rise dramatically from the sea and plain of Co Down to 2 796ft/852m Slieve Donard, and extend westwards to Carlingford Lough and north into rolling foothills. The Kingdom of Mourne, the strip of land between the mountains and the sea, is a region of small fields divided by drystone walls where for centuries a life of farming and fishing continued largely undisturbed by external events. Nowadays the mountains and coast are a favourite holiday area, with good beaches and lovely scenery enjoyed by hill walkers and climbers. ▯ *10-14 Central Promenade* ☎ *028 43722222* ▯ *28 Bridge St, Kilkeel* ☎ *028 41762525*

▶ **Orient Yourself:** The Mourne Mountains are bounded by the Newry–Downpatrick road, A 25, and the coast road, A 2

- **Don't Miss:** Castlewellan Forest Park
- **Also See:** DOWNPATRICK, DUNDALK, NEWRY

Excursions

Inland

Murlough National Nature Reserve

2mi/3.2km E of Newcastle by A 2. (NT) ⏲ *Park: dawn to dusk. Information Centre: Jun to Sep 10am-6pm; mid-Mar to May, Sat-Sun, Bank Hols 10am-6pm.* ⬚ *£2.50 car.* 🅿 ☎ *028 43751467*

The magnificent sand dunes between the Carrigs River and Dundrum Bay, which reach a height of 100ft/30m, provide sanctuary to migratory birds and a broad range of plants. There are traces of early human habitation, including an ancient tripod **dolmen** (8ft/2.5m high).

Dundrum Castle★

4mi/6.4m E of Newcastle by A 2; in Dundrum turn left uphill to car park. (HM) ⏲ *Open Apr to Sep Tue-Sun 10am (2pm)-7pm; Oct to Mar Sat-Sun 10am (2pm Sun) - 4pm.* 🅿 ☎ *028 90543034*

The ruins north of the town show how the castle's strategic postion and natural defences were supplemented by an impressively deep rock-cut ditch. Building was probably initiated by John de Courcy c 1177, so that the approach to the Lecale peninsula and Strangford Lough could be defended. There is an unusual circular keep (fine

Address Book

SIGHTSEEING

Mourne Countryside Centre – *87 Central Promenade, Newcastle* – Provides information and organises a programmme of hill walks in the summer months, including the **Mourne International Walking Festival** *(last weekend in June)* which starts from Newcastle or Warren Point ☎ *028 43724059*

For coin ranges, see the Legend on the cover flap.

WHERE TO STAY

⊜🛏**The Cuan** – *Strangford - 9.5mi/15km NW by A 25* - ☎ *028 4488 1222 - www.thecuan.com* ✗ 🅿 Well located for Strangford Lough, golfing, sailing and walking, this comfortable guesthouse with an established restaurant will suit most needs.

⊜🛏**Slieve Croob Inn** – *119 Clanvaraghan Rd, Castlewellan, BT56 8BN – 5.2mi N by A 25 off B 175 - 7 rm -* ☎ *028 4377 1412 - info@slievecroobinn.com - www. slievecroobinn.com. Closed 25 Dec* ✗ 🅿 Rustic inn with its exposed timbers. The bedrooms are simple yet pleasantly decorated. Various options for meals.

SPORTS AND LEISURE

There are bathing beaches at Newcastle and Cranfield.

Castle and Islands Park, *Newcastle*. – Swings, slides, Slippery Dip, 9-hole pitch and putt course, tennis, boating.

Tropicana, *Newcastle*. – Heated outdoor sea-water pools, giant water slides, bouncy castle, adventure playground, supervised crèche and kiddies' club ☎ *028 43725034*

Coco's Indoor Adventure Playground, *Newcastle*. – Snake slides, free fall, assault course and soft play activity area ☎ *028 43726226*

Soak Seaweed Baths –*Newcastle* ☎ *028 43726002 - www.soakseaweedbaths.co.uk* Pamper yourself with revitalising steam bath with seaweed.

EVENTS AND FESTIVALS

The **Boley Fair**, traditional sheep fair, in Hilltown *(Tuesday after 12 July)*.
The **Maiden of Mourne Festival** in Warrenpoint in early August.
Fiddlers' Green Festival – Folk festival at the picturesque town of Rostrevor *(last week in July)* – ☎ *028 4173 8738 - www.fiddlersgreenfestival.com*

Mourne Mountains

NITB, Belfast

views from the parapet) and Lower Ward, added between the 13C and 15C, enclosing the remains of a once-grand house built by the Blundell family in the 17C.

Tollymore Forest Park★
Open 10am-dusk. £4 car. www.forestserviceni.gov.uk
The main mansion at the heart of this vast landscaped desmesne straddling the salmon-rich River Shimna is long gone, but several follies and bridges are preserved in the province's first Forest Park (1955). There is a hermitage, the extravagantly decorated Gothic and Barbican Gates, and the church-like Clanbrassil Barn (**information centre**); trails thread past splendid specimen trees, and through an avenue of Himalyan cedars, an azalea walk, and conifer plantations. The local fauna includes foxes, otters, badgers, red squirrels and pine martens, moths, butterflies and many birds.

Castlewellan Forest Park★★
4mi/6.4km N of Newcastle by A 50. Open 10am-dusk. £2 pedestrian, £4 car - www.forestserviceni.gov.uk
Castlewellan, a spacious and elegant little market town was laid out in 1750 around its two squares by the Earl of Annesley.
The **forest park** is based on the desmesne developed by the Annesley family from the mid-18C, its splendid tree collection forming the basis of the national **arboretum**. The Annesleys, descendants of an Elizabethan army captain, were successors in this part of Ulster to the Magennis clan, who lost their landholdings after the 1641 rising. The core of the estate is not so much the Scottish baronial style castle built in granite and now used as a conference centre, but the superb **Annesley Gardens**, enclosed by a wall and ornamented by two fountains. The mile-long lake provides excellent fishing, while along its shores a 3mi/5km **Sculpture Trail** features pieces created from natural materials. There is an ice-house on the south shore and a pagan standing stone, now covered with Christian symbols, on the north bank. From the highest point, Slievenaslat (8 96ft/273m) provides magnificent views of the Mourne Mountains. The largest and longest permanent hedge **Maze** was opened in 2001.

Legananny Dolmen
11mi/18km N of Newcastle by A 50 and side roads from Castlewellan.
The dolmen consisting of a huge slanting capstone delicately balanced on three unusually low supporting stones, is sited in a theatrical setting on the southern slope of Slieve Croob (1 745ft/532m) with a magnificent view of the Mourne Mountains.

Brontë Country

Among the rolling northern foothills of the Mourne Mountains stands the ruined cottage *(plaque)* where Patrick Brunty (O'Pronitaigh), the father of the famous literary sisters, Charlotte, Emily and Anne, was born in 1777. He may have changed to Brontë before leaving Ireland in 1802 to study theology at St John's College, Cambridge, inspired perhaps by Lord Nelson who was made Duke of Brontë (1799), after a place in Sicily, by Ferdinand, King of Naples, in recognition of his assistance in recapturing Naples from the French.

Brontë Centre

1.5mi/2.5km N of Rathfriland, off B 25 in Drumballyroney (sign).   *Open 17 Mar to Sep Fri-Sun, Bank Hols noon-4.30pm or by appointment.*   *£3.*   *028 40623322 - www.banbridge.com*

The hamlet's little white schoolhouse and church now function as an interpretative centre for the life and work of Patrick Brontë and his three famous daughters. A signed **tour** *(10mi/16km)* highlights other sites in the area associated with the family.

Drumena Cashel and Souterrain★

A good number of the Early Christian farm enclosures, or cashels, have survived in the Mourne Mountains. This well-preserved example consists of an oval space encircled by a drystone wall, containing the foundations of a house and a T-shaped underground tunnel, called a souterrain, which can be entered.

Silent Valley Reservoir★

  Visitor Centre: Open Jul to Aug 11am-6pm; May-Jun, Sep Sat-Sun 11am-6pm.   *£3 car. Shuttle to/from Ben Crom £1.20 return.*   *0845 7440088 - www.newry-andmourne.gov.uk*

The Mourne Mountains have few natural lakes, so the reservoirs supplying Belfast and Co Down since 1933 have altered the landscape, many would say for the better. The Silent Valley scheme on the Kilkeel River took 10 years to complete, and holds 136 million cubic metres of water. The catchment is protected by the extraordinary 22mi/35km linear **Mourne Wall**, beautifully constructed in rough mountain granite between 1910-22, providing seasonal relief work to as many as 2000 local men. There is a pleasant walk *(2hr there and back on foot)* to the dam which provides a superb **view**★ of the reservoir below Slieve Binnian (2 441ft/744m). From the east end of the dam the path continues north to **Ben Crom Reservoir** (3mi/4.8km), while the path at the opposite end returns down the valley past **Sally Lough**, through a grove of conifers and over a wooden footbridge spanning the Kilkeel river.

Spelga Pass and Dam★

From the dam there is a superb **view** north over the foothills of the Mourne Mountains to the rolling hills of Co Down. The reservoir (fine angling for brown trout), flooded the summer pastures known as Deer's Meadow in 1959.

Crocknafeola Forest

The small coniferous forest stands beside the road which traverses the Mourne Mountains from north to south skirting the west face of Slieve Muck (2 198ft/670m).

Driving Tour

Along the coast

Newcastle

The town "where the mountains of Mourne sweep down to the sea", immortalised in verse by Percy French, began to develop in the early 19C when seaside holidays became fashionable. From the tiny harbour a long promenade of hotels, shops and amusement arcades face onto the long sandy beach of Dundrum Bay. Beyond the red-brick bulk of the Slieve Donard Hotel, built by the railway company in 1898, lie the championship links of the Royal County Down Golf Club.

The town's Roman Catholic church (1967), **Our Lady of the Assumption**, is a modern circular structure with striking stained glass.

Donard Park on the banks of the Glen River, is a good point from which to start the steep but steady climb to the summit of **Slieve Donard**, named in honour of Donard, a local chieftan supposedly converted to Christianity by St Patrick.

▶ *From Newcastle take A 2 south.*

Bloody Bridge

This was where a group of government prisoners was murdered by a man called Russell, seized by a fear of attack, on their way from Newry to Downpatrick to be exchanged for captured rebels at the time of the 1641 uprising.

Annalong

From A 2 turn S by the Police Station towards the shore.

The early-19C **cornmill**★ (restored), driven by a back-shot breast-shot water-wheel is the last of some 20 mills in the Kingdom of Mourne which once milled wheat and oats or scutched flax in the 17C/18C. The Exhibition Room describes the history of milling; the tour of the mill and its functioning machinery is fascinating. ♿ ☉ *Open Apr to Sep Wed-Mon 2-6pm.* ☞ *£2.15.* ☎ *028 4376 8736 (07739527036 for tours)*

Kilkeel

The little town at the mouth of the Kilkeel River, is full of interest, with stepped pavements and many different levels, but its true colours are really seen when the boats of Northern Ireland's largest fishing fleet land their catch at the quayside.

Narrow Water Castle

Greencastle

The ruins of an Anglo-Norman stronghold, probably built in the mid 13C, are set on a low outcrop of rock extending into Carlingford Lough. The **Royal Castle**, consisting of a large rectangular keep within a four-sided walled enclosure with D-shaped corner towers, was surrounded by a moat cut in the rock. It was beseiged by Edward Bruce (1316) and used as a garrison in Elizabethan times. From the top of the keep there is a fine view to Cranfield Bay (*good sandy beach – ideal for bathing*), up Carlingford Lough and the mountains of the Cooley Peninsula in the Republic. (HM) *Open Jul to Aug Tue, Fri-Sun 2-6pm, Wed-Thu 10am-1pm. 028 90543037 - www.ehsni.gov.uk*

Rostrevor Forest Park

The pine forest covering the south bank of the Kilbroney River and the steep north-west slopes of Slieve Martin (597ft/182m), is ideal for walking – to the **Cloghmore**, a great glacial boulder, and to the **viewpoint**★ high above Rostrevor Bay.

Rostrevor

This attractive little town on Carlingford Lough enjoys a temperate climate allowing palm trees and mimosa to thrive.

Warrenpoint

The town is both a port equipped to take container traffic, and a pleasant resort, with a vast central square, used for markets and festivals, and a promenade facing south down Carlingford Lough between the Mourne Mountains and the Cooley Peninsula.

Narrow Water Castle Keep★

2mi/3.2km N of Warrenpoint on A 2. Open Jul to Aug Tue, Fri-Sat 10am-1pm, Wed-Thu 2-6pm.

The castle keep occupies a strategic position on a promontory commanding the narrows at the mouth of the Newry River where it enters Carlingford Lough. It was built in the 1650s as an English garrison at the cost of £361 4s 2d. Although restored, it is an excellent example of a **tower house** complete with **bawn.**

The Elizabethan Revival castle *(private)* is only open for private receptions.

LOUGH NEAGH★

Ten rivers converge on the broad and tranquil lough, the largest body of fresh water in the British Isles (153sq mi/400m2) but it is drained by only one, the Lower Bann, which flows north to discharge into the sea just downstream from Coleraine. Despite its size, the lake is never more than 50ft/12m deep, and has little impact on the surrounding flat countryside. Only in Antrim Bay is the shore lined with woodland; elsewhere it is low and marshy, virtually roadless, and sometimes infested with (non-biting) midges. Together with its tiny northern neighbour, Lough Beg, Lough Neagh is a site of international importance for wintering wildfowl, and nature reserves have been established on many of its islands.

▶ **Orient Yourself:** Lough Neagh lies about 15mi/24km W of Belfast between M 1 and M 22. There is no continuous shore road, only a few points where minor roads reach the water's edge

🕭 **Also See:** ANTRIM, ARMAGH, BELFAST, LISBURN, SPERRIN MOUNTAINS.

Excursions *In clockwise order starting from the south-east corner*

Lough Neagh Discovery Centre
South shore; Oxford Island; sign at Junction 10 on M 1. 🕭🕑 *Open Apr to Sep 10am-6pm (7pm Sun); Oct to Mar 10am-5pm.* 🍴☎ *028 38322205 - www.oxfordisland.com*
This modern visitor centre, surrounded by lakeside meadows provides information on the wildlife, history and management of the lake; great views from the mezzanine level of the restaurant. Five hides and several footpaths *(4mi/7km)* through the reedbeds, wildflower meadows, woodland, and marina in Kinnego Bay, provide ample opportunity to watch out for birds.

Address Book

GETTING AROUND

The Loughshore Trail, a relatively flat route, ideal for cycling and walking, is composed of 128mi/206km miles of quiet lanes, which run alongide or close to the lough shore. It forms Route 94 of the National Cycle Network and incorporates a short section of Route 96 by Lough Beg. *www.loughshoretrail.com*

SIGHTSEEING

Lake Cruises are available from **Kinnego Marina** on the south shore. *Master McGra takes 12 passengers Apr to Oct Sat-Sun afternoons. Prior booking essential.* ☎ *028 3832 7573 or 077 7481 1248.*
The are also cruises from **Sixmilewater Marina** in Antrim. Occasionally there is also a **Bann cruise** between Antrim and Castlerock *(35mi – 6/7hr).*

SPORTS AND LEISURE

Watersports are available at the marinas at Antrim, Ballyronan and Kinnego and at the Craigavon Watersports Centre.
There is an **RSPB reserve** at Portmore Lough (southeast) and **nature reserves** at Reas Wood in Antrim, at Oxford Island, at Peatlands Park, at Washingbay Wetlands near Dungannon and at Randalstown Forest.
Fishing Permits are available from tackle shops and from the Fishery Conservancy Board in Portadown. ☎ *028 38334666 - www.fcbni.com*
Permits and **gillie services** for the Lower Bann are available from Bann System Ltd, Coleraine ☎ *028 70344796 - www.bannsystem.com*

Lough Neagh Discovery Centre

Lough Neagh

Peatlands Park

South shore; sign at Junction 13 on M 1. ♿🕐 *Open 9am-9pm (5pm Oct to Easter). Info centre and railway: open Jun to Aug noon-5pm; Sep to Easter Sat-Sun, Bank Hols noon-5pm.* ∞ *£1.* ☎ *028 3885 1102*

This old hunting park is the best place in the North to learn about Ireland's long relationship with peat: the **narrowgauge railway** installed by the Irish Peat Development Company provides a scenic tour of the site; **turf cutting** by hand and machine is demonstrated at the outdoor turbary station, while the **bog garden**, two small lakes, an orchard and woodland – in part designated a National Nature Reserve – provide nature lovers with a place to enjoy the unusual flora and fauna.

Maghery

Sited where the River Blackwater enters the lough, the village has a lakeside country park from which Coney Island, a densely wooded island, can be visited by boat.

Ballyronan

West shore. The little marina, lake shore and beach are a great draw.

Kinturk Cultural Centre

♿🕐 *Open 2-5pm, 7.30-11pm.* ∞*£1. Boat trips and guided tours.* 🍴 🅿 ☎ *028 8673 6512*

Detailed information *(video, echibition)* about the long-established local eel industry in and around Lough Neagh.

Ardboe Cross★

E of Cookstown by B 73.

The finest high cross of its kind in Ulster stands in an evocative spot at the entrance to a graveyard around the ruins of a 17C church. It is extensively carved with scenes

---

The Empire of the Eel

The waters of Lough Neagh and its tributaries teem with every kind of freshwater fish: rudd, roach and pike, pollan (freshwater herring) and the rare dollaghan (a kind of salmon-trout). There are giant pike in Lough Beg, bream in the Blackwater, trout and salmon in the Bann. But the lough is particularly famous for its eels which hatch far away in the Sargasso Sea, and swim across the Atlantic to the Bann to spend 12-14 years in the lough before heading back to their birthplace to die. Many, however, are caught and exported from the cooperative fishery at Toome to connoisseurs abroad, who relish them both smoked or unsmoked.

from the Old and New Testaments, probably in the 10C to mark the site of Ardboe Abbey, founded around the 6C and associated with St Colman.

From Ardboe Point there is an extensive **view**＊ of Lough Neagh: Slieve Gallion and the Sperrin Mountains *(northwest)*, Slemish *(northeast)*, Divis Mountain *(east)*, and the Mourne Mountains *(southeast)*.

Bellaghy
North shore; in Bellaghy, 4mi/7km N of A 6.

The 17C **bawn** (restored) was built by the Vintners' Company in 1619; its exhibition relate to local history, the Ulster Plantation and the poetry of Bellaghy-born Seamus Heaney. *(HM)* ◷ *Open Easter to Aug 10am-6pm; Sep to Easter Mon-Sat 9am-5pm, including Bank Hols.* ◷ *Closed Christmas to New Year.* ⊗ *£2.* ☎ *028 7938 6812*

Churchtown Point
The low promontory has a holy well and the ruins of Cranfield Church, which once attracted scores of pilgrims.

Seamus Heaney

The poet and Nobel Prize winner Seamus Heaney (b 1939) was born at his family's farm near Bellaghy. Much of his work, notably his Lough Neagh cycle, is marked by memories of the landscapes and people of his youth. His feelings for his homeland and respect for those who, like his father, were bound to it by hard physical work, are echoed in his writing:

"Between my finger and my thumb
The squat pen rests.
I'll dig with it."
Digging (1966)

NEWRY

POPULATION 21 633

Newry (An Tiúr) occupies a commanding position in the "Gap of the North" or Moyry Gap, between the line of hills that separates Ulster from the plains of Meath. A location that has brought destruction and prosperity to the place, as armies marched through on their way north or south. In the 18C Newry was linked by canals to Lough Neagh and to the sea at Carlingford Lough, becoming for a while the busiest port in the North. Those days are long gone but its road and railway links to both Belfast and Dublin enable shoppers to come from both sides of the border. 🛈 *Bank Parade* ☎ *028 30268877 - www.newryandmourne.gov.uk*

▶ **Orient Yourself:** Newry is situated on the main road (A 1/N 1) between Belfast and Dundalk, just north of the border

◔ **Also See:** ARMAGH, DUNDALK, MONAGHAN, MOURNE MOUNTAINS

A Bit of History

Newry's history began with the foundation in 1157 of a Cistercian abbey. Turbulent times have erased most of the old town, including the castle built by the Anglo-Norman John de Courcy, and all the strongholds that succeeded it. In the 16C, the abbey accommodated Sir Nicholas Bagenal, Marshal of Ireland, who built St Patrick's Church (1578) on the hill to the east of the town centre: the first Anglican church to be built in Ireland, bearing its founder's coat of arms in the porch.

In 1731 work began here on the first inland canal in the British Isles, linking Newry via fourteen locks to Lough Neagh. Thirty years later, a ship canal was dug to provide the town with an outlet to Carlingford Lough and the Irish Sea. The town prospered from the trade in linen, coal, building stone and emigrants, as the Georgian town houses and multi-storey quayside mills testify. In 1956, the inland canal was closed and the ship canal became redundant when modern port facilities were provided downstream at Warrenpoint. Today it provides for recreational use.

Visit

Newry Cathedral
Newry has been the seat of the Roman Catholic diocese of Dromore since about 1750. Its cathedral, designed by Thomas Duff in 1825 and dedicated to St Patrick and St Colman, was the first Roman Catholic cathedral to be built in Ireland following the Act of Emancipation. Inside, it is vivid with stained glass and colourful mosaics.

Newry and Mourne Museum
   Open Mon-Fri 10.30am-1pm, 2-4.30pm. ☎ *028 30266232*
The modern Arts Centre beside the Town Hall straddles the river and thus has one foot in Co Armagh and one in Co Down. The museum deals competently with the archeology and history of the area. It has a lovely early 18C panelled room recalling prosperous times, and Nelson's cabin table from HMS Victory.

Excursion

Cullyhanna
15mi/24km W of Newry by B30 and N by A29 and a minor road (left).
The **Cardinal O'Fiaich Centre** is devoted to the life of Tomás O'Fiaich (d 1990), a local boy who became Cardinal-Primate of all Ireland. It charts his career as student, priest, professor, scholar with recorded interviews, video and personal memorabilia.
   Open Mon-Fri 1-5pm; Bank Hols 10am-6pm or by appointment. ⊛ *£2.50.* ☎ *028 30868757*

Driving Tour

Slieve Gullion★ *Round tour of 27mi/43.5km – 1 day*

This "enchanted mountain" (B Kiely), together with its attendant circle of lesser heights known as the Ring of Gullion, designated an Area of Outstanding Natural Beauty in 1991, dominates the countryside to the west of Newry. It is intimately associated with the legendary Cuchulain, hero of the epic *The Cattle Raid of Cooley (Táin bo Cuainlge)* and is rich in prehistoric remains.

▷ *From Newry take A 25 W; after 1.5mi/2.4km turn right onto B 133 to Bessbrook.*

Bessbrook
This early and fascinating example of a planned industrial village has terraces of granite-built, slate-roofed cottages neatly ranged round three sides of two grassy squares. The settlement, complete with churches, schools, shops and a community hall but no pub, was built in 1845 by the Quaker linen manufacturer John Grubb Richardson for his flax workers. Bessbrook later inspired the Cadbury family to build the far larger model settlement of Bournville near Birmingham.

▷ *From Bessbrook take B 112; turn right onto A 25. W of Camlough village turn left onto B 30.*

Cam Lough
From the road there is a fine view of the narrow lake in its deep trough between Camlough Mountain (1 417ft/423m) and Slieve Gullion.

▶ *At the crossroads turn left onto a narrow road along the west side of Cam Lough.*

Killevy

An ancient graveyard, overhung with beech trees, surrounds the ruins of two **churches**, standing end to end. The eastern building is medieval; the western one is earlier (12C) although the west wall, which is pierced by a doorway below a massive lintel, may be 10C or 11C. A granite slab in the northern half of the graveyard is said to mark the grave of St Monenna (also known as Darerca and Bline) who founded an important early nunnery here in the 5C. This later became an Augustinian convent until it was suppressed in 1542. A path north of the graveyard leads to a holy well.

▶ *Continue S for 1.5mi/2.4km; turn right onto B 113.*

Slieve Gullion Forest Park★

🅿 *8mi/13km Scenic Drive: steep gradients and difficult bends.*

The pines, larches and spruce of the Forest Park clad the lower slopes of the south-west face of Slieve Gullion. The visitor centre housed in old farm buildings provides inforamtion about the park and displays old hand tools.

After climbing through the forest, the Scenic Drive emerges on the open slopes of Slieve Gullion; on the left is an extensive view over the treetops; on the right is the path, waymarked in white, to the top of the south peak of Slieve Gullion (1 894ft/573m) marked by a cairn; another cairn crowns the lower north peak. The Drive swings left downhill and doubles back along the southwest slope, through the trees and rocks, to a **viewpoint**★ overlooking a section of the **Ring of Gullion**.

▶ *At the exit turn right onto B 113 and immediately turn left. After 1.5mi/2.4km turn right; after 1mi/1.6km park at the T-junction.*

Kilnasaggart Stone

Most of Ireland's cross-decorated pillar-stones are in the west of the country but this granite example (7ft/2.15m high) in its hedged enclosure *(across two fields)* is the earliest dateable one of its kind, its crosses carved around AD 700. The pillar itself, which marks the site of an Early Christian cemetery, may in fact be much older, a prehistoric standing stone converted to a new use. It also bears an inscription in Irish stating that the site was dedicated under the patronage of Peter the Apostle by the son of Ceran Bic, Ternohc, who died c 715.

▶ *Return to B 113; turn right towards Newry; after 5mi/8km turn left to Ballymacdermot Cairn (sign).*

Ballymacdermot Cairn

Beside the road *(right)* on the south slope of Ballymacdermot Mountain are the remains of a Neolithic court grave: two burial chambers with an antecham-ber and a circular forecourt enclosed in a trapezoidal cairn. Fine **views** extend southwest across the Meigh plain to Slieve Gullion and the Ring of Gullion.

▶ *Continue for 1mi/1.6km.*

Kilnasaggart Stone

P Thebault/MICHELIN

Bernish Rock Viewpoint★★
The view sweeps over Newry to the Mourne Mountains on the eastern horizon.

▶ *Return downhill to Newry.*

PORTRUSH

POPULATION 5 703

Easily accessible by road and rail from Belfast, Portrush has been one of the North's most popular seaside resorts since early Victorian times, the natural qualities of its sandy beaches and the nearby coastline are now supplemented by a host of man-made attractions. The town is laid out on a little peninsula which ends in Ramore Head, a notable haunt of bird watchers. *Dunluce Centre, Sandhill Drive ☎ 028 70823333 (Apr-Sep)* *Railway Rd, Coleraine ☎ 028 70344723*

▶ **Orient Yourself:** Portrush is situated north of Coleraine, between Portstewart and Ballycastle, on the coast road, A 2
Don't Miss: Dunluce Castle, Gortmore Viewpoint and Magilligan Strand
Especially for Kids: a day at the beach and one at Leslie Hill Open Farm
Also See: GIANT'S CAUSEWAY, LONDONDERRY, LOUGH NEAGH, SPERRIN MOUNTAINS

Visit

The **Dunluce Centre,** housed in the same prominent pavilion as the Tourist Information Centre, contains lavish revisions of traditional end-of-the-pier entertainments for all ages. *Open Easter week, Jul to Aug 10.30am-6.30pm; Jun noon-5pm (6.30pm Sat-Sun); Sep to May, Sat-Sun noon-5pm (6.30pm Apr-May). Combined ticket ☎ £8.50; individual facilities. ☎ £3.50-4.50. ☎ 028 70824444 - www.dunlucecentre.co.uk*
The **Countryside Centre**, located in an old Victorian bath-house, provides an introduction to the ecology and marine life of the locality; visitors can observe the denizens of the seabed from within the "wreck" of the Nautilus. *Open Jul to Sep 10am-5pm. ☎ 028 70823600 - www.ehsni.gov.uk*

Driving Tours

East of Portrush *7.5mi/12km*

▶ *From Portrush take A 2 E.*

Controversy and Conservation

West of Portrush the coast is interrupted by the Bann estuary; beyond is a long sand dune extending into Lough Foyle. East of the town, more sand dunes give way to strangely weathered and cave-riddled limestone cliffs, and the extraordinary volcanic rock formations of the Giant's Causeway. This geologically important sectio of the north Antrim Coast has been designated as a National Nature Reserve. Deatiled analysis of the rocks at Portrush provided the key to a long-standing controversy about the origin of such features as the Giant's Causeway.

Ph.Hurlin/MICHELIN

Dunluce Castle

Dunluce Castle★★

(HM)🕐 *Open Apr-Sep Mon-Sat 10am-6pm, Sun noon (2pm Apr-Jun, Sep)-6pm; Oct-Mar, Tue-Sun 10am (2pm Sun) to 4pm. 🖾 £1.50. ☎ 028 20731938; www.northantrim.com*
There can be few more romantic sights than the jagged outline of ruined Dunluce Castle, perched on its isolated rock stack 100ft/30m above the sea. For years it was the seat of the Irish branch of the Scottish MacDonnell clan, known as "Lords of the Isles"; the most notable leader was Sorley Boy MacDonnell, a constant iritant to both the native Irish and the English. Despite the use of artillery, the latter failed to expel him permanently from Dunluce, and his descendants were eventually made Earls of Antrim. In the 17C they modernised the castle to provide more comfortable accommodation but when the kitchen collapsed into the sea, they abandoned it.
Beyond the drawbridge and the late-16C gatehouse with its Scottish-style turrets and crow-step gables, stand the two 14C towers and south wall. The upper yard is dominated by the 17C **great hall**, built in grandiose style with bay windows on the west front. The cobbled **lower yard** is surrounded by service buildings including the bakery. From here there is a superb **view** of the Causeway Coast.

▷ *Continue E on A 2.*

Bushmills

The most prominent feature in the village is the distinctive caps of the **Bushmills Distillery** kilns. The original licence to distil was granted to Sir Thomas Phillips in 1608, although references to a local distillery date back to 1276. Water drawn from St Columb's Rill, a tributary of the River Bush which rises in peaty ground, is used to produce two blended whiskeys and one malt. The tour includes the main stages in the production of whiskey: mashing, fermentation, distillation, maturing in oak casks, blending and bottling. Tasting takes place in the Potstill Bar; a small museum has been created in the old malt kilns. 🖾 *Apr to Oct 9.30am (noon Sun) -5.30pm (last tour at 4pm); Nov to Mar Mon-Fri 10.30am, 11.30am, 2.30pm,3.30pm, Sun 1.30pm, 2.30pm, 3.30pm.* 🕐 *Closed Good Fri, 12 Jul, Christmas and New Year. No children under 7. 🖾 £5.* 🅿☎ *028 20733218 - www.bushmills.com*

Inland from Portrush *15mi/24km*

From Portrush take A 29 inland to Coleraine.

Coleraine

At the head of the Bann estuary, Coleraine is Co Londonderry's second largest town, now an important shopping and commercial centre for the area, and home to the province's second university (1968). The main attractions are the river and its estuary, the quayside, occasional regattas, a large-scale marina, and a bird sanctuary.

▶ *From Coleraine take B 67 E via Ballybogy for 5.5mi/9km.*

Benvarden★

🕐 *Open Jun to Aug, Bank Hols noon - 5.30pm.* ⬤ *£3.50.* ☎ *028 20741331 - www. benvarden.com*

Benvarden House, home of the Montgomery family since 1798, opens its garden and grounds to the public every summer. One of Ireland's most attractive walled gardens (2 acres/0.8ha), parts of which may date back to the original fortified enclosure, features rose beds, a formal hedged garden, a vinery and a pergola walk. Beyond are the neatly laid out kitchen gardens, with Victorian hothouses and the old gardener's bothy. A wild garden and azalea walk lead down to the River Bush, which is spanned by a Victorian stone and cast-iron bridge, rare of its type in Ireland.

▶ *Return to Ballybogy. Turn left onto B 62 towards Ballymoney; from the by-pass roundabout follow the sign.*

Leslie Hill Open Farm

Kids 🕐 *Open Jul-Aug 11am (2pm Sun)-6pm; Jun Sat-Sun 2-6pm; Easter to May Sun, Bank Hols 2-6pm.* ⬤ *£3.50.* ☎ *028 27666803 - www.lesliehillopenfarm.co.uk*

This mixed-farming estate has been in the ownership of the same family since the mid-18C, so its buildings and implements provide a vivid picture of farming evolution. Horse-drawn vehicles, rarebreeds, red deer provide a good day out for children. A track, hidden from view from the imposing Georgian house by a ha-ha, leads to the walled garden with its pit-house, hot wall, and the remains of the heating arrangements for growing peaches.

West of Portrush *20mi/32km*

▶ *From Portrush take A 2 W.*

Portstewart

Less exuberant than its larger neighbour, Portstewart was a fashionable watering-place in the 19C and has kept something of its Victorian atmosphere. It has a picturesque harbour and the very prominent O'Hara's Castle, a Gothic-style mansion (1834) transformned into a Dominican college. From the promenade, paths lead west along the cliffs to Portstewart Strand *(2mi/3.2km)*. Regular exhibitions are held at the Flowerfield Arts Centre.

▶ *Continue W on A 2 via Coleraine; 1mi/1.6km beyond Articlave at the Liffock crossroads turn left into the car park.*

Hezlett House

Castlerock, on the NW corner of the crossroads. (NT) Tour (40min): Jul to Aug Wed-Sun, Bank Hols noon-5pm. £2.80. 028 70848728 - www.nationaltrust.org.uk
Hezlett House, built in 1691 probably as a clergyman's residence, is a long, single-storey thatched cottage with battered, rough-cast walls, an attic and cruck truss roof. It was taken over by the Hezlett family in 1761.
Visitors are led through the tiny kitchen, pantry, dining room, bed-sized bedrooms and parlour and up into the attic, where the servants slept. Furnishings date from the 19C and include balloon chairs (with holes for women's bustles) and prayer chairs, allowing women to kneel in hoop skirts while retaining their dignity. A small museum in the outbuildings shows Victorian farming implements.

▶ *Continue W on A 2.*

Downhill Estate★

(NT) Grounds: open dawn-dusk. Mussenden Temple: open Sep Sat-Sun 11am-5pm. £3.80 car. 028 70848728 - www.nationaltrust.org.uk
The Earl Bishop's building activities still mark this stretch of the Co Londonderry coast, though his castle, rebuilt after the fire of 1851, is now a roofless shell. From the

Earl Bishop

Known as the Earl Bishop, Frederick Augustus Hervey, Bishop of Derry (1730-1803), was also an unusually enlightened prelate, an advocate of church reform and a supporter of emancipation for Dissenters. He became the 4th Earl of Bristol on the death of his brother. Bad health dictated long spells on the Continent, where many a Hotel Bristol is named after him. A flamboyant character, fabulously rich, he was arrested by Napoleon's police as a spy, and enjoyed a particularly scandalous affair with the mistress of the King of Prussia: he was described as "a bad father, a worse husband, very blasphemous in his conversation, and greatly addicted to intrigue and gallentry".

A passionate builder, traveller and collector of art and antiquities, he is responsible for Ickworth Place in Suffolk and a palatial residence at Ballyscullion on Lough Beg (never completed; its portico now fronts St George's Church in Belfast). **Downhill Castle** was designed in 1772 by his favourite architect, Michael Shanahan, to house his huge art collection: largely destroyed by fire in 1851.

Mussenden Temple

imposing **Bishop's Gate** a charming glen planted with flowers and shrubs, a path leads up to the cliff top from where there is a splendid **view** of the coast.

Little of the castle remains, but the **Mussenden Temple**★ erected as a memorial to his cousin, Mrs Mussenden, clearly suggest the Earl Bishop's taste. This elegant Classical rotunda perched precariously on the very edge of the high cliffs, is modelled on the Temple of Vesta at Tivoli. Built of local basalt and faced with sandstone from Ballycastle in 1785, the building was used as a library by the Bishop, who allowed the local Roman Catholic priest to say Mass in the basement.

▶ *Continue W on A 2.*

Beyond the Lion Gate, the sea and the strand become visible: where once the Bishop held horse races, the present generation indulges in surfing. The Bishop's Road across the Binevenagh Mountain was built as a short cut home from Limavady.

▶ *Bear left into the Bishop's Road.*

Gortmore Viewpoint★★

High up on the northeast slope of Binenvenagh Mountain, there is a superb **view** of Magilligan Strand across the mouth of Lough Foyle towards the Inishowen Peninsula; in the 19C it was used as the base line for the Ordnance Survey of Ireland.

▶ *Return downhill; turn left onto A 2.*

Magilligan Strand★★

The long stretch of golden sand dunes (6mi/10km) is equipped with sports facilities at Benone. Much of the land is reserved for military purposes. The Point, where a Martello Tower (1812) was built during the Napoleonic Wars to guard the narrow approach to Lough Foyle, is now a Nature Reserve.

SPERRIN MOUNTAINS★

These lonely smooth-topped mountains dividing the Londonderry lowlands from northeastern Ulster rise to their highest point in Sawel Mountain (2 224ft/678m). Composed of schist and gneiss, they were once covered in magnificent forests but their upper slopes are now grazed by sheep and clad in blanket bog and purple heather, and woodland is confined to the deep gorges worn by mountain streams. Over the moorland hover birds of prey; the rare hen harrier is sometimes seen, and the Sperrins are the only site in Ireland where cloudberry grows. The rocks contain minute deposits of gold, the extraction of which gives rise to periodic controversy about the future of these mountains which have largely remained outside the mainstream of modern life. ⓘ *Burn Rd, Cookstown* ☎ *028 86766727* ⓘ *7 Connell St, Limavady* ☎ *028 77760307* ⓘ *1 Market St, Omagh* ☎ *028 82247831* ⓘ *Abercorn Sq, Strabane (Apr-Oct).* ☎ *028 71883735 - www.sperrinstourism.com*

▶ **Orient Yourself:** The Sperrin Mountains are bounded to the west by A 5 between Londonderry and Armagh and bisected by A 29 between Armagh and Coleraine, and by A 6 between Londonderry and Belfast

◉ **Don't Miss:** Ulster American Folk Park celebrating Irish and American history

◔ **Also See:** DUNGANNON, LONDONDERRY, LOUGH NEAGH

A Bit of History

In the 17C certain areas were granted to the London city livery companies – Drapers, Skinners, Grocers and Fishmongers – who brought in new settlers mainly from Scotland, to inhabit their new towns and villages. Initially the land was let through local landlords on the rundale system; by the early 19C the region was overpopulated so assisted emigration was introduced; the land was re-allocated in holdings of 20–30 acres/8–12ha of neatly-hedged fields; model farms were established to promote modern methods; roads and bridges, churches, schools and dispensaries were built.

Driving Tours

Uplands and Coast [1]

▶ *From Londonderry take A 2 eastwards; turn right.*

Eglinton
This elegant little village (1823-25) with its **Courthouse** was developed by the Grocers' Company around a tree-shaded green beside the Muff River which tumbles down through **Muff Glen**, a narrow tree-lined valley of pleasant walks.

Ballykelly
This community was established early in the 17C by the Fishmongers' Company. The model farm on the north side of the road consists of a two-storey block linked to two one-storey pavilions by curtain walls enclosing a farmyard. Opposite is the Presbyterian Church (1827). The Anglican Church (1795) was one of several built by the Earl Bishop of Derry.

Limavady
The town takes its name from the Irish for Dogleap since the original settlement was farther upstream (2mi/3.2km) by the 13C O'Cahan castle in what is now the Roe Valley Country Park. It was re-founded as Newtown-Limavady in the 17C by Sir Thomas Phillips, Chief Agent of the City of London in Ulster. It is now a pleasant Georgian

market town where the famous song, *Danny Boy* or *The Londonderry Air*, was noted down by Jane Ross (1810–79) who lived at 51 Main Street *(plaque)*.

▶ *Take B 68 south.*

Roe Valley Country Park★

(HM) ⊙ *Park: open daily. Visitor Centre: open Easter to Sep 9am-6pm; Sep to Easter Mon-Fri 9am-5pm.* ☎ *028 7722074 - www.ehsni.gov.uk*

The country park extends along a stretch *(3mi/4.8km)* of the wild thickly wooded valley, where the peaty red River Roe runs over rocks and through gorges on its way north to the sea. The **Visitor Centre** at the Dogleap Bridge provides information on the local flora and fauna, old industries and on the 17C Plantation. As well as great natural beauty and scenes of the O'Cahans' legendary exploits, the park preserves evidence of early industrial activity: bleach greens, weirs and mill races, and 18C water-powered mills for sawing wood, scutching flax, weaving and beetling linen. An unusual feature is the stone-built **Power House** (1896), the site of early success in generating hydroelectric power.

▶ *Take B 192 south to Burnfoot.*

Bovevagh Church

In the churchyard of a ruined medieval church stands a **mortuary house** similar to the one at Banagher *(see above)*; its ruined state reveals the cavity, which contained the body, and the hand hole in the east end through which the faithful could touch the relics.

▶ *Continue south; turn left onto A 6 and make a detour east.*

Address Book

🕯 *For coin ranges, see the Legend on the cover flap.*

WHERE TO STAY

⊜ **Ballyhenry House** – *172 Seacoast Rd, Limavady - 0.75mi N by B 48 - 3 rm - ☎ 028 77722657 - michaeljkane@hotmail.co.uk* 🅿 Attractive farmhouse B&B in Roe Valley. Ideal for outdoor activities (fishing, riding, golf, walking around farm estate.

⊜⊜**B&B Tullylagan Country House** – *40B Tullylagan Rd, Sandholes, Cookstown - 4mi S by A 29 -15 rm ☎ 028 8676 5100 - www.tullylagan.co.uk.* ✗🅿⚲ Peaceful country house on the Tullylagan River. The interior has a Georgian feel and the bedrooms all have an individual personality; evening meals ⊜⊜.

WHERE TO EAT

⊜⊜**Lime Tree** – *60 Catherine St, Limavady - ☎ 028 7776 4300 - info@limetreerest.com -* ⊙ *Open for dinner, Tue-Sat 6pm-9pm; early bird option Tue-Fri 6-7pm .* ⊙ *Closed 1 week Feb, 1 week July, 1 week Nov, 25-26 Dec.* Seasonal produce, modern Irish cuisine; good wine list. Booking recommended.

SPORTS AND LEISURE

The **Ulster Way**, a long-distance footpath, passes through the eastern slopes.

The Owenkillew and the Glenelly are both good trout streams. The many good angling streams flow north and west down the River Roe and the Foyle tributaries into the Foyle estuary or southeast into Lough Neagh.

TRACING ANCESTORS

Ulster-American Folk Park – *Centre for Migration Studies: Mon-Fri 10.30am-4.45pm*

Glenshane Pass★

The pass between Mullaghmore (1 818ft/555m – south) and Carntogher (1 516ft/462m – north) carries the main Belfast-Londonderry road through the Sperrin Mountains. The northern approach through dramatic mountain scenery overlooks Benady Glen on the River Roe; the southern approach provides a **panoramic view**★★ across Lough Neagh in the mid-Ulster plain to Slemish.

▶ *Continue east on A 6. At the north end of the main street turn right into Bank Sq.*

Maghera

This little town at the foot of the Glenshane Pass has a picturesque ruin – **St Patrck Church** (c 10C) boasts an outstanding west door added c 12C, with inclined jambs, wonderful floral and animal decoration and a lintel carved with an elaborate Crucifixion scene. In the graveyard stands a rough pillar stone, carved with a ringed cross, which, according to tradition, is the grave of St Lurach, who founded an important monastery on this site in the 6C. *Key with Megherafelt TIC.* ☎ *028 79631510*

▶ *Return west on A 6.*

Dungiven

Before it was redeveloped by the Skinners' Company, Dungiven was the base of the fierce O'Cahan clan. Just outside the town is an imposing natural strongpoint above the River Roe, the site of a pre-Norman monastery and ruined Augustinian **priory**. The church remains are impressive, but the main attraction is the magnificent O'Cahan **tomb** of the chieftan Cooey-na-Gal, who died in 1385; it consist of an effigy beneath a traceried canopy, protected by heavily armed Scottish mercenaries in kilts, known as "gallowglasses". Similar tombs dating from the 15C survive in western Scotland. In the 17C Sir Edward Doddington, who constructed the walls of Londonderry, built himself a house in the cloister.*(HM)* *Check with Megherafelt TIC.* ☎ *028 79631510.* North of the path is a **bullaun**, a hollowed stone originally used for grinding grain – it now collects rainwater which is deemed to cure warts, hence the rags tied to the overhanging tree.

▶ *In Dungiven turn left into a minor road.*

Banagher Church

In the graveyard of the ruined church(c 1100) stands a 12C **mortuary house,** built of dressed stone probably to house relics disturbed by the addition of a chancel to the church. The panel on the west gable depicts a figure with a hand raised in blessing and bearing a crozier. According to tradition it is the tomb of St Muiredach O'Heney and sand from his tomb brings good luck.

▶ *Return to A 6 or take B 74 west through Feeny and Claudy to rejoin A 6.*

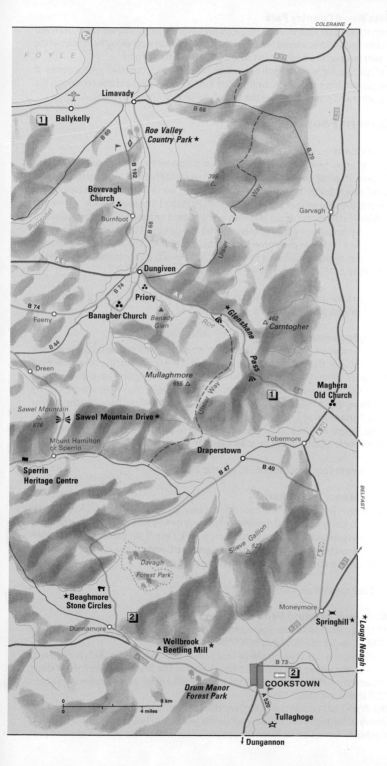

Ness Wood Country Park

From the car park walk through the picnic area into the wood. The waterfall (30ft/9m) is unfenced; children should be accompanied. Woodland walk along both sides of the stream meeting at a bridge about 600yd/548m from the car park.

The spectacular waterfall (*an eas* in Irish) was created, together with a series of gorges, potholes and rapids, by the River Burntollet eroding a channel through the metamorphic schist rock since the end of the last Ice Age.

Eastern Foothills 2

Cookstown

Once an important linen centre, Cookstown is now an important market centre for the area. Its most notable feature is the extraordinarily long and very broad main street which, under 10 different names, extends north from the River Ballinderry towards the silhouette of Slieve Gallion (1 732ft/528m). The result of one of the most ambitious attempts at urban planning ever imposed on the Irish landscape, devised c 1750 by James and William Stewart, after the original Plantation settlement of Cookstown had been destroyed in the rebellion of 1641. The new street extended south to their own property at Killymoon Castle *(private)* which was redesigned by John Nash in 1803; its grounds are now a golf course.

▷ *From Cookstown take A 29 south; bear left into B 520. Turn left on a blind corner into the car park; 10min there and back on foot.*

Tullaghoge Fort

The tree-crowned earthworks of this hillfort are replete with memories of the ancient rulers of Ulster, having enclosed the residence of the O'Hagans: the chief justices of the old kingdom of Tyrone. It was here that the rulers of Tyrone were inaugurated, the last of them being Hugh O'Neill in 1593. Their stone throne was broken up by Lord Mountjoy in 1602. The **view** from the fort is extensive: southwest to the circular walled graveyard at Donaghrisk where the O'Hagans were buried; east towards Lough Neagh; north to Slieve Gallion with the River Ballinderry in the foreground and Killymoon Castle in the trees by the river.

▷ *Return to Cookstown; take A 505 west for 2.5mi/4km.*

Drum Manor Forest Park

&♿⏰ *Open 10am-dusk.* ⊛ *£1 pedestrian, £3 car.* ♨ *(Jul-Aug)* 🅿

The old country house of Drum Manor has long been a ruin, but its walled gardens and open parkland now form part of Forest Park. One of the gardens has lent itself perfectly to conversion into a **butterfly garden**t, while in the ruins of the manor house an attractive **flower garden** has been created.

▷ *Continue west on A 505; turn right (sign).*

Wellbrook Beetling Mill★

(NT) 🐾 *Tour: Jul to Aug 1pm-6pm; Apr to Jun, Sep Sat-Sun, Bank Hols 1-6pm.* ⊛ *£3.10.* 🅿☎ *028 86748210/028 86741735*

Beetling is the last stage in the production of linen where the cloth is beaten to close up the weave and give it a smooth sheen. The first mill at Wellbrook came into operation in September 1767; the present mill, known as no 6, dates from about 1830 and worked until 1961.

The drying loft contains an excellent display on the production of linen and the history of the Irish linen industry, while the lower floor houses the seven **beetling machines** turned by an external wooden water-wheel. The amount of noise pro-

Beaghmore Stone Circles

duced by two beetling engines operating for a few minutes explains why deafness was common among beetlers, who worked from early morning to nine at night.

▶ *Continue west on A 505; at Dunnamore Bridge turn right across the river.*

Beaghmore Stone Circles★

Mid-Ulster is particularly rich in prehistoric stone circles. This site, used in Neolithic times, has seven from the Bronze Age, comprising quite small stones set on, rather than in, the ground. Six circles are arranged in pairs, with a cairn and a row of stones near the point of intersection. The area enclosed in the seventh circle is studded with close-set stones known as "Dragons' Teeth" – used to calculate the rising and setting of the sun and moon.

▶ *Continue north; turn right into minor road which joins B 47.*

Draperstown

This pleasant little town is a busy market centre in the heart of Sperrin Mountain country. A classic settlement from the time of the Ulster Plantation in the early 17C.

▶ *From Draperstown take B 40 east; turn right onto A 29 to Moneymore.*

Springhill★

(NT) ⚬ ⚬ *Tour: Jul to Aug 1pm-6pm; Apr-Jun-Sep, Sat-Sun, Bank Hol Mon 1-6pm. Last admission 1hr before closing.* ⊗ £4.30. ⊟ P ☎ *028 86748210*

This attractive country house was the family home of the Conynghams, who came to Ulster from Ayrshire early in the 17C. Built around a deep courtyard flanked by service buildings, it is a rare survivor of the kind of comfortable residence built by Plantation families at this time, despite the difficult and sometimes dangerous conditions. The property was altered and enlarged by subsequent generations of Conynghams, who usually followed military careers.

Family portraits hang throughout the house, which is furnished with **fine 18C and 19C furniture**. Note the splendid oak **staircase** with a yew handrail. The older rooms contrast with the more spacious interiors added later like the early 19C dining room graced by an Italian marble chimney-piece presented by the notorious Earl Bishop of Londonderry. The gun room collection includes flintlocks used during the Siege of Derry and a pair of pikes from the Battle of Vinegar Hill.

The courtyard buildings now house a **costume collection** of some 2300 articles from the 18C-20C, displayed in rotation.

▶ *From Moneymore take A 29 south to return to Cookstown.*

Central Heights ③

▶ *From Omagh take B 48 north*

Gortin Glen Forest Park
🕐 *Open 10am-dusk.* 🚶£1 pedestrian; £3 car 🅿 ☎ *028 81648217*
The coniferous woodland park is part of the larger Gortin Forest, a commercial plantation. The forest drive *(5mi/8km – one direction only)* offers great vistas over the Sperrin Mountains. Information on trails and where to see Sika deer is supplied in the Nature Centre.

▶ *From B 48 turn right.*

The **Oak Lough Scenic Road** ★ loops round a cluster of lakes, the delight of canoeists, and provides a fine **view** of Gortin on the Owenkillew River.

▶ *Turn left onto B 46. In Gortin turn right onto B 48; after crossing the river turn right onto a minor road; in Scotch Town turn left.*

The **Barnes Gap** carries the road through a narrow cleft in the hills between the valleys of the Owenkillew and Glenelly Rivers.

▶ *At the T-junction turn right; at the next T-junction turn left; cross the river at Clogherny Bridge; turn right; turn right onto B 47.*

Sperrin Heritage Centre
🕐 *Open Apr to Oct 11.30am (2pm Sun) to 5.30pm (6pm Sat-Sun). Last admission 45min before closing.* 🚶 *£2.60.* ☎ *028 81648142 - www.strabanedc.com*
The Centre, on the B47 linking Strabane with Draperstown, is sensitively designed to fit with three adjoining cottages. Videos, computers and exhibitions enable visitors to explore the local flora and fauna, history and culture.

▶ *Continue east on B 47; in Sperrin / Mount Hamilton turn left.*

The **Sawel Mountain Drive** ★, a narrow unfenced road along the east face of Sawel Mountain (2 229ft/678m), the highest peak, passes through the wild and austere beauty of the open moorland; the **views** ★★ are spectacular.

▶ *Continue east on B 47; in Sperrin / Mount Hamilton turn left. Beyond Dreen turn left onto B 44 ; turn left onto B 48 to return to Omagh via Plumbridge.*

Western Valleys ④

Omagh
The former county town of Co Tyrone is normally a quiet market town, built on a steep slope overlooking the point where two rivers, the Camowen and the Drumragh, join to form the Strule. Sadly, the place won international notoriety in 1998 as the site of the greatest single atrocity of Northern Ireland's Troubles, when an intransigent republican grouping exploded a bomb in the town centre, killing 29 people.

▶ *From Omagh take A 5 north.*

Ulster-American Folk Park★★
♿🕐 *Open Mon-Sat, 10.30am-6pm (last admission at 4.30pm), Sun and Bank hols, 11am-6.30pm (last admission at 5pm); Oct to Easter, Mon-Sat, 10.30am-5pm (last admission at 3.30pm).* 🚶 *£4.50.* 🍴✕ 🅿☎ *028 82243292 - www.folkpark.com*

Of all the establishments in Ireland celebrating the country's intimate links with America, this extensive open-air museum is perhaps the most evocative. Opened in 1976 as part of the American bicentennial celebrations, it is laid out around the ancestral cottage from which **Thomas Mellon**, of the banking dynasty, emigrated with his family at the age of five in 1818. There is also a Centre for Migration Studies, with a library, extensive database, and facilities for research.

Conestoga Wagon, Ulster American Folk Park

The Matthew T Mellon Information Centre and the **Emigrants' Exhibition** give the historical context for mass emigration, citing life stories of particular individuals who settled in the New World. Various other buildings, some replicas, others transferred from elsewhere in Ulster or America, are laid out in chronological order starting with the typical 18C and 19C **Ulster buildings** like a humble cabin from the Sperrins, a complete "Ulster Street" lined with shops, workplaces, and Reilly's pub-cum-grocery. The cottage in which Thomas Mellon was born in 1813 was built by his father with his own hands; it was transported here in 1976 to form the nucleus of the park. The **Ship and Dockside Gallery** marks the transition to America, and features the brig Union moored at the Belfast quayside. The **American Street** with its all-important General Store has a replica of the 1870 First Mellon Bank of Pittsburgh, shielding a series of log cabins and a complete mid-18C stone dwelling, brought from frontier territory in Pennsylvania, where it was built by an emigrant from Co Donegal.

In the workshops and cottages local people in **period costume** demonstrate the old crafts: cooking, spinning, weaving, the making of baskets, candles and soap; blacksmithing and carpentry; turf fires burn throughout the year.

Newtonstewart

The village is set near the confluence of the River Mourne and the River Strule. On a nearby hilltop stands **Harry Avery's Castle**, two D-shaped towers from a 14C O'Neill stronghold. There are fine views of the surrounding countryside.

Sion Mills

This model village was established by the three Herdman brothers, who in 1835 started a flax-spinning operation in an old flour mill on the Mourne. The buildings are an appealing mixture of Gothic Revival terraced cottages in polychrome brick, and black and white half-timbered edifices, of which the most striking is Sion House, and the Church of the Good Shepherd, a splendid Italianate Romanesque building (1909). By contrast, the Roman Catholic church, St Teresa's, is an uncompromisingly modern structure (1963) with a striking slate mural of the Last Supper.

Strabane

This small town stands at the confluence of the Finn and the Mourne as they join the Foyle, which defines the borders of Co Londonderry and Co Donegal.

In the 18C Strabane was famous for printing: this is celebrated behind the bowed Georgian shopfront of **Gray's Printery** *(49 Main Street)*, where a 19C printing shop has been preserved with its 19C hand- and foot-operated presses. *(NT)* 🚻☕ Tour: *Apr to May, Sep Sat 2-5pm; Jun Tues-Sat 2-5pm; Jul to Aug 11am-5pm.* 💷 £2.80. ☎ 028 71880055/028 86748210 - www.nationaltrust.org.uk

Two local apprentices made their mark in the USA: John Dunlap (1747–1812), working for Gray's Printery, printed the American Declaration of Independence in his newspaper the *Pennsylvania Packet*; James WIlson became editor of a Philadelphia newspaper after leaving for America in 1807.

The **Wilson Ancestral Home** is a whitewashed thatched cottage on the south side of town, where James Wilson is honoured less than his grandson, **President Woodrow Wilson**. The house contains some of the original furniture, including a cupboard bed by the kitchen fire and curtained beds in the main bedroom. Wilsons still live in the modern farmhouse behind the cottage. *Tour:Jul to Aug Tue-Sun 2-5pm or by appointment.* ☎ *028 71382204 - www.strabanedc.com*

▶ *Continue on this road; in Plumbridge turn right onto B 48 to return to Omagh.*

STRANGFORD LOUGH★

This inland sea, 18m/29km long with its 80mi/142km coastline, has a tranquillity and unspectacular beauty which is disturbed only when the tides rip through the narrow channel linking it to the Irish Sea. Strangford Lough was formed when the sea level rose at the end of the Ice Age, drowning the drumlins which are the most characteristic features of its landscape or converting them into countless whale-backed islands. The lough lends itself to sailing and boating, supports an exceptional wealth of bird-life, while its shores and islands are rich in historical remains. *31 Regents St, Newtownards* ☎ *028 91826846* *The Stables, Portaferry* ☎ *028 42729882 (Easter to Sep)*

▶ **Orient Yourself:** Strangford Lough lies SE of Belfast and is ringed by the A 20, A 21, A 22 and A 25

▶ **Don't Miss:** an excursion to Castle Ward

▶ **Especially for Kids:** Exploris

▶ **Also See:** BANGOR, DOWNPATRICK, LISBURN, MOUNT STEWART

A Bit of History

The old Irish name for the lough was Lough Cuan but the name bestowed by the Vikings – "violent fjord" – prevails, acknowldeging the regular spectacle of 350 million tonnes of sea water racing through the strait between Portaferry and Strangford village as the tide changes. Conditions in the lough itself vary between the exposed eastern shore on the Ards Peninsula and the sheltered western shore.

The whole of the Lough is a **Marine Nature Reserve**, the first in Northern Ireland managed by public bodies like the National Trust and the Royal Society for the Protection of Birds.

Driving Tour

Newtownards

An ancient priory predates the modern dormitory town annexed to Belfast which was refounded in Plantation times. Today, the spacious market square, a handsome Georgian town hall in Scrabo stone and a distinctive market cross (1635) survive from the 17C, as do the unremarkable priory ruins and the burial vault of the Londonderry family.

There is a fine collection of of 13C **cross slabs**★ inscribed with foliage crosses at **Movilla Abbey**, however, once one of the most important abbeys in Ulster *(2mi/3.2km NE by A48, B172 and Old Movilla Road (right); entry through the graveyard).*

▶ *From Newtownards take A 20 along the east shore of the lough.*

Grey Point
Crawfordsburn Country Park
BELFAST
Belfast Lough
A 2
BANGOR
Groomsport
Copeland Islands
NORTH
A 2
Donaghadee
A 48
Somme Heritage Centre
★ Ballycopeland
Millisle
CHANNEL
BELFAST
Newtownards
A 21
A 2
Movilla Abbey
A 20
Scrabo Country Park
Ballyferis Point
Comber
A 20
ARDS
MOUNT STEWART ★★★
A 22
A 21
▲ Temple of the Winds
Ballywalter
Wildfowl and Wetlands Trust ★
★ STRANGFORD
Grey Abbey ★
B 5
A 22
Mahee Castle
Mahee Island
PENINSULA
Burr Point
Nendrum Monastery ★
Kircubbin
A 2
Sketrick Castle
LOUGH
Portavogie
A 20
Rowallane Gardens ↘ Hillsborough ★
Killyleagh
A 22
BELFAST
Delamont Country Park
★ Audley's Castle
Rowallane Gardens ↙ BELFAST
Audleystown Cairn
Portaferry
B 7
★★ Castle Ward
Strangford
★ Quoile Countryside Centre
A 25
★ Inch Abbey
B 2
Raholp
Saul
St Tassach's Church
Quoile
Downpatrick
Slieve Patrick
Kilclief Castle
NEWCASTLE
A 25
Struell Wells ★
Ballyquintin Point
LECALE PENINSULA
Killard Point
Stone Circle
IRISH
B 1
A 2
Ballynoe
Ardtole
SEA
A 2
Killough
Ardglass ★
Dundrum Bay
Church
St John's Point
STRANGFORD LOUGH

0   5 km
0   3 miles

Grey Abbey★

(HM) ⚓ *Closed for refurbishment (2006).* 🅿 ☎ *028 90546552*
The Cistercian abbey was established in 1193 by Affreca, the wife of John de Courcy, for monks from Holm Cultram Abbey in Cumbria: its church, one of the first in Ireland to exhibit traces of the dawning Gothic style, has a magnificent **west door** (1220-30) with elaborate moulding and dog-tooth decoration. Damaged in the Elizabethan wars, the abbey church was restored and served as the parish church. The small **visitor centre** displays descriptions of monastic life and the abbey; a herb garden stocks medicinal plants typical of a Cistercian garden.

▷ *Continue S on A 20.*

Portaferry

A busy coastal town until the mid 19C, Portaferry is now a yachting and sea angling centre. Two handsome Georgian houses on the waterfront contain the marine biology centre of Queen's University, Belfast. **Portaferry Castle**, was probably built early in the 16C by the Savage family. **Exploris**★ presents the varied marine life of Strangford Lough and the Irish Sea. 🧒 🕐 *Open Apr to Aug, 10am (11am Sat, noon Sun)-6pm; Sep to Mar, 10am (11am Sat, 1pm Sun)-5pm. Mar to Sep:* 💶 *£6.70; Oct to Feb:* 💶 *£5.40.* ☎ *028 42728062 - www.exploris.org.uk*

▷ *Take the car ferry across the strait to Strangford.*

Strangford Castle

At the heart of this picturesque harbour town stands a 15-16C **tower house**. An internal wooden stair climbs the three storeys to a very narrow roof walk from where there is a fine **view** of the ferry running between the Narrows and Portaferry. *(HM)* 🕐 *Key at house opposite - www.ehsni.gov.uk*

▷ *Make a detour (2.5mi/4km) S by the coast road (A 2).*

Kilclief Castle

(HM) ♿🕐*Open Jul to Aug, Tue, Fri, Sat 2-6pm; Wed-Thu 10am-1pm.* ☎ *028 91811491*
The gatehouse style **tower house**, with two defensive projections was built to guard the entrance to the Narrows.

▷ *From Strangford take A 25 W.*

Castle Ward★★

(HM) ♿🕐 *Grounds: open 10am-8pm (4pm Oct to Apr). House:* 👣 *tour Jul to Aug 1-6pm; Sep, Sat-Sun 1-6pm. Last tour at 5pm. House, grounds and wildlife centre:* 💶 *£5.50; Grounds and Castle:* 💶 *£3.50.* 📷☎ *028 44881204 - www.nationaltrust.org.uk*
This uniqe Great House surrounded by superb parkland overlooking Strangford Lough is an odd but endearing architectural compromise between the conflicting tastes of Bernard Ward, later the first Lord Bangor, and his wife Anne. The main facade is Palladian, the garden front is Gothick. The interiors exhibit a similar dichotomy. The entrance to the **house** (1760-75) opens into the hall exuberantly decorated with stuccowork. The rooms on the northeast side reflect the Gothick style favoured by Lady Bangor – the boudoir **fan vaulting** is modelled on the Henry VII's Chapel in Westminster Abbey; window panels in the saloon are deemed to be 17C Flemish. By contrast, the **dining room** on the Classical side of the house has 18C panelling and Chippendale chairs (c 1760).
When the new house was built, the formal gardens were replaced by a naturalistic landscape of grass, trees and deer park around such features as the **Temple Water,** created in 1724, and the **ice house** on the east bank, close to where the former early

Gothick Boudoir, Castle Ward

A von Einsiedel/National Trust Photographic Library

18C house stood. The Walled Garden, which originally provided the house with cut flowers and produce now contains pens for the **Wildfowl Collection**.

The 17C **tower house**, known as Old Castle Ward on the lake shore, was the first dwelling built on the estate by a Ward; today it is surrounded by farmyard buildings – the original 18C mill, once a tidal mill, was later adapted to be powered by the Temple Water. One building houses the **Strangford Lough Wildlife Centre**.

▶ *On foot from the north entrance to Castle Ward estate or by minor road W of Castle Ward estate. Drive through the gate to the car park.*

Audley's Castle★

The ruins of this 15C "gatehouse" type of **tower house**, stand on a spit of land projecting into Strangford Lough. It was built by the Audley family, who sold it in 1646 to the Wards of Castle Ward. The hamlet of Audleystown was demolished in the 1850s and the inhabitants are thought to have emigrated to the USA.

Ward Family

Late in the 16C Bernard Ward from Capesthorne in Cheshire bought the Castle Ward estate from the Earls of Kildare. In 1610 Nicholas Ward built a tower house, Old Castle Ward, by Strangford Lough. In the 18C the Ward estates extended from Castle Ward to the coast of Dundrum Bay; nothing remains of the 18C house built by Michael Ward, a good landlord, who promoted the linen trade, developed the lead mines on his estate, built the new town and harbour of Killough and became a Justice of the Court of the King's Bench in Ireland. In 1812 the property passed to Robert Ward, who prefered to live at Bangor Castle. In 1827 the 3rd Viscount Bangor (a title bestowed in 1781) started restoring the estate. In 1950 the house was received by the state in lieu of death duties and presented to the National Trust.

Audleystown Cairn

Walk across the fields. The cairn, which is revetted with drystone walling, is a dual court tomb with a forecourt at each end opening into galleries. Excavations in 1952 revealed 34 partly burned skeletons, Neolithic pottery and flint implements.

▶ *Continue W on A 25.*

Quoile Countryside Centre★

In 1957 a barrage was built at Hare Island excluding the sea from the Quoile estuary, turning the tidal flats into a freshwater lake with sluice gates. The (494 acres/200ha) Nature Reserve has woodland, grassland and reedbed habitats enjoyed by birds and otters.

From **Quoile Quay**, which was built in 1717 by Edward Southwell and served as a port for Downpatrick until 1940, the road reaches **Quoile Castle**, a late-16C tower house inhabited by the West family until the mid 18C. The **visitor centre** provides descriptions of the local history, flora and fauna. &🕐 *Open Apr to Aug, 11am-5pm; Sep to Mar, Sat-Sun 1-5pm. Castle island hide 10am-4pm.* 🅿☎ *028 44615520 - www. ehsni.gov.uk*

▶ *From Downpatrick take A 7.*

Inch Abbey★

2mi/3.2km NW of Downpatrick by A 7; after 1mi/1.6km turn left.
The abbey on an island in the marshes is now accessible by road. The daughter house of the Cistercian abbey at Furness in Lancashire, was founded c 1180 by John de Courcy. Among the ruins are the remains of the 13C church and detached buildings presumed to be an infirmary *(southeast)*, a bakehouse and a guesthouse.

▶ *From Downpatrick take A 22 N.*

Delamont Country Park

🕐 *Open 9am-dusk* ⌣ ☎ *028 44828333 - www.delamontcountrypark.com*
The park containing a walled garden with formal beds, extends to the shore of Strangford Lough. A spacious bird hide is ideal for bird watching; the longest mini-ature railway in Ireland, boat trips and an adventure playground are more fun.

▶ *Continue N on A 22.*

J Cornish/National Trust Photographic Library

Drumlins in Strangford Lough

Killyleagh

The picturesque turreted **castle** redesigned in 1850 by Charles Lanyon, has two circular towers (13C and 17C). The original castle, built by de Courcy, was acquired by the O'Neills, destroyed by General Monk in 1648 and then rebuilt by the Hamiltons, Earls of Clanbrassil and later Viscounts Clandeboye. Killyleagh was the birthplace of **Sir Hans Sloane**, whose collection of curios, books and manuscripts formed the nucleus of the Natural History and British Museums in London.

▶ *Continue N on A 22; bear right into minor road along the shore.*

Sketrick Castle

The approach to Sketrick Island is guarded by the ruins of a massive four-storey tower house which collapsed in a storm in 1896.

▶ *Continue N on minor road along the shore.*

Mahee Island Nendrum Monastery★

(HM)🕐 *Open Apr-Sep, Tue-Sun, 10am (2pm Sun) to 7pm; Oct-Mar, Sat-Sun 10am (2pm Sun) to 4pm.* 🅿 ☎ *028 91811491 - www.ehsni.gov.uk*
This inspiring Early Christian site stands on an island in the lough now linked by causeways to a chain of islands. Nendrum was excavated and partly restored in the 1920s. A visitor centre tells the story of the three concentric enclosures (cashels) defined by drystone walls and the monastery founded in the 5C by St Mochaoi (Mahee), sacked by Vikings and reestablished in the 12C by the Anglo-Norman John de Courcy, who staffed it with Benedictine monks from Cumbria. In the 14C it was abandoned. The remains of the monastic church (10C) with an east end built by Benedictines (12C) stands in the central enclosure; middle area contained the school and monastic workshops, while the extensive outer enclosure accommodated the guesthouses, dwellings, gardens, orchards, pastures, arable fields, and a tide-driven mill.

▶ *Continue N on minor road along the shore.*

Wildfowl and Wetlands Trust (Castle Espie Centre)★

♿🕐 *Open Mar to Oct, Mon-Fri 10.30am-5.30pm (5pm Sep-Oct), Sat-Sun 11am-5.30pm; Nov to Feb, 11am-4pn (4.30pm Sat-Sun)* ☕🅿☎ *028 91874146 - www-wwt.org.uk*
The protected area on the west shore of Strangford Lough includes freshwater lakes, flooded clay and limestone quarries. These are now home to endangered species bred in captivity and a broad range of wild species. In winter, thousands of wildfowl arrive here from the Arctic.

▶ *Continue N on A 22; in Comber take A 21; turn left up steep minor road.*

Scrabo Country Park

(HM)🕐 *Tower: open Apr to Sep, Sat-Thur 10.30am-6pm.* 🅿☎ *028 91811491 - www. ehsni.gov.uk*
The upper end of Strangford Lough is dominated by **Scrabo tower** on Scrabo Hill, the centrepiece of a popular country park. The dolerite, a form of volcanic lava extruded at the same time as at the Giant's Causeway, has protected the underlying sandstone from erosion. Both rocks have been quarried in the past, the dark dolerite for Mount Stewart, the light sandstone for many Belfast buildings. Both were used in the 135ft/41m high tower, which was built in 1857 to commemorate the 3rd Marquess of Londonderry (1778-1854), a compassionate man who showed great concern for his tenants during the Great Famine.
There is a video and display about the park in the tower, from where the **view**★★ *(122 steps – viewing maps)* extends to the Scottish coast, the Isle of Man.

MAPS AND PLANS

LIST OF MAPS

TOWN PLANS

Republic of Ireland

Northern Ireland

PLANS OF MONUMENTS

Republic of Ireland

Northern Ireland

LOCAL MAPS

Republic of Ireland

Northern Ireland

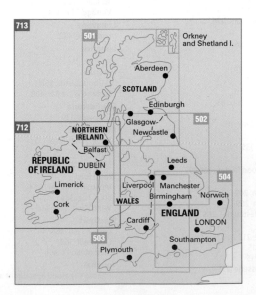

COMPANION
PUBLICATIONS

A map reference to the appropriate Michelin map is given for each chapter in the Selected Sights section of this guide.

MICHELIN MAP 712 – IRELAND:

- Scale 1 : 400 000 - 1cm = 4km - 1in : 6.30 miles   covers the Republic of Ireland and Northern Ireland, and the network of motorways and major roads. It provides information on shipping routes, distances in miles and kilometres, town plans of Dublin and Belfast, services, sporting and tourist attractions and an index of places; the key and text are printed in four languages.

MICHELIN TOURIST AND MOTORING ATLAS GREAT BRITAIN & IRELAND:

- Scale 1 : 300 000 - 1cm = 3km - 1in : 4.75 miles (based on 1 : 400 000)   covers the whole of the United Kingdom and the Republic of Ireland, the national networks of motorways and major roads. It provides information on route planning, shipping routes, distances in miles and kilometres, over 60 town plans, services and sporting and tourist attractions and an index of places; the key and text are printed in six languages.

MICHELIN MAP 713 – GREAT BRITAIN AND IRELAND:

- Scale 1 : 1 000 000 - 1cm = 10km - 1inch : 15.8 miles   covers the whole of the United Kingdom and the Republic of Ireland, the national networks of motorways and major roads. It provides information on shipping routes, distances in miles and kilometres, a list of Unitary Authorities for Wales and Scotland; the key and text are printed in four languages.

INTERNET:

- Users can access personalised route plans, Michelin mapping on line, addresses of hotels and restaurants listed in The Red Guide and practical and tourist information through the internet:

    www.ViaMichelin.com

Legend

Selected monuments and sights

◉ ⇒	Tour - Departure point
🏛️🏛️ ⵜ ⵜ	Ecclesiastical building
▨ ▬ ⵛ	Synagogue - Mosque
▰	Building
■	Statue, small building
ⵜ	Calvary, wayside cross
◎	Fountain
●━●■■	Rampart - Tower - Gate
✕	Château, castle, historic house
⁙	Ruins
∪	Dam
✿	Factory, power plant
☆	Fort
∩	Cave
◳	Troglodyte dwelling
⚓	Prehistoric site
▼	Viewing table
Ⅲ	Viewpoint
▲	Other place of interest

Special symbols

M3	Motorway
A2	Primary route
🌳	Forest, Country Park, National Park

Sports and recreation

🐎	Racecourse
⛸️	Skating rink
≋ ▨	Outdoor, indoor swimming pool
🎥	Multiplex Cinema
⛵	Marina, sailing centre
⬡	Trail refuge hut
▢━■━■━▢	Cable cars, gondolas
▢┼┼┼┼▢	Funicular, rack railway
🚂	Tourist train
◆	Recreation area, park
🐎	Theme, amusement park
Ψ	Wildlife park, zoo
✾	Gardens, park, arboretum
◉	Bird sanctuary, aviary
🚶	Walking tour, footpath
😊	Of special interest to children

Abbreviations

C	County council offices
H	Town hall
J	Law courts
M	Museum
POL.	Police
T	Theatre
U	University

Highly recommended	★★★	
Recommended	★★	
Interesting	★	

Additional symbols

🛈		Tourist information
═══	═══	Motorway or other primary route
❶	❶	Junction: complete, limited
⊨══⊨	══	Pedestrian street
I ═ ═ ═ ═ I		Unsuitable for traffic, street subject to restrictions
⊓⊓⊓⊓	‑ ‑ ‑ ‑	Steps – Footpath
🚆	🚉	Train station – Auto-train station
🚌	S.N.C.F.	Coach (bus) station
‑‑‑‑‑		Tram
Ⓜ		Metro, underground
P-R		Park-and-Ride
♿		Access for the disabled
✉		Post office
☎		Telephone
✉		Covered market
•✗•		Barracks
△		Drawbridge
℧		Quarry
✗		Mine
B	F	Car ferry (river or lake)
🚤		Ferry service: cars and passengers
⇌		Foot passengers only
③		Access route number common to Michelin maps and town plans
Bert (R.)...		Main shopping street
AZ B		Map co-ordinates

Places to stay and places to eat

Republic of Ireland= €

Hotels- price categories:

⊖	<90 €
⊖⊖	90 to 140 €
⊖⊖⊖	140 to 220 €
⊖⊖⊖⊖	>220 €

Restaurants- price categories:

⊖	<20 €
⊖⊖	20 to 50 €
⊖⊖⊖	50 to 80 €
⊖⊖⊖⊖	>80 €

Northern Ireland= £ Sterling:

Hotels- price categories:

⊖	<£60
⊖⊖	£60 to 95
⊖⊖⊖	£95 to 150
⊖⊖⊖⊖	>£150

Restaurants- price categories:

⊖	<£15
⊖⊖	£15 to 35
⊖⊖⊖	£35 to 55
⊖⊖⊖⊖	>£55

20 rooms :	Number of rooms
⊑ *€4.50*	Price of breakfast when not included in the room price.
100 beds	Number of beds (youth hostel, university residence).

🚫💳	No credit cards accepted
P	Reserved parking for hotel patrons
🏊	Swimming Pool
▦	Air conditioning
♿	Rooms accessible to persons of reduced mobility

All prices are given in € in the Republic of Ireland and in £ Sterling in Northern Ireland. Prices quoted include VAT unless otherwise specified. Service charge may be expected.

507